THE AGE OF THE
STORYTELLERS
British Popular Fiction Magazines
1880-1950

THE AGE OF THE STORYTELLERS

British Popular Fiction Magazines 1880-1950

MIKE ASHLEY

THE BRITISH LIBRARY
AND
OAK KNOLL PRESS

© 2006 Mike Ashley
The Introduction and entry on *The Strand* are joint copyright
© 2006 David Pringle and Mike Ashley

First published 2006 by
The British Library
96 Euston Road
London NW1 2DB
and
Oak Knoll Press
310 Delaware Street
New Castle
DE 19720

Cataloguing-in-Publication Data
is available from both The British Library
and the Library of Congress

ISBN 0–7123–0698–6 (BL)
ISBN 1–58456–170–X (OKP)

Designed and typeset by Mike Ashley
Cover designed by Bob Elliott
Printed in England by Antony Rowe Ltd

CONTENTS

Illustrations in text	vii
Acknowledgements	x
Introduction by David Pringle and Mike Ashley	1
User Guide	17
Chronology	20
Colour Plates	38
Section 1: Primary Magazines	39

Adventure-Story Magazine • Air Stories • All-Story Magazine • Argosy • Best-Story Magazine • The Blue Magazine • Cassell's Magazine • Chapman's/Crampton's Magazine • The Charing Cross Magazine • The Club Room • The Corner Magazine • The Crusoe Mag. • The Detective Magazine • Empire Frontier • English Illustrated Magazine • Everybody's Magazine • Fantasy • The Golden Mag./Golden West • The Grand Magazine • The Green Magazine • The Happy Mag. • The Holborn Monthly Magazine • Hush • Hutchinson's Magazine • The Idler • The Jolly Mag. • The Lady's Magazine • Lady's Realm • Lloyd's Magazine • The London Magazine • The Ludgate Monthly • The Magpie • The Merry Mag. • The Minster • Modern Stories • Mystery and Detection • Mystery Stories • Mystery-Story Magazine • Nash's Magazine • The New Magazine • The Novel Magazine • Pall Mall Magazine • Pan • Pearson's Magazine • The Premier Magazine • The Realm • The Red Magazine • Romance • The Royal Magazine • Sievier's Monthly • The Sovereign Magazine • Standard Stories • The Story-Teller • The Strand Magazine • The Sunny Mag. • Tales of Wonder • Tip-Top/Regent Magazine • 20 Story Magazine • The Universal Magazine • The Violet Magazine • War Stories • Weekly Tale-Teller • Western Adventures • The White Magazine • The Windsor Magazine • Wings • Woman at Home • World Stories • The Yellow Magazine • Yes or No

Section 2: Other Magazines 242

Argosy • Atalanta • Badminton Magazine • Belgravia • Black and White • The Black Cat • Blackwood's Magazine • The Boy's Own Paper • Britannia and Eve • The Butterfly • The Captain • Chambers's Journal • Chums • Colour • The Cornhill Magazine • Eureka/The Favorite Magazine • Fry's Magazine • Gaiety • Good Housekeeping • Good Words • The Graphic • Harper's Bazaar • Harper's Monthly Magazine • Home Chimes • Horlick's Magazine • The Illustrated London News • The Imp • Lambert's Monthly • London Society • Longman's Magazine • Lovat Dickson's Magazine • Macmillan's Magazine • The Master Thriller • Nash's Illustrated Weekly • The Osborne • Outward Bound • The Passing Show • Pearson's Story-Teller • Pearson's Weekly • The Quiver • Sandow's Magazine • The Savoy • Scoops • The Search Light • Short Stories • The Sketch • The Smart Set • The Sphere • The Sunday/ Story Journal • The Sunday Strand • T.P.'s Magazine • Temple Bar • The Temple Magazine • The Thriller • Thrills • Tit-Bits • To-Day • Woman • Woman's Journal • The World and His Wife • The Yellow Book

Summary of Editors and Publishers 274

Bibliography 290

Index 294

ILLUSTRATIONS IN TEXT

Where known, cover artists' names are noted in brackets.

The Strand Magazine, January 1891 (George Haite)	1
The Story-Teller, April 1908 (David Whitelaw)	2
Robert Louis Stevenson	4
The Boy's Own Paper, 4 October 1879	7
Sherlock Holmes drawn by Sidney Paget for *The Strand*, July 1891	11
Pearson's Magazine, April 1902 (Gambier)	12
Strand Magazine, November 1939	15
Illustration by Anthony Gilbert for "The Return of Long John Silver" in *The Strand*, December 1949	16
Adventure-Story Magazine, January 1926 (E.M.)	41
Air Stories, January 1940 (S. Drigin)	43
All-Story Magazine, January 1927 (Leo Bates)	45
The Argosy, May 1933	47
The Blue Magazine, October 1921	50
John Cassell	52
Cassell's Family Magazine, August 1893	53
Heading for "In the Chains of Crime" from *Cassell's Magazine*, June 1898	54
Cassell's Magazine, March 1908	55
Cassell's Magazine, January 1913 (Cyrus Cuneo)	56
Chapman's Magazine, general cover design	58
Crampton's Magazine, May 1902	60
The Corner Magazine, March 1927	63
The Crusoe Mag., July 1924	65
Illustration by Inder Burns for "Linckes' Great Case" in *The Detective Magazine*, 2 March 1923	67
Empire Frontier, January 1930 (Charles Crombie)	68
Illustration by Walter Crane for "A Herald of Spring" in *The English Illustrated Magazine*, April 1884	70
Illustration by John Collier for "Wooden Tony" in *The English Illustrated Magazine*, December 1890	71
Everybody's Story Magazine, January 1911 (Harold Goldman)	77
Everyone's, January 1914 (Persis Kirmse)	78
Fantasy #3, 1939 (S. Drigin)	79
The Golden Mag., June 1926	80
The Grand Magazine, February 1905	81
The Grand Magazine, May 1939 (Edward Ormond)	85

vii

The Happy Mag., November 1938 (D.L. Ghilchik)	87
The Evesham Monthly Magazine, April 1903 (P. Lancaster)	89
Hush, December 1930	90
Hutchinson's Story-Magazine, September 1928	92
Heading by Dudley Hardy for "The Idler's Club" for *The Idler*, February 1892	95
The Idler, July 1899 (S.H. Sime)	97
The Idler, June 1904 (G.K. Chesterton)	99
The Lady's Magazine, November 1901	101
The Lady's Realm, November 1896	103
Lloyd's Story Magazine, May 1917 (Filmore)	107
The London Magazine, November 1909	111
Heading by Hilda Cowham for "The Railway Children" in *The London Magazine*, January 1905	113
Frontispiece to "The Scarlet Plague" for *The London Magazine*, June 1912	115
Illustration by Warwick Reynolds for "When the World Was Young" in *The London Magazine*, June 1926	116
The New London Magazine, September 1931	117
The Ludgate Monthly, November 1891	118
Illustration by Ernest Prater for "The Deeds of Michael Niel" in *The Ludgate*, February 1898	120
The Magpie, August 1912	122
The Merry Magazine, April 1929	123
Mystery-Story Magazine, April 1924	127
Nash's Magazine, June 1911	129
Nash's and Pall Mall Magazine, July 1916 (Harrison Fisher)	131
Illustration by John R. Flanagan for "Zanzibar" in *Nash's and Pall Mall Magazine*, August 1923	134
Nash's—Pall Mall, December 1936 (Philip Zec)	136
The New Magazine, May 1909	138
The Novel Magazine, November 1909	142
The Novel Magazine, April 1919 (E. H. Thomas)	145
Illustration by Aubrey Beardsley to "The Black Art" for *Pall Mall Magazine*, June 1893	147
Illustration by Aubrey Beardsley to "The Kiss of Judas" for *Pall Mall Magazine*, July 1893	148
Illustration by Abbey Altson to "A Beauty to Her Mirror" for *Pall Mall Magazine*, December 1894	148
Pall Mall Magazine, October 1927 (Edmund Dulac)	154
Pan, April 1924 (Tom Purvis)	156
Pearson's Magazine, March 1902 (Popini)	159
Heading by Cosmo Rowe for "The War of the Worlds" for *Pearson's Magazine*, April 1897	161
Pearson's Magazine, February 1925 (Howard Elcock)	166
Illustration by John Campbell for "The Problem of Uncle Meleager's Will" for *Pearson's Magazine*, July 1925	167
The Premier Magazine, May 1914 (Cyrus Cuneo)	169
The Premier Magazine, March 1923 (Dorothy Morgan)	172

The Red Magazine, 1 March 1910	176
The Red Magazine, 18 February 1921 (Hawley Morgan)	178
Romance, July 1924 (J. Dewar Mills)	180
The Royal Magazine, August 1902	182
Illustration by E. H. Shepard for "Kanga Comes to the Forest" for *The Royal Magazine*, October 1926	185
The New Royal, December 1930; *The Royal Pictorial*, November 1934; *Screen Pictorial*, July 1937	186
The Sovereign Magazine, November 1919	188
Standard Stories, October 1925	190
The Story-Teller, April 1907 (David Whitelaw)	191
The Story-Teller, November 1930	194
George Newnes	196
The editorial offices of *The Strand* from the December 1892 issue	198
Sidney Paget's first illustration of Holmes and Watson for *The Strand*, July 1891	199
A. Conan Doyle in feature "Portraits of Celebrities at Different Times of their Lives" from *The Strand*, December 1891	200
The Strand Magazine, July 1917	203
Alfred Leete's depiction of Jeeves in *The Strand*, June 1916	204
The Strand Magazine, October 1941	205
Tom Purvis's illustration of Sherlock Holmes for *The Strand*, February 1947	206
The Sunny and Gaiety Mag., June 1929	209
Tales of Wonder, Autumn 1940 (Harry Turner)	210
Tip Top Stories, July 1924 (C. Loneragan)	211
20 Story Magazine, March 1930 (Edgar Spenceley)	213
The Violet Magazine, 16 April 1926 (Dudley Cowes)	217
Weekly Tale Teller, 28 May 1910 (Dudley Cowes)	219
Western Adventures, June 1936 (W. Gale)	221
The Windsor Magazine, January 1905	223
Illustration by Stanley L. Wood for "Dr Nikola" in *The Windsor Magazine*, January 1895	224
Illustration by Maurice Greiffenhagen for "Ayesha" in *The Windsor Magazine*, January 1905	226
The Windsor Magazine, February 1937 (John Campbell)	229
The Woman at Home, October 1901	231
The Home Magazine, January 1923	235
The Yellow Magazine, 15 May 1925	237
Yes or No, 5 December 1908	239

Acknowledgements

A work of this kind cannot be completed without a considerable amount of help from others, either in checking or pursuing facts or in providing access to source materials. First and foremost thanks must go to David Pringle, without whom this book may not have existed. In establishing the "Fictionmags" internet discussion group to encourage research into the "Standard Illustrated Popular Magazine", as he calls them, David encouraged me to pursue work that I had commenced years before. David also composed the introduction to this book and contributed the entry on *The Strand* as well as those on *Boy's Own Paper*, *Chums*, *The Captain* and *The Thriller*.

I must thank staff at the British Library for their help and guidance, in particular Frances Lill, for helping to identify holdings and unwrinkling the whole research process, Arthur Cunningham, who first saw the potential of this project, and David Way for steering me through the minefield. Thanks also to Kelvin Ithell, Stewart Gillies and Sharon Foster at the British Library; Vanessa Corrick and Richard Bell at the Bodleian Library, Oxford; Yvonne Marr at the National Library of Scotland, and Toni Richardson at the Library of Congress.

My thanks also go to the following. Dennis K. Lien at the University of Minnesota for his help in identifying major US library holdings and, along with Richard Bleiler of the University of Connecticut and Victor Berch of Brandeis Library, Boston, in responding to a welter of queries on writers and newspaper sources. Jack Adrian for helping to clarify many of the obscure by-ways of popular fiction magazines. George Locke of Ferret Fantasy for allowing access to many of his magazines plus commenting on the final copy and providing freely of his deep knowledge of popular fiction. John Eggeling for his knowledge of the minutiae of the popular fiction world and for his help in tracking down some of the more obscure magazines. Stephen Holland for his detailed knowledge of the world of boys' fiction and the crossover with popular magazines and story-papers and in sharing data on lesser known writers. Dr Aubrey Wilson for his help with Ernest Bramah. Bill Contento for maintaining the "FictionMags" Index, plus Michael Saler, Michael Ward, Phil Stephensen-Payne, Jess Nevins, Morgan Wallace and other members of the "FictionMags" internet discussion group for data on magazine contents and covers and in helping identify variances between British and American editions. Finally thanks to Margaret Rose and Chloe Veale at the History of Advertising Trust for their help in checking their archives and, in particular, the *Advertisers' Protection Society Monthly Circular*.

INTRODUCTION

THE AGE OF THE STORYTELLERS

"The 'age of the Story Tellers', initiated by Stevenson with *Treasure Island* in 1883 and ushered in by Rider Haggard with *King Solomon's Mines* two years later, was already becoming rather overblown by the end of the century. A host of followers ... were pouring out romances and adventure stories in an ever thickening stream."
— Roger Lancelyn Green, Introduction, *The Prisoner of Zenda* by Anthony Hope, 1966

This book seeks to explore a major aspect of what, following Roger Lancelyn Green's lead, was the "Age of the Storytellers". Its subject is the popular (as distinct from the "literary") fiction magazine which proliferated in Britain from 1880 to 1950 in the wake of the success of *The Strand Magazine*. Its purpose is to provide a history and appreciation of these magazines, to explore their contribution to the growth of popular fiction and, hopefully, to spread an awareness of their existence and the role they played in developing writers and establishing the popular categories of fiction. This introduction sets the context in which the magazines grew and prospered, and a series of A-Z entries discusses in detail each of the 144 titles (70 in the main section and 74 shorter entries in the subsidiary section) which were the primary British popular fiction magazines.

The Strand defines the era, for it was this magazine that established the pattern for its competitors, and it was the last of the original magazines to survive. Most other survivors disappeared during the Second World War, which is the real cut-off point of this volume. *The Strand* managed to survive until 1950, but it was a shadow of its former self and had shrunk into the digest format which became the new norm for the relatively few fiction-carrying magazines of the 1950s and '60s. Thus the core of this Guide covers those magazines whose heyday was in the period 1890-1940 but viewed within the context of the Age of the Storytellers from 1880 to 1950.

These magazines fall into two closely-related groups. *The Strand* itself, starting in 1891, and its most successful imitators – *The Windsor*, *Pearson's*, *The London* and, to a lesser degree, *Pall Mall* – were among the breed of monthly general-interest family magazines that were printed on high-quality glossy paper, allowing for a profusion of photographs, illustrations and fine art. Because they were priced at just sixpence – later ones even less – they brought the world into the reach of millions. They were modelled to a large extent on the American magazines *Harper's* and *Century Illustrated*, though they had their own forerunners in Britain, especially *The English Illustrated Magazine*. Some of these, most notably *Nash's*, metamorphosed in the 1920s into the large, flat glossy format, which became known as the "big slick" magazine, and was heavily (literally) supported by advertising. At the heart of the success of these magazines was their short fiction, especially the popular story series so well defined by the Sherlock Holmes adventures by Arthur Conan Doyle. In establishing their popularity these magazines ushered in the era of the short story, particularly those built around iconic heroes and villains. So much of the popular fiction that typifies the late Victorian and Edwardian periods, and the Roaring Twenties, first appeared in these magazines. The success of this first group encouraged the second. In the mid-Edwardian period the major publishers experimented with magazines consisting solely of short stories, mostly un-illustrated and usually printed on poorer-quality paper, either newsprint or pulp. *The Novel* was the forerunner and, to some extent, *The Grand*, but it was *The Story-Teller*, in 1907, that established this trend and over the next few years there was a huge eruption of all-fiction monthly magazines.

These are the periodicals covered in this book. They are the magazines that are either all-fiction, or where the fiction is uppermost and, over the magazine's lifetime, the most significant element. They are also, for the most part, monthlies, though some had fortnightly schedules for part of their run. A few weekly magazines are included because they were special, but they are the exception. These are the magazines which fall under the above definitions that were published in Britain and had their significant years in the period 1890 to 1940. Amongst them are a few titles, such as *Cassell's* and *English Illustrated*, which began before 1890 and, others like *The Strand* or *The Quiver*, which continued beyond 1940. There are no entries for magazines whose life was over by 1890, or soon after, and likewise none where their main existence was after 1940.

Some of these magazines, particularly *The Strand* and *Nash's* are very well known, and have been written about elsewhere, but many are long forgotten and some, like *The Club Room*, are so rare that no complete run is known to exist. The majority of these magazines have not been covered in any reference book. Although some may be referred to in author biographies or discussions of popular fictional characters the degree of coverage is superficial at best. Who now recalls that it was in *The Story-Teller* that Sax Rohmer's Fu Manchu first appeared? Or *Hutchinson's Magazine* that first presented Sapper's Bulldog Drummond? Or *The Home Magazine* where Richmal Crompton's "Just William" first got into mischief, or *The Premier Magazine* where Rafael Sabatini's Captain Blood raised the skull-and-crossbones? Without these magazines cultivating and tilling the soil, could these characters, and many others, ever have taken root and flourished?

This is the first reference book to study these magazines in the context of their period and provide a comprehensive survey and analysis. The entries concentrate on the fiction but also seek to give an all-round picture through their non-fiction features and artwork. It provides in

INTRODUCTION

both colour and black-and-white, the most extensive reproduction of cover art, ever made for these periodicals, revealing their rich variety. The Guide is the culmination of many years' research and of many more years' fascination with the world of popular-fiction magazines. Hopefully it will encourage further interest and research from others in broadening our knowledge and understanding of the magazines, their publishers, editors, artists and writers, and in bringing back to life a world that has for too long been forgotten.

*

In the peculiarly modern age of mass production and mass communications which began in the last quarter of the nineteenth century, before film, radio and television were established, the prime medium for popular storytelling was the printed word. Whether in book or magazine form, printed storytelling vied only with the popular stage – drama, music-hall, and song – for the attention of the fast-rising urban and suburban populations of late-Victorian Britain. The theatre, like the later cinema, lay outside the private home; one had to go to the trouble and expense of visiting a playhouse, or a picture house; hence the main medium for the absorption of commercial storytelling within the home was the printed word, the book and the magazine; and of these two forms, given the relatively long production time of the book, the magazine was the more immediate and "newsworthy". The popular magazine, whether weekly or monthly, was the vehicle for the latest stories by the latest authors; it was the medium through which written tales passed on their way towards becoming books. Insofar as it was "domestic", the function of the magazine in late-Victorian and Edwardian times was exactly equivalent to the later functions of radio and television: it brought storytelling, along with pictures, news, information and other diversions, *into* the home, and did so in regular, packaged ways. It shared its "domesticity" and its immediacy, only with the newspaper and, in the days before radio and TV, newspapers also ran a good deal of fiction. The dividing line between newspaper and magazine is by no means clear – the two tend to blur into each other, particularly in the area of "weeklies" – but in this book we deal primarily with the more permanent end of the periodical market, the monthly magazine, as a vehicle for fiction, and we look only glancingly at the similar function of weekly and daily papers. Fiction dominated this period and it was as much a selling factor for daily and weekly newspapers as it was for monthly magazines, but it is impossible to cover them all in one volume. Newspapers have been the subject of many books and analyses whereas the monthly fiction magazines have hitherto been almost ignored.

If we take Roger Lancelyn Green's conceit of an "Age of the Storytellers" seriously – and here we do, because it coincides with the era of the popular fiction-bearing magazines described in this book – then we need to ask when that age began and ended. Robert Louis Stevenson's rousing pirate tale *Treasure Island* did indeed appear in book form in 1883, but it had first seen print as a serial, "The Sea Cook, or Treasure Island" under Stevenson's pseudonym of Capt. Geo. North, in the weekly *Young Folks* from 1 October 1881 to 28 January 1882. *Young Folks*, which also serialised Stevenson's "The Black Arrow" (30 Jun-20 Oct 1883) and "Kidnapped" (1 May-31 Jul 1886), was a children's paper published from London by fellow Scot, James Henderson. It ran from 1871 to 1897 under various titles (ending as the cosy-sounding *Folks at Home*), and would be completely forgotten today were it not for the connection with Stevenson. So the "beginning" of Lancelyn Green's putative Age of the Storytellers can be pushed back to 1881.

Treasure Island was not quite Stevenson's first work of fiction: his first story-collection, *New Arabian Nights* (1882), had preceded. The contents of that volume were varied, but its centre-piece, the story-cycle which gave the book its name, had first appeared as "Latter-Day Arabian Nights" during 1878, in another weekly called *London*. This now-obscure publication, which ran for 114 issues from February 1877 to April 1879, was edited by the redoubtable William Ernest Henley, an English poet and *litterateur* whom Stevenson (*left*) had befriended when the former was undergoing prolonged hospital treatment in Edinburgh, in the mid-1870s. Henley's formidable, dominating personality, as well as his physical ailments (he had had a leg amputated), made a deep impression on the young Stevenson, and he had Henley very much in mind when he created the memorable character of Long John Silver, the one-legged hero-villain of *Treasure Island*. So, in some sense, does the seed for the Age of the Storytellers date back to Stevenson's first meeting with W. E. Henley in an Edinburgh hospital in 1875?

Perhaps. In later years, while working as an editor for Cassell, Henley was to be the one who eased the way to book publication of both Stevenson's *Treasure Island* and Haggard's *King Solomon's Mines* (with the assistance of another famous man-of-letters and propagandist for the new kind of "romance", Andrew Lang); while at *The National Observer*, Henley was to publish Rudyard Kipling's *Barrack-Room Ballads*, plus early stories and poems by W. B. Yeats; and while at *The New Review* he was to serialise H. G. Wells's *The Time Machine*, Arthur Morrison's *A Child of the Jago* and many other works. But whatever Henley's input, he was clearly less important to the nascent Age of the Storytellers than the talented writer he first "adopted", R. L. Stevenson. There were to be other editors in Stevenson's life, besides Henley. Stevenson's début short story, "A Lodging for the Night," appeared in the magazine *Temple Bar* in October 1877, and it is a small masterpiece. It contains atmospheric descriptions of a snowbound city (Paris), nice handling of a very ambiguous hero (François Villon, a great poet but a bad man), and many excellent hard-hitting details – especially striking is the scene where Villon steals some coins from a frozen-dead prostitute. According to Walter Allen's study, *The Short Story in English*, this piece marks the beginning of the modern British short story – Stevenson created the field, claims Allen. Of course, there were notable French and American and Russian short-story writers before Stevenson, but there were few people in Britain producing significant short stories – significant in the "modern" sense, as Allen, and a fairly wide critical consensus, defines it.[1]

---

[1] That is not to say that no one was writing short stories, only that the form had not developed in adult fiction in Britain as it had in America, France or Russia. In Britain writers who dabbled with the short story did so in imitation of the form elsewhere, especially in gothic or supernatural fiction, emulating the works of Hoffmann and Poe, or in terms of the fairy tale or folk tale, inspired in particular, after 1843, by the stories of Hans Christian Andersen. The majority of short fiction prior to 1877, whether it be by Charles Dickens, Bulwer-Lytton, Margaret Oliphant, Mrs Gaskell, Wilkie Collins, George MacDonald or Sheridan Le Fanu, owed more to Continental or folk roots than to any independent imaginings.

INTRODUCTION

Another, much longer, Stevenson story was "The Pavilion on the Links", which appeared anonymously as a two-parter in *The Cornhill Magazine* (Sept-Oct 1880). This story appealed so strongly to a young acolyte (another Edinburgh man) called Arthur Conan Doyle that more than a quarter of a century later he was moved to write:

> That story stamped itself so clearly on my brain when I read it in *Cornhill* that when I came across it again many years afterwards in volume form, I was able instantly to recognise two small modifications of the text – each very much for the worse – from the original form. They were small things, but they seemed somehow like a chip on a perfect statue. Surely it is only a very fine work of art which could leave so definite an impression as that [...] How well I remember the eagerness, the delight with which I read those early tales in *Cornhill* away back in the late seventies and early eighties. They were unsigned, after the old unfair fashion, but no man with any sense of prose could fail to know that they were all by the same author. [2]

It was because he had such a large impact on other writers to come that Stevenson makes an appropriate figure with which to begin any account of the Age of the Storytellers. Both the above-mentioned tales were reprinted in his first collection, *New Arabian Nights*, alongside the story-cycle Henley had commissioned for his paper, *London*. So the stories in that volume had appeared in various magazines, over a five-year period prior to 1882. If this, together with the 1881-1882 serialisation of Stevenson's first novel, represents the beginning of the Age we are trying to pin down, then it seems fair enough to nominate "1880" as the starting point.

Spurred on by Stevenson (and by lesser lights like Talbot Baines Reed and F. Anstey – the latter's popular first novel, *Vice Versa; or, A Lesson to Fathers*, appeared in 1882) – it was becoming an age of shorter novels. The High Victorian "three-decker" did not die the death until the mid-1890s; but, for those with eyes to see, its days were numbered from the early 1880s onwards. With publishers like Cassell and Longman, single-volume novels were becoming the fashion — brevity and speed were replacing the old ponderousness (and of course brevity was to lend itself to successful publication in magazine form). Discussing Stevenson's influence in the 1880s, Roger Lancelyn Green refers to:

> the great divide between the ponderous and consciously annotated historical novels of the Lytton and Ainsworth school and the well-digested, light and speedy historical romances of Doyle and Weyman and Haggard and Crockett that were so soon to rout the old guard: the lissom rapier driving the cumbersome broadsword from the field. [3]

In the area of the most crowd-pleasing fiction, a new publisher, Arrowsmith of Bristol, was to achieve a considerable success with its "shilling shockers" — short novels on sensational themes, and so called because they were priced, in paperback, at only one shilling (this at a time when the official price of a new three-decker was still three guineas, or 63 shillings). The shockers began with *Called Back* by "Hugh Conway" (the author's real name was Frederick John Fargus). Published initially in an 1883 Arrowsmith Christmas annual, then reprinted as a shilling softcover in 1884, this sensational story of murder, amnesia, Siberian exile, political assassination and detection made a tremendous hit. It was translated all over Europe, a

---

[2] Arthur Conan Doyle, *Through the Magic Door*, 1907 (chapters VI and XII).
[3] Roger Lancelyn Green, *Teller of Tales*, 1965, p. 153.

dramatised version ran for a year and the novel sold over 350,000 copies in four years[4]. Conway was also adopted by one of the new illustrated monthlies, *The English Illustrated Magazine* which, with its profusion of artwork and mix of fact and fiction, helped lay the groundwork for the Standard Illustrated Popular Magazines to follow.

Other shockers, from Conway's and others' hands, followed in profusion. Perhaps the most successful of them, later that decade, was Fergus Hume's *The Mystery of a Hansom Cab* (1887 in Australia; 1888 in Britain). So great was the vogue, and so great the potential rewards, that up-and-coming writers like Stevenson and Conan Doyle were tempted to try this new form. Stevenson's *Strange Case of Dr Jekyll and Mr Hyde* (1886) was conceived and written as a shilling shocker (although, in the event, it was published by Longman, not Arrowsmith). At about the same time as Stevenson's horrific novella appeared, in early 1886, the as-yet unknown Conan Doyle sat down to write his own attempt at a brief shocker, entitled *A Study in Scarlet* and featuring a detective hero called Sherlock Holmes. In May 1886 he submitted it to Arrowsmith, for possible publication in their popular line. Two months later, unaccountably, they rejected it. Doyle tried other publishers and finally, in October, Ward, Lock & Co. wrote to him: "We have read your story 'A Study in Scarlet', and are pleased with it. We could not publish it this year, as the market is flooded at present with cheap fiction, but if you do not object to its being held over to next year we will give you £25 for the copyright." Doyle accepted[5]; and it was indeed to be another year before the first Holmes novel appeared from Ward, Lock as their *Beeton's Christmas Annual* for 1887.

The shockers rarely had prior magazine serialisations – though they were usually published, whether in Christmas annuals or straight into paperback, with the immediacy and cheapness of magazine fiction. For a slightly more elevated market, Arrowsmith, like other publishers of the day, soon commenced a hardcover line of modestly-priced one-volume novels, and a number of these *were* taken from magazines. "Arrowsmith's 3/6 Series" began with *Three Men in a Boat* by Jerome K. Jerome (1889), a humorous yarn which had run in a monthly magazine called *Home Chimes* (another forgotten publication, but of minor note in that Jerome, in his up-and-coming years, wrote a good deal for it). Number 11 in the series was to be another classic of humour, *The Diary of a Nobody* by George and Weedon Grossmith (1892), originally published as a series of sketches in the weekly *Punch*. Number 18 in the series, however, had made no prior magazine appearance: it was *The Prisoner of Zenda* by Anthony Hope (1894), an adventure story which founded an entire popular-fiction sub-genre, the Ruritanian romance. These three books have since sold in the millions and have probably never been out of print, in one edition or another, in over a century – not a bad record for one small publisher situated far from London, down Bristol way. And these books, in their differing fashions, help define what Lancelyn Green meant by the Age of the Storytellers. Clearly it was an age not so much of great and weighty literature (the preceding, High Victorian, period had been such an age) as of remarkably enduring "minor" works – a range of popular fiction, from *Treasure Island* to *Three Men in a Boat*, from *Vice Versa* to *The Prisoner of Zenda*, which has enjoyed an enormous afterlife, not only in terms of staying in print and continuing to draw readers a

---

[4] John Sutherland, *Longman Companion to Victorian Fiction*, p. 222.
[5] In 1887 £25 had the purchasing power of around £2,000 today.

century after the books were written (a huge achievement in itself) but also in terms of repeated adaptation to other media – stage, film, radio and TV.

So the Age of the Storytellers, from 1880, is marked by the growing frequency of such books. But what of magazines? A number have already been mentioned, monthlies like *The Cornhill* and *Temple Bar*, and weeklies like *London* and *Young Folks*. These all had pre-1880 origins, and belong essentially to the preceding age (hence we do not give them all major coverage in the present book). Among newer publications, a frequently mentioned landmark, harbinger of much of the popular journalism to come, was George Newnes's *Tit-Bits*, a lower-class (but aspiring) penny weekly launched from Manchester in October 1881. *Tit-Bits*, which became a raging success, was filled in the main not with news but with oddments and anecdotes. It was to publish a good deal of serial fiction in its time, and its publisher was to go on to found the crucial monthly of the Age of the Storytellers, *The Strand Magazine*, but *Tit-Bits* is not otherwise of great importance to our narrative. Nor are its fiction-carrying imitators such as *Cassell's Saturday Journal* (from 1883), Alfred Harmsworth's *Answers* (from 1888) and C. Arthur Pearson's *Pearson's Weekly* (from 1890) – although, as an aside, it is worth stressing that Messrs Harmsworth and Pearson were to become very influential publishers of magazines and papers of other types: in the context of British periodicals, Newnes, Harmsworth and Pearson were the essential triumvirate of publisher-entrepreneurs who were to put their stamp on the entire period we are discussing.

A case can be made, though, for the importance to popular fiction of another weekly, one which had been founded more than two years before *Tit-Bits*. It has one of those titles which, like *Punch* and *The Strand*, and very few other periodicals, has passed into legend. It is a name which many people still recognise, even though the publication in question has been dead for a long time – *The Boy's Own Paper*. Launched by the Religious Tract Society (which tried to keep its identity secret from its readers) on 18 January 1879, *The Boy's Own* (or *BOP* for short) was by no means the first story paper for young male readers – there had been countless examples since about 1850, most of them shoddy and downmarket, believed to be of dubious morals, and known colloquially as "penny dreadfuls" or "penny bloods". But the *BOP* is notable for being the first "improving" weekly for boys that turned out to be genuinely popular and long-lived. As such, it was to be an important part of the Age of the Storytellers.

The *BOP*'s star contributor in its early years was Talbot Baines Reed, a young man of the Christian Socialist persuasion. He was in much the same tradition as the mid-century Muscular Christians, Charles Kingsley and Thomas Hughes, who wrote such long-lived Victorian "boys' books" as *Westward Ho!* (1855) and *Tom Brown's Schooldays* (1857). An anonymous story by Reed led the paper's very first issue, and soon he emerged as its most esteemed writer of serials. Not only his first, "The Adventures of a Three-Guinea Watch", but such later novels as "The Fifth Form at St Dominic's" (1881-1882), "The Willoughby Captains" (1883-1884), "The Master of the Shell" (1887-1888) and "Tom, Dick and Harry" (1892-1893) were run through the paper and then issued in hardcover by the RTS, which kept them in print for many decades. These were school stories, and perhaps the most entertaining examples of that peculiarly British genre. As late as the 1950s and 1960s, some of us who grew up in those decades still read them, or saw adaptations of them on TV (*The Fifth Form at St Dominic's* was a four-part serial from the BBC in 1961). Alas, Talbot Baines Reed died at the age of 41 in 1893.[6]

Perhaps it is also worth pointing out that Victorian boys' books – and their distaff equivalent, "girls' books", sometimes produced by the same writers – were not intended, in the main, for young children. Rather, they were meant for those vital readerships that today we would refer to as teenagers and young adults. According to some accounts, *The Boy's Own Paper* in its opening years was read by young men in their early 20s as well as by their younger siblings. It should also be borne in mind that many of these "boys" and "girls" were in fact workers. A privileged few attended fee-paying schools to the age of 18 or thereabouts, but the vast majority left school at 12 or 14 to become factory hands, "office boys", domestic servants, "shop girls" and "mill girls". Before the Education Act of 1870, many British youngsters had no formal schooling at all – although, thanks to Sunday schools and various charitable and self-help organisations, a majority could read, even before 1870. The boys' book, a phenomenon which could be said to have begun in the 1840s with the later novels of Captain Frederick Marryat (principally a writer for adults), and which gathered steam in the 1850s with the appearance of a flow of works by three specialist big producers, W. H. G. Kingston, T. Mayne Reid and R. M. Ballantyne, catered to this huge and very impressionable audience. A second wave of successful boys'-book writers – G. A. Henty, G. Manville Fenn (one-time editor of *Cassell's Magazine*), Gordon Stables and many others (including Jules Verne in translation) – formed a minor but not unimportant part of the Age of the Storytellers, and contributed to the *BOP* and its rivals.

Although often decried today as paternalistic, jingoistic and even racist, the Victorian and Edwardian boys' (and girls') book can be viewed as a significant literary movement. Most certainly it did much, for better or for worse (and some of us would argue for better), to form the opinions and attitudes, the mind-sets, of several generations of Britons -- not to mention Americans and, for that matter, "colonials" in places like Canada, Australia, India and South Africa. The relatively high prestige of the boys' book a century and more ago is testified by the number of writers for adults who at least occasionally bent their pens to the production of such works, and who, in so doing, produced some of the most influential examples of the form. After all, Robert Louis Stevenson wrote *Treasure Island* as a boys' book, and the impulse to do so undoubtedly came from fond memories of his own childhood reading (he was born in 1850). Stevenson placed a poem, "To the Hesitating Purchaser", at the head of his novel, and in it he mentioned: "Buccaneers and buried Gold / And all the old romance, retold / ... [of] Kingston and Ballantyne the brave..." (Although Kingston had died in 1880, Ballantyne's career was by no means over when Stevenson's novel appeared in book form in 1883 – he was to remain active until his death in 1894.) The Age of the Storytellers, post-1880, could almost be defined

---

[6] As an aside, it is worth noting that in America some of his serials were published by Frank Munsey in his boys' weekly, *The Golden Argosy* (launched 1882) – the same publication that, in 1896, Munsey converted into the first true pulp magazine, *The Argosy*. It is strange, but rather appealing, to think that the *BOP* and Talbot Baines Reed may have been a contributory factor in the growth of the field of American "pulp fiction".

INTRODUCTION

as consisting of those writers who had grown up with the Victorian boys' book and who, although their literary aims may have been higher, were unashamed of trying to recapture some of the pleasures of the books of their youth. Other unabashed examples are Rider Haggard, with *King Solomon's Mines* (1885) – dedicated, in part, to "all the big and little boys who read it", although none of Haggard's later works were slanted towards youngsters; Rudyard Kipling, with *"Captains Courageous"* (1897) and *Kim* (1901); J. M. Barrie, with his play *Peter Pan, or The Boy Who Wouldn't Grow Up* (1904) and its associated books, and Conan Doyle, with *The Lost World* (1912).

Indeed, a feeling that the boys' book may have been in some mysterious way essential to the achievements of the Storytellers was expressed by one of the last editors of *The Strand Magazine*, Reginald Pound, when he lamented, in the 1940s:

> Conan Doyle ... was among the last of the nation's professional story tellers in the old tribal sense. He had that narrative power which seems to have vanished. Literary agents try to 'sell' me other names, but they cannot shake me in a conviction ... that what can be called our racial story tellers are dying out. Merit can be found in some ... but they lack the grand magisterial manner of Rider Haggard, Conan Doyle, John Buchan, W. J. Locke, Anthony Hope, William Le Queux, and others like them. [...] Stories of action and romance gave way between the wars to studies of character and motive by the new men like A. E. Coppard and H. E. Bates, who could not write a boys' story if they tried. And the essence of the narrative writers' success was that they wrote what were really boys' stories.[7]

But to return to *The Boy's Own Paper*: for a publication with moralistic designs on its readers, it did surprisingly well, soon achieving a circulation in the hundreds of thousands which it managed to maintain for many decades, only entering its period of long, slow decline after 1913 when it went monthly. In fact, together with its sister publication, *The Girl's Own Paper* (launched 3 Jan 1880), it became a great British institution – rather like Penguin Books or the BBC in the twentieth century – and is still widely referred to today, in conversation and in journalism, by people who are far too young ever to have seen a copy. The *BOP* was the most famous, but of course it was never alone: in its wake sprang up other boys' papers such as *The Union Jack* (1880-1883); *Chums* (1892-1934); the Newnes monthly *The Captain* (1899-1924), which published P.G. Wodehouse's early school stories; and a whole slew of weeklies launched by the energetic Alfred Harmsworth, later Lord Northcliffe, founder of the Amalgamated Press, including the revived *Union Jack* (1894-1933; renamed *Detective Weekly*, 1933-1940), home of Sexton Blake; *Pluck* (1894-1916); *The Boys' Friend* (1895-1927); *The Girls' Friend* (1899-1931); *The Gem* (1907-1939); *The Magnet* (1908-1940), home of Billy Bunter; *Triumph* (1924-1940); *The Modern Boy* (1928-1939), home of Robert Murray Graydon's Captain Justice; *The Thriller* (1929-1940), home of Leslie Charteris's The Saint; *The Girls' Crystal* (1935-1953); and many, many more. Thousands of issues, millions of pages of excitement, wonder and laughter.

So vigorous were Harmsworth's publications, and the continuing independents such as the *BOP* and *Chums*, not to mention the later products of another weekly fiction factory, the Dundee-based company of D. C. Thomson (*Adventure*, 1921-1961; *The Rover*, 1922-1973; *The Wizard*, 1922-1964; *The Hotspur*, 1933-1959; etc.), that specialised pulp-fiction monthlies on

---

[7] Reginald Pound, *A Maypole in the Strand*, p. 11.

the American model never really took off in Britain: the crucial juvenile section of the British fiction-reading public was already well catered for. (There were of course a number of British pulps – *The Grand Magazine*, *The Novel Magazine*, *The Story-Teller*, *The 20-Story Magazine*, *Hutchinson's Mystery-Story Magazine*, etc., all of which have entries in this book – but they rarely won the enduring affections of a mass public in a way that the best of story papers did.) And alongside, and intermingling with, all these story papers, the boys' book in hardcover form continued to thrive: novels by Harry Collingwood, Herbert Strang, Fenton Ash (Frank Aubrey), Percy F. Westerman, Gunby Hadath, A. Harcourt Burrage, Frank Richards (Charles Hamilton), Captain W. E. Johns, Angus MacVicar and numerous others (including a legion of girls'-book writers) continued to appear throughout the first half of the twentieth century and even into the 1950s and 1960s. The death in 1968 of Captain W. E. Johns, whose Biggles air-adventures were serialised in *The Boy's Own Paper* in its waning days, perhaps marks the end-point for the traditional British boys' book. It was a tradition which lasted rather more than a hundred years, and which now seems to have been killed off by films, radio, comics, television, role-playing games and paperback-original media-spinoff novels. Or perhaps it would be more appropriate to say that it has been killed off by a hundred-and-one social and historical changes, the steady grind of time which crushes all our shared fantasies. Although this was a tradition based in weekly story papers and young people's hardcover "gift books" rather than in adult monthlies, it was an important part of the popular fiction we attempt to map in this book.

But, for all the significance of boys' and girls' papers, the central periodical of the Age of the Storytellers was, of course, an adult monthly, *The Strand Magazine*. Whilst drawing upon the development of British magazines since *The Cornhill* in 1860, *The Strand* looked for its inspiration to the American magazines, many of which had British editions printed in London. *Harper's Monthly* was the first, its "European edition" being published by Sampson Low since December 1880. It was followed by *Century Illustrated Magazine* and *Scribner's Monthly* in November 1881 and January 1887 respectively. These soon had their impact in Britain. The title of Macmillan's *English Illustrated Magazine*, launched in October 1883, was a reassertion of the qualities of British magazine production in retaliation to the *Century Illustrated Magazine*, and its presentation was to show all that was best of the British Arts and Crafts movement. W. T. Stead, who had worked with George Newnes during the 1880s until he founded *Review of Reviews* in January 1890, called the *Century Illustrated* "one of the best, if not the very best, and most widely circulated periodicals in the whole world. In every respect it is admirable and its general get-up is as near perfection as is possible…"[8] Further American influence came with the appearance of the British edition of *Lippincott's Magazine* from Ward, Lock in February 1890, for although its early issues were not so profusely illustrated, its editor, Joseph Stoddart, was building the magazine's reputation on British writers. He had commissioned Arthur Conan Doyle and Oscar Wilde to write short novels which were to be published complete in each issue, the results being Doyle's second Holmes story "The Sign of the Four" and Wilde's study in evil, "The Picture of Dorian Gray".

Perhaps the final straw was the dramatic change in the magazine *Cosmopolitan*. This had been started by a minor publisher in Rochester, in upstate New York, in 1886 but was fading fast when it was bought in 1889 by John Brisben Walker and its offices moved to New York.

---

[8] W. T. Stead, *Index to the Periodicals of 1890* (London: Review of Reviews, 1891), p. 127.

INTRODUCTION

Walker invested a small fortune, giving the magazine a major facelift and promotion. He famously set Elisabeth Bisland off around the world in November 1889 in a race against Nellie Bly from the *New York World*, both of whom were trying to emulate Jules Verne's Phileas Fogg. Bisland's illustrated articles were a significant attraction in *Cosmopolitan*. Writing eighteen months later, W. T. Stead remarked that *Cosmopolitan* is "more smart, more up to date, than any of its rivals, and it is more profusely illustrated." This included photographs.

The ability to reproduce photographs in magazines was a novelty of the 1890s, and one which *The Strand* used to its advantage, but the first issues, in 1891, contrast sharply with earlier magazines in a number of other ways (one of which was price – at just sixpence, it was half the cost of most other middle-class magazines which had usually been priced at a shilling, as had the British edition American titles). There is a greater density of line drawings and wash, particularly for the fiction (photographs were to be used mainly for non-fiction), approaching Newnes's aim of "a picture on every page". In this *The Strand*, and the magazines that followed, were to encourage the emergence of a host of British illustrators, including Charles Crombie, Warwick Goble, H. R. Millar, Warwick Reynolds, W. Heath Robinson, Ernest H. Shepard, J. A. Shepherd, Sidney H. Sime,

"THE PIPE WAS STILL BETWEEN HIS LIPS."

Steven Spurrier, Stanley L. Wood, Lawson Wood, Mabel Lucie Attwell, and of course, Sidney Paget, renowned as the illustrator of the Sherlock Holmes stories (*shown above*).

Above all, there are short stories, and plenty of them. Newnes sometimes has been criticised, in retrospect, for filling the first year's-worth of *The Strand* with translated stories by European authors such as Pushkin, Daudet and Maupassant (and occasional Americans like Frank R. Stockton and Bret Harte); but it may be argued this was a sensible and, at the time, rather revolutionary policy. This way the early *Strand* introduced British readers to the modern short story as such; for prior to 1890, and despite such pioneers as Stevenson and Kipling, this was mainly an American and Continental (French, German, Russian) form of writing. But, as argued in the entry on *The Strand* in this book, the magazine's greatest innovation was the *series short story* – a tight form, usually numbered and run in consecutive issues, essentially invented by Conan Doyle in July 1891 for his first Sherlock Holmes story-series. (He had a few pointers from the long-dead Edgar Allan Poe, but the Chevalier Dupin trilogy of stories had been an "accidental" near-series, appearing in three different American magazines over a period of several years in the 1840s, rather than a series proper.[9]) The Doyle-perfected

---

[9] There had been some numbered story series in earlier magazines, such as the "Noctes Ambrosianae" by John Wilson and others, and "The Shepherd's Calendar" by James Hogg, both of which ran in *Blackwood's* in the 1820s. But these were not tight sequential six- or twelve-part series with a common background and an intrinsic story arc, but loosely connected tales and episodes linked together by a common narrator. Arguably only Samuel Warren's "Passages from the Diary of a Late Physician" also in *Blackwood's* (began Aug 1830 in 18 parts) comes close to the later series sequence established by Doyle but it did not set a precedent. The popularity of the series in book form had been established by Anthony Trollope starting with *The Warden* (Longman, 1855), the first of his Barchester novels.

magazine short-story series was so explosively popular that literally scores of writers emulated it almost immediately – and not only in detective fiction but in other genres too: a few examples are C. J. Cutcliffe Hyne with his Captain Kettle seafaring adventures and Kate and Hesketh Prichard with their Don Q bandit capers (both in *Pearson's Magazine*); and ultimately P. G. Wodehouse with his Jeeves-and-Wooster comedies in *The Strand* (and the American weekly, *The Saturday Evening Post*).

This book concentrates, for the most part, on *The Strand* and its progeny. These fall broadly into two types of monthly: the Standard Illustrated Popular Magazine, of which *The Strand* was the model, and which was the forerunner to the later larger "slick" magazines (see the entry for more discussion of this); and the "all-fiction" (or nearly so) pulp-paper magazine, an off-shoot of the more generalist (and smoother-papered) standard magazines. The first type arose with

The Strand in 1891 (although we include here entries on its predecessors – *Cassell's Magazine*, founded in 1867, and *The English Illustrated Magazine*, founded in 1883) and was soon copied by *The Windsor*, *Pearson's*, *Harmsworth's*, *The Royal* and others. The second type arose around 1905-1907 with *The Novel Magazine* and *The Story-Teller*, and rapidly inspired imitators, from *The Red* and *Everybody's* to a slew of post-war titles including *The Blue*, *Adventure-Story* and *20-Story*. The first type flourished mainly in the years up to 1914, and the others mainly in the years after 1914 and up to the beginning of World War II in 1939 (see the "Chronology" for a schedule of magazine births and deaths). However, it should not be assumed that one type simply replaced the other. The standard illustrated magazines, or "proto-slicks", of 1891-1914 carried on, some of them, just as long as the "pulps" did, not least *The Strand* itself, which remained essentially unchanged until 1941 (it staggered through its last eight-and-a-bit years, to 1950, in a quite different format, that of the new "digest-sized" magazines).

From 1907 to 1941, both forms of magazine – proto-slick and pulp – existed side by side, complementing each other, and with much overlap of content, writers like Agatha Christie, E. Phillips Oppenheim or P. G. Wodehouse contributing with ease to both. The only differences were that the proto-slicks were printed on good-quality paper and had more variegated content, non-fiction as well as fiction, while the pulp magazines were printed on rougher paper and largely eschewed non-fiction. The smoother-papered magazines also attracted more advertising (printed on fore-and-aft pages, separate from the main body of the magazine itself) – which, of course, was the point of the higher-quality paper. One could claim that the fiction in the proto-slicks was more "literary" than that in the pulp magazines; but plenty of counter examples could be adduced. G. K. Chesterton's finely crafted Father Brown stories first appeared in a pulp, *The Story-Teller* (from 1910), then moved to the proto-slicks and slicks.

On the whole, Britain failed to develop a distinct "field" of pulp magazines in the way that America did. In the US "pulp fiction", meaning primarily popular and generic fiction published originally in pulp-paper magazines, has gained an almost mythological status; but not so in Britain, except by contagion from the US (the average British reader today, questioned about pulp magazines, would probably reply that they were an American phenomenon, and be quite

INTRODUCTION

unaware that there were any UK pulps). We have speculated above that this may have been partly because of the strength of the juvenile story-paper tradition in the UK; but there may be other reasons, for example the relatively slow development in Britain of the "slick" magazine (which in America made the pulps all the more conspicuous by sharp contrast); or, indeed, it may have been due in part to the very prestige, persistence and unchangingness of *The Strand* until World War II. It is because of this interpenetration of the two types of magazine, proto-slick and pulp, and because of the lack of an awareness in Britain of any real distinction between them, that we think it appropriate to deal with the two kinds together in this book.

Of course, other types of fiction-bearing magazine have arisen in the UK since the magazines we describe here – and these are (or were) also of two (much more sharply divided) kinds. On the one hand, there is what is known in American parlance (dating from the 1920s) as the "big slick" (a British illustrator, the late Alfred Bestall, referred to them endearingly as "the big shinies") – i.e. magazines which take a larger, flatter format, usually on quality paper, and have fully integrated advertising (rather than fore-and-aft). On the other hand, there is (or was) the so-called "digest-sized" magazine, taking its small format from *The Reader's Digest* in 1922 and pioneered, as far as fiction is concerned, in America by *Ellery Queen's Mystery Magazine* (from 1941). Both these latter-day formats began to become reasonably common in Britain in the 1930s, overlapping in time with the then-surviving proto-slicks and pulps; both came fully into their own after World War II, and especially from the 1950s onwards. The UK version of *Good Housekeeping* was an early example of a "slick" and *Lilliput* an early example of a "digest" (matched in America by the broadly similar *Coronet*). But, with a few exceptions, we don't deal in this book with magazines of these later formats. The exceptions are those magazines of the older types which metamorphosed into slicks or digests – *Nash's Pall Mall* is the leading example of the former case (from 1923); and *The Strand* itself the leading (if unhappy) example of the latter (from 1941).

*

To return to a question raised earlier: if the Age of the Storytellers began in 1880, ten years before *The Strand Magazine*, when did it end? In the classic sense, the sense intended by Roger Lancelyn Green, it clearly came to an end in 1914, the year of the outbreak of the Great War, which had a considerable effect on British publishing, as on so many things. *The Strand*, *Pearson's*, *The Windsor* and numerous other magazines, continued to appear, but the world around them was changing. For one thing, it was no longer Britain's world; in economic, as well as literary, terms it was fast becoming America's world. After 1914, the big money, and the big magazines, were in the States, and British writers increasingly aimed their efforts at selling transatlantically. Also, around 1914, competition from another medium of entertainment, the cinema, began to intensify (although arguably it would not be until the coming of the talkies, in the late 1920s, swiftly followed by mass radio in the 1930s, that new media began to draw audiences away from reading to an extent that really mattered). Moreover, the essential writers of the Age of the Storytellers were ageing or, in some cases, already deceased. One could argue that the "big five" of the Storytellers' generation – those who combined popularity with real imaginative quality and an ability to produce long-lasting works – were Robert Louis Stevenson (1850-1894), H. Rider Haggard (1856-1925), A. Conan Doyle (1859-1930), Rudyard Kipling (1865-1936) and H. G. Wells (1866-1946). Of the survivors, all had done their best work by 1914. They were to go on writing into the 1920s and 1930s, even into the 1940s in Wells's case, but none of their later fiction had much impact on the world – at any rate, not when compared with the sort of impact they had made decades earlier. A writer like Doyle could still command high rates, and his appearance in an issue of *The Strand* might still bump up the magazine's circulation; but the imaginative force was gone. The same was true of Kipling and Wells (less so of Haggard, whose reputation had slumped by the time of the war – although he continued writing, for a shrinking audience, until his death in 1925).

Much the same was true of most of the other writers who collectively define the Age of the Storytellers in our retrospective imaginations – F. Anstey, Hall Caine, S. R. Crockett, Kenneth Grahame, Robert Hichens, Anthony Hope, E. W. Hornung, C. J. Cutcliffe Hyne, W. W. Jacobs, Jerome K. Jerome, Andrew Lang, Arthur Machen, A. E. W. Mason, L. T. Meade, Henry Seton Merriman, Arthur Morrison, Edith Nesbit, Barry Pain, Gilbert Parker, Arthur Quiller-Couch, W. Pett Ridge, H. de Vere Stacpoole, Bram Stoker, Stanley J. Weyman, Oscar Wilde – the list could go on and on. Some of these people continued to write – Hyne and Mason, like Wells, were active as late as the 1940s – but the magic had evaporated. On the other hand, there were younger writers who had begun their careers in the 1890s or 1900s, and who therefore were fully a part of the Age of the Storytellers, who did go on to flourish in the 1920s and later. They include E. F. Benson, Algernon Blackwood, John Buchan, G. K. Chesterton, Lord Dunsany, Jeffery Farnol, R. Austin Freeman, Edgar Jepson, Baroness Orczy, Sax Rohmer, Rafael Sabatini, Edgar Wallace, P.G. Wodehouse and P. C. Wren. And they were joined by a new cadre of popular writers who began their careers around the time of World War I or soon after. So perhaps we need to posit a second half to the Age of the Storytellers, a "silver age" to the previous half's "golden age". *The Strand Magazine* lasted until 1950, so maybe that makes an appropriate final cut-off point for the Storyteller Age. As it happens, the 70-year period covered by this book (*The Strand*'s 60 years plus ten beforehand) divides neatly into two approximate 35-year periods, pivoting around the year the world changed, 1914.

So let us imagine that the years 1915-1950 were a Silver Age of the Storytellers. It was a period still rich in fiction-carrying magazines (at least up until 1939), and, thanks to new printing techniques and intensified marketplace competition, they were more colourful than ever, with brighter and more varied covers and more lavish internal illustrations. If anything, fiction dominated these magazines more than before the War, with the illustrated features that had so popularized *The Strand* and its imitators now taking a back-seat or shifting into the slicks or more specialist magazines. Spurred on by the success of *The Story-Teller*, other magazines had adopted the all-fiction approach, including the venerable *Cassell's*, so that by the 1920s there was a profusion of general fiction pulps, including *The New Magazine, The Premier, The Red, The Blue, 20-Story Magazine* and *Hutchinson's* (which switched from standard to slick to pulp). Even *The Strand* and especially *Pearson's* adopted a similar guise, making the Roaring Twenties the last haven of the popular fiction magazine.

Other magazines became specialist in the fiction they published. In titles like *Adventure-Story* (from 1922), *The Detective Magazine* (1922), *The Happy Mag.* (1922), *Mystery-Story* (1923), *Romance* (1923), *The Jolly Mag.* (1927), *Hush* (1930), *Air Stories* (1935) and *Tales of Wonder* (1937) – we begin to see the division of popular fiction into the modern, labelled genres we have since come to take for granted: crime fiction, the humour, the love story, science-fiction, etc. Women's magazines, starting from the *Strand*-imitation, *Woman at Home*

INTRODUCTION

in 1893, continued to flourish from the 1920s on and increasingly these entered the territory of the "slicks" with magazines like *The Home Magazine, Good Housekeeping, Britannia and Eve* and *Woman*, which allowed great exposure to advertisements to which women responded better than men. Such "genre-fication" of mass-market fiction was a noted feature of the Silver Age.

Character series, Holmes-style, continued to proliferate, introducing some, like William Brown, Hercule Poirot (*right*), Fu Manchu or Winnie-the-Pooh, who have lived on in popular memory. In addition to the survivors of the pre-1914 old guard, the writers who filled these magazines often enjoyed great, sometimes immense, popularity – Margery Allingham, Michael Arlen, Stacy Aumonier, H. C. Bailey, John Dickson Carr, Leslie Charteris, Peter Cheyney, Agatha Christie, Richmal Crompton, E. M. Delafield, Ethel M. Dell, Daphne du Maurier, C. S. Forester, Stella Gibbons, Bruce Graeme, Graham Greene, L. Patrick Greene, Georgette Heyer, E. M. Hull, W. E. Johns, Gerald Kersh, Compton Mackenzie, Ngaio Marsh, A. A. Milne, J. B. Priestley, Arthur Ransome, "Sapper", Dorothy L. Sayers, Hugh Walpole, Henry Williamson, Dornford Yates – and alongside them the

evergreen P. G. Wodehouse (who would write until he dropped, in 1975). If these names, collectively, do not have quite the lustre of the generations of writers who established themselves before 1914 – well, that may be in the eye of the beholder. Agatha Christie, the *Guinness Books of Records* tells us, is the bestselling fictionist of "all time", not only in Britain but around the world, with over a billion books sold. As for fictional characters who have entered common mythology, perhaps C. S. Forester's Horatio Hornblower and Wodehouse's Jeeves and Wooster, with a few others, deserve to stand in the same pantheon as Long John Silver, Dr Jekyll and Mr Hyde, Sherlock Holmes, Mowgli, Fu Manchu, A. J. Raffles and Count Dracula, though one gets the feeling one may be straining to be generous.

The trouble with the Silver Age writers is that they were varying the templates rather than creating them. Most later detectives are faint echoes of the great Sherlock, just as most later science-fiction monsters are mere shadows of Wells's Martians, Morlocks and Dr Moreau. The authors of the Golden Age of the Storytellers created all the templates, and in a sense, wrote all the scripts, for the twentieth century. The Silver Age writers were able to embroider a little on that achievement, but they could not match it.

The other problem with the Silver Age is that it was increasingly in decline unlike the Golden Age, which was full of promise. Despite a flourish in the 1920s, when there were more fiction magazines in print than at any other time, the end was in sight. The Depression of the 1930s was an economic factor that culled many magazines, but it was accompanied by changing habits for those who had greater leisure time. The growth in cinema and the radio cut deeply into what once was valuable reading time, and greater freedom and other pursuits, particularly for men, cut into reading habits. Cheap books, especially the growth in paperbacks during the 1930s, took over from magazines. The biggest single example for this came when Walter Hutchinson closed his magazine empire in 1929 to invest in large-scale cheap book production. The thirties saw a massive increase in bargain books with the novel supreme and the bumper anthology superseding the magazine. Men's reading habits changed whilst women's magazines reduced the emphasis on fiction in favour of household features and celebrity. The women's "slick" magazines became the new magazine standard and these demanded high advertising revenues something the general fiction magazine could not support. Some titles, such as *The London*, *The Royal* and even *Pearson's* made a half-hearted attempt to adapt, but rapidly went under. It was only with huge investment that new titles like *Britannia and Eve* could survive. Other companies turned either to the specialist markets – particularly women and young adults or later, with *Men Only* and *Lilliput*, a much changed men's market.

What economics or fashion had not already blighted, the Second World War ended. Of our primary magazines only *The Strand* survived, though a few other old warhorses like *Blackwood's*, *Chambers's Journal*, even *The Quiver*, coped by appealing to their loyal readers. But the Silver Age was really over by 1940, and *The Strand*'s final years scarcely glowed.

Yet, in a neat squaring of the circle, the very last serial *The Strand Magazine* ran (Dec 1948-Feb 1949), and which may therefore be said to have brought the Age of the Storytellers to a close, was a condensation of John Connell's forthcoming novel *The Return of Long John Silver*. The author, a journalist whose birth name was John Henry Robertson (Connell was his mother's maiden name) also won an important literary award, the James Tait Black Memorial Prize, in that same year, 1949. The award was not for his novel but a biography, *W. E. Henley* (1949). We may safely assume that John Connell's researches into the life of the late-Victorian poet and editor, the original "model" for Long John Silver, had also inspired him to write a sequel to Stevenson's *Treasure Island*, a sequel which concentrated on the life of the peg-legged old pirate at the story's heart. Thus, to stretch the point to its ultimate, one could argue that the Age of the Storytellers began and ended with William Ernest Henley.

By March 1950, almost all the magazines covered in this book were gone. They had few replacements. The favoured media of today, cinema, radio and television, owe an immense amount to them and to the writers they nurtured. They should be remembered.

David Pringle & Mike Ashley
June 2005

USER GUIDE

Content
This book is divided into two main parts plus several subsidiary sections. The main part consists of seventy entries in A-Z format covering the major fiction magazines. These are magazines where fiction was over 50% of the magazine's content (based over its whole run) and was thus the enduring image of the magazine. Needless to say whilst most magazines fit comfortably within this section there are always borderline cases. Likewise there are many other magazines in which fiction was less than 50% of the content and yet where that fiction may have been significant, at least for a period, and one of the major attractions of that magazine. Since they also contributed to the Age of the Storyteller it is difficult to exclude these titles and so there is a second section, with shorter entries to catch those titles of interest which fall through the net of the primary section. This second section also includes the longer-running magazines such as *Blackwood's, The Cornhill* and *Chambers's Journal*, which were really the product of the Victorian age and were already old when *The Strand* appeared and yet which continued through and way beyond the Age of the Storyteller to linger like living fossils into the Television Age.

In addition to these two main sections there is a Chronology, to set the magazines and their fiction into an historical timeline, plus an Index to Editors and another to Publishers. Both indices and the chronology relates to all of the magazines in both main sections.

Format for entries
Heading. At the start of each entry under Primary Magazines is listed the total number of issues published plus the dates and volume numbers of the first and last issues. Dates are also given for issues where there is a title change or other significant variation. Note that months in the Heading are written out in full but elsewhere all months are abbreviated to their first three letters (Jan, Feb, etc) or four for September (Sept).
Supplemental. After each entry are a series of notes and data sources. These are in a standard format, and the extent of detail varies depending on the scale and complexity of the magazine. Most of it is self explanatory, but the following provides some notes for help.
Frequency: Identifies frequency of publication with dates for any changes.
Publisher: Name of publisher with dates of any changes. Unless specifically stated, the place of publication is London.
Editors: Names of editors and, where known, the dates of their tenure. All too few editors were named so it is not always possible to cite specific issues. If not known, years are stated rather than months, but if an approximate month is known it is stated with a question mark.

Format/Size: Indicates the size and nature of the magazine and the dates of any changes. This heading also covers changes in pagination, though where this gets complicated pagination is given a separate heading. Most magazines are bound in signatures which rise in multiples of 4, 8, 16, 32 and so on, so it is quite common for a magazine to have, for example, 112 pages one month and 116 another or 108. These small changes are not noted, but are expressed as 108/112, etc. Only significant and sustained changes are noted. Christmas issues were often considerably larger but these are not noted separately.

There are no standard recognised words or phrases for magazine sizes, and their bindings can vary significantly from book sizes such as quarto, octavo and so on. To simplify matters in this Guide we have used a common set of phrases to distinguish between the size and format of the magazine, as follows:

Standard. The size and format adopted by the regular magazines from *The Strand* onwards. Most of these were printed on high quality coated paper (though many had to reduce to newsprint during the First World War). They usually have substantial advertising sections fore and aft. If the magazine was printed on cheap paper, either newsprint or pulp, it is described as "Standard, pulp". The standard size was 240 x 165mm (9½ x 6½ inches), though some may be slightly smaller. Further details will be found in those entries.

Slick. The size and format adopted by *Nash's* and *Home Magazine* which became the new standard size for most glossy general interest women's magazines. It measures 280 x 220mm (11 x 8⅔ inches). These magazines are always on heavy coated stock and have integrated advertisements.

Digest. The size made popular by *Reader's Digest* and to which many magazines turned during and after the Second World War. Usually 190 x 130mm (7½ x 5 inches). These magazines may be on glossy paper but most are on good quality newsprint. Advertising is less and is usually integrated.

Pocket-book. The size taken by most popular paperbacks in the forties and fifties, measuring 180 x 110mm (7 x 4⅓ inches). The pages are almost always good quality book paper.

Tabloid. The size adopted by most of the regular daily newspapers. It was a common size for the early boys' papers, and the paper could be either "slick" or newsprint. The dimensions can vary and here it covers a range from 450 x 360mm (17¾ x 14¼ inches) to 360 x 260mm (14¼ x 10¼ inches). The larger extremes are sometimes called *folio*.

Price: This is the cover price of the magazine shown in old pence. One shilling is the equivalent of five pence today. Christmas and Summer special issues would sometimes be more expensive but this one-off variance is not noted.

Other editions: This provides details of any variant editions, usually American.

References: Cites any significant source for further data on the magazine, including Indexes.

Anthologies: Lists any multi-author anthologies that have been compiled wholly from the magazine under discussion.

Holdings. Lists any significant library holdings. It covers complete or near-complete runs and only lists smaller runs if that magazine is rare and these are the only runs known.

Collecting points. Brief note on the general availability of magazines plus notes on bindings.

This degree of detail is not included for the magazines listed in the second section, though this does record the number of issues, with start-finish dates, and details of publishers and editors.

Circulation data.
Formal circulation data is seldom published and publishers may mask true sales figures by referring to print runs or gross sales rather than nett sales, which include returns. In 1904 the Advertisers' Protection Society (A.P.S.) was established with the express purpose of obtaining accurate sales figures. These, together with reports and analysis were published in *The A.P.S. Monthly Circular*, which ran until 1920 after which the Society was reincorporated as *The Incorporated Society of British Advertisers* and the magazine became *The I.S.B.A. Monthly Circular* which ran until 1922. All circulation figures quoted are from this source unless otherwise stated.

Illustrations.
Every effort has been made to include one or more representative covers of each magazine within the entry (in black and white) and in the colour plates. It has not always been easy to find covers in good condition. Bound volumes of magazines usually lack the covers, and even those with covers included may be bound too tight or are too fragile to allow reproduction of the cover. Many covers on single issues have faded or suffered from the ravages of time or have dealer's stamps or other marks. Whilst good copies have been used wherever possible, it was thought that any cover reproduction was better than none, so that in a few instances poorer quality covers have been used. In other instances the publisher's volume binding has been used where it is of more interest and of better quality than the individual magazine. The majority of these covers come from my own collection but a few have been provided by the British Library and the Bodleian Library, Oxford.

*

Every effort has been made to ensure that the information in this Guide is both complete and accurate and hopefully any inadvertent errors have been kept to the minimum. One of the hardest areas for completeness is information on magazine editors and the dates of their tenure. Few magazines identified their editors and some data published in reference books and market reports of the day are contradictory. There are some gaps in this information and the compilers of this book welcome any feedback which may help update these facts. Similarly it has not been possible to check all libraries for magazine holdings though where long runs were known to exist via WorldCat and other sources these were double-checked for accuracy. The holdings at the British Library and the Bodleian have all been personally verified. Nevertheless there may be errors in some listings and other major holdings may have been overlooked. Feedback on significant library or private holdings is welcomed.

CHRONOLOGY

The following charts the key dates relating to the magazines covered in this Guide. The first column lists significant dates for the magazines themselves (first/last issues, name/publisher changes and so on). The second column lists key stories in the magazines plus a few other selected stories and events (e.g. author's/editor's/ artist's deaths) in the wider literary world. Magazine dates cited relate to the cover date although in most cases the magazine was on sale up to three weeks prior to that date.

Magazine event (relating to magazines in this Guide)	Date	Key stories and other significant events
first issue *The Boy's Own Paper* (18th)	**1879** Jan	
	1881 Oct	"Treasure Island" by Robert Louis Stevenson begins, *Young Folks* (1st); first issue of George Newnes's *Tit-Bits* (22nd)
first issue *Longman's Magazine*	**1882** Nov	
first issue *The English Illustrated Magazine*	**1883** Oct	first issue *Cassell's Saturday Journal* (6th)
	1884 Feb	Society of Authors founded (18th)
	1885 Sept	*King Solomon's Mines* by H. Rider Haggard published (30th)
	1886 Jan	"The Mayor of Casterbridge" by Thomas Hardy begins, *The Graphic* (2nd)
	Oct	"She" by H. Rider Haggard begins, *The Graphic* (2nd)
	Nov	first issue of *The British Weekly* (5th)

CHRONOLOGY

Magazine event		Key stories and other significant events
	1887	
	Jan	"Allan Quatermain" by H. Rider Haggard begins, *Longman's Magazine*
first issue of *Atalanta*	Oct	
	Nov	First Sherlock Holmes novel, "A Study in Scarlet" by A. Conan Doyle, *Beeton's Christmas Annual*
	1888	
	Jun	first issue of Harmsworth's *Answers* (2nd)
	Aug	"Three Men in a Boat" by Jerome K. Jerome begins, *Home Chimes*
	Oct	Stanley J. Weyman's first historical novel, "The House of the Wolf" begins, *English Illustrated Magazine*
	1889	
first issue *Magazine of Short Stories* (12th)	Jan	
	1890	
first issue of *Lambert's Monthly*	Jan	
	Feb	"The Sign of the Four" by A. Conan Doyle, *Lippincott's Magazine*
	Jun	"The Picture of Dorian Gray" by Oscar Wilde, *Lippincott's Magazine* "The Story of the Glittering Plain" by William Morris begins, *English Illustrated Magazine*.
	Jul	first issue *Pearson's Weekly* (26th)
	1891	
first issue *The Strand Magazine*	Jan	
first issue *Black and White* (6th)	Feb	
last issue of *Lambert's Monthly* and first issue *The Ludgate Monthly*	May	
	Jul	"The Adventures of Sherlock Holmes" begins, *The Strand*; "Tess of the d'Urbervilles" by Thomas Hardy begins in *The Graphic* (4th)
	1892	
	Jan	last issue *Tinsley's Magazine*
first issue *The Idler*	Feb	
first issue *The Search Light*	Mar	first issue *Ludgate Weekly Magazine* (5th) first issue *The Million* (26th)
first issue of *Chums* (12th)	Sept	
Edward Arnold takes over publication of *The English Illustrated Magazine*	Oct	last issue *Ludgate Weekly Magazine* (1st)

21

Magazine event	1893	Key stories and other significant events
first issue *The Sketch* (1st)	Feb	first important female fictional detective, Loveday Brooke, created by C. L. Pirkis, appears in *The Ludgate*
first issues of *The Pall Mall Magazine* and *The Butterfly*	May	
Magazine of Short Stories taken over by Pearson's and retitled *Short Stories* (15th)	Jul	
Illustrated London News assumes publication of *English Illustrated Magazine* first issue *The Woman at Home*	Oct	
Pall Mall Magazine runs first colour plate; first issue of weekly *To-Day* (11th)	Nov	"Rikki-Tikki-Tavi" by Rudyard Kipling, *Pall Mall Magazine*
	Dec	Doyle kills off Sherlock Holmes in "The Adventure of the Final Problem", *The Strand*.
	1894	
	Jan	"Trilby" by George du Maurier begins, *Harper's Monthly* "The Collaborators", first important story by Robert S. Hichens, *Pall Mall Magazine*
last issue *The Butterfly*	Feb	
	Mar	Martin Hewitt series by Arthur Morrison begins, *The Strand*
first issue *The Yellow Book*.	Apr	
last issue *The Search Light*	Sept	
	Dec	death of Robert Louis Stevenson (3rd)
	1895	
first issues of *The Windsor* and *The Minster*	Jan	first appearance of Dr Nikola in "A Bid for Fortune" by Guy Boothby, *The Windsor*
	Mar	last issue of *All the Year Round* (30th)
first issue *Chapman's Magazine*	May	*The Time Machine* by H. G. Wells published after running in *The New Review* (Jan-May)
Jerome K. Jerome becomes sole editor of *The Idler*; first issue of *Badminton Magazine*	Aug	first story by Walter de la Mare, "Kismet", *The Sketch* (7th)
first issue of *Pearson's Story-Teller* (9th)	Oct	
Black & White acquire *The Ludgate*	Nov	
	1896	
first issues *Pearson's Magazine* and *The Savoy*	Jan	"A Grey Sleeve", Stephen Crane's British debut in *English Illustrated Magazine*
last issue *The Minster*	Mar	The Publishers' Association founded
	Jun	Captain Kettle appears in "Stealing a President" by Cutcliffe Hyne, *Pearson's Magazine*

CHRONOLOGY

Magazine event	(1896)	Key stories and other significant events
Lord Hamilton assumes sole editorship of *The Pall Mall Magazine*; first appearance of a readers' letter column in a monthly magazine in *The Windsor*	Sept	
first issue *The Temple Magazine*	Oct	
first issues of *The Lady's Realm* and *The Osborne*	Nov	
Max Pemberton becomes editor of *Cassell's Family Magazine*; last issue *The Savoy*	Dec	
	1897	
	Jan	first issue of *Country Life*
first issue *Eureka*; last issue *The Yellow Book*	Apr	"The War of the Worlds" by H. G. Wells begins in *Pearson's Magazine*
last issue of *The Osborne*	May	
	Jun	"The Invisible Man" by H. G. Wells begins in *Pearson's Weekly* (12th); death of Margaret Oliphant (25th)
Cassell's Family Magazine retitled *Cassell's Magazine*	Dec	
	1898	
first issue *The Black Cat*; J. M. Dent take over publication of *The Idler*	Feb	
	Mar	death of Aubrey Beardsley (16th)
first issue *Physical Culture* (later *Sandow's Magazine*)	Apr	
	Jun	first appearance of Raffles in "In the Chains of Crime" by E. W. Hornung, *Cassell's Magazine*
first issue *The Harmsworth Monthly Pictorial Magazine*	Jul	
W. R. Russell takes over publication of *The Idler*	Aug	
last issue of *Atalanta*	Sept	
	Oct	R. Austin Freeman's first story, "The Resurrection of Matthew Jephson", *Cassell's Magazine*; W. Somerset Maugham's first story, "Don Sebastian", *Cosmopolis*; first issue *The New Penny Magazine*
first issue *The Royal Magazine*; *Chapman's Magazine* retitled *Crampton's Magazine*	Nov	
last issue *London Society*	Dec	first known story by Rafael Sabatini, "The Red Mask", *The Ludgate*; "Stalky and Co." series by Rudyard Kipling begins in *The Windsor Magazine*

23

THE AGE OF THE STORYTELLERS

Magazine event	1899	Key stories and other significant events
	Jan	"When the Sleeper Awakes" by H. G. Wells begins in *The Graphic* (7th)
	Feb	"Heart of Darkness" by Joseph Conrad begins in *Blackwood's Magazine*
The Butterfly reappears	Mar	
first issue *The Captain*; *Physical Culture* retitled *Sandow's Magazine*	Apr	
Arthur Lawrence becomes editor of *The Idler*	May	
last issue of *Belgravia*	Jun	first issue *The Penny Pictorial Magazine* (10th)
New Century Press takes over publishing *The Black Cat*	Jul	"The Lost Continent" by C. J. Cutcliffe Hyne begins, *Pearson's Magazine*
	Oct	death of Grant Allen (28th)
	Dec	first story by Ethel M. Dell, "In Her Majesty's Service", *The Ludgate*
	1900	
first issues of *The Charing Cross Magazine*, *The Sunday Strand* and *The Sphere* (27th)	Jan	
first issue *The Universal Magazine*; *The Butterfly* folds again	Feb	
last issue *The Black Cat*	Mar	
last issue *The Charing Cross Magazine*	May	
Horace Marshall takes over publication of *The Idler*	Aug	
Sidney Sime becomes editor of *The Idler*; New Century Press ceases and *Crampton's Magazine* passes to new publisher	Sept	
	Nov	death of Oscar Wilde (30th)
	1901	
first issue *The Lady's Magazine*; George R. Halkett becomes editor of *The Pall Mall Magazine*	Jan	"The Eternal City" by Hall Caine begins in *The Lady's Magazine*; "Kim" by Rudyard Kipling begins in *Cassell's Magazine*; "The Purple Cloud" by M. P. Shiel begins in *The Royal Magazine*
Dawbarn & Ward take over publication of *The Idler*	Feb	
The Ludgate merges with *The Universal* as *The Universal and Ludgate Magazine*	Mar	
	May	"The Old Man in the Corner" series by Baroness Orczy begins, *The Royal Magazine*
	Aug	"The Hound of the Baskervilles" begins in *The Strand*; sales allegedly hit 500,000
	Sept	last issue of *The Argosy*

CHRONOLOGY

Magazine event	(1901)	Key stories and other significant events
T. Fisher Unwin takes over publication of *The English Illustrated Magazine*	Oct	
The Harmsworth Magazine finally becomes *The London Magazine*	Nov	
	1902	
last issue *The Universal Magazine*	Jan	
Robert Barr resumes editorship of *The Idler*	Apr	
	Jun	"The Adventures of Romney Pringle" by "Clifford Ashdown" begins in *Cassell's Magazine*
Chatto & Windus takes over publication of *The Idler*	Oct	
Last issue *Crampton's Magazine*	Dec	
	1903	
	Feb	"Pro Patria", Somerset Maugham's first story in *Pall Mall Magazine*
Hutchinson takes over publication of *The English Illustrated Magazine*; first issue *The Holborn Monthly Magazine*	Apr	
	Jun	death of W. E. Henley (11th)
	Aug	death of artist Phil May (5th)
last issue *The Temple Magazine*	Sept	
	Nov	first story by Arthur S. Ward ("Sax Rohmer") "The Mysterious Mummy", *Pearson's Magazine*
	Dec	first issue *The Bystander* (9th)
	1904	
first issue *Horlick's Magazine*	Jan	
first issue *Yes or No* (19th)	Mar	
first issues of *The Realm* and *Fry's Magazine*; last issue *The Holborn Monthly Magazine*	Apr	
last issue of Pearson's *Short Stories*	Jun	"The Club of Queer Trades" by G. K. Chesterton begins in *The Idler*; "The Loot of Cities" by Arnold Bennett begins in *The Windsor Magazine*
The Lady's Magazine retitled *The Lady's Home Magazine*	Jul	
last issue *The Realm*	Sept	
	Oct	P. G. Wodehouse's first appearance in an adult magazine, "An Afternoon Dip", *Pearson's Magazine*
first issue *The World & His Wife*	Nov	

Magazine event	1905	Key stories and other significant events
Pall Mall Magazine drops cover price to 6d; *Sandow's Magazine* becomes a weekly and drops fiction	Jan	H. G. Wells's "Kipps" and Joseph Conrad's "The Mirror of the Sea" both begin, *Pall Mall Magazine*; "The Railway Children" by Edith Nesbit begins, *The London Magazine*
first issue *The Grand Magazine*	Feb	death of Guy Boothby (26th)
last issues of *The Home Magazine of Fiction* and *Horlick's Magazine*	Mar	
first issue *The Novel Magazine*	Apr	
Charles Morley becomes editor of *The Pall Mall Magazine*; last issue of *To-Day* (19th)	Jul	
	Sept	death of George MacDonald (18th)
last issue, *Longman's Magazine*	Oct	Edgar Wallace publishes *The Four Just Men*
	Dec	Mabel Lucie Attwell's artwork appears in *Pearson's Magazine*
	1906	
Pearson's Magazine begins crusading articles, "Pressing Problems of the Day"	Jan	"Puck of Pook's Hill" by Rudyard Kipling begins, *The Strand Magazine*
	Feb	first story by Arthur Ransome "The Pipe from the Rue Pignon", *Temple Bar*
Good Words merges with *Sunday Magazine*	Apr	
	Jun	death of George Griffith (4th)
last issue *Temple Bar*	Dec	"Vaiti of the Islands" by Beatrice Grimshaw begins, *Pearson's Magazine*
	1907	
	Jan	first story by Oliver Sandys (as Olive Bree), "A Woman", *The Novel Magazine*
first issue *The Story-Teller*.	Apr	"The Adventures of Arsène Lupin" by Maurice Leblanc begins, *The Story-Teller*
first issue *The Imp*	Jun	
last issue *Macmillan's Magazine*	Oct	
	1908	
	Jan	H.G. Wells's "The War in the Air" begins, *Pall Mall Magazine*; *The Blue Lagoon* by H. de Vere Stacpoole, published; death of Sidney Paget (29th)
	Feb	first issue *The Magnet* (15th)
first issue *The Red Magazine*	Jun	
	Dec	first appearance of Raymond Chandler with poem "The Unknown Love", *Chambers's Journal* (19th); first Dr Thorndyke story, "The Blue Sequin" by R. Austin Freeman, *Pearson's Magazine*

CHRONOLOGY

Magazine event	1909	Key stories and other significant events
first issue *Sievier's Monthly*	Jan	
first issues *The White Magazine* and *The Sunday Journal* (8th; retitled *The Story Journal* from Sept)	Mar	
first issues *Nash's Magazine* and *The New Magazine*	Apr	death of F. Marion Crawford (9th)
first issue *Weekly Tale-Teller* (8th)	May	
	Jun	"The Adventures of Lady Molly of Scotland Yard" by Baroness Orczy begins, *Cassell's Magazine*
The Pall Mall Magazine adds 'The Pall Mall Story Book' section; last issue *The White Magazine*	Jul	Edgar Wallace's first important magazine story, "The Barford Snake", *Pall Mall Magazine*; death of Oswald Crawfurd (31st)
Newnes takes over publication of *Woman at Home*	Aug	death of George Manville Fenn (26th)
	Sept	first Sanders of the River story by Edgar Wallace, "The Wood of Devils", *Weekly Tale-Teller* (25th)
first issue *Everybody's Story Magazine*; Stanley Paul take over publication of *The Lady's Realm*	Nov	
	1910	
	Jan	"The Brain", the first Smiler Bunn story by Bertram Atkey, *The Grand*
The Red Magazine switches from monthly to twice-monthly schedule	Mar	
	Apr	death of Mark Twain (21st)
last issue *The World & His Wife*	May	first story by Dornford Yates, "Temporary Insanity", *Punch* (25th)
The Sunday Strand merged with *Woman at Home*	Jun	deaths of O. Henry (W.S. Porter) (5th) and Sir George Newnes (9th)
	Sept	first Father Brown series by G. K. Chesterton, *The Story-Teller*; "The Babes in the Wood" by Dornford Yates, *Pearson's Magazine*
first issue *T.P.'s Magazine*	Oct	
last issue *Sievier's Monthly*	Nov	
	1911	
	Jan	"The Lodger" by Marie Belloc Lowndes, *Nash's Magazine*
National Magazine Company formed and takes over publication of *Nash's Magazine*	Feb	"The Common Law" by Robert W. Chambers begins, *Nash's Magazine*
last issue *The Idler*	Mar	

Magazine event	(1911)	Key stories and other significant events
	May	start of Craig Kennedy series by Arthur B. Reeve, *Nash's Magazine*
last issue *The Imp*	Nov	death of W. Clark Russell (8th)
	1912	
Everybody's Story Magazine becomes *Everyone's Story Magazine*; *Black and White* merges with *The Sphere* (13th)	Jan	
Cassell's Magazine relaunched in pulp format as *Cassell's Magazine of Fiction*; Newman Flower takes over as editor	Apr	sinking of the *Titanic*, with deaths of Jacques Futrelle and W. T. Stead (15th); death of Bram Stoker (20th)
	May	Talbot Mundy's first appearance in a British magazine with "The Soul of a Regiment", *Grand Magazine*
last issue *T.P.'s Magazine*	Jul	
first issue *The Magpie*	Aug	
	Oct	first appearance of Dr Fu Manchu in "The Zayat Kiss" by Sax Rohmer, *The Story-Teller*; death of Robert Barr (21st)
	1913	
Iliffe & Co. take over publication of *The Pall Mall Magazine*	Jan	
	Apr	"The Methods of Moris Klaw" by Sax Rohmer begins, *The New Magazine*
last issue *The English Illustrated Magazine*	Aug	
first issue *The Club Room*; *Everyone's Story Magazine* relaunched as family paper, *Everyone's*; *Boy's Own Paper* switches from weekly to monthly publication	Nov	
	1914	
last issue *Everyone's*	Apr	
first issue *The Premier Magazine*; probable date for last issue *The Club Room*	May	
first issue of *Colour*; last issue *The Story Journal* (31st)	Aug	
last issue *Pall Mall Magazine*, merges with *Nash's Magazine*	Sept	
	Nov	"The First Hundred Thousand" by John Hay Beith ("Ian Hay") begins, *Blackwood's Magazine*
last issue *The Magpie*	Dec	

CHRONOLOGY

Magazine event	1915	Key stories and other significant events
	Jan	death of Peter Keary (29th)
	Feb	death of Mary E. Braddon (4th)
first issue *The Passing Show* (20th)	Mar	death of Walter Crane (14th)
	May	sinking of *Lusitania*, with deaths of Elbert Hubbard and Justus Miles Forman (7th)
	Jul	"The Thirty-Nine Steps" by John Buchan begins, *Blackwood's Magazine*
	Aug	"The Wanderings of Prosper Fair" by Bertram Atkey begins, *The Red Magazine* (2nd); death of Richard Marsh (9th)
	1916	
	Jan	Jeeves and Wooster debut in "Extricating Young Gussie" by P. G. Wodehouse, *The Strand*.
last issue *Weekly Tale-Teller* (29th)	Apr	
last issue *The Lady's Realm*	May	
	Aug	"The Historical Nights Entertainment" by Rafael Sabatini begins, *Premier Magazine*.
	Nov	death of Jack London (22nd)
	Dec	death of J. W. Comyns Carr (12th)
	1917	
fiction magazines raise prices across the board to 7d.	Feb	
The Mother's Magazine retitled *Lloyd's Magazine* and becomes primarily a fiction magazine last issue of *The New Fry's Magazine*	Jul	
	Sept	death of Bonavia Hunt (12th)
	1918	
The Red Magazine reverts to monthly schedule; last issue of *Yes or No* (27th)	Apr	
Woman at Home retitled *The Home Magazine*	Jun	
	Dec	"Jeremy" series by Hugh Walpole begins, *The Story-Teller*
	1919	
first trial issue of *Pan*; *The Red Magazine* reverts to twice-monthly schedule	Feb	first appearance of William in "Rice-Mould" by Richmal Crompton, *The Home Magazine*
	Apr	first issue *John o'London's Weekly* (12th)

29

Magazine event	1919	Key stories and other significant events
The Premier Magazine switches from monthly to fortnightly schedule; first issue *Nash's Illustrated Weekly* (14th)	Jun	
first issues of *The Blue Magazine* and *Hutchinson's Story Magazine*	Jul	
The Red Magazine switches to fortnightly schedule from twice monthly	Aug	
	Sept	first appearance of Bulldog Drummond, created by "Sapper", *Hutchinson's Story Magazine*
first issue *The Sovereign Magazine*; first formal issue of *Pan* (8th)	Nov	*The Sheikh* by E. M. Hull published; first issues of *Eve* and *The London Mercury*
	1920	
	Feb	Agatha Christie's first novel, "The Mysterious Affair at Styles" begins, *The Times Weekly* (27th)
The Home Magazine experiments with large flat slick format until Aug issue	Mar	death of Charles Garvice (1st)
last issue *Nash's Illustrated Weekly* (10th)	Jul	"The Man Who Knew Too Much" series by G. K. Chesterton begins, *The Story-Teller*
Pan switches from weekly to monthly schedule	Aug	
first issue *Outward Bound*	Oct	
	Nov	"Scaramouche" by Rafael Sabatini begins, *The Sovereign Magazine*
	Dec	Captain Blood first appears in "Brethren of the Main" by Rafael Sabatini, *The Premier* (3rd)
	1921	
Yes or No revived (28th)	Feb	last issue *Cassell's Saturday Journal* (19th)
Lloyd's Magazine retitled *Lloyd's Story Magazine* and switches to pulp format	Jun	
Pan revamped as *Pan: The Fiction Magazine* and relaunched in standard format	Jul	
first issue *The Yellow Magazine* (23rd)	Sept	
first issue *Gaiety*	Dec	death of Sir Arthur Pearson (9th)
	1922:	
	Jan	"The Return of Clubfoot" by Valentine Williams begins, *Premier Magazine* (24th)
	Feb	first crossword puzzle in a British magazine, *Pearson's Magazine*

CHRONOLOGY

Magazine event	(1922)	Key stories and other significant events
first issue *Good Housekeeping*	Mar	
last issue of revived *Yes or No* (24th)	Apr	
	May	"The Secrets of Dr. Taverner" by Dion Fortune begins, *The Royal Magazine*
first issue *The Happy Mag.*; *The Home Magazine* briefly retitled *The Ladies' Home Magazine* until Oct issue and switches to large flat slick format	Jun	
first issues of *The 20-Story Magazine* and *The Violet Magazine*	Jul	
	Aug	death of Alfred Harmsworth, Viscount Northcliffe (14th)
first issues of *Adventure-Story Magazine* and *The Corner Magazine*	Sept	"Aliens", early nature story by Henry Williamson, *The Story-Teller*
	Oct	"Taipan", *Pearson's*, Somerset Maugham's first new story in Britain for thirteen years
first issues of *The Green Magazine* (7th) and *The Detective Magazine* (24th)	Nov	
	Dec	first Hercule Poirot serial, "The Girl With the Anxious Eyes" by Agatha Christie starts, *The Grand Magazine*
	1923	
last issues of *Lloyd's Story Magazine* and *Badminton Magazine*	Jan	first issue of the revived *The Queen* (4th)
first issue *Mystery-Story Magazine*; *Everywoman's Weekly* becomes the monthly *Romance*	Feb	
The Premier Magazine revamped as a slick magazine in standard format on monthly schedule	Mar	first Hercule Poirot short story, "The Affair of the Victory Ball" by Agatha Christie, *The Sketch* (7th)
Nash's and Pall Mall Magazine switches to large flat slick format	Apr	
	May	"A Trap for the Unwary", Agatha Christie's first non-Poirot short story, *The Novel Magazine*
first issue *Tip Top Stories*; last issue *The Green Magazine* (18th)	Dec	
	1924	
last issues of *The Captain* and *Outward Bound*	Mar	
first issue of Hutchinson's *Woman*	Apr	death of Marie Corelli (21st)
last issue *Pan*	May	death of Edith Nesbit (4th); possibly Peter Cheyney's debut in *Mystery-Story*

Magazine event	(1924)	Key stories and other significant events
first issue *The Crusoe Mag.*; *Tip Top Stories* retitled *The Regent Magazine*	Jun	"Tales of the Long Bow" series by G. K. Chesterton begins, *The Story-Teller*
first issue *The Merry Mag.*	Jul	
Hutchinson's Magazine switches to large flat slick format	Aug	death of Joseph Conrad (3rd)
Alice Head becomes editor of *Nash's–Pall Mall*	Sept	death of J. Y. McPeake (19th)
	Dec	"The Painted Veil" by W. Somerset Maugham begins, *Nash's–Pall Mall*; "Blackshirt" by Bruce Graeme begins, *The New Magazine*
	1925	
	Jan	"Tarka's Last Hunt" by Henry Williamson, *20-Story Magazine*; "The Seven Sleepers", first novel by Francis Beeding, begins, *The Corner Magazine*; death of artist Harry Furniss (14th)
Hutchinson's takes over publication of *The Regent Magazine*	Feb	"Sons of the Sheikh" by E. M. Hull begins, *Pearson's Magazine*; Cassell's *P.M.* (formerly *The Penny Magazine*) relaunched as *Cassell's Popular Magazine*
The Regent Magazine merges with *The Sovereign Magazine*	Mar	
last issue *The Detective Magazine* (8th)	May	death of Sir Henry Rider Haggard (14th)
first issues *Standard Stories* and *The Sunny Mag.*	Jul	first Lord Peter Wimsey story, "The Problem of Uncle Meleager's Will" by Dorothy L. Sayers, *Pearson's Magazine*
	Aug	last issue *Cassell's Popular Magazine*
	1926	
	May	General Strike (3rd-12th)
first issue *The Argosy*; *The Crusoe Mag.* relaunched as *The Golden Mag.* last issue *Standard Stories*	Jun	Winnie the Pooh first illustrated by E. H. Shepard, *The Royal Magazine*
first issue *Best-Story Magazine*	Aug	
17th, last issue *The Yellow Magazine*	Sept	
first issue *All-Story Magazine*; *The Premier Magazine* reverts to pulp format	Oct	
Berry Brothers purchase Amalgamated Press	Nov	death of Clement King Shorter (19th)
	Dec	Harley Quin series by Agatha Christie begins, *The Story-Teller*; death of artist Warwick Reynolds (15th)

CHRONOLOGY

Magazine event	1927	Key stories and other significant events
Publication of Cassell's magazines *The Argosy, Cassell's Magazine, The Corner Magazine, The New Magazine, The Quiver* and *The Story-Teller* passes to Amalgamated Press	Feb	
final issue *The Sovereign Magazine*.	Apr	final Sherlock Holmes story, "The Adventure of Shoscombe Old Place", *The Strand*; "It" by Elinor Glyn begins, *Nash's Magazine*;
first issue *The Jolly Mag.*; *Nash's Magazine* and *Pall Mall Magazine* return to separate publication	May	
	Jun	death of Jerome K. Jerome (14th)
The Golden Mag. relaunched as *The Golden West*; last issue *Romance*	Jul	
first issue of the British *Golden Book Magazine*	Aug	
Harry Golding becomes editor of *The Windsor Magazine*	Sept	
Adventure-Story and *Mystery-Story* combine as *Adventure & Mystery-Story Magazine*	Oct	death of William Le Queux (13th)
Gaiety merges with *The Sunny Mag.*; first issue *Woman's Journal*	Nov	
probable last issue *The Jolly Mag.*	Dec	first appearance of Miss Marple in "The Tuesday Night Club" by Agatha Christie, *The Royal Magazine*
	1928	
last issue *All-Story Magazine*	Jan	death of Thomas Hardy (11th)
first issue *World Stories*	Apr	
last issue of British *Golden Book Magazine*	May	
first issue of *Britannia* (28th)	Sept	
last issue *Golden West Magazine*	Dec	death of Stacy Aumonier (21st)
	1929	
first issue of *The Thriller* (9th)	Feb	
last issue *Best-Story Magazine*	Apr	
Britannia and *Eve* merge	May	
last issue *Adventure & Mystery-Story Magazine*; *Hutchinson's Story Magazine* reverts to standard format	Jun	
Woman merged with *Hutchinson's Story Magazine*	Jul	

Magazine event	(1929)	Key stories and other significant events
Empire Frontier created out of *Frontier Stories*; last issue *The Blue Magazine*; *The Red Magazine* reverts to monthly schedule	Aug	
Nash's Magazine and *Pall Mall Magazine* re-merge as *Nash's–Pall Mall*; first British edition of *Harper's Bazaar*	Oct	
last issue *Hutchinson's Story Magazine*	Dec	
	1930	
last issue *The Merry Magazine*	Feb	
	Mar	death of D. H. Lawrence (2nd)
	May	death of William J. Locke (15th)
first issue *Hush*	Jun	
	Jul	death of Sir Arthur Conan Doyle (7th)
The London Magazine relaunched as *The New London Magazine* in large flat format	Nov	
last issue *The New Magazine*; *The Royal Magazine* relaunched as *The New Royal Magazine* in large flat format	Dec	
	1931	
last issue *The Home Magazine*; merges with *Homes & Gardens*	Jan	
last issue *The Premier Magazine*	Mar	death of Arnold Bennett (27th)
last issue *Hush*	Jun	
	Aug	death of Sir Hall Caine (31st)
	Dec	death of artist Maurice Greiffenhagen (26th)
	1932	
	Feb	death of Edgar Wallace (10th)
Passing Show revamped into a full colour story tabloid (26th)	Mar	
last issue of *Colour*	May	
The New Royal Magazine retitled *The Royal Pictorial* with drop in fiction content	Jun	"Early Morning", last story by Arnold Bennett, *The Story-Teller*
Empire Frontier merged with *All Star*; last issue *The Graphic* (14th) (retitled *The National Graphic* for last 12 issues)	Jul	
last issue *Cassell's Magazine*	Dec	
	1933	
	Jan	death of John Galsworthy (31st)
last issue *The Sunny and Gaiety Mag.*	Apr	

CHRONOLOGY

Magazine event	(1933)	Key stories and other significant events
last issue *The New London Magazine*	May	
last issue of *All Star Western & Frontier Magazine*	Jun	"Over the River", last novel by John Galsworthy, begins, *The Story-Teller*
first volume of the *Master Thriller* series	Jul	
first issue *Lovat Dickson's Magazine*	Nov	
	Dec	"Incident in Azania" by Evelyn Waugh, *The Windsor Magazine*; death of Robert W. Chambers (16th)
	1934	
	Jan	death of artist Harrison Fisher (19th)
first issue of *Scoops* (10th), folds 23 June	Feb	first issue of *New Stories* from Blackwell's
first issue *Wings*; last issue of *Chums*	Jul	
first issue *Modern Stories*	Aug	
first issue *Mystery and Detection*	Sept	"Department of Dead Ends" series by Roy Vickers begins, *Pearson's Magazine*
	1935	
The Royal Pictorial becomes *The Royal Screen Pictorial*	Jan	death of H. Greenhough Smith (14th)
last issue *The Corner Magazine*	Feb	
first issue *Air Stories*; last issue *World Stories*	May	
last issue of *Lovat Dickson's Magazine*	Jun	
	Jul	"Mr. Pond" series by G. K. Chesterton begins, *The Story-Teller*
last issue *Mystery and Detection*; first issue *War Stories*	Oct	
	Dec	first issue of *Men Only*
	1936	
last issue *Wings*	Jan	death of Rudyard Kipling (18th)
first issue *Western Adventures*; probable last issue *War Stories*	Feb	
first issue *Mystery Stories*	Mar	first issue of *New Writing* from Bodley Head
	Apr	last issue, *New Stories* from Blackwell's
possible last issue *Western Adventures*	Jun	death of G. K. Chesterton (14th)
The Story-Teller relaunched in glossy format	Nov	
fiction phased out of *Screen Pictorial*	Dec	
	1937	
The Story-Teller reverts to pulp format	May	first issue *Courier*
first issue *Tales of Wonder*	Jun	

THE AGE OF THE STORYTELLERS

Magazine event	(1937)	Key stories and other significant events
	Jul	first issue *Lilliput*
	Aug	death of "Sapper" (H. C. McNeile) (14th)
last issue of *Nash's–Pall Mall*, merged with *Good Housekeeping*	Sept	death of Ivor Nicholson (9th)
	Oct	first issue of *Parade* from Odhams Press
last issue *The Story-Teller*	Nov	
last issue *The Novel Magazine*	Dec	first issue *Penguin Parade*
	1938	
	Feb	death of artist C. E. Brock (28th)
	Jun	death of Sir Arthur Spurgeon (9th)
first issue *Fantasy*; first volume *Nash's Annual*	Jul	
	Dec	first professional appearance by Arthur C. Clarke, "Man's Empire of Tomorrow", *Tales of Wonder*; Doctor Dogbody series by James Norman Hall begins, *The Windsor*
	1939	
last issue *The Passing Show* (25th)	Feb	
	Apr	last issues of *Pearson's Weekly* (1st) and *The London Mercury*
Pearson's converts to large flat size	May	
last issue *Fantasy*	Jul	death of artist Louis Wain (4th)
last issues of *The Red Magazine* and *The Windsor Magazine*	Sept	death of Ethel M. Dell (17th)
last issues of *Pearson's Magazine* and *The Violet Magazine*	Nov	
last volume of the *Master Thriller* series	Dec	
	1940	
The Argosy relaunched in large digest form as *Argosy of Complete Stories*	Feb	death of John Buchan (11th)
The Thriller becomes *War Thriller* (9th)	Mar	
last issues of *Air Stories* and *The Grand Magazine*; *The Happy Mag.* now digest size	Apr	
last issues of *The Happy Mag.* and *War Thriller* (10th)	May	
The Quiver drops to small digest format	Aug	
last issue *The 20-Story Magazine*	Oct	*The Bystander* merges with *The Tatler* (30th)
	Dec	Penguin *New Writing* series begins

CHRONOLOGY

Magazine event	1941	Key stories and other significant events
	Jan	death of John Oxenham (23rd)
	Sept	last issue of *Parade* from Odhams Press
The Strand Magazine switches to digest format	Oct	
	Nov	death of P. C. Wren (22nd)
	1942	
last issues *Mystery Stories* and *Tales of Wonder*	Feb	
Boy's Own Paper changes to digest format	Aug	
	1943	
	Jan	death of artist Warwick Goble (22nd)
	Sept	deaths of W. W. Jacobs (1st) and Elinor Glyn (23rd)
	1944	
	Sept	death of W. Heath Robinson (13th)
	1946	
	Feb	death of E. Phillips Oppenheim (3rd)
	Aug	death of H. G. Wells (13th)
Nash's Annual revived	Dec	
	1947	
	Nov	death of Baroness Orczy (12th)
	1948	
	Jul	death of artist G. E. Studdy (25th)
	Nov	death of A. E. W. Mason (22nd)
	1949	
last issue of revived *Nash's Annual*	Dec	
	1950	
	Feb	deaths of Rafael Sabatini (13th) and Sir Max Pemberton (22nd)
last issue *The Strand Magazine*, merges with *Men Only*	Mar	
	Apr	death of Warwick Deeping (20th)
	Jul	death of Robert S. Hichens (20th)
	Sept	death of artist Harry Rountree (26th)

COLOUR PLATES

Magazine covers are reproduced in chronological order of the magazine's first appearance. Covers used, whilst usually representative of the magazine's early period, may not always date from the first few years. Cover artists are noted in brackets where known.

Plate 1. *Cassell's Family Magazine*, November 1897 (Hurst); *The English Illustrated Magazine*, July 1893; *The Strand Magazine*, volume 1 (1891); *The Ludgate*, volume 9, new series (1900); *The Idler*, volume 1 (1892); *The Pall Mall Magazine*, August 1898 (Sambourne); *The Woman at Home*, December 1899; *The Minster*, October 1895; *The Windsor Magazine*, September 1903 (Hare).

Plate 2. *Chapman's Magazine*, volume 5 (1896); *Pearson's Magazine*, October 1902 (S. L. Wood); *The Lady's Realm*, April 1901; *The Harmsworth London Magazine*, August 1901 (C. Dawson); *The Royal Magazine*, August 1899 (E. Read); *The Charing Cross Magazine*, January 1900; *The Universal Magazine*, November 1901 (R. Pannett); *The Lady's Magazine*, November 1903; *The Holborn Monthly Magazine*, May 1903.

Plate 3. *Yes or No*, 8 February 1913; *The Realm*, title page, 1903; *The Grand Magazine*, February 1916; *The Novel Magazine*, October 1907; *The Story-Teller*, December 1907 (Whitelaw); *The Red Magazine*, November 1918 (H. Morgan); *Sievier's Monthly*, March 1909 (R.J.R.); *The White Magazine*, March/April 1909; *Nash's Magazine*, April 1909 (L. Wood).

Plate 4. *The New Magazine*, November 1911 (A. Morrow); *Weekly Tale-Teller*, 7 August 1909; *Everybody's Story Magazine*, April 1910 (H. Copping); *The Magpie*, October 1912; *The Club Room*, November 1913 (S. Abbey); *The Premier Magazine*, December 1915 (C. Cuneo); *Lloyd's Story Magazine*, November 1921 (E.M.H.); *The Blue Magazine*, November 1923 (E.M. Cockroft); *Hutchinson's Magazine*, April 1922.

Plate 5. *The Sovereign Magazine*, November 1920 (W.S.B.); *Pan*, February 1921 (E. A. Cox); *The Yellow Magazine*, 23 September 1921 (H. Morgan); *The Happy Mag.*, August 1934 (D. L. Ghilchik); *The 20 Story Magazine*, January 1935 (Woods); *The Violet Magazine*, December 1937; *Adventure-Story Magazine*, December 1922; *The Corner Magazine*, May 1928; *The Green Magazine*, 7 November 1922 (H. Morgan).

Plate 6. *The Detective Magazine*, 29 August 1924 (C. P. Shilton); *Mystery-Story Magazine*, July 1923; *Romance*, October 1924 (J. Dewar Mills); *Tip Top Stories*, May 1924 (D. Colquhart); *The Crusoe Mag.*, January 1925; *The Regent Magazine*, September 1924 (A. Brunton); *The Merry Mag.*, August 1924 (A. Ferrier); *Standard Stories*, February 1926 (Doco); *The Sunny Mag.*, September 1932 (T. Henry).

Plate 7. *The Argosy*, June 1926; *The Golden Mag.*, September 1926 (T. Henry); *Best-Story Magazine*, March 1927; *All-Story Magazine*, November 1927 (L. Bates); *The Jolly Mag.*, November 1927; *The Golden West*, July 1927; *World Stories*, October 1932 (S. Waite); *Empire Frontier*, January 1932 (Blick); *Hush*, November 1930 (A. Bowyer).

Plate 8. *Wings*, August 1935 (S. Bradshaw); *Modern Stories*, October 1934 (Youngman Carter); *Mystery and Detection*, October 1935 (Blick); *Air Stories*, July 1936 (S. Drigin); *War Stories*, February 1936 (Forester); *Western Adventures*, April 1936 (C. Caney); *Mystery Stories*, March 1936 (J. Nicholson); *Tales of Wonder*, Autumn 1939 (J. Nicholson); *Fantasy*, #2, 1939 (S. Drigin).

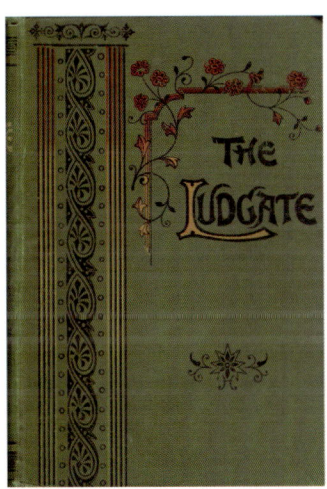

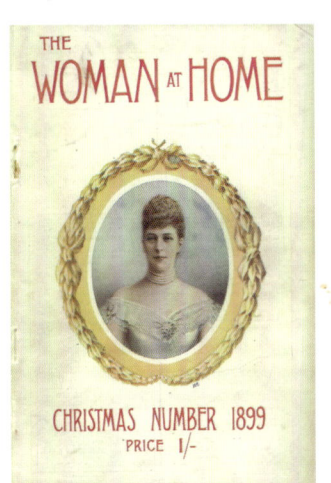
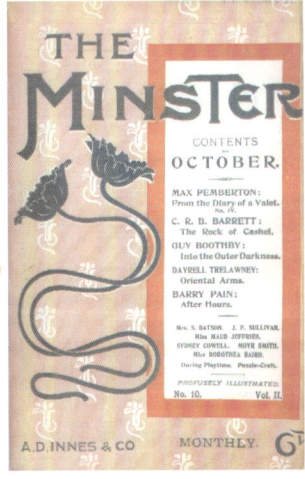
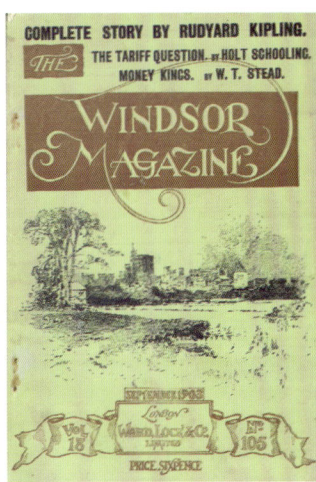

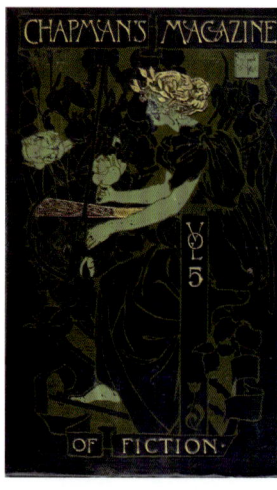  

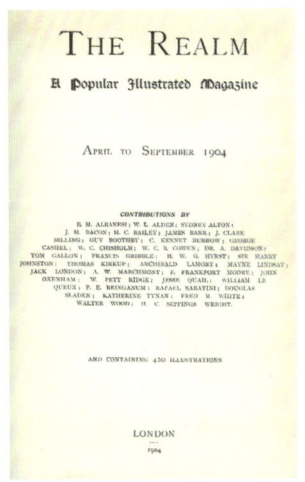
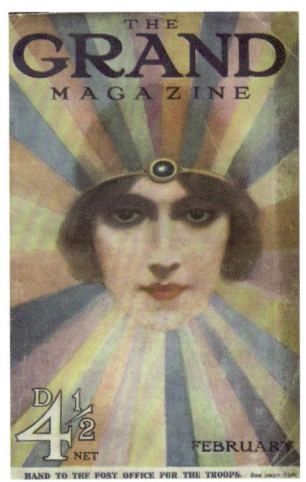

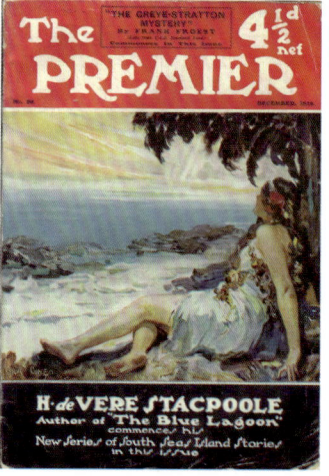

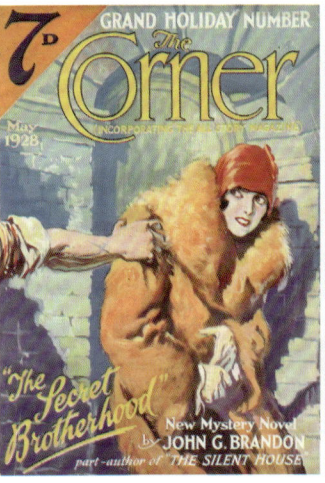

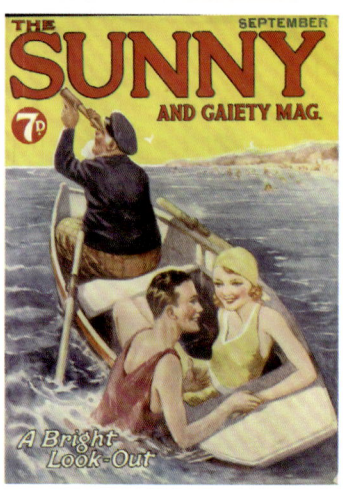

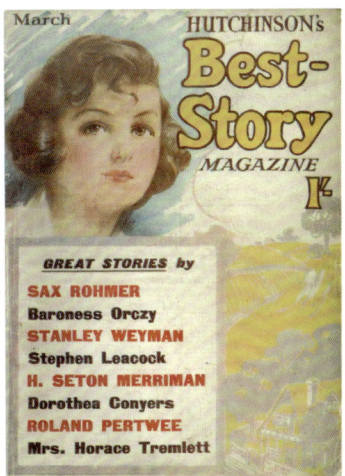

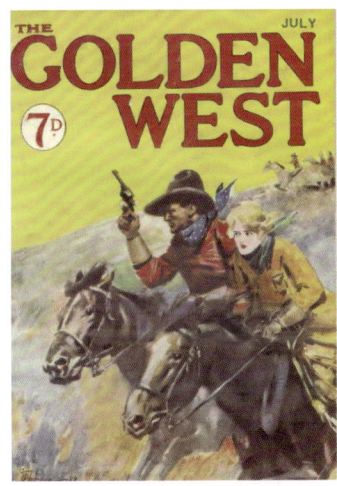
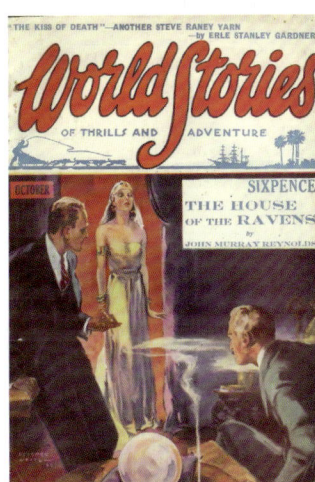
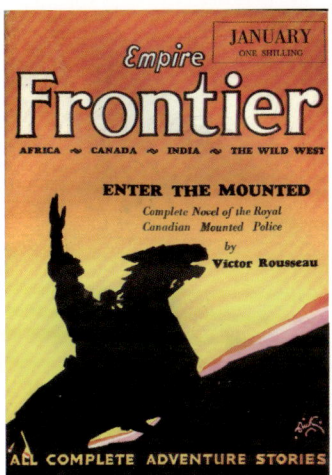

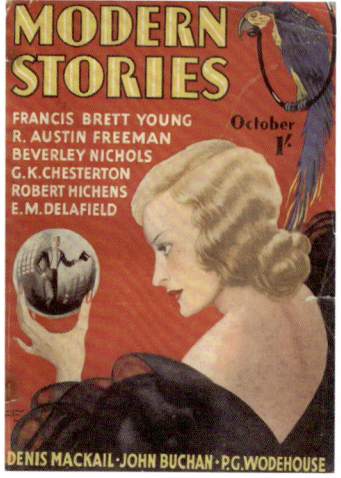
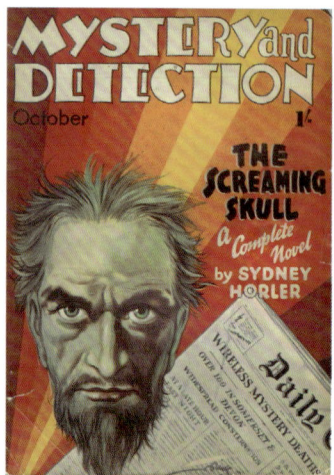
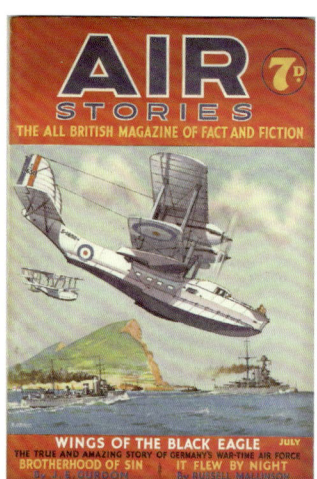
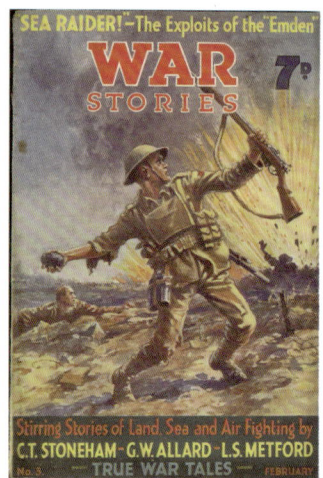
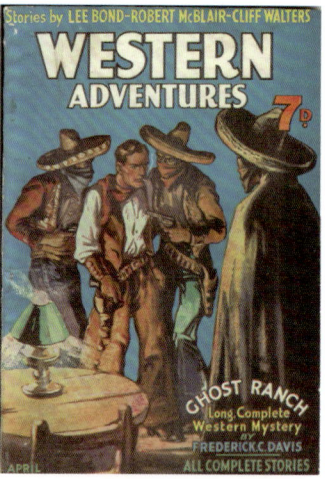

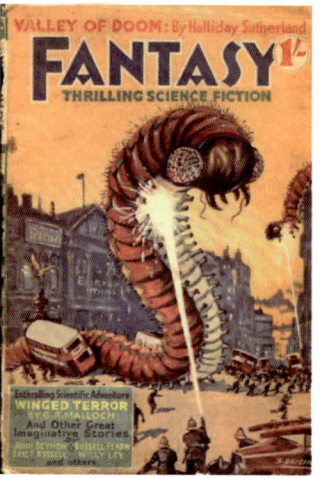

SECTION ONE

PRIMARY MAGAZINES

SECTION ONE

PRIMARY MAGAZINES

ADVENTURE-STORY MAGAZINE
81 issues. Volume 1, Number 1, September 1922 to Volume 10, Number 60, September 1927 (60 issues). Merged with *Mystery-Story Magazine* to form ADVENTURE & MYSTERY STORY MAGAZINE, Volume 1, Number 1, October 1927 to Volume 4, Number 21, June 1929 (21 issues).

In 1922 publisher Walter Hutchinson hired writer E. Charles Vivian to edit two specialist fiction magazines, *Adventure-Story* and *Mystery-Story*. Vivian had previous experience on *The English Review*, *Land and Water* and the aviation magazine *Flying*. He had also just completed a lost-race novel in the style of H. Rider Haggard, "City of Wonder", which became the first serial to run in *Adventure-Story*, to considerable reader acclaim.

Adventure-Story had a wide remit. A market report at the time said that it required:

> …stories of action and adventure the whole world over, packed with plot and local colour; stories of the sea, the Wild West, the Tropics, etc. The more unusual the setting and stronger the plot, the more suitable is the story for this magazine. The love element is only necessary where it acts as the mainspring of adventure, and adventure *must* dominate sentiment in every story accepted.[1]

The emphasis of plot over character shows that this magazine had no pretense to sophistication, but was copying the popular American adventure pulps – *Argosy*, *Adventure*[2], *Blue Book* and, more significantly, *Action Stories*, which had started in September 1921 with Hutchinson launching a British edition in April 1923. The first issue of *Adventure-Story* also included C.M. Eddy's "Moonshine" from *Action Stories*. Hutchinson was well aware of the popularity of the adventure story following the success of Rafael Sabatini's "Scaramouche" in *The Sovereign Magazine* the year before. By 1923, Hutchinson was the main British publisher of the American-style pulp magazine.

The early issues of *Adventure-Story* relied upon reprints from American pulps with work by Edison Marshall, H. Bedford-Jones, Anthony M. Rud, Frank L. Packard, Ben Ames Williams, Johnston McCulley, Harold de Polo and J. Allan Dunn. They had developed a sturdy action-orientated form of story that did not sacrifice character and was at home equally in the better

---

[1] Michael Joseph, *Short Story Writing for Profit* (London: Hutchinson, 1923), p. 197.
[2] The Ridgway Company, publisher of *Adventure*, brought an action against Hutchinson to stop the use of the word "Adventure" in the title but the action was dismissed (*The Times*, 15 June 1923, p. 5).

quality magazines as the pulps. The same applied to some of the British writers whom Vivian acquired, including Sapper, who led the first issue, C. Lestock Reid, F.A.M. Webster, and the much travelled and now American resident A. R. Wetjen. The experiences of these writers during the War and their subsequent travels provided them with a never-ending stream of plots, which the creative penny-a-word pulpster could often rework to good effect.

Not all contributors were middle- or even low-brow. Vivian was able to call upon Oliver Madox Hueffer, the younger brother of Ford Madox Ford (whom Vivian had worked with at the *English Review*), who provided four strange mysteries, starting with "Asking for It" (Jan 1923). Stanley J. Weyman, then approaching seventy, but having a twilight revival, provided one of his last historical novels, "The Traveller in the Fur Coat" (Sept 1923-Feb 1924).

One of the most prolific contributors was Vivian himself, doubtless trying to stretch his limited budget and earn a little extra above Hutchinson's parsimonious wage. He wrote two more lost-world novels, "Field of Sleep" (May-Aug 1923) and "People of Darkness" (Feb-May 1924), in between which he squeezed the Sabatini-esque historical novel "Count Gaspar" (Dec 1923-May 1924), plus plenty of strange stories under a variety of pen names. Vivian enjoyed the unusual and for *Adventure-Story*, the more exotic the setting the better.

The mood changed slightly under his successor. Oscar Cook had been a District Officer in British North Borneo and he too enjoyed the exotic, though with less of the fantastic. His issues emphasised the danger and grimness of strange places, primarily in the Far East, India or Africa. He recruited a number of ex-colonials to produce authentic tales of adventure including former rubber-plantation manager Edmund Snell, colonial officer Hilton Brown, American big-game hunter Gordon MacCreagh, and those queens of the South Seas, Elinor Mordaunt and Beatrice Grimshaw. Cook also captured the master, H. Rider Haggard, albeit posthumously, with "The Treasure of the Lake" (Dec 1925-Sept 1926). Hilton Brown later became a producer for BBC Radio, and Cook published works by two other radio pioneers, Lance Sieveking and (in *Mystery-Story*) Eric Maschwitz. This was not a coincidence. All three were clients of the Curtis Brown Literary Agency where Cook's wife, Christine Campbell Thomson worked.

Cook remained with Hutchinson's for only a year. Under his successors, Meredith Dixon and Miss G. Gilligan, *Adventure-Story* lost much of its exotic flavour and became too similar to *Mystery-Story*. Hutchinson made a deal with Bernarr Macfadden whereby Hutchinson was able to reprint stories from Macfadden's magazines, especially *Ghost Stories*, along with its posed photographs and pseudo-realism. The last serial of interest was "Sing Sing Nights" (Feb-Apr 1927) by the eccentric Harry Stephen Keeler, regarded by some as his most successful novel.

The increasing similarity between the two magazines led to their merger from October 1927. Though the *Adventure* element led the title, it was *Mystery-Story* that was bolder on the cover, and mystery fiction predominated, including the Partners-in-Crime series featuring Tommy and Tuppence by Agatha Christie (Feb-Aug 1928). Original adventure stories were few and far between, but included some fine south-sea romances by Beatrice Grimshaw, westerns by Johnston McCulley, and unusual stories by Douglas Newton, H. R. Wakefield and J. Russell Warren. In this form *Adventure & Mystery-Story Magazine* survived a further sixteen issues before Hutchinson culled all his magazines.

Under Vivian, *Adventure-Story* was one of the more unusual British fiction magazines but it faded rapidly and, with isolated exceptions, later issues lacked originality. Nevertheless the sheer rarity of the magazine makes it one of the most collectable of British pulps.

Frequency: Monthly, but combined issue Jun/Jul 1926.
Publisher: Hutchinson.
Editors: E. Charles Vivian, 1922-24; Oscar Cook, 1925; Meredith V. Dixon, 1926; Miss G. Gilligan, 1927.
Format/Size: Standard pulp. Page count, 96, rose to 160, Aug 1925, dropped to 128, Mar 1926.
Price: 7d.
References: "The Trail of Adventure and Mystery" by Mike Ashley, *Pulp Vault* #10 (May 1992), pp. 4-14. The first 27 issues were indexed by Tom Moriarty in *Lore*, August 1966. Also indexed on CD-ROM *Science Fiction, Fantasy & Weird Fiction Magazine Index (1890-2001)* by Stephen T. Miller & William G. Contento (Locus Press, 2002).
Holdings: *Substantial run, UK*: Bodleian has all issues except Sept 1926 (*Call Number*: Per. 25612 d.23) • British Library has Sept 1922, Sept 1923, Feb 1925–Sept 1927 and Dec 1928 only (*Shelfmark*: PP.6004.got).
Collecting points: Extremely rare. Isolated issues surface infrequently at high cost. No known volumes in publisher's binding. Only one full run known in private hands.

***

ADVENTURE & MYSTERY STORY MAGAZINE *see* ADVENTURE-STORY MAGAZINE

***

AIR STORIES
60 issues. Volume 1, Number 1, May 1935 to Volume 10, Number 4, April 1940.

Air Stories was a magazine of aviation fiction, similar to *Wings*. All its stories were about aircraft and their pilots, with an emphasis on the First World War, the escapades of air aces and the Royal Flying Corps. The editor, T. Stanhope Sprigg, came from a family of journalists. His father, Stanhope Sprigg, had been the founding editor of the *Windsor Magazine*, whilst his brother, Christopher, earned a reputation as a poet. With his brother, Sprigg founded Airways Publications in 1924 to publish the technical magazine *Airways*. By 1931, when he obtained his pilot's licence, they were also publishing the monthly *Aircraft Engineering*, the weekly *Flying* and the annual *Who's Who in British Aviation*. He approached Newnes in 1934 with the idea of producing a group of specialist fiction magazines all of which eventually appeared: *Air Stories*, *War Stories, Western Adventures* and *Fantasy*.

Sprigg's knowledge of the subject helped give access to many key writers and he assembled a strong line-up. Leading the first issue was Arch Whitehouse, one of the leading writers of aviation fiction. Though resident in America, where he produced reams of stories for the pulps,

Whitehouse had been born in Britain and had joined the RFC in 1916. He brought two series to *Air Stories* that had been running in the American pulps. "One Man's War", in the first issue, intro-duced British readers to the "Coffin Crew", four daring RFC "warriors" who take on the more dangerous missions; whilst in "The Sky-Bandit Strikes" (Jul 1935) and sequels, playboy millionare and mystery pilot Kerry Kean, alias the "Griffon", took on the Master Criminal of the Age. Whitehouse also employed the alias Jack Townsend to by-line stories already published under his own name in the American pulp *Flying Aces*. Whitehouse's stories were standard American pulp action fiction but which did not skimp on accuracy or detail.

From the first issue, Sprigg ran extracts from V. M. Yeates's novel *Winged Victory* (Cape, 1934) as a three-part serial under the title "Cundall of the Camels". Hailed as the finest novel of the Great War in the Air, it was a thinly disguised autobiography of Yeates's heroic escapades in the RFC. Most contributors to the magazine were current or former pilots, many of them war veterans. Some, such as George Fielding Eliot, William Maclanachan ("McScotch") and Oliver Stewart, went on to become reporters or commentators upon the armed services and acquired a sharp, reportorial eye. Most, however, wrote for the thrill of it and some of their work was only a cut above boys' adventure material. The best of these was undoubtedly W. E. Johns though, sadly for collectors, there were no stories featuring Biggles in *Air Stories*. His contributions began with "Aerial Enemy No. 1" (Jan-Mar 1936), a three-part serial published in book form as *Sky High* (Newnes, 1936), which features Johns's other popular hero, "Steeley" Delaroy, an aristocratic air ace who rights wrongs as a "Robin Hood of the Air".

Another regular was Captain John E. Gurdon, one of the great air aces of the War who was in the same Squadron as Whitehouse. Gurdon had been involved in one of the most famous dogfights of the War, when he and another pilot took on twenty enemy planes between them, downing eight. The incident is covered in Gurdon's serial, "Winged Warriors" (Feb-Apr 1936). With "The Loop of Death" (Aug 1936) Gurdon began a series about Secret Service agent Alistair Kinley, later collected as *The Monkey Trick* (Newnes, 1936).

Other regular contributors included G. M. Bowman, Captain John E. Doyle, Edward Green (a Canadian pilot whose stories dealt with aerial combat against problems and disasters in northern Canada), J. H. Stafford (whose stories are set in such trouble spots as Palestine and the North-West Frontier) and, perhaps the most popular, Wilfrid Tremellen. Tremellen, another air ace, strove for authenticity. Whether it is a story about a dare-devil pilot on a lone mission ("The Penalty is Death", Feb 1936) or pilot hi-jinks ("The Macaroni Cup", May 1936), there is a strong sense of character and place. Tremellen never achieved the success of Johns or Whitehouse, but his stories remain amongst the more fondly remembered in *Air Stories*.

Some readers asked for air stories of the future. Generally Sprigg avoided science fiction in *Air Stories*, but he did publish a serial, "Campaign in the Clouds" (Oct-Dec 1935) by David Martin, about a future aerial invasion of England. He also published "The Fourth Dimension" (Apr 1940) by Stuart Martin, in which a pilot temporarily disappears into another dimension, but this story was probably a hangover from *Fantasy*.

Air Stories published much more than fiction and lived up to its occasional cover tag, "Flying Fiction and Facts". Each issue had a feature on World War I flying aces by Alfred H. Pritchard and, from the second issue, there was a regular book review column and a question-and-answer feature. Readers were keen to collect the cover paintings, all of which were by Serge Drigin, so Sprigg ensured that the painting remained free of print. Sprigg responded to readers' requests, establishing a feature about model aircraft, by James Hay Stevens (from Oct 1935) and introducing a correspondence club (from Oct 1936). The editorial column, "Contact", also included readers' letters and feedback on specific issues, occasionally reuniting former wartime colleagues and revealing personal flying experiences. Other features included an eyewitness account of the first aerial invasion of England ("The Terror That Flew by Night" by John L. Miller, Jun 1935), the serialised autobiography of German air ace Ernst Udet ("Ace of the Black Cross", Sept-Dec 1936) and A. H. Pritchard's long study of Britain's air services during the War ("Warriors of the Air" (Apr-Jul 1938).

The mainstay artist was Serge Drigin, but other regulars included George Blow and Stanley Bradshaw. There were standard features on specific aircraft, most illustrated in meticulous detail by A. C. Leverington. The result was a package that appealed to all enthusiasts of aerial combat and adventure and of new developments in flight.

When Britain entered the Second World War *Air Stories* continued, censorship not initially a problem despite its coverage of new military developments and with stories now focusing on current rather than past war in the air. The only significant change was that authors dropped any reference to rank in their by-lines. But the magazine's days were inevitably numbered. Sprigg, who was a member of the Royal Air Force Reserve, was mobilised at the outbreak of War and it became impossible to continue the magazine.

Frequency: Monthly.
Publisher: George Newnes.
Editor: T. Stanhope Sprigg.
Format/Size: Standard pulp, 96 pages.
Price: 7d, rose to 9d, Apr 1938, returning to 7d, Aug 1939.
Holdings:
Complete run, UK: Bodleian (*Call Number*: Per. 25613 d.156).
Substantial run, UK: British Library is missing Feb, Jul, Nov 1936; Aug, Nov 1937; Feb, Sept 1938; Jan, Aug, Sept, Dec 1939; Feb, Mar 1940 (*Shelfmark*: PP.6004.tan).
Collecting points: Individual issues are still relatively easy to find and it is possible to build a full run, though prices are rising. No copies seen in publisher's binding.

* * *

ALL [STAR] DETECTIVE STORIES *see* EMPIRE FRONTIER

* * *

ALL STAR WESTERN AND [EMPIRE] FRONTIER MAGAZINE *see* EMPIRE FRONTIER

* * *

ALL-STORY MAGAZINE
16 issues. Volume 1, Number 1, October 1926 to Volume 3, Number 16, January 1928.

All-Story took over the publication slot from Harmsworth's *Yellow Magazine*, but it was an entirely different product. It appeared in that transitional period when fiction magazines were reorientating upon the growing women's market whilst trying to keep their traditional readership. Magazines like *Nash's* and Hutchinson's *Woman* showed a move towards the glossy format full of advertising. *All-Story* did not go that way, but it upgraded the image of *The Yellow Magazine* to a standard size on better quality paper. It was heavily illustrated, with attractive, gaudy covers by Leo Bates, all depicting a romantic or enjoyable moment. Whilst it tried to retain some of the old romance of adventure, the emphasis was on love stories. *All-Story* was thus a mixture of love and intrigue aimed at the newly liberated woman. It described its contents as "Vivid stories of love and life today".

Central to many of these stories are women establishing their place in society. A typical example is "Where the Blue Roads Meet" by Joanna Cannan in the first issue, with its young modern woman determined to take control of her life. Douglas Newton provided a series, under the generic title "Pandora, if You Please" (Oct 1926), about bachelor girl, Pandora Sway, a beautician who sets out to remove wrinkles not just from her client's faces but also their lives. The liberation of women clearly upset the protagonist in Selwyn Jepson's "Girls Are So Different" (Feb 1927) when he returns from years abroad and cannot cope with the modern girl. Ethel Mannin looked at the artistic society in Paris in "Bohemia" (Mar 1927) while in "Her Allegiance" (May 1927) I. A. R. Wylie considers the significance of love and intellect. The femme fatale appears in J. D. Beresford's "The Two Sirens" (Oct 1927) and Fannie Hurst's "The Vampire" (Dec 1927), whilst the domineering woman gets her comeuppance in F. Morton Howard's amusing "Low Tide" (Aug 1927). Wallace Irwin's "Scarlet" (Oct 1926) is representative of the more torrid love story, which has since become formulaic. The story blurb says it all: "A woman with a past, a man without scruple, a foolish wife and a headlight."

In "Madonna of the Pueblos" (Oct 1927) Tom Gill contrasts English society with that in Mexico with a clash between generations. The story is typical of many with exotic settings. "The Gods Arrive" (Feb 1927) by Kathlyn Rhodes is set in fashionable Helouan, Egypt; Alice Perrin's "The Victim" (Apr 1927) is a tale of "love and hate in the jungle"; Elinor Mordaunt's "Mac's Wife" (Jun 1927) is set in Zanzibar, and Dorothy Black's "And if Your Song-Bird Disappears" (Nov 1927) takes place in the mystique of Mandalay. The magazine was ideal for W. Somerset Maugham's stories of oriental intrigue, such as "The Yellow Streak"[1] (Sept 1927), based on a true experience. Sax Rohmer was present with his Chinatown story "The Dance of the Veils"[2] (Nov 1926). Readers were taken to the Canadian forests in "The Knight-Errant" (Feb 1927) by G. B. Lancaster, but the most popular example of the outdoor story was

---

[1] Reprinted from *Nash's Magazine*, October 1925.
[2] Reprinted from *The Sovereign Magazine*, June/July 1920.

James Oliver Curwood's talies about Kazan, a domesticated dog that turns feral, reprinted from *The Story-Teller* in 1913. Perhaps as much as a third of the stories were reprints though they were not identified as such. Some, like W. J. Locke's "A Christmas Mystery" (Dec 1926), where three men become involved with the birth of a child on Christmas Eve, had often been reprinted in books and magazines since it first appeared in the *American Magazine* in 1909. Robert W. Chamber's novel of a girl as victim to destiny, "The Dark Star" (Jun-Nov 1927), had not been out of print since its first book publication in 1917.

All-Story published little outright supernatural fiction, though weird elements feature in some stories by Elinor Mordaunt, Eden Phillpotts, Alice Perrin and Edgar Wallace. There were other mystery and detective stories by E. Phillips Oppenheim and Michael Kent. Arnold Bennett, Marjorie Bowen, Robert W. Chambers and Hugh Walpole were other major names showing that *All-Story* was a magazine of quality fiction.

Considering the quality of the stories and authors one might expect the magazine to thrive, but by the end of the twenties the fiction-magazine bubble had burst and only the most original and best financed would survive. Had *All-Story* been upgraded to a slick, it might have continued, for a while, but it was only ever a side-line to Amalgamated Press's main magazines and, considering its scarcity, sales must have been low. After sixteen issues it merged with *The Corner Magazine* – an about turn as *The Corner* was a traditional adventure magazine.

Frequency: Monthly.
Publisher: Amalgamated Press.
Editor: possibly W. A. O'Donnell.
Format/Size: Standard newsprint, 96 pages.
Price: 6d, rose to 7d, Apr 1927.
Holdings: *Complete run, UK*. British Library (*Shelfmark*: PP.6004.taf); Bodleian (*Call Number*: Per. 25612 d.84). *Complete run, Australia*. University of Queensland (*Reference*: PR1309.S5 C6).
Collecting points: Extremely rare. No full run known in private hands.

* * *

THE ARGOSY

571 issues. Two series. Volume 1, Number 1, June 1926 to Volume 26, Number 164, January 1940. New series as ARGOSY OF COMPLETE STORIES (as ARGOSY from April 1945), Volume 1, Number 1, February 1940 to Volume 35, Number 2, February 1974; merged with *Books and Bookmen*.

By 1926 short stories were appearing in their thousands in British and American periodicals. Keeping track of them was impossible. The previous decade had seen a growth in anthologies selecting the best fiction. E. J. O'Brien's annual *Best Short Stories* from American magazines began in 1915, complemented by a British volume from 1922. George H. Doran assembled *The World's Best Short Stories of 1925*, selected by the editors of the leading American magazines. The Review of Reviews Company launched *The Golden Book* in January 1925, which had an editorial board that selected the world's best stories for each monthly issue.[1] Taking their cue from this Cassell's began their own magazine of the world's best short stories, *The Argosy*. This had nothing to do with the American magazine *The Argosy*, published by the Munsey

---

[1] A British edition of *Golden Book* ran from Aug 1927-May/Jun 1928. See Section 2.

Company, which had started the pulp-magazine revolution in 1896. Neither was it related to the Victorian magazine, *The Argosy* (*see Section 2*). Cassell's *Argosy*, launched at the height of the magazine boom, would be its lone survivor outliving every other popular magazine, including *The Strand*. Remarkably the magazine's first issue came out in the same week as the General Strike in May 1926 and many felt it would fall at the first hurdle, but it survived and went from strength to strength.

In his foreword the editor said that the sole purpose of *The Argosy* was, "to give only the world's best stories", adding: "There are so many fine stories [which] one would gladly read if it were always possible to find them. The *Argosy* will find these stories for you …"[2] As a consequence *The Argosy* was predominantly reprint, though the option for original stories was retained. *The Argosy* rarely indicated whether a story was a reprint but usually proclaimed the new ones. Most readers would recognise the magazine's first serial, "Dracula" by Bram Stoker, as a thirty-year old classic, and would suspect that many other stories, especially those by Maupassant, Jerome K. Jerome and O. Henry were reprints. To many it did not matter. What was important was that Cassell's editorial team, led at the start by E. V. Odle, were seeking stories of quality and merit. Austin Clarke, who became Odle's assistant in 1929, recalled that "The task of finding good stories in collections and files of old magazines was easy yet tantalizing, for the short story as a literary form is little more than a century old."[3] So much excellent fiction had been published over the previous three or four decades

(they seldom went earlier) that *The Argosy* could always guarantee a quality line-up.

The Argosy did run some new items. Eden Phillpotts's "Something to Talk About" (Dec 1926) is listed as "A New Play" and had no other publication before inclusion in *Three Short Plays* (Duckworth, 1928). *Argosy* published other new plays by Clemence Dane, W. W. Jacobs and Thornton Wilder. Likewise John Galsworthy's "Told by the Schoolmaster" (May 1927) was promoted as "John Galsworthy's Latest Story".[4] *Argosy* ran many new poems by W. B. Yeats, Walter de la Mare, Alfred Noyes, John Drinkwater and W. H. Davies. It also ran the pre-book serialisation of the novels "Flowering Wilderness" by John Galsworthy (Sept-Dec 1932) and "Five Silver Daughters" by Louis Golding (Dec 1933-Jul 1934). It occasionally ran a new short story, such as Stacy Aumonier's "Second Subject" (Sept 1932), plus many translated especially for the magazine, such as Stefan Zweig's "Letter from an Unknown Woman" (Jan 1933). There were several original essays and reminiscences such as Newman Flower's "The Arnold Bennett I Remember" (Jan 1934) and Edward J. O'Brien's short series "Modern Masters of the Short Story" (Aug 1934-Jan 1935). A careful analysis of the magazine could reveal other original contributions.

---

[2] *The Argosy*, June 1926, p. 16.
[3] Austin Clarke, *A Penny in the Clouds* (Routledge & Kegan Paul, 1968), p. 187.
[4] This was its first British appearance though it had just appeared in America in the charity volume *Samples* (Boni & Liveright, 1927).

Occasionally *Argosy* included little extras. The third issue (Aug 1926), ran a long lost poem by Lewis Carroll, "The Lady of the Ladle", which had previously appeared only in *The Whitby Gazette* for 31 August 1854. It also ran several series such as the "World's Great Mystery Stories", "World's Great Love Stories" and "World's Best Short Novels". In later series it invited authors to contribute their own comments, so that in the "Great Fiction Characters" series that began in August 1929, W. W. Jacobs, Hugh Walpole, Cutcliffe Hyne and others penned a few words on how their famous characters originated.

Its selection of authors was mostly British or American, with a smattering of European – usually French and Russian. The expression "world's best" was arguably an exaggeration, as only one or two translated stories appeared each issue. In most cases Cassell drew from their own archives. After the magazine was transferred to Amalgamated Press in December 1926 the archive grew, but editor Clarence Winchester cast his net wide and could always boast major names in every issue. Stacy Aumonier, Arnold Bennett, Robert W. Chambers, Noël Coward, Arthur Conan Doyle, Thomas Hardy, Gilbert Parker, Sax Rohmer, Rafael Sabatini, H. de Vere Stacpoole, H. G. Wells and Oscar Wilde are just a few of the names reprinted in the first year, and every story writer of note appeared during the magazine's run.

Originally *The Argosy* was not illustrated and featured the same sailing-ship cover, with occasional variations. Over time a few illustrations appeared, mostly for the lead story, but from the December 1933 issue the magazine was redesigned. A new cover was introduced featuring photographs of various authors, and several illustrated features were added. This was evidently unpopular as the standard cover was restored after just two issues though the pictorial features continued, and rather more stories were illustrated. Clearly what had become a well-established format was not to be trifled with. During the pre-War years, *The Argosy* was remarkably consistent in format and content. It presented a varied mix of material, some of which reflected the public mood of the day, but most of which was simply good quality fiction.

However, by 1940 the Wartime restrictions were starting to bite. Most of the fiction magazines had fallen by the wayside – *The Argosy* would absorb one of the last survivors, *The Red*. At this time *The Argosy* chose to restyle itself. A new series started in February 1940 in a slightly smaller format with an increased page count. Otherwise it continued just as before. *The Argosy* survived well beyond the closing date of this volume, but though it later shrunk to pocket-book size, it remained consistent in its original aim of presenting the best stories from around the world. By the time of its demise in 1974 it was the last survivor in Britain from the age of the popular-fiction magazine.

Frequency: Monthly but no issue for Aug 1959, and issues combined for Jan/Feb 1971, in both cases due to industrial action.
Publishers: Cassell to Feb 1927; thereafter Amalgamated Press (Fleetway Publications from Oct 1959 and absorbed within IPC Magazines from Feb 1969).
Editors: Clarence Winchester (1926-40), Harold W. Snoad (1941-44), Dorothy M. Sutherland (1945-64), Laurence Hammond (1965-74).
Format/Size: First series, standard pulp; page count mostly 152, dropped to 140/144, Oct 1931; 128, May 1937; 112, Feb 1938. Second series was in a large digest format reducing to digest from Oct 1943. First five issues 192 pages; thereafter varied considerably between 160, 144 and 128.

Price: 1/- to Sept 1941; 1/3d to Oct 1947; 1/6d to Apr 1956; 2/- to Dec 1958; 2/6d to Jun 1964; 3/6d to Jul 1970; 4/- (20p) to Apr 1971; thereafter 25p.
Holdings:
Complete run, UK. Bodleian (*Call Number*: Per. 25612 d.64 to Jun 1929; Per. 25612 d.229 for remainder).
Substantial run, UK. • British Library is missing Jul-Dec 1934, Jul 1936-Jan 1940, Mar 1940-Apr 1941, Oct 1969, Apr 1970, Sept 1970, Jul 1971 (*Shelfmark*: PP.6004.tad). • National Library of Scotland (*Shelfmark*: HP1.88.883 SER) has run from Jun 1926–Mar 1960.
Collecting points: Post-war issues remain comparatively common but pre-war pulp issues are becoming scarcer. They usually surface in single issues.

* * *

BEST-STORY MAGAZINE
33 issues. Volume 1, Number 1, August 1926 to Number 33, April 1929.

As the title suggests, *Best-Story* was primarily a reprint magazine, hot on the heels of *Argosy*, but a much bigger offering, most issues running to 192 pages. Its bright covers promised romance and intrigue, and though its appearance was pure pulp, it presented a wide selection of authors including John Buchan, Thomas Burke, E. F. Benson, Marjorie Bowen, Robert Hichens, Oliver Onions, Sax Rohmer, Hugh Walpole and H. G. Wells. It ran a high proportion of mystery and supernatural stories. With the first issue it began serialisation of Fergus Hume's classic 1886 novel, "The Mystery of a Hansom Cab" and stories stretched back at least as far as 1821 with William Maginn's macabre "The Man in the Bell" (Oct 1927). Many stories were reprinted from Hutchinson's other magazines, some as recent as Margery Lawrence's "Robin's Rath" (Jul 1927) from the November 1923 *Hutchinson's Magazine*. The magazine ran no illustrations and its only other feature was "The Lighter Side", where the editor encouraged readers to submit humorous anecdotes or jokes, which seemed oddly out of place. Whilst the stories were all entertaining, and the equal of any reprint anthology, the magazine was expensive for what it offered. Nevertheless it was evidently cheap to produce and Walter Hutchinson kept it going for nearly three years until he closed his magazine operations.

Frequency: Monthly.
Publisher: Hutchinson.
Editor: Evelyn Hornibrook.
Format/Size: Standard pulp, page count 224, first issue; 192, Sept 1926; 144, May 1928.
Price: 1/-.
Holdings: *Complete run, UK.* British Library (*Shelfmark*: PP.6004.tae); Bodleian (*Call Number*: Per. 25612 d.76).
Collecting points: Increasingly rare and almost impossible to assemble a substantial run.

* * *

THE BLUE MAGAZINE
121 issues. Volume 1, Number 1, July 1919 to Number 121, August 1929.

Despite the title, *The Blue* was not related to Amalgamated Press's *Red Magazine*. It was an independent title from Walbrook & Co. in Whitefriars Street, London, with editorial offices in Charing Cross Road. It was one of the first new pulp magazines to appear after the War and though similar to *The Red* in appearance, it was closer to Cassell's *New Magazine* in content. It ran all fiction, no articles or illustrations, though it later ran photographs of actors and later still a "Who's Who" gallery of contributors. The editor was not named in the magazine or in market reports. According to magazine authority Jack Adrian[1] the owner was Frank Sellicks who may also have been the editor at the outset, but later editorial remarks suggest there were two joint editors.

Lacking the financial backing of the bigger publishers, *The Blue* seldom published stories by major writers but prized its reputation for stories of originality, regardless of the author's renown. Writing in the April 1927 issue, the editors proudly claimed to have published the first stories by P.C. Wren, F.A.M. Webster and C. Lestock Reid. In fact all three had sold stories elsewhere before their appearances in *The Blue*, but Webster and Reid established their reputations there. Wren's first appearance, "At Oxford" (Jul 1919) is little more than a humorous school story, but "The Old Knife" (Jan 1920) is more in line with the military stories for which Wren became famous.

Webster and Archibald Pechey, who wrote under the alias "Valentine", were the most prolific contributors. Webster, athlete and traveller, contributed mostly empire and mystery stories. His most popular were the "Old Ebbie" series (began Feb 1922) about Ebenezer Entwhistle, a chemist whose knowledge of pharmaceuticals is such that he is frequently consulted by the police. Ebbie ran through three series all of which made it into book form. Another book, *The Odyssey of Husky Hillier* (Chapman, 1924), about an African adventurer who takes on international cases, had also run in *The Blue* during 1923. Surprisingly Webster's other main series, "Max Cramer–Master in Crime" (Jul 1927-May 1928), is uncollected. Webster and C. Lestock Reid cornered the market for stories set in darkest Africa, whilst Elinor Mordaunt explored the South Seas and Edmund Snell, chose the Far East and Indonesia.

Valentine's stories were usually light-hearted, parodying the humorous if challenging mores of twenties' society, and particularly the emerging independence of young girls. His first serial for the magazine, "Cuddl'ums" (Jan-Jul 1920), was about an affectionate but innocent young girl who makes her way through life because everyone adores her. Valentine, who created the intriguing story title "The House With Someone Always Round the Corner" (Nov 1921), also looked at men cast on the scrapheap following the War and turning their skills to whatever is required in the series "Substitutes, Ltd." (Feb-Jun 1921).

---

[1] See Adrian's introduction to *The Occult Files of Francis Chard* by A. M. Burrage (Chester: Ash-Tree Press, 1996), p. xv.

The emergence of the liberated woman during the twenties was a frequent theme in *The Blue*, though never enough to tip it into being a women's magazine. Most of its contents were slanted towards men. A key feature was its regular series, right from the first issue with Arthur Applin's wartime spoof on the Arabian Nights, "Some Nights and One". Most series were either adventure or mystery, though there was an interesting historical series by Guy Thorne, covering key literary events, such as Shakespeare's inspiration in "The Dark Lady" (Oct 1920). There were several Club-story series of which the most unusual was "The Drug Club" (Sept 1922-Feb 1923) by Howel Evans, where a drug frees the good side of an individual. Edward Woodward produced a series about an investigator who takes on crimes that have baffled the police in "The Amazing Mr. Abukir" (Aug 1923-Jan 1924). There were two series about investigators of the supernatural: Ella Scrymsour's "Sheila Crerar, Psychic Investigator" (May-Oct 1920) and A. M. Burrage's "The Strange Adventures of Francis Chard" (Feb-Nov 1927). The June 1922 issue is also of interest for the posthumous appearance of William Hope Hodgson's borderline science-fiction story, "A Timely Escape".[2]

The occasional surprise name surfaces, such as actress Hermione Gingold who collaborated with her then husband, Eric Maschwitz, on a revenant story, "The Bed" (Aug 1923). Maschwitz also contributed several Grand Guignol stories. Stacy Aumonier, who in the 1920s was regarded as one of the premier short-story writers, contributed one of his typically matter-of-fact episodes, "And Life Went On" (Sept 1925). Alec Waugh contributed several stories reflecting his finely crafted observations on people and relationships, starting with "An Unfinished Story" (Sept 1921), which was more suited to the growing market of slick magazines than the pulps. Other writers of interest include Marjorie Bowen, Beatrice Heron-Maxwell, Edgar Jepson, Ethel Mannin and Esmé Wynne-Tyson.

Rare amongst magazines, *The Blue* revealed its circulation figures as a lure to advertisers. The December 1921 issue carried fully audited figures from the first issue showing that during its first six months it had an average circulation of 32,765 rising to just under 35,200 over the next six months. Though a respectable figure for a newly established magazine it was about a third that of its rivals.

Early covers were drab and uninspiring, but they went through rapid changes from portraits or photographs of then famous actors to a variety of modernist and avant-garde paintings, reflecting the excitement and daring of the "roaring twenties". This trendiness was exaggerated when the editors chose to reprint French stories in their original language, starting with "La Vengeance á Domicile" by J.-H. Rosny, aîné (Mar 1929). Perhaps *The Blue* had pretentions of becoming a slick magazine or a literary review. At this same time it changed publisher and the indications are that further changes were afoot, but instead the magazine soon ceased, one of many victims of a blight that hit fiction magazines at the end of the twenties.

Frequency: Monthly, but combined Jul/Aug 1928 issue.
Publisher: Walbrook to Jun 1926; William Southern, Jul-Dec 1926; F. J. Parsons for The Blue Magazine Company, Jan 1927-Jul/Aug 1928; Link House, Sept 1928-Aug 1929.
Editor: Possibly Frank Sellicks to 1926; others not known.

---

[2] According to Sam Moskowitz in the Hodgson collection *The Haunted Pampero* (Grant, 1991), Hodgson was paid ten guineas for this story. At 5,000 words this suggests that *The Blue* paid a halfpenny a word, a very basic rate for the period.

Format/Size: Standard pulp, page count 96, rose to 104, Feb 1928; 128, Sept 1928.
Price: 7d, rose to 9d, Feb 1920; 1/-, Sept 1920.
Holdings: *Substantial run, UK.* British Library is missing only the first issue and that for Oct 1928 (*Shelfmark*: PP.6018.tal).
Collecting points: Rare, though occasional single issues appear. Publisher's binding was in plain blue cloth, unindexed, in half-yearly volumes. Only one full run known in private hands.

* * *

CASSELL'S MAGAZINE

789 issues in four series. First series: Volume 1, Number 1, April 1867 to Volume 3, Number 32, November 1869; 32 issues. New series, Volume 1, Number 1, December 1869 to Volume 9, Number 60, November 1874; 60 issues. Relaunched as CASSELL'S FAMILY MAGAZINE, Volume 1, Number 1, December 1874 to Volume 24, Number 12, November 1897; retitled CASSELL'S MAGAZINE, Volume 25, Number 1, December 1897 to Volume 53, Number 6, March 1912; 448 issues. Relaunched as CASSELL'S MAGAZINE OF FICTION, Number 1, April 1912 to Number 249, December 1932; 249 issues.

Cassell's Magazine superseded the weekly *Cassell's Illustrated Family Paper*, which had appeared in 1853 as one of the earliest publications of John Cassell (*left*). An ardent temperance reformer, Cassell established his publishing business to help educate and enlighten the masses. The didactic overtones of *Cassell's*, and its even more religious companion, *The Quiver* (see Section 2), were in tune with High Victorian evangelism. The forerunner of *Cassell's Magazine* does not concern us in detail but its emphasis on moral rectitude and Victorian values cast a long shadow over the publishing company, and *Cassell's* for the rest of the Victorian era.

When *Cassell's Magazine* was launched, as a monthly, under the editorship of William Moy Thomas there was an attempt at a more liberal policy. Like its predecessor it was illustrated with engravings, many of which Cassell had acquired through a cost-sharing arrangement with Hachette in France. Although the initial investment was high, Cassell's were able to re-use these plates many times over. Newman Flower recalled how old plates were still being used fifty years later. The magazine tried to appeal to the readership of *All the Year Round*, where the main contributor, after Dickens, was Wilkie Collins. Thomas turned a hand to his own form of "sensation" novel, "A Fight for Life" (1868). It fell on stony ground and Thomas left after only a year.

His successor, John Lovell, did no better and although his successor, Hugh Haweis, also served only a year, it was under him that the magazine began to grow. Haweis was a clergyman and, like Cassell, believed in the morally improving quality of fiction, but recognised this could be achieved equally through the "sensation" novel as with the overtly didactic. It was Haweis who brought to *Cassell's* both Wilkie Collins and J. Sheridan Le Fanu, whilst Charles Reade, was secured soon after by Haweis's successor, the popular novelist George Manville Fenn. Under Haweis, *Cassell's* circulation rose to 200,000. But he didn't entirely sell out to popular demands. He became famous for editing the phrase "Damn it" out of Collins's serial "Man and Wife" in 1869. Fenn was less prudish, knowing a shocking story when he saw one, but he probably went too far when he serialised Reade's "A Terrible Temptation" in 1871. Similar to the work of Mary Braddon, this lurid novel was Reade's attack upon lunatic asylums, but the establishment of the day found it too disgraceful. The *Saturday Journal* remarked that it cast "shame on the professedly decent journals which are publishing the loathsome production." *The Times* warned mothers about letting their daughters near it. Although this notoriety boosted sales of the book, it reflected poorly on *Cassell's* image. In due course Fenn left to follow a successful career as a writer of boys' books and *Cassell's*, now retitled *Cassell's Family Magazine*, with dull lifeless covers, sank into mediocrity under new editor Bonavia Hunt.

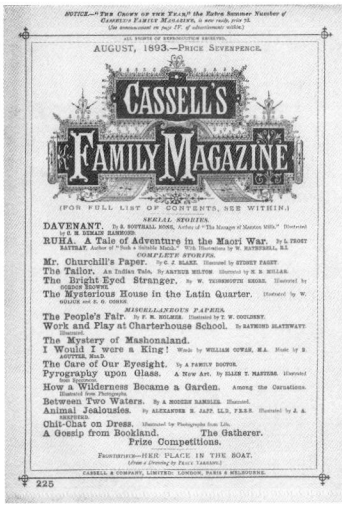

Hunt was a "safe bet". He had joined Cassell's in the same year that John Cassell died and, like Cassell, was a religious man and a dedicated educationalist – founder of Trinity College, London in 1872. He had been editor of *The Quiver* since 1865, founded Cassell's children's magazine, *Little Folks* in 1871, and assumed editorial control of *Cassell's* in 1874, where he remained for twenty-two years. His main interest, though, was *The Quiver*, where he was editor for forty years. As a result *Cassell's Family Magazine* languished. In the words of Cassell's historian, Simon Nowell-Smith, the magazine gave its readers "a dead level of romance and adventure, varied at most by sociological purpose but never touched with inspiration."

Little that was published during Hunt's editorship remains memorable. The primary contributors were former editor George Manville Fenn, Lucy Farmer (with her chronicles of Cardewe Manor), Henry Frith (one of the few authors to show originality), John Berwick Harwood, whose works, along with Frank Barrett's, were the closest Hunt came to anything sensational, and L. T. Meade (who really only flowered after Hunt's tenure ended). One of the reasons that *Cassell's* remained relatively innocuous was that in October 1883 Cassell's had started *Cassell's Saturday Journal* in response to the success of Newnes's weekly *Tit-Bits*. A more liberated paper, it published (usually anonymously) a greater range of exciting and adventurous fiction. Occasionally writers would spill over from the *Journal* into *Cassell's*, and in this way *Cassell's* published early stories by Arthur Conan Doyle, "Touch and Go" (Apr 1886), and C. J. Cutcliffe Hyne.

Hunt was set in his ways and took little notice of the success of *The Strand*. In this he was encouraged by Cassell's General Manager (since 1887), Wemyss Reid. A political journalist, Reid had little interest in popular fiction and, along with the firm's other "greybeards", looked back on Cassell's educational and religious heritage in the belief that they were always in the right. It was not until the emergence of *The Windsor Magazine*, that the hierarchy at Cassell took some notice. They retained Hunt at *The Quiver*, where he was best suited, but from December 1896 brought in Max Pemberton, the founding editor of Cassell's successful boys' magazine, *Chums*, to work the same magic with *Cassell's*. From Pemberton's first issue the magazine changed format, increasing its page count to 112 and introducing more pictures, though most were still sketches or engravings from Cassell's archives around which authors were being asked to write new stories. Photographs remained a rarity. A year later the name reverted to *Cassell's Magazine*, distancing itself from the home-and-hearth image that "*Family*" implied. *Cassell's* slowly remodelled itself on *The Strand*, with popular articles, novelty features and children's stories in addition to the regular diet of fiction.

It took a while for Pemberton to build his stable of writers, though he was able to rely on established names such as Grant Allen and L. T. Meade plus emerging writers A.E.W. Mason and Horace Annesley Vachell. Meade was a good example of a popular writer who was acceptable to both the new and the more traditional "Sunday" reader. To *Cassell's* she brought a new series, "A Master of Mysteries" (Jun-Nov 1897), the adventures of John Bell, "ghost explorer" written with Robert Eustace. One of Pemberton's new regulars was Halliwell Sutcliffe, regarded by some as the successor to R. D. Blackmore, with his brooding stories set in the remote moors and dales. Sutcliffe also wrote historical stories, a strong feature of *Cassell's*, always evoking a sense of the past. There remains a feeling when reading any issue of *Cassell's*, that whereas *The Strand* and most other new popular magazines concentrated on the town and the present, *Cassell's* looked to the rural and the past. It gave *Cassell's* an archaic, period feel that set it apart from its rivals, more for ill than for good.

There were a few contributors who bucked that trend with forward-looking stories – Robert Barr, L. J. Beeston, Henry A. Hering, Fred M. White, Cutcliffe Hyne – but most, like Ouida, Anthony Hope, H. Seton Merriman, even William Le Queux at times, seemed happy with this tapestry of the past. Pemberton also contributed several historical novels and secured H. Rider Haggard's novel of the crusades, "The Brethren" (Dec 1903-Nov 1904). Perhaps the most memorable serial that Pemberton acquired was Rudyard Kipling's "Kim" (Jan-Nov 1901).

One writer who did capture the public imagination, giving *Cassell's* a character that could rival Sherlock Holmes and Captain Kettle, was E. W. Hornung. He created the gentleman-thief A.J. Raffles, a burglar with a code of ethics. Published in bookform as *The Amateur Cracksman* (Methuen, 1899), the series ran in *Cassell's* (from Jun 1898) as "In the Chains of Crime". It introduced a character who has long outlived its creator and become synonymous with the honourable villain.

Pemberton was unable to secure the second series of Raffles stories but he did the next best thing in acquiring the early work of R. Austin Freeman. He had first appeared in *Cassell's* under his own name with a naval story, "The Resurrection of Matthew Jephson" (Oct 1898). He adopted the alias Clifford Ashdown in collaboration with J. J. Pitcairn. Their first two series, "The Adventures of Romney Pringle" (Jun-Nov 1902) and "Further Adventures" (Jun-Nov 1903), featured another gentleman-thief. Both these and "From a Surgeon's Diary" (Dec 1904-May 1905), were a big success and paved the way for Freeman to cast off his pseudonymity and create the memorable character of Dr John Thorndyke. Unfortunately *Cassell's* missed out again as the Thorndyke stories went to *Pearson's*, but they did secure the rights to another gentleman-thief series, "The Chronicles of the Burglar's Club" by Henry A. Hering (Jun-Nov 1904).

It was not until Sir Wemyss Reid died in 1905 that further advances could be made. The new General Manager, Arthur Spurgeon, was determined to root out the stubborn traditionalists and over thirty members of staff were dismissed in his first year. Pemberton, who had liked Reid, resigned, as did Bonavia Hunt from *The Quiver*. David Williamson, who had previously edited *The Windsor* and *The Temple*, was brought in to edit *Cassell's* and *The Quiver*. From December 1905 both magazines received a facelift. The old engravings were phased out, there was an increase in photographs and new drawings and a wider range of articles on topical subjects. The size was increased to 144 pages and colour, which had been introduced in the Christmas 1903 issue, was brought cautiously to the monthly, initially on special pages where old paintings were reproduced, but then with two-tone pictures within the magazine. For two years (1906/7) *Cassell's* experimented with top quality stock for the reproduction of photographs and coarser book paper for the stories.

Although *Cassell's* was always playing catch-up with the popular magazines, Williamson attracted some major names. Of special interest were the serialisation of Conan Doyle's "literary autobiography" "Through the Magic Door" (Dec 1906-Nov 1907), G. K. Chesterton writing about what he felt was "My Ideal Magazine" (Dec 1906), H. Rider Haggard's new African adventure, "Benita" (Dec 1905-May 1906) and Joseph Conrad's "Il Conde" (Aug 1908). Williamson also acquired the Thinking Machine stories by Jacques Futrelle starring Professor S.F.X. van Dusen (left), which began in the December 1907 issue.

More changes were afoot. Spurgeon continued to purge *Cassell's* of its old guard and brought in further new blood. Newman Flower, who would later edit *Cassell's*, started an all-fiction pulp magazine *The Story-Teller*, with profitable results. Spurgeon also hired American journalist James Walter Smith as General Editor. Boston born-and-bred, but long resident in London, Smith had compiled the American edition of *The Strand* for the past twelve years. Williamson remained with *The Quiver*, but was replaced on *Cassell's* by Stanhope W. Sprigg, working under Smith.[1] In his history of the House of Cassell, Simon Nowell-Smith is dismissive of Smith stating that "this experiment produced no lasting results" and the magazine's circulation continued to drop to around 34,000. There was no improvement in the magazine's content and, if anything, a monotony set in. The covers, which under Williamson had been bright, became drab, the page count reverted to 112, the contents were predictable and there was little to capture the public imagination. The only series of note was Baroness Orczy's "The Adventures of Lady Molly of Scotland Yard" (Jun 1909-May 1910).

Spurgeon felt the need for drastic changes. He asked Newman Flower to take over *Cassell's* and introduce some radical thinking. The changes were fundamental. Relaunched as *Cassell's Magazine of Fiction and Popular Literature*, it was, to all intents, a new magazine. Declaring

---

[1] Sprigg is listed as editor in the 1910 edition of *The Writers' and Artists' Yearbook*, suggesting he held that rôle during 1909. Nowell-Smith makes no reference to him and implies that Smith took over directly from Williamson. Most likely, Sprigg was Smith's sub-editor.

itself "The Largest Magazine in the World", it ran to 260 pages, on lower quality paper, and reduced its cover price from sixpence to fivepence. It claimed that each issue would run some twenty short stories, four or five articles, a complete novel, and a fashion section.

The first new issue, dated April 1912, included an article on divorce by H. G. Wells, stories by I.A.R. Wylie, Frank Shaw, Alice and Claude Askew, Fred M. White and C. Randolph Lichfield, and a complete novel, "The Valehampton Riddle" by T. W. Hanshew, featuring Cleek, the master of disguise. Nor was this a one-off. *Cassell's* remained at five pence and delivered what it promised until wartime restrictions caused the price to rise and the page count to drop. By then *Cassell's* had achieved its aim. The magazine's circulation had risen five-fold. The cover of the April 1918 issue, which featured a scoop with Manfred Von Richthofen's "My Fights on the Western Front", proclaimed "The Most Widely Read of All British Magazines". They also launched a bumper *Cassell's Winter Annual*.[2]

Under Spurgeon and Flower Cassell's operations came back into profit. Flower rose through the ranks, becoming a director in 1915 and ultimately Managing Director and President of the Company. Although he remained closely attached to *The Story-Teller*, he stepped back from the other magazines and a succession of sub-editors ran *Cassell's* through the war and into the 1920s.

What Flower had recognised was that by 1911 fiction magazines had fallen into two main camps. There was the glossy general-interest magazine, dominated by *The Strand* and *The London*, and there was the new breed of all-fiction magazine, where *The Story-Teller* led the way. Changing *Cassell's* so dramatically was a risk, but a calculated one, as Flower sensed that here was a market looking to be dominated. These cheaper magazines – the dawn of the pulp magazine in Britain – appealed to a wider, less demanding readership who enjoyed sensational drama, adventure, mystery and romance, material that could be produced by a second-tier of reliable but less expensive writers. Big names could be included now and again, but this was the age of the pulpsmith. The kind of material that *Cassell's* now offered by the cartload included new Scarlet Pimpernel stories by Baroness Orczy, work by Sax Rohmer (whose Dr Fu-Manchu series was running in *The Story-Teller*), swashbuckling historical adventures by Rafael Sabatini, sea stories by Captain Frank Shaw, the Jimmie Dale stories (another gentleman burglar) by Frank L. Packard, plus occasional appearances by H. de Vere Stacpoole, G. K. Chesterton (including a new series of Father Brown stories in 1925), Alfred Noyes, Robert W. Chambers and enough big guns to keep every one happy.

After the War *Cassell's* benefited from the public's desire for escapist reading material and the magazine prospered during the early twenties. It increased its size from July 1922 to 160 pages and was able to boast that it was "The Biggest Magazine on the Bookstalls" (though by

---

[2] The first volume appeared in December 1915 and ran to 320 pages, possibly the largest single issue of a pulp magazine. It included a novel by Andrew Soutar and stories by H. G. Wells, Arnold Bennett, Ruby M. Ayres and others, plus colour cartoons by Lawson Wood. All stories appear to be reprints. Wartime restrictions delayed the next *Annual* until November 1920. Two further annuals appeared before it was dropped and the pages of *Cassell's Magazine* increased. A *Cassell's Holiday Annual* was issued in 1926.

then the large slicks like *Nash's* could challenge that). Whilst *The Story-Teller* was the primary magazine at Cassell's for mystery and adventure and *The New* shifted towards women's fiction and romance, *Cassell's* followed the middle road. In the immediate post-war years it boasted several major names, amongst them Arnold Bennett, Warwick Deeping, Sax Rohmer, Robert W. Chambers and Zane Grey. It ran features by or about almost every Crown Head of Europe. By 1926 it also experimented with returning to higher quality coated stock, but only briefly. *Cassell's* had enough sales to sustain itself, and though it was never in the front rank, it was firmly in the second.

In October 1920, the controlling share in *Cassell's* was acquired by the Berry Brothers, William and Gomer (later Lords Camrose and Kemsley) and in November 1926 they also acquired Amalgamated Press. For a brief period they presided over the biggest magazine publishing operation in Britain. In 1927 they recarved the cake with all magazines passing to Amalgamated Press whilst Cassell's became solely a publisher of books.

At Amalgamated Press *Cassell's* came under the editorial wing of Clarence Winchester who had responsibility for a dozen fiction magazines. It was too many, with a number of titles in direct competition. The early thirties saw a steady process of integration. From January 1931 *Cassell's* absorbed *The New Magazine* but, at the end of 1932, *Cassell's* was absorbed in turn by *The Story-Teller*. Its final years had seen a mixture of romance and adventure from the pens of E. Phillips Oppenheim, Horace Annesley Vachell, Rudyard Kipling, plus several American-based writers including Achmed Abdullah, H. Bedford-Jones, A. R. Wetjen and Albert Payson Terhune. It ran a couple of early features on Alfred Hitchcock, including "An Autocrat of the Film Studio" (Jan 1928) which shows Marie Belloc Lowndes watching the filming of her famous story, "The Lodger". Cassell's went with a bang, though. Its final enlarged Christmas issue ran the short novel, "The Laughing Pearl" by Bruce Graeme, featuring yet another gentleman thief, Richard Verrell, known as Blackshirt.

At times it is hard to understand how *Cassell's* survived for 65 years, but it was a mixture of dogged determination and eventually learning from trends and stealing from rivals. In that sense, like its most famous character and recurring motif, it was the Raffles of magazines.

Frequency: Monthly.
Publisher: Cassell to Feb 1927; then Amalgamated Press.
Editors: William Moy Thomas, Apr 1867-Mar 1868; John Lovell, Apr 1868-Mar 1869; H. R. Haweis, Apr 1869-Mar 1870; George Manville Fenn, Apr 1870-Nov 1874; Bonavia Hunt, Dec 1874-Nov 1896; Max Pemberton, Dec 1896-Nov 1905; David Williamson, Dec 1905-Nov 1908; Walter Smith, Dec 1908-Mar 1912 (assisted by Stanhope W. Sprigg, 1909-1910); Newman Flower, Apr 1912-1922; Charles Vivian, 1922-24; Clarence Winchester, 1924?–Dec 1932.
Format/Size: Large standard, 80 pages. Switched to standard size, 108/112 pages, Dec 1896. From Apr 1912 became standard pulp. Page count 288, dropped to 256, May 1912; 224, Nov 1914; 192, May 1916; 160, Mar 1918; 144, Apr 1918; 128/132, Aug 1918; rose to 148/152, Apr 1919; dropped to 136/140, Mar 1920, 128/132, May 1920; rose to 160, Jul 1922; dropped to 144, Nov 1928, 136, Sept 1931, and 128, Jun 1932.
Price: 6d, rose to 7d, Nov 1874; returned to 6d, Dec 1896; 5d, Apr 1912; rose to 6d, Jun 1916; 8d, May 1917; 9d, Jan 1918; 1/-, May 1918.
References: *Just As it Happened* by Newman Flower (Cassell, 1950); *The House of Cassell* by Simon Nowell-Smith (Cassell, 1958). Fiction only from Dec 1874 to Oct 1910 indexed in *Cassell's*

Family Magazine: Indexes to Fiction by Sue Thomas (University of Queensland, Victorian Fiction Research Guide #12, 1987).
Other editions: An American edition, dated one month later than the English, ran from Jan 1884-Dec 1907.
Holdings:
Substantial run, UK. British Library is complete except for Dec 1903-May 1904; Dec 1904-May 1905; Jun-Nov 1908; Jan-Jun 1914; Dec 1919; Jul-Dec 1923; Jan-Jun 1925; Jan and Dec 1927; Nov and Dec 1930 (*Shelfmark*: PP.6004.da). • The Bodleian run is sub-divided. *Cassell's* (*Family*) *Magazine* is complete (*Call Number*: Per. 256 d.256). *Cassell's Magazine of Fiction* is near complete, missing issues for Jan 1915, Feb-Oct 1932 (*Call Number*: Per. 25611 d.5). • Cambridge University Library has *Cassell's Magazine*, 1867-1908 (*Classmark*: L900.b.91). • National Library of Scotland run of *Cassell's* (*Family*) *Magazine* is missing Jun 1898-Aug 1911 (*Shelfmark*: Y.16). It has no copies after Mar 1912.
Substantial run, US: Boston Public Library has issues from 1867-1922. • Library of Congress has issues Apr 1867-Mar 1912 (*Call Number*: AP4.C3). • New York Public Library has run Nov 1867-Jan 1907, incomplete.
Collecting points: Publisher's binding is red cloth and between 1896 and 1912 is especially attractive in decorative art nouveau boards. Most volumes until 1912 are relatively common but thereafter are scarce and only a few single issues tend to surface, seldom in good condition.

* * *

CHAPMAN'S MAGAZINE OF FICTION

92 issues. Volume 1, Number 1, May 1895 to Volume 11, Number 2, October 1898; 42 issues. Retitled CRAMPTON'S MAGAZINE from Volume 11, Number 3, November 1898 to Volume 19, Number 92, December 1902; 50 issues.

Chapman's Magazine took its name from the venerable Victorian publisher Chapman and Hall. It was the brainchild of Oswald Crawfurd who had become the company's chairman upon the retirement of Frederic Chapman. The son of a diplomat, Crawfurd had been the British consul in Oporto from 1866-1890, but had always been a devotee of literature and the arts and had written several books and served as editor of *Black & White*. Charming, suave and something of a lady's man, Crawfurd had winning ways and though Frederic Chapman, who remained as Managing Director, did not always agree with Crawfurd's plans, Crawfurd usually got his way – and this became absolute after Chapman's death in March 1895. Chapman and Hall already published the relatively successful *Fortnightly Review* which, after a radical period under Frank Harris, had become more sedate under W. L. Courtney. Crawfurd proposed an all-fiction companion and *Chapman's Magazine of Fiction* appeared in May 1895.

Flying in the face of recent trends, *Chapman's* was unillustrated and carried nothing but fiction. Crawfurd, a traditionalist, modelled his magazine on the old-style monthlies such as *The Cornhill* and *Longman's* and perhaps *Belgravia* which had become all-fiction in 1886, all magazines that were suffering from the new competition. Crawfurd no doubt believed that his magazine, whilst not destined for a high circulation, would appeal to the literary and critical establishment and, to this end, he sought to acquire the best new quality fiction. Unfortunately Crawfurd had a higher view of his abilities than he possessed. Writing in *A Hundred Years of Publishing*, Arthur Waugh observed that:

> Crawfurd was a kindly, amiable man, with a genuine love of literature, but he was an amateur in everything he essayed. He went at his work with all an amateur's enthusiasm, but he had not the solid, expert knowledge and experience to check his judgment.

The result was a magazine that Crawfurd intended to appeal to a literary readership but with contents more suited to a popular fiction audience. The first few issues, for instance, contained material that would not have been out of place in *The Strand* or *The Idler*. Bret Harte, darling of the British literary circuit and, like Crawfurd, a former consul, contributed his new novel, "In a Hollow of the Hills" (May-Nov 1895). Stanley J. Weyman, whose popularity had surged with his historical novel *A Gentleman of France* (1893), contributed an historical play, set during the siege of Paris, "For the Cause" (May 1895). The discoverer of Weyman, James Payn, then editor of *The Cornhill*, but a devotee of sensational fiction, contributed a brief ghost story "A Noiseless Burglar" (May 1895). Crawfurd's mistress and protégé, Violet Hunt, who was only just establishing herself as a writer, contributed a serial, "A Hard Woman" (May-Nov 1895) and there were other contributions by S. R. Crockett, Flora Annie Steel, George Gissing, Frank R. Stockton, Brander Matthews, E. W. Hornung and Eden Phillpotts. Crawfurd also published work by Stephen Crane, whose "The Bride Comes to Yellow Sky" (Jan 1898) is regarded as amongst his best stories. It was a solid, if slightly eclectic, selection, but packaged in the wrong garb and not necessarily reaching the readership to which it would most appeal

In fact the early issues of *Chapman's* have more appeal for those interested in ghost stories and crime fiction. These include, in the 1895 Christmas issue, Violet Hunt's "The Story of a Ghost", B. M. Croker's "Number Ninety" and Arthur Machen's "The Red Hand". In addition to a short series of detective stories, "The Experiences of Inspector Battle" by George Ira Brett (May-Jun 1895), there was "The Long Arm" (Aug 1895) by Mary E. Wilkins, one of the first stories based on the notorious Lizzie Borden case. E. F. Benson contributed "My Friend the Murderer" (Oct 1895) and, blending the criminous with the grotesque, was M. P. Shiel with "The Case of Euphemia Raphash" (Dec 1895). Crawfurd also published the first of the exotic Kai Lung stories by Ernest Bramah, "The Story of Yung Chang" (Oct 1896).

There were several unusual mood stories, most rather downbeat, such as Mark Sale's "How Hepzibah Shut the Gates of Paradise" (Sept 1895) and Mary Gaunt's bleak story of a suicide, "Where No Hope is Left" (Jan 1896). Even Jerome K. Jerome's attempt at levity, "A Man of the World" (Jan 1896) is ultimately a depressing story about the boredom of an aesthete. Crawfurd contributed several stories himself, mostly under the alias Joseph Strange, including a play, "The Newer Woman" (Jul 1895), set in the future and parodying female emancipation.

Chapman's thus established a magazine of challenging and unusual fiction, somewhat in the vein of *Pall Mall Magazine* and *The Yellow Book*, but lacking the artistic daring of the latter and the financial base of the former. His selection of material was, at the outset, inventive and reliable. He chose for the delight of the idea, the type of "clever" story that was emerging in the USA in *The Chapbook* and *The Black Cat*, but which had yet to establish itself in Britain.

Crawfurd may thus be seen as a traditionalist in style, but a radical in outlook. It was a magazine that has appeal in hindsight, but which failed to hold a readership in its day.

Crawfurd persevered with *Chapman's* for three years and then, tiring of the in-house criticism levelled at him, resigned and took the magazine with him. Although a man of  independent means he had sunk much money into *Chapman's* which left him in financial straits. He turned to writing, but also wished to continue editing and sold *Chapman's Magazine* to New Century Press. This small firm had launched the *New Century Review* in 1897 and was seeking to broaden its magazine base. New Century took over *Chapman's* and renamed it *Crampton's Magazine* from November 1898.

Nothing else changed. The magazine continued in its own individual way only now, with less money to hand, there were less well known names – Beatrice Heron-Maxwell and Walter Besant amongst them. Crawfurd relied more on his new writers, Violet Hunt, Ernest Bramah and E. R. Punshon. Unfortunately the magazine lost such direction as it had. Whereas its main appeal had been Crawfurd's interest in the unusual, the content now became more predictable, with an increase in domestic stories and romances.

Crawfurd remained with the magazine for most if not all of the next three years but the turbulence in his private life suggests he was no longer providing the magazine with the attention it needed. New Century Press closed down its operations in September 1900 and the magazine passed to new owners in what was a period of some disruption.[1] The new editor, according to the *Literary Year-Book*, was George Perris, also editor of *Concord* and known for his interest in international affairs. He noted that the "wave of interest in the New Short Fiction" which had buoyed *Chapman's Magazine* aloft in the mid-nineties had now subsided and that whilst *Crampton's* would continue to publish short stories it would also run non-fiction. Such items as "Life in the Antarctic" by Frederick A. Cook (Oct 1900), "An Audience with the Emperor of China" by Sheridan P. Read (Nov 1900) and the debate, "The Yellow Peril: Is it a Reality?" (Jun 1901), soon dominated *Crampton's*, making it more of a review than a popular magazine. There was some fiction of note, including Stephen Crane's last story, "The Squire's Madness" (Oct 1900), completed by his widow; "The Life-Monger" (Jul-Aug 1901), one of Bertram Atkey's earliest stories; and the novel, "Love's Renewal" by the French writers "J.H. Rosny" (Jul-Dec 1901).

The change seems to have been welcomed as the editor reported that copies were sold out within days of publication, but interest must have faded rapidly as it changed hands again in December 1901. The new editor, the ebullient Harold Tremayne, injected new life into it and introduced a range of more popular writers. Edith Nesbit, Mrs Croker and Alice Perrin all appeared in the first issue, and Louis Wain contributed the first of a series of articles, "The Story of My Work", which suffered only from not being illustrated. Nesbit also contributed a new Oswald Bastable story, "An Object of Value and Virtue" (Feb 1902). With "The Delirium

---

[1] An apology for errors "owing to the changes first of Proprietorship and Editorship and then of Printers" was published in the September 1900 issue. The October editorial referred to the "sudden" change. The identity of the new proprietor is not known.

of Nine Stars" (Feb 1902), a tale of drugs and murder, Fred M. White began a series of dramatic stories. There were stories by "Rita", Louis Becke and Richard Marsh. Sidney Dark began a series of "Pen Pictures" with a profile of Conan Doyle (Feb 1902) and there were two symposia on the subject of "My Ideal", with Marie Lloyd writing on her ideal man.

Just as the magazine was reawakening, Tremayne, who was primarily a parliamentary reporter and was looking for vehicles to promote his own activities, resigned in order to pursue work with the Tariff Reform League. *Crampton's* folded with the December 1902 issue.

Chapman/Crampton's was a magazine out of its time, inadequately financed and edited with too much individual idealism and too little regard for the market. It should still be better remembered because of the authors it helped promote but commercially it was a failure. Ironically within a few years of its demise more adequately financed all-fiction magazines emerged and prospered – *The Grand*, *The Novel* and *The Story-Teller* – and Crawfurd, who continued to write fiction, lived just long enough to see it. He died in 1909 aged seventy-five.

Frequency: Monthly.
Publisher: Chapman & Hall to Oct 1898; W. R. Russell for the New Century Press, Nov 1898-Sept 1900; publisher unstated, Oct 1900-Nov 1901; Anthony Treherne, Dec 1901-Dec 1902.
Editors: Oswald Crawfurd, May 1895-Sept 1900(?); George H. Perris, Oct 1900-Nov 1901; Harold Tremayne, Dec 1901-Dec 1902.
Format/Size: Standard, unillustrated; 112 pages, rose to 120 pages for *Crampton's*, dropped to 88/92, May 1900; rose to 120, Dec 1901; dropped to 112, May 1902; 96, Sept 1902.
Price: 6d.
References: Arthur Waugh, *A Hundred Years of Publishing* (Chapman & Hall, 1930), pp. 188-194.
Holdings:
Complete run, UK. Bodleian (*Call Number*: Per. 256 d.124). • Cambridge University Library (*Classmark*: L996.c.44). • National Library of Scotland (*Shelfmark*: U.410).
Substantial run, UK. British Library has volumes 1–5 (May 1895-Dec 1896), and volume 7 (May-Aug 1897) but is missing all issues of *Crampton's* (*Shelfmark*: PP.6004.gmp).
Substantial run, US: Princeton University Library has volumes 1-12, May 1895-Apr 1899. • New York Public Library has volumes 1-11, May 1895-Oct 1898.
Collecting points: Volumes of *Chapman's* occasionally surface especially the first two usually bound as one volume, but copies of *Crampton's* are much less common.

***

THE CHARING CROSS MAGAZINE
8 issues. Volume 1, Number 1, January 1900 to Volume 1, Number 8, August 1900.

At the turn of the nineteenth century the New Century Press was alive with ideas. Besides the *New Century Review* it had *Crampton's Magazine* for fiction, *The Windmill* and *The Butterfly* for art and literature, and *The Black Cat* story paper. *The Charing Cross Magazine* sought to fit somewhere in the middle, being a popular, illustrated magazine running a bit of everything. The magazine promoted itself as bright and healthy, decrying the "morbid sentiment" of recent years, and this was evidenced by the pictorial feature "Beauties of the American Stage" in the first issue and "Some Pantomime Characters" in the second. However, most articles and stories were downbeat. There was an article on "Buddhist Funeral Rites and Ceremonies", Mabel

Quiller-Couch's story "Two Years Hard Labour", and the serial, "A Baptism of Fire" by Fritz Ormsby, about a man who through a good deed is left a fortune but on whom suspicion falls. Similarly downbeat, but more unusual, was "The Crime Bacillus" (Apr 1900) by P. Beaufoy, about a virus that turns people into criminals.

The magazine had some interesting features – a blood-and-thunder sensation story, "The Mystery of Seven Deaths" by Francis St Clair (Mar 1900), an illustrated article, "Shall We Fly?" (Mar 1900), a weird mystery, "The Poison Glasses" by Harold W. Wild (Jun 1900) and an inventive series, "The Confessions of a Private Secretary" by Dagney Major (Jul-Aug 1900) – but it always looked to be struggling. The company was under financed and by September 1900 had ceased operating. The contents of a September issue were listed in the concurrent issue of *Crampton's Magazine*, but it is uncertain whether it ever appeared.

Frequency: Monthly.
Publisher: The New Century Press.
Editor: Not identified, but possibly Edwin Oliver.
Format/Size: Standard, 118/120 pages, dropped to 96, Jun 1900 and 80, Jul 1900.
Price: 3d.
Holdings:
Complete run, UK. Bodleian (*Call Number*: Per. 2705 d.116).
Substantial run, UK. British Library has Jan-May 1900 (*Shelfmark*: PP.6018.pda).
Complete run, US: Library of Congress (*Call Number*: Microfilm 82/5495).
Collecting points: Extremely rare.

* * *

THE CLUB ROOM
Total issues unknown, possibly 7. Number 1, November 1913 to uncertain (May 1914 ?)

This periodical called itself "A Magazine for Adult Minds", the editor complaining that the "public are 'fed-up' with 'slapper' literature and ask instead for a more comprehensive form of fiction for adult minds." It was a direction already being waymarked by *The Magpie*. Examples in the first issue include "The Prodigal's Brother" by Max Rittenberg (who was probably the editor) about a man's reaction to the return of his wayward brother, and "Her Little Son" by Howard P. Rockey, a tense story about a mother's fitness to rear her child. The first issue also had a powerful story of murder and revenge, "The Unwritten Law" by Andrul and a borderline science-fiction story where a scientist attempts to enhance a beggar's psychic capabilities, "The Man Who Knew" by Joseph Groves.

The magazine ran to at least May 1914, but only the first issue has been seen. Although it was a companion to *The Lady's Realm*, it shared none of that magazine's gloss and style. Printed on crude pulp paper it sold for just threepence and the editor urged the readers to patronise the advertisements in order to bolster revenue. Presumably, despite the strength of the first issue's fiction, the support was wanting.

Frequency: Monthly.
Publisher: Amalgamated Magazine Company.

Editor: not identified by possibly Max Rittenberg.
Format/Size: Slim pulp, 72 pages.
Price: 3d.
Holdings: British Library has first issue only (*Shelfmark*: PP.6004.sen). No other holdings are known.
Collecting points: Exceedingly rare. Only first issue known.

***

THE CORNER MAGAZINE
149 issues. Volume 1, Number 1, September 1922 to Volume 25, Number 149, February 1935.

The Corner was a cheaply produced pulp magazine, selling for sevenpence, which fitted, both in mood and cost, between the weekly story-papers and the shilling fiction monthlies. It kept costs low by reprinting many stories, perhaps as much as a half of its overall content, either from American sources or Cassell's own archives. It had no pretensions to grandeur but instead pandered to sheer escapism, providing a diet of unsophisticated adventure, mystery and romance fiction. Nevertheless it was exciting and popular, outliving its parent *Cassell's Magazine*, and its contents include much of interest and several surprises.

Although the magazine sought to appeal to both men and women – its very title suggests a cosy, relaxing read and it even included a women's advice column, "Melisande's Corner Causerie" – the bulk of its contents consisted of mystery stories and high adventure. Two authors stand out as its most prolific contributors. Representing Britain was Captain Frank H. Shaw who appeared in almost every issue, mostly with stirring sea stories similar to those he provided for the boys' adventure magazines. His most original series was "Blackbeard's Descendant" (Nov 1923-May 1924), about a female sailor who is a distant descendant of the notorious buccaneer. Representing America (though Swedish by birth) was Herman Landon. *The Corner* reprinted almost the entire series featuring gentleman burglar, the Picaroon, which had been running in the American pulp *Detective Story Magazine* since 1921. The character was modelled unashamedly on Frank Packard's Jimmie Dale, some of whose stories were also reprinted in *The Corner* during 1927.

Other adventure writers include H. Bedford-Jones, F.A.M. Webster, Marr Murray, and Albert R. Wetjen all with their usual fare. Top adventure writer Talbot Mundy appeared with three stories, all from American pulps, including "For Liberty!" (Aug 1934), in which freedom fighter Dick Anthony leads an army into Persia. Regular contributors of mysteries include J. Allan Dunn, Bruce Graeme and Edgar Wallace, the latter with his little known series about masked avenger, "The Earl of Nowhere" (from Aug 1929) reprinted from *The New Magazine*. Almost rivalling Landon's Picaroon for popularity were Johnston McCulley's stories about twins Peter and Paul Selbon who were swindled out of a fortune by unscrupulous financiers and who in "The Avenging Twins" (May-Oct 1924; also from *Detective Story Magazine*) sought their revenge.

Sax Rohmer, then at the height of his fame, appeared with the serial "Grey Face" (Jul 1924-Feb 1925), announced as "the Greatest Mystery Ever Written", and which Rohmer's biographer Cay Van Ash likewise called "one of the finest things written."[1] During 1926 a hit stage play was *The Bat* by Mary Roberts Rinehart and Avery Hopwood, based on Rinehart's 1908 novel, *The Circular Staircase*. *The Corner* ran the original novel under the title "The Bat" (Sept 1926-Feb 1927). Gaston Leroux, as popular then as now because of *The Phantom of the Opera*, appeared with the first English translation of "Man of a Hundred Masks" (Jan-Jul 1930). Of historical import was the publication of the first novel by Francis Beeding, an adventure of international intrigue, "The Seven Sleepers" (Jan-Jun 1925).

Other occasional contributors include Peter Cheyney, Warwick Deeping, Melville Davisson Post and Val Gielgud. Rafael Sabatini put in a solitary appearance with his mystery story "The Avenger" (Dec 1924). *The Corner* did not run much historical fiction, though there were a couple of French Revolution adventures, including S. Walkey's "When Romance Blossomed" (Aug 1925). Although the magazine was all fiction, it ran one non-fiction series by Charles Kingston about historical villains under the heading "Six Super-Rogues" (Jun-Nov 1927).

There were plenty of love stories for the female readers, with the primary contributor being Berta Ruck. This included her enterprising series, "Love Affairs of a Large Family" (Jan-Apr 1925). Ruby M. Ayres and Ethel M. Dell also appeared. The other main genre was sport stories, mostly by Sydney Horler (football and boxing) and Edward Woodward (horse-racing). There were occasional humorous stories, including some contributions by music-hall veteran George Robey, stories of the theatre by Guy Fletcher and the infrequent cowboy story, including an appearance by the prolific Max Brand, "No Partners" (Jan 1924).

The Corner liked to proclaim itself as "the biggest and brightest" sevenpenny magazine. It preferred novelettes, sometimes run as serials, and even when the page count dropped to 96 it continued to concentrate on longer stories, proclaiming them as "two novels each issue". As a counterbalance was the regular feature, "Told in the Corner Tales", which ran two or three very short stories, often with a neat twist. Until the final year, when art shifted to line-drawing fillers and silhouettes, all stories were illustrated though with no artists credited. Keen eyes, though, will find the signatures of H. M. Brock, Albert Morrow, Stanley L. Wood and Fred Bennett. Most covers are also anonymous but Lawson Wood provided occasional seasonal paintings.

The closest rival to *The Corner*, especially after *The Blue* and Hutchinson's *Adventure-Story* folded, was *The Red Magazine* and when Cassell's titles passed over to Amalgamated Press in 1927 *The Corner* and *The Red* became stable-mates. There were several mergers at this time and *The Corner* absorbed Amalgamated Press's *All-Story Magazine* in February 1928, though the latter's more sophisticated romance and human experience stories made only a brief flirtation in *The Corner*. Although there are no circulation data the figures must have been high for *The Corner* to survive as long as it did. It provided a more exciting mix of adventure and mystery than its close companions and outlived most of them. The decision to close it must have been sudden as the March 1935 issue, on sale on February 7, was announced but never appeared. Instead the promised stories appeared in the March *Red Magazine*, on sale on February 20. Despite its popularity *The Corner* is amongst the most forgotten of a number of neglected magazines, and it deserved a better fate.

---

[1] Cay Van Ash and Elizabeth Sax Rohmer, *Master of Villainy* (London: Stacey, 1972), p. 154.

Frequency: Monthly
Publisher: Cassell's, to Apr 1927; then Amalgamated Press.
Editors: Charles Vivian, 1922-24; Clarence Winchester, 1925-35.
Format/Size: Standard pulp, 128 pages, dropped to 96, Feb 1929.
Price: 7d.
Holdings: *Substantial run, UK*. British Library holding is on microfilm and is missing issues Sept 1922-Aug 1923 and Mar 1932-Feb 1933 (*Shelfmark*: PP.6018.tav; *Microfilm*: MIC.C.345). The Bodleian has issues Sept 1922-Jun 1929 (*Call Number*: Per. 25612 d.11) plus restricted access to Jul and Dec 1929 (*Call Number*: Hogan 856).
Collecting points: Very rare. Occasional single issues appear.

* * *

CRAMPTON'S MAGAZINE *see* CHAPMAN'S MAGAZINE OF FICTION

* * *

THE CRUSOE MAG.

24 issues. Volume 1, Number 1, June 1924 to Volume 4, Number 6, May 1926. Relaunched as *The Golden Mag.*

The Crusoe Mag. led a somewhat chequered career in various guises. It was a companion to *The Happy Mag.*, but whereas that contained stories of homely fun for the whole family, *The Crusoe* was aimed at younger readers. The format was identical to *The Happy* with stories set in small type, illustrated by R. H. Evens, Charles Crombie, Reginald Glossop and others, juxtaposed with cartoons, humorous sketches, jokes and anecdotes. A section, "The Bosun's Den", provided hints on handicraft, hobbies and sports, showing that the magazine was aimed more at boys than girls. The title was intended as being synonymous with adventure, as per Robinson Crusoe and Robert Louis Stevenson. John Hunter's opening serial, "Thunder Island", a story of hidden treasure, was typical of the "ripping yarns" that *The Crusoe* sought to publish.

It is perhaps surprising, then, that the real hit of the magazine was the Esme stories by A. M. Burrage. These began with the serial, "Poor Dear Esme" in the first issue. Esme Geering is a young boy who has to disguise himself as a girl when the original Esme, who was in her uncle's care, disappears. The serial is set at a girl's school and was such fun that Burrage continued the Esme stories, though with Esme back as a boy at the boy's school. Esme became to *The Crusoe* what Richmal Crompton's William Brown was to *The Happy*. Both series were illustrated by Thomas Henry.

The other hit of *The Crusoe* was the series about reporter-detective Selston Leigh by Stacey Blake and were imitations of his own Moreton Stowe stories from *The Big Budget* twenty years earlier. Other stories in *The Crusoe* followed the standard boys' adventure formula, the magazine's title giving rise to a high quota of sea stories or ones set on remote islands. Other regulars included T. C. Bridges, Peter Gladwin and Augustus Muir (whose series about Pickering, the accident-prone insurance clerk, were also popular but have dated badly).

After two years *The Crusoe* was relaunched as *The Golden Mag.*, which was identical in all but name, but was intended as a move towards becoming a western magazine. *The Crusoe* had clearly not been as successful as *The Happy* or *The Sunny* and the fault may be that whilst it looked like a family magazine it aimed itself primarily at boys who already had a profusion of other magazines. *The Golden* would fare no better (see separate entry).

Frequency: Monthly.
Publisher: Newnes.
Editor: A. C. Marshall
Format/Size: Standard pulp, 92 pages.
Price: 7d.
Holdings: *Complete run, UK.* British Library (*Shelfmark*: PP.5993.mbd); Bodleian (*Call Number*: Per. 2533 d.165).
Collecting points: Becoming increasingly uncommon but individual issues still surface. Bound volumes are uncommon.

* * *

THE DETECTIVE MAGAZINE
65 issues. Volume 1, Number 1, 24 November 1922 to Volume 5, Number 65, 8 May 1925.

The Detective Magazine was Britain's first specialist crime-fiction magazine, though it was preceded by several near-specialist boys' papers like *The Union Jack Library* and *Detective Library*. It was printed on a mixture of pulp paper and slightly coated stock of sufficient quality to carry photographs. In appearance it was similar to its stable-mate *The Premier*, with which it originally alternated on a fortnightly schedule and with which it ultimately merged. It was edited by crime afficianado George Dilnot who also contributed copiously. Dilnot's fascination with criminology meant that the magazine ran a large quota of non-fiction, often as much as half the issue. These included reminiscences by leading detectives and specialists of the day. The noted police pathologist, Bernard Spilsbury, wrote on "Science – Ally and Antagonist" in the first issue. Various former Superintendents and Chief Inspectors wrote about their greatest cases, and there were articles on specialist forensic work, such as "Dentists as Detectives".

There were various competitions set to entrap readers. Chief amongst these was a new serial by Edgar Wallace, "Flat 2", which ran in four parts. After the third part readers were asked to submit their solution to the mystery before Wallace's finale appeared.

Inevitably much of the fiction fell into various series. The first issue started Octavus Roy Cohen's stories about overweight private detective Jim Hanvey, which was then running in America in the *Saturday Evening Post*. With the second issue Mrs Wilson Woodrow began a series about lawyer-turned-criminal Heywood Achison, and Austin Philips provided something original with his Post Office sleuth, Stephen Staplehurst. The magazine's first major serial, Valentine Williams's "The Orange Divan" (30 Mar-20 Jul 1923) featured Inspector Manderton of the Yard. Other characters to appear in later issues included Arthur B. Reeves's scientific detective Craig Kennedy, Oliver Madox Hueffer's crafty villain, Monsieur Letruc, and Clarence B. Kelland's bibliophile and criminologist Alpin Stone. There was a Sherlock Holmes parody with Sheerluck Combs, "Sheer Luck Again" by Stanley Rubinstein (13 Apr 1923). One of the surprises in the magazine is an early mystery by Georgette Heyer, "Linckes' Great Case" (2 Mar 1923, right). There is also a brief serial by Harry Stephen Keeler, "The Strange Visitor" (26 Sept-10 Oct 1924), which includes E.W. Hornung's characters Raffles and Bunny. They were deleted in the book version presumably after objections from Hornung's estate.

Although it did little to develop crime fiction, it was an entertaining magazine with a varied mix of fact and fiction and it is surprising that it did not last longer – especially as the editor revealed that "many members of the present and past Government were among subscribers to *The Detective Magazine*."[1] Perhaps with such a profusion of fiction magazines in the mid-1920s – almost half the magazines covered in this Guide were on the stalls in 1925 – it was difficult for a specialist one to find a sufficient share of the market.

Frequency: Fortnightly.
Publisher: Amalgamated Press.
Editor: George Dilnot.
Format/Size: Standard pulp, 100 pages.
Price: 7d.
Holdings:
Complete run, UK. Bodleian (*Call Number*: Per. 25612 d.15).
Collecting points: Plain bound volumes occasionally appear but these lack covers and single issues are preferred. It is highly sought after so issues are expensive.

***

EMPIRE FRONTIER

99 issues. Began as THE FRONTIER, April 1925; retitled FRONTIER STORIES, January 1928; retitled EMPIRE FRONTIER, August 1929 to June 1932; relaunched as ALL STAR WESTERN AND EMPIRE FRONTIER MAGAZINE, Volume 1, Number 1, July 1932 to Volume 2, Number 5, June 1933.

During the 1920s and 1930s several of the American pulps had separate British editions (*see* Section 2). In a few instances British reprints took on a life of their own. Some, like *World Stories*, were always a separate entity, but others are more complicated, and it does not come any more labyrinthine than the pulp *Empire Frontier*. The British publisher, World's Work, was a subsidiary of the American company Doubleday, and took its name from Doubleday's magazine, *The World's Work*, which had appeared in July 1901, with a British edition started in December 1902. In March 1910 Doubleday took over an ailing magazine, *Short Stories*, and soon found they had a success on their hands. The British edition started in March 1920 was

---

[1] "Hue and Cry", *The Detective Magazine*, 27 April 1923, p. 100.

also a success. Doubleday launched two further all-fiction magazines, *The Frontier* in October 1924 and *West* in January 1926. These both received British editions, in April 1925 and August 1926 respectively, all three selling well. Doubleday admitted his surprise, remarking: "All of which is astonishing to me, because both of these magazines are most strikingly American in every sense of the word. Many of the phrases used must be entirely unintelligible to the English readers; but somehow they like it, and we are very glad that they do."[2]

All three magazines consisted primarily of western stories, which in the mid-twenties were in vogue. Even though *Short Stories* and *The Frontier* ran other mystery and adventure stories, the covers almost always portrayed cowboy scenes. *The Frontier*, which became *Frontier Stories* in December 1926, published a wide range of adventure stories, including north-west stories, sea stories, tales of Darkest Africa and of the Foreign Legion.

The British edition ran about six months behind the American. As it became established it took on its own personality. The American editorial, "The Trading Post", was substituted for a British one with its own features and, from June 1929, a separate letter column was started, encouraging feedback from British readers through-out the Empire. One view that was strongly expressed was that the magazine ran too many stories of the American frontier, and not enough set in the rest of the world. The British editor therefore decided to broaden the coverage and, from August 1929, it was retitled *Empire Frontier* and promised to publish stories set in the outposts of Empire. "The Trading Post" was suitably retitled "The Outpost" in December 1929. *Empire Frontier* was now a separate magazine in its own right, no longer a copy of its American parent. Its contents remained all reprint, but they were now drawn from a wider range of magazines. These included not only the American pulps *Argosy*, *Danger Trail*, *The Popular*, *Adventure Trails* and, of course, *Short Stories*, but also from British magazines. Somerset Maugham's "The Yellow Streak" (Oct 1929) had previously appeared in *Nash's* (Oct 1925), and H. de Vere Stacpoole's "Kitiwik" (Sept 1930) had been in *The London* (Apr 1926).

Two or three Westerns still appeared each issue, but stories were now set all over the globe. J. D. Newsom continued his Foreign Legion stories, but for most of its life *Empire Frontier* was dominated by four authors all British by birth but American resident. With "Shark Teeth" (Sept 1929), Albert R. Wetjen brought his noted Shark Gotch of the South Seas series to *Empire Frontier*. Most of L. Patrick Greene's stories were set in Rhodesia, where he had been a government official. His series about "The Major" had previously run in *The Grand* and *20-Story Magazine*, but switched to *Empire Frontier* from January 1930, which depicted the Major on its cover in all his monocled glory (*see above*). Hugh B. Cave became a popular contributor of stories set in Borneo, starting with "Borneo Brag" (Jan 1931). Victor Rousseau, who had several westerns in the magazine, introduced a series tailor-made for *Empire Frontier*, featuring Thorne the Empire Builder. "Pawns of Empire" (Jun 1931) and "The Throne Maker" (Jul 1931) saw him cutting a swathe through turbulent parts of the globe.

---

[2] F. N. Doubleday, *The Memoirs of a Publisher* (Doubleday, 1972), p. 155.

The changes proved popular with positive feedback from readers all over the world and a significant increase in sales. In the November 1929 issue the editor was confident of hitting the 100,000 mark. But other signs were less encouraging. In July 1930 the page count dropped and from October a standard cover was introduced, showing a cowboy silhouetted against a setting sun. These seemed unnecessary cost-cutting exercises if the magazine was such a success.

A further complication arose when World's Work started a new magazine, *All Star*, in April 1931, the British edition of Doubleday's *Star Magazine* (begun Nov 1930). *All Star* ran similar adventure stories to *Empire Frontier* – in fact some of the contents of *Star Magazine* were from *The Frontier*. In effect it was a direct competitor. The American parent magazine ceased in October 1931, but in Britain *All Star* continued[3] until July 1932 when it merged with *Empire Frontier* under the unwieldy title *All Star Western and Empire Frontier Magazine*. "Empire" was dropped from the fourth issue. On the contents page the stories were grouped as either "Western Stories" or "Frontier Stories", though this was dropped by the fourth issue as not all stories fitted into either category. Within a few issues the mix grew with mystery stories, war and air stories. It was vibrant and entertaining, but no longer representative of its title or cover. What had seemed a profitable and worthy venture as *Empire Frontier* had become confusing.

The situation was further aggravated by the bankruptcy of William Clayton, whose pulps had been a source for some of the reprints, and the sale of his magazines. In June 1933 *Empire Frontier* ceased publication. World's Work used the slot to relaunch it as *All-Star Detective Stories*, a reprint of a Clayton pulp which had been acquired by Dell Publishing. They retitled it *All Detective Magazine*, under which title World's Work continued the magazine in Britain as a direct reprint. Thus an enterprising experiment that grew out of a western magazine and ended up a detective magazine having worked its way round the globe, came to an end.

Frequency: Monthly.
Publisher: The World's Work, Kingswood, Surrey.
Editor: Not known.
Format/Size: Standard pulp, 176 pages; became large flat pulp, 96 pages, May 1926; reverted to standard pulp, 176 pages, Feb 1927. As *Empire Frontier*, standard pulp, 192 pages, dropped to 176, Oct 1929; 128, Jul 1930. As *All Star Western and Empire Frontier*, standard pulp, 176 pages, dropped to 128, Mar 1933.
Price: 1/-.
Holdings: *Substantial run, UK*. The British Library has a full run of *Empire Frontier*, but is missing the Feb-Dec 1927 issues of *The Frontier* (*Shelfmarks*: PP.6018.the for *The Frontier/Empire Frontier*; PP.6004.tai for *All Star* in its various incarnations). • The Bodleian has a near full run of *The Frontier/Frontier Stories*, missing only the first issue (*Call Number*: Per. 25612 d.53), plus a full run of *Empire Frontier* (*Call Number*, Per. 25612 d.53) and *All Star* (*Call Number*: Per. 25613 d.13). • Cambridge University Library has a complete run of *All-Star* through its various changes (*Classmark*: L996.c.2) but none of *The Frontier* or *Empire Frontier*.
Collecting points: The British edition of *Frontier Stories* is more common than *Empire Frontier* and its successors but occasional issues do surface.

***

---

[3] It became *All Star Western Story Magazine* in December 1931 and supplemented the remaining stories from *Star Magazine* with others from *Short Stories* and elsewhere.

THE ENGLISH ILLUSTRATED MAGAZINE

359 issues. Two series. Volume 1, Number 1, October 1883 to Volume 28, Number 234, March 1903. New series, Volume 29, Number 1, April 1903 to Volume 49, Number 125, August 1913.

The appearance of the *English Illustrated Magazine* in 1883 heralded the transition from the literary and often unillustrated magazine of the High Victorian period to the popular illustrated magazine of the late Victorian period. It was the idea of publisher Alexander Macmillan, but the development was in the hands of Joseph Comyns Carr. Despite his barrister training, Carr had passed into literary journalism and become an art critic and editor. He was editing *Arts and Letters*, the English edition of the French *L'Art*, which was not a financial success, when Macmillan asked him to produce a similar magazine for them. Macmillan already published the highly successful *Macmillan's Magazine*, where the emphasis was on fiction and literary essays. The *English Illustrated Magazine* was to be an artistic miscellany with a far broader remit. Comyns Carr was helped by Emery Walker, pioneer of the Arts and Craft Movement, who advised on format and oversaw the production of the engravings.

The magazine ran to only 64 pages and sold for a shilling, the standard cost for most of the literary monthlies, but the value for money was high because of the lavish production. It was liberally illustrated with high-class engravings on almost every page. Many works of art were reproduced for which new engravings were undertaken. The result was one of the most beautiful of the Victorian magazines. Special features included verse written and illuminated by Walter Crane (*left*), and art by Harry Furniss, Randolph Caldecott, Herbert Railton, Heywood Sumner, Laurence Alma-Tadema, Charles Whymper and Henry Ryland. The magazine ran some of the earliest artwork by Louis Wain, Albert Morrow and Hugh Thomson.

The magazine was designed around traditional artistic values and revelled in studies of nature, arts, crafts, literature and architecture. The first issue included a poem by Algernon Swinburne, essays by Grant Allen on the dormouse, Comyns Carr on Rossetti, F. W. Maitland on the old Law Courts, and a lecture by T. H. Huxley on oysters. One of the major features of the magazine, and now of great historical importance, was its study of notable landmarks and localities. There were articles on the Fens, Dartmoor, Cornwall (a series by Mrs Craik), Bruges, Bath, Clovelly, and a fascinating series by W. Outram Tristram on old coaching routes. These articles not only described but illustrated buildings and settings which no longer exist, or have been radically altered. The core of the magazine was its features on arts and crafts. This included not only studies of major artists like Rossetti, Joshua Reynolds, Gainsborough and Burne-Jones, but such crafts as lace-making, casting bronzes, etchings and hair fashion. Of particular interest is a feature on bookbinding by Cobden-Sanderson (Jan 1891).

The magazine attracted work by both new and major writers. Robert Louis Stevenson contributed "The Character of Dogs" (Feb 1884). J. M. Barrie penned one of his earliest essays, "Gretna Green Revisited" (Jan 1886). Flinders Petrie wrote on the fledgeling science of archaeology (Mar 1886). Oscar Wilde contributed "London Models" (Jan 1889) and George Bernard Shaw appeared with "Wagner in Bayreuth" (Oct 1889).

Fiction, though not the primary content, was far from ignored. Each issue usually ran one short story plus a serial. Charlotte M. Yonge contributed the first serial, the historical novel "The Armourer's Prentices" (Oct 1883-Sept 1884), but the real discovery of the first year was Stanley J. Weyman. Weyman had previously sold a few stories to *Chambers's Journal* and *The Cornhill*, and James Payn of *The Cornhill* advised him to write historical fiction. His first sales to *English Illustrated* were light contemporary romances, starting with "The Story of a Courtship" (Dec 1883), but encouraged by Comyns Carr he completed the first of many rousing historical novels, "The House of the Wolf" (Oct 1888-Mar 1889).

Comyns Carr was close friends with Frederick Fargus, who wrote as "Hugh Conway" and who, at the time that *English Illustrated* was launched, was having a phenomenal success with his murder mystery *Called Back*. Fargus, unfortunately, had only two years to live and Carr published his final works, including the novel, "A Family Affair" (Oct 1884-Sept 1885), which Fargus completed only days before his death.

Thomas Hardy was one of Macmillan's major authors, often contributing to *Macmillan's Magazine*, but an early Casterbridge episode, "Interlopers at the Knap" appeared first in *English Illustrated* (May 1884). Henry James's contributions started with "The Author of Beltraffio" (Jun-Jul 1884), which, in considering the conflict between the artistic world and "outsiders", was ideally suited to the magazine's ethos.

A fair proportion of the fiction had a fey otherworldliness, a tone set from the first issue with William Black's "The Supernatural Experiences of Patsy Corig", based on Celtic folklore. There was also J. H. Shorthouse's mystical "The Little Schoolmaster Mark" (Nov 1883), described as a "spiritual romance", and a revised version of the Earl of Lytton's novel of guilt, "The Ring of Amasis" (Oct 1889-Apr 1890[1]).

Two stories, however, stand out during the magazine's first decade. The first is William Morris's serial "The Story of the Glittering Plain" (Jun-Sept 1890). Morris, who had become a close friend of Emery Walker, had contributed several poems to *English Illustrated*, but this was his first full-length fantasy. Fantasy historian L. Sprague de Camp stated that "Morris was trying to revive the kind of medieval prose narrative that had perished with the publication of *Don Quixote*."[2] The novel could thereby be considered as the culmination of Comyns Carr's ideals with *English Illustrated*, to publish material that reflected the traditions and values of the great works of the past, albeit, as with all of Morris's prose romances, viewed through rose-tinted glasses. The other profound story was "Wooden Tony" by Mrs. W. K. (Lucy) Clifford (Dec 1890). Like all good

WOODEN TONY: AN ANYHOW STORY.
By MRS. W. K. CLIFFORD.
Illustrations by the HON. JOHN COLLIER.

fairytales it has a far deeper meaning and should be appreciated by a wider readership. It deals with the suffocating oppression of the Victorian moralistic regime, which sought to suppress

---

[1] This was originally published in 1863 under the alias Owen Meredith, because Lytton's father, the more famous Lord Lytton, had forbidden him to use the family name because it was so poor.
[2] L. Sprague de Camp, *Literary Swordsmen and Sorcerers* (Sauk City: Arkham House, 1976), p. 40.

the creative imagination of young Tony who ultimately has to conform. Here was another story tailor-made for the magazine.

Other renowned contributors during the 1880s, of both fiction and essays, were Wilkie Collins, W. E. Norris, Bret Harte, D. Christie Murray, Mary Molesworth, Margaret Oliphant, W. Clark Russell and F. Marion Crawford. The latter was one of Macmillan's own favourite writers and *English Illustrated* serialised, amongst others, "Sant' Ilario" (Oct 1888-Sept 1889) and "The Witch of Prague" (Oct 1890-Sept 1891).

Charles Morgan, in considering the early days of the magazine observed:

> Though it was the first of the illustrated monthlies, it is scarcely to be regarded as a forerunner of the popular magazines that followed it, for its tendency was from the outset a little nostalgic; it looked to old cities, old and stately houses and the old coaching-days for its subjects; and its chief surviving interest is in its employment of artists and engravers during the decade immediately preceding the conquest of the illustrated press by photography.[3]

Morgan is certainly correct in describing the general reflective nature of the magazine, a mood it would retain for most of its existence. But its rôle cannot be entirely discarded as not having any influence upon the popular magazines of the 1890s. Its very existence was part of the evidence of change. As David Reed has observed,[4] the format and design adopted by *English Illustrated* was one already developed in the United States by *Harper's New Monthly* and *Scribner's Monthly* during the 1870s. A European edition of *Harper's* was launched in London in 1880 which emphasised the difference in production between American and British periodicals. George Newnes was likewise influenced by *Harper's* and *The Century* (which *Scribner's* had become) when he launched *The Strand* in 1891, but it was *English Illustrated* which first developed the techniques in a British magazine. The magazine's title thus speaks for itself, showing this was what the English could do using its century-old skills.

During its first decade *English Illustrated* underwent several changes. Carr retired[5] and was succeeded by fellow barrister Clement Kinloch Cooke. Cooke had travelled extensively in his early years and encouraged the publication of articles on distant places, especially Australia and New Guinea, and which caused him to publish several early pieces by Gilbert Parker. His interests in sport led to articles on cricket (by W. G. Grace, June 1890) and football (by C. W. Alcock, January 1891). The appearance of the magazine changed. Although the articles were highly illuminated the stories featured less illustration. This was almost certainly a sign that the ornate flamboyance of the 1880s was proving too great for Macmillan's budget. During 1892 most engravings were phased out in favour of simple line drawings, though photographs also made their first appearance in a series of articles about railways.

It was also during 1892 that the magazine parted company with Macmillan's. It was sold to the firm of Edward Arnold, the first of five changes in publishers the magazine would endure.

---

[3] Charles Morgan, *The House of Macmillan, 1843-1943* (Macmillan, 1943), pp. 124-5.
[4] David Reed, *The Popular Magazine in Britain and the United States 1880-1960* (British Library, 1997), p. 95.
[5] In *Some Eminent Victorians* (Duckworth, 1908), Comyns Carr notes (p. 158) that he was editor of *English Illustrated* for three years but elsewhere (pp. 159-60) refers to being editor when Weyman's "The House of the Wolf" was serialised (Oct 1888-Sept 1889). There was a significant change in the magazine's format and content from October 1889, which suggests an editorial change. James Thorpe in *English Illustration: The Nineties* (Faber, 1935), p. 144, also confirms 1889.

Arnold restored some of the magazine's production values with more engravings, but this retrospective stance, whilst staying true to the magazine's origins, was noticeably out of step with the new popular magazines. These included not only *The Strand* and *The Idler* but, from May 1893, *English Illustrated*'s own imitator *Pall Mall*.

English Illustrated remained attractive (though not as beautiful as its first few years) and a bastion of traditional values, but it had anchored itself to a rock whilst the rest of the world moved away. This did not materially affect the articles, which continued to consider nature, art and culture, but it made the selection of fiction more challenging. Cooke, an eminently capable editor, continued to publish the more traditional domestic and historical stories, whilst he used the new strain of fiction to highlight changes. The most potent example is E. Douglas Fawcett's serial "Hartmann the Anarchist; or, the Doom of the Great City" (Jun-Sept 1893). Written in the style of Jules Verne, it is about an inventor who creates a fleet of super airships with which he intends to destroy the governments of the world and set up a new world-wide regime based on socialist principles. The serial is strikingly illustrated by Fred T. Jane, who later established such seminal reference works as *Jane's Fighting Ships* (1898). At one point the narrator, a fellow socialist, makes a statement that could easily have been a motto for *English Illustrated*. "We must not . . . see the graces of high life, art and culture, fouled by the mob, but the mob elevated into a possession and appreciation of the graces."[6]

Cooke steadily embraced the scientific developments that were transforming the world. The same issue that began the Fawcett serial started a series "The Romance of Modern London", written and illustrated by Fred T. Jane, who had a message for any Luddites amongst the magazine's readers. Talking, in this instance, about the structure of railway stations he remarks:

> It is a sample of the beauty that comes of age, which is ever reckoned a beautifier of everything, except possibly the fair sex. For aught we know the ancient Egyptians growled at their pyramids and temples as unsightly modern erections.[7]

Thus were vocalised the tensions between the old and the new that beset *English Illustrated*. It clearly plagued Edward Arnold who realised what an expensive and intractable legacy they had taken on. Within a year they sold the title to Sir William Ingram, the proprietor and publisher of the *Illustrated London News* (*ILN*). With the change came a new editor, Clement Shorter, who also edited *ILN* and its companion, *The Sketch*. Both Ingram and Shorter were realists and champions of the new technology. Whilst they appreciated the values of the past, they were not slaves to them. Under their regime the *English Illustrated* blossomed anew.

The main benefit of the change was having access to the resources of the Ingrams, the printing facilities of the *ILN* and the distribution network. By sharing overheads the production quality of the *English Illustrated* increased. There was no need to return to the old form of expensive engravings because the *ILN* had one of the most advanced printing presses in Britain. The magazine was now published on heavier duty coated stock with photogravure plates and photographs. From November 1894 occasional issues ran a colour frontispiece and the Christmas issues ran extra colour plates – as many as sixteen in the December 1898 issue which has to rank as one of the most beautiful issues of any of the Victorian monthly

---

[6] E. Douglas Fawcett, "Hartmann the Anarchist", *English Illustrated Magazine*, June 1893, p. 641.
[7] Fred T. Jane, "The Romance of Modern London", *English Illustrated Magazine*, June 1893, p. 659.

magazines. The magazine used the plates not only to illustrate stories but relevant features, such as a new fashion column, "Fine Feathers", from January 1899.

Having improved its presentation, *English Illustrated*'s next problem was in sustaining readers with a good mix of features and stories. To some extent Shorter returned to the pattern of the early issues, running features on stately homes, famous localities, personalities and nature. Richard Garnett contributed "Shelley in Italy" (Dec 1894) and Philip Norman "Historic London Houses" (Jan 1895). "Morning Calls" was an occasional series where visits were made to the homes of famous people, starting with William Morris (Apr 1895). There was a somewhat condescending, though interesting, series, "How the Other Half Lives", which looked at the jobs of manual workers and artisans. Despite the superior tone, which betrays the social standing of *English Illustrated*, the articles were a fascinating insight into the work of policemen, market porters, railway workers and sewermen of the 1890s. Another series was on the life of Horatio Nelson, "Our Great Naval Hero" (from Nov 1896), written by Clark Russell. Shorter may have been taking a leaf from the book of American S.S. McClure. The circulation of his magazine, *McClure's*, almost tripled when it ran a series about the life of Napoleon.

For a period Shorter captured stories by many major names. Some, like Gilbert Parker and Stanley J. Weyman were already contributing to the *ILN*. Weyman's work included the popular serial "From the Memoirs of a Minister of France" (Oct 1894-Sept 1895) and there were stories by Katharine Tynan, Cutcliffe Hyne, George Gissing, Violet Hunt, Morley Roberts, Clark Russell and E. Phillips Oppenheim. Shorter also arranged with American publishers to reprint stories from American magazines. *English Illustrated* was the first English magazine to run a story by Stephen Crane, "A Grey Sleeve" (Jan 1896). There were stories by Julian Hawthorne, Mary E. Wilkins, Joel Chandler Harris, Robert W. Chambers, Brander Matthews, Frank R. Stockton and Harriet Prescott Spofford.

This concentration of talent, quality of production and diversity of material had its effect and Shorter reported in the March 1897 issue that over the previous three years the circulation of *English Illustrated* had more than doubled. A primary reason was benefiting from the *ILN*'s distribution network, but *English Illustrated* had responded well to its opportunities and was enjoying a golden period. Curiously, just when the magazine was at its most beautiful, the title was modified. On the February 1899 issue it was shown as *The English (Illustrated) Magazine*, whilst from March to September the type size for 'Illustrated' was considerably reduced so that it appeared as *The English Illustrated Magazine*. The implication is that the Ingrams may have been considering changing the title to *The English Magazine* and dropping all artwork. It was during this period that the colour plates stopped, and no colour featured in the magazine at all after March 1899. At this same time the quota of short fiction in the *ILN* was increased, further suggesting that they may have been considering phasing fiction out of the *English Illustrated*.

It seems that despite having produced a magazine of considerable high quality, the Ingrams were uncertain about how to sustain it. Rapidly, from April 1899, the quality of the magazine deteriorated. Shorter's interests were now elsewhere. In 1900 he established a new company to publish *The Sphere* and revive *The Tatler* and from September 1899 *English Illustrated* was left to Bruce Ingram, who also took over *ILN* and *The Sketch*. *English Illustrated* became an increasing burden and was publishing little of interest. The magazine had never established any regular fiction series, unlike *The Strand* or *Pearson's*. A few series did appear towards the end of Shorter's tenure including "In Tight Places" (Oct 1897-Jun 1898), about amateur detective

Lionel MacNaughten-Innes, by Major Arthur Griffiths and "Robin Hood and His Merry Men" by Barry Pain (Mar-Sept 1898), but neither raised much interest. Ingram introduced "The Adventures of Archibald P. Batts, Millionaire" by Emeric Hulme-Beaman (May-Oct 1900) and a short and irregular series, "Maggie Drew, Cowboy" by Philip Verrill Mighels (from Nov 1900). The last was the most original, but did nothing to set readers alight.

The end was in sight, and from October 1901 *English Illustrated* was sold to T. Fisher Unwin. Initially Unwin was able to incorporate some interesting names. H. G. Wells contributed a couple of articles. M. P. Shiel appeared with two stories of which "Ben" (Jan 1902), about the vilification of a local backward boy, is especially strong. Harry Furniss wrote "Some Confessions of an Illustrator" (Dec 1901). From October 1901 W. Pett Ridge began a regular column of gossip and anecdotes, and there were stories from George Moore, Richard Marsh and Maxim Gorki. Paul Kruger, the former President of the Transvaal, contributed a piece about his early days as a big-game hunter (Dec 1902), but perhaps the most interesting article was a feature on the Turin Shroud, "Do We Possess Christ's Photograph?" (Jul 1902), translated from the French of Paul Vignon.

Unwin supported the magazine for two years before they sold it to Hutchinson's, whereby it became a companion to *The Lady's Realm*. The two magazines had similarities and evidently Hutchinson's decided to make *English Illustrated* the more literary. They introduced a review column by Edward Bennett and, most useful for literary researchers, ran a series of "Birthday Portraits". These selected authors whose birthdays fell that month and provided a capsuled appreciation of their work, a photograph and a detailed bibliography. Such bibliographies were rare at this time and make these issues of special interest. Authors covered include Swinburne (Apr 1903), J. M. Barrie (May 1903), Thomas Hardy and W. B. Yeats (Jun 1903), George Bernard Shaw (Jul 1903), F. Anstey and W. E. Henley (Aug 1903), W. W. Jacobs (Sept 1903), George Gissing (Nov 1903), Rudyard Kipling (Dec 1903), Alfred Russell Wallace (by G. K. Chesterton, January 1904), George Meredith (Feb 1904) and Andrew Lang (Mar 1904).

Hutchinson's failed to match their literary contents with other items of interest. Within two years the magazine was sold again, this time to the Central Publishing Company. Details of this company are hard to find and it may have been run by the new editor, Oscar Parker, a drama critic and theatre enthusiast who wrote a regular column, "The London Stage", for the magazine. He introduced his own book review column and developed further columns covering music, fashion, humour, the motor-car and even caravanning.

Under Parker *English Illustrated* became more of a general interest than a literary magazine, but the quality was uneven and Parker was unable to attract any major names. There were occasional items of interest, most especially "The Lost Land of King Arthur" (Apr-Sept 1907), a six-part series by J. Cuming Walters, beautifully illustrated by Bernard Munns. Other unusual series were "Hindu Tales and Fables" (from May 1907), translated from the Sanskrit by Henry Francis, and "Horse Tales" (from Oct 1910), reminiscences of a famous London horse-dealer by George Cox. Arnold Golsworthy provided the highly amusing "Another History of England" (Feb 1911), a forerunner to *1066 and All That*. The growing interest in air travel was the basis for H. T. Webster Worrell's series about a secret-service agent, "The Chronicles of Henley Brandon, Aviator" (Jan-Jun 1913). But otherwise the magazine had fallen into a rut. There was yet another set of articles on towns which had been covered many times before, discussion of authors such as Charles Dickens and George Eliot, and features on such household objects as keys, vases, knives and forks.

At the time that Central had taken over *English Illustrated* its circulation had been estimated by the Advertisers' Protection Society at only 5,000. It is unlikely that the magazine's sales subsequently increased and it must have been running at a loss. That it survived so long is remarkable. Its demise was inevitable and it was no doubt hastened by a court case brought by W. Pett Ridge. In June 1913 he sued *English Illustrated* for libel because they had published a story, "The Man Who Had a Conscience" (Jul 1912), that was not by him but carried his name. It transpired that the story had been submitted by an aspiring writer who seemed unaware of the legal implications of using another's name. Ridge maintained that the poor quality of the story had injured his reputation and the court agreed. He was awarded damages of £150.[1] During the case it was reported that the editor had been ill for some time and that stories were being accepted by the Company Secretary. This combination of costs, circulation and illness with no adequate cover was more than sufficient to bring the magazine to an end. Its final years did nothing to enhance its former glory. Under Comyns Carr and Shorter the magazine had two periods of greatness, and published sufficient material of merit to be highly regarded. If it had folded in 1900 it would have kept that reputation instead of dying a long and lingering death.

Frequency: Monthly.
Publisher: Macmillan until Sept 1892; Edward Arnold, Oct 1892-Sept 1893; Illustrated London News/Ingram Brothers, Oct 1893-Sept 1901; T. Fisher Unwin, Oct 1901-Mar 1903; Hutchinson, Apr 1903-Feb 1905; Central Publishing, Mar 1905-Aug 1913.
Editors: J. W. Comyns Carr, Oct 1883-Sept 1889, Clement Kinloch-Cooke, Oct 1889-Sept 1893, Clement King Shorter, Oct 1893-Aug 1899; Bruce Ingram, Sept 1899-Sept 1901; Hannaford Bennett, Oct 1901-Mar 1903; unknown, Apr 1903-Feb 1905; Oscar Parker, Mar 1905-Aug 1913.
Format/Size: Standard. Page count 64, rose to 70, Oct 1888; 88, Apr 1893; 94, Oct 1894; 112, Oct 1896. Fluctuated between 96/112, Apr 1898-Sept 1899; thereafter 96/100.
Price: 1/- until Sept 1893; then 6d.
Other editions: The simultaneous American edition was retitled *New Illustrated Magazine* from Feb 1897-Sept 1901.
References: *The House of Macmillan* by Charles Morgan (Macmillan, 1943), pp. 124-6; *The Popular Magazine in Britain and the United States, 1880-1960* by David Reed (University of Toronto Press, 1997), pp. 95-6.
Holdings:
Complete run, UK/Eire. British Library (*Shelfmark*: PP.6004.gld). • Bodleian (*Call Number*: Per. 2705 d.223); National Library of Scotland (*Shelfmark*: M.159). • University of Aberdeen, Queen Mother Library (*Call Mark*: Per 050 Eng). • Trinity College, Dublin (*Call Number*: Per 91-142).
Substantial run, UK. Cambridge University Library has volumes 1-40 (Oct 1883-Mar 1909) (*Classmark*: L996.b.21). • University of Birmingham has volumes 1-11 (Oct 1883-Sept 1894), 13-14 (Apr 1895-May 1896) and 23 (Apr-Sept 1900). • Leeds University Library has volumes 1-10 (Oct 1883-Sept 1893), 12 (Oct 1894-Mar 1895), 14-15 (Oct 1895-Sept 1896), 18-21 (Oct 1897-Sept 1899) and 27 (Apr-Sept 1902).
Complete run, US. Library of Congress (*Call Number*: AP4.E5 and on microfilm). • Boston Public Library (*Ref*: 5385.1 and on microfilm). • California State Library. • California State University,

---

[1] Equal to £10,000 at today's value. The full case is reported in *The Times* (London), 13 June 1913.

Long Beach (*Ref*: AP4.E5). • Florida State University (on microfilm). • Los Angeles Public Library. • New York Public Library (*Call Number*: ZAN-5397 on microfilm). • New York University (on microfilm). • University of California at Davis. • University of Connecticut (on microfilm). • University of Rhode Island (*Call Number*: EBP:458-467 on microfilm). • University of Rochester (*Call Number*: E245 4580467 on microfilm). • Rutgers University (on microfilm).
Substantial run, US. University of Minnesota has all but final volume (49).
Complete run, Canada. University of Calgary Library (*Call Number*: A.51.304).
Collecting points: Publisher's binding is in green decorative cloth, with a de luxe binding with gilt decoration. Early volumes are very common but are uncommon from 1910 onwards. Single issues are also uncommon.

* * *

EVERYBODY'S STORY MAGAZINE

54 issues. Two series. Number 1, November 1909 to Number 48, October 1913. Retitled EVERYONE'S STORY MAGAZINE from Number 27, January 1912. New series as EVERYONE'S from Number 1, November 1913 to Number 6, April 1914.

In 1908 Flora Klickmann took over the editorial reins of the *Girl's Own Paper*, where she would remain for the next twenty-three years. One of her early projects was to develop a new magazine of wider family interest. *Everybody's Story Magazine* was issued as a cheap unillustrated pulp rather than the standard glossy tabloid format used by both *Boy's Own Paper* and *Girl's Own Paper*. The cover of the first issue, showing a man trying to revive a young woman who has swooned, suggests an air of intrigue and possible romance, which reflects the overall mood of the magazine. The stories are all light, moral and guaranteed not to shock. They include light romances either with a touch of mystery, as in Joseph Hocking's "The Abbot's Treasure", or humour, as in Albert Payson Terhune's "A Honeymoon in Paris". There's a sports story, a "story of nautical humour" and a "missionary adventure", though this last, "Kallala's Test" by Charles Henry, is full of the racial prejudices of the period. Of historical interest is a story of an attempt to fly a plane across the Pacific, "The Fall of Icarus" by Ernest Protheroe. There is also an amusing detective story, "The Madness of Toppy McGee" by Owen Johnson, in which McGee tries everything to stop being a detective. Perhaps the most daring was "Number Nine" by Mrs George de Horne Vaizey, about a suffragette. As Klickman gave pains to demonstrate, there was nothing to offend in these stories. Even the presence of Bram Stoker in the second issue should raise no concern as "The Way of Peace" was not a horror story but a humorous tale of Irish life.

The magazine was fond of series. "Phineas Tooper: Dealer in Queer Lots" by Charles Henry (Jun 1910-Apr 1911) was clearly based on Sherlock Holmes. Others included "The Meteoric Career of Barry Webbling" by William Freeman (Jan-Dec 1911) about a man who loses his money and undertakes a series of unusual jobs; "Dr Marlow's Patients" by Ralph Dundas (Dec 1911-Jun 1912) about a physician; "Our Lady of France" by Draycott M. Dell

(Oct 1912-Jul 1913), set during the French Revolution; and "Strange Yarns of a Ship's Doctor" by E. Forster Marshall (Nov 1912-Oct 1913). Some of the better known authors to contribute included Beatrice Heron-Maxwell, Francis Brett Young, Elia W. Peattie, Phyllis Bottome, Bruno Lessing, Frank L. Packard, Ernest Bramah and Annie Swan (as "David Lyall"), but for the most part contributors were better known in the story-papers or women's magazines.

In 1912 the magazine changed its title to *Everyone's Story Magazine* following a challenge in the courts by the publishers of the American magazine *Everybody's*, but it was evident that  there was a more fundamental problem. Most of the stories were a little above boys' adventure yarns yet they were packaged as light romance for women. Circulation figures are not available, but comparative data for both *Girl's Own Paper* and *Boy's Own Paper* suggest that *Everybody's/Everyone's* would not have sold more than 30,000 copies. In November 1913 the magazine was completely revamped and issued in glossy tabloid form, looking the same as *Girl's Own*, and now entitled simply *Everyone's*. Despite the makeover, though, it remained a family version of the girls' and boys' magazines with heavily illustrated features on such pursuits as mountaineering, motor-cycling, boatbuilding and flying. Fiction took a back seat with formulaic stories of romance or adventure. One of the few original stories was "Out of the Night" about an aerial burglar, by Harry Harper and noted aeronaut Claude Grahame-White. In its new form *Everyone's* looked and felt superfluous and lasted only one volume. Flora Klickman would achieve much with her magazines for girls and young women, but *Everybody's* has to be regarded as one of her lesser endeavours.

Frequency: Monthly.
Publisher: Religious Tract Society.
Editor: Flora Klickmann.
Format/Size: Pulp, 128 pages. As *Everyone's*, flat slick small tabloid, 64 pages.
Price: 4½d.
Holdings: *Complete run, UK*. British Library on microfilm (*Shelfmark*: PP.6018.tah; *Microfilm*: PB Mic C.1866).
Collecting points: *Everybody's* is very uncommon whilst the plain bound volume of *Everyone's* is slightly easier to find.

***

EVERYONE'S [STORY MAGAZINE] see EVERYBODY'S STORY MAGAZINE

***

THE EVESHAM MONTHLY MAGAZINE see THE HOLBORN MONTHLY MAGAZINE

***

FANTASY

3 issues. Volume 1, Number 1 [1938] to Volume 1, Number 3 [1939].

When T. Stanhope Sprigg launched *Air Stories* in 1934 he proposed several other magazines including one of science fiction. He explained: "*Fantasy* originated in my own long-standing interest in science fiction, plus my conviction that there was a real need for a British science-fiction magazine in this country which, at that time, was overrun with American sf 'pulp' magazines dumped over here in vast quantities."[1] It took four years for Newnes to give the green light, possibly because they were uncertain of the market in Britain following the disaster of *Scoops*, a juvenile weekly story paper from Pearson's (Newnes's sister company) in 1934. In the meantime World's Work issued *Tales of Wonder* in 1937, the success of which may have caused Newnes to change its mind. They were still cautious as *Fantasy* was not given a regular schedule and the delay meant that Sprigg assembled only three issues before the outbreak of War.

This was a shame as *Fantasy* was a good magazine. Marred only by the science-fiction stereotypes of the period, the contents were on a par with the best of the American magazines. This was partly because British writers – especially John Russell Fearn, John Beynon Harris (writing here as John Beynon and later better known as John Wyndham) and Eric Frank Russell – were already selling to the top American pulps. The story plots were typical of the period, especially in the light of the darkening shadows of War. There were super weapons in John Beynon's "Beyond the Screen" (#1) and "The Trojan Beam" (#2) and in Eric Frank Russell's "Mightier Yet" (#3). "Valley of Doom" (#2) by Halliday Sutherland tells of an apparently ideal state created by eugenics. In "Climatica" (#2) by John Russell Fearn, attempts to control the weather in Britain prove cataclysmic. And there are plenty of threats to Earth by alien invaders in such stories as "Winged Terror" (#2) by G. R. Malloch (a reprint from *Pearson's Magazine*, Feb 1931) and "Invaders from the Void" (#3) by George C. Wallis.

As in *Air Stories*, Sprigg used regular features, including science-fact articles by P. E. Cleator and German rocket specialist (then resident in the USA), Willy Ley.

It is certain that Sprigg would have developed *Fantasy* into a first-class magazine but he had scarcely unfurled his wings when War intervened. With only three issues it is easy to relegate *Fantasy* to the backwaters of science fiction but, after the disaster of *Scoops*, it showed that Britain was capable of producing a quality science-fiction magazine. It would be nearly ten years before John Carnell reharnessed British sf with *New Worlds*.

Frequency: Irregular.
Publisher: George Newnes.
Editor: T. Stanhope Sprigg.
Format/Size: Standard pulp, 96 pages.
Price: 7d.

---

[1] Private letter, Sprigg to Mike Ashley, 19 August 1974.

Holdings:
Complete runs, UK. British Library (*Shelfmark*: PP.6018.th); Bodleian (*Call Number*: Per. 254399 d.62); Leeds University Library (*Ref*: S/F A-0.01 FAN).
Substantial run, UK. Cambridge University Library has issues 1 and 3 (*Classmark*: L999.c.3.1307).
Collecting points: Reasonably common though increasingly expensive.

* * *

THE FRONTIER / FRONTIER STORIES see EMPIRE FRONTIER

* * *

THE GOLDEN MAG.

22 issues. Volume 1, Number 1, June 1926 to Volume 3, Number 13, June 1927; 13 issues. Relaunched as THE GOLDEN WEST from July 1927, Volume 1, Number 1 to Volume 4, Number 9, December 1928. Retitled (on cover only) GOLDEN WEST MAGAZINE from January 1928.

The Golden Mag. was a direct continuation of *The Crusoe Mag.* (see entry). Although it reverted to Volume 1, most of the features and stories ran over. A. M. Burrage continued his stories of schoolboy "Esme" Geering; John Hunter his various juvenile island adventures, this time a series, "Hurricane Island" and K.R.G. Browne his humorous stories of family problems, whilst Stacey Blake began a school series about cadets at Marlborough. There was also the "nutshell" story, a one-page vignette, probably finished at the last minute to fill space and invariably written by Philip Atkey (as Barry Perowne) who initially served as editor.

But *The Golden Mag.* did make one significant change. It was moving towards being a western pulp. Its cover, by Charles Crombie, showed an American Indian about to ambush a wagon train. It illustrated Zane Grey's serial, "The Roaring U.P. Trail", about the building of the Union Pacific Railway. Though written for adults[1], it was perfectly suited to the teenage audience where *The Crusoe* and now *The Golden* were targeted. The hobbies and handicrafts feature, "The Bosun's Den", from *The Crusoe*, became suitably "Round the Campfire".

The first few issues, however, lacked conviction for the new direction as they consumed *The Crusoe*'s inventory, with stories about a shipwreck in Tasmania and perils amongst the natives of Borneo. With the next two issues the covers reverted to the form of *The Crusoe* and *The Happy* – indeed Thomas Henry's cover for September 1926 depicts Richmal Crompton's William, though he's not in the magazine.

This continued for thirteen issues. *The Golden Mag.* was *The Crusoe* in all but title, and felt like a magazine in limbo. With the July 1927 issue, however, it reverted again to Number 1 and became *The Golden West*. The decision must have been sudden as the line-up for that issue has a few hangovers, such as Burrage's Esme and Browne's humorous serial, but the shift towards

---

[1] Originally serialised in *Blue Book*, June 1917-January 1918.

the western was significant. A couple of stories, those by Murray Leinster and Jack Bechdolt, were reprints from America, but most were attempts by British boys' writers to produce their version of the cowboy story. This remained for a few more issues with the quota of home-grown material steadily decreasing.

The complete split came with the April 1928 issue, when it became a straightforward British edition of the American *Golden West Magazine*. That magazine had been issued by Golden West Publishing in New York in January 1927 and continued monthly until August 1929. Newnes must have licensed the title from them and when they found that their own version was not working, they switched to reprinting the US original. Though this was publishing stories by James Oliver Curwood, Clarence E. Mulford, Charles Alden Seltzer, Albert Bigelow Paine and even Damon Runyon,[2] it seems this did not work either. The British edition folded after nine issues in December 1928.

Frequency: Monthly
Publisher: George Newnes.
Editor: Possibly Reeves Shaw.
Format/Size: Standard pulp, 96 pages.
Price: 7d.
Holdings: *Complete run, UK.* British Library (*Shelfmark*: PP.5993.mbd); Bodleian (*Call Number*: Per. 2533 d.181 for *Golden Magazine*; Per. 25612 d.103 for *Golden West*).
Collecting points: Extremely rare.

* * *

THE GRAND MAGAZINE
422 issues. Volume 1, Number 1, February 1905 to Volume 77, Number 422, April 1940.

The Grand ought to have the honour of being the first of the new generation of all-fiction pulp magazines that set the world alight in the late Edwardian age, just as its elder sister, *The Strand*, had revolutionised magazines in the 1890s. Yet, despite appearing two months before *The Novel* and two years before *The Story-Teller*, *The Grand* was not the ground-breaking publication one might expect. In laying it before the public its publisher, George Newnes, believed that "a large number of the reading public sometimes prefer to let their imagination picture the scenes described rather than that the letterpress should be interrupted." He appeared to be taking a retrograde step, returning to the unillustrated all-text magazines of the Victorian period. In fact he was seeking to create a stepping-stone between *The Strand* and the cheap weekly novelettes and story papers, most of which were also unillustrated. Newnes was hoping to provide more sophisticated reading for an otherwise less discerning readership.

---

[2] "The Breeze Kid's Big Tear Off", October 1928.

What his editor, H. Greenhough Smith, and sub-editor, Alderson Anderson, produced was, to all intents, a more people-orientated version of *The Strand*. The emphasis was not on fiction, which comprised less than a third of the first volume. Rather it was on the kind of popular article and symposia that so characterised *The Strand*. Amongst its features were "Both Sides" where individuals took opposing views on a subject; "Under the X-Rays", where specialists analysed a controversial subject in depth; and "Interesting People" which discussed personalities in the news. There were such symposia as "My First Time in Print" (May 1905) or the long-running "The Secrets of Success" with contributions from celebrities. "The Grand Kaleidoscope" was a miscellany that highlighted scientific developments and curiosities, and encouraged contributions from readers. "The Causeries of the Grand Club" was an excuse for gossip and *bon mots* and was clearly modelled on the "Idlers' Club" in *The Idler*.

There were plenty of individual articles. George Bernard Shaw appeared in the first issue with "The Theatre of the Future" and Mrs Belloc Lowndes considered the difference between the French and English attitudes towards marriage in "Love and Matrimony" (May 1905). One of the more significant articles during these early years was H. G. Wells's series, "New Worlds for Old" (Jul 1907-Mar 1908), which discussed the changing shape of society and the rise of socialism. Features sought to be provocative to encourage reader feedback. Both the uncredited article, "Real Experiences in the Supernatural", and John Oliver Hobbes's "Who Has the Best Time – A Man or a Woman?" in the first issue, brought a wave of reader response which formed the basis for subsequent features. The fiction also generated reaction. The second issue reprinted Frank R. Stockton's puzzle story "The Lady or the Tiger?", and asked readers for their solutions. This resulted not only in a lively discussion but further puzzle stories.

A key feature which ran for three years (and was resurrected in the late twenties) was "My Best Story" selected by the authors who provided a brief introduction explaining why. Arthur Conan Doyle opened the first issue with his 1891 story "A Straggler of '15" and later issues included W. W. Jacobs, H. G. Wells, Max Pemberton and Mary E. Braddon. Of particular interest was the story from Barry Pain. In the June 1905 issue Pain had selected "The Kindness of the Celestial" as his best published story but remarked that he believed "The Night of Glory" was his best, but it had been rejected by every magazine. Smith asked to see the story and ran it in the next issue. Otherwise little fiction stood out in the early issues. Usually two or three stories per issue were reprints, including translations from European authors. *The Grand* made great play out of discovering the writer Henry Normanby who appeared in every issue during the first year but, good though these stories were, Normanby made little impact. Two other relatively new authors in the June 1905 issue would go on to much greater glory: P. G. Wodehouse and William Hope Hodgson.

In this way *The Grand* continued for three years, usually interesting but seldom remarkable. By 1908, though, it was taking note of the opposition. Both *The Novel* and, more significantly, *The Story-Teller*, had done what *The Grand* should have done, which was to create a market for the popular all-fiction magazine, and in particular the more action-orientated story. Better late than never, it switched policy with the April 1908 issue, rechristening itself *The Grand Magazine of Fiction*. From here on it was all fiction but it had already lost the lead. It experimented with running a "complete novel" (usually about fifty pages) backed up by a dozen or so short stories. All this soon changed, however, to placing the emphasis on story series, the concept that had revolutionised fiction in *The Strand* twenty years before. For the most part the big-name authors vanished and *The Grand* became the home for the second string of reliable, creative and above all populist fictioneers.

One of the earliest successes was the series featuring Smiler Bunn by Bertram Atkey. Bunn was a chancer, a forerunner of all lovable rogues, who tried all manner of devious yet ingenious schemes. Starting with "The Brain" (Jan 1910), the Bunn stories appeared frequently in *The Grand* for the next twenty years and established Atkey's reputation. Another regular was F. St Mars, the best known alias of Frank Atkins, Jr., under which name he contributed a string of wildlife stories starting with "The Master of the Situation" (Nov 1910). L. J. Beeston became known for his historical war stories, especially the series "Dagobert's Children" (Aug 1911-Jun 1912), about the Franco-Prussian War. "The Count's Hand" (Apr 1911) was regarded as such a definitive war story that it was reprinted in the October 1914 issue, at the outbreak of World War I. H. C. Bailey was also a regular, mostly with historical naval stories, including the series "The Sea Captain" (Jan-Dec 1912) set during the days of Sir Francis Drake. Jeffery Farnol's Regency stories also appeared at this time, whilst Ruby M. Ayres and Winifred Graham provided stories of light romance and human drama. Unlike other magazines there were remarkably few stories dealing with female suffrage. New editor Charles Wingham seemed to like the off-trail and unusual story. "In the Days of Calamity" (Jan-Apr 1911) was a short series by Gerald Grant set in 1925 which saw Britain subject to one disaster after another. "1930" by Mayne Royal (Aug 1911) almost has the Earth destroyed by a rogue star. In "The Airboard Strike" (Nov 1911) Donovan Bayley portrays a global airmail service in 1965 that is brought to an end by a strike. For a brief period one such unusual story appeared in almost every issue.

Two major authors who did not desert *The Grand* were Baroness Orczy and H. G. Wells. Orczy contributed several Scarlet Pimpernel series, starting with "Eldorado" (Jun 1912-Apr 1913), and H. G. Wells appeared with two of his novels of social barriers and human relationships, "The Passionate Friends" (Mar-Nov 1913) and "Bealby" (Aug 1914-Mar 1915). Two other significant authors of the pre-war years were Jack London and Talbot Mundy. London contributed several south-seas stories, starting with the serial "Adventure" (Mar-Jun 1911) and including the series "Sun Tales" (May-Nov 1912). "The Soul of a Regiment" (May 1912) marked the first appearance of Talbot Mundy in a British magazine, though he had been selling to the American pulps for over a year. The story had appeared in *Adventure* (Feb 1912) and became not only one of that magazine's most popular stories but the one that made Mundy's name, causing him to be ranked alongside Kipling and Haggard. He became a regular in *The Grand* over the next few years with his military stories. One other writer worthy of mention is F. Tennyson Jesse. With "A Corner in Confetti" (Jun 1914) and "Cupid and the Cinema" (Sept 1914), she contributed two spin-offs from her unusual picaresque novel *The Milky Way* (1913).

Like most of the magazines, with the outbreak of War *The Grand* became consumed by war stories. These included the last work by S. R. Crockett, the series "Peter the Renegade" (Oct 1914-Mar 1915), set during the Peninsular War. One of the main contributors of war stories, certainly in the first year of the War, was Colonel (later Major-General) Ernest Swinton who wrote under the alias "Ole-Luke-Oie". Robert Tanacre, Lloyd Osbourne, John Margerison, Lewis Ricci ("Bartimeus"), F. Britten Austin, William Le Queux and H.C. McNeile ("Sapper") were all regulars. Beatrice Heron-Maxwell wrote a poignant tale of a wounded soldier in "Kegs" (Nov 1914), but perhaps the story which best summed up the effect of War on British society was Robert Tanacre's "The Innocence of Innocence" (Feb 1915).

The War stories were soon tempered by, and later overshadowed by, escapist fiction and it was during these years that the fascination for the South Seas and other lands took hold. H. de Vere Stacpoole led the way with "The Pearl Fishers" (Dec 1914-Sept 1915), followed by Beatrice Grimshaw's series "The Kris-Girl" (Aug 1915-Jan 1916) and, for pure escapism, Leslie Beresford with "Khûm" (Sept-Nov 1915), about a lost land in the Himalayas. A regular illustrated cartoon feature, "The Lighter Side of War", began (Sept 1916), with work by W. Heath Robinson, H. M. Bateman and Lawson Wood.

By the end of the War fantasy and romantic adventure had given way again to historical stories and a greater emphasis on women's fiction. Rafael Sabatini dutifully combined the two in "The Fortunes of Casanova" (Mar-Aug 1918). Baroness Orczy likewise contributed "The Triumph of the Scarlet Pimpernel" (Jun 1921-Jan 1922). Elinor Glyn provided a rare non-fiction series, "The Philosophy of Love" (from Aug 1919), where she advised women on coping with men. Suitably passionate was the romance "A Woman's Heart" (May-Sept 1920), translated from the French of Paul Bourget. *The Grand* was not so dominated as some magazines with the post-War fascination with spiritualism, though Marie Belloc Lowndes contributed one such occult series, "The Ivory Gate" (from Apr 1920).

Part of this change was as a result of a new editor. Reeves Shaw, who had been editor of *The Captain*, now took on *The Grand* and developed several new magazines, including *The Humorist* and *The Happy*. His fondness for humorous fiction saw *The Grand* become more bright and breezy. The cartoon feature had become "The Lighter Side of Things" after the War, and though briefly replaced by a theatre section, it soon returned and remained throughout the twenties. One benefit was the return of P. G. Wodehouse, with the serials "Jill the Reckless" (Sept 1920-Jan 1921) and "Leave it to Psmith" (Jul-Dec 1923). Though Wodehouse remained a *Strand* regular, he appeared in *The Grand* throughout the twenties and thirties.

Assisting Shaw was writer Alice Grant Rosman, and it was through her that *The Grand* became a major market for women writers. This included Agatha Christie, for whom *The Grand* was her biggest British market after *The Sketch*. Her first appearance was with the Poirot serial, "The Girl With the Anxious Eyes" (Dec 1922-Mar 1923)[3]. It published over a dozen of her stories including the first of the Harley Quin episodes, "The Passing of Mr. Quin" (Mar 1924). Berta Ruck, May Edginton, Oliver Sandys, Violet Quirk, Philippa Southcombe, Mildred Cram, Marjorie Bowen, Fanny Heaslip Lea, E. L. White, even Sarah Bernhardt, were all regulars, filling perhaps half the magazine. Much of the other half was filled with light romance and humour by male writers – Arthur Applin, A. M. Burrage, H. C. Bailey, Michael Kent and Gilbert Frankau – whilst A.E.W. Mason, E. Phillips Oppenheim, Sax Rohmer, Valentine Williams and Edgar Wallace provided the more mysterious fare. Wallace's contributions included the series "The Man Who Saw Evil" (1924-25), better known as *The Mind of Mr. J. G. Reeder* (Hodder, 1925). There were also plenty of stories from American writers, including the prolific Max Brand.

In 1927 Rosman returned to full-time writing and Harry Leggett become acting editor. He would take on full duties when Shaw took over editorship of *The Strand* in 1931. From here on the magazine lost the predominance of women's fiction, and though it remained orientated towards the women's market, it featured more adventure fiction. Leggett introduced some cost-

---

[3] Better known in book form as *The Murder on the Links* (Bodley Head, 1923).

saving features. The "My Best Story" feature returned in October 1927 and *The Grand* began to reprint other items, including a selection of the best Sherlock Holmes stories. Reprints would continue throughout the rest of the magazine's life though they were rarely identified as such. For a while cover art was dropped, replaced by a list of names, and internal illustrations were phased out. Both of these returned in the thirties. For a while the magazine looked more like Cassell's *Argosy*, which had become successful on a sole diet of reprints.

For a while the zest went out of *The Grand* but it returned in the early thirties with a strong line-up of contributors including W. Somerset Maugham, Hugh Walpole, Warwick Deeping, Michael Arlen and A. E. Coppard, whilst P. C. Wren, Dorothy L. Sayers and Robert Hichens appeared occasionally. The mainstay authors, however, were H. de Vere Stacpoole, Beatrice Grimshaw, Dorothy Black, John Russell, Francis Brett Young, Edgar Jepson, James Francis Dwyer and I.A.R. Wylie, almost all with romantic or exotic stories. The magazine struck gold in 1934, in what proved to be its final year of greatness. It acquired British serial rights to Agatha Christie's "The Murder on the Orient Express" (Mar-May 1934), which ran alongside P. G. Wodehouse's, "Right Ho, Jeeves" (Apr-Sept 1934).

By the late thirties it was becoming harder to distinguish between the new and reprint fiction. Some was of comparatively recent vintage. For example, Dennis Wheatley's "The Snake" (Feb 1937) had appeared only three years earlier in *Nash's Magazine* (Dec 1933). The magazine had cut both its price and page-count during the thirties but by the end of the decade it no longer seemed the same value for money. A series of lacklustre covers harmed the magazine's image, though it restored stronger action covers in 1937. At the same time it absorbed its old rival *The Novel*. Its days were numbered, however, and soon after the outbreak of War, it was merged with *The Strand*, its final issues almost entirely reprint.

The Grand never rose to the heights of its elder sister, and never fulfilled its early potential. It ran some excellent stories, but mostly because it benefited from its relationship with *The Strand*. It did not establish an independent identity to rival *The Story-Teller*, even though the capacity was there. It remained a magazine content to be a competitor rather than the lead.

Frequency: Monthly but combined March/April 1910 issue.
Publisher: George Newnes.
Editors: Alderson Anderson, 1905-10; C. W. Wingham, 1911-20; Reeves Shaw, 1920-31 (assisted by Alice Rosman, 1923-27; and H. W. Leggett, 1927-31); Leggett alone 1932-40.
Format/Size: Standard pulp. Page count, 176, dropped to 160, Sept 1906; 152, May 1907; briefly 168/172, May-Aug 1909; dropped to 144/148, Nov 1909; 128/132, Jan 1915; 112/116, Feb 1916; 92, Feb 1918; 72/76, Jun 1918; rose to 80/84, Feb 1919; 96, Apr 1919; 104/108, Jun 1919; 122, October 1922; 128/132, Nov 1922; dropped to 96, Jul 1932.
Price: 4½d; then 6d, Dec 1916; 8d, Jan 1918; 10d, Jun 1918; 1/-, Jun 1920; dropped to 7d, Jul 1932.
Holdings:
Substantial run, UK. British Library has issues Feb 1905-Jul 1908; Sept 1911-Jun 1912; November 1912-Jun 1915; Mar-May 1916; Sept 1918; Sept 1919; Mar-Aug 1920; Mar 1921-Aug 1922; May,

Jul 1923, Jan 1924; May 1931; Mar 1933-Feb 1935 (*Shelfmark*: PP.6004.gmo). • Bodleian has run from Feb 1905-Jun 1936 (*Call Number* Per. 2705 d.174). • National Library of Scotland has issues from Feb 1905-Jan 1906 only (*Shelfmark*: U.446). No library holds any issues after Jun 1936.
Substantial run, Australia. University of Queensland has issues from Nov 1916-Apr 1940 with the exception of Mar-Aug 1918 (*Reference*: PR1309.S5 G7).
Partial run, US. There are no substantial runs in the US. University of Rochester has volumes 1-12, Feb 1905-Feb 1911 only; The University of California, Southern Regional Library Facility has volumes 1-6, Feb 1905-Jan 1908 only.
Collecting points: Early publisher's binding is in blue decorative boards until 1911, thereafter in red blind-stamped boards. Bound volumes are still fairly common until 1915 but thereafter are rare, as are the single issues, though these are still fairly common from the 1930s.

***

THE GREEN MAGAZINE
30 issues. Volume 1, Number 1, 7 November 1922 to Volume 5, Number 30, 18 December 1923.

The Green Magazine was the fourth of the colour-titled fiction magazines released by Amalgamated Press after *The Red*, *The Yellow* and *The Violet*. As its title suggests it was aimed at fiction of the great outdoors – nature, exploration and sport. The first issue was heavily biased towards sport, with stories of boxing, golf, football, fishing and, unusually, a romance of the curling rinks. This still left room for a nature story by H. Mortimer Batten, a sea story by Guy Thorne and a romance of the South Seas by Owen Oliver. Sports stories had not featured highly in *The Red* or *The Yellow*, though they were a staple diet of the boys' magazines issued by Amalgamated Press and which were compiled in the same department as *The Green*. As a consequence many of the same writers were recruited and it was inevitable that the sports stories would read only a little above boys' magazine level.

Finding good sport stories with sufficient variety was not easy and it was not long before *The Green* broadened its policy to include more adventure stories. Douglas Newton provided a rousing sea story, "The Impossible Brute" (30 Jan-10 Apr 1923). E. Charles Vivian's contributions included a smuggling tale in South America, "Breaking the Monopoly" (24 Apr 1923), and an adventure in Darkest Africa, "The Magic of Hubble" (19 Jun 1923). Andrew Murray penned the series "The Exploits of Cap'n Nat Silver" (from 22 May 1923). *The Green* even searched for adventures in the distant past with Sir Ernest Low's "The Sabre-Tooth" (13 Feb 1923) and "The Kheddah" (20 Nov 1923). Sports stories still appeared, mostly by John G. Brandon, but within a few months *The Green* was also running humorous stories, romances and mysteries. Its last serial, beginning in the final issue, was "The Master Criminal" by J. Jefferson Farjeon, continuing in *The Yellow*, with which *The Green* merged.

As most of the stories were written by the same stable of writers, it was impossible for them to deliver sufficient quality and variety for all the magazines. Soon after *The Green* had appeared Amalgamated Press launched another fortnightly, *The Detective Magazine*, so that along with *The Premier* and *The London*, each month saw thirteen issues of fiction magazines. It was roughly an issue every other day and clearly not only could the writers not produce sufficient variety, but there were not sufficient readers. *The Green* was too similar to its companions and had added nothing to the overall pool of magazine fiction. The few good stories it published would have served better in *The Red* or *The Yellow*.

Frequency: Fortnightly.
Publisher: Amalgamated Press.
Editor: John Stock.
Format/Size: Small pulp, 112 pages.
Price: 7d.
Holdings:
Complete run, UK. Bodleian (*Call Number*: Per. 25612 e.1626).
Other run, UK. The British Library has issues #13, 14, 15, 17 and 21 only, all on microfilm (*Shelfmark*: PP.6018.taw; *Microfilm*: Mic.C.329).
Collecting points: The rarest of the 'coloured' titles. Issues seldom appear.

* * *

THE HAPPY MAG.

236 issues. Two series. Volume 1, Number 1, June 1922 to Volume 36, Number 214, March 1940. New series, Volume 1, Number 1, April 1940 to Volume 1, Number 2, May 1940. Also 13 Christmas Extras (1923-1935) and 7 Summer Holiday Extras (1933-1939).

A Gentleman of the Old School!

The Happy Mag. was one of the many humourous fiction magazines that flourished during the twenties and its success encouraged imitators such as *The Merry* and *The Jolly*. The magazine had a standard format that hardly changed during its eighteen-year life. Approximately a third of the magazine was given over to humorous anecdotes, jokes, cartoons and sketches. Popular artists such as Graham Simmons, Arthur Ferrier, Alfred Leete, Thomas Henry, Will Owen and Gilbert Wilkinson provided most of the illustrations, with Lawson Wood also painting several of the covers. There was a children's comic strip, "Peter Rabbit and the Baby Bunnies" by Harrison Cady, showing that the magazine was intended for all the family, especially mothers.

The other two-thirds consisted of humorous tales and light romances. Michael Kent, K.R.G. Browne, F. Morton Howard, Evadne Price and Holloway Horn were regulars, as were Will Scott, Edward Woodward, A. M. Burrage and May Edginton, all with their own brand of sparkle. But one author took over *The Happy* and made it special – Richmal Crompton. With the seventh issue (Dec 1922), her stories featuring troublesome schoolboy William Brown were transferred from *The Home Magazine*. Apart from a brief hiatus in late 1923, when Crompton was laid low with poliomyelitis, she produced a William story a month for ten years and the pace slackened only slightly thereafter. *The Happy* published 202 William stories, only one of which was a reprint, plus other occasional features. Thomas Henry painted regular William covers and occasional cartoon spreads, including all-colour plates in the Christmas specials.

The magazine was so closely associated with William that it is easy to forget it published anything else but there is much that is unexpected in the magazine. From the first issue it serialised Bertram Atkey's Smiler Bunn novel, "The Man With the Yellow Eyes". It also featured an Edgar Wallace story, "The Sentimental Crook". Charles Dana Gibson was present with a series of two-page spreads. The September 1922 issue launched the career of Georgette Heyer with "A Proposal to Cicely". Leslie Beresford created a spoof Zorro character in, "Bravados the Bandit" (Apr 1923). Keble Howard contributed some of the magazine's best material. These include an amusing motoring series, "Muriel, the Motor, and Me!" (May-Dec 1924), illustrated by Will Owen, and the desert-island spoof, "Bravo, Belinda!" (Feb-Oct 1926). Oliver Sandys and E. J. Rath also contributed serials. Perhaps most surprising is that *The Happy* gave the first UK serialisation to "Tarzan and the Golden Lion" (Aug 1923-Apr 1924) by Edgar Rice Burroughs, with several excellent illustrations by E. P. Kinsella.

Starting in 1923 *The Happy* also published a Christmas Extra, which was simply a bigger version of the monthly issue. In 1933 Newnes switched to publishing a Summer Holiday extra so that for most of its life *The Happy* saw thirteen issues a year. *The Happy* was really a half-way house between the emerging comic books and the standard magazines and with the rapid growth in comics during the 1930s the market for *The Happy* dwindled. It was probably the William stories that kept it alive. When wartime restrictions began to bite, *The Happy* was converted to a digest-size magazine, along the lines of *Lilliput*, a change that *The Strand* would soon follow. It survived in this form for only two issues.

The Happy is one of those rare magazines that is associated with one author and character but which, despite a noticeable repetition of formula, contains much else of harmless fun.

Frequency: Monthly
Publisher: George Newnes
Editors: Reeves Shaw, 1922-31 (assisted by Philip Atkey, 1925-27); Herbert Shaw, 1932-40.
Format/Size: Standard pulp, 92 pages, until Mar 1940; digest, 126pp, Apr- May 1940. Christmas and Summer Extras, 132pp.
Price: 7d. (Extras, 1/-).
References: Entry in *The William Companion* by Mary Cadogan (Macmillan, 1990), pp. 105-108.
Holdings: *Substantial run, UK.* The British Library is missing only volume 7, Jun–Nov 1925 (*Shelfmark*: PP.6018.tas; *Microfilm*: Mic.C.353). • The Bodleian has run from Jun 1922–Mar 1933 (*Call Number*: Per. 25612 d.8).
Collecting points: Both bound volumes (in blue) and single issues are fairly common, avidly collected by William fans who have thus preserved copies but which also makes them expensive.

***

THE HARMSWORTH [MONTHLY PICTORIAL] MAGAZINE *see* THE LONDON MAGAZINE

***

HARMSWORTH'S RED MAGAZINE *see* THE RED MAGAZINE

***

THE HOLBORN MONTHLY MAGAZINE
13 issues. Volume 1, Number 1, April 1903 to Volume 3, Number 1, April 1904.

Although the cover bore the title *The Holborn Monthly Magazine*, the contents page was headed "Our Magazine", and declared that it was a magazine for women. It appeared at a time when women's magazines were growing and *The Holborn* had little new to offer. There were the inevitable columns on fashion, toiletry, food, health, the home and the theatre, whilst covers portrayed women at leisure, but not everything seemed aimed at women. There was a piece about Prince Albert of Monaco, "A Prince of Deep-Sea Science" (May 1903), and one by Robert Peary, "Hunting on Great Ice" (Aug 1903). Several issues ran drawing-room sketches, such as John Oliver Hobbes's "The Land of Regrets" (May 1903). Cosmo Hamilton contributed a poignant romance, "Till the End of Time" (Jun 1903); there was a moving Japanese story, "Love of a Geisha Girl" by Onoto Watanna (Sept 1903), and Seamus MacManus injected much needed light relief with "How Dark Patrick Saved the Bank of Ireland" (Sept 1903). Louis Wain and Penrhyn Stanlaws were amongst the artists, and Robert Barr contributed a serial, "The Mystery of Castle Stormax" (Oct 1903-Mar 1904), but the only item that now makes the magazine of interest was the historical series by Rafael Sabatini, "The Fortunes of Lal Faversham" (Oct 1903-Mar 1904).

The novelty of this magazine was that it was syndicated as an accompaniment to local newspapers, with the magazine retitled accordingly. Identical issues appeared as *The Evesham Monthly Magazine* on sale with the *Evesham Journal*, and doubtless other versions exist. This idea[1] does not seem to have helped sales and it folded after a year.

Frequency: Monthly.
Publisher: The Magazine Publishing Company.
Editor: Not known.
Format/Size: Small standard, 72 pages.
Price: 4d dropping to 2½ locally.
Holdings:
Complete run, UK. Bodleian (*Call Number*: Per. 2705 d.152).
Substantial run, UK. The British Library has all issues but the first issue is unreadable. (*Shelfmark*: PP.6018.tf).
Collecting points: Very uncommon, though the first issues surface occasionally.

***

THE HOME MAGAZINE *see* WOMAN AT HOME

***

---

[1] This concept was pioneered by *The Dawn of Day* (1878-1939; retitled *The New Day*, 1929) which was circulated to churches and distributed with the local parish magazine.

HUSH
13 issues. Volume 1, Number 1, [June] 1930 to Volume 3, Number 13, June 1931.

Hush was a pulp magazine issued by William Collins as part of their Detective Story Club imprint. Although Edgar Wallace was credited as editor, the real editor was journalist and criminologist George Dilnot, who earned a reputation as being the only crime-fiction writer to have helped Scotland Yard solve a murder. Both Wallace and Dilnot have a regular presence in the magazine, which was composed almost entirely of reprints. Wallace's stories came from his collection *48 Short Stories* (Newnes, 1929), whilst Dilnot had a series "The Inside of Scotland Yard" (Jul 1930-Jun 1931), adapted from his book *The Story of Scotland Yard* (Bles, 1926). Also of interest were several new articles by Wallace that had arisen out of his recent trip to the United States, which had included a whistle-stop tour of Chicago's underworld. The first two issues ran "The Gang Wars of Chicago" and "Murder Men of Chicago" followed by "A Day in Sing Sing" (Dec 1930).

Despite its shoddy appearance, the magazine reprinted some good stories. These included Arthur B. Reeve's Craig Kennedy stories from *The Panama Plot* (Harper, 1918; Collins, 1920), and stories from G.D.H. and M. Cole's *Superintendent Wilson's Holiday* (Collins, 1928), *The Malachite Jar* (Collins, 1930) by J. S. Fletcher and *Tales of Mynheer Amayat* (Newnes, 1930) by H. de Vere Stacpoole. Of particular interest are several Miss Marple stories by Agatha Christie. These had run in *The Royal Magazine* in 1928 but did not appear in book form until *The Thirteen Problems* (Collins, 1932), so this was another pre-book publication. Some of the lesser-known stories may be original to the magazine. *Hush* gave no indication either way.

The magazine lasted for only thirteen issues and was cut abruptly as a fourteenth was announced. The anthology *The Big Book of Detective Stories* (Clowes, 1932), issued as part of that publisher's "Big Value" series, contained stories all from *Hush* (though this was not acknowledged). Being predominantly reprint *Hush* added nothing to the development of crime fiction but because of the Wallace and Christie associations has become highly collectable.

Frequency: Monthly.
Publisher: William Collins for the Detective Story Club.
Editor: Nominally, Edgar Wallace, but actually George Dilnot.
Format/Size: Standard pulp, 128 pages.
Price: 6d.
References: Contents listing in *Search & Research* #1 (Nov 1973), pp. 13-14.
Holdings:
Complete run, UK. Bodleian (*Call Number*: Per. 25612 d.160).
Other, UK. Cambridge University Library has issues 1-3, 13 (*Classmark*: L996.c.4).
Collecting points: The first four issues are numbered but undated. Copies are very rare.

* * *

HUTCHINSON'S ADVENTURE-STORY MAGAZINE and HUTCHINSON'S ADVENTURE & MYSTERY STORY MAGAZINE
see ADVENTURE-STORY MAGAZINE

***

HUTCHINSON'S MAGAZINE see HUTCHINSON'S STORY MAGAZINE

***

HUTCHINSON'S MYSTERY-STORY MAGAZINE see MYSTERY-STORY MAGAZINE

***

HUTCHINSON'S STORY MAGAZINE

125 issues. Volume 1, Number 1, July 1919 to Volume 21, Number 6, June 1929; 119 issues. Retitled HUTCHINSON'S MAGAZINE April 1920, though kept former name on contents page. Relaunched as HUTCHINSON'S STORY MAGAZINE from Volume 1, Number 1, July 1929 to Volume 1, Number 6, December 1929; 6 issues.

Hutchinson's, under the dictatorial rule of Walter Hutchinson, called itself the "largest publisher in the world". It published a huge quantity of cheap books of variable quality which sold in their tens of thousands throughout the world. Walter Hutchinson had little time for quality – he would often reject a book as being "too highbrow" – but he wanted his firm to be recognised by its peers. Hutchinson decided to launch *Hutchinson's Story Magazine* to serve as a showcase for authors published by the firm and helped promote forthcoming books.

Its first issue, dated July 1919, was in standard format, on medium quality paper, selling for 9d. No editorial persona was present: Hutchinson did not want his staff – who were hired and fired with intemperate regularity – becoming public personalities and kept them anonymous. It is therefore difficult to ascertain who edited the magazine but it may initially have fallen to Hutchinson's production manager Erle Lunn before the magazine department was re-established a year or two later. Then Eric Maschwitz became the managing editor until he moved to the fledgling BBC.

Initially, the magazine serialised four or five novels per issue, phased down to one or two after a year. *Hutchinson's* could boast many popular authors including H. de Vere Stacpoole, Baroness Orczy, Stacy Aumonier and H. Rider Haggard, all in the first issue. *Hutchinson's* ran three serials by Haggard: "She Meets Allan" (Jul 1919-Mar 1920), "Wisdom's Daughter" (Mar 1922-Mar 1923) and "Heu-Heu, or The Monster" (Jan-Mar 1924). Along with Stacpoole, whose "A Man of the Islands" (Apr-Sept 1920) was also serialised, his work typified the popular, escapist, romantic adventure that Hutchinson liked to publish. Similar contributors included A.E.W. Mason, Robert Hichens and the two most prolific – Edmund Snell and "Sapper" (H. C. McNeile). Sapper's Bulldog Drummond first appeared in the September 1919 issue. For women, on the light romance side, there were Ruby M. Ayres, Berta Ruck and Gilbert Frankau, later joined by Ethel M. Dell and Philip Gibbs.

Initially the magazine was all-fiction, with some cartoons, humour and a children's page. It also ran poetry. The children's section was dropped once it became clear it was not really a family magazine but one where the emphasis was on dashing adventure and romance with more than a touch of mystery. It became a regular market for weird and uncanny stories of which its primary contributor was E. F. Benson. He had nearly thirty stories in the magazine, frequently announced on the cover as "Another Spook Story". The tag line lent itself to Benson's collection *Spook Stories* from Hutchinson in 1928. Other contributors in this vein

were Lewis Spence, Margery Lawrence, Elliott O'Donnell and, with the Grand Guignol theatre at the height of popularity in the twenties, Izak Goller, Gaston Leroux and E. Charles Vivian. A particular coup was presenting a previously unpublished fairy play by Oscar Wilde, "For Love of the King" (Oct 1921), though its authenticity was later challenged and it is now believed a forgery.

From April 1920 the magazine dropped the "Story" in its title to become *Hutchinson's Magazine*. This change was appropriate for the restyling of the magazine in August 1924 when it switched from standard size to the large flat format. There had been a steady change amongst the leading magazines, encouraged by the success of *Good Housekeeping*, to turn to the 'slick' photogravure format heavily supported by advertising. At the same time as *Hutchinson's* converted, it launched a slick companion, *Woman* (Apr 1924-Jul 1929). Initially *Hutchinson's* retained the lesser quality paper, and though it improved steadily over time it was never wholly 'slick'. Nevertheless the large format was intended as a sign of sophistication and with the change *Hutchinson's* included more features and articles in order to promote a wider family appeal. It was profusely illustrated with high quality artwork by M. Mackinlay, L. R. Brightwell, Reginald Cleaver, and Lindsay Cable, plus some of the last work by Warwick Reynolds. It ran cartoons by W. Heath Robinson, features about gardens, sport, motoring and radio, plus articles about major writers. It ran a couple of stories by D. H. Lawrence, and serialised Joseph Conrad's last (incomplete) novel, "Suspense!" (Feb-Aug 1925). But otherwise the mix of fiction was much as before – Rafael Sabatini, H. de Vere Stacpoole, Sapper, Edmund Snell and E. C. Vivian – showing that it remained a magazine of rousing adventure and mystery albeit clothed in a more sophisticated dress. For a period *Hutchinson's* was a close rival, in terms of sheer entertainment, to *Pearson's* and *The Story-Teller*, but never equalled the sophistication of *Nash's Pall Mall* or *The Windsor*.

At the outset Hutchinson's claimed a "circulation" of 200,000, though this was probably the initial print run. A more credible figure of 93,228 for average net sales during 1921 was revealed to the Advertisers' Protection Society. Details of its later circulation are not known but, as with most of the fiction magazines, it had almost certainly declined by the late twenties. Its core stable of writers never deserted it, despite Walter Hutchinson's unpredictable moodswings. The magazine ran more illustrative features, especially of the stage and screen, plus such popular non-fiction series as Lord Birkenhead's studies of major trials (from Oct 1926) and Sir Cecil Harcourt-Smith's feature "Art Treasures of the Nation" (Mar-Dec 1928).

In April 1929 it revamped its contents page, grouping its fiction under such headings as "Adventure and Mystery", "Romance and Drama", "Humour", "Children's story" and so on. This was evidently a forerunner to the merger, in June 1929, with its companion magazine *Adventure & Mystery Story*. It also reverted to the standard size with a downgrade to pulp paper and a return to its original title, *Hutchinson's Story-Magazine*. Most artwork was dropped, a sure sign of tightening belts. Many of the big names remained along with Arnold Bennett, Sax Rohmer, James Hilton, Agatha Christie and Warwick Deeping.

The new format lasted only six issues and with its passing in December 1929, Hutchinson closed down its magazine division and concentrated on book production. Although the heyday of the fiction magazine had faded by the end of the twenties, *Hutchinson's* was not itself a failure. It is likely it could have continued and sustained a viable circulation if Walter Hutchinson had determined to support it financially, but he had lost interest in magazines. It always gave good value, and much of its fiction was readable and enjoyable, but it is today mostly remembered for its 'spook stories' by E. F. Benson, its serials by Rider Haggard, and for launching Bulldog Drummond on the world.

Frequency: Monthly, but no issue for Jul 1926.
Publisher: Hutchinson.
Editors: Details incomplete. Possibly Erle Lunn, 1919-21; Eric Maschwitz, 1922-23; Meredith V. Dixon, 1926-27; Evelyn Hornibrook, 1927-29; Miss G. Gilligan in 1929.
Format/Size: Standard, book-quality paper. Page count 128; from Jan 1920 varied between 104/116 (sometimes included adverts in page count); rose to 140/144, Jan 1924. Switched to large-format semi-slick, 128 pages, from Aug 1924; dropped to 112, Jan 1925 (but 128, Jan-Aug 1926), 88, Jan 1928, rose to 96, Aug 1926, 112, Oct 1928. Reverted to standard pulp, 176 pages, from Jul 1929.
Price: 9d, rose to 1/-, Mar 1920.
References: Robert Lusty, *Bound to be Read* (Jonathan Cape, 1975); Richard Joseph, *Michael Joseph: Master of Words* (Ashford Press, 1986).
Holdings: *Complete run, UK*. British Library (*Shelfmark*: P.P.6018.tak); Bodleian (*Call Number*: Per. 25611 d.56).
Collecting points: Very rare. Individual issues surface infrequently but no long runs.

***

THE IDLER

228 issues. Two series. Volume 1, Number 1, February 1892 to Volume 21, Number 8, September 1902; 126 issues. New series, Volume 22, Number 1, October 1902 to Volume 38, Number 102, March 1911; 102 issues.

Although most closely associated with Jerome K. Jerome, *The Idler* owed its existence and its survival for almost two decades to its founder, Robert Barr. Born in Scotland, but raised in Canada, Barr settled in Detroit after his marriage in 1876 and became a journalist. He worked for the *Detroit Free Press*, where his antics to gain news – ranging from rifling mail bags to crossing a river on ice floes – earned him a reputation as an enterprising reporter. He returned to England in 1881 to start a British edition of the *Free Press*, an idea that had also occurred to

William Dunkerley, later better known as the writer John Oxenham. Dunkerley needed an excuse to escape from the family food-import business and the opportunity came when he teamed up with Barr. They formed a good partnership and the British edition of the *Detroit Free Press* was a great success during the 1880s. As its popularity faded at the end of the decade the team decided on a new venture.

Barr was keen to publish a monthly illustrated magazine, a desire re-energised with the appearance of *The Strand*. He and Dunkerley formed a new company. The idea was for Barr to be the editor, Dunkerley the business manager, and to have a major literary name as a figurehead, who would be labelled as editor but who would simply lend his name to the venture and provide a monthly column. Their first choice was Barr's friend Mark Twain, but they could not reach a financial agreement. Both J. M. Barrie and Rudyard Kipling were considered but the final choice was Jerome K. Jerome, then in the first flush of fame following the success of *Three Men in a Boat*. Jerome had also been considering starting a magazine and was highly enthusiastic. From the start there was a clash of egos over who was the real editor. This proved beneficial to *The Idler* – a title suggested by Jerome – because their editorial ramblings gave it a strong personality. It was rare for magazines to betray an editorial persona at that time. But Barr (sometimes writing as Luke Sharp) and Jerome vied with each other through their various contributions to be the wittiest and the result was a lively, friendly, welcoming magazine.

Jerome's concept of the "idler" was not the same as laziness. He had had some success with his book of musings, *Idle Thoughts of an Idle Fellow* (Field & Tuer, 1886), where he demonstrated the positive side of unhurried contemplation. *The Idler* was planned as a magazine that would provide food for thought in a relaxing and congenial way.

The magazine was awash with advertising and, according to Jerome, proved profitable from the start, with a respectable circulation.[1] Although there were pictures on almost every page, the illustrations did not dominate the magazine as in *The Strand*. They were there to illustrate the text, not adorn it. The primary artists were George Hutchinson and Dudley Hardy, joined later by Fred Pegram, Stanley L. Wood and John Gülich. The emphasis was on the written word and the joy of language.

The first issue was a more compact size than that adopted by *The Strand*. It led with the serial "An American Claimant", Mark Twain's sequel to *The Gilded Age*. It concerns a harebrained American inventor's aspirations to an English earldom and in vivacity, originality and, at times, pure wackiness, set the mood which *The Idler* wanted to achieve – a magazine that was creative but did not take itself too seriously. In the same tone was "Choice Blends", where photographs of various personalities were overlaid to produce composite creations. There were a series of spoof excuses for an interview with Mark Twain because Robert Barr (writing as Luke Sharp) refused to interview him for fear of Twain's wrath and financial demands.

Of special import was "The Idlers' Club", which became the backbone of the magazine. It was a symposium where various contributors voiced their views on a given topic or anything that took their fancy. Once *The Idler* was launched Barr held afternoon teas to which authors and others were invited and George Burgin, the magazine's sub-editor, would keep track of

---

[1] Precise circulation details from the 1890s are not available but Jerome wrote, "In circulation *The Idler* is second to only one other English magazine ..." (*The Idler*, August 1895, p. 97). This suggests a figure anywhere between 100,000 and 200,000.

discussions and somehow compile a thread into the "Idlers' Club" miscellany.[2] In later issues the column became a bit too regimented but at the outset it was casual, often wayward and always challenging. In addition to the editors the main contributors were Barry Pain, Israel Zangwill, Eden Phillpotts, George R. Sims, W. L. Alden and Conan Doyle. Topics ranged from childhood to smoking (in which there is an early comment about the link between smoking and cancer[3]) and everything else in between. The first "Idlers' Club" high-lighted the matter of the magazine's readership. Barr commented upon the benefits arising from the education system since the 1871 Education Act, whose first beneficiaries were now of working age. Barr also determined that *The Idler* should attract and develop new writers, joking that contributors to the first issue – Mark Twain, Bret Harte and Andrew Lang – would not remain unknown for long.

The essays were always witty, sometimes verging on the flippant. An off-hand remark by Grant Allen in the September 1892 issue, commenting adversely on Walter Besant's attitude to publishers, brought a quick riposte from Besant. Jerome contributed a series about music-hall stars which, along with other features on the stage, reflected Jerome's thespian background. The fiction was also invariably light-hearted, notably Barr's parody of Sherlock Holmes, "The Adventures of Sherlaw Kombs" (May 1892). Even stories that may at first appear serious were, at a deeper level, satirising society or scientific development. Conan Doyle's "The Los Amigos Fiasco" (Dec 1892), shows how the over-zealous use of an electric chair makes the victim immortal. Jerome also contributed the serial "Novel Notes" (May 1892-Apr 1893). Somewhat in the vein of *Three Men in a Boat*, it is about four men who endeavour to write a novel and recount experiences which they believe will be the basis for the book. Similar was Conan Doyle's autobiographical "The Stark Munro Letters" (Oct 1894-Nov 1895) and Israel Zangwill's satire on Jewish society, "The King of Schnorrers" (Aug 1893).

Jerome did not want the magazine to be entirely light-hearted. He wanted it to explore popular literature and culture and he instigated a number of informative series. In "My First Book" noted authors looked back at how their literary careers began. They included Walter Besant, R. M. Ballantyne, Hall Caine, Rudyard Kipling, Conan Doyle, H. Rider Haggard, W. Clark Russell, Marie Corelli and Robert Louis Stevenson. "Lions in Their Dens" (from Jan 1893) featured the home life of leading personalities in stage, politics and art, including George Grossmith, George Newnes, Lord Charles Beresford, Father Ignatius and Henri Rochefort.

Jerome also featured ghost and mystery stories such as "A Spectre's Dilemma" by Eden Phillpotts (Mar 1892) and "Rutherford the Twice-Born" by Edwin Lester Arnold (May 1892). There were mystery stories by Fergus Hume and Rodriguez Ottolengui and, most notably, "The Case of Lady Sannox" by Conan Doyle (Nov 1893). There were oriental stories by H. N. Crellin and sea stories by Clark Russell. Robert Barr contributed several unusual stories. "The

---

[2] Burgin's memories of these events are recorded in *Many Memories* (Hutchinson, 1922), pp. 94-107.
[3] See *The Idler*, November 1892, p. 456.

Doom of London" (Nov 1892) depicts a London destroyed by a suffocating fog. "The Fear of It" (May 1893) has a survivor cast ashore on an unknown island where the inhabitants worship the dead. "The Revolt of the –" (May 1894) is a satire on the growth of female emancipation and considers a future rôle reversal. It may have encouraged the Idlers' Club discussion, "How to Court the Advanced Woman" (Sept 1894),[4] with a frontispiece by Aubrey Beardsley.

In "The Idlers' Club" for June 1894 contributors developed a mini-story around a given plot. This may have sparked the idea for "The Mystery of Black Rock Creek" (Oct 1894), a round-robin story with chapters written in turn by Jerome, Phillpotts, E. F. Benson, F. Frankfort Moore and Barry Pain. It was followed by "Tales of Our Coast", a series set around Britain's coast, each story by a different author. Gilbert Parker began the series but the best known story was "The Roll-Call of the Reef" (Jun 1895) by Arthur Quiller-Couch. Each story was illustrated by Frank Brangwyn, and it was from this time that art became more dominant.

It had been evident during 1894 and into 1895 that *The Idler* was changing. Jerome did not always want to be labelled as a humorist and wanted to inject items of greater import. As early as the May 1893 issue he had started Sophie Wassilief's serial "Memoirs of a Female Nihilist". There was also an increased in illustrated poetry, starting with "The Story of Ung" (Dec 1894) by Kipling. He introduced a regular book review column by W. L. Alden (from Sept 1894) and began a series about famous men with an article on the boyhood of Sir Henry Irving (Jan 1895). He also gave greater exposure to artists with features on Frank Brangwyn (Mar 1895), H. R. Millar (Oct 1895) and Louis Wain (Jan 1896).

The notebooks of William Dunkerley identified the growing rift. His daughter Erica noted:

> Unfortunately, almost from the beginning, the magazine was in troubled waters. And the reason was to be found in the fact that – in Jerome and Barr – it had two captains, both of them rather strong-willed, both desirous without doubt of steering the ship to success, but with widely differing views as the best course to take.[5]

Not only were there artistic and literary divisions, but Jerome insisted on paying the authors, many of them close friends, high wordage rates despite Dunkerley, as business manager, maintaining that payment should be left to him. Frustrated, Barr and Dunkerley thought they could divert Jerome's interests by giving him a newspaper to edit, so that Barr could take back *The Idler*. However, Jerome had the capacity to handle both[6] and threw himself into editing the weekly *To-Day*, the first issue of which appeared on 11 November 1893, with equal vigour. Barr had only doubled the problem. In the end he gave up the fight, remaining as proprietor and leaving Jerome to edit *The Idler* single-handedly from the August 1895 issue.

From that issue several changes were immediately apparent. Jerome converted the magazine to the more familiar standard size, thereby losing some of the intimacy of the compact edition, but allowing for greater use of artwork. Initially it became a magazine of two halves. The first was liberally illustrated with specific features and photographs. The second half was virtually devoid of illustration, consisting of many brief stories and columns. In his editorial, Jerome noted that he was not trying to appeal "to the masses" but to the "growing

---

[4] *The Idler* had a chiefly male readership. Barr did consider *The Lady's Idler*, and prepared a registration copy in January 1894, but did not pursue it. Thereafter there was a slight increase in articles for women.
[5] Erica Oxenham, *Scrap-book of J.O.* (Longmans, Green, 1946), p. 38.
[6] Thanks to help from his private secretary, the young Ernest Bramah.

public which possesses literary tastes and artistic sympathies." It was another year before the art content became a significant part of the magazine, but then it blossomed with many reproductions of fine art, and regular in-depth features on major artists, past and present.

However, in broadening the magazine's coverage, Jerome diluted the original potent mix. Despite the major authors he published – amongst them Kipling, H. G. Wells, Anthony Hope, George Gissing, Stanley Weyman and William Le Queux – he failed to sustain the market against the growing number of rivals. Sales began to fall, leading Dunkerley to insist upon cutting rates to authors. Jerome would have persevered but a legal case put an end to it all. In April 1897 *To-Day*'s financial editor provoked a libel suit from a company promoter, Samson Fox. The case was a minor one, but still ran for a record sixteen days in the High Court, and although Fox won he was awarded only a farthing in damages, and each party was charged with costs. Jerome, who had put much of his own money into *To-Day*, found he had a debt of £5,000.[7] Barr was forced to sell the paper. It was acquired by Horatio Bottomley, with Barry Pain as editor. Barr found a new publisher for *The Idler*, J. M. Dent, and a new editor, Edwin Oliver, but within a year the magazine was sold to the artist Sidney Sime.

Despite their clashes, *The Idler* had been better under the joint editorship of Barr and Jerome than Jerome alone, though throughout his tenure Jerome could be proud of his work. This is especially true of the number of new writers he encouraged, amongst them W. W. Jacobs, Eden Phillpotts and Barry Pain. The magazine was charged with a creative spark, which flickered out after Jerome's departure.

Under a new proprietor, *The Idler* strove to continue its mix of bohemianism and literary culture. Sime's partner, Arthur Lawrence served as editor for the first year, with Sime as art editor. With such talent, it should have succeeded, but although both its price and page count increased the magazine remained underfunded. Although Sime had inherited a considerable sum of money, he found that in purchasing the magazine he had also acquired huge debts and it was draining him of his resources.[8]

Sime wished to develop the artistic element and the magazine became beautifully illuminated with art nouveau so typical of the *fin de siècle*. The magazine reflected much of the exotic delight of the period, especially the interest in *chinoiserie*, something that would remain, to a lesser degree, for the rest of the magazine's life. There was an increase in fine line pen-and-ink drawings of exceptional quality, including work by Arthur Layard, Stephen Reid, Celia Levetus and Sime himself. Looking through an artistic eye, James Thorpe regarded *The Idler* as "one of the few examples of the best achievement of English magazine production during the nineties."[9]

The fiction, however, though plentiful, was for the most part, undistinguished. There were historical romances, such as Fred Wishaw's serial "At the Court of Catherine the Great" (Feb

---

[7] Jerome recalled that the debt was £9,000 in *My Life & Times* (Murray, 1926, p. 147), but Dunkerley's notes record it as £5,000, *Scrap-Book of J.O., op. cit.*, p. 45.

[8] The General Review and Magazine Company set up to take over *The Idler* went into receivership in October 1899.

[9] James Thorpe, *English Illustration: The Nineties* (Faber, 1935), p. 161.

1898-Jan 1899), a charming Christmas fantasy in Laurence Housman's "The Love-Child" (Jan 1899), and Harold MacGrath's Ruritanian-style adventure "The Puppet Crown" (Mar 1901-Jan 1902) which, surprisingly, was unillustrated. But otherwise there was little of note. Of more interest were a number of articles on crimes and criminals, including "True Stories from the Underworld" by Josiah Flynt and Francis Walton (from Feb 1901) plus assessments of the *cause célèbre*, the Dreyfus Case.

The appearance of a contest story, "A Cornish Mystery" (Jun 1901), asking readers to contribute the next episode, was a sign of desperation. Such ideas are never successful and are always an indication of financial problems. Sime had grown tired of the magazine. With much relief but at great financial loss, he sold it back to Robert Barr, who immediately tried to re-invigorate the magazine with some of its former flair and audacity. *The Idler* passed through several publishers until Barr restored it to Chatto & Windus. Having dwindled to 96 pages, within a year it increased to 126 pages with over twenty pages of advertising.

Initially Barr acquired what material he could by purchasing stories from American magazines, primarily *McClure's*. Barr had a long-standing relationship with S. S. McClure and had helped him when he launched *McClure's Magazine* in 1893 – indeed, *McClure's* had been planned as a US edition of *The Idler*. Now it was McClure's opportunity to reciprocate, providing Barr with top quality stories. For a while most stories had American settings, with many frontier stories such as "The Forest Runner" by Stewart Edward White (Aug 1902) and "Billy the Buck" by Henry Wallace Phillips (Sept 1902). There were several Klondike stories by Jack London, plus contributions from Cyrus T. Brady, Josephine Dodge Daskam and Sarah Orne Jewett. Barr reprinted one of F. P. Dunne's early Mr. Dooley stories, "Mr. Dooley Guesses About Women" (Feb 1903), but failed to follow the series through to develop the success that came later in *Nash's*. Barr also secured the first British publication of the Darby O'Gill stories by Herminie Templeton with "Darby O'Gill and the Good People" (Jul 1902).

Compared to the American stories the British material was rather tame. There were stories of the Scottish scamp Wee Macgregor by J. J. Bell, a couple of ghost stories by Elliott O'Donnell, early tales by Berta Ruck who also illustrated stories, and Barr's completion of Stephen Crane's novel, "The O'Ruddy" (Jan-Jul 1904), but most of the stories were brief and inconsequential. From the home market Barr was acquiring mostly non-fiction. Besides the usual literary and travel items, there were such forward-looking pieces as Frank Fayant's "Flying Across London" (Oct 1902) and a feature on how Alphonse Bertillon solved a crime through fingerprints in the sensationally entitled, "Sherlock Holmes Outdone" (Jan 1903).

At last, though, Barr achieved a scoop, publishing G. K. Chesterton's new series "The Club of Queer Trades" (Jun-Dec 1904). Barr hoped this series would turn round *The Idler*'s fortunes. In that month's "The Idlers' Club" he noted that he had arranged for extensive advertising about the series, firmly believing that there must be at least half-a-million readers in Britain who would want to read it. He also recognised that the cost of printing a further 300,000 copies was prohibitive, so he limited himself to printing an extra 10,000 copies. The implication is that the print run for *The Idler* was already 200,000, but this is questionable. The Advertisers' Protection Society assessed the circulation during 1907 as only 10,000,[10] a long way from Barr's inference. An answer may be that when Barr referred to printing an "extra" 10,000 he

---

[10] See *The A.P.S. Monthly Circular*, November 1907.

was, in effect, hoping to double his sales to 20,000. Nevertheless this low circulation was not enough to support a heavily illustrated magazine with major authors.

Chesterton's series was evidently not the breakthrough that Barr had hoped. He tried desperately to secure stories that would capture the public mood. There were the "Billy" stories by Margaret Westrup, the "Pinch and Potty" stories by W. C. Yarcott and the excellent mystery series "The Tracer of Lost Persons" by Robert W. Chambers (Oct 1906-Apr 1907). Barr acquired several stories by O. Henry, and ran the atmospheric series "Carnacki the Ghost-Finder" by William Hope Hodgson (from Jan 1910). *The Idler* ran one of the earliest stories by F. Tennyson Jesse, "The Dog Decides" (Feb 1911). It even dared run a story by Aleister Crowley, "The Drug" (Jan 1909). Barr contributed many stories of his own, including the medieval adventure novel, "Prince Roland" (Dec 1909-Aug 1910), issued in book form as *The Sword Maker* (Mills & Boon, 1910). Although these and others proved  popular with readers, they failed to develop the magazine's circulation. The effort proved injurious to Barr's precarious health. Illness forced him to suspend the magazine with the March 1911 issue. He died of dropsy brought on by a weak heart in October 1912, aged 62.

The Idler ran enough good quality material to have kept its memory alive during the twentieth century, though this owes as much to the reputation of Jerome K. Jerome as to its own achievements. Had it been able to continue as it had begun it would have succeeded as the *enfant terrible* of the 1890s: mischievous and clever without being reckless and *risqué*.

Frequency: Monthly, but no issues for Feb or Mar 1902.
Publisher: Chatto & Windus, Feb 1892-Jan 1898; J. M. Dent, Feb-Jul 1898; W. R. Russell, Aug 1898-Jul 1900; Horace Marshall, Aug 1900-Feb 1901; Dawbarn & Ward, Mar 1901-Sept 1902; Chatto & Windus, Oct 1902-Sept 1906; The Idler [Robert Barr], Oct 1906-Mar 1911.
Editors: Jerome K. Jerome with Robert Barr, Feb 1892-Jul 1895; Jerome alone, Aug 1895-Nov 1897; Barr alone, Dec 1897-Sept 1898; Edwin Oliver, Oct 1898-Apr 1899; Arthur Lawrence and Sidney H. Sime, May 1899-Feb 1901; not known (possibly Clement Dawbarn or H. Snowden Ward), Feb-Sept 1902; Robert Barr, Oct 1902-Oct 1911.
Format/Size: Small standard (demy octavo, 21cm x 13.5cm). Page count 118/124, rose to 144, Oct 1894; dropped to 126, Jul 1895. Standard (royal octavo, 23.5cm x 16cm), 96/100 pages, from Aug 1895, rose to 160, Feb 1896, dropped to 142, Aug 1896, 100/104, Feb 1900; 92/96, Feb 1901; rose to 126, Oct 1902; dropped to 112 (with slight variances) from Oct 1903.
Price: 6d, though raised to 1/- during Sime's editorship.
References: Fiction only covered in *Indexes to Fiction in The Idler* (Victorian Fiction Research Guide #23), by William Thesing and Becky Lewis (University of Queensland, 1994).
Holdings:
Complete run, UK/Eire. Bodleian (*Call Number*: Per. 2705 d.238). • Cambridge University Library (*Classmark*: L996.c.41). • National Library of Scotland (*Shelfmark*: U.425). • Trinity College, Dublin.
Substantial run, UK. British Library has all issues except Aug 1897-Jan 1898 and Feb-Mar 1911 (*Shelfmark*: PP.6004.gmi).

Complete run, US. The University of California, Southern Regional Library Facility • Free Library of Philadelphia (*Call Number*: 052 119). • All others on microfilm. Library of Congress (*Call Number*: AP4.I2). • Boston Public Library. • Florida State University. • Illinois State University. • Los Angeles Public Library. • New York Public Library. • New York University. • University of California at Davis. • University of California, Riverside. • University of Connecticut. • University of Rhode Island. • University of Rochester. • Rutgers University.
Collecting points: Publisher's binding is plain olive green. Early volumes to 1896 are common but thereafter are increasingly rare. The Sime issues are highly prized.

* * *

THE JOLLY MAGAZINE
8 issues. Volume 1, Number 1, May 1927 to perhaps Number 8, December 1927.

The Jolly Mag. was a continuation of *The Sovereign* which, in its final few issues had switched from an adventure to a humour magazine. To keep the names alive, *The Jolly* carried on its cover the line "incorporating Sovereign & Regent Magazines" even though the magazine bore no similarity to those titles apart from completing the crime serial, "Black Star's Return" by Johnston McCulley. *The Jolly* was a blatant imitation of *The Merry Mag.* and *The Sunny Mag.*. It opened with a miscellany of jokes and cartoons, and ran various humorous columns and features, mostly short and today very dated. There was a regular column by Stephen Leacock, "Afternoon Adventures at My Club" and contributions from various music-hall celebrities – Jack Buchanan, Claude Hulbert and Flotsam and Jetsam were in the early issues. H. M. Bateman wrote and illustrated a regular feature.

Amongst all this whimsy was a mixture of stories, three or four an issue but sometimes long enough to fill almost half the magazine. They include a series of light-hearted romances by Richmal Crompton, starting with "Journey's End" (May 1927), and various amusing tales or light romances by Eden Phillpotts, Berta Ruck, Ethel Mannin, Anthony Armstrong, Phyllis Hambledon and Max Pemberton. *The Jolly* may have raised a smile now and then, but it contains little of significance. It does not seem to have survived its first year. It may have continued until Hutchinson closed down his magazine operation but, if so, no later copies seem to have survived.

Frequency: Monthly.
Publisher: Hutchinson.
Editor: Probably Miss G. Gilligan.
Format/Size: Standard pulp, 96 pages.
Price: 7d.
Holdings: *Partial run, UK*. British Library (*Shelfmark*: PP.6018.tbc) and Bodleian (*Call Number*: Per. 25612 d.140) both have issues May-December 1927 only.
Collecting points: Rare. Only occasional single issues surface.

* * *

THE LADY'S MAGAZINE

51 issues. Volume 1, Number 1, January 1901 to Volume 9, Number 51, March 1905. Retitled THE LADY'S HOME MAGAZINE from Volume 8, Number 43, July 1904; became LADY'S HOME MAGAZINE OF FICTION from Volume 9, Number 49 (Jan 1905) and THE HOME MAGAZINE OF FICTION from Volume 9, Number 50 (Feb 1905).

For most of its life *The Lady's Magazine* seldom settled at being any one thing, yet it ended up forming the basis for the first British popular all-fiction magazine. At the outset the editor stated that no British monthly magazine for women had achieved one-tenth the circulation of the most popular equivalent in the United States, *The Ladies' Home Journal*, with a circulation of a million. Noting that Britain had half the population of the USA, the editor declared, "I shall not rest satisfied till the circulation of the *Lady's Magazine* is half-a-million." Maybe this is why the magazine changed its publishing policy so often, possibly alienating as many readers as it fostered.

A near scandal at the outset should have helped sales. The serial, "The Eternal City" by Hall Caine, not only reconsiders the whole future of the Holy See, but has the startling revelation that the lead male character is the illegitimate son of the Pope. The editor had no problem with this, having introduced the novel by saying, "I have, of course, read the whole of 'The Eternal City', and I can assure you that it is quite the strongest and the most charming story that Mr Hall Caine has written." Clearly her publisher, C. Arthur Pearson, disagreed. The serial was suddenly dropped from the June 1901 issue with a statement saying in part, "Differences have arisen between [the proprietors] and the author as to the suitability of the story for *The Lady's Magazine*, and the proprietors have, in consequence, commenced proceedings against Mr. Hall Caine." The novel went on to be a million-seller, but it is unlikely that the magazine benefited from the matter. On the contrary, it had demonstrated that the publisher was not prepared to be controversial and readers could conclude that they would settle down to a magazine of humdrum normality. Caine's serial was replaced by the more homely "The Cat's Paw" by Mrs Croker.

The Lady's Magazine looked identical to both *The Lady's Realm* and *Woman at Home*, with the same features on fashion, health, beauty and cooking. As in many other magazines it opened with an article on artists and their work, looking mostly at painters of children, women or animals, and occasionally at female artists. There were the inevitable articles about royalty and high society, though not as many as in *The Lady's Realm*. If anything, *The Lady's Magazine* considered more unusual pursuits with articles on lady balloonists, lady bookbinders, even lady tobogganists.

About half the issue was fiction, including a "storyette" feature, the only item to remain throughout the magazine's life. Although it ran several simple love stories, there was generally a good mixture of the humorous, historical and dramatic. Early contributors included J. J. Bell, F. Frankfort Moore, Frank Norris, Flora Annie Steel, Ernest Seton-Thompson and the Baroness von Hutten. With "Celia's Engagement" (Jan 1901), Rosalie Neish began a long-running series about the high-spirited Celia and the problems she foisted upon family and friends. Other notable contributors included Marie Belloc, who wrote mostly on fashion, and J. A. Middleton, who wrote on art and contributed many poems.

The editor clearly enjoyed stories and features about the Orient, starting with Clive Holland's story, "Mousmé" (Dec 1901), illustrated by Arthur Rackham. There were several contributions by Onoto Watanna, including the short serial "The Japanese Nightingale" (May-Jun 1902). Starting from July 1903 the magazine ran a series of covers portraying Oriental scenes. They are amongst the most beautiful covers to appear on any magazine at this time, yet there was no reference to them within the magazine and no artist was credited,.

From May 1902 the magazine underwent several changes. Although recognising the popularity of fiction, the number of stories was reduced to make way for several new features, including theatre gossip, etiquette, "the man at home" (a light-hearted series started by Rosalie Neish considering the plight of the undomesticated male) and a children's section, "Playtime". For a while the magazine issued a small supplementary children's magazine, *Wonderland* (Oct 1902-Apr 1903). From September 1902 the magazine also offered a free pattern with each issue. Although fiction took a back seat, *The Lady's* published work by several noted American writers including Herminie Templeton, Josephine Dodge Daskam, Justus Miles Forman and Ellis Parker Butler.

However, fiction fought back. From May 1903 the full title became *The Lady's Magazine of Fiction and Fashion* and most features were dropped. Leading the revival was L. G. Moberly, already a regular contributor of poems and storyettes and now the chief contributor of series, starting with "Adventures of a Lady Courier" (Mar-Aug 1903). Later series include "The Experiences of a Lady Doctor" (Sept 1903-Feb 1904), "My Six Daughters" (Aug 1904-Jan 1905) and the serial, "The Woman with the Awful Eyes" (Mar-Aug 1904). Other series include "The Chronicles of Lady Gwen" by J. K. Prothero (Sept 1903-Feb 1904), about the adventures of an actress, and "True Tales of Monte Carlo" by Mrs C. N. Williamson (Apr-Sept 1904). Amongst American contributors, *The Lady's* ran Anna Katherine Green's mystery serial, "The Amethyst Box" (Jun-Aug 1903) and short stories by Tudor Jenks, Gelett Burgess and Mary E. Wilkins. Historically the most interesting series was "The Chronicles of Addington Peace" (Aug 1904-Jan 1905) by B. Fletcher Robinson, included in Ellery Queen's *Queen's Quorum* of keystone detective books.

The magazine at last had some zest and though most of the fiction was imitative of material elsewhere, it was starting to develop. From November 1904 the title metamorphosed through *Lady's Home Magazine of Fiction* to *The Home Magazine of Fiction* by February 1905. It was now almost all fiction, including a new series by Moberly, "Episodes in the Life of a Lady Nurse" (from Jan 1905), and a dramatic serial by Louis Tracy, about people shipwrecked on a lighthouse, "The Pillar of Light" (began Dec 1904).

At this stage the directors at Pearson's, felt the magazine's rôle needed to be broadened. They believed the title was cumbersome and no longer related to the woman's market. So in March 1905 *The Home Magazine* was dropped and the following month *The Novel Magazine* was launched, with more pages and at a lower price. In announcing the change the editor wrote: "Fiction has always played a strong part in our cast – it will now play the leading rôle, for *The Novel Magazine* will be practically devoted to it, and will be the only British all-fiction magazine." From a magazine of health hints, beauty treatment and fashion, was born the movement for a revolution.

Frequency: Monthly.
Publisher: C. Arthur Pearson.
Editor: K. Maud Bennett.
Format/Size: Standard. Page count 112, dropped to 100/104, Jul 1901; rose to 118/120, May 1902; back to 100/104, Sept 1902; rose to 120, Jan 1905.
Price: 6d.
Holdings:
Complete run, UK. Bodleian (*Shelfmark*: Per. 2705 d.128). • Cambridge University Library (*Classmark*: L448.c.7).
Partial run, US. No substantial runs are known. University of Texas at Austin, Harry Ransom Center has Volumes 1-4, Jan 1901-Dec 1902 (*Call Number*: R115Clad).
Collecting points: Extremely rare, though single issues occasionally surface. Those featuring Fletcher Robinson's series are most prized.

* * *

THE LADY'S REALM

235 issues. Volume 1, Number 1, November 1896 to Volume 39, Number 235, May 1916.

The Lady's Realm carved a niche as a leading Society monthly magazine that also ran popular fiction. It was designed for the upper and aspiring middle classes and for its first few years did not veer from its course of reminding everybody of their position in Society. The magazine revolved around status, decorum and quality breeding. This was evident not only in its articles, which included features on the Crown Heads and nobility of Europe (and beyond), and its columns, which covered fashion, society weddings, engagements, gossip, beauty hints and cuisine, but also its fiction. The first issue included Marie Corelli's "Jane", about a girl's debut into Society whilst the second issue ran "The Return of Dodo", featuring E. F. Benson's character from his successful first Society novel.

Most of the contributors were titled ladies: the Countess of Warwick, the Countess of Malmesbury (on "The Domestic Servant Problem"), the Countess of Munster; if you were not in Society, it must have been difficult to sell to the magazine. The publisher, George Hutchinson, was a social climber (his son, Walter, was even worse), though George had to wait till 1912 to receive his knighthood. The founding editor, William H. Wilkins, had been Private Secretary to the Earl of Dunraven and was later a biographer of Edward VII, but his presence in the magazine was remote. He rarely contributed an editorial, and even the one in the first issue was sewn in separately. It summed up the magazine's position quite clearly:

> It will deal with all subjects of interest to ladies and, while it will touch on matters affecting Society, it will contain nothing to which objection can be taken. It will be essentially a magazine for the refined and cultured home.

In sustaining its "refined" image it was, at least in its early years, perilously close to being a religious "home" magazine. Although in appearance it looked like yet another *Strand* imitation – its six-monthly bound volumes always boasted "over 500 illustrations" on the cover – it was nothing like *The Strand* in content or, for that matter, like the other *Strand*-imitation woman's magazine, *Woman at Home*. Its contents were so rigid in following Victorian decorum that today many of its articles and stories read like museum pieces, lacking any life or vitality. It was not until the Edwardian era that the magazine would loosen its starched-collar and corset and breathe a little. Even then its format and general content remained much the same.

The real value of the magazine is in its photographs. There can scarcely be any member of the English aristocracy or European royalty not photographed or discussed in the magazine, either in a feature article or a society column. It is evident that the contributors, at least those amongst the nobility, found it difficult to see beyond their own circle. When, at the turn of the century, several were asked to look to the future, their thoughts clung to the continuation of luxury, pleas to resolve the servant problem, and hopes that legislation will be introduced to stop marriages between "degenerates".

The magazine rarely gave any coverage to its contributors, but there was the occasional feature on authors. The first to be so honoured was Frances Hodgson Burnett who wrote of her early days in "How I Served My Apprenticeship" (Nov 1896). In "Marie Corelli and Her Work" by Mrs Tom Kelly (Jan 1898), Corelli maintained the fabrication that she was adopted by her stepfather. One wonders whether she would have been allowed into the portals of the magazine if the editor (and the readers) knew that she was the illegitimate child of a servant girl. Others to receive special treatment were E. Thorneycroft Fowler (May 1900), Mrs Katherine Thurston (Apr 1905), Mark Twain (Feb 1908), Elinor Glyn (May 1908) and Selma Lagerhof (Feb 1910). One unusual feature was that most articles during the magazine's early years ran the signatures of authors at the end of their contribution.

Most of its fiction had historical settings, particularly the serials, which were often stretched out over a full year. These include Mary E. Braddon's "In High Places" (Nov 1897-Oct 1898), set during the reign of Charles I, F. Frankfort Moore's Regency novel, "A Nest of Linnets" (Nov 1900-Oct 1901) and H. Rider Haggard's "Fair Margaret" (Nov 1906-Oct 1907), set in the sixteenth century. These stories reflect the retrospective mood of the magazine, frequently looking back to supposedly better times.

Most other stories were Society dilemmas. Arabella Kenealy's novel, "Charming Renée" (Nov 1899-Oct 1900), deal with a mother's concern about her daughter's marriageable status. "The Splendid Porsenna" (May-Oct 1899), a serial by Mrs Hugh Fraser involves a debutante's "coming-out", set in fashionable Rome (Paris and Rome feature frequently in many stories). Mrs Fraser's maiden name was Mary Crawford, and she was the sister of novelist F. Marion Crawford, which may account for the unusual appearance of a vampire story in the magazine, his "The Dead Smile" (Dec 1899). Vampires aside, the magazine published several strange stories, such as the series, "The Relations: What They Related" (Feb-Nov 1902) by G. M.

Robins. There were also such symposia as "Do Ghosts Appear?" (Jan 1902) and "Do the Dead Return?" (Nov 1903).

The magazine occasionally ventured into the area of sensational fiction, such as Mrs Campbell Praed's "Miss Crosson's Familiar" (Jul 1897), though it was as likely to parody it. At the end of Violet Fane's overly dramatic "The True Story of a Midnight Murder" (Apr 1899) we discover that the murder victim is a mosquito. The magazine could, at times, publish the most syrupy of religious fantasies, of which E. F. Benson was a culprit in "The Everlasting Silence" (Jan 1898). It did, however, publish some fine fantasies ostensibly for children, but of benefit to all. These include, during the magazine's flirtation with the Orient, "Buddha's Crystal" (Mar 1904), a beautiful Japanese fairy tale written and translated by Yei Theodora Ozaki. They also include several stories by Walter de la Mare of which "The Dutch Cheese" (May 1908) is the best known. De la Mare sold ten stories to *The Lady's Realm*, starting with "The Quincunx" (Jan 1906) and it remained his sole market for the next two years.

Change did come gradually to the magazine. It began to discuss more adventurous occupations for women, such as "A Lady's Adventures in Unknown India" by Isabel Savory (Nov 1899-Apr 1900). Annesley Kenealy wrote about "A Lady's Adventures in a Balloon" (Nov 1903) and August 1904 saw the start of "Careers for Women". Most of these appeared following a change in editorship to Edward Keble Chatterton. A drama critic, Chatterton introduced a column "Plays and Players". He broadened the magazine's parameters whilst retaining its Society status. The covers improved and there was more discussion of popular art. The magazine had always featured classical art but now it included material by or about Willy Pogany, Harry Rountree, Charles Sykes and W. Heath Robinson. It published stories by Jack London, Ernest Bramah, H. de Vere Stacpoole, Phyllis Bottome and I.A.R. Wylie, at last pushing aside the titled ladies. Even a servant was allowed to contribute "A Servant on the Servant Problem" (Nov 1909), though in deference to her employer she remained anonymous. One of E. F. Benson's stories at this time, "The Puce Silk" (Nov 1907), is of interest as it includes a lady called Lucia, albeit not the same as the Lucia of his later famous series (which started with *Queen Lucia* in 1920).

Although the suffragette movement had by and large been ignored by *The Lady's Realm*, most Society ladies not being supporters, by the late Edwardian period that was no longer possible. The magazine's response, however, was to lampoon it. Frank Finn contributed "The Suffragette Movement in the Animal World" (May 1909) whilst George Buckingham dared to ask the question, "If the Women of England Went Out on Strike" (Jan 1910). He even dared to answer by suggesting little would change. Mrs George Crichton Miln countered with "The He-Suffragette" (Dec 1912).

The cost of producing *The Lady's Realm* must have been high. The circulation in 1906 was reported as 35,000, dropping to 31,000 by 1911. Although it usually ran over thirty pages of advertising, it is unlikely this covered the cost of production. In 1909 Hutchinson's sold the magazine to Stanley Paul who, a year later, licensed it to editor Vere Smith of the Amalgamated Magazine Company. A retired military man, Smith seems to have run the magazine as a hobby more than a commercial proposition.

Whilst staying true to its roots, under Smith the volume of fiction increased. Bernard Capes contributed the series, "The Adventures of Gilead Balm in Search of the Truth" (Dec 1909-Oct 1910), in which Balm investigates cases arising from newspaper agony columns. H. G. Wells's novel, "Marriage" (Feb-Dec 1912) was not only good material for *The Lady's Realm* but an ideal example of the dilemmas arising for women in society in their choices between work and marriage, independence or motherhood. "The Betrothal of Maria Mullens" by Mrs Crichton Miln (Sept 1912) was one of several stories of the day to explore the Mormon sect and its attitude towards women. Max Rittenberg turned to fantasy to satirise developing social conventions in a series, "Modern Arabian Days" (Sept 1912-Mar 1913). Rittenberg became a regular contributor and it is possible that Vere Smith delegated the editing of the magazine to him. It even had a companion title, *The Club Room* (see entry).

In its final years *The Lady's Realm* ran more general fiction, opening its pages to F. Britten Austin, W. L. George and W. Pett Ridge; there's even an early story by American mystery writer Earl Derr Biggers. But despite these changes, the magazine stuck rigidly to its class values. Once the nation was enveloped in War it seemed even more fixed in the past. Falling circulation, escalating costs and Vere Smith's own failing health brought the magazine to a belated close. In its final year a greater emphasis on fashion and the theatre, and a cut in the amount of fiction, might just have saved the magazine without the economic strife of the War. Ironically, in slick form, had it survived, it would have thrived in the 1920s, as it was a direct forebear of the classier women's magazines like *The Home Magazine* and *Good Housekeeping*.

Frequency: Monthly.
Publisher: Hutchinson, Nov 1896-Oct 1909; Stanley Paul, Nov 1909-Oct 1910, who licensed the magazine to Amalgamated Magazine Company, Nov 1910-May 1916.
Editors: William Henry Wilkins, Nov 1896-Oct 1902; E. Keble Chatterton, 1904-1906; Vere Smith, 1907-1911; thereafter possibly Max Rittenberg.
Format/Size: Standard, 112/120 pages, dropped to 76 pages from May 1915.
Price: 6d.
References: Fiction only from Nov 1896 to Oct 1914 indexed in *The Lady's Realm: Indexes to Fiction* by Sue Thomas, M. Versteeg & J. Huddleston (University of Queensland, Victorian Fiction Research Guide #5, 1981).
Anthologies: *The Lady's Realm: a Selection from the monthly issues, November 1904 to April 1905*, with introduction by Lady Georgina Coleridge (London: Arrow Books, 1972), non-fiction only.
Holdings:
Complete run, UK. Bodleian (*Call Number*: Per. 2705 d.76). • National Library of Scotland (*Shelfmark*: U.423) have complete runs.
Substantial run, UK. British Library has Nov 1896-Dec 1907, Nov 1908-Oct 1909, Nov 1912-Oct 1913 (*Shelfmark*: PP.6004.og). • Cambridge University Library has volumes 1-24, Nov 1896-Oct 1908 (*Classmark*: L448.c.6). • Bradford City Library has volumes 10-36 (May 1901-Apr 1915).
Substantial run, US. Library of Congress has volumes 1-36, Nov 1896-Oct 1914 (*Call Number*: AP4.L229 on microfilm). • Chicago Public Library has volumes 1-34, Nov 1896-Oct 1913. • University of Minnesota Libraries has volumes 1-36, Nov 1896-Oct 1914. • University of Rochester has volumes 1-36, Nov 1896-Oct 1914.
Substantial run, Australia. University of Queensland Library has volumes. 1-35, Nov 1896-Apr 1914 (*Reference*: AP4.L229).
Collecting points: Early volumes in the publisher's maroon binding are common, but later ones (in green binding after 1910) are scarce, especially the final two years. Single issues are very rare.

***

LLOYD'S MAGAZINE

67 issues. Converted from THE MOTHER'S MAGAZINE and ran from Volume 29, Number 356, July 1917 to Volume 34, Number 422, January 1923. Retitled LLOYD'S STORY MAGAZINE from June 1921.

Edward Lloyd was a great entrepreneur in the stimulation of popular and cheap reading material for the masses. Since 1835 he had produced a mass of penny serial fiction, which earned him a fortune. In November 1842 he began *Lloyd's Illustrated London Newspaper* in rivalry to the *Illustrated London News*, and in 1876 he purchased the *Daily Chronicle*, turning it into London's first daily newspaper. He died in April 1890, just months before the launch of *The Strand*, otherwise he might well have created his own popular illustrated monthly. In 1916 the *Daily Chronicle* and *Lloyd's Weekly News* were purchased by a new consortium that became United Newspapers and it was only after this, a quarter of a century after his death that a magazine bearing his name appeared, and even then the origins of *Lloyd's Magazine* are complicated.

In 1887 Lloyd's had started *Baby: The Mother's Magazine* to provide a range of advice to young mothers. It ran no fiction, apart from the occasional children's story – indeed, *The Writers' and Artists' Year-Book* advised strongly against submitting any. In November 1915 it changed its name to *The Mother's Magazine* and began to run serials, such as Silas Hocking's "His Own Accuser", along with the occasional short story, all high on romance and slanted towards the young mother. Of war interest was "A Red Cross Nurse in the Balkans" by Alice and Claude Askew (Mar-Oct 1917).

With the May 1917 issue, the now retitled *Lloyd's Mothers' Magazine* incorporated a special 32-page "complete novel" supplement. They included such romantic stories as "Dr. Fabian's Wife" by Mark Allerton, "Won by a Wager" by May Wynne and "The Finger of Fate" by L. G. Moberly. Though bound in, they were separately paginated and printed on coarser pulp paper rather than the magazine's slightly coated stock. The stock soon changed to light green, standing out from the rest of the issue. The company had just started *Lloyd's Weekly War Novels*, and these thin books were in the same format.

In July 1917 the title shrank to *Lloyd's Magazine*, but it clearly displayed "incorporating The Mothers' Magazine and Baby" on the cover. Though this was dropped in December, it remained on the magazine's masthead for the rest of its existence. Readers used to traditional and homely words of wisdom on motherhood must have been shocked upon receiving the August 1917 issue to discover a war story by Edgar Wallace and an article about Rasputin, "Dark Forces in Statecraft", by Sax Rohmer. Rohmer was a regular contributor for the next few issues, writing about his travels in Egypt under the heading "Phryné in Pharaoh-Land".

At no time did *Lloyd's* ever identify its editor, but it is almost certain a new editor would have seen through this transition to establish the magazine's new identity. The first editorial announcement about the changes did not appear until May 1918, containing bold proclamations of making *Lloyd's* "the first magazine in Great Britain". The editor later credited with seeing through these changes was Louis Vincent, a Catholic journalist and novelist.

As 1917 became 1918 the quota of fiction increased, but it was not until mid 1919 that the magazine shook off its old image. The first issue where the fiction outweighed the non-fiction was for December 1917, with stories by Keble Howard, Marjorie Bowen, May Wynne and Guy Thorne, amongst others. If there was any doubt that the magazine was shifting its readership towards a more male-oriented market one need only consult the January 1918 issue. Douglas Newton contributed "The Ultimate Aeroplane", about a super aircraft that would bring an end to all wars. A. Demain Grange contributed a strange story, "The Sixth Sense", whilst Sax Rohmer wrote about dead pharaohs in "The Unwrapped Mummy" whilst Hartley Withers pondered on whether the old sovereign coin was lost forever, replaced by the pound note. There were still features for women but these were now taking into account new developments and the changing rôle of women. There was an unusual story in the February 1918 issue, "The Human Experiment" by Owen Oliver, provoked by the interest in eugenics. It explored the difference between intelligence and instinct by having a group of children raised in isolation on a remote island.

Healthy doses of romantic fiction remained in the magazine but this was now buttressed by stories and features looking ahead to the post-war years and a new decade. The pseudonymous "Onlooker" considered the wonders that science would bring in "Twenty Years After the War" (May 1918), including equality of the sexes and an early concept of cable television. There was a column (albeit short-lived), "Popular Science and Invention" by C. Basil Barham, a feature on the future of air transport, "Pathways in the Air" (Mar 1919) by Ignatius Phyre, and a long serial by William Le Queux about a future master-criminal of the air, "The Terror of the Air" (Oct 1919-Jun 1920).

Alongside this were many war-influenced stories and articles. E. Phillips Oppenheim explored the psycho-social effects of not having played a full part in the War in his serial "Mr Lessingham Goes Home" (May-Nov 1918). Lady Troubridge looked at the effect of the war on the class system when a former footman returns home in "William" (Aug 1918). Commander Locker-Lampson revealed his wartime experiences in "Condemned by the Kaiser" (May-Nov 1918), whilst May Bateman's "The Massacre of the Innocents" (Oct 1918) was a harrowing account of the wartime toll in child and infant deaths. "The Whistling" (Oct 1918) by Martin Swayne was a most unusual story telling of an inexplicable whistling that pervades the whole Earth causing a cessation in hostilities. There was a feature on spiritualism by May Bateman in the March 1919 issue which brought a response from Sir Arthur Conan Doyle.

Amidst the romantic stories and wartime reflections there were the occasional humorous pieces, horror stories, tales of the wilderness and mystery stories. *Lloyd's* could even boast a new novel by Joseph Conrad, "The Arrow of Gold" (May 1919-Feb 1920). Written under trying circumstances this is not regarded as one of Conrad's best works, but its reflective nature suited the post-War mood and it was a major name to capture.

By mid 1919 *Lloyd's* had successfully made the transition to a popular general interest magazine. It introduced several illustrated features, such as "People You Might Like to Meet", with profiles and photographs. A film and theatre column was started and there were articles on sport, including "Women in Sport" (Sept 1919) by former athlete F.A.M. Webster. The magazine was buoyant, running poetry and light society fiction, sometimes experimental, with a smattering of major names. J. D. Beresford, Max Pemberton, H. de Vere Stacpoole, Katharine Tynan, even Zane Grey, each put in an appearances or two. There were a few regular series. A. M. Burrage revealed the romantic adventures of Peter Pry (Mar-Aug 1920), followed by the exploits of Captain Dorry (Mar-Jul 1921), a soldier of fortune turned roguish adventurer. F.A.M. Webster contributed a series of East African adventures,[1] which proved highly popular and were issued by the United Press as *The Curse of the Lion* (1922). In "Beryl of 'The Movies'" (Jan-Jun 1921) Cecil H. Bullivant told of the amusing and sometimes dangerous exploits of a young actress in the burgeoning film industry, a subject which fascinated most readers and provided material for occasional features.

However, this quality production lasted barely two years before the magazine transformed again, in June 1921, into an all-fiction pulp, retitled *Lloyd's Story Magazine*. Reginald Poole had just been appointed as overall fiction editor for United Newspapers, and it is probable he dictated the direction of the magazine, though Vincent remained the editor. Poole had previously worked for Amalgamated Press and became better known as a writer of boys' adventure fiction. Whilst he did not convert *Lloyd's* into a boys' magazine, the emphasis shifted to more formulaic fiction, rather than the stronger character-based work that Vincent had been developing. Evidently *Lloyd's* had aimed its sights too high and moved out of the publisher's traditional arena. Poole was to bring it back into line.

A few of the same writers remained, most notably F.A.M. Webster, who broadened his coverage by writing not only further African stories but ones with settings in India and the Far North. The editor made great play at having secured two sequels to successful works. From J. Storer Clouston came the latest sequel to his perennially popular *The Lunatic at Large* (1899), the equally humorous "Mr. Essington at Large" (Jun 1921-Jan 1922); whilst George Randolph Chester provided "The Son of Wallingford" (Jun-Nov 1921), portraying the adventures of the heir to Get Rich-Quick Wallingford.[2] The most popular contributions in the new *Lloyd's* were the sports stories by the late Charles Van Loan. These started with the racetrack exploits of Old Man Curry, which had originally run in *Collier's Weekly*, and were followed by boxing stories collected in *Taking the Count* (Doran, 1915) and the golfing stories collected as *Fore!* (Doran, 1918), some of which had run in the *Saturday Evening Post*. These showed that whilst *Lloyd's* may have shifted from glossy to pulp, there was no corresponding drop in quality, simply a shift to the more 'popular' end of the range.

Many of the stories were escapist, so typical of the 1920s, and included a quota of the highly popular south-seas adventures of the period by Holloway Horn, "Seamark", Edward Cecil and inevitably Beatrice Grimshaw. There was a variety of oriental or near-eastern stories, all with suitably evocative titles. H. de Vere Stacpoole took readers on a tour of coasts and islands in a series of adventures that added to his reputation for slightly *risqué* stories, one of which, "The Chilean Girl" (Jul 1922), was heralded as "racy" and may even have encouraged that issue's daring cover of a bare-backed young lady. Although in his sixties, the endlessly inventive Horace Annesley Vachell provided an intriguing series, "Lucky Wendover" (Dec

---

[1] One of these stories, "Treasure in the Wilderness" (Nov 1920), refers to the main character having contributed to *The Yellow Magazine* (as Webster did to *The Blue Magazine*). The title was snapped up a few months later by the Amalgamated Press.
[2] The original series had run in *Cosmopolitan* in the USA and *Nash's* in Britain.

1921-May 1922) which concerns a man, wealthy but bored, who takes on work from a psychiatrist to help investigate the more unusual cases.

Romantic fiction was not forgotten, though Fannie Heaslip Lea and Ethel L. White, who dominated the first half of *Lloyd's* existence, were less in evidence. Nevertheless, Lea's "Love-in-a-Mist" (Sept 1922) was the epitomé of the sentimental love story. Instead the stories, and covers, emphasised either the modern girl and the dangers of the 1920s, or the true romance of exotic locations and the demands faced by loving couples. A fine example is the story of the love of an American Indian for a white girl in "The Laughter of John Lamewolf" by Leslie H. Gordon (Mar 1922). A. M. Burrage provided an enjoyable slant on the light romance with his series "Lovers, Ltd." (Sept 1922-Jan 1923) about an agency which helps stalled love affairs come to fruition.

Lloyd's remained heavily illustrated throughout the pulp period, though the reproduction left a lot to be desired and often devalued the quality of the work of Warwick Reynolds, C. E. Brock, Alfred Leete and others. The covers reflected a variety of moods, but moved away from the usual woman-of-fashion to more exciting, active portrayals of the mood of the twenties.

The appearance of such writers as E. F. Benson, Eden Phillpotts (whose daughter, Adelaide, debuted in the Nov 1921 issue), Sapper and Thomas Burke showed that *Lloyd's* was prepared to challenge the leading magazines. The overall quality was above average and in the final few issues there was a return to better quality paper and a bolder design. But, whatever the intentions, it ended abruptly when United Newspapers dropped all their adult fiction line. *Lloyd's* ended with its January 1923 issue, before the conclusion of Mary Roberts Rinehart's long-running serial, "The Breaking Point".

Although *Lloyd's* could offer something for everyone, it lacked the prestige of *The Strand*, the energy of *Pearson's* or the flair of *Nash's*. *Lloyd's* never really established a character. It seemed to be striving to be *The Royal* at one stage and *Pearson's* at another but for most of the time was like a superior *Blue*. Nevertheless it deserves to be better remembered and it remains one of the more undervalued of the fiction magazines.

Frequency: Monthly.
Publisher: United Newspapers.
Editor: Louis Vincent.
Format/Size: Standard, changing from glossy to pulp from Jun 1921. Pagination: 56/60, settling at 68/72 to Mar 1920; rose to 84/88, Apr 1920; 90, Aug 1920; 106/110pp, Jun 1921.
Price: Price 6d; rose to 8d, May 1918; 1/-, Apr 1920.
Holdings:
Complete run, UK. British Library (*Shelfmark*: PP.5992.ec). • Bodleian (*Call Number*: Per. 1778 d.41).
Partial run, UK. Cambridge University Library has issues Mar 1917-Oct 1918 only (*Classmark*: L448.c.4).
Complete run, US: Hofstra University.
Collecting points: Extremely rare. Single issues seldom appear on the market and no bound volumes are known.

* * *

THE LONDON MAGAZINE

417 issues. Various title changes and series. Began as THE HARMSWORTH MONTHLY PICTORIAL MAGAZINE Volume 1, Number 1, July 1898 to Volume 4, Number 24, July 1900. Retitled THE HARMSWORTH MAGAZINE from Volume 5, August 1900 to Volume 6, Number 36, July 1901. Retitled THE HARMSWORTH LONDON MAGAZINE from Volume 7, August 1901 and THE LONDON MAGAZINE from November 1901. A new series began with Volume 25, Number 147 (also numbered 1), November 1910. Continued to Volume 65, Number 240, October 1930. Retitled THE NEW LONDON MAGAZINE, new series, Volume 1, Number 1, November 1930 to Volume 6, Number 31, May 1933.

Although *The London Magazine* would become the biggest selling popular monthly magazine of the Edwardian period, it was issued almost as an afterthought, and seldom seemed to be high on the agenda of its creator, Alfred Harmsworth. Harmsworth (Lord Northcliffe from 1905) had found his first success with *Answers* in 1888, and during the 1890s he established a huge publishing empire, ranging from comics and juvenile story-papers, of which *Comic Cuts* was the most successful, to newspapers. He took over the *Evening News* in 1894, launched the *Daily Mail* in 1896, *The Daily Mirror* in 1903 and eventually took over *The Times* in 1908.

In the midst of this huge empire appeared *The Harmsworth Monthly Pictorial Magazine* in July 1898. Although Alfred wrote the editorial, he made it clear that the "experiment" was headed by his brother Cecil. It was an experiment because the magazine was priced at just threepence, half the price of the other standard monthlies. He remarked that it was only possible to do this because the magazine is "a small incident in an organisation controlling four daily journals and nearly thirty weekly periodicals." This portrayed the magazine as just one fish in a huge shoal, and the fact that it had been allocated to Cecil suggests that Alfred may not have expected the magazine to last. Cecil lacked the flair of his two elder brothers. One of the biographers of the Harmsworths says of Cecil that "he seems to have been written off as a disaster at an early stage."[1]

Harmsworth's appeared long after the major players in the popular monthly magazine stakes had claimed their territory. There was nowhere new for *Harmsworth's* to go and, apart from seeking to undercut the other magazines, it had nothing new to offer. The first few issues contained the same features that had been pioneered by *The Strand*, with plentiful photographs, portfolios of works of art, novelty items, short stories – none especially outstanding – and pictorials. Alfred Harmsworth had stated that the magazine would not resort to the hype and bluster of other magazines in promoting major writers but would, instead, rely on new writers. In fact over the next few years *The Harmsworth/London* would be as active in promoting itself and its contributors as any magazine, perhaps more so. But initially it published few major authors – Cutcliffe Hyne, S. Baring-Gould, William Le Queux and Richard Marsh being the few exceptions. Some who went on to become major names, sold early work here, including

---

[1] Paul Ferris, *The House of Northcliffe* (Weidenfeld & Nicolson, 1971), p. 53

Rafael Sabatini. There is a short story by Winston Churchill, "Man Overboard!" (Jan 1899). Otherwise most stories are by unknowns or by Harmsworth's growing stable of writers.

Neither did the magazine do anything to establish a popular story series, the device which had established *The Strand*. Instead, what emerges is a sense of fun, with such items as novelty pictorials showing London on holiday with notable landmarks transplanted to other localities in Britain, or humorous features such as Dan Leno playing cricket. There was also an emphasis on wealth. Harmsworth's market had clearly been the working and lower-middle classes who enjoyed the penny and halfpenny weeklies and for whom *The Harmsworth* might provide some social aspirations. So there were features on expensive hobbies, such as "A £10,000 Toy" (Aug 1898), about a miniature railway set, or "Postage Stamps Worth Fortunes" (Sept 1898) or "Mice Worth Their Weight in Gold" (Jan 1899) or "How American Millionaires Live" (Aug 1901). This was likewise reflected in the fiction. Richard Marsh's "That £500 Prize" (Aug 1898) or "The Cruise of the Searchlight" by J. L. Hornibrook (May 1899), about what befell the richest woman in the world. The July 1900 issue contrasted "Pictures Worth Fortunes" with "Seven Days Hard", looking at the treatment of convicts.

In content *The Harmsworth* was no comparison to its major rivals, and yet it rapidly secured a commanding circulation. By 1903 the magazine published its audited circulation figures for the first eight months, all in excess of 350,000.[2] This was a similar figure to that proclaimed, but never supported, by *The Strand*. As *The Harmsworth* had nothing comparable to offer it must have reached these figures partly because it was so cheap and because it benefited from the distribution network of the Harmsworth Brothers. Harmsworth had to increase the cover price by a halfpenny from the second issue because retailers objected to their reduced share of the costs, but it was still the cheapest magazine available for its size. *The Royal* also started out at threepence, but was a smaller magazine and, within a year, increased its price to fourpence.

One other factor that may have affected sales was that *The Harmsworth* went on sale in the middle of the month as dated on the cover, rather than at the start of that month, with the schedule slipping further as issues progressed. The third issue, though dated September, did not appear until the 29th of that month. As a result the November issue became the Christmas one and remained on sale a couple of weeks longer, meaning there was no December issue. The schedule remained erratic and did not settle until April 1906.

More changes were afoot. In August 1900 the magazine truncated its cumbersome title to *The Harmsworth Magazine*. In December 1901 Alfred and Harold Harmsworth combined their publishing imprints as one company, the Amalgamated Press. The magazine became *The Harmsworth London Magazine* just before this change and *The London Magazine* from November 1901. The title page retained the fuller title for another two years but it was no longer the official title.[3]

Cecil Harmsworth stepped back from the magazine quite early, more interested in launching a political paper, the *New Liberal Review*. His assistant, Percy Parker, took over the editorship but did little to bring it alive. After three years the rôle passed to Charles Sisley, a more accomplished editor who strove to give the magazine a separate identity. This was difficult with so much competition and it was a while before Sisley could secure any major names,

---

[2] Harmsworth had claimed a sale of 877,000 for its first issue (*The Times*, 22 August 1898, p. 11).
[3] The Harmsworths liked to keep their name in their magazine titles. *The Red Magazine* was still called Harmsworth's *Red Magazine* on its cover well into the 1930s.

resorting instead to reprinting a story by Marie Corelli ("The Song of Miriam", January 1903) and reproducing a facsimile of Rudyard Kipling's corrected page proofs (Aug 1902). He acquired some fiction from Robert Barr, and reprinted works by Frank R. Stockton and Frank T. Bullen from American magazines. He tried to secure some character series that could be associated with the magazine. His first, "The Doings of Vigorous Daunt" by Australian writer Ambrose Pratt (Aug 1902-Apr 1903), illustrated by Stanley L. Wood, was rather too similar to the ripping yarns in Harmsworth's boys' papers, but would have appealed to the same people who enjoyed Captain Kettle in *Pearson's*. More significantly Sisley managed to acquire Arthur Morrison's Martin Hewitt from *The Windsor* with "The Red Triangle" (Nov 1902-Apri 1903).

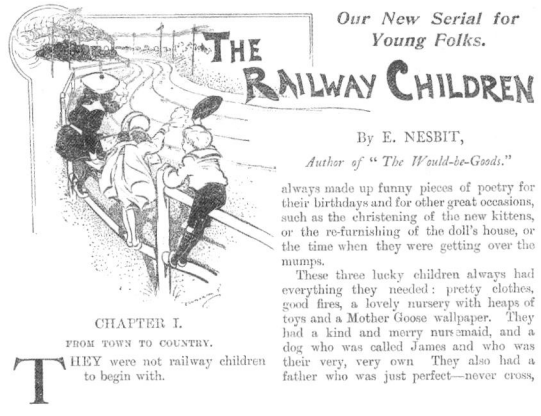

Eventually some bigger names were lured to *The London*. H.G. Wells contributed "Mr Skelmersdale in Fairyland" (Feb 1903), and Thomas Hardy both "A Mere Interlude" (May 1903) and "The Melancholy Hussar" (Sept 1903). Edith Nesbit, whose children's stories made her the darling of *The Strand*, also turned to *The London* for her new series about Oswald Bastable, later collected as *The New Treasure Seekers* (1904). It was Sisley who commissioned Nesbit to write her best known book and arguably the most popular serial *The London* published, "The Railway Children" (Jan 1905-Jan 1906).

In December 1903 *The London* increased its page count, at the same time raising its cover price. The increased income allowed it to refresh its appearance – the quality of photographic reproduction and artwork improved significantly. Although it ran the occasional colour frontispiece it did not go for all-out colour for another three years. Instead it tried to induce better known names to the magazine and their entourage steadily grew. In addition to Rafael Sabatini and Cutcliffe Hyne, there were stories by J. J. Bell, J. S. Fletcher, W. W. Jacobs and A.E.W. Mason. *The London* also ran one of James Branch Cabell's early stories, "The Rhyme to Porringer" (Aug 1905) from *Collier's Weekly*.

Despite these changes, *The London* still lacked a heart. This was true to some extent as, despite his hard work, Sisley's heart was really in the weekly *Penny Pictorial*, which he had founded. Sisley did not get much support from Harmsworth and was annoyed he was sidelined and Harmsworth gave the editorship of *The London* to John A. Hammerton. Hammerton had been employed by Harmsworth to develop a popular encyclopedia as a part-work. Harmsworth was sitting on the decision, leaving Hammerton with nothing to do. It was an awkward handover, resulting in Sisley throwing in his job and moving to Cassell. Hammerton felt he had been passed a poison chalice. "They were not easy years," he later commented, adding, "I was at any moment prepared to step aside and let somebody else take over its responsibility."[4]

This was the start of a period of three almost "caretaker" editors, serving under the erratic control of Lord Northcliffe. Hammerton remarked that "The truth was that Northcliffe himself

---

[4] J.A. Hammerton, *Books and Myself* (Macdonald, 1944), p. 191.

did not know how *The London* ought to be edited, although he repeatedly told me that if he could do it himself for a month or two he would double the circulation."[5]

Hammerton had taken over at a difficult time. The advent of cheap sixpenny paperbacks had eaten considerably into the sales of magazines. Sales fell by half between 1903 and 1907, and it was all too easy to attribute this to the editor. In fact under Hammerton sales began to claw back and the magazine took on a glow that had been missing. He may not have wanted the rôle but he devoted himself to it. The magazine now sported a full colour cover and frontispiece and more two-tone colour pictorials. Hammerton stated in his editorial to the April 1906 issue – the one that got the magazine back on schedule[6] – that he wanted to make *The London*, "a thing of beauty."

Hammerton still had trouble securing major names. Arthur Quiller-Couch's historical novel "Poison Island" (Feb 1906-Feb 1907) reportedly proved popular. Joseph Conrad contributed an article, "London's River" (Jul 1906), and Arnold Bennett a short story, "From One Generation to Another" (Oct 1906). There were further contributions by A.E.W. Mason, Mary Braddon, Rafael Sabatini, Gilbert Parker, Cutcliffe Hyne and Joseph Conrad. Hammerton also acquired a number of speculative articles. "The Call of Another World" (May 1907), looked at our fascination with Mars and the prospect of life there, with some intriguing pictures. The article was uncredited but came hot on the heels of Camille Flamarrion's "Where is the Earth Going To?" (Feb 1907). *The London* capitalized on the fascination with the conquest of the air, one of Northcliffe's passions, and ran a special two-part feature, "The Airship Age" (Oct-Nov 1907). There was also a special aeroplane issue in November 1909 (*pictured on page 111*).

Harmsworth was dissatisfied, however. He wanted an Americanised approach. Hammerton stepped aside, recommending Eric Scott as someone who might follow that route. Scott lasted for about as long as Hammerton and was succeeded by Comyns Beaumont. Beaumont made a few changes, but he was too much his own man for Harmsworth. His main acquisition was the Arsène Lupin serial, "813" by Maurice Leblanc (Feb-Oct 1910).

It was not until David Whitelaw took over in November 1910 that a harmony emerged between publisher and editor to their mutual satisfaction. Whitelaw had worked at Cassell's, helping launch *The Story-Teller*, and understood what makes a magazine tick. Harmsworth recognised the value of the fiction but also wanted a magazine that made a statement, and pushed for reform. During 1910 *The London* published several crusading articles, rivalling the table-thumping by C. Arthur Pearson at *Pearson's Magazine*. These included "The Dawn of a New Ireland" by F. E. Green (Jun 1910), where an agricultural revolution was helping rebuild the country, and "The Leviathan" (Oct 1910), in which Harold Shepstone questioned how far new whaling techniques were pushing the animals to extinction.

The big change came with the November 1910 issue, which was wholly revamped. The changes were sufficiently significant to relaunch the magazine in a new series. It was enlarged with several colour plates and a complete "novel" (usually about 30-35 pages). Headlining the magazine were a series of articles drawing attention to issues facing Britain. The first two were a clever harmony between fact and fiction. Conan Doyle contributed two historical stories using themes as parallels to potential problems. "The Last Galley" (Nov 1910), about the

---

[5] Hammerton, *ibid*.
[6] Although there are only eleven issues dated 1906 *The London* did not miss a month. The March issue appeared on 15 March, the April/May issue on 15 April and the June issue on 20 May.

withdrawal of the last of the Roman legions, was accompanied by an introduction by Doyle, "A Warning to Britain", commenting on how a mighty power can fall if it does not remain alert. "The Passing of the Legions" (Dec 1910), drew parallels between Britain and current unrest in India, an issue explored further in F. A. McKenzie's article "Lest We Forget." Other headline articles included "Can Man Take the Strain?" (Nov 1910), wondering how people were coping with the stress of modern life, "Over-Eating" (Dec 1910) and "Black Plague in England?" (Mar 1911), advocating the extermination of rats. Public health was one of Harmsworth's *cause célèbres* and the subject of several articles, including a two-parter from Upton Sinclair, "Starving for Health's Sake" (Feb-Mar 1911). There was a highly controversial article on children with mental and physical afflictions, "Stamping Out the Diseased" (Jan 1911), suggesting ways of purifying the bloodstock. These and similar articles had an immediate, if short-lived effect on sales. Data made available to the Advertisers' Protection Society, of which Harmsworth was one of the few strong advocates, showed circulation increasing from around 150,000 to just under 200,000, though it began to fall away again after the initial enthusiasm.

The complete "novel" feature was well received. Whitelaw attracted several major names, including Joseph Conrad with "A Smile of Fortune" (Feb 1911) and "Freya of the Seven Isles" (Jul 1912). During the first two years of Whitelaw's editorship *The London* became vibrant. There was work from H. de Vere Stacpoole, P.G. Wodehouse, Robert W. Chambers, Jack London, Sax Rohmer, Talbot Mundy and Rudyard Kipling. Arnold Bennett produced the sequel to *The Card*, "The Regent" (Nov 1912-July 1913). F. St Mars began a series of nature stories with "King of Pilots" (Nov 1912), all of which were illustrated by Warwick Reynolds, a partnership that lasted till St Mars's early death in 1921. Shackleton wrote about "The Race for the South Pole". There was a much appreciated series by John Foster Fraser, "The Discovery of London" (from Nov 1911) which looked at many forgotten and unusual aspects.

Whitelaw's fascination for the unusual led to some pioneering stories. There were articles on the power of the mind with "Auto-Suggestion" (Jan 1912) and mental science (Mar 1912); a distinctive series by Max Rittenberg, "The Strange Cases of Dr Xavier Wycherley" (Feb-Jul 1911), about a psychologist; and weird tales from Barry Pain, Algernon Blackwood and William Hope Hodgson. Some authors, mindful of the social upheavels, looked to the future. Kipling's "As Easy as A.B.C." (Mar 1912), a sequel to "With the Night Mail", which had appeared in *The Windsor*, looked at how international communications could control society. Jack London's "The Scarlet Plague" (Jun 1912, *right*) depicted a world almost destroyed by plague with scattered remnants trying to rebuild civilisation. It was a powerful counterpoint to Charles G. D. Roberts's series, "In the Morning of Time" (May-Oct 1912), which looked at the emergence of primitive man and the creation of societies. Other warning features included as "In the Case of War" by Hilaire Belloc (May 1912), "Race-Culture or Race-Suicide?" by Henry Forman (Jul 1912) and "The Big, Big Blunder" by Viscount Mountmorres (Mar 1913), about the senselessness of war.

When War came, *The London*, like all magazines, was filled with articles on its progress, propagandistic stories and much escapist fiction. H. G. Wells lead the way with a look at the cost of the conflict, "The Reckoning for the War" (Dec 1914). Walter Wood reworked the success he had had at *The Royal*, with eye-witness accounts of major events in "True Stories of the Great War" (from Dec 1914), whilst naval expert John Margerison, explored the war at sea.

During the War some of the sparkle left *The London*. This was partly inevitable because of the conflict, but just before the War Whitelaw had launched a new all-fiction magazine, *The Premier*, which syphoned away some of the unusual fiction. It left *The London* publishing rather more routine war fiction and romances. It had a few surprises, such as luring Cutcliffe Hyne's Captain Kettle away from *Pearson's* for the series "Captain Kettle's Bit" (May-Dec 1918), but rather more typical was the homely concern of Martha Jane Linnedale, the village shopkeeper and busybody in Orme Agnus's long running series that began with "The Strategy of Martha Jane" (Nov 1916). So popular was this character that Agnus replicated her with a seventeenth-century wise woman in "Witchcraft" (Dec 1918). In similar vein were the "Fallen Star" stories by Stacey Blake (from May 1918), about an actor who falls on hard times but whose homely philosophy and strength of character see him through.

By the end of the War and especially into the twenties, *The London* had become almost indistinguishable from *The Strand* and *The Windsor*, running many of the same authors with the same blend of light humour, romantic adventure and daring mystery. For a brief period from May 1920 *The London* experimented with an illustrated children's section, "The Jolly Times", in two-tone colour, but this looked out of place and was soon dropped. Nevertheless, during the twenties *The London* ran some significant material. It serialised John Buchan's adventure novel "Huntingtower" (Mar-Aug 1922). It ran an early story by Stephen Vincent Benét, "The Sobbin' Worm" (Aug 1926). With "My Adventure in Jermyn Street" (Jan 1927), it began an occasional series by radio broadcaster, A. J. Alan. It also ran several of A. A. Milne's Winnie the Pooh stories starting with "Tigger Comes to the Forest" (Aug 1927). There was a new Beau Geste story by P. C. Wren, "Buried Treasure" (Aug 1928) and a new Bulldog Drummond serial by Sapper, "Temple Tower" (Nov 1928-Jul 1929). At the end of the twenties it ran several pieces by Rudyard Kipling, including "The Church That Was at Antioch" (Aug 1929), and a new Stalky & Co. story (Sept 1929).

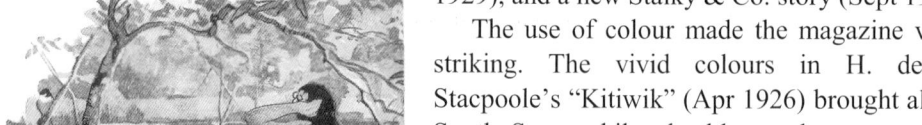

The use of colour made the magazine visually striking. The vivid colours in H. de Vere Stacpoole's "Kitiwik" (Apr 1926) brought alive the South Seas, whilst the blue and orange tones in Warwick Reynolds's pictures for F. Britten Austin's "When the World Was Young" (May-Nov 1926, *right*) suggested far-off days. They were amongst Reynold's last work as he died at the end of 1926 aged only 46. Austin was one of *The London*'s regulars during the twenties producing a number of stories set in either pre-history or mythological periods. Another regular was A. M. Burrage, who appeared in almost every issue with either a romance, a mystery, a ghost story or a school story. Gilbert Frankau, Andrew Soutar, Eden Phillpotts, Selwyn Jepson and Marjorie Bowen were amongst other regulars and, towards the end of the twenties, Whitelaw published some of the unusual Solange Fontaine stories by F. Tennyson Jesse.

But for every memorable story or article there were as likely to be three or four routine tales or features on cricket, tennis, bridge, dancing, even choosing a trousseau. *The London* gave increasing coverage to film stars with suitably dashing pictures of Ronald Colman, John Gilbert or the latest heart-throb. It did not follow *The Royal* into becoming a film magazine, but it did lean heavily towards stage, screen and stardom. With a growing women's readership it was inevitable that *The London* would make the change to the large flat semi-slick format and, in November 1930, it transformed into *The New London*. David Whitelaw oversaw the change but then retired gracefully. There seemed little heart in it. It was promoted as a bold new move, but was essentially following the trend towards a greater women's magazine market. *The London* did not go all the way into becoming a full flat slick, using a smooth, near matt paper rather than gloss. It ran for a little over two years in this form, the emphasis as much on film and fashion as on fiction. Amongst its more noteworthy items was the last fiction written by Lily Adams Beck, under her alias E. Barrington, the series, "Love Stories of the Queens of England" (from Nov 1930), beautifully illustrated by Fortunio Matania. There were also stories from Arnold Bennett, Gilbert Frankau, Selwyn Jepson and Sax Rohmer, but these all rather blended into the background. The experiment had not worked and from June 1933 the magazine was merged with *The Story-Teller*.

The London was an example of a magazine that could become a market leader simply by substantial funding rather than content, but once established it lived up to its reputation, thanks mostly to the skills of David Whitelaw.

Frequency: Monthly, but combined November/December 1898 and April/May 1906 issues.
Publisher: Harmsworth. Reincorporated as the Amalgamated Press from August 1901.
Editors: Cecil Harmsworth, 1898-1902 (assisted by Percy L. Parker); Charles Sisley, 1902-5; J. A. Hammerton, 1905-7; Eric Clement Scott, 1907-9; Comyns Beaumont, 1909-10; David Whitelaw, 1910-31; Francis Ward, 1931-33.
Format/Size: Standard. Page count 112, dropped to 96, Oct 1898, rose to 112, Jul 1902, 120, Feb 1904, 144/152, Nov 1910, dropped to 130/136, Jul 1914, 112/116, Jul 1916; 88, Jul 1917; 80, Sept 1918; rose to 88/90, Apr 1919; 96, Sept 1919 and 116/120, Aug 1922. Changed to large flat format, 108/112 pages, Nov 1930, reducting monthly to 72 pages, Jul 1931 and 52 pages, Mar 1932.
Price: 3d, first issue only; 3½d, Aug 1898; 4½d, Dec 1903; 6d, Nov 1910; 7d, Feb 1917; 8d, Dec 1917; 9d, Feb 1918; 1/-, May 1918; 6d, Nov 1930.
References: Passing references in *The Romance of the Amalgamated Press* by George Dilnot (Amalgamated Press, 1925), *A Bonfire of Leaves* by David Whitelaw (Bles, 1937) and *Books and Myself* by J. A. Hammerton (Macdonald, 1944).
Indexes: Fiction only to 1915 in *Indexes to Fiction: The Harmsworth Magazine later The London Magazine* by Sue Thomas (University of Queensland, Victorian Fiction Research Guide #10, 1984).

Holdings:
Complete run, UK. Bodleian (*Call Numbers*: Per. 2705 d.85 and Per. 2705 c.67 for *New London*).
Substantial run, UK. British Library is missing issues for Nov 1920, Jan-Jun 1921 and Jan-Jun 1922 (*Shelfmark*: PP.6018.ta). • Cambridge University Library has volumes 1-21, Jul 1898-Feb 1909 (*Classmark*: L996.c.45). • National Library of Scotland has issues Jul 1898-May 1901 and Aug 1903-Oct 1930 (*Shelfmark*: NJ.710).
Complete run, US: New York Public Library.
Substantial run, US. Library of Congress has all issues to Oct 1930 (*Call Number*: AP4.L5) but no copies of *New London*.
Collecting points: The publisher's binding of bi-annual volumes, with index, is in light green decorative cloth. Early volumes are still common as are some from the 1920s but the Wartime issues are rare as are issues of *The New London*.

* * *

THE LUDGATE MONTHLY

118 issues. Two series. Volume 1, Number 1, May 1891 to Volume 9, Number 54, October 1895. New series, Volume 1, Number 1, November 1895, to Volume 11, Number 64, February 1901. Retitled LUDGATE ILLUSTRATED MAGAZINE from volume 8 (Nov 1893) and THE LUDGATE from New Series, Volume 1 (Nov 1895). Merged with *The Universal Magazine* from March 1901.

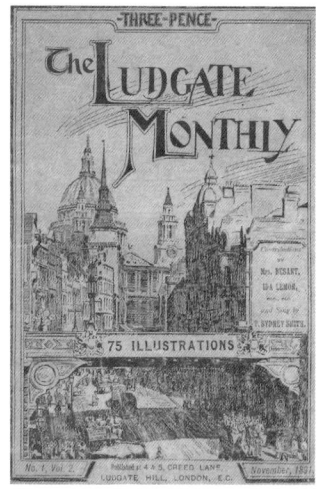

The first new magazine to appear in the wake of *The Strand*, though it was not initially an imitator. It was a slim 64 pages, styled more closely on *Cassell's Family Magazine*, and with the same moralistic zeal, though undercutting its rivals by selling for only threepence. It was in some ways a successor to the story paper *Lambert's Monthly*, which folded the same month.

In an introductory note the editor, Philip May (not to be confused with artist, Phil May), called it "an illustrated family magazine" and intoned that its articles will be "both interesting and instructive." As for its fiction, this would "… have some lesson to teach or good cause to plead."[1] This was particularly true of that issue's "A Serpent's Tooth" by Florence Marryat which the editor said, "reminds children of the duty which they owe to their parents." The editor also tells us that the children's story, "Laura and Her Rival" by Leopold Wagner, "entreats children to be kind to their pets", whilst John A. O'Shea's story set during the Franco-Prussian War, "Hans and Hamet", "aptly describes the horrors, the miseries and the crimes of war." The first issue was also able to boast a new story by Rudyard Kipling, then still on the lower rungs of his climb to fame, and we are told that "The Last Relief" "pleads for those who are doing their duty for their country." There was a series about the work of the Salvation Army, "Life in Darkest London" by James Greenwood, which the editor patronisingly highlighted "will induce many to sympathise with the poor, whose suffering are so acute in the vast metropolis." The early issues are not quite as sanctimonious as the editor's comments suggest, but it is evident that he wanted to promote a family magazine that was both educational and morally improving.

---

[1] "Introduction", *The Ludgate Monthly*, May 1891, p. 2.

Little can be found about the editor. In an article about the River Thames (Jul 1891), he revealed that he had been born at Kingston, Surrey, before the current bridge had been built. Since that was completed in 1828, May must have been born in the early 1820s and was thus in his seventies when *The Ludgate* was launched. This may account for the retrospective and overly didactic mood of the magazine in its early years. It may also account for the magazine's first serial, "A Life's History" by May himself, episodic musings of the life of an old man.

The Ludgate settled into a pattern. Each issue carried the words and music of a popular song (a feature later picked up by *The Strand*), an article about an area of beauty in Britain one about more distant lands. There was an article about sport (which was invariably cricket, including a piece by W. G. Grace on "The Cricket of the Future" in the second issue), and a military article or story. The December 1892 issue began a series on British regiments. Each issue ran a children's story, which, by the fourth volume, had developed into the series, "Tales from Dreamland" by May Cumberland. These features remained fairly constant throughout May's editorship, with the addition of a series on Public Schools, which began with volume four and which became the most popular item in the magazine. A specific feature for women was initiated, "Whispers from the Woman's World" by Florence May Gardiner, plus a society and theatrical gossip column, "Incidents of the Month".

Within the first year May declared that the magazine had the "largest circulation of any threepenny magazine in the United Kingdom" and a companion *Ludgate Weekly* was launched in March 1892, edited by Charles Ogilvie. The *Weekly* lasted only a few issues, however, and with the fourth volume, in November 1892, *The Ludgate* converted into a more standard monthly increasing its size to 112 pages and raising its price to sixpence.

The fiction was usually either light domestic or military but there were occasional surprises that bucked the otherwise doctrinal tones. Two such were by literary critic D F. Hannigan. In "The Extraordinary Case of Mr. Ebenstal" (Aug 1891) a man discovers that his wife is of serpentine origin, while "Old Doctor Rutherford" (Oct 1891) is about immortality. The December 1892 issue ran one of Mrs Riddell's ghost stories, "Hartford O'Donnell's Warning", whilst the special *Christmas Annual* was "The Woeful Story of Mr. Wobbley, Comedian" by Henry Herman, one of the earliest novels to feature invisibility. Perhaps the most significant series in the early issues was "The Experiences of Loveday Brooke, Lady Detective", by C(atherine) L. Pirkis (Feb-Jul 1893) featuring the first important female private detective.

Further series included "Mr. Fordham's Strange Cases" by Hubert Grayle (Apr-May 1893), "Revelations of a London Pawnbroker" by Paul Seton (Aug 1893-Jan 1894) and "At the Sign of the Blue Anchor" (Oct 1893-Mar 1894), a series of travellers' tales by Charles J. Mansford. The reformatting, plus the popular-style series, showed how the magazine was now imitating *The Strand*. Always profusely illustrated, *The Ludgate* increased its quota. It also ran two of the earliest sketches by Sidney H. Sime (Apr and Jun 1892 issues. In recognition of this change the magazine revised its name to *The Ludgate Illustrated Magazine* from November 1893.

Just when Philip May ceased to be the editor is not certain as no editorial credits were given. He had certainly gone by November 1894, and though he had some signed contributions during 1894 he could have handed over editorial reins earlier.[2] If so, his successor is not known, but it may have been he effected the changes into a *Strand* look-alike. The new editor

---

[2] His parting may coincide with the change of publisher in May 1894.

also had a penchant for unusual stories. Several psychic tales appeared of which the most interesting was the series, "The Memoirs of Dr. Francis Wiseman" by Paul Seton (Apr-Nov 1894), purported accounts from private papers that formed "an astounding narrative of the invisible and supernatural." During 1895 *The Ludgate* ran longer stories, most of the rousing adventure kind, such as the story of the Wanderers' Club, "Peter Longfellow's Adventures" by Colin Carre, and several mysteries by Guy Clifford.

During 1895 *The Ludgate* was taken over by *Black and White*, the slick weekly society paper that had started only a few months before *The Ludgate*, in February 1891. *The Ludgate* came under the editorship of James Nicol Dunn. The magazine increased in size to Imperial Octavo (18cm x 27.5cm) which gave greater scope for illustrations. Over the next year *The Ludgate* became swamped with photographs and features. A six-page "Fashions of the Month" began, and there was a regular section (26 pages in the first issue) with photographs of recent events, personalities, and theatre news. There were caricatures of authors by "GRIP" (Alfred Brice) which included George Du Maurier (Nov 1895) and Arthur Conan Doyle (Dec 1895).

The new production process allowed for the facsimile of letters and *The Ludgate* began an occasional feature reproducing the monographs of celebrities who had responded to certain questions. In the first issue authors nominated which of their works they either most liked or disliked, with letters from Walter Besant, Conan Doyle, Stanley Weyman, Anthony Hope and S. R. Crockett. The idea was repeated with artists in the February 1896 issue. All the old features passed away. A new column for women and the family was started by Muriel Babbington-Bright, "The Bonbonnière", which was usually a clever anecdotal reflection on events. To encourage reader involvement they ran a contest for the best story or novel plot, the best artwork, photographs and verse, and these were published regularly in later issues. Fiction became lost for a while amongst the illustrative features, though Eden Phillpotts had several amusing stories, much like those he was contributing to *The Idler*, and Barry Pain contributed a quirky romance, "The Octavo of Claudius" (Sept 1896-Aug 1897).

The orgy of photographic excess ended as abruptly as it had started after three volumes. From May 1897 the magazine reverted to the standard size and a degree of editorial balance returned. Lowry succeeded in blending the best intentions of the original *Ludgate* with the

"THE INDIAN CLEFT HIM THROUGH THE SKULL."
(See "The Deeds of Michael Hirst," page 174.)

more exciting, bolder endeavours of its later years. Back came articles on cricket whilst those for women and children were dropped, showing an obvious reorientation within the market. Back came some of the crusading articles with which the magazine had started, such as "Cry of the Children" by Frank Hird (from Oct 1897), about the plight of working children. There were a large number of highly illustrated travel articles on places all over the world to the extent that *The Ludgate* could have substituted for the *National Geographic*. There were also articles on authors, artists and, most especially, the theatre and music-hall. These remained for the rest of the magazine's life.

It is now that we see the biggest change in the fiction, moving away from the moralistic tales of the early issues towards the unusual and sensational. This is shown graphically in two drawings in the February 1898 issue. Ernest Prater's frontispiece for the military series "The Deeds of Michael Niel" by F. Norreys Connell, shows a Gurkha cleaving an army officer's skull (*opposite*), whilst in Edwin Pugh's "Crazy Madge", Grenville Maton portrays Madge finding her lover, a highwayman, hanging from a tree.

This change may mark the shift from Dunn's editorship to Lowry's.[3] From here on there are more unusual stories. In "The Vampire Bat", Sydney Travers (Jul 1898) suggests that "thought" is the vampire because it drains a person of spontanaiety and individuality. In "The Tragedy of the Wedding" (Oct 1898), Stanley Percival explores the unscrupulous use of hypnotism. The collaborative team of C. Ranger Gull (later better known as Guy Thorne) and Reginald Bacchus cornered the market for the unusual in *The Ludgate*. Starting with "The Dragon of St Paul's" (Apr 1899), where an explorer revives the frozen body of a prehistoric flying monster, the duo contributed a series of bizarre often gruesome stories. The most extreme was "The Children of Pain" (Nov 1899) which reveals the mistreatment meted out by the son of a circus owner to the human "freaks" in the company.

It was into this climate of the unusual that two authors who were to become big names made their magazine debuts. Rafael Sabatini contributed three swashbuckling historical stories, starting with "The Red Mask" (Dec 1898), whilst a teenage Ethel M. Dell appeared with a story of the Afghan War, "In Her Majesty's Service" (Dec 1899).

It seems unfair that at the moment when *The Ludgate* had found its metier, it should fail but, following a brief change of publisher, the magazine was sold again, in 1900, to Alexis de Beck, who merged it with his magazine *The Universal*. *The Ludgate's* title continued in that magazine, but none of its features was retained. *The Ludgate* has been relegated to a footnote in literary history, saved only by Pirkis's female detective, but it had far more to offer, and its sheer diversity over the relatively short space of ten years made it one of the most exciting magazines of the 1890s.

Frequency: Monthly.
Publisher: F. J. Lambert on behalf of The Ludgate Company until April 1894; Horace Marshall, May 1894-Oct 1895. New series: W. J. P. Monckton, on behalf of Black and White, Nov 1895 to Mar 1898; F. V. White, on behalf of Black and White, Apr 1898-Oct 1900; Jules de Meray, Nov 1900-Feb 1901.
Editors: Philip May, May 1891-Apr (?) 1894; editor uncertain, May 1894-Oct 1895; James Nicol Dunn, Nov 1895-1897; Henry D. Lowry, 1897-1898/9; Charles Hyatt-Woolf, 1898/9-Feb 1901.
Format/Size: Standard. Page count 64, rose to 112, Nov 1892. New series, large standard (imperial octavo), 106/112 pages, dropped to 96, May 1898.
Price: 3d until October 1892, thereafter 6d.
Holdings:
Complete run, UK/Eire. Bodleian (*Call Number*: Per. 2705 d.253). • Cambridge University Library (*Classmark*: L900.b.94). • National Library of Scotland (*Shelfmark*: U.411). • Trinity College, Dublin (*Call Number*: 65.pp.18).
Substantial run, UK. British Library has volumes 1 (May-Oct 1891), 3-9 (May 1892-Oct 1895) and New series, volumes 2-10 (May 1896-Jul 1900) (*Shelfmark*: PP.6004.glo).

---

[3] Lowry's *Who's Who* entry says he edited *The Ludgate* until 1898 but the *Literary Year-Book* shows him as editor during 1899.

Complete run, US: Library of Congress on microfilm (*Call Number*: 05419). • University of Connecticut on microfilm.
Collecting points: Most volumes in a succession of different publisher's bindings can be found without much difficulty at reasonable prices except the final volume.

* * *

THE MAGPIE
28 issues. Volume 1, Number 1, August 1912 to Volume 5, Number 28, December 1914.

The Magpie does not conform with any of the standard fiction magazines proliferating in 1912. It was narrower, slightly taller and slimmer, the first issue only 52 pages plus advertising. The uncredited cover, a rather sketchy, static example of art deco, was standard on the first few issues. The pages were thick pulp, full of text unleavened by illustration. The price was threepence, evidently seeking to undercut the other monthlies, but first impressions were of a magazine trying to add some culture to the penny weeklies without being lost amongst the regular sixpenny monthlies.

Its strength lay not in its looks but its content. The first issue brought with it a bevy of names – Elinor Glyn, O. Henry, Arthur Morrison, E. Œ. Somerville and H. de Vere Stacpoole. Uppermost in their's and other's stories is the power of story-telling – real stories and real characters by masters of their craft. The publisher, was evidently trying to capture a slice of the fiction-magazine market, and splashed out on major writers rather than on looks. The editor was Alders Anderson, who had run *The Grand* for Newnes and had a wealth of experience. The magazine adopted the slogan, "Live stories for Clever People", a phrase that links it to the *Smart Set* school of fiction. Certainly it published a high level of intelligent rather than sensational fiction, without being too "literary".

For the first few issues *The Magpie* lived up to its standards. Contributors included Oliver Madox Hueffer, Edgar Jepson, Compton Mackenzie, Barry Pain and Max Rittenberg. It ran Gouverneur Morris's powerful horror story, "Back There in the Grass" (Sept 1912) and the series by George A. Birmingham collected in book form as *The Adventures of Dr. Whitty* (1913). It also ran some of the earliest stories by Roy Vickers, "The Exploits of Sefton Kyle"[1] (Mar-Apr 1913). The critics liked the magazine, *The Times* noting *The Magpie* was "a particularly good specimen."[2] The magazine commented that its readers "numbered by tens of thousands", and it provided a "circulation" figure of 50,000 for its first year to the Advertisers' Protection Society, though net sales may have been closer to 30,000.

Whatever the reason, the magazine passed from Everett's to Horace Marshall. Under them it prospered. From October 1913 the page count nearly doubled and the price rose by half. The covers became flamboyant and colorful. Anderson continued to seek unusual material. In his June 1914 editorial he attacked those who equated "popular" with "sub-standard". "Most

---

[1] Vickers later used his detective's name Sefton Kyle as a personal pseudonym.
[2] *The Times*, 2 June 1913, p. 3.

popular publications," he wrote, "are conducted on the assumption that the intelligent portion of the public is an altogether negligible quantity." He paraphrased an unnamed source that had estimated there were only 30,000 discerning readers in the whole of England, but Anderson argued that based on *The Magpie*'s circulation that figure needed revising.

Anderson's own discernment meant that the fiction in *The Magpie* remained of a high standard. Stories include "A Coincidental Correspondence" by Upton Sinclair (Dec 1913), "The Strange Case of Mr Todmorden" a clever mystery by F. Britten Austin (Dec 1913) and a powerful psychological study, "The Man Who Cut Himself" by F. J. St Aubyn (Jul 1914). In "The Making of a Man of Genius" (Dec 1914), Herbert Jenkins raised the question of what constituted greatness.

Despite the critical success of *The Magpie*, or perhaps because of it, Anderson found it difficult to continue the magazine into the War years. His editorials became downbeat and he began to reprint examples of tough war fiction, including an extract from Tolstoi's *War and Peace*. Consigned to an early grave, and with copies extremely rare, *The Magpie* has been forgotten, but it was a good example of what a strongminded, literary editor could achieve.

Frequency: Monthly, but no issue for Nov 1914.
Publisher: Everett & Co., to Oct 1912; thereafter Horace Marshall.
Editor: Alderson Anderson.
Format/Size: Slim standard pulp (24.6cm x 15cm), 52 pages, rose to 64/68, Sept 1912; 110/112, Oct 1913.
Price: 3d, rose to 4½d, Oct 1913.
Holdings: *Complete run, UK*. Bodleian (*Call Number*: Per. 25611 d.8).
Collecting points: Very rare, though occasional single issues surface at reasonable prices.

***

THE MERRY MAG.
68 issues. Volume 1, Number 1, July 1924 to Volume 12, Number 68, February 1930. Title revised to THE MERRY MAGAZINE from August 1927. Merged with *The Red Magazine*.

The Merry was Amalgamated Press's response to Newnes's *The Happy Mag*. In looks it was identical but, lacking the draw of Richmal Crompton's William stories, the publisher built the magazine around the then top music-hall entertainer, Leslie Henson. He contributed a humour column, remaining identified with the magazine until December 1927, though the fabrication that he also edited it ceased after the first year.

Some of *The Happy*'s regulars also wrote for *The Merry*, such as A. M. Burrage and F. Morton Howard, to which were added Rowan Glen, Edward Woodward, Richard Starr, William Freeman, Herbert Allingham and Pearkes Withers, sufficient to make the magazine look like a light-hearted version of *The Violet*. Light romance was a staple element rather than simple humour. Cartoons and jokes did not festoon the magazine as in *The Happy*, but many of the same artists appeared, especially Lindsay Cable, Graham Simmons, Arthur Ferrier (who did most of the early covers) and Leonard Shields. Most later covers were by P. B. Hickling, Reginald Glossop and Norman Keene.

Edgar Wallace appeared in two issues with "The Fearful Four" (Feb 1925) and "The Will and the Won't" (Jul 1925). Howel Evans contributed a series with a mischievous heroine, "Woffles" (from Jul 1924), whilst F. Morton Howard doubled the trouble in "The Merry Twins" (from Jul 1925). Herbert Allingham contributed a Wodehousian series about a millionaire buffoon, "Entertaining Archie" (from Aug 1928). Perhaps the cleverest series began as "The Ways of Wanda" by Peter Warrington (from August 1926) and then switched the viewpoint as "The Perversities of Peter" by Wanda Warrington (from Feb 1927).

Towards the end *The Merry* introduced a film column (from Dec 1928) and ran profiles of film stars. The emphasis shifted to romantic fiction. There was a spoof on Elinor Glyn's *It* in, "Absolutely No IT!" by Royal Brown (Jan 1929). The magazine remained light-hearted ephemeral fun, but with the end of the twenties, it was merged with *The Red Magazine*.

Frequency: Monthly.
Publisher: Amalgamated Press.
Editor: Nominally, Leslie Henson (until June 1925). Actual editor not known.
Format/Size: Small pulp, 96 pages.
Price: 7d.
Holdings: *Substantial run, UK.* Bodleian has all issues to Apr 1929, except Dec 1924 and Jan 1925 (*Call Number*: Per. 2705 e.585).
Collecting points: Very uncommon. Occasional single issues surface.

***

THE MINSTER
15 issues. Volume 1, Number 1, January 1895 to Volume 3, Number 3, March 1896.

The Minster is difficult to classify. It had only three volumes but all were very different. It began as a church magazine, evolved from *The Newbery House Magazine*, "a monthly review for churchmen and churchwomen", which lasted from 1889 to 1894. *The Minster* was full of articles and features on saints, the clergy and good causes, but found room to include one or two short stories per issue. George Gissing, James Payn, Anthony Hope and Stanley Weyman were amongst the contributors, but were as easily passed by. Its most interesting feature was a series by Linley Sambourne, "The Progress of Black and White Art" (from May 1895), which continued into the new volume.

With that volume, the mood changed. It shifted from its ecclesiastical base towards the world of popular fiction. Max Pemberton began a series about the adventures of a baronet, "From the Diary of a Valet". Barry Pain contributed a humour column. There were travel articles, items on royal wedding dresses, railways, dreams, newspaper production – all the miscellany one came to expect from the regular magazines. The fiction was somewhat bland, favouring the historical or moralistic, though with occasional surprises, such as a love story by Guy Boothby ("Misplaced Affections", Aug 1896).

With the third volume all changed again. It was acquired by the Artistic Publishing Company, run by L. Raven-Hill, who wanted "to make *The Minster* the first English magazine, not merely in the excellence of its literary and artistic matter, but also in its reproduction and printing." Edited by Ernest Bramah, the change was remarkable. Their first issue (Jan 1896) featured stories by W. L. Alden, W. W. Jacobs and Eden Phillpotts. The next proclaimed itself "the Biggest Magazine in the World", though its 166 pages included two supplements and the advertisements. At the back of one supplement was a musical score by Gordon Craig. Sime had illustrations in both this and the third issue, which reverted to the standard size. It included Arthur Waugh's study "The Oxford of Fiction" plus H. G. Wells's clever story, "The Lost Inheritance". Unfortunately that was the final issue. The Artistic Publishing Company ran out of money. *The Minster* is a yet another example of a magazine that became too ambitious but lacked the wherewithal.

Frequency: Monthly.
Publisher: A. D. Innes, to Dec 1895; Artistic Publishing Company, Jan-Mar 1896.
Editor(s): First two volumes, unknown; third volume, Ernest Bramah.
Format/Size: Standard, mostly 106/112 pages; but Feb 1896 issue 166 pages.
Price: 6d.
Holdings:
Complete run, UK. British Library (*Shelfmark*: PP.6004.glu).
Substantial run, UK. Bodleian (*Call Number*: Per. 2705 d.50) and Cambridge University Library (*Classmark*: L900.c.106) both have issues for January-December 1895 only.
Complete run, US. Library of Congress (*Call Number*: AP2.M48).
Collecting points: The first volume surfaces occasionally but the other two are rare.

※ ※ ※

MODERN STORIES

Number 1, August 1934 to ? (1935?); total number of issues not known.

Modern Stories was an imitation *Argosy* all-reprint magazine showcasing the best short stories. It included work by G. K. Chesterton, Warwick Deeping, Agatha Christie, P. C. Wren, John Buchan, E. M. Delafield and others, plus articles by P. G. Wodehouse originally written for *Vanity Fair*. The editor promised to publish new stories, but copies of later issues are rare and it is not certain just how much new material appeared, if any. It was initially very popular, but does not seem to have survived its first year, though the exact number of issues is unknown.

Frequency: Monthly.
Publisher: World's Work, Kingswood.
Editor: Not known.
Format/Size: Standard pulp, 128 pages.
Price: 1/-.
Holdings: None known.
Collecting points: Rare.

***

MYSTERY AND DETECTION
9 issues. Number 1, [September] 1934 to Volume 2, Number 3, October 1935.

One of several pulp reprint magazines issued by World's Work in the mid-thirties as a spin-off from the *Master Thriller* series where the first *Tales of Mystery and Detection* had appeared in March 1934. The contents included old classics, such as G. K. Chesterton's Father Brown and R. Austin Freeman's Dr Thorndyke; more recent classics, such as Dorothy L. Sayers's Peter Wimsey and F. Tennyson Jesse's Solange, plus lesser known material. The quality was high, but little that was not already available in the bumper hardcover anthologies of the thirties. Despite the strong names in each issue, which also included H. C. Bailey, Thomas Burke, Algernon Blackwood, Oliver Onions, E. Phillips Oppenheim and Edgar Wallace, the magazine offered nothing new. It was soon phased out in favour of its companion *Mystery Stories*.

Frequency: Irregular, then monthly from Number 3 (Apr 1935).
Publisher: The World's Work, Kingswood, Surrey.
Editor: Possibly H. Norman Evans.
Format/Size: Standard pulp, 128 pages.
Price: 1/-.
References: Indexed in *Science Fiction, Fantasy & Weird Fiction Magazine Index (1890-2001)* by Stephen T. Miller and William G. Contento (Locus Press, 2002).
Holdings: *Partial run, UK*. Bodleian has first two issues only (*Call Number*: Per. 25613 d.67).
Collecting points: Rare; less common than *Mystery Stories*. No full run known.

***

MYSTERY STORIES
25 issues. Volume 1, Number 1, [March] 1936 to Number 25, February 1942.

A companion title to *Mystery and Detection*, *Mystery Stories* was a mixture of new stories and reprints, but drew mostly from lesser known British sources or American pulps. The issues were a mixture of mystery and weird fiction, most of them following the formulaic pattern of the day. Contributors included Vincent Cornier, R. Thurston Hopkins, Garnett Radcliffe, Francis H. Sibson, Edmund Snell, Edgar Wallace and F.A.M. Webster. Amongst new material were two stories by L.T.C. Rolt, "New Corner" (#20, 1940) and "The Mine" (Feb 1942). *Mystery Stories* is an uneven mix of standard potboiler fare and the occasional gem.

Frequency: Quarterly.
Publisher: The World's Work, Kingswood.
Editor: H. Norman Evans
Format/Size: Pulp, 128 pages, dropped to 80, in 1940.
Price: 1/-.
References: Indexed in *Science Fiction, Fantasy & Weird Fiction Magazine Index (1890-2001)* by Stephen T. Miller and William G. Contento (Locus Press, 2002).
Holdings: *Partial run, UK*. British Library has issues #22-#25 only (*Shelfmark*: PP.6004.tap).
Collecting points: Uncommon but single copies surface occasionally.

***

MYSTERY-STORY MAGAZINE

55 issues. Volume 1, Number 1, February 1923 to Volume 10, Number 55, September 1927. Merged with *Adventure-Story Magazine* to form ADVENTURE & MYSTERY STORY MAGAZINE.

Mystery-Story Magazine has acquired a near legendary status amongst collectors of pulp magazines. It is extremely rare and is of special interest to collectors of the American pulps *Weird Tales* and *Ghost Stories*, because there was a significant exchange of stories between them. Like its companion, *Adventure-Story*, its contents were a mixture of new material and stories selected from the American pulps.

Britain's first specialist mystery-fiction pulp, *The Detective Magazine*, had appeared from Amalgamated Press in December 1922, followed by Hutchinson's *Mystery-Story* two months later. It was started, according to one publicity blurb, "to supply the needs of lovers of gripping mystery and detective stories." Though there was no shortage of British mystery writers but it was probably cheaper to acquire ready-made material from the American pulps. It is likely that Hutchinson had an arrangement with American publisher Bernarr Macfadden, as not only did Hutchinson's publish a British edition of Macfadden's money-spinner *True Story Magazine* from December 1922, but *Mystery-Story* carried stories from Macfadden's obscure tabloid magazine *Midnight Mysteries*. There were doubtless similar arrangements with other US publishers, including Street and Smith, who published *Detective Story Magazine*, and Rural Publishing, who produced *Weird Tales*.

A market report requested stories of "murder, robbery, impersonation, a ghost story with 'atmosphere', a spiritualistic yarn with a new idea behind it – anything, in fact, in which lurks a mystery."[1] Editor E. C. Vivian had a penchant for supernatural fiction and, as a result, the magazine ran plenty of ghost and weird stories including work by Elliott O'Donnell and Lewis Spence, plus two British writers who would establish reputations in America, Arlton Eadie and G. G. Pendarves. Vivian also contributed to the magazine, under his own name and various pseudonyms, including Galbraith Nicholson, under which name ran the serial "The Tiger's Tear" (Nov 1923-Apr 1924) about an accursed jewel.

Many of the contributors are little known outside the magazine which suggests most may be new writers interested in weird fiction. It resulted in some singularly unusual stories which is what makes *Mystery-Story* such an interesting magazine. Two examples will suffice. "Siblett's Tree Lady" (Sept 1923), by O'Brien Bell, is about a soldier during the First World War who uses an ancient willow tree as a lookout post where he encounters the dryad of the tree who has been wounded by the "iron bees" of the enemy. "Sink of the World" (Nov 1923) by R. W. Alexander is in the form of a diary kept by a man on board ship which is disabled by gun fire and drifts into a strange fog-bound world of giant birds and intelligent apes. The magazine allowed authors to spread their imaginative and creative wings and produce fiction that was beyond the parameters of the standard magazines.

---

[1] Michael Joseph, *Short Story Writing for Profit* (London: Hutchinson, 1923), p. 199.

On the mystery side the work was more traditional. There were several series. In "The Professor's Problems" (Apr-Nov 1923) Francis D. Grierson created forensic scientist Professor Wells in imitation of Freeman's Dr Thorndyke. There was also a brief series about a Holmesian consulting detective in "Concerning Mr. Rumm" by Ronald M. Newman (Apr-May 1923). More dramatic and verging on the hard-boiled were several of Lemuel de Bra's Chinatown Secret Service stories reprinted from the American *Blue Book*, starting with "Tears of the Poppy" (May 1923). There was also a series of articles by E.W.D. Cuming on "Forgotten Crimes" (Jul-Dec 1923) which considered major murder cases.

Not only were the stories as atmospheric and sensational as possible, but so were the covers. Bright, gaudy and full of action, they reflected Hutchinson's desire for colour. Hutchinson once admonished one of his editors for buying a lacklustre picture, saying, "If I have to pay four guineas for a wrapper design I want more paint on it."[2]

According to Vivian's biographer, Peter Berresford Ellis, *Mystery-Story* and *Adventure-Story* "became Britain's top-selling popular fiction magazines."[3] Even so, whilst Vivian had acquired some original and unusual stories he had not been able to attract many major names. During his tenure contributors included such reliable second-tier writers as F.A.M. Webster, Robert W. Sneddon, E. R. Punshon – plus a few surprises – Richard Hughes, Lance Sieveking and an early story by Peter Cheyney ("A Double, Double Cross", May 1924). Vivian also published Michael Joseph's much-reprinted horror story, "The Yellow Cat" (Jun 1924). Joseph later remarked that "If the *Mystery-Story Magazine* had refused it, I should almost certainly not have sold it elsewhere. It is too gruesome for the ordinary fiction magazines."[4]

Vivian's successor, Oscar Cook, had a fondness for the *conte cruel*, as did his wife Christine Campbell Thomson (who wrote under the name Flavia Richardson). They both contributed several grim stories, such as "When Hell Laughed" (Jan 1926) by Campbell Thomson, about the dire consequences of a man meddling with the occult. Christine Campbell Thomson worked for the literary agent Curtis Brown and through her Cook acquired stories by better known writers. Thus during his year as editor the magazine's profile grew with contributions by Mrs Belloc Lowndes, Margery Lawrence, Sax Rohmer and the Earl of Birkenhead (who, from April 1925, contributed a series on famous historical trials).

If under Cook the emphasis was on the macabre, under his successor, Meredith Dixon, it shifted back towards the supernatural. It was now that the arrangement with Bernarr Macfadden had greatest effect. Macfadden had started *Ghost Stories* in July 1926, and many of its stories were reprinted in *Mystery-Story*, usually with the dramatically posed photographs that Macfadden used to imply a factual basis. For a while, running into 1927, parts of *Mystery-Story* read more like a spiritualist's confession magazine. The stories were less original than during Vivian's editorship. Nevertheless Vibart, and his successor, Miss Gilligan, also attracted a variety of well known writers, not all of whom would seem immediately at home in such a sensational pulp. These included William Le Queux, Stacey Aumonier, Arnold Ridley (with

---

[2] Robert Lusty, *Bound To Be Read* (London: Cape, 1975), p. 50.
[3] Peter Berresford Ellis, "Master of Mystery", *Million* 1:6 (November/December 1991), p. 25.
[4] Michael Joseph, *The Magazine Story* (London: Hutchinson, 1928), p. 118.

the story behind his hit stage play "The Ghost Train", Jun/Jul 1926), John Galsworthy (with the story of his play "Escape", Nov 1926) and actress Hermione Gingold. Other occasional contributors included Edgar Wallace, Sax Rohmer, Ursula Bloom and Baroness Orczy.

Mystery-Story could almost certainly have continued for several more years, but responding to Hutchinson's publishing whims, it merged with *Adventure-Story* in October 1927. It is a magazine that has more of interest than of quality, and the researcher will find some truly unusual stories amongst the lesser material. Although it has a somewhat inflated reputation it is a fine example of the adaptability of a single title to publishing opportunities and public tastes. It is the closest Britain came to a weird-fiction pulp in the pre-war years and was also the closest in content and form to the American pulps whilst retaining its own personality.

Frequency: Monthly, but combined June/July 1926 issue.
Publisher: Hutchinson.
Editors: E. Charles Vivian, 1922-1924; Oscar Cook, 1925; Meredith V. Dixon, 1926; Miss G. Gilligan, 1927.
Format/Size: Standard pulp, 96 pages, rose to 128 in 1926.
Price: 7d, rose to 1/- in 1926.
References: "The Trail of Adventure and Mystery" by Mike Ashley, *Pulp Vault* #10 (May 1992), pp. 4-14. Also indexed in CD-ROM *Science Fiction, Fantasy & Weird Fiction Magazine Index (1890-2001)* by Stephen T. Miller & William G. Contento (Locus Press, 2002).
Holdings: *Complete run, UK*. Bodleian (*Call Number*: Per. 25612 d.22).
Collecting points: Very rare and probably impossible now to build a complete run. Less common than *Adventure-Story* but also more desirable.

* * *

NASH'S MAGAZINE [NASH'S–PALL MALL]

341 issues. As NASH'S MAGAZINE, Volume 1, Number 1, April 1909 to Volume 10, Number 6, September 1914; 66 issues. Merged with *Pall Mall Magazine* as NASH'S AND PALL MALL MAGAZINE but continued numbering from *Pall Mall*, Volume 54, Number 258, October 1914 to Volume 79, Number 407, April 1927; 150 issues. Reverted to NASH'S MAGAZINE, Volume 79, Number 408, May 1927 to Volume 83, Number 436, September 1929; 29 issues. Again merged with *Pall Mall Magazine* as NASH'S—PALL MALL from Volume 84, Number 437, October 1929 to Volume 99, Number 532, September 1937 (briefly retitled NEW NASH'S PALL MALL MAGAZINE October to November 1935 only); 96 issues. Merged with *Good Housekeeping*. Revived as NASH'S ANNUAL, Summer 1938 and December 1946 to Winter 1949/50 (5 issues).

Nash's Magazine is second only to *The Strand* in being the most influential British popular fiction magazine. If one were to take seriously the words of its founder Eveleigh Nash, we may imagine he believed this from the outset. "The day will come," he purportedly told one of his prospective advertisers, "when *Nash's Magazine* will have the biggest sale of any British magazine."[1] As he wrote that twenty-one years later we must take his word for it as being remarkable foresight rather than convenient hindsight. The truth was that the original *Nash's Magazine* was nothing spectacular, but it did benefit from Nash's skill at promotion. To launch the magazine Nash arranged for a coach-and-four to travel through central London, causing chaos in the traffic, its passengers dressed in the Regency costume of Beau Nash, and the carriage bedecked in the cover design of the first issue by Lawson Wood (*see over*).

The Times went so far as to call it "the best sixpennyworth of fiction that has ever been offered to the public."[2] Apparently sales were excellent, Nash reporting a circulation of 150,000, though this was probably not net sales. A few months later figures were given as 75,000. *Nash's* was not as groundbreaking as its publisher liked to make out. His idea was simply to put out an unillustrated magazine carrying fiction by the best authors selling for sixpence. This was what *The Grand* and *The Novel* had been doing for four years, and *The Story-Teller* and *The Red* for over a year – and they were cheaper. The difference was that whereas these magazines tended to publish "popular" fiction, Nash promised "a high standard of literary merit". In fact there was little to distinguish between "literary merit" and "popular" fiction as evidenced by the main reason for the magazine's success, the serialisation of H. Rider Haggard's new novel, "Queen Sheba's Ring". This lost-race adventure set in Ethiopia was a return to Haggard's most popular territory ater a few years writing historical novels. It was unadulterated popular fiction and, of course, the public loved Haggard at his best.

Nash had other strong names in these early issues: Rudyard Kipling, Anthony Hope, George R. Sims, William Le Queux, Edith Nesbit and A.E.W. Mason. And despite his claims for literary distinction he was not averse to publishing unusual stories such as Flora Annie Steel's fantasy of pre-history, "The Birth of Fire" (Jul 1909), or "The Voice in the Night", a highly atmospheric horror story of the sea by William Hope Hodgson (Jan 1910).[3] Generally, though, *Nash's* contents were fairly restrained. Most were light romances, society stories or high-society mysteries, such as William Le Queux's series about Lady Sybil Sheringham, known as Tibbie, who proves a remarkable sleuth. Katharine Tynan had a Napoleonic story, "Mounseer" (Jul 1909) whilst B. M. Croker contributed one of her typical stories of Irish life, "The Spare Bed" (Nov 1909).

Although launched as an all-fiction magazine, Nash soon introduced a series of articles by historian Martin Hume, "True Stories of the Past" (Oct 1909-Mar 1910), which proved highly popular. Recognising the power of a "scoop", Nash upgraded the quality of the paper from poor wood-pulp to "white wove", in order to reproduce the photographs accompanying Robert Peary's revelations "The Discovery of the North Pole" (Feb-Mar 1910). It was now that the magazine showed its real potential. Nash secured the rights to Kipling's new series of Puck of Pook's Hill stories – the first had run in *The Strand* – starting with "Gloriana" (Mar 1910), illustrated by H. R. Millar. It also ran possibly its most memorable story, "The Lodger" (Jan 1911), Mrs Belloc Lowndes's "Jack the Ripper"-inspired novelette.

Despite these moments sales continued to drop. Nash declared a circulation of 60,000 by early 1911. The increased production costs must have eaten into any profits and Nash had been unable to secure sufficient advertising revenue. He sold the title, later remarking that "I only

---

[1] Eveleigh Nash, "Coming of Age, 1909-1930", *Nash's–Pall Mall*, July 1930, p. 31.
[2] *The Times*, 1 April 1909, p. 7.
[3] It had earlier appeared in America in the November 1907 issue of *The Blue Book Magazine*.

sold *Nash's Magazine* because I was a private person and not a company." Had he let the magazine lapse it would scarcely be remembered but, as a consequence of the sale, *Nash's* would pass into history.

The purchaser was American newspaper millionaire William Randolph Hearst, who had established a publishing empire in the United States through such papers as *San Francisco Examiner* and the *New York Journal*. He had revolutionised the popular magazine when he transformed *Cosmopolitan* in 1905, using it as a vehicle for popular crusades. The term "muckraking" was applied to those exposés that upset the established social and political conventions. Two early enquiries into corruption in the Senate and child labour boosted *Cosmopolitan*'s sales, which would treble in less than ten years. Hearst sought to do the same in Britain, through *Nash's*. He established the National Magazine Company with editorial offices in Fleet Street. The managing director was James Young McPeake, a 42-year-old Irish journalist who had transformed the *Dublin Evening Mail*, whilst the overseeing editor was Perriton Maxwell, who had been the editor of *Cosmopoliton* since 1906.

The first exposé was "Barbarism in Britain" (Mar 1911) about child cruelty, written by the Director of the NSPCC. Later features covered the divorce rate, poverty in Britain and the nation's health. There were also such celebrations as the coronation of George V (Jun 1911), the Prince of Wales's investiture (Jul 1911), and the relationship between Britain and the United States and their domination of world affairs (Aug 1911). These articles were liberally illustrated with dramatic photographs, charts and a creative use of space and design facilitated by the new half-tone printing techniques. The artwork within the magazine was exceptional, with work by Charles A. Winter, Will Foster, Anton O. Fischer, Charles Dana Gibson and Chandler Christy, and the quality of reproduction was second to none. The covers were by Harrison Fisher, famed for his romantic pretty-girl image. These were so popular that they became collectable in their own right, with *Nash's* offering reproductions on art paper.[4]

Although the exposés were the bait that lured people to *Nash's*, it was the fiction that was the hook. Maxwell relied on the same stable of writers he had used at *Cosmopolitan*, providing long-running serials and series that kept bringing the readers back. The number of key writers was quite small – Robert W. Chambers, Jack London, Arthur B. Reeve, George Randolph Chester and Bruno Lessing – but between them they represented the range of expression that Hearst wanted to portray. Primary in this was Robert W. Chambers. He had recently moved from the historical novel to exploring the tensions of modern life and the consequences of female emancipation. Starting with "The Common Law" (Feb-Dec 1911[5]) Chambers wrote a series of novels that focused on these social changes and which considerably enhanced his

---

[4] During the Great War some 500,000 copies of Fisher's pictures were sold separately. See *Nash's–Pall Mall*, July 1930, p. 32.

[5] This serial had been running in America in *Cosmopolitan* from November 1910. Chambers was paid £3,000 for the serial rights (presumably both US and UK). See *New York Times*, 5 February 1911, "Literary Notes from London".

reputation. Chambers's work was echoed in a controversial trilogy by Virginia Van de Water: "Why I Left My Husband" (Sept 1911), "Why I Left My Wife" (Dec 1911) and "Why I Left Home" (May 1912). Divorce and marital strife was much in the news at this time when the Royal Commission set up in 1909 to consider the subject finally presented its report. *Nash's* ran data from the report (Apr 1911) plus a symposium of views by Thomas Hardy, Leonard Huxley, Hall Caine and others (Mar 1912) and an opinion from G. K. Chesterton, "Divorce vs Democracy" (May 1912). There was a sense from the start that the new *Nash's* was aware of the issues of the day and not afraid to view them from all angles. Other social issues emerged in the stories of Bruno Lessing, the pen name adopted by Hearst editor Rudolph Block. Lessing wrote stories set in the Jewish ghettos (anglicised for publication in *Nash's*) which raised matters of race, religion and poverty.

The other thread is represented by George Randolph Chester and Arthur B. Reeve. Chester had created the character Get-Rich-Quick Wallingford, the first series of which had run in the *Saturday Evening Post* in 1907. *Cosmopolitan* secured the second series and, to allow British readers to catch up, *Nash's* ran both series back to back from May 1911. Wallingford was a dodgy but lovable business man who looked for the quick scheme to make money, and always stayed just the right side of the law. He passed rapidly into American folklore and became the epitomé of the entrepreneurial spirit, a positive view that Hearst was keen to project. The same could be applied to Craig Kennedy, the scientific detective, whom Arthur B. Reeve created in a long series of stories starting in the March 1911 *Cosmopolitan* and running just two months later in *Nash's*. Although Kennedy had some of the character of Sherlock Holmes, he was a man of the day, not the Victorian era, and used modern scientific developments in his research. He too was entrepreneurial, demonstrating the potential of the technological advance with which American industry was closely associated. *Nash's* ran several features on the most famous American scientific pioneer, Thomas Edison, starting with "A New World Ahead of Us" (Mar 1911). *Nash's* also promoted the pioneering spirit through the stories of Jack London. Starting in the August 1911 issue was a long series featuring Christopher "Smoke" Bellew who takes his chances in the Klondike gold rush. Through these features *Nash's* showed that it not only understood the problems of today but was looking ahead to solutions and progress.

Nash's strove to promote a positive attitude. It opened each issue with a short essay in the form of a meditation. These were always uplifting, though often challenging. Most were by Elbert Hubbard, beautifully illustrated by Charles A. Winter. There were also regular poems by Ella Wheeler Wilcox. Readers of *Nash's* therefore felt that here was a magazine which understood the world and was prepared to do something about it. In so doing it did not ignore traditional values. There were plenty of features that cherished our literary and artistic heritage. August Rodin, Charles Dickens, Arnold Bennett, Israel Zangwill, for example, were all the subject of highly illustrated articles. McPeake also acquired some of the papers of Charlotte Brontë and published extracts from her juvenilia "Tales of the Islanders" (Dec 1911).

Many of the stories and features were usually published in *Cosmopolitan* a month or two earlier, almost to the extent that *Nash's* could be considered a British edition of *Cosmopolitan*. The traffic was not all one-way, though. For instance, McPeake secured an article by Dickens's son A. Tennyson Dickens, "My Father and His Friends", which appeared in the September 1911 *Nash's* and the January 1912 *Cosmopolitan*. This two-way exchange would grow as *Nash's* established itself.

Overnight *Nash's* moved from a second-rate fiction magazine to a high quality, challenging, vibrant and above all positive channel for entertainment and information at no increase in price. Circulation blossomed. Sales had bottomed out at around 40,000 when acquired from Nash, but doubled by the end of 1912 and with the September 1913 issue passed the 100,000 mark.

Having established a winning pattern, *Nash's* built on it. New authors were added to the inner coterie. Compton Mackenzie, Gouverneur Morris, Elinor Glyn, Booth Tarkington (whose stories about young scalliwag Penrod Schofield began in the January 1914 issue), Rudyard Kipling, John Galsworthy and William J. Locke all became regulars over the next few years. E. Phillips Oppenheim, who was another of the regulars from the start, maintained a remarkable record of appearing in virtually every issue throughout this decade with a variety of thriller and mystery series.

With the October 1914 issue *Nash's* absorbed *Pall Mall Magazine*. Although *Pall Mall* has been sold by its original proprietor William Waldorf Astor to Iliffe in 1912, it had been his fortune that had sustained the magazine for twenty years, so it seems rather fitting that it was another American's fortune that saved the magazine. The original hope was to sustain *Pall Mall* as a separate title, but the outbreak of War stopped that. The combined *Nash's and Pall Mall Magazine* continued the volume numbering of *Pall Mall*, so that *Nash's* suddenly leapt from volume 10 to volume 53. In all other respects the magazine remained *Nash's*.

The outbreak of War led to an inevitable flurry of articles, including a special War issue (Sept 1914) with essays by Hilaire Belloc, Chesterton, R. H. Benson and George Bernard Shaw. Two months later Jerome K. Jerome, W. W. Jacobs, May Sinclair, F. Anstey, Barry Pain and others contributed to "The War as Viewed by Famous British Authors".

War-inspired articles were uppermost during the first year but then settled to a steady trickle. *Nash's* tried to present a feeling of solidarity and continuity. It still ran the occasional crusading article, with pieces on child education, vaccination and feminism vs masculinism, but these became more low-key. In light-hearted vein F. Peter Dunne contributed a series of humorous reflections on various topics through the eyes of his philosophical Irish bar owner, Mister Dooley. From the start the Hearst *Nash's* had run a monthly photogravure section on the theatre, depicting actors and actresses of the day. This feature would develop during the War. *Nash's* also serialised George Bernard Shaw's "Pygmalion" (Nov-Dec 1914).

Otherwise it was fiction to the fore. Throughout the War the same team of writers appeared, though Jack London was lost after his death in 1916. Frances Hodgson Burnett and Edna Ferber were added to the line-up. One of the more surprising discoveries of *Nash's* was Enid Blyton with the poem "Have You – ?" (Mar 1917). The war inevitably affected the fiction, producing such memorable tales as Kipling's "Mary Postgate" (Sept 1915), and E. P. Oppenheim's series about diplomat Ambrose Lavendale, "The Man Who Could Have Ended the War" (from Mar 1916). But the most noticeable change was with the rising interest in spiritualism. The key that opened the door was an essay by Estelle Stead, daughter of W. T. Stead, "War the Great Awakener" (Nov 1916). This began a thread that continued long after the war and included Marie Corelli's novel "The Young Diana" (began Oct 1917), about a method to perpetuate youth, Conan Doyle's series of articles "The Vital Message" (May-Oct 1919) and several essays by Basil King, starting with "The Abolishing of Death" (Sept 1919).

The War also had its effect on the publishing of *Nash's*. It retained a monthly output but paper restrictions meant that it had to reduce both the quality of the paper from July 1916, and the number of pages, which had almost halved by September 1918. At the same time the price doubled. Yet its circulation continued to rise undaunted, doubling in sales and passing through the 200,000 mark in 1917 during which year it overtook *The London Magazine*, to become the bestselling British monthly fiction magazine. Ever since Hearst had taken over *Nash's* it had borne the banner "Great Britain's Greatest Magazine" and now that was no idle boast. Wartime sales peaked in early 1918 at just over 240,000 and then began to slide. This was almost certainly due to paper rationing limiting the number of copies that could be printed but after the War sales remained at about the same level. Despite the quality of its contributions there was a degree of predictability with the magazine. The same stable of writers, with only a few newcomers, could provide only so much originality. The flair and excitement that had crackled with expectation when Hearst had taken over had settled to a reliable but inevitable pall.

At the start of the 1920s some changes occurred. The magazine had always emphasised strong character stories with a heavy romantic involvement, but most of these were written by men. In the twenties a greater quota of women contributed. Frances Hodgson Burnett, Helen McCormack, Josephine Daskam Bacon, I.A.R. Wylie, Sheila Kaye-Smith, Fanny Heaslip Lea and Fannie Hurst were amongst a new stable of writers who, if not as regular as the old guard, were frequent enough to recharge the batteries. Other writers put in frequent appearances – Ben Ames Williams, H. G. Wells, G. K. Chesterton, Somerset Maugham, James Oliver Curwood – sufficient that although Bruno Lessing, E. P. Oppenheim and others continued to appear, the magazine was signalling a change. There was also a change from social dramas to more adventurous stories – a sign that the "roaring twenties" were emerging. A major scoop was to acquire "The Desert Healer" (Dec 1922-May 1923), the new novel from Edith Maude Hull, author of *The Sheikh* (1919).

The big change came with the April 1923 issue when *Nash's* switched from the old standard size to become a fully-fledged slick. The British edition of *Good Housekeeping* had been launched by Hearst in March 1922 in the full flat format which was becoming the new standard size in the United States. *Nash's* was the first magazine that was primarily fiction orientated to make the change, though *The Home Magazine* had experimented with it in 1920. One of the consequences of the change was to integrate the advertising with the main body of the text – what is called "overmatter" – rather than have an advertising section at the front and the back. This allowed for greater flexibility with the advertising, leading to higher rates and thus more income.

The change allowed for more creative use of artwork. The style of John R. Flanagan was ideal for the exotic fiction now emerging, such as his work for William Ashley Anderson's "Zanzibar" (Aug 1923, *right*). *Nash's* would declare stories as being of the "Far East" or "Far West". There were Somerset Maugham's stories set in the Orient, Cynthia Stockley's stories of the African veldt, John Russell's tales of the South Seas, Achmed Abdullah's tales of Arabia and India and Gouverneur Morris's strange tales in remote places. There were stories of rural America by Irvin S. Cobb and westerns by Frederick Bechdolt and a rare appearance by the pioneer western writer Owen Wister ("Sun Road", Sept 1924). H. G. Wells returned to science fiction, as a vehicle for another of his social studies, with "The Dream" (Oct 1923-May 1924). Rudyard Kipling visited the mystical in "A Madonna of the Trenches" (Sept 1924), whilst Winston Churchill began a series contemplating the fate of civilisation in "Will Mankind Commit Suicide?" (Sept 1924). Even the more traditional stories took a turn for the bizarre. There were more violent murder mysteries and tales of revenge such as "A Streak of Personality" by Richard Washburn Child (May 1923) and "Homeward Bound" by Perceval Gibbon (Jul 1923), whilst G. K. Chesterton's ever popular Father Brown stories became even more "impossible"[6].

Somerset Maugham contributed one of his most controversial serials, "The Painted Veil" (Dec 1924-Jul 1925), in which his thinly disguised characterizations of real people and events led to a lawsuit. Maugham not only revised the story for book publication, but made revisions as it was serialised, which makes the magazine appearance all the more interesting. The editor had to preface later instalments with the now familiar statement: "The Editor begs to inform readers that the characters in this story are purely imaginary and that no reference or allusion is intended to apply to any living person or persons." The controversy stimulated circulation, as Alice Head recalled in her autobiography, where she also remarked that "I shall always regard it as one of the most outstanding novels ever published."[7]

Alice Head had taken over as editor following the death of James McPeake in September 1924. Although McPeake had edited *Nash's* capably, increasing the circulation sixfold, the twenties were a time of change. Head had previously been editor at *Woman at Home* and knew the women's market. She had served as an assistant to McPeake since 1917, but now received Hearst's full blessing. However she was also spending much of her time editing *Good Housekeeping* and to help in the overall management of the magazines she employed Ivor Nicholson. McPeake's son, Alan, also became involved as art editor. Between them they achieved a good balance of fiction and features appealing to both male and female readers.

The female element was dominated in the twenties by Anita Loos who had shot to fame with *Gentlemen Prefer Blondes*. She contributed a sequel to *Nash's*, "Why Not Brunettes?" (Oct 1926-Oct 1927) and also became a columnist. Elinor Glyn remained a regular contributor, including the serial "It" (Apr-Jun 1927), which when transformed for the cinema made the career of Clara Bow as "the 'It' girl". Gertrude Atherton and Arnold Bennett locked horns in a debate guaranteed to raise controversy, "Are Men/Women Mentally Lazy?" (Mar 1928).

For a brief period from May 1927 the old *Pall Mall* was revived as a story magazine and *Nash's* continued in its own right, but they were reunited in October 1929. Apart from retaining a few of its features, such as Edmund Dulac's crossword puzzles, *Pall Mall* was lost within *Nash's*. The title remained *Nash's—Pall Mall*, but the *Pall Mall* logo was often hidden by the cover art and internally the magazine was called simply *Nash's*.

The number of non-fiction features had increased since 1925. Amongst them were several literary reminiscences by Sir Philip Gibbs, the Earl of Birkenhead and J. D. Beresford. In 1927 St John Ervine began an occasional series of literary sketches. Stephen Leacock became a regular contributor, including his well-known essay "Save Me From My Friends" (Jan 1928). Arnold Bennett wrote about "Fear of Middle Age" (May 1928) and the Earl of Birkenhead looked at "The World in 2029" (from Mar 1929). A particularly chilling article was by Sinclair

---

[6] This series (began Dec 1923) appeared in book form as *The Incredulity of Father Brown* (1926).
[7] Alice M. Head, *It Could Never Have Happened* (Heineman, 1939), p. 181.

Lewis's wife, Dorothy Thompson, who raised a genuine dilemma in her life in "Should I Have Killed This Man?" (Dec 1929). She later contributed an insightful article, "I Saw Hitler!" (May 1932), which concluded what an insignificant man he was. The most controversial article about Hitler, however, was Robert Bernay's "Little Man, What Now?" (Sept 1933), which led to *Nash's* being banned in Germany.

By the end of the 1920s Head was devoting almost all her time to *Good Housekeeping* and its spin-off books. Ivor Nicholson moved on to establish his own publishing house. Ivor Brown, who had assisted on *Pall Mall* now assisted on *Nash's*, but in 1930 George Doran, the American publisher who had sold his company to Doubleday and retired to England, took over the editorial rôle. He operated out of the Savoy Hotel where he frequently entertained writers, and his wide network of contacts established a new circle of contributors. Amongst them were A. J. Cronin, Edgar Wallace, Sinclair Lewis, John Masefield, Damon Runyon, Warwick Deeping and Ernest Hemingway. Beverly Nicholls and Aldous Huxley became regular columnists. Doran acquired a new Scaramouche novel, "The Kingmaker" (May-Dec 1931), from Rafael Sabatini, and a new Miss Marple series from Agatha Christie, but perhaps his most bizarre scoop was an article by Benito Mussolini, "Where Will Science Lead Us?" (Nov 1930).

During the 1930s *Nash's* was the highest paying fiction magazine in Britain and attracted all the major writers. It was arguably at its peak during Doran's ebullient editorship. However, affected by poor health, he returned to the United States in 1933 and was succeeded by another American, Richard Meadland. Meadland was young and energetic but, without Doran's circle of contacts, his issues lack the diversity. David Low began a series of foldout paintings with text by Rebecca West, "The Modern Rake's Progress". A. J. Cronin, Henry Williamson, Osbert Sitwell, Geoffrey Household and Alexander Woollcott were amongst the contributors, as well as emerging writers Pamela Frankau, Pamela Hansford Johnson and Mazo de la Roche. There was a Simon Templar story by Leslie Charteris, "The Golden Journey" (May 1934), several Ellery Queen stories and three "novelisations" by H. G. Wells of films derived from his stories,

"Things to Come" (Oct 1935), "The Man Who Could Work Miracles" (Jan 1936) and "The New Faust" (Dec 1936). *Nash's* also ran Ernest Hemingway's noted ambiguous story, "The Short, Happy Life of Francis Macomber" (Oct 1936).

One of the noticeable changes came with the death of Harrison Fisher in 1934. He had provided over two hundred covers for *Nash's* (most originally painted for *Cosmopolitan*) since 1911, and had established the cover image of the pretty girl. Both *Cosmopolitan* and *Nash's* sought to continue that, eventually settling on Bradshaw Crandell to provide a more up-to-date "pin-up" style image. However for a while *Nash's* broke from that mould with a series cartoon-style covers by Philip Zec starting with the December 1936 issue (*left*).

Meadland sought to change the format of *Nash's* from October 1935 with new features and more emphasis on non-fiction. He introduced a letter column and what becomes strikingly evident is the high proportion of women readers and the growing demand for features for women. Meadland complied but, as a consequence, *Nash's* became less appealing to men and more like *Good Housekeeping*. Although *Nash's* retained a high circulation it also had expensive production costs and by 1937 was no longer viable. Much to the regret of Alice Head and others, it merged with *Good Housekeeping* from October 1937. The decision must have been sudden as the only announcement was a special flyer inserted in the last issue.

To keep control of the name, the publisher issued a large format *Nash's Summer Annual* in 1938 with 80 pages on uncoated stock. It ran the usual mix of articles and stories with material by Stella Gibbons, Alec Waugh, Gerald Heard and Ellery Queen but, apart from the photogravure theatrical supplement was lacking in artwork. Shelved during the war *Nash's Annual* was revived as a Christmas release in 1946 and sustained for four winters, each with between 72 to 84 pages in full colour. Contributors included Stuart Cloete, H. E. Bates, John Hersey, V. S. Pritchett, C. S. Forester and A. A. Milne. Each issue proclaimed the hope that the monthly magazine would be revived. But it never was. Historically that is all to the good, as it means *Nash's* remains burned on the twenties and thirties as the high spot of British popular fiction.

Frequency: Monthly.
Publisher: Eveleigh Nash to Jan 1911; thereafter National Magazine Company.
Editors: James Eveleigh Nash, 1909-11; Perriton Maxwell, 1911-15; J. Y. McPeake, 1915-24; Alice Maud Head, 1924-30 (assisted by Ivor Nicholson, 1924-28, Ivor Brown, 1929-30); George Doran, 1930-33; Richard L. Mealand, 1933-37.
Format/Size: Standard pulp; paper changed from wood pulp to quality white weave in Feb 1910; from Mar 1910 issues were mixture of coated full gloss stock and white weave; turned full glossy stock from Oct 1911. Increased to large flat slick from Apr 1923.
Pagination: 160, dropped to 144, Nov 1909; 128, Jan-Feb 1910; 112, Mar 1910; 96, Feb 1911; rose to 120, Mar 1911; 128/132, Oct 1911; 136/140, Jan 1912; dropped to 128, Sep 1914; 112, Jul 1916; 96, Jun 1917; 88, Apr 1918; 78/80, Sep 1918; rose to 92/108 (varied by issue), Mar 1919; 116, Jun 1922. With large format, 140/152 (with variations), from Apr 1923; 124/128, Mar 1929.
Price: 6d; rose to 7d, Feb 1917; 8d, May 1917; 10d, Feb 1918, 1/-, Jun 1918.
Holdings:
Complete run, UK. Bodleian (*Call Number*: Per. 2561 d.66); • Cambridge University Library (*Classmark*: L996.b.36 to Dec 1922; L996.b.28 thereafter).
Substantial run, UK. British Library is missing issues for May, Jun, Aug, Sept 1909; Jan 1915; Jan, Apr, Jun-Aug 1919; Feb-Oct 1920; Sept, Oct 1923; May-Dec 1927; Jan-Dec 1929; Jan-Jul, Sept, Nov 1930; Jan, Feb, Apr-Dec 1935; Jan-Dec 1936; Jan-Sept 1937 (*Shelfmark*: PP.6004.goe). • National Library of Scotland has run Oct 1914-Sept 1937 (*Shelfmark*: K.373).
Complete run, US. Free Library of Philadelphia (*Call Number*: 050 P18).
Substantial run, US. Library of Congress has first series, Apr 1909-Sept 1914 (*Call Number*: AP4.N13); and intermittent thereafter on microfilm (*Call Number*: 05419) missing many single issues, most between Aug 1928 and Sept 1930 and none after Feb 1935. Many other libraries have this same incomplete run on microfilm including Boston Public Library, University of Connecticut, Florida State University, Illinois State University, University of Massachusetts, New York University, University of Rhode Island, University of Rochester, Rutgers University. • New York Public Library has Apr 1909-Mar 1912 and Oct 1914-Sept 1937, incomplete.
Substantial run, Canada. University of Toronto, Robarts Library, has microfilm run as cited above.
Collecting points: Volumes of the original *Nash's* are uncommon. Copies of the Hearst *Nash's* are more common in both bound volumes (which include contents pages) and single issues and a complete run can still be amassed over time. The later annuals are rare.

***

THE NEW MAGAZINE
260 issues. Volume 1, Number 1, April 1909 to Volume 44, Number 260, December 1930.

With the success of *The Story-Teller*, Cassell's issued a new magazine slanted towards the women's market. The rather uninspiring title, *The New Magazine*, was reminiscent of *The Novel Magazine* (where 'novel' meant 'new') which had started the all-fiction magazine ball rolling. Although the same price as *The Story-Teller*, *The New* was fifty pages smaller, but made up for this by running illustrations and a sixteen-page photogravure supplement, "Stage and Stalls", with photographs of leading actors and actresses. This was a feature that had caught on in America in magazines like *Red Book* and was already used in Britain by *The Royal*. The photographs were usually in a shade of green or blue, allowing the feature to be advertised as "colour". It changed to "Play of the Month" in July 1910 and thereafter, apart from a few changes during the War years, remained a standard part of the magazine. Surprisingly, despite this shop-window display, few of the magazine's stories related to the stage.

The last sixteen pages were devoted to a section called "Woman's Kingdom", covering fashion and various domestic matters. This ran until June 1918, when it fell victim to paper shortages, though by then seemed out of place with the "new woman" readership. Throughout its life, except for a few moments of doubt, *The New* was never a love-story magazine and certainly not a "home" magazine. The emphasis was on excitement, adventure and mystery, with dashes of humour and light romance.

At the outset *The New* was part of the Edwardian mindset and took a while to be sure of its readership. It mixed society stories with shop-girl romances and sports stories but it was evident, from the price and the recurring theme of individuals trying to better themselves, that *The New* was being pitched at the lower-middle and upper-working classes. Though the intended market was primarily female, it published sufficient mystery and adventure stories to interest men, and in both cases younger men and women.

The most prolific contributor was Frank H. Shaw. He frequently had two or three stories per issue, most with a naval background but as Grenville Hammerton he contributed the first main series, "The Affairs of Montagu Fleming, M.D." about a doctor detective. In "The Vengeance" (Aug 1909) he produced a powerful story of revenge and mental torture, which demonstrated that *The New* was far from being a docile, unsensational magazine. In fact most early issues carried tales of revenge, revolution and secret societies. In "A Tale of the Terror" (Apr 1910) Baroness Orczy managed to include all three. Of interest is the "Old Pawray" series by Frank Howel Evans (Oct 1909-Feb 1910). It features a detective called Monsieur Poiret, a French policeman retired from the Secret Service and living in London. It has been conjectured that this may have subconsciously inspired Agatha Christie's Poirot.[1]

---

[1] See Margaret Osoba, "The Strange Case of Monsieur Poiret", *Book and Magazine Collector* #195, June 2000, pp. 27-36.

With "The Stolen Rubens" (Jun 1909), editor Newman Flower switched Jacques Futrelle's Thinking Machine stories from *The Story-Teller*, presumably to boost a cross-over readership. Also switched across were Maurice Leblanc's Arsène Lupin series, starting with "The Confessions of Arsène Lupin" (May 1911). It is sometimes the case that an editor will switch a popular series to a new magazine to help boost sales, but such evidence as exists shows that the circulation of *The New* was healthy from the start and remained so well through the War years.[2] It is as likely that with his dextrous editing, Flower had such an abundance of good material that he was able to share it between his magazines simply to meet deadlines and contractual obligations. Flower also switched Sax Rohmer from *Cassell's* with "The Methods of Moris Klaw" (Apr 1913-Jan 1914). Rohmer became a regular contributor including a new Fu Manchu series (Jun 1915-Mar 1916), later collected as *The Devil Doctor* (Methuen, 1916), and, after the War, the potent anti-drug novel, "Dope" (Mar-Sept 1919).

The other prevailing theme was of the emerging independent young woman. Tom Gallon contributed two such series, "Peggy-Wake of Nowhere" (Dec 1910-Mar 1911) and "The Card in the Window" (Apr-Sept 1912), both depicting determined women coping with the world. William Le Queux used the changing social rôle of women to clever effect in "The Indiscretions of a Lady's Maid" (from Feb 1911), but the series that made the most impact was "Life of Youth" by Olive Wadsley (Mar-Aug 1914), about a smart young woman determined to prove herself in a man's world. Wadsley repeated the theme in a slightly more humorous way, better suited to wartime, "Romance" (Mar-Sept 1915).

Frank Shaw, writing as Frank Hubert, explored the other side of the coin, highlighting the importance of the woman-at-home for troops in battle in "Letty's V.C." (Jul 1911). Shaw may also have been the author of the uncredited series "Muriel Bracebridge: Adventuress" (from May 1912). The changing shape of society was also evident in I.A.R. Wylie's poignant series, "The Paupers of Portman Square" (Apr-Sept 1911) about a former well-to-do family who fall on hard times, whilst J. J. Bell's "The Agitator" (Mar 1910) considered the rise of socialism.

The War changed the mood in *The New* as it did in all magazines. There was an initial rush of war-related stories – many by Frank Shaw, but also by Talbot Mundy, S. Walkey, Roland Pertwee and the soon-to-be-famous "Sapper". William Le Queux chose a woman to be his secret agent in "The Silk Purse" (Sept 1915). In "The Coward" (Feb 1916), W. Townend wrote a particularly powerful story of shell-shock and the psychological effect of War. These were tempered by humorous stories and light romances, but steadily gave way to more escapist fiction. One of the most popular post-war themes was stories of the South Seas. *The New* revelled in these, not just after the War but during. It was Olive Wadsley again who led the way with "The Garden of Eden" (Oct 1915), soon followed by Andrew Soutar with the series "Lost Days" (Apr-Jun 1916). The covers, which hitherto had been rather static portraits of women or photographs of actresses, now became highly colorful and enticing, depicting island paradises or exotic lands. Scarcely an issue passed between 1916 and the mid-twenties when the covers, usually by Albert Morrow, did not depict scenes in the South Seas or the Far East. Another favourite motif was the shipwrecked girl alone on a beach or a raft facing unknown odds,

---

[2] The Advertisers' Protection Society noted a circulation figure of 150,000 for *The New*'s first issue, but these were probably gross figures for issues despatched. The first audited figures gave net sales of 96,997 as the average for the year to September 1913. This dropped to 74,720 over the next year, but rose to 103,201 for 1915 and 105,027 for 1916.

almost always illustrating a story by Shaw, Soutar, Wadsley or the other prolific post-War contributor of sea stories, Albert R. Wetjen.

The other escapist area was historical fiction, and *The New* had an especial fondness for stories of the French Revolution and Napoleonic period. Marjorie Bowen, S. Walkey, Claire Pollexfen and inevitably Frank Shaw were amongst the primary contributors and the ever-reliable Max Pemberton contributed a stirring tale of Napoleon's hundred days, "A Daughter of Destiny" (Dec 1918). Baroness Orczy also contributed a new Sir Percy Blakeney story, "How Jean-Pierre Met the Scarlet Pimpernel" (Dec 1916).

Although most of the contributors to *The New* were stock writers from the Cassell stable, some stories were imported from American magazines including those by Samuel Hopkins Adams, John Kendrick Bangs, Edna Ferber, Edith Miniter, Stephen Leacock and Mary Roberts Rinehart. One major British name to adorn the magazine in the immediate post-war years was Robert S. Hichens who, hoping to recapture the success of his *Garden of Allah* (Methuen, 1904) produced another North African adventure, "The Tocsin" (Dec 1919-Feb 1920). Alfred Noyes, who was a regular in *The Story-Teller* also put in a few appearances as did Stacy Aumonier, Horace Annesley Vachell (with a "Quinneys" story, "The Jade Bouddha", December 1920) and music-hall star George Robey.

The big hit of the immediate post-war years, however, brought *The New* back to the independent woman. Old stager Bertram Atkey created the character of Winnie O'Wynn, a bright, single and wily young girl who manages to run rings around men. The series (began Dec 1920) proved such a success that Atkey continued it for the rest of the decade. In between *The New* ran other Atkey stories including a *Sheikh*-imitation desert romance "Harvest of Javelins" (Jan-Oct 1922). Also a success were two serials by Ethel M. Dell, "The Obstacle Race" (Apr 1921-Apr 1922) and "The Unknown Quantity" (May 1924-Apr 1925). Both are reckoned amongst her more mature romances produced at the height of her popularity. Along with the south-seas romances, which continued to dominate *The New*, Dell and Atkey's works epitomised the magazine's immediate post-War years: stories of passion, adventure, freedom and success – all that the young woman wanted.

In September 1924 *The New* increased in size to 174 pages, proclaiming itself "the biggest magazine on the stalls." The extra room allowed it to run a genuine full-length novel starting with the Scarlet Pimpernel in "Jasper Tarkington's Wife", better known in book form as *Pimpernel and Rosemary*. Other novels included Compton Mackenzie's "The Old Man of the Sea" (Oct 1924) and Edgar Wallace's "Big Little Brother" (Mar 1925), though *The New* also reprinted some works from their archives. Ernest Bramah resurrected his blind detective Max Carrados for a new series (Dec 1925-Feb 1926), but probably the most popular mystery series was Bruce Graeme's "Blackshirt" (Dec 1924-Jul 1925) about gentleman cracksman Richard Verrell. It was so successful that it sold over a million copies in book form.

The New managed to continue its unusual stories for a while after it was transferred from Cassell's in 1927. Kobold Knight created the fascinating character of Dr Sun, the Doctor of Souls (from Apr 1927), whilst Sax Rohmer came up with one of his most bizarre series, "The Zone Spider"[1] (Dec 1927-Jun 1928), but these became the exception rather than the rule. With the switch to Amalgamated Press the magazine was rebranded "The Magazine of Humour and

---

[1] This became the first half of the book *The Emperor of America* (Cassell, 1929).

Romance". It was given bright, cheerful covers by Lawson Wood and Thomas Henry. It secured a new P. G. Wodehouse serial, "The Small Bachelor" (Nov 1926-May 1927), plus a sequel to W. A. Darlington's successful *Alf's Button*, "Alf, Bill and a Carpet" (from Dec 1926).

However, *The New* did not fit easily with the new publisher's line-up. Amalgamated Press simply had too many magazines competing for the romance and adventure market, which had also passed its peak by the end of the twenties. Forced to change, *The New* became an odd hybrid of strange mysteries, light romance and humour with work by K.R.G. Browne, Berta Ruck and F. Morton Howard. It also reprinted more stories from the archives. Despite securing a third series from Graeme, "Blackshirt Again!" (Dec 1928-May 1929), the magazine developed an identity crisis which affected its sales. It went rapidly downhill and after December 1930 was merged with *Cassell's*.

The New had always played third fiddle to *The Story-Teller* and *Cassell's* but now and then its melody came to the fore. It was a title to watch but it has become the forgotten Cassell magazine and thus still holds surprises for the researcher.

Frequency: Monthly, but combined issue for Jul/Aug 1926.
Publisher: Cassell to Apr 1927; then Amalgamated Press.
Editors: Newman Flower to 1922; Charles Vivian, 1922-24; Harold Wimbury 1924-27; Clarence Winchester, 1927-30.
Format/Size: Standard pulp. Page count 128 (plus 16 unnumbered photo supplement); rose to 144, Jul 1910; dropped to 112, May 1916; 96, Apr 1918; 80, Aug 1918; rose to 96, Apr 1919; 108/112, Nov 1919; 100/104, Apr 1920; 110/112, Jan 1923; 176, Sep 1924; dropped to 142/146, May 1925; 136/138, Jan 1929.
Price: 4½d, rose to 6d, Aug 1916; 8d, Jun 1917; 9d, Feb 1918; 1/-, May 1918.
Holdings: *Substantial run, UK*. British Library has all issues except Oct 1914-Mar 1915, Jul 1916, Aug 1918, May, Jul 1919, Aug 1923, Jan-Jul 1927; Dec 1930 (*Shelfmark*: PP.6004.god). • The Bodleian has a run Apr 1909-Jun 1929 (*Call Number*: Per. 2561 d.64).
Collecting points: Early bound volumes in green publisher's binding occasionally surface but later individual issues are rare, especially from the 1920s. Bound volumes are undated and can only be identified by the number of stars on the spine.

***

THE NOVEL MAGAZINE
393 issues. Volume 1, Number 1, April 1905 to Volume 66, Number 393, December 1937.

The Novel was the first all-fiction British pulp magazine. It appeared two months after Newnes launched *The Grand*, but though *The Grand* later became an all-fiction magazine, its early issues were a miscellany of fiction and fact. *The Novel* was a replacement for Pearson's *The Home Magazine of Fiction* (see *The Lady's Magazine*), which had switched to all fiction for its last few issues. The man in charge of this change was Percy Everett, Pearson's Editorial Director, who remained the magazine's managing editor for the first few years.

The Novel, as the name implies – relating to "novel" as in "new", not in terms of novel-length stories – was experimental, which shows in the presentation of the contents. Rather than a straightforward selection of stories, Pearson's introduced them from different angles. There

was a "My Best Story" feature introduced by the author. Coincidentally *The Grand* had introduced the same feature, which limited the choice, so *The Novel* concentrated on Pearson's authors, including J. J. Bell, Winifred Graham, Cutcliffe Hyne, Baroness Orczy, B. Fletcher Robinson, Rafael Sabatini, and P. G. Wodehouse during the first three years.

"Stories in Verse" might seem of limited appeal, yet this remained throughout Everett's editorship. One of the first features to be dropped ran extracts from classic works grouped under a particular theme, beginning with "Cupid in Fiction", portraying moments of high romance. A feature that lasted longer than one might expect was "Books in Brief" where, instead of a review section, a writer converted a novel into a short story. Since this was guaranteed to reveal the ending, it would spoil any reader's interest in the book, but it evidently proved popular. The most durable feature was "Half-Minute Stories", humorous anecdotes which remained the magazine's light relief well into the 1930s.

Besides a children's section, "Our Pinafore Pages", which soon faded away, there were two other features which were more enterprising. "Masterpieces of Foreign Fiction" may have been a cheap way of acquiring fiction – in fact about a third of contents of the early issues consisted of reprints in some form or another – but it introduced readers to stories they might not otherwise see. Over the first few years there was scarcely a country in Europe left untouched – there was even a story translated from the Welsh – plus plenty from further afield, including Tibet.

The other feature, which began with the September 1906 issue, was devoted to "First Stories". The editor had commented generally on the number of submissions he had been receiving and devoted several early editorials to advising contributors on the do's-and-don'ts of writing. Through his editorials Everett established an encouraging rapport and new stories poured in. With each new story Everett provided an instructional comment on its strengths and weaknesses. Amongst the hopefuls were a young Oliver Sandys (later Countess Barcynska), then writing under her stage name of Olive Bree (Jan 1907), and Margaret Chute, who became a regular film-and-theatre columnist (Jul 1907).

The remaining fiction, which averaged around ten to twelve stories per issue, fell fairly evenly between mysteries and stories of romance or domestic strife, along with a few adventure or historical stories. The magazine's first serial was "Bardelys the Magnificent" by Rafael Sabatini, his third published novel. Morgan Robertson took readers to sea in "A Latter-day Jonah"; there was intrigue in James Barr's "The Ambassador to the Court of St James" and suspense in a short serial, "The Pillar of Light" by Louis Tracy, carried over from *The Home Magazine*. There was a detective serial from Anna Katherine Green, a war story from Paul Marstone and a domestic tragedy from Carolyn Wells, otherwise all stories were romances.

The big guns had been brought in for the first issue but thereafter, apart from reprints and serial episodes, most of the contributors were unknowns or known for their domestic fiction in women's story-papers. To some extent *The Novel* was a monthly version of a weekly story-paper: no illustrations and, at fourpence, the equivalent of four weeks' worth of penny papers. This may have been the core of the magazine's success in that it was cheap enough to be within the grasp of domestic and manual workers, but with sufficient prestige, through its better known authors, to have a veneer of quality. As a gimmick Pearson's offered to refund the fourpence to any who applied on a form provided in the first issue, arguing it was cheaper to do that than to spend thousands on advertising.

The editor's rapport and undisguised sincerity would also have endeared the magazine to readers who might not otherwise consider the glossier sixpenny monthlies. Over the first two years the editor reported a steady increase in sales. No official circulation figures were ever published but the Advertisers' Protection Society estimated a net sales figure of 55,000 for 1907. This was unchallenged by Pearson's, but was probably on the low side, as all indications from the editorials are that this must have increased significantly over the next few years.

Reprints aside a few authors of note contributed to the early issues. P. G. Wodehouse was still establishing his reputation when he appeared with "Between the Innings" (Jul 1905), and Alice Perrin contributed a tense story of a tiger hunt, "The Spell of the Jungle" (Aug 1905). Ethel M. Dell, who would remain a regular, scored one of the magazine's first successes with a story of romantic intrigue, "The Secret Service Man" (Oct 1906). Others included Alice and Claude Askew, Ruby M. Ayres, J. S. Fletcher, Edgar Jepson and I.A.R. Wylie.

Reprints were seldom noted as such. Conan Doyle's early sensational novel, *The Mystery of Cloomber* (1888) was serialised from December 1908. Some readers may have assumed J. M. Barrie's "A Lady's Shoe" (Apr 1907) was new[1]. This mystery, with its either/or ending, allowed the editor to set a contest for readers to suggest how the story might have ended and this, and similar competitions, became a regular feature over the next few years.

Many stories came from American magazines. The first story in the first issue, an ebullient romance, "No Cinderella" by Harold MacGrath, came from the *Saturday Evening Post*. Doubtless Pearson's were able to get British serial rights in bulk at a cheap rate, and *The Novel*, for most of its life, always gave the appearance of being published "on the cheap". One of the first American authors to appear regularly in *The Novel* was Ambrose Bierce, starting with "An Occurrence at Owl Creek Bridge" (May 1905). Upton Sinclair's autobiographical novel "The Journal of Arthur Stirling" was serialised from September 1906.

The lesser-known names did not mean that all stories were the work of amateurs, and Everett was not prepared to lower his standards. He confided in one of his editorials that he had rejected a story from someone who said they would kill themselves if the story did not sell. He admitted to watching the newspapers closely over the next few days. But it also meant Everett selected some unusual stories with no other obvious market. "Lovely Mum" by Eva M. Bosanquet (May 1905) had apparently been rejected by others because it was "needlessly cruel" and "not sufficiently plausible", even though this potent story of child abuse at a boarding school was based on true events. "An Island Adventure" by J. Sackville Martin (Oct 1907) chronicles the disintegrating effects of being shipwrecked upon a misogynist and a woman. "The Truth" by H. C. Ransom (Nov 1909), follows a day in the life of a man who endeavours to speak only the truth – some ninety years before the film *Liar! Liar!*

One story in *The Novel* at this time is of historical interest: the Dr Thorndyke case, "The Willowdale Mystery" by R. Austin Freeman (Aug 1910). This was the first of his "inverted" detective stories where the reader sees the crime committed and then follows through the

---

[1] First published in *Black & White*, 6 February 1892.

investigation. Everett, presumably uncertain as to how the form would be accepted, ran this story in *The Novel* before he ran the others [eventually collected as *The Singing Bone* (1912)] in *Pearson's*, and thereby established a key date in crime-fiction history.

Such stories, though, were the exceptions and by and large it is clear that *The Novel*, unlike its partners *Pearson's* or *The Royal*, was intended as entertainment for the less discerning masses. Its contents demonstrated it was every bit as much the family magazine as *Pearson's* or *The Strand*, but at a lower level of disposable income.

From 1912 changes took place in the magazine. Charles Vivian[2], who had been an assistant editor on *Pearson's* since 1910, was promoted to the editorship of *The Novel*. He dropped most of Everett's special features and most of the reprints, other than from American sources. He later took a survey to check what type of fiction readers most liked. Top of the list was detective stories followed by love stories, humour, uncanny tales and stories of the stage.[3] Amongst the detective series were "Chronicles of Dennis Chetwynd" by Henry J. Fiddler (from Aug 1912) and "Paul Beck, Detective" by M. McDonald Bodkin (from Feb 1914), which continued sporadically for some years. Talbot Mundy put in a rare appearance in *The Novel* with a long murder story, "The Charles Street Mystery" (Oct 1913). Winifred Graham, a regular contributor, had caused a sensation with her violent anti-Mormon book, *Ezra the Mormon* (1907). *The Novel* serialised the sequel, "In the Meshes of the Mormons" (began Nov 1912), where a young girl is abducted by the sect.

There was a significant increase in weird stories. When Vivian took over he published at least one strange story per issue. With the April 1913 issue this became a regular "uncanny tale" slot which ran for the next ten years and included stories by A. M. Burrage, Michael Kent, Elliott O'Donnell, E. R. Punshon, Violet Quirk, Robert W. Sneddon, H. de Vere Stacpoole and Roy Vickers. Two anthologies were compiled from the series.

Perhaps the most "uncanny tale" *The Novel* ran, albeit unintentionally, was "The White Ghost of Disaster" by Mayn Clew Garnett. This appeared in the June 1912 issue, which went to press two months before, just days before the *Titanic* disaster. Yet this story, about a liner striking an iceberg with terrible consequences, has a remarkable number of similarities, including the same speed of the ship.[4]

Edgar Wallace became a contributor almost the moment Vivian took over, with a "Sanders of the River" story "The Education of the King" (Feb 1912[5]). He remained a regular for the next decade, writing the wartime series, "Clarence – Private" (Dec 1914-Jun 1915) and "The Fighting Scouts" (Oct 1918-May 1919), about Scots airman Tam o' the Scoots. Sax Rohmer also contributed a long serial, "The Quest of the Sacred Slipper" (Sept 1913-Apr 1914) which did not appear in book form until 1919.

Under Vivian, *The Novel* had come alive but his opportunity to develop the magazine was curtailed by the outbreak of War. Vivian signed up. He was replaced by Arthur Applin before he too, was called up, when Roy Vickers took over. Vickers was of a similar mind to Vivian

---

[2] Not to be confused with mystery and adventure writer E. Charles Vivian.
[3] Results reported in the March 1914 issue.
[4] The story had appeared in America in the May 1912 issue of *The Popular Magazine*, which had already been printed at the time of the incident. The story can be found in *The Wreck of the Titanic Foretold?*, edited by Martin Gardner (Prometheus Books, 1998).
[5] Originally published in *Weekly Tale-Teller*, 22 January 1910.

and maintained the status quo, keeping a balance of mystery and romance stories alongside the inevitable demand for war-related fiction. E. Phillips Oppenheim contributed an espionage serial, "The Double Traitor" (Jan-Aug 1917), Marjorie Bowen delved into "Crimes of Old London" (from Nov 1917) and W. A. Williamson (who would later edit *Pan* and *20-Story Magazine*) began a series about poet-detective Christopher Strain with "The Poet and the Postage Stamp" (Nov 1918). Berta Ruck, Ruby M. Ayres and Clare Thornton provided most of the romance and Ellis Parker Butler sustained the light relief with occasional help from W. Heath Robinson.

Vickers handed the reins back to Vivian during 1919, probably with the April issue, though the transition was too smooth to notice. It was in that issue that the editor proclaimed that *The Novel* aimed to be full of "bright, readable, up-to-date stories. You will not find yarns of Tudor days or war stories of the Roman invasion. Nor will you find the very 'high-brow' tale, all character drawing and analysis." The cover reflected female liberation with a woman aeronaut (*right*), and over the next year most covers portrayed women in new guises. The feminist angle was strong and received a further boost with the serialisation of Elinor Glyn's sequel to her notorious *The Visits of Elizabeth* (Duckworth, 1900), "Elizabeth's Daughter" (Feb-May 1919), announced as promising "demure naughtiness and delicious worldly wisdom."

In a flood of post-war escapism the stories emphasised adventure, mystery and intrigue. From Beatrice Grimshaw, the Queen of the South Seas, came "The Terrible Island" (Jun 1919-Jan 1920). Edgar Wallace started a series about Wise Simon, police reporter (Jul 1919) and, with "The Vanishing Colonel" (Feb 1920) Keble Howard began an unusual series about a retired colonel turned detective, who can render himself invisible. The "uncanny tale" slot continued and there were other unusual stories, one of the best being "Something" by Albert Payson Terhune (Dec 1919). A renowned dog enthusiast, Terhune wrote a poignant war story of a collie with a psychic link to his master in the trenches. Equally powerful was "The Destroyer" by Michael Kent (May 1920) where an inventor discovers a way to destroy all matter absolutely and wonders how he might best use it.

In 1922 Vivian left to take over editorship of *Cassell's Magazine*, and the magazine's golden days were over. He was succeeded by Miss N. W. Kennedy. The change in *The Novel* was abrupt. The uncanny feature stopped and although a few weird stories appeared, including those by Ursula Bloom, Agatha Christie[6] and Richmal Crompton, *The Novel* became a magazine of romance fiction. There was occasional humour from F. Morton Howard and Evadne Price, with her series about ten-year-old terror, Jane Turpin. There were adventure and mystery stories, mostly imported from America, by Sewell Peaslee Wright, Albert R. Wetjen and Vingie E. Roe, plus the early stories about "The Major" by L. Patrick Greene, but these were seldom more than one per issue. Stories of romantic intrigue, the perils of marriage and domestic strife dominated. Fannie Hurst, Ethel Mannin, Kathlyn Rhodes, Phyllis Hambledon,

---

[6] Christie's "A Trap for the Unwary" (May 1923) was her first non-Poirot short story.

Berta Ruck and especially Ruby M. Ayres were now the main contributors. It reprinted W. Somerset Maugham's popular novel, "The Painted Veil" (from Dec 1925), with the text revised from its original run in *Nash's* the year before. There were occasional surprises. Alec Waugh contributed "A Long Weekend" (Dec 1935), and the aviatrix Amy Johnson contributed "All Aboard, London – Paris" (Jun 1937), which was more of a travelogue than a story. Some stories sought to get beneath the veneer of romance. Ella Scrymsour's "Man's Law" (Oct 1934) follows the trial of a long-abused wife who takes revenge on her husband, but finds the law biased. But otherwise a dust of predictability settled over the magazine.

It remained profitable, partly by using many reprints and increasing the print size whilst reducing the page count, but *The Novel* had become an anachronism, unable to match the lure of the glossy slicks. At the end of 1937 it merged with its old rival *The Grand*. *The Novel* was never a sophisticated magazine but it was a pioneer and, during its first decade, established a strong bond with its readers that must have inspired hundreds of would-be writers. By so doing it paved the way for the fiction pulps that were to follow.

Frequency: Monthly.
Publisher: C. Arthur Pearson.
Editors: Percy W. Everett, 1905-11; Charles Vivian; 1912-14; Arthur Applin, 1914; Roy Vickers, 1915-18; Charles Vivian, 1919-22; Miss N. W. Kennedy, 1923-37.
Format/Size: Standard pulp. Page count 144, dropped to 134/136, Oct 1906; 118/120, Oct 1914; 100, Jun 1916; 112, Dec 1916; 84, Jun 1917; 72, by Jul 1918; 76/80, Dec 1918; 96/100, Jun 1919; thereafter fluctuated between 96-108.
Price: 4d; rose to 4½d, Sep 1911; 6d, Dec 1916; 7d, Dec 1917; 10d, by Jul 1918; back to 9d, Feb 1919; rose to 10d, Nov 1920; back to 9d, by Jan 1923; dropped to 7d, by Oct 1935.
Anthologies: *Uncanny Stories* (London: Pearson, 1916), *More Uncanny Stories* (London: Pearson, 1918), both volumes combined and reissued as *Ghost Stories and Other Queer Tales* (London: Pearson, 1931). All anonymous but probably compiled by Roy Vickers or Percy Everett.
Holdings:
Substantial run, UK. British Library run is on microfilm and is missing May 1911, Oct 1917-Jun 1918, Aug 1918, Oct, Dec 1920, Jan, Feb 1921, Oct 1921–Dec 1922, Oct, Nov 1924, Feb-Jun 1925, Jan-Jun 1928, Oct 1934-May 1936, Jul-Sept 1936 (*Shelfmark*: PP.6018.taa; *Microfilm*: Mic.C.1839). • The Bodleian is missing Apr 1913-May 1919, Aug 1919, Sep 1928, Jun 1933, Oct and Dec 1934, Apr and Sep 1935, Jul 1936-Dec 1937 (*Call Number*: Per. 2561 d.28). • National Library of Scotland has issues Apr 1905-Mar 1906 only (*Shelfmark*: U.446).
Partial run, US. There are no substantial runs in the US. The University of California, Southern Regional Library Facility has volumes 1-8, Mar1905-Apr 1909 only.
Substantial run, Australia. University of Queensland has all issues except Jul-Dec 1910 and Jan-Jun 1934 (*Reference*: PR1309.S5 N6).
Collecting points: The publisher's bound volumes in attractive pink decorative cloth are rare. Individual issues surface infrequently and long runs are uncommon, especially the wartime issues. No complete run is known.

* * *

THE PALL MALL MAGAZINE

286 issues. Volume 1, Number 1, May 1893 to Volume 54, Number 257, September 1914; 257 issues. Merged with *Nash's Magazine* as *Nash's and Pall Mall Magazine* (see under *Nash's Magazine*) but revived as PALL MALL MAGAZINE for new series, Volume 1, Number 1, May 1927 to Volume 5, Number 5, September 1929; 29 issues.

Pall Mall was one of the most attractive of the popular monthly magazines of the 1890s. Although it appeared in the wake of *The Strand*, it was no imitation, and might have appeared regardless of *The Strand*'s success. If it had any progenitor it was *The English Illustrated Magazine*, as both celebrated beautiful artwork, and championed the aesthetic movement.

Pall Mall was the literary companion to the *Pall Mall Gazette*, a newspaper that had been acquired in 1892 by the American millionaire William Waldorf Astor. Astor had moved to London and wished to be involved in the newspaper world as a means of promoting his political views. He had converted the *Gazette* from a radical to a conservative paper and, in the process, had replaced most of the editorial staff. The new editor, Henry Cust, was, however, no mere puppet and legend has it that *Pall Mall Magazine* was born because Cust refused to publish certain material from Astor, advising that it was better suited to a general-interest magazine. Astor, though, had further motives. He was a highly cultured man, with a passion for art and fine living. *Pall Mall Magazine* became his indulgence, an opportunity to explore, encourage and enjoy all aspects of art and literature.

Astor agreed a publishing arrangement with the firm of George Routledge, but it remained his property.[1] Their production was first class, both in the individual monthly issues and the high-class bound volumes in their distinctive blue and gold bindings designed by Linley Sambourne. The agreement assured that Astor would underwrite any losses arising and the magazine gave the impression of there being no expense spared. H. G. Wells described Astor's attitude as "fine regardlessness of expenditure."[2]

Astor secured not one editor, but two, Lord Frederick Hamilton and Sir Douglas Straight. All three were members of the Carlton Club and both Hamilton and Straight were old Harrovians. Hamilton, though only thirty-six, had already had a varied career in the Diplomatic Service and had been a Member of Parliament since 1885. Straight, still only forty-eight, had recently retired as the High Court Judge at Allahabad. He had served as a newspaperman before being called to the bar and had written several pseudonymous books in the 1860s. Hamilton records nothing of his days with *Pall Mall* in his trilogy of autobiographies and Straight also kept quiet on the matter so there is no record of how their rôles were divided.

---

[1] There is no mention of the magazine in F. A. Mumby's *The House of Routledge* (Routledge, 1934), suggesting that this was solely a business arrangement and Routledge's had no other relationship with it.
[2] H. G. Wells, *Experiment in Autobiography* (London: Gollancz, 1934), p. 373.

Recollections by writers, however, suggest that Hamilton worked on the artistic presence of the magazine, whilst Straight commissioned the articles and fiction, with doubtless much overlap.

It was evident from the start that the magazine was not aimed at the same market as *The Strand*. It was priced at 1/-, and its emphasis on artistic and literary quality set it above the more populist magazines. From the outset, *Pall Mall's* identity was shaped by its illustrated and literary features, most noticeably the poetry that opened each issue, illuminated by artists of the pre-Raphaelite or art nouveau schools. The artwork, especially that by Vera Christie and Abbey Altson, was decidedly *risqué* if never overtly erotic, but it certainly put the magazine beyond the purview of most mild-mannered readers. Starting in the first issue was a series of articles on alchemy, "The Black Art" by James Mew, which included artwork by Aubrey Beardsley. Beardsley also illustrated a wonderfully decadent vampire story, "The Kiss of Judas", by X.L., alias of the notorious Julian Field (*below*).

Pall Mall delighted in encouraging the exotic. There were poems by Paul Verlaine and Hamilton Aïde. One poem, "A Beauty to Her Mirror" by H. N. Robbins (Dec 1894), was set in reverse type so it could be read only in a mirror. It was accompanied by one of Altson's resplendent nudes (*right*). Articles included "Strange Cities of the Far East" by George (later Lord) Curzon (from Jun 1893) and "Sir John Mandevile, Liar" by George Layard (Feb 1894), about the lure of alien cultures. Stories likewise

emphasised the strange and unusual, like "The Soul of Daphne" by Katherine Carmarthen (Jul 1893, illustrated by Housman), "Parpon the Dwarf" by Gilbert Parker (Mar 1894) and several by Astor himself. Astor's stories were either of the supernatural or set in ancient worlds, especially Egypt. Amongst its more overt supernatural stories was one of M. R. James's first ghost stories, "Lost Hearts" (Dec 1895), M. P. Shiel's "Huguenin's Wife" (Apr 1895), and Robert S. Hichens's "A Reincarnation" (Aug 1895). It was *Pall Mall* that began Hichens's reputation. Though he had sold earlier stories, Douglas Straight recognised his talent when he bought "The Collaborators" (Jan 1894). When Hichens submitted his novel, "The Green Carnation", which satirised the aesthetic movement, Straight, knowing it was unsuitable for the magazine, recommended it to publisher William Heinemann. It was a huge success.

As a counterbalance to the exotic were reactionary political and social discussions. A regular column was "Vexed Questions" where contributors considered issues such as Irish Home Rule, the payment of MPs, and the need for the Labour Party. Israel Zangwill was the first of several literary columnists producing a monthly causerie. These would later include Arthur Quiller-Couch, W. E. Henley and G. K. Chesterton. There were also many articles on military exploits, particularly the fall of Napoleon and the rise of Wellington.

The magazine was distinctive in setting its text in one column rather than two per page, a format that allowed the best use of illustrative material which could flow across the page.

Astor, anticipating that the magazine would grow and develop, gave it the motto "*vires acquirit eundo*", from Virgil's *Aenead*, meaning "she gains strength as she goes."

This all gave the magazine an elitist feel, like an exclusive club, becoming closely associated with the aesthetic movement.[3] It thus rose above most of the popular magazines, but likewise remained aloof from the more decadent magazines like *Yellow Book*. It also had a measured, leisurely feel. Many of its stories and features were longer than those in the punchier *Strand*, clearly intended to be read by men of leisure. It did, at times, allow women and children into its portals, though even here some of the children's stories, such as "Princess Crystal's Quest" by Dorothy Stephens (Jan 1895), were presented as literary fantasies, providing an opportunity for extravagant artwork.

Yet, despite this exclusiveness, *Pall Mall* was not totally removed from the world of popular literature. It did not develop the popular story series, which had established the *The Strand* and was imitated by its rivals, but it did publish stories by Arthur Conan Doyle and Cutcliffe Hyne. It also ran historical fiction by Stanley J. Weyman, Irish fiction by Bram Stoker, and a drawing-room play by Mary E. Braddon. It also published one of H. Rider Haggard's novels, although "Joan Haste" (Sept 1894-Jul 1895), about the problems of a girl locked in a marriage, was not typical of his work. More typical of *Pall Mall's* fiction was one of George Meredith's late serials, "Lord Ormont and His Aminta" (Nov 1893-Jul 1894) and Thomas Hardy's story "An Imaginative Woman" (Apr 1894).

Early in *Pall Mall's* life there was an adverse reaction, particularly amongst the American literary establishment, to Astor investing in a British publication. Zangwill raised the point in one of his "Without Prejudice" columns (May 1894), noting that many American magazines, such as *Harper's, Century, Scribner's* and *Lippincott's*, were well supported in Britain and that it was high-time a British magazine should benefit from American money. The problem, however, was more about Astor subsidising a British magazine rather than supporting his own country's publications. The lavishness of the early issues – it ran colour plates from the November 1893 issue[4] – must have seen the magazine running at a loss, despite its high cover price. Also the magazine became known for its generous payment. Wells noted that "the rate of pay was exceptionally good for the time,"[5] whilst Horace Annesley Vachell, then just emerging as a writer, recalled that in addition to encouragement from Hamilton he was sent "the biggest cheque I had ever received for a short story."[6] Rider Haggard was offered £1,500 (close to £100,000 today) in advance of his writing the serial "Joan Haste".[7] Nevertheless, records in the Routledge archives suggest that after the first year the magazine was making a profit, as Routledge owed Astor a return of £5,205 on the magazine's sales.

Despite its elitism, *Pall Mall* was a remarkable production in its first few years, and even though little of its fiction stands out, the whole was greater than the sum of its parts. Unfortunately this did not continue through the rest of the decade. This may in part be due to the departure of Douglas Straight in 1896 when he took up editorship of the *Pall Mall Gazette*

---

[3] There was a detailed article, "The Aesthetes", in the January 1895 issue.
[4] The *Illustrated London News* had used colour as early as 1855 but it was not common in the popular fiction magazines. Newnes had also used colour in *The Million* launched in 1891.
[5] Wells, *Experiment in Autobiography*, p. 373.
[6] Letter by Vachell to *Pall Mall*, May 1927, p. 2.
[7] See D. S. Higgins, *H. Rider Haggard, The Great Storyteller* (London: Cassell, 1981), p. 154.

in February. Although George R. Halkett came on board as art editor, Hamilton was faced with acquiring all the magazine's contents and the overall quality dropped. It was always beautiful but seemed of less substance. A few items stand out, in some ways because they were untypical of the content. There was Anthony Hope's Ruritanian adventure, "Rupert of Hentzau" (Dec 1897-Jul 1898), matched by Cutcliffe Hyne's "Prince Rupert the Buccaneer" (Apr-Jul 1898). Although Edith Nesbit's stories of Oswald Bastable, which began with "Good Hunting" (Apr 1898), were a delight, they felt as if they had escaped from *The Strand*. Yet the Nesbit stories, along with H. G. Wells's sequence, "A Story of the Days to Come" (Jun-Oct 1899), were a sign of a change that would make *Pall Mall* more populist in the coming years. Hamilton must also be acknowledged for publishing some of the earliest weird fiction by Algernon Blackwood ("A Haunted Island", April 1899) and Walter de la Mare ("The Giant" as Walter Ramal, June 1899). He also published Robert Louis Stevenson's posthumous novel, "St. Ives" (Nov 1896-Nov 1897), completed by Quiller Couch.

Hamilton stepped down as editor in December 1900. It must have been a sudden decision as it is noted only by a slip inserted into the issue. The note, probably written by Astor himself, thanks Hamilton for having "done so much to maintain the best traditions of English periodical literature." The key word is "traditions". Throughout the 1890s *Pall Mall* had sought to maintain a literary and artistic standard in a rapidly changing world. That image made *Pall Mall* special, but it would not last long into the new century.

George Halkett, the art editor, now took over full editorial duties, working under managing editor Frederick Higginbottom. It was a challenging rôle. Entering a new century, Halkett needed to sustain the literary and artistic standards of the magazine yet incorporate the best of the new. He succeeded remarkably well. The most obvious immediate change, albeit superficial, was a shift to two columns a page. This, and its affect on the artistic format of the magazine, made it appear conformist and in keeping with *The Strand* and its rivals, though it was still closer to *English Illustrated* and *Cassell's* in content and appearance.

The magazine also became more forward-looking. This reflected the zeitgeist of the *fin de siècle*, and *Pall Mall* endeavoured to get to grips with scientific advance. Articles appeared on "Signalling to Mars", the development of the submarine, prehistoric monsters, how long our coal reserves would last, and Polar exploration – all within Halkett's first few months.

Halkett also tried to remove some of the elitism and make literature more accessible. One of his best ideas was to include a series of lively interviews of literary figures conducted by William Archer. Called "Real Conversations", these were so brightly transcribed that the reader felt in the room. Following Arthur Wing Pinero (Mar 1901) came Thomas Hardy (Apr 1901) talking about supernaturalism, George Moore (Jul 1901) bemoaning the degradation of art, W. S. Gilbert (Sept 1901) revealing his anti-hunting views and publisher William Heinemann (Apr 1902) questioning the need for literary agents.

Alongside these, Halkett commissioned William Sharp to write a series on "Literary Geography", which explored locations with strong literary associations. Halkett also introduced "The Round Table", which allowed contributions from anyone about anything. Although at the outset its main purpose was to promote political or literary views the feature developed into a miscellany of debate, anecdotes, poetry, caricatures and even short fiction. Max Beerbohm was a regular contributor. G. K. Chesterton, who had started a "Books to Read" column in

September 1901, was more likely to appear in "Round Table", putting forth his views about various authors' careers, including H. G. Wells, Victor Hugo and Bret Harte.

Halkett also liked to develop controversial issues. He reopened the debate on who the real author of Shakespeare's plays might be;[8] he ran several articles on how vulnerable England was to invasion, plus features on reincarnation and whether there was life on Mars. Perhaps the most notorious item was W. E. Henley's attack upon the memory of Robert Louis Stevenson in his review of Graham Balfour's biography, *The Life of Robert Louis Stevenson* (Methuen, 1901).[9] It brought a howl of protest and caused *Pall Mall* to publish a letter in response.

Halkett continued to promote the magazine's artistic importance and develop new talent. He had already introduced Sidney H. Sime and W. Heath Robinson during his days as art editor and was quick to commission work from Edmund Dulac, Ernest H. Shepard, Arthur Rackham and Charles Robinson. Their style was ideal for the exotic image *Pall Mall* still wished to present, and particularly for the increasing number of children's stories it was running. Edith Nesbit now appeared regularly although her main home remained at *The Strand*. At the same time, though, much of the artwork was being supplanted by photographs. Halkett appreciated the potential of the medium in the hands of creative photographers. He used new printing techniques to the full to run many evocative location shots in major cities.

With the emphasis on presentation, literary discussion and provocative articles, fiction took something of a back seat. With a few exceptions, *Pall Mall* ran little of lasting merit during Halkett's editorship. The exceptions include Conrad's tense sea story and character study "Typhoon" (Jan-Mar 1902), George Moore's "Home-sickness" (Sept 1902), and, with "White and Yellow" (Feb 1905), the start of a string of stories by Jack London.

The January 1905 issue contained a number of highlights. There was a new poem by Thomas Hardy, the start of Conrad's series of sketches, "The Mirror of the Sea", a new series of Raffles stories by E. W. Hornung and the first episode in H. G. Wells's new serial, "Kipps". Arnold Bennett recorded in his journal that according to Wells, Halkett had been hesitant about accepting "Kipps", uncertain that *Pall Mall's* readership "were interested in quite such a narrow range."[10] Although Halkett was not so misguided as to reject "Kipps", it suggests that his understanding of literature was not as sharp as his understanding of art. Yet he had successfully guided *Pall Mall* into the early years of the twentieth century and had removed many of the trappings that had made it elitist. *Pall Mall* was at its most exuberant during Halkett's editorship.

Those early 1905 issues were the last Halkett was to edit. *Pall Mall* underwent a fundamental change in order to compete directly with the sixpenny monthlies. From January 1905 it reduced its cover price to sixpence and increased its print run to 200,000.[11] Halkett oversaw the change along with his successor Charles Morley, the nephew of John Morley who had been editor of the once radical *Pall Mall Gazette* during 1881-83 and also of *Macmillan's Magazine*. Charles had also served on the *Gazette*, but was much less radical than his uncle. If anything, he was ultra conservative. As a journalist rather than artist, Morley switched the balance in *Pall Mall's* content. Within two years of his assuming control the magazine had

---

[8] "Did Lord Bacon write Shakespeare's Plays?" by George Stronoach (Feb 1902).
[9] "R.L.S." by W. E. Henley (Dec 1901).
[10] see Vincent Brome, *H. G. Wells* (Longmans, Green, 1952), p. 74.
[11] As reported in *The Times*, 23 December 1904.

become almost identical to all the other popular monthlies on the stands. Although illustrations remained an integral part, the art element was reduced, replaced by sketches or photographs.

The quota of fiction increased considerably, although much of it was still not by major names. Nevertheless the magazine could boast Joseph Conrad, serialising both "Gaspar Ruiz" (Jul-Oct 1906) and "The Duel" (Jan-May 1908); Eden Phillpotts, whose Dartmoor stories now appeared regularly; and Cutcliffe Hyne, with his serial, "The Trials of Commander McTurk" (Sept 1905-Jul 1906). Edith Nesbit continued her children's stories and there were contributions from Arnold Bennett, Somerset Maugham, E. F. Benson, Fiona Macleod, Oliver Onions, A.S.M. Hutchinson, the Baroness von Hutten, Ernest Bramah, Jack London, Arthur Morrison, R. Austin Freeman, Rafael Sabatini, E.M. Forster, Walter de la Mare and John Masefield. It also ran "The Barford Snake" (May 1909), which Edgar Wallace regarded as his breakthrough sale, though he had been selling to *Ideas* and other papers for several years.

An article about H.G. Wells and his work in the December 1907 issue served as a prelude to the serialisation of "The War in the Air" (Jan-Dec 1908). The novel, along with the harrowing illustrations by A. C. Michael, fed the growing fascination with the conquest of the air, the subject of an article by Count Zeppelin in the June 1909 issue. The fascination with air travel contrasted oddly with the historical fiction that still dominated *Pall Mall*, in particular the stories and novels by H. C. Bailey. These included the Elizabethan, "Raoul, Gentleman of Fortune" (May-Dec 1906), "The God of Clay" (Jan-Dec 1907) about Napoleon, the series, "The Pageant of England" (May-Oct 1908), and "The Lonely Queen" (Jul-Nov 1910) about Elizabeth I.

The switch in emphasis on fiction took a strange turn from the July 1909 issue. The magazine added a "Pall Mall Story Book" supplement. Initially 22 pages it grew, settling at 64 pages with occasional fluctuations. This was an unillustrated section tucked away at the back of the magazine, consisting entirely of short stories, mostly very short, and published on cheap paper. This was Morley's approach to capturing the public's interest in all-fiction magazines, following the success of *The Novel* and *The Story-Teller*. Most of the stories were light and inconsequential though there were some good pieces by Thomas Burke, Charles G.D. Roberts, E. R. Punshon, J. S. Fletcher and May Wynne. What made it strange was that stories also appeared in the main glossy part of the magazine, with the added bonus that those were illustrated. The result was a two-tier magazine with the impression that those in the "Story Book" were lesser items – as indeed many were. The experiment lasted on and off for over three years. During this period *Pall Mall* was one of the thickest magazines on the stands (rivalled only by the revamped *Cassell's Magazine* after April 1912). It maintained an average of 186 pages per issue and 250 for the Christmas specials –270 pages for December 1912.

By then other changes were in hand. Despite cutting its costs, *Pall Mall* was running at a loss and Astor called it a day. It was reported that he had only sustained it because his wife was fond of the magazine,[12] but in October 1912 he sold it to the firm of Iliffe & Sons for a reputed £1,250. He retained the *Pall Mall Gazette* and the more profitable *Observer* for two more years until he sold these in a fit of pique.[13]

---

[12] See *A.P.S. Monthly Circular*, November 1912.
[13] See *New York Times* 14 July 1914 (pp. 1, 3) for details of a quarrel that erupted between Astor and his son and daughter-in-law that led to the peremptory sale of both papers.

Iliffe was a small firm that produced specialist magazines and guide-books. It had launched *The Autocar* as far back as 1895 and had employed the young Alfred Harmsworth as editor of *Bicycling News* in 1886. It also published *The Aero*, one of Britain's earliest aeronautical magazines, and these specialist publications remained its main output for most of its life. The acquisition of *Pall Mall* was thus somewhat unusual and suggested that Iliffe was looking to expand. Edward Iliffe later became Baron Iliffe and a major newspaper magnate. Although Charles Morley's name had disappeared from the magazine's masthead in 1907 he had continued to edit the magazine to the last Astor issue, but he did not pass over to the new publisher. He was probably succeeded by Hubert Fitchew who is recorded as editor in 1914.

Under Iliffe a balance was restored between fiction and articles with a stronger level of contributor. Both Hilaire Belloc and T. P. O'Connor became columnists and there were features on sport and the theatre. G.K. Chesterton transferred his Father Brown stories from *The Story-Teller* with "The Wisdom of Father Brown" (from May 1913). Charles G. D. Roberts contributed tales about the days when Earth was young, and there were stories by Marjorie Bowen, H. Rider Haggard, W. J. Locke, Oliver Madox Hueffer, P. G. Wodehouse, Compton Mackenzie, Rafael Sabatini and H. de Vere Stacpoole.

The magazine celebrated its twenty-first anniversary in May 1914 when the editor remarked on its "illustrious tradition", and that it was "based on the assumed existence of intelligent and cultivated people." Iliffe was endeavouring to recultivate the idealism and elitism of the original *Pall Mall*, albeit with less ostentation. Plans were afoot to considerably increase its size and the volume of fiction. The editor announced the plans in the July 1914 issue, remarking that the August issue would become "the largest sixpenny monthly magazine in the world." In addition the paper would change from coated stock to non-coated and the loss of high quality pictures suggests that *Pall Mall* was seeking to follow the route taken by *Cassell's Magazine*, and change to an all-fiction pulp.

But it didn't happen. A week after that issue went on sale *Pall Mall* was sold to Hearst's National Magazine Company, which also ran *Nash's Magazine*. When the August issue arrived on the 17 July, it was the same format as before and announced that from the next issue *Pall Mall* would merge with *Nash's*. Hearst had wanted the title, but with the threat of War the likelihood of paper rationing would make running the two magazines difficult. Just five days after the sale, the assassination of Archduke Ferdinand propelled the world into the Great War. That would change the face of publishing forever, and *Pall Mall* was one of the first casualties.

There was a huge outcry from the reading public and *Pall Mall* had a reprieve for just one issue. A belated September issue appeared on September 1, clearly assembled in a hurry, as only half the pages were numbered and at least one story, "In the Bilges" by Frank Chase, had been set in type for *Nash's*. There was one further Father Brown story, "The God of the Gongs" but most of the stories previously announced still did not appear, amongst them Conrad's "The Spoiled Smile".[14]

Although *Pall Mall* ceased to exist after September 1914, it continued in name in *Nash's and Pall Mall* for another twenty-three years. *Nash's* assumed the volume numbering of *Pall Mall* so one could argue, technically, that it was *Nash's* that had folded and *Pall Mall* continued, but in practice the magazine took on the guise of *Nash's*.

---

[14] This appeared in the US as "Because of the Dollars", *The Metropolitan Magazine*, September 1914.

When the editor announced the merger with *Nash's* he said of *Pall Mall* that "During the twenty-one years of its existence it has published more important contributions to English literature by more important authors than all the other British monthly magazines combined. The history of the *Pall Mall Magazine* is the history of the best contemporary literature in these islands." He may be excused his hyperbole, but it remains true that *Pall Mall* set itself high standards and for much of its lifetime came close to attaining them regardless of fashion in the rest of publishing. But despite Astor's fortune, which could have sustained *Pall Mall*, it could not exist in total isolation and had to reflect the changing demands of the public, and it was this that most adversely affected the magazine. Its editors and publishers clung to Astor's ideals whilst trying to adapt to the mainstream, and the pieces never quite fitted together. The result was a melange that contained some of the best works of art and literature alongside some of the most idiosyncratic and self-indulgent. Surprisingly the end result retained a unique if disjointed appeal. Of all the popular fiction magazines of the period 1890-1914, the *Pall Mall* was the exception that proved the rule.

*

It was not the last the world would see of *Pall Mall*. In a somewhat misguided experiment in May 1927 *Nash's* split and *Pall Mall* re-emerged. In the intervening years *Nash's—Pall Mall* had upgraded to become a large flat glossy slick magazine and had gained an equally handsome companion *Good Housekeeping*. When *Pall Mall* was revived it was issued in the old standard format on near-pulp stock with no illustrations. It was still priced at 1/-, as was

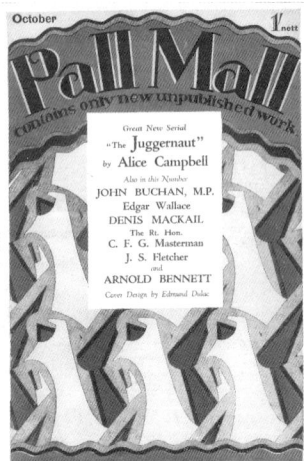

Nash's, which continued in the fully illustrated slick format, so *Pall Mall* was immediately at a disadvantage on the stands. 1927 was a difficult time to launch a fiction magazine, even one with such a venerable name. The other magazines were fading and within the next few years most would fold or switch to the large flat format. *Pall Mall*'s move was a backward step.

The emphasis was on fiction, though ironically one of its more popular features were a non-fiction series by Helena Normanton about major criminals and another by Elinor Glyn on the nature of romance. The magazine promoted the fact that its fiction was all new, a swipe at the number of reprints being used in magazines at this time. The mixture was typical – light romance, domestic tragedies, adventure stories, crime and mystery and even the occasional western. The magazine had an initial success with the serialisation of Arnold Bennett's new novel, "The Vanguard" (May-Dec 1927). Other highlights in the first few issues include D. H. Lawrence's "Two Blue Birds" (Jun 1927), comparing the consequences of female emancipation upon two different women, and John Buchan's adventure series (Sept 1927-May 1928) later collected as *The Runagates Club* (Hodder, 1928). From the August issue, Edgar Wallace appeared with a series featuring Detective Oliver Rator – "the Orator" – of C.I.D., whilst Maurice Leblanc contributed a "bogus" Arsène Lupin series featuring the equally duplicitous character of Jim Barnett (Dec 1927-Aug 1928). There were stories by Valentine Williams, Robert Hichens, Storm Jameson and one of Leslie Charteris's early pre-Saint stories "Bright Young People" (Jan 1928).

As one might have expected *Pall Mall* tried to present an unusual cover, the one visual element it could promote. *Pall Mall* went for an all out *art deco* design by Edmund Dulac. The design – a series of interlocking grids – remained the same on each cover but the colours within the grids changed. From the following February *Pall Mall* presented new primitive covers by Freda Beard and Stella Steyn. Steyn's work reflects her time in Paris where she had become the friend of James Joyce. As with the original *Pall Mall*, these covers may have attracted the artistic establishment but would not have broadened the magazine's appeal.

Sales evidently remained low, and, with the August 1928 issue, *Pall Mall* had a complete facelift and reverted to the large slick format. It now looked exactly like *Nash's* with only its brash Steyn covers to distinguish it. Fiction remained dominant, but a host of features and articles now bristled forth, all highly illustrated and decorated. The fiction was much as before, but with occasional Beau Geste stories by P. C. Wren, a detective serial by A. E. W. Mason and humour by Ben Travers. There was even a regular crossword puzzle designed by Edmund Dulac, who was an ardent cruciverbalist. There were articles by and about P. G. Wodehouse, features for men and women on fashion, motoring, the theatre and cinema, on auction bridge and even a careers department.

Ivor Nicholson, working with Alan McPeake and later assisted by Ivor Brown, was doing his best to produce an all-round family magazine, but the main market, male readers, steadfastly stayed away. The cover slogan which had hitherto boasted "contains only new unpublished work" changed, on the November 1928 issue, to "a magazine men can read", but it failed to attract. The problem was simple and unavoidable. The main market for the slick magazine was women and both *Nash's* and *Good Housekeeping*, which had pioneered the slick magazine in Britain, had a strong image and loyal readership. *Pall Mall* was superfluous. Eventually Nicholson admitted defeat and the magazine was absorbed back into *Nash's* from October 1929, to make way for the British edition of *Harper's Bazaar*.

The second incarnation of *Pall Mall* has been overlooked by many. Though not as provocative or as exciting as the original magazine, and though it remained in the shadow of *Nash's*, it ran a good range of stories and articles and deserves to be better remembered.

Frequency: Monthly.
Publisher: George Routledge, May 1893-Dec 1912; Iliffe & Sons, Jan 1913-Aug 1914; National Magazine Co., Sep 1914, and May 1927-Sept 1929.
Editors: Lord Frederick Hamilton and Douglas Straight, May 1893-Aug 1896; Hamilton alone, Sept 1896-Dec 1900; George R. Halkett, Jan 1901-Jun 1905; Charles Morley, Jul 1905-Dec 1912; Hubert Fitchew, Jan 1913-Sept 1914; Ivor Nicholson, May 1927-Sept 1929.
Format/Size: Standard. Pagination varied at outset from 128 for first issue through 160, settling at 176 in 1894. Thereafter (with slight variances) 160, May 1895; dropped to 144, Jan 1897; 128, Jan 1905; varied between 156-186, Jul 1909-Dec 1912; 144, Jan 1913; 128, Sep 1914. When revived, varied between 120-136, May 1927-Dec 1928; 112, Jan-Sept 1929. Switched to large format slick, Aug 1928.
Price: 1/- to Dec 1904; dropped to 6d, Jan 1905. When revived, 1/-.
References: Albert Kinross, "Coming of Age", *Pall Mall Magazine*, May 1914, p.574.
Holdings:
Complete run, UK/Eire. British Library (*Shelfmark*: PP.6004.gln). • Cambridge University Library (*Classmark*: L996.c.35, first series; L996.b.27, second series).

Substantial run, UK. Bodleian has all except the Sep 1914 issue (*Call Number*: Per. 2705 d.24, first series; Per. 25612.d.94, second series). • Both National Library of Scotland (*Shelfmark*: K.373) and Trinity College, Dublin (*Call Number*: 32.f.31-83) have first series only, May 1893-Sep 1914.
Complete run, US. Library of Congress (*Call Number*: AP4.P17 and on microfilm). • Boston Public Library (*Ref*: EBP 732-745). • University of California at Davis (*Ref*: AP4.E25). • University of Connecticut (on microfilm). • Free Library of Philadelphia (*Call Number*: 050 P18). • New York University (on microfilm). • University of Rochester (on microfilm).
Substantial run, US. University of Minnesota Libraries has first series, May 1893-Jun 1914. • University of California at Berkeley, Pennsylvania State University and Rutgers University all have first series, May 1893-Aug 1914 (lacking only Sep 1914) on microfilm.
Complete run, Canada. University of Toronto, Robarts Library (*Call Number*: AP4.P17).
Collecting points: The Victorian volumes in their art nouveau blue-and-gold publisher's binding are plentiful. The Edwardian volumes, in darker blue binding, are less plentiful but not uncommon. The Iliffe issues are uncommon and surface more often as single issues. The late 1920s revival is extremely rare.

***

PAN

84 issues. Three series. Volume 1, Number 1, February 1919 to Number 3, June 1919; 3 issues. Relaunched as PAN: A JOURNAL FOR SAINTS AND CYNICS, Volume 1, Number 1, 8 November 1919 to Volume 5, Number 3, June 1921; 46 issues. Revamped as PAN: THE FICTION MAGAZINE, Volume 6, Number 1, July 1921 to Volume 11, Number 35, May 1924; 35 issues. Incorporated with *20-Story Magazine*.

Pan did not start as a fiction magazine but as a magazine of mischievous art and humour. Author and drama critic, W. A. Darlington, who was an assistant at Odhams Press in 1919, recalled that *Pan* was intended to "outdo all its rivals in wit, daring and beauty."[1] Its advice to authors also revealed its individuality: "A clever, smart, Bohemian atmosphere is sought after, and war is declared on cant and snobbishness."[2]

In the immediate post-war years, Odhams underwent much change under new managing director, J. S. Elias, later Lord Southwood. Darlington recalled, they "were carrying out a process of trial and error which was fascinating to watch . . . New papers were being projected, old ones were being galvanised into new life."[3] Odhams were already running *John Bull, The Passing Show* and *The World* and were launching *Ideal Home Magazine*. The brains behind most of this was the entrepreneurial journalist William Comyns Beaumont. Beaumont issued three trial issues of *Pan* which, though it promised to go full colour on a weekly basis, gave no hint of its potential. It consisted mostly

---

[1] W. A. Darlington, *I Do What I Like* (London: Rockliff, 1950), p. 207.
[2] *The Writers' and Artists' Yearbook, 1921* (London: A. & C. Black, 1921).
[3] W. A. Darlington, *ibid*, p. 206.

of half- or full page cartoons by Tom Cottrell, Lindsay Cable, G. E. Studdy and Starr Wood, plus a couple of ultra-short stories and scattered verse.

When it was relaunched in November it was in full colour throughout, with a beautiful cover by H. Pizer. The prime purpose of the magazine was as a humour miscellany, rather like *Punch*, but with the style and appearance of the Christmas issues of *The Sphere*. It consisted mostly of regular columns, cartoons and short features with the briefest of short stories. "Brevity is the soul of it", Beaumont noted in his market guidelines. Regular columnists included J. B. Morton, T.W.H. Crosland and Basil Macdonald Hastings whilst the mainstay artists were George Whitelaw, Steven Spurrier, H. M. Bateman, Kay Edmunds, Gilbert Wilkinson and before long, Tom Purvis, who later became renowned for his art deco travel posters. He was the primary cover artist for the rest of *Pan*'s existence. The reported circulation was around 100,000 for its first three issues and the fourth dropped only just below at 99,142.

At this time the stories were a minor element. Their purpose was to be sharp, witty and clever and they were almost all stories of amusing society incidents. Authors included Keble Howard, Lady Kitty Vincent, Barry Pain and Will Scott. When it switched from weekly to monthly in August 1920 it also increased in size and though several columns grew, there was space to fill. The number and length of short stories increased. Stacy Aumonier, Elinor Mordaunt and Douglas Newton joined the ranks and then, most tellingly, P. G. Wodehouse. *Pan* serialised "Three Men and a Maid" (Feb-Sept 1921). The balance of fiction to features shifted. This may have been a response to falling sales. Despite its auspicious start, *Pan*'s sales by the end of 1920 had dropped to 25,000, far too low to support the high production costs.

As a consequence all changed from the July issue, which was announced as a "special all-fiction number". *Pan*'s switched to a standard-size all-fiction magazine, retaining the quality paper but dropping the colour art and features. It was probably at this time that editor William Williamson took over, as the light banter in the editorial column remains consistent for the rest of the magazine's run. From here on it was an entirely new magazine.

Pan evidently saw fiction as its salvation. There had been a huge upsurge in fiction magazines in the immediate post-war years and Odhams leaped into the market, first with *Pan* and later with *20-Story* and *Romance*. Unique amongst magazines *Pan* grouped its stories on the contents page by subject and not in page order. So the opening story, "Menena" by Douglas Newton, set in the Amazon jungle, was labelled "Adventure" and appeared half-way down the contents page. The top three stories were all labelled "Love". Other categories were "Business", "Romance", "Satire", "Detective", "Humour", "Underworld" and "Novelty", a catch-all for anything, including any non-fiction features. These labels changed from issue to issue. It's an early example of the genrefication of fiction.

Though flexible the categories provide a useful clue to readers' tastes. The divide between "love" and "romance" was often fuzzy. Today these terms are synonymous and that shift occurred during the twenties. Hitherto "romance" had been more closely associated with adventure fiction, and that transition is evident here. For instance, in that first all-fiction issue the three stories labelled "love" are clearly all about male-female relationships. In the "romance" category is an historical story of love and intrigue, "In the Time of Her Lovers" by L. J. Beeston, the kind that Georgette Heyer would become famed for. Just two years later the stories labelled "romance" in the November 1923 issue are both love stories, such as "The Wife Who Came by Post" by Dale Collins, about a mail-order marriage.

By the same token the stories labelled "adventure" might also be crime or romance. "The Stark Robbery" by Halliwell Sutcliffe (Aug 1921), about a man on the run and the woman who saves him, fell into all three categories. Somewhat unhelpfully Will Scott's series about the philosopher-tramp Giglamps, who helps solve crimes, was usually listed under "romance", but occasionally under "humour" and only once under "detective". There was no category for the ghost story and these, which were uncommon, usually appeared under "crime". There was a category for "grand guignol", which was very popular in the early twenties, and which featured several stories by the French writer Maurice Level, including the noted "Night and Silence" (Jan 1922). By the end of the magazine's run, though, that category was not used and any such macabre story was labelled "drama".

The breakdown by category is useful in identifying what the public wanted and how the editor promoted the contents. Of the 503 stories and serial episodes published in the all-fiction issues of *Pan*, over a third (35.8%) were described as "love" or "romance" and a fifth (19.9%) as "adventure". These accounted for over half the contents and their share increased as the magazine progressed. Crime stories accounted for less than a sixth (14.9%) and that steadily decreased over the magazine's life apart from the last few issues. The only other category of any size was "humour", which accounted for a tenth (10.3%), and that was also on the decrease. Adventure and romance, by the broadest of definitions, dominated.

Each issue of *Pan* proclaimed that its policy was "to print each and every story because it is worth printing – whether the Author is famous or obscure." Their writers' guidelines also said, "unknown artists and authors encouraged", and authors' names were never promoted on the cover. Nevertheless major names did appear. With the completion of Wodehouse's serial, James Oliver Curwood's novel, "The Flaming Forest" (Sept 1921-May 1922), began, recounting an adventure of the North-West Mounted Police. That same issue marked the first of several stories by Earl Derr Biggers, "The Girl Who Paid Dividends", set in the film industry. There were two early stories by Stephen Vincent Benét,[4] plus stories by Richard Harding Davis, Roland Pertwee, A. P. Herbert and Edgar Wallace. Michael Arlen appeared with the mystery story "The Ancient Sin" (May 1923). There were adventure stories by Austin J. Small under his own name and as 'Seamark', including the Alaskan adventure serial "Frozen Gold" (Dec 1922-Oct 1923). There were romances by Ethel Lina White and early nature stories by Henry Williamson, beginning with "Raskil, the Wood Rogue" (Nov 1922). Perhaps the best known story to appear in *Pan* is "The Most Dangerous Game" by Richard Connell (Mar 1924)[5] about a man shipwrecked on an island who becomes the human prey in a hunt. It has been filmed at least three times, the first as *The Hounds of Zaroff* (1932).

Pan carried several pages of advertising, especially for the Christmas issues, which had the unusual feature of a 28-page section of the best adverts for the year, under the banner "A Pageant of Advertising". Yet despite this revenue *Pan* was clearly not paying its way. After the May 1924 issue it was merged with *20-Story Magazine*. Williamson had admitted many

---

[4] "Jerry and James and John" (Jul 1923) had just been published in America in the June 1923 issue of *Red Book*, but an earlier source for "Sir Willie of the Valley" (Mar 1923) has not yet been traced.
[5] It also appeared in *Collier's Weekly* for 19 January 1924.

months before that he considered all submissions equally for either magazine, so they were almost interchangeable except that *Pan* had the prestige of the better quality paper and illustrations. Despite its short life, *Pan* was a strikingly diverse and entertaining magazine that provided bright and original fiction.

Frequency: First series, monthly (but no April or May). New series, weekly to 3 Jul 1920, monthly from Aug 1920.
Publisher: Odhams Press.
Editors: W. Comyns Beaumont, 1919-20; A. D. Peters, 1920-21; W. A. Williamson, 1921-24.
Format/Size: First series: tabloid, 24 pages. Second series: tabloid, 36/40 pages to 3 Jul 1920; 56/60, Aug 1920. From Jul 1921, standard size on coated stock, 96 pages; rose to 112, Oct 1921; 128, Jul 1922; back to 96pp, May 1924.
Price: 6d, rose to 1/-, 20 Mar 1920.
Holdings:
Complete run, UK. British Library has all three series (*Shelfmark*: PP.6018.tam).
Partial run, UK. The Bodleian has first series only (*Call Number*: Per. 2706 c.21).
Collecting points: Extremely rare. Individual issues seldom surface and there are no known publisher's bound volumes.

***

PEARSON'S MAGAZINE

527 issues. Volume 1, Number 1, January 1896 to Volume 88, Number 527, November 1939. Merged with *The Strand Magazine*.

C. Arthur Pearson had been a business manager with George Newnes for nearly six years, working mostly on *Tit-Bits*, before he established his own company in 1890 and launched *Pearson's Weekly*. It was profitable from the start and the company grew. Pearson experimented briefly with the monthly anthology *The Search Light*, from 1892-4, but concentrated on the cheap end of the market for five years before launching his sixpenny illustrated all-new monthly. By the time *Pearson's Magazine* appeared, on 1 January 1896, it was a late entry. *Pearson's* needed to establish an identity without being seen as another reflection of *The Strand*.

Pearson was uncertain about the first issue, noting his dissatisfaction in his editorial and stating that there was "room for improvement". With one exception, that first issue had little to distinguish it from the other monthlies. It opened with an overview of recent prominent painters in a feature, "Artists and Their Work", which would remain, in one form or another, the lead feature in most issues over the next thirty years. Archibald Forbes began a short series, "The Bravest Deed I Ever Saw". "In the Public Eye" focused on topical individuals, including the Sultan of Turkey and William Waldorf Astor. "What It Costs" launched another short series which considered the investment required for major undertakings. There was an illustrated poem by Norman Gale – identical to a feature in *The Windsor* – plus a humorous poem, "The Great Water Joke", written and illustrated by *Strand* regular J. F. Sullivan. There was a humour column from another *Strand* and *Idler* regular, W. L. Alden, which, under various titles, ran for the first three years. There was also a drawing-room sketch published each month for the first volume, by Walter Besant and Walter Herries Pollock.

Even amongst the fiction there were the same names – Anthony Hope, Bret Harte, Robert Barr – with the same type of fiction they were contributing to the other monthlies. All, that is, except for the series by Allen Upward, "Secrets of the Courts of Europe". Purporting to be confidential revelations made by a former British ambassador to a journalist, and with familiar places and settings, with only the names withheld or changed, this gave every impression that it could be based on the truth, and was manna to all devotees of secret histories. Upward, a barrister who failed to become an MP, is unjustly forgotten today. His conspiratorial series hit just the right level amongst the growing market of middle-class readers that Pearson wanted to tap, and was the main factor in the early success of the magazine.

Pearson was a hands-on publisher in the early days, and he claimed to have personally edited *Pearson's* during its first four years.[1] He would certainly have dictated the direction of the magazine and made the final decisions, along with the help of his business manager Peter Keary, but the day-to-day management of the magazine was down to Pearson's Editorial Director, Percy Everett. Pearson's formula was simple, and though he retained a miscellany of features and stories on a range of subjects, the heart of the magazine was built around adventure, awe and excitement. He was fortunate in that he had three other contributors, besides Upward, whose work helped set *Pearson's* apart from its rivals. These were Cutcliffe Hyne, George Griffith and H. G. Wells.

Hyne must feature at the head of this list as he created the character who became most closely associated with *Pearson's*, Captain Kettle. According to the *Times* obituarist, Kettle was second only to Sherlock Holmes in popularity amongst the reading public at that time, and it was thus Hyne who boosted *Pearson's* circulation and cemented its reputation. Kettle had first appeared as a secondary character in a serial in *Answers*. Harmsworth suggested that he develop the character but did not back this with any significant offer. Hyne turned his sights on *Pearson's*. His first appearance was with "London's Danger" (Feb 1896), a warning story, which would become another feature of *Pearson's*. Hyne then submitted a Captain Kettle story, "Stealing a President" (Jun 1896). Here Kettle was centre stage and this pugnacious, belligerent, self-centred yet dependable character, who operated by his own set of jingoistic standards, became an instant hit. Kettle was a merchant seaman with a boat for hire who becomes involved in all manner of dubious projects, but always saves the day and thereby grows in power and status. Part of the attraction of the character is his ability to survive against all odds. Pearson commissioned Hyne to produce a series of six stories for which he paid fifty guineas a story. "The Adventures of Captain Kettle" began in the February 1897 issue, and was so successful that a second series followed immediately. Kettle was in almost every issue until June 1899 and reappeared with "More Adventures of Captain Kettle" from January 1902. He remained a recurrent feature well into the years of the First World War.

---

[1] C. Arthur Pearson in "Twenty-One Years Old", *Pearson's Magazine*, January 1917, pp. 65-67.

Hyne was a fixture even without Kettle. "The Lost Continent", set during the final days of Atlantis, was serialised between July and December 1899. Then came the somewhat rambling "Tales of a Steam Hotel" (Jul-Dec 1900), and a return to form with "McTodd in the Arctic" (Jan-Jun 1901). McTodd was a rather less irascible version of Kettle, and when Hyne revived Kettle in later issues he brought McTodd on board as a counterbalance.

Pearson would later acknowledge that Hyne, and in particular Kettle, was the main factor in the magazine's success. The character appealed to Pearson as representing the true British spirit, able to stand up and fight when circumstances required. Throughout its formative years *Pearson's* would push this message. During the two decades before the First World War there was concern in Britain about the imperial designs of the Kaiser and whether Britain was prepared. This need to be ahead of the game was reflected in many of the magazines but especially so in *Pearson's*. As a consequence *Pearson's* became the most amenable market to future war and invasion stories, which was where George Griffith and H. G. Wells featured.

Griffith had already featured in *Pearson's Weekly* and its companion *Short Stories* with serials warning of Britain's vulnerability to attack by those with advanced weapons, starting with "The Angel of the Revolution" (1893). Griffith's contributions to the monthly, both under his own name and as Levin Carnac, were mostly articles and short stories which highlighted areas of public concern. These included "War on the Water" (Feb 1896) about the conflict between two major fleets of ironclad warships, "A Photograph of the Invisible" (Apr 1896), on the public's caution over X-Rays and "A Corner in Lightning" (Mar 1898) on concern over the power of electricity. Griffith also took readers on a tour of the solar system in "Stories of Other Worlds" (Jan-Jun 1900). But it was Wells who took the big step and with "The War of the Worlds" (Apr-Dec 1897), which combined the concerns of foreign invasion and scientific superiority, he produced not only the most memorable serial that *Pearson's* ever published but also his most famous novel. Wells also contributed "In the Abyss" (Aug 1896), "The Sea Lady" (Jul-Dec 1901) and "The Valley of the Spiders" (Mar 1903).

Between them Wells and Griffith did much to alert readers to what science had to offer and that, combined with the *fin de siècle* anticipation of the new century meant that, for a while, *Pearson's* ran more science fiction and speculative articles than any of its competitors. The launch of an American edition of *Pearson's* in March 1899 saw an influx of American writers. Wardon Allan Curtis considered the potential for brain transplants between human and dinosaur in "The Monster of Lake La Metrie" (Sept 1899), whilst Edward Olin Weeks showed the entrepreneurship of the inventor in "The Master of the Octopus" (Oct 1899). This story was a satire on the works of the great Thomas Alva Edison and there were features on both Edison ("The White Magician", May 1898) and Nikolai Tesla ("The New Wizard of the West", May 1899) to further spark the imagination. There were also articles on "How Will the World End?" (Jul 1900), "The Origin of the Sun and its Planets" (Dec 1900), "Prehistoric Monsters" (Dec 1900) and, most remarkably, speculation about television in "Seeing by Wire" by Cleveland

Moffett (Oct 1899). One of the best-remembered series was the 'Doom of London' sequence (Jan-Jul 1903) by Fred M. White where each story looked at a potential threat to London, including blizzard, smog, pollution and plague. These stories and their striking illustrations by Warwick Goble brought home to readers the vulnerability of London and paved the way for later crusading issues.

Captain Kettle and scientific progress were the main elements of *Pearson's* success, but not to the exclusion of other factors. The magazine continued to milk the delight in secret histories. Allen Upward wrote two series of factual "Historical Mysteries" (Jan-Jun 1900) and masqueraded as an international spy under the alias "A.V." for the series "Underground History" (Jan-Jun 1903). One could include R. M. Bucke's article, "Shakespeare Dethroned" (Dec 1897) into this category of revisionist history, where he states his case for Bacon as the author of the plays. Add to this a long series of statistical features by J. Holt Schooling where he stripped Britain down to its basics, and you see *Pearson's* providing its readers with a wealth of material with which to reinterpret the world about them.

There were also sufficient major names to capture new readers. Amongst Rudyard Kipling's sporadic appearances were "Captains Courageous" (Dec 1896-Apr 1897), several stories set in India, including "The Tomb of His Ancestors" (Dec 1897) beautifully illustrated in colour by Paul Hardy, and a few of his Just-So stories, beginning with "How the Leopard Got His Spots" (Apr 1902). In imitation of Kipling, A. Sarath Kumar Ghosh presented the "Indian Nights Entertainment" (Jan-Jun 1902). Arthur Conan Doyle contributed an intermittent and short-lived series, "Tales of the High Seas" (from Jan 1897). Bret Harte provided a clever Sherlock Holmes parody in one of his "condensed novels", "The Stolen Cigar Case" (Dec 1900), featuring Hemlock Jones. Robert Barr and Halliwell Sutcliffe contributed several historical stories as did Max Pemberton, whose series "Zoë" (Jul-Dec 1901), set in the early Byzantine Empire, was unusual for its time.

Everett was good at attracting new writers. Even if he did not discover all of the following, he certainly provided their main initial market. These include Baroness Orczy ("The Traitor", December 1898), Rafael Sabatini ("The Coward", May 1900) and A. Sarsfield Ward, better known as Sax Rohmer ("The Green Spider", October 1904). Starting in January 1904 the magazine ran occasional contests for new writers and amongst one of the earliest runners-up was Algernon Blackwood ("Testing His Courage", September 1904). P. G. Wodehouse also made his first appearance outside the boys' magazines, with "An Afternoon Dip" (Oct 1904).

Pearson had enticed the young adventurer and sportsman Hesketh Prichard to contribute a series of ghost stories that were presented as if true, complete with photographs. "Real Ghost Stories" (from Jan 1898), written in collaboration with his mother as E. and H. Heron, introduced occult investigator Flaxman Low. Prichard also created the character of Spanish Brigand Don Q for *The Badminton Magazine* (1898) and Everett asked for more for *Pearson's* starting with "The Chronicles of Don Q" (from Jul 1903). The character resurfaced many times up to Prichard's death in 1922. The editor acknowledged that Don Q was almost as popular as Captain Kettle, both helping to build *Pearson's* circulation during the Edwardian era.[2]

---

[2] *Pearson's* sales figures were never released. They alluded to a "circulation" of 200,000 in 1905, reduced to 150,000 in 1906, both probably print runs. The A.P.S. suggested sales of 100,000 in 1907, and this was not challenged.

The appearance of *Pearson's* was also important. Unlike most of its competitors, *Pearson's* did not go for a standard, static cover. Each featured a new portrait or illustration, usually contrasting shades of red against a yellow background. Internally the magazine was liberally illustrated, just like *The Strand*, with a picture or photograph on every page and though it was never as artistic as *English Illustrated* or *Pall Mall*, it always lead with a feature on the nation's art and ran several colour plates, mostly in the Christmas issues. The paintings by Abbey Altson to illustrate Lewis Spence's "To Venus, the Evening Star" (Dec 1897) were amongst the most beautiful in any of the monthly magazines.[3] *Pearson's* featured many regular magazine artists including Stanley L. Wood, Lawson Wood, Will Owen and occasionally Arthur Rackham. *Pearson's* also used some of the earliest work by Mable Lucie Attwell, whose engaging drawings of young children ran for several issues from December 1905 onwards.

The quality of the magazine's production was further enhanced during the early 1900s when it exchanged stories and articles with American magazine publishers. This was prompted by the interplay with the American edition of *Pearson's*. As a consequence Jack London, Hamlin Garland, Charles G. D. Roberts and Frank Savile, amongst others, appeared, as well as artists Charles Livingston Bull, E. S. Blumenschein and Charles Dana Gibson. Readers were treated to stories of American Indian life, such as "A Warrior's Daughter" by Zitkala-Sä (Nov 1902), and a series about cowboy Long Jim by D. F. Seton Carruthers. They were also reminded of the social gulf between black and white Americans in the controversial story "The Black Hands" by Albert Bigelow Paine (Dec 1903[4]) in which, following an accident and a botched operation, a white man is transformed into a black man. There were also adventure stories, such as Cyrus Townsend Brady's serial "Sir Henry Morgan, Buccaneer" (Dec 1904-Jun 1905), and humorous stories, like Ellis Barker Butler's "Miss Millie's Creche" (Dec 1904).[5]

The use of American stories and articles, especially when printed from American plates, caused a problem over the use of American spelling. One reader queried why *Pearson's* had spelled "traveler" the American way, and the editor's response, that American spelling made sense and should we not revise English spelling, incurred the wrath of hundreds of readers.

During the Edwardian period *Pearson's* developed a lighter tone. Although the scientific-warning story remained it was balanced by light-hearted items and outdoor features. P. G. Wodehouse became a regular contributor. From the July 1905 issue a new miscellany of humour was introduced, "The Merry Thought", which remained to the magazine's final issues. That same issue was designated an "Outdoor" number and ushered in a series of special issues covering transport, sports, Nelson (Oct 1905, on the centenary of Trafalgar) and commerce.

Although Arthur Pearson had been more involved with his newspaper, the *Daily Express*, since 1900, he launched a series of crusading issues during 1906 under the banner "Pressing Problems of the Day". The first was "The Waste of Infant Life" (Jan 1906) which argued that over half of infant deaths were preventable. Others included the prevalence of insanity, the "frenzy" of football, the housing problem, cigarette smoking amongst juveniles and industrial

---

[3] Artist James Thorpe was less positive. He wrote, "From an artistic point of view *Pearson's Magazine* in these early years formed an almost perfect example of how not to do it", adding, "even when excellent illustrations were supplied these were often ruined by over-reduction, carelessly made or mutilated blocks and the use of unpleasant coloured inks." *English Illustrations: The Nineties* (Faber, 1935), p. 180.
[4] This had first appeared in the September 1903 US edition.
[5] Both had previously run in *McClure's*.

accidents. These issues brought a large response and the editor established a regular column, "Sparks from Our Anvil", to review the feedback and actions arising. An issue that kept recurring was women's suffrage, started by the symposium "What will be the Future of Women?" (Sept 1906). *Pearson's* sought to remain impartial so when it ran "Votes for Women" by Sylvia Pankhurst (Mar 1909) it also ran "Why Women Do <u>Not</u> Want the Vote" by E. L. Somervell. The latter brought a hostile reaction from many readers, not all women.

The other change that became apparent from 1906 onwards was the increase in exotic adventure fiction and detective fiction. One of the most popular themes in romantic adventure in the 1910s and 1920s was stories set in the South Seas. There had been a few in earlier issues, such as Louis Becke's "Susãni" (Sept 1900), but the real trigger was the series, "Vaiti of the Islands" (Dec 1906-May 1907) by Beatrice Grimshaw. Grimshaw was an Irish lady who had served for a while as a journalist in London but yearned to escape and in 1906 achieved her desires by settling in New Guinea. Over the next thirty years she produced a huge quantity of rather idealised romantic south-sea fiction. The first series was followed by "Queen Vaiti" (Apr-Sept 1908) and "When the Red Gods Call" (Dec 1910-Jun 1911).

Prior to 1908 *Pearson's* had published some detective fiction, including several episodes of Robert Barr's Eugene Valmont, but this series was also running in *The Windsor*, and *Pearson's* had nothing like Sherlock Holmes to call its own. This all changed with "The Blue Sequin" by R. Austin Freeman (Dec 1908), heralding the appearance of scientific detective Dr John Thorndyke. Thorndyke was the prototype of the forensic detective, applying all the latest scientific knowledge in solving the crime. The emphasis on science made the series ideal for *Pearson's*, which enhanced the stories by running photographic evidence within the stories. Soon Freeman took the detective story one step further. In "The Case of Oscar Brodski" (Dec 1910) he split the story into two, the first half showing the crime being committed and the second revealing how Thorndyke solved it. This became known as the "inverted" detective story, best known from the *Columbo* television series.

Freeman's forensics and Grimshaw's paradise islands often ran side by side in *Pearson's*, the one showing the full application of science, the other an escape from it. Thorndyke's character was so dominant that it allowed little room for any rivals, although Hesketh Prichard's series about woodsman detective November Joe (from Jul 1912) was sufficiently different to gain a following. It was not until after the War that *Pearson's* detective fiction would blossom into full flower.

Pearson's had a few literary surprises during this period. It ran a serial by H. Rider Haggard, the mystical "The Ghost Kings" (Oct 1907-Jun 1908), which Haggard had worked on with Rudyard Kipling. It published one of the earliest stories by Dornford Yates, the light romance "The Babes in the Wood" (Sept 1910). It printed a previously unpublished poem by Robert Louis Stevenson, "From Wishing Land" (Dec 1907), written in 1889. The Christmas 1909 issue published a short story by Napoleon, set in ancient Bagdad. Apparently written in 1787 it had been published in France in 1821 but had not previously been translated. *Pearson's* also ran a three-part account by Ernest Shackleton, "Nearest the South Pole" (Sept-Nov 1909).

From March 1910 *Pearson's* was back on the campaign trail, starting with "On the Edge of the Unknown", a series about spiritualism conducted by William Marriott, with further investigations carried out by Pearson's staff. In his editorials, Everett took several mediums to task and reported that one had even left the country after their exposure. For once *Pearson's* was not even-handed, especially as no one responded to their challenge for firm evidence. However fourteen years later, under John R. Wade, *Pearson's* saw fit to run Conan Doyle's "Adventures in the Spirit World" (Mar-Apr 1924).

Anticipation of the return of Halley's Comet caused *Pearson's* to publish "The Danger of the Comet" by E. C. Andrews (Dec 1909). This opened the floodgates to another series of warning articles. "Where Will the Enemy Land?" (Feb 1910) considered weaknesses in Britain's defences. "The Great White Plague" (Apr 1910) drew attention to the problems of consumption. In March 1911 the magazine introduced an "Educational Supplement" to deal with problems of education and raising of children. But the shouting really began with the "Wake up, England" campaign launched in September 1911. "Our Pig-Headed Farmers" looked at how much food we import due to slack farming in Britain. In the next issue Baden-Powell attacked apathy in "Workers or Shirkers". Later articles examined food contamination, the number of foreign seamen manning British ships, and weaknesses in the British army.

This concern was inevitably reflected in the fiction. The newly elected Member of Parliament for Kensington, Alan Burgoyne, contributed several stories about future naval warfare, starting with "The Way of the Navy" (Sept 1909) and including "The Death Dive: The Story of the World's Last Naval Battle" (Oct 1911). "The Two Punctures" (Feb 1912) by the pseudonymous "Secret Service" (possibly Upward again) revealed a plot to destroy the British Empire which was allegedly based on real events. In "The Great Drought" (Aug 1912) Fred M. White returned to his stories of doom, this time inspired by the exceptionally dry summer of 1911. In "Up Above"[6] (Dec 1912) John N. Raphael considered how an invisible alien vessel could visit Earth and abduct humans and animals for experimentation.

All of this stopped when War broke out. There were no "we told you so" recriminations. Instead *Pearson's* began publishing war-inspired fiction almost immediately, with rousing items like "Pro Patria" by F. Britten Austin (Oct 1914) and "Rejoining at Once" by Cutcliffe Hyne (Dec 1914). One of the more impressive stories was "The Red Days" by H. de Vere Stacpoole (Aug 1915), a purportedly true account of the war based on the diary of a Prussian officer. There were the inevitable articles by Hilaire Belloc and, equally inevitably, Captain Kettle came out of retirement for "Kettle on the War-path" (from Oct 1915). Early in 1917 Hyne suggested to the British naval authorities a method of blockading harbours by means of cruisers filled with concrete. The idea was not adopted but Hyne used it in the story "The McTodd Plug" (Dec 1917). The same idea was then used by the British Navy to blockade Zeebrugge and Ostend in May 1918.

Towards the end of the War the amount of war-related fiction decreased to be replaced by more light-hearted and inspiring items. There was an increase in the number of nature-study features. *Pearson's* had always been strong on these and there was scarcely an issue that did not include at least one such study by S. L. Bensusan or F. St. Mars. Now H. Mortimer Batten and later Henry Williamson continued the tradition, with illustrations by Harry Rountree or Warwick Reynolds. George Robey contributed a series of "After Dinner Stories" (from Sept 1919), illustrated by H. M. Bateman.

It took a while for *Pearson's* to recover after the War. The magazine had reduced considerably in size and paper quality. To their credit Pearson's had maintained all three of its

---

[6] The story was freely adapted from *Le Péril Bleu* by Maurice Renard (Paris: Michaud, 1911).

fiction magazines, *Pearson's*, *The Royal* and *The Novel*, despite the paper rationing, but this had taken its toll and for a while the heart had fallen out of the magazine. It was time for an editorial change and John Reed Wade injected a new zest.

The most notable change in *Pearson's* during the twenties and thirties was the injection of light-hearted stories and features, including the whacky invention pictures by W. Heath Robinson. *Pearson's* also introduced a puzzle page and in so doing made history by publishing the first crossword puzzle in a British magazine, in the issue for February 1922.

The featured writer was Denis Mackail who from 1925 onwards appeared almost every month with witty stories reflecting the carefree upper-middle class attitude of the twenties. In similar vein were the Mrs Bindle stories by Herbert Jenkins, which ran occasionally through 1921/22, and W. A. Darlington's amusing fantasy about the young snoot Egbert who, in "The Afflictions of Egbert" (Oct 1923-Mar 1924), is transformed into a rhinoceros when he upsets a wizard. The series was cleverly illustrated by George Studdy, the creator of "Bonzo". There were amusing stories by Richmal Crompton, Roland Pertwee, Barry Perowne, Bertram Atkey and Anthony Armstrong. Leslie Henson recalled "My Laugh Story" (from Jan 1926), but perhaps the most memorable series was H. M. Raleigh's accounts of the misadventures of Lord Grebe of Slyme Court (from Aug 1932). Raleigh was one of the better imitators of Wodehouse, and the master himself was tempted back to *Pearson's* with two serials, "Laughing Gas" (Aug-Oct 1935) and "Summer Moonshine" (Sept 1937-Apr 1938).

When not making you smile *Pearson's* was whisking you away to exotic places. Beatrice Grimshaw and H. de Vere Stacpoole continued their many and varied series set in the South

Seas, though Stacpoole ventured into the Amazon in "Deep in the Forest" (Jan 1927). Edmund Snell took us to the tropics, Albert R. Wetjen took us to sea, Garnett Radcliffe to the North-West Frontier, Zane Grey to the Wild West, P. C. Wren to the foreign legion and Elizabeth Marc, really Princess Nusrat Ali Mirza, gave us romance amongst the Eskimaux. The strange oriental mystery "The Taipan" (Oct 1922), saw Somerset Maugham's first appearance in a British magazine for thirteen years; it was chosen by E.J. O'Brien as one of that year's best stories. All these displayed the passion of the twenties for blending the dream-like exoticism of far off places with the allure of forbidden desire. None was better at that than E. M. Hull whose *The Sheikh* had been the bestseller of 1921. *Pearson's* secured the sequel, "Sons of the Sheikh" (Feb-Nov 1925), announced with a rare photograph of Hull trying to blend into the Arabian desert.

Like Hull, Lady Dorothy Mills was a great traveller and she recounted her Saharan expedition to Timbuctoo (Aug 1923), whilst Rosita Forbes took us to Abyssinia (Jan 1927) and Howard Carter revealed an experience related to the discovery of Tutankhamun's tomb in "The Tomb of the Bird" (Nov 1923). Lieutenant-Commander Richard Byrd contributed "The First Flight to the North Pole" (Feb 1927), whilst editor John R. Wade looked ahead to "The Conquest of the South Pole by Air" (May 1931).

Most of the adventure storytellers were seasoned travellers, none more so than Australian James F. Dwyer. His stories span the world, but perhaps his most touching was his retelling of the birth of Christ in "The White Camel That Saw Jesus" (Dec 1934). Dwyer recalls that Wade was concerned over the title, thinking it might affront some readers, but unable to think of an alternative he ran it and had not a single complaint.[7] Others who turned their travels into tales include Reginald Campbell, whose life as a "teak-wallah" in Siam, generated a series starting with "The Shikaree's Vengeance" (Mar 1928), and William J. Makin who gave us the adventures of Red Head of Arabia, a blending of Lawrence of Arabia with Robin Hood in a long-running series that began with "Red Head of the Red Sea"[8] (Nov 1932).

There was still room for the more traditional love story, mostly by Alicia Ramsay, Ethel Lina White, Alice Grant Rosman or Clare Thornton. There were not many historical series at this time but one that made up for that consisted of several new stories about Captain Blood by Rafael Sabatini, starting with "The Blank Shot" (Jan 1930), vividly portrayed on the cover by Joseph Greenup. There was not much in the way of science fiction, either, but another dramatic Greenup cover, showing a giant caterpillar destroying London, heralded "The Winged Terror" by G. R. Malloch (Feb-Apr 1931). Some writers merged mystery and adventure. "Sapper" had been one of *Pearson's* discoveries, when he submitted stories from the trenches. Although *Pearson's* missed out on the Bulldog Drummond stories, which went to *Hutchinson's*, they published many of his stories of international intrigue, including "The Chronicles of Jim Maitland" (from Aug 1922), and the adventures of Ronald Standish (from Jun 1935).

Mystery and detective fiction blossomed in *Pearson's* during the twenties. It was here that the first Lord Peter Wimsey short stories by Dorothy L. Sayers appeared, starting with "The Problem of Uncle Meleager's Will" (Jul 1925). *Pearson's* failed to capture any series from Agatha Christie but did run the occasional non-series story, such as "The Edge" (Feb 1927), written just before her notorious disappearance. Another well known series was Roy Vickers's "Department of Dead Ends" (from Sept 1934). Less well known and deserving better attention are the impossible crime stories by Vincent Cornier. Cornier had first sold to *The Story-Teller*, but *Pearson's* tied him down and he became a regular contributor from "Dust of Lions" (Apr 1933). From January 1932 Douglas Newton contributed his original series about police detective Paul Toft, who solves his cases by intuition. Throughout this period *Pearson's* presented a series of true-crime articles by H. Ashton-Wolfe who was allowed unprecedented access to the French police archives.

The Problem of Uncle Meleager's Will
By DOROTHY L. SAYERS
Illustrations by John Campbell

Adventure, mystery and humour dominated *Pearson's*, and is the image that its covers projected. Although it also published a few stories by J. B. Priestley, Alec Waugh, Stacey

---

[7] James Francis Dwyer, *Leg-Irons on Wings* (Melbourne: Georgian House, 1949), p. 208.
[8] This series was running concurrently in the USA in *Blue Book*, where the British Intelligence Officer, Paul Rocher, was known more effectively as the Red Wolf of Arabia.

Aumonier and James Hilton, and articles by Winston Churchill, these were marginalised. *Pearson's* was the closest to a slick American adventure magazine that Britain produced.

In the July 1936 issue Stephen King-Hall considered the huge social revolution that was happening in Britain. A few years earlier John Logie Baird had discussed the future of television (Jan 1931) and a little later William J. Makin discussed the desire amongst nations for supremacy of the radio airwaves (Aug 1937). If anyone had looked ahead they would have seen the seeds of change in these articles which would signal the downfall of the fiction magazine. *Pearson's* was itself changing to market demands. It had modernised its appearance in November 1935, with more stylised artwork, often in two-tone colour. Then in May 1939 it changed completely to the full flat size, though the glossy paper was downgraded to newsprint. The covers became light-hearted sketches by Edgar Norfield, and the humour section was expanded. Fiction remained but there were more photographic features and life-style articles. Cyril Hare, Donald Barr Chidsey, W. E. Johns (who edited these issues) and H. M. Raleigh all contributed. The new format was short-lived. With the outbreak of war *Pearson's* was merged with *The Strand*.

The pleasure of *Pearson's* over its entire life was that it never took itself seriously and was there for fun and escapism. It used its position, through stories and articles, to alert the public to the need for change, but it never sought to be pretentious like *The Windsor*, or superior like *Pall Mall*, or ground-breaking like *The Strand*. Rather it took elements of all these and mixed them in the way that gave the most enjoyment, in which it succeeded well for over forty years.

Frequency: Monthly.
Publisher: C. Arthur Pearson.
Editors: C. Arthur Pearson, 1896-99; Percy W. Everett, 1900-11; Philip O'Farrell, 1912-19; John Reed Wade, Jan 1920-Apr 1939; W. E. Johns, May-Nov 1939.
Format/Size: Standard until Apr 1939 then switched to large flat size for final seven issues. Page count fluctuated between issues but in general was 112/120 to Jun 1916; 92/96, Jul 1916; 80/84, May 1917-May 1918 and Jan 1919; 70/72, Jun-Nov 1918; 96/100, Feb 1919; 128, Jun 1927; 108/112, Jan 1928; 100/104, Mar 1934; 108, May-Nov 1939.
Price: 6d; rose to 7d, Feb 1917; 8d, Sept 1917; 9d, Jan 1918; 1/-, Jun 1918.
Other editions: A separate US edition ran from Mar 1899-Apr 1925 (313 issues). It began as a straight reprint but after its sale to J. J. Little in 1902 it developed a separate identity under editor Arthur Little. From 1908, with new editor E.J. Clode, it ceased its connection with the British parent, becoming a cheaply produced radical review, a role further developed under editors Frank Harris (1916–1922) and Alexander Marky (1922-1925).
References: *British Literary Magazines, Volume 4, The Modern Age, 1914-1984* edited by Alvin Sullivan (Westport, CT: Greenwood Press, 1986).
Holdings:
Complete run, UK. National Library of Scotland (*Shelfmark*: U.425).
Substantial run, UK. British Library has all issues except Jan 1897-May 1898, Apr, Jun 1936; Jan 1937-Nov 1939 (*Shelfmark*: PP.6004.gmq). • The Bodleian has run from Jan 1896-May 1936 (*Call Number*: Per. 2705 d.69). • Cambridge University Library has volumes 1-27, Jan 1896-Jun 1909 only (*Classmark*: L996.c.32).
Complete run, US. Library of Congress (*Call Number*: AP4.P35).

Substantial run, US. University of Minnesota Libraries have vols. 1-81, Jan 1896-Jun 1936.

Collecting points: The publisher's attractive six-monthly bound volumes with art nouveau decoration are very common for the first decade but less common until the 1930s. Individual issues have the advantage of the pictorial covers and whilst uncommon do surface randomly.

* * *

THE PREMIER MAGAZINE

256 issues. Three series: Number 1, May 1914 to Number 159, 6 February 1923; 159 issues. New series, Volume 1, Number 1, March 1923 to Volume 7, Number 43, September 1926; 43 issues. Third series, Number 1, October 1926 to Number 54, March 1931; 54 issues.

The Premier was arguably the leading magazine of adventure and mystery fiction of the First World War, taking the mantle from *The Story-Teller*, which David Whitelaw had also helped launch. Whitelaw had moved to Amalgamated Press in 1911 to edit *The London Magazine*, but his passion was to create an all-fiction pulp like *The Story-Teller* and his opportunity came late in 1913. Although Amalgamated Press already had one all-fiction magazine, *The Red*, that fell into the department that handled the story-papers and comics. *The Premier* came under the prestigious magazine department and, with the might and finances of the Amalgamated Press to call upon, Whitelaw was able to produce a significant magazine.

The first issue was a substantial 176 pages printed on heavy quality pulp stock so that it was half-an-inch thick and, with a cover price of 4½d, promised value for money. The wordage was also substantial as the typeface was small, so that even allowing for illustrations and advertisements, it must have run in excess of 100,000 words.

Whitelaw selected a strong line-up and the cover, by Cyrus Cuneo, illustrated, in all its fearsome glory, a scene from Sax Rohmer's new series, "Brood of the Witch-Queen". Rohmer was rapidly becoming a major name, thanks to his Fu Manchu stories, and Whitelaw had managed to lure him away from the Cassell to *The Premier*. In his biography of Rohmer, Cay Van Ash noted that "throughout the following six years Rohmer's fiction was a mainstay of the magazine, contributing much to the latter's popularity."[1] The other significant author in the first issue was Rafael Sabatini, with a tale of the Spanish Inquisition, "The Heresy of Don Ramon". Though already an established name, it was through his involvement with *The Premier* that Sabatini would become world renowned in later years. It was here that Sabatini composed the stories that became the three-volume *The Historical Nights' Entertainment*, and it was also here that Captain Blood first raised the skull-and-crossbones.

Two other names appeared in the second issue who would become regulars. William Le Queux began a series of espionage stories, "House of a Thousand Secrets", published in book form as *The German Spy* (Newnes, 1914), whilst American writer Albert Payson Terhune contributed a short novel of lost treasure, "The Treasure of Suleiman". Terhune was a close

---

[1] Cay Van Ash, *Master of Villainy* (Stacey, 1972), p. 297.

friend of Whitelaw's and was best known for his dog stories, which became a feature of *The Premier*. The third issue marked the first contribution by A. M. Burrage, who was already a regular in *The London* and whom Whitelaw ranked "among the foremost of our short-story writers."[2] Burrage would contribute some of his best ghost stories to *The Premier*.

Amalgamated Press reported sales of 242,720 for the first issue, a remarkable figure considering that *The London*, which was then the bestselling of the fiction monthlies, was selling 140,000.[3] When sales settled *The Premier* was reportedly selling around 120,000, which raises questions over the original data. Nevertheless it was a respectable figure and about the equal of its rival, *The Story-Teller*.

The magazine ran line drawings with most of its stories, usually as headings but occasionally within the story. The reproduction is seldom of top quality and did not improve until the magazine switched to the art paper format in 1922, but there are nevertheless several top magazine illustrators present, amongst them H. M. Brock, Gordon Browne, Fred Bennett, E. H. Shepard and H. R. Millar.

As with any new venture the editor tried an experiment to capture reader interest. He commissioned Max Pemberton and Arthur Quiller-Couch to write a story in which a murder is left unsolved. He then sent the proofs of Pemberton's story to G. K. Chesterton to have Father Brown solve the murder, while Baroness Orczy set Lady Molly onto the task of solving Q.'s mystery. The first two ran in the October and November 1914 issues, whilst the second pair ran in the July 1915 issue. Whitelaw felt that "the results were admirable"[4], but did not repeat the experiment.

Within four months of launching *The Premier*, Europe spiralled into war. It was fortunate that *The Premier* survived.[5] Whitelaw recalled the immediate effects:

> Staffs were depleted by the call to arms, advertisements – the life-blood of magazinedom – fell away, paper, for any other than national purposes, was difficult to procure and the great reading public had to be given the fare the peculiar circumstances demanded. Make-ups were ruthlessly torn apart, love stories and domestic dramas filed away for use in happier times, literary agents were besieged for authors who could write of the clash of arms with some semblance of knowing what they were writing about.[6]

W. Douglas Newton, who had predicted a forthcoming conflict in *War* (Methuen, 1914), had jumped the gun, so to speak, and submitted "Battle" (Nov 1914), which proved a rather timely story. Hilaire Belloc began a series of stories set during the French Revolution with "The Flight to Varennes" (Dec 1914) and there were any number of spy and historical war stories. However Whitelaw soon realised that what readers wanted was not the realism of War but escapism and *The Premier* provided that in abundance with adventures historical, exotic, oriental, mysterious, supernatural and even scientific.

---

[2] David Whitelaw, *A Bonfire of Leaves* (London: Bles, 1937), p. 117.
[3] See *The A.P.S. Monthly Circular*, July 1914. At its General Meeting on 16 December 1914, Amalgamated Press reported that *The Premier* had become "the most widely read fiction magazine in this country, with a larger circulation than any similar magazine." (*The Times*, 17 December 1914, p. 14.)
[4] Whitelaw, *ibid.*, p. 162.
[5] Plans were well advanced by Universal Press to launch *The Piccadilly Magazine* in September 1914, with stories acquired for the first issue, but it was shelved permanently upon the declaration of War.
[6] Whitelaw, *ibid.*, pp. 114-115.

One of the most popular subjects in the fiction magazines during the War years and well into the twenties were stories with a south-seas setting, as far away from the conflict in Europe as possible. This had been popularised by H. de Vere Stacpoole with *The Blue Lagoon* (1908) and he would frequently return to the theme. Stacpoole became a regular in *The Premier* starting with "Pearl Island" (Aug 1914). The cover of the December 1915 issue displayed a picture of a south-sea paradise and announced Stacpoole's new series in bold letters. This was "The Luck of Captain Slocum" about a slightly disreputable but lovable fortune-seeking old captain in the Pacific. Whitelaw also attracted the three other major writers of exotic eastern and south-seas adventures, James Francis Dwyer, Beatrice Grimshaw and Achmed Abdullah.

Abdullah had a hit with his first appearance, a series run under the title "The Scarlet Mark" (Mar-Jul 1916), better known under its book title *The Red Stain* (Simpkin, 1916).[7] Abdullah was mining a vein similar to that of Sax Rohmer's. A secret cult of the goddess Kali is endeavouring to pit East against West controlled by an oriental mastermind. Read at a time when the full impact of the First World War was being realised in Britain the series struck a responsive chord and a second series, "The Trail of the Blue Eyes", followed immediately. It ran alongside the first of Rafael Sabatini's "Historical Nights Entertainment" and Sir Arthur Quiller-Couch's "Tales of the Spanish Main" (Jun 1916).

James Francis Dwyer's stories were not only exotic but had a vibrant atmosphere of the fantastic. "The Cross of Fire" (Oct 1915) blended the south-seas adventure with a tale of lost Crusader treasure. "The Gorge of Kala" (Jul 1916) is a near-eastern fantasy about a chasm haunted by the soldiers of Tamerlane, whilst "The Reckoning" (Jun 1916) is a Celtic fantasy. Dwyer enjoyed confronting the everyday with the heroic as in "The Man Who Fought a Battleship" (Mar 1917) where one man single-handedly holds a battleship at bay.

The other main feature of *The Premier* during the war years was crime and mystery fiction. Frank Froest, the recently retired head of C.I.D. at New Scotland Yard contributed a serial, "The Greye-Stratton Mystery" (Dec 1915-Apr 1916), which followed the authentic workings of the detective service. William Le Queux appeared with "'Cinders' of Harley Street" (Dec 1915-Aug 1916), a series of medical mysteries, purporting to be accounts from the diary of a recently deceased physician. L. J. Beeston's "The Master Touch" (from Nov 1916) featured Acton Dawes, a thief turned detective, and there were any number of one-off crime stories, often intermingled with unusual or supernatural stories. In addition to Sax Rohmer and James Francis Dwyer, William Hope Hodgson, Vincent O'Sullivan, Jerome K. Jerome, Morley Roberts and Guy Thorne were amongst a dozen or more writers who contributed weird fiction.

The announcement "Earth to be Annihilated" for the story "The Moon Maker" by Arthur Train and Robert W. Wood (Feb-Jun 1917), must have caused some concern, coming as it did at the height of the War. This was one of the earliest science-fiction stories about astronauts trying to save the Earth from collision with an asteroid. Whitelaw enjoyed science fiction and published several by Guy Thorne, including "The Air Pirate" (Jun-Aug 1919), one of a number of immediate post-war stories which considered mastery of the air. Leslie Beresford became a regular contributor of science fiction in the 1920s, including his short novel "The Moon Men" (24 Sep 1920), in which the Earth is invaded, and "The Winged Terror" (7 Oct 1921), in which pterodactyl eggs are hatched.

---

[7] This series had run in the American pulp *All-Story* under the title "The God of the Invincibly Strong Arms" (18 Sept-16 Oct 1915).

The post-war interest in spiritualism only served to increase the number of weird stories in *The Premier*. Gerald Biss's werewolf story, "The Door of the Unreal" was serialised from February to April 1919. The earliest of F. Tennyson Jesse's Solange stories, which blended the detective story with a psychic awareness, began in the November 1918 issue. The issue for 26 September 1919 saw the start of Mrs Champion de Crespigny's series about psychic detective Norton Vyse and the end of J. D. Beresford's series "The Symbol", in which the narrator reveals various past lives of man's passion for gold over the millenia. Beatrice Grimshaw also wrote a south-seas story of past lives in "Through the Back Door" (19 Dec 1919). Starting from the issue for 9 April 1920 Elliott O'Donnell began a series, "Famous Hauntings".

The war had taken its toll on *The Premier*. The magazine had lost almost half its pages and yet doubled in price. It had also dropped in circulation, but not too drastically. Average sales in 1919 were just under 74,000. Amalgamated Press must have been sufficiently satisfied to double the magazine's frequency to twice a month from June 1919, and then fortnightly.

The Premier's content changed little with historical stories and exotic adventures to the fore. Baroness Orczy brought the Scarlet Pimpernel to the magazine with "The First Sir Percy" (5 Dec 1919-26 Mar 1920) whilst Rafael Sabatini introduced Captain Blood in "Brethren of the Main" (3 Dec 1920-11 Mar 1921). Whitelaw revealed that William Le Queux had been a pioneer researcher into radio and his series "Messages of Mystery" (25 Feb-29 Jul 1921) considered how radio might be used in the future. One of the most popular spy stories of the War had been *The Man with the Clubfoot* (Jenkins, 1918) about Dr Adolph Grundt, head of the Kaiser's secret service. Valentine Williams brought him back in "The Return of Clubfoot" (24 Jan-2 May 1922).

Writers Abdullah, Grimshaw, Dwyer, Rohmer and Stacpoole continued to appear though there was a noticeable change as the emphasis shifted away from adventure towards the romantic. In its post-war marketing for authors *The Premier* referred to itself as requiring "stories of love and adventure", and although adventure and mystery remained uppermost, an increasing number of light romance and humorous stories appeared. This may have been an

effort to capture the growing women's market but if so this did not happen. *The Premier's* circulation continued to dwindle, reaching around 54,000 during 1921. It had the audacity to label itself "The Leading Fiction Magazine" on the cover of the issue for 23 September 1921 even though its sales were below its stablemate *The Red*, then averaging 88,000, and its closest rival *The Story-Teller*, then averaging 94,000.

The time came for a facelift and with the issue for March 1923 *The Premier* changed into a standard slick monthly, looking like its partner *The London*, and likewise selling for a shilling. It was abundant with advertising and heavily illustrated. During 1922 the covers of *The Premier* had also changed to portraying women rather than depicting scenes from stories. The early twenties had seen a rapid increase in glossy magazines designed for general home readership, especially the new professional middle classes, but aimed chiefly at women.

The new *Premier* was an attractive product clearly aimed at women. The lead serial was by Robert W. Chambers, "The Girl from Paris"[8], a story full of the verve of the twenties, but with more than a hint of the occult. Most of the remaining stories were either fantasies or mysteries but with a strong romance element. There were also stories of the modern women and more stories of light humour, such as the tales of the Happy Rascals by F. Morton Howard. The issue reflected the transition from post-war to roaring twenties, which much flair and excitement seasoned with mystery and the bizarre.

To begin with, the revamped *Premier* felt a little like a sheep in wolves' clothing, with the nature of the contents too similar to the previous incarnation. But the transition was soon over and during 1924 there was an increase in non-fiction features, more elaborate artwork (including two-colour separations) and a greater variety of fiction. The romantic element, however, tended to remain superficial. Most stories, aside from the regular mystery and supernatural pieces, were either sporting stories or about humorous antics, very typical of twenties fiction. Amongst the new authors, of special interest are Richmal Crompton, who first appeared with "Sar' Ellen" (Mar 1925), a story of motherly devotion, Albert Wetjen, who produced sea adventure stories starting with "Heaven Island" (May 1923), and Alice Perrin, whose three contributions began with an Indian ghost story, "Ann White" (May 1923).

Central to the magazine, though, remained its mystery and off-trail stories. Several series appeared which deserve to be better known. Albert Payson Terhune contributed "The Adventures of Hester Gregg" (Sept-Dec 1924) about an old spinster with such remarkable deductive powers that she is nicknamed Sherlockette. The series preceded Agatha Christie's Miss Marple by four years. J. B. Harris-Burland, one of the most prolific contributors to *The Premier* created two original series: "The Secrets of Sallowby" (Sept 1923-Feb 1924) about the investigations of an antiquarian bookseller, and "The Quests of Quickerell" (Dec 1924-Jul 1925), featuring mysteries encountered by a genealogist. George Dilnot, a journalist who had been allowed special access to Scotland Yard's files, contributed several non-fiction series, such as "Woman of the Underworld" (from Aug 1924) and "Master Minds of Crime" (from Nov 1925). The more regular appearance of Dilnot was due to the cessation of *The Detective Magazine*, which had merged with *The Premier* causing the June and July 1925 issues to be entitled *The Premier and Detective Magazine*.

The Premier's period as a general-interest slick magazine did not last long. Circulation figures are not available but it must be deduced that they did not compensate for the extra cost, despite the increased cover price and profusion of advertisements. From March 1926 most of the features faded away and the reversion to an all-fiction magazine was a prelude to changing back to pulp format in October 1926. Whitelaw heralded the change as if he were welcoming back an old friend.

> The keynote of the stories will be, as ever since the magazine began, *virility*. For many years the *Premier* had held pride of place among the magazines devoted to fiction by reason of the vivid, human interest of the stories. Love, romance, adventure – all have place in *The Premier*.

---

[8] Retitled *The Talkers* for book publication from Doran (1923) and T. Fisher Unwin (1925).

Despite this promise the final incarnation of *The Premier* is lacklustre compared to its former two lives and, despite some highlights, has a feel of a magazine running out of steam. Apart from the ever-present humorous tales by F. Morton Howard and a few old friends like Andrew Soutar and Albert Payson Terhune, most of the original contributors have gone, or appear irregularly. The exotic adventure story had all but vanished, apart from the work of Beatrice Grimshaw and Edmund Snell. There were occasional sea stories, mostly by Captain Dingle, but otherwise the magazine had returned primarily to mystery stories, supported by weird tales, sports stories and romantic melodramas.

A few new authors began to appear, amongst them Oscar Schisgall, Octavus Roy Cohen H. Bedford-Jones, Sewell Peaslee Wright, Melville Davisson Post and Edison Marshall, showing that Whitelaw was now buying heavily into second serial rights from American magazines. Amongst the British authors it was now that A. M. Burrage contributed the majority of his ghost stories, Evadne Price became a regular contributor of light romance and Stephen Phillips contributed a couple of adventure stories. Playwright Basil Macdonald Hastings contributed three detective stories all, unfortunately, appearing just after his all-too-early death.

Otherwise there was little of note in *The Premier* and it was no longer the presence it had been nearly twenty years before. After the March 1931 issue it merged with *The Red Magazine*.

Frequency: Monthly, but fortnightly from issue 63 (Summer 1919) to 159 (6 Feb 1923).
Publisher: Amalgamated Press.
Editor: David Whitelaw.
Format/Size: Standard. First Series was pulp, page count 176, dropped to 160, Nov 1914; 144, May 1916; 136, Jun 1916; 120, May 1917; 84, Jun 1918; rose to 120, Mar 1919; dropped to 112, 29 Aug 1919; 108, 21 Feb 1922; 100, 21 Mar 1922. Second Series was standard, slick, 124 pages. Third Series reverted to standard pulp, 96 pages.
Price: 4½d, rose to 6d, Feb 1917; 7d, Dec 1917, 8d, Mar 1918; 9d, May 1918; back to 7d, 24 Jan 1922. Second Series was 1/-. Third Series dropped to 6d, rose to 7d, Apr 1927.
References: *The Premier Magazine 1914 to 1931: an annotated checklist* by George Locke (London: Ferret Fantasy, 1999). This book, the only complete annotated guide to a British fiction magazine, also carries a selection of twenty stories from the magazine.
Holdings: *Substantial run, UK.* The Bodleian has a run from May 1914–Jun 1929 (*Call Number*: Per. 25611 d.18). • British Library has only (on microfilm) Feb 1918, 7 Nov 1919; 7 May 1920; 6 May 1921; 12 Aug 1921 (*Shelfmark*: PP.6004.gol; *Microfilm*: Mic.C.327).
Collecting points: Extremely rare and only occasional single issues surface. Only one complete run known in private hands.

* * *

THE REALM
6 issues. Volume 1, Number 1, April 1904 to Volume 1, Number 6, September 1904.

The Realm was the ambitious companion to *The Lady's World*, aiming at a wider family readership. Its timing was disastrous. The period 1904/05 saw a fifty percent slump in sales of popular magazines and it is unlikely *The Realm* succeeded in capturing any significant share of the market. To do so it had to contain something special, but instead it was a copy of all that was available elsewhere, a standard mix of popular articles, stories and features all highly illustrated. The nation's fascination with the East was reflected in several articles about Japan and Korea. Intrigue with the Dark Continent led to such articles as F. C. Selous's "Lion Stories" and Sir Harry Johnston's "The Pygmy Races of Africa", plus James Barr's story "The Death of the Man-Eater". Fascination with scientific advance and warfare were covered by "The Conquest of the Air" by J. M. Bacon and "Torpedoes in Action" by Walter Wood.

The headline stories were Tom Gallon's serial of shady dealings, "Poverty's Diamonds", and William Le Queux's series about the court of Louis XIV, "The Cardinal's Eye", but of more historical interest are two uncollected early stories by Rafael Sabatini, "The Face of the Clock" and "The Devourer of Hearts", plus several stories by James Barr, especially "This Black Bear", set in northern Canada. Jesse Quail, who may have had a hand in editing the magazine, contributed several interesting items including an astronomical column, "The Stars Month by Month". There were also profiles of "Brains in Business" and "Health and Science Notes". Ten years earlier *The Realm* might have made a mark, but the publisher soon realised their mistake and closed the magazine after six issues.

Frequency: Monthly.
Publisher: Macdonald & Martin.
Editor: Not known, possibly Jesse Quail.
Format/Size: Standard, 100/102 pages.
Price: 3d.
Holdings: None known.
Collecting points: Very rare. Individual issues not known but the publisher's bound volume in red may surface infrequently.

* * *

THE RED MAGAZINE

620 issues. Volume 1, Number 1, June 1908 to Volume 101, Number 620, September 1939. Cover showed title as THE HARMSWORTH'S RED MAGAZINE for many years.

Although *The Red Magazine* was published by the same company as *The London*, it would be misrepresentative to call the two magazines companions. They were as different as champagne and chips. They came from different offices within Amalgamated Press. *The London* was in the senior editorial department run by Eric Scott, whilst *The Red* was allocated to the boys' magazine department run by Hamilton Edwards. As a consequence *The Red*, though designed as an adult all-fiction magazine, ran many stories by boys' adventure writers and often read only a little above a boy's story-paper. That may even have been the secret of its success.

The Red was almost certainly started as a result of the success of *The Story-Teller* at Cassell's, and was part of the first wave of all-fiction magazines. Unlike the others, which followed the standard size, *The Red* was slightly stunted, almost an inch shorter, but it made up for this in the use of bulky pulp paper which made the first issue's 170 pages over half-an-inch thick. Since it sold for only 4½d (less than two pence in today's money and the equivalent today of £1.40) it gave the impression of considerable quantity for the money. The cover was unillustrated, merely listing the names of contributors, a design that would remain for eight years. Similarly, although the stories were illustrated they were only hasty sketches. The magazine was clearly produced on the cheap, and the real test was in the value of its fiction.

The magazine was edited for the first twenty years by John Stock, though early issues were co-edited with Albert Broadwell. The first issue simply claimed "openness", that it would run a wide variety of stories and encourage new writers. To that end there was a story competition, offering £100 for the best story under 8,000 words. The contestants had to submit stories under an alias and put their real names in a sealed envelope so as to avoid any bias. The winner, whose story "The Gun" appeared in the January 1909 issue, was Frank Howel Evans. Second place, with "The Sea Urchin and the Prince" (Feb 1909), went to Ethel M. Dell, the leading writer of romantic fiction of the day.

The first issue ran eighteen stories, leading with a series, "My Lady of Mystery" by Jacques Futrelle, famous for the Thinking Machine stories. Another series, "Mulberry Wharf" by H. B. Marriott-Watson, was set in London's dockland. An analysis of stories in the first volume shows that some 30% fell into the category of romantic fiction and 16% equally for adventure stories and general slice-of-life dramas. 12% were mystery and intrigue and 10% were humour. This mixture would not change much over the next few years, though at different times adventure fiction (including westerns and science fiction) or romantic fiction would dominate.

During the first year the headline stories were crime and mystery fiction. The big scoop was the serialisation of Gaston Leroux's "The Perfume of the Lady in Black" (Mar-May 1909), the sequel to Leroux's immensely popular "The Mystery of the Yellow Room" (Daily Mail, 1908), then selling in its tens of thousands. To complete it before its book release, *The Red* ran it in three enlarged issues still at the standard price. Precise sales figures for these issues are not available, but Amalgamated Press claimed average "circulation" figures of around 150,000 for the year which, if true, would certainly place *The Red* amongst the top-selling magazines. When accurate audited figures were released from 1910 onwards, they showed net sales in the 90,000+ region, still very satisfactory. Whatever the exact figures, Amalgamated Press must have been satisfied with sales as, from March 1910, they issued the magazine twice monthly. Sales did not diminish, and it was clear *The Red* had found its place in the market and would remain there for over thirty years.

Apart from a few major names, which in the first two years included Jack London, Oliver Onions, Leonard Merrick, Rafael Sabatini, Barry Pain, O. Henry and F. Frankfort Moore, the bulk of the fiction was by a few regulars. Four in particular stand out and between them they must have accounted for over a tenth of the magazine's contents, pre-1920. They were James Barr, Coutts Brisbane, Bertram Atkey and Roy Norton.

James Barr was the brother of Robert Barr, the editor of *The Idler*. He had been born and raised in Canada, a locale he frequently used for his fiction, much of which was either adventure or romantic intrigue. Although much of his work was serious, he could produce light-hearted material, and could always be relied on for something different. He caused a stir with a series that plotted such changes as may occur if the plans of the socialists came to pass.

"His Grace of Brackenshire" (1 Apr 1911), considered the fate of the peerage, "When Women Won" (15 Apr 1911), concerned female suffrage, "The Passing of Doctor Evening" (1 Jun 1911) explored the nationalisation of the health service and "The Return of the Emigrants" (15 May 1911), considered the impact of too much emigration.

Coutts Brisbane and Reid Whitley were the pseudonyms of Australian R. Coutts Armour, who had settled in London and wrote primarily for the boys' magazines. Both names appeared regularly in *The Red*. Most of these were humorous spoofs – Brisbane could be considered the magazine's court jester. He could write serious fiction if he chose, usually warning stories, such as "As It Was in the Beginning" (15 Dec 1914) which considered the potential for global famine. But most of his stories were satires on society, such as "Mixed Piggles" (1 Dec 1910) in which certain people are changed into pigs, or the series "The Roman Nights" (7 Jan-4 Feb 1921), where he lampoons modern society through situations in ancient Rome.

Bertram Atkey was the champion of the series, and he rattled out one after the other. His most popular character was Prosper Fair, a college lecturer who grows tired of the pressures of life and becomes a gentleman of the road. Starting in "The Wanderings of Prosper Fair" (2 Aug 1915), Fair acquires a donkey and a caravan and sets off on his travels. The series was so popular that Atkey returned to him time and again. "The Pyramid of Lead" (6 Jun-1 Aug 1924) is a clever murder mystery involving Fair. In "The Backslidings of Mr Hobart Honey" (1 Jul-1 Nov 1916) Atkey created the character of Hobart Honey who, through some mysterious pills, sends his consciousness back to different eras in time. "Hercules Makes Good" (1 Jun-1 Sep 1917) dealt with the Labours of Hercules written in the style later associated with Thorne Smith, whilst "The Experiment of Toto" (Oct 1918) introduced what he called the "unnatural nature" series, about strange creatures of legend.

Roy Norton was an adventure writer, pure and simple. Most of his contributions were westerns or frontier stories, including a long-running occasional series about two cowboys, David and Goliath. He was not averse to wilder flights of fancy. "The Garden of Fate" (15 Aug-15 Oct 1910) is an Arabian adventure. "The Glyphs" (31 Oct-12 Dec 1919) and its sequel "The Secret City" (6 Feb-2 Apr 1920) involve a lost Mayan city, whilst "The Shaman" (22 Dec 1922-16 Feb 1923) involves the discovery of a lost village in northern Alaska.

Other regular contributors of adventure stories were James Francis Dwyer, Stuart Martin and Leslie Beresford. Throughout the War years the emphasis was on humour, romance and escapism. When not relying on the bizarre spoofs of Coutts Brisbane or Bertram Atkey, more down-to-earth humour was available from F. Morton Howard and A. E. Ashford, both of whom could write in the vein of P. G. Wodehouse. As for romantic fiction, Ethel M. Dell and May Edginton were the primary contributors, though light society stories and human relationships featured strongly in the stories by Anthony Greenwood, Edgar Jepson, Michael Kent, Selwyn Jepson, E. Norman Torry, Florence Howard-Burleigh and Phyllis Hambledon. Another popular author was William Hope Hodgson who contributed some of his best weird stories of the sea, such as "The Derelict" (1 Dec 1912) and "The Finding of the Graiken" (15 Feb 1913), before settling for more routine sea stories and historical fiction.

Most issues usually ran at least one nature story. The main contributors were F. St. Mars and Charles G. D. Roberts, though later H. Mortimer Batten joined the fold, and *The Red* also reprinted several of the wilderness stories by James Oliver Curwood. There were occasional sports stories, though these were syphoned off into *The Green Magazine* in the early twenties.

Besides the usual suspects were occasional big names. Robert W. Chambers contributed several serials including the light romantic fantasy, "The Green Mouse" (15 Mar-1 Jun 1910) and "Ailsa Paige" (1 Dec 1910-15 Feb 1911), a romance of the American Civil War. H. Rider Haggard appeared with "Red Eve" (1 Dec 1910-1 Mar 1911), a harrowing historical novel about the Black Death. For more light relief was R. Austin Freeman's "The Exploits of Danby Croker" (15 Feb-1 May 1911). E. W. Hornung contributed a series, "The Crime Doctor" (from 15 Aug 1913), whilst H. de Vere Stacpoole appeared with a somewhat uncharacteristic novel, "The Man Who Lost Himself" (15 Oct-1 Dec 1917) about an individual who finds he has exchanged characters with a rich man. Also of interest is "Dormant" (began 15 May 1911), an adult romance by Edith Nesbit, based on the Sleeping Beauty legend. Nesbit's biographer Julia Briggs observed that "Though *Dormant* was written for adults, its structure and symbolism belong to the world of her children's writing."[1] That describes many of the stories in *The Red*, which were pure escapism for adults.

Towards the end of the War, during which time the price had risen and the page count dropped, *The Red* returned to a monthly schedule, but not for long. After just nine months, from February 1919 it reverted to twice monthly and a few months later it switched to fortnightly. Throughout the War *The Red* had sustained a remarkably consistent level of circulation of around 95,000, and by the end of the War had exceeded 100,000. The last recorded figures, for the first six months of 1921, gave an average net sale of 88,337.

The variety of stories in *The Red* remained much the same after the War, though romance fiction came more to the fore. This was evident from the lead stories and serials, which were mostly romances. For a while Ethel M. Dell alternated with one of *The Red*'s discoveries, Margaret Pedler. Although all but forgotten today, Pedler was a major writer of romances between the Wars. She had contributed short stories since 1915 before starting a long run of serials with "The Splendid Folly" (15 Jul-1 Oct 1917). The one that made her reputation was "The House of Dreams" (1 Jul-17 Oct 1919) where a young couple fulfil a gypsy's prophecy. Pedler was one of the pioneer Mills-and-Boon authors. Another young contributor during 1921, though solely of poetry, was Ursula Bloom.

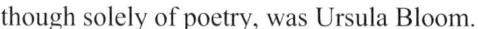

It was during this period that *The Red* gained three companions. First, in September 1921, was *The Yellow*, which syphoned off some of the more unusual stories, allowing *The Red* more space for romantic fiction. The demand for more light romance led to *The Violet* from July 1922, which allowed adventure fiction to regain ground. Finally there was *The Green*, from November 1922, which went for sports and outdoor stories. *The Red* remained the bastion around which the others revolved, and for a while it gave *The Red* more scope to explore what was most important to readers. This diversity accounts for the variety of the covers, which variously reflected romance fiction, adventure or humour. A symbolic cover was that for 18 February 1921 by Hawley Morgan (*above*), which portrayed a globe about which were depicted various types of stories.

---

[1] Julia Briggs, *A Woman of Passion* (London: Penguin Books edition, 1989), p. 346.

The fight for supremacy between romance and adventure continued throughout the first half of the twenties, with Edmund Snell, Roy Norton, Charles Saxby and Leslie Beresford keeping the flag flying for intrigue, and Margaret Pedler, Ethel M. Dell, E. Norman Torry and Florence Howard-Burleigh keeping hearts fluttering. By 1925 women's fiction began to dominate, leading to at least one surprise appearance, "One of my Oldest Friends" by F. Scott Fitzgerald (4 Jun 1926) from *Woman's Home Companion* (Sept 1925).

Both *The Yellow* and *The Green* folded after a few years. Although *The Violet* continued, *The Red* still ran a high quota of romance fiction, and reflected this in the covers. In 1928 the magazine introduced a woman's column by Elizabeth Craig. From here on *The Red* was essentially a woman's magazine. New writers included Olive Wadsley, Edna Ferber, Ruby M. Ayres and Alice Perrin. From August 1929 it reverted to a monthly schedule and, after twenty years, changed its format to the standard pulp size, though only 96 pages. It continued to run humorous fiction, absorbing *The Merry Mag.* from March 1930. During the 1930s *The Red* was a remarkable survivor, absorbing all its companions, including its one-time rival *The Story-Teller*. It also absorbed *The Premier*, at which point David Whitelaw briefly became editor. He soon passed the baton to Francis Ward who had wrapped up the final issue of *The New London*. Under Ward and even more so Clarence Winchester, *The Red* drew heavily on reprints from the publisher's vast archive and from American pulps, so it retained little of its original character. Eventually *The Red* reached a stage when reprints were so dominant that it might as well be a reprint magazine. As a consequence it merged with the one companion it could not absorb, the reprint magazine *Argosy*, which Winchester also edited.

At 620 issues, *The Red* was one of the most prolific British fiction magazines. It cannot ever be said to have been ground-breaking, but it probably provided more escapist fun and romance than any of its rivals, especially during the War years.

Frequency: Monthly, but twice-monthly 1 Mar 1910-15 Mar 1918 and again 1 Feb 1919-1 Aug 1919, then fortnightly from 8 Aug 1919-9 Aug 1929.
Publisher: Amalgamated Press.
Editors: John Stock, 1908-26(?), jointly with A. H. Broadwell until at least 1909; W. A. O'Donnell, 1926(?)-31; David Whitelaw, 1932; Francis Ward, 1933-35; Clarence Winchester, 1936-39.
Format/Size: Small standard pulp until Sept 1929 then switched to standard pulp. Pagination fluctuated during the first year from 192 to 168/170; dropped to 160, Jun 1909; 144, Mar 1910; 128, Jul 1916; 96, 15 Apr 1917; rose to 112, 1 Feb 1919; returned to 96, 13 Aug 1926.
Price: 4½d, rose to 6d, Aug 1917; 7d, Apr 1918; dropped to 6d, 24 Sept 1926, reverting to 7d, 25 Mar 1927.
References: George Locke, "Fantasy in The Red Magazine", *Search & Research*, November 1973, pp. 1-9.
Holdings:
Complete run, UK. British Library on microfilm (*Shelfmark*: PP.6018.tad; *Microfilm*: MiC.C.1830). *Substantial run, UK*. The Bodleian has a run to #488 (8 Mar 1929), missing also issues #147 (15 May 1915), #290 (22 Jul 1921) and #343 (3 Aug 1923) (*Call Number*: Per. 2561 e.5907).
Collecting points: Random single issues are common but long runs are rare. The publisher's own bound file copies, preserving the wrappers, were disposed in auction but the run was broken up.

* * *

THE REGENT MAGAZINE see TIP TOP STORIES OF ADVENTURE & MYSTERY

***

ROMANCE
54 issues. Volume 1, Number 1, February 1923 to Volume 7, Number 54, July 1927.

Although launched as a new magazine, *Romance* was a continuation of a story paper that had started out as *Mrs Bull* in 1910 and changed name twice to become *Everywoman's Weekly* from 27 March 1915.[1] The last change accounts for *Romance's* subtitle as "Everywoman's Story Magazine". At the time *Romance* appeared the word "romance" was undergoing a shift from meaning a tale of adventure to a tale of passion. *Romance* is a good example of this transition, as almost all its stories are love stories, but many are also adventure stories.

This was only too evident from the first issue which opened with an announcement depicting *Romance* as "The Magic Gateway" promising "sanctuary from a wearisome world" in "the Land of Dreams Come True". This was no better demonstrated than in the opening story, "Amanu, Who Was a King" by "Seamark", where a typist in London finds love with a Polynesian king. "Wild Honey" by Jeremy Lane took advantage of the fashion for desert romances inspired by E.M. Hull's *The Sheikh* whilst Morgan Johnson's "The Folly of Guido" takes us back into a romantic historical setting. A more prosaic escapism was in "Lucy's Errand" by Roy Heather where a shop-girl finds romance with an earl.

This type of fiction dominated the early issues whose content was more than adequately reflected on the covers by J. Dewar Mills with their passionate glances and smouldering kisses, and the illustration of knightly derring-do which adorned the contents page. Somewhat more down to earth, but a chance to breath between the dreams, were an advice column, fashion features, a cookery column and a rather idealised view of the drudgery of housework in "The Romance of Housekeeping". All of this was a hangover from the *Everywoman's* days.

Perhaps the strangest content of the first few issues was the serial "The Venus Girl" by Leslie Beresford, about a girl who is sent from the planet Venus to stimulate passion amongst Earthly humans. What could have become a sleazy sex novel instead becomes a battle of wills between the girl and her human paramour.

Romance continued in this form until the closure of its sister publication *Pan*. Thereafter *Romance* started a film supplement of screen stars plus a frontispiece of an attractive young starlet. The stories remained a mixture of saccharine love and escapist romance, but now

---

[1] *Mrs. Bull* was a paper started on 29 October 1910 as an emancipated woman's companion to Horatio Bottomley's *John Bull*. The early issues carried no fiction but it soon changed into a small tabloid story-paper, aimed at the housewife. It broadened its outlook with a title change to *Mary Bull* on 1 March 1913, adopting the sub-title "Everywoman's Weekly" from 17 May that year.

included some bigger-name authors: Ruby M. Ayres, Berta Ruck, Marjorie Bowen and Elinor Glyn. James Oliver Curwood contributed his adventures of the Far North and there were occasional items from Edgar Wallace, L. Patrick Greene, Reginald Campbell, Octavus Roy Cohen and an early story by Erle Stanley Gardner, "Beyond the Limit" (Nov 1925) from *Sunset* (Apr 1925). With the January 1925 issue it began a feature which adapted a current stage play or musical into a short story, starting with "The Pelican". It usually ran the adapted story under the name of the leading actor, so that although "The Pelican" had been written by F. Tennyson Jesse and H. M. Harwood, it was shown as adapted by the actress Josephine Victor. This allowed for a number of interesting names to appear, including Fay Compton, Athene Seyler and Evelyn Laye, as well as the occasional proper credit for Ivor Novello and Noël Coward.

Despite its evident allure *Romance* was no contest against the growing number of women's slick magazines. In a surprise move, Odhams sold the title to the publisher of *The Blue Magazine*. *Romance* now took on an even stronger feel of an adventure magazine with many of *Blue*'s regular contributors. F.A.M. Webster began a series, "The Queen's Confidant" (Mar 1927), about a man who saves a princess from an assassin. C. Lestock Reid, Beatrice Heron-Maxwell and Eric Maschwitz all appeared in its last few issues. But *Romance* did not have a happy ending. After its chameleonesque existence since 1910, it folded in July 1927. It remains a magazine of sugar and spice that occasionally surprises the taste buds.

Frequency: Monthly.
Publisher: Odhams Press to Jan 1927; thereafter F. J. Parsons for The Blue Magazine Co.
Editor: Philippa Preston, 1923; W. A. Williamson, 1924; Miss F. C. MacKenzie, 1925-26; J. Hoole, 1926-7?
Format/Size: Standard pulp, 128 pages. Dropped to 112, Aug 1923; 96, May 1924; returned to 112, Jul 1924 and 126/128, Aug 1924 with minor fluctuations.
Price: 7d, rose to 9d, Jul 1924; 1/-, Jan 1926.
Holdings: *Substantial run, UK*. British Library has a run on microfilm up to Jun 1926 (*Shelfmark*: PP.6018.tax; *Microfilm*: Mic.C.335). The British Library run of *Mrs Bull / Mary Bull / Everywoman's Weekly* is complete and held at Colindale. • Bodleian has run to May 1927 (*Call Number*: Per. 25612 d.16). The Bodleian also has a full run of *Mrs Bull/Mary Bull* (*Call Number*: N. 2474 c.11) and of *Everywoman's Weekly* (*Call Number*: Per. 2705 d.315).
Collecting points: Very rare.

***

THE ROYAL MAGAZINE

491 issues, but only 434 as a fiction magazine. Two series: Volume 1, Number 1, November 1898 to Volume 64, Number 385, November 1930; 385 issues. Revamped as THE NEW ROYAL MAGAZINE, Volume 1, Number 1, December 1930 to Volume 2, Number 18, May 1932; 18 issues. Retitled THE ROYAL PICTORIAL, Volume 2, Number 19, June 1932 to December 1934; 31 issues. Thereafter became a film magazine as THE ROYAL SCREEN PICTORIAL (January to June 1935) and SCREEN PICTORIAL (July 1935 to September 1939).

The Royal was launched by C. Arthur Pearson soon after Harmsworth's had issued *The Harmsworth Magazine*, and was the last new standard illustrated popular magazine of the

1890s, the decade that had revolutionised the popular magazine. With more than a dozen competitors, there was little that *The Royal* could do but imitate, intentionally or otherwise.

Priced at threepence, the same as *The Harmsworth*, it sought to undercut the more expensive monthlies and appeal to a lower middle class family. The surprising fact about the launch of *The Royal* was that it claimed an initial print run of one million copies, which posters declared throughout London a whole month in advance. The editorial says that it took 65 machines 24 days to print and the final run weighed 300 tons. In a single pile it would have reached almost five miles high. Pearson tried to imply that *The Harmsworth* had failed at threepence, but also argued that to sustain that low cover price the magazine needed a "colossal circulation".[1] No accurate sales data are available for any of the magazines at this time, but later estimates suggest they sold anywhere between 150,000 and 250,000 – the latter for the special Christmas issues. It was unlikely, even at threepence, that *The Royal* would sell any more than this, and there was no later editorial claim about the success of the first issue.

Some of the novelty features, such as "The Curiosity Shop", "Snapshot Interviews" and "Some People and Parents", were variations on themes common in all the popular magazines. *The Royal* sought to outdo *The Strand* and even its elder brother, *Pearson's*, on the scale of photographs used. "The Art of the Camera", in one form or another, would remain its lead feature for the next decade. From July 1899 it added "Our Stereoscopic Gallery", printing pairs of photographs and provided a special viewer so they could be seen in 3-D.

The 1890s had been a revolutionary decade for the once genteel Victorian, and certain contents of *The Royal* would have disturbed some households. The second issue ran a feature on the electric chair at Sing Sing prison, "Death by Electrocution", including a photograph of the execution. The next issue ran "Modern Instruments of Torture". There were features on accidents and disasters, a crypt of skulls, detonators and an overly voyeuristic "A Peep Into an Imbecile Training College". *The Royal* was evidently not for the faint-hearted even though it ran a children's play, "The Seven Little Dwarfs" (Feb 1899), a story of a circus, and a story of moral courage, "Æolf the Martyr" by A. W. Marchmont (Nov 1898).

If the shock tactics worked it is likely that *The Royal* attracted a predominantly male readership even though the title – which, unlike *The Windsor*, showed no regal affiliation – might have been intended to attract a female readership. There was an article on dolls in the May 1899 issue, and Edgar Jepson contributed a light-hearted story of a child, "The Heroic Polly" (Jun 1899). But generally the stories and articles were violent. "Juliette" (Aug 1899), was one of Baroness Orczy's earliest pre-Scarlet Pimpernel stories set during the French Revolution. T. V. Crosby's "The Blood of Abel" (Sept 1899) was about Charles I's executioner. Guy Boothby's "The Woman of Death" (Nov 1899-Sept 1900) was about a secret organisation that sponsored duels to the death. Rafael Sabatini sold many of his early stories to *The Royal*, starting with the suggestively entitled "The Curate and the Actress" (Nov 1899).

---

[1] See the display advertisement in *The Times*, 12 October 1898, p. 11.

The magazine threw itself into coverage of the Boer War with both details of events and stories set in the conflict. This bias in the magazine was noted by the editor. Responding in the June 1901 issue to a comment about the comparatively modest covers, he said he was "an editor who has ever manfully striven to delete anything too sweet from the pages of his magazine." These overly bellicose contents eventually ran their course culminating with M. P. Shiel's serial of the destruction of most life on Earth, "The Purple Cloud" (Jan-Jun 1901). This novel is violent from start to finish – the lead character is a murderer and racist – and is stark in its imagery. Once that novel finished the magazine phased out almost all violent fiction.

It's probable that at this stage there was a change in editor. Although Pearson was a hands-on editor, *The Royal* does not betray his mark, and he was otherwise involved with the launch of the *Daily Express*. The magazine shows more the hand of Peter Keary. He also edited *Pearson's Weekly*, which had been noted for its many war-related novels. Keary also became involved with the *Daily Express*, so that by 1901 *The Royal* was left in the hands of Percy Everett. He worked with a series of assistants. The first was explorer Ernest Shackleton, who remained less than a year. His successors were A.S.M. Hutchinson, Rudolf Besier and F. E. Baily, the last later taking over full editorship.

The magazine introduced a humour column from the May 1901 issue. First called "Risms and Rhythms", which the editor admitted was a clumsy title, it changed to "Caps and Bells" and remained a standard feature over the next 28 years. The new lead feature became "From the Stalls", which also remained for the rest of the magazine's life. It carried photographs and commentary on leading actors and actresses and was thus a foretaste of *The Royal*'s ultimate fate as a film magazine.

Under Everett *The Royal* had its first popular success with a series of detective stories by Baroness Orczy now known collectively as "The Old Man in the Corner", but initially run as "London Mysteries" (May-Oct 1901), starting with "The Fenchurch Street Mystery". The success of the first series led to two more, "Mysteries of Great Cities" (Apr-Oct 1902) and "The Old Man in the Corner" (Apr 1904-Mar 1905). In the third series Everett inserted a line to warn readers when the solution was about to be revealed so that they could pause and work it out for themselves. It was a device Ellery Queen would adopt thirty years later.

Orczy stopped after three series when she turned to writing the Scarlet Pimpernel, a work not offered to any of Pearson's magazines. With her departure *The Royal* lost its main star. Although the magazine ran stories by many who would become major names, at this stage they were little known and the works were not those for which they became famous. R. Austin Freeman had a couple of minor stories. Victor L. Whitechurch had a few railway stories, but it was not until the July 1905 issue that they would develop into a detective series with Thorpe Hazell, Railway Detective. P. G. Wodehouse appeared with several cricketing stories, starting with "Jackson's Extra" (Jun 1904). Sax Rohmer, then still known as A. Sarsfield Ward, appeared with the story of a hoax, "Who Was the Rajah?" (Nov 1905). Though these are historically interesting, none of them was of much significance at the time, and *The Royal* was really only playing second fiddle to *Pearson's*. It even had the embarrassment of publishing a plagiarism, "The Tenth Cartridge" by Charles W. Miller (Feb 1905), a direct copy of C. J. Cutcliffe Hyne's "The Ransom".[2]

---

[2] From *The Paradise Coal-Boat* (Bowden, 1897).

The only real success of *The Royal* at this time was a non-fiction series, "Survivors' Tales of Great Events". Starting in February 1905 this ran for 82 issues until December 1911. Walter Wood interviewed survivors of major events, mostly military engagements, and presented their recollections as first-person accounts. The series began with the battle of Rorke's Drift and included the Charge of the Light Brigade, Gettysburg, the Indian Mutiny and even back to the Battle of Waterloo. Later episodes broadened coverage to major disasters.

By 1906 there was a further change in the magazine. A new editorial hand was at play. Everett was distracted, working on *The Novel* and developing *The Scout* for the Boy Scout movement, in which he became heavily involved. Francis Baily took over as acting editor. *The Royal* now ran a greater number of stories and features for women. Ethel Lina White, Ruby M. Ayres, the young I.A.R. Wylie, Jessie Pope and Berta Ruck all became regulars. In response to a reader's enquiry about what kind of stories *The Royal* ran, the editor remarked that "*The Royal* attempts above all to amuse" – a distinct change from eight years earlier – and noted that 90% of the stories submitted were either humorous or romantic. The sensational type of story had apparently "dried up". A new series of tips for women was introduced, "The Woman Beautiful" by Augusta Prescott, superseded by "The Perfect Woman" by Maude Odell (Mar 1909). Love stories, many of an overly saccharhine taste, became the order of the day, although "A Waltz Dream" (Oct 1908) by Daisy Mace Edginton, billed as "a girl's thrilling experience with a dancing baboon", may have taken things a little too far.

The Royal also ran a new series of Paul Beck detective mysteries by McD. Bodkin (Mar-Oct 1907), and Brinsley Moore attempted a series with a twist about a Hindu conjuror and fortune-teller, "Chander Rao, Criminal Expert" (from Oct 1909), but neither of these had much heart in them. What was developing under the surface were stories about the "new woman" and women's suffrage. May Edginton's series "Meg Morton: Fortune Hunter" (Jun-Nov 1911) is about a lone girl who is determined to make her way in the world. There is a remarkable episode in "A Romance of the South Downs" by Fox Russell (Oct 1911) in which the male character discovers that the girl he felt the need to protect can well look after herself. When attacked by villains she knocks them out in true "Emma Peel" style.

Women's stories – not just romances, but stories of independent women – dominated the magazine and grew when Francis Baily became full editor in 1912. He married May Edginton that year and she may well have influenced him in the type of material he ran. Not that he needed much influencing. Baily remained editor of the magazine for fifteen years, apart from a year away during the War. In all that time he contributed many articles and stories both championing and challenging the rôle of the "New Woman". There was no doubt that after a violent start and a rather mixed first decade, *The Royal* had found its niche as the voice of the woman's movement.

That is not to say that it avoided exciting "men's" fiction. *The Royal* was still a general-interest magazine and much of what men enjoyed would also interest the soon-to-be liberated woman. Baily's skill as an editor was in juxtaposing the mix of fiction to produce something that appealed to the whole readership. On the one hand there was Talbot Mundy's serial of German intrigue in India, "The Winds of the World" (from Dec 1915), William Le Queux's series of a radio operator working for the Secret Service, "The Mystery of the Five Beans" (from Sep 1915), John Margerison's many submarine stories and Charles G. D. Roberts' tales of law-and-order in the Canadian backwoods. On the other hand Baily himself wrote several series featuring the modern girl. These included "The Meanderings of Mary" (from Jan 1916), concerning a go-ahead young girl with a passion for motor-cycling, and "Her Feet Beneath Her Petticoat" (from Dec 1917) about a flapper. There were articles asking such questions as "Do Women Really Fall in Love?" (Mar 1916), "Should Girls Wear Trousers?" (Jul 1916), "Will the War Alter Marriage?" (Jan 1917) and "Will the Skirt Go?" (Oct 1917). Baily secured a series of articles by Horatio Bottomley. Although the first picked up on the growing interest in spiritualism, "Are They Really Dead?" (Feb 1917), most of the others dealt with women's liberation. These included "Should Women be Conscripted?" (Mar 1917) and "Why Not a Women's Parliament?" (May 1917). This last matter was returned to after the war by Lady Bonham-Carter in "If Women Ruled" (May 1924), looking at an all female parliament.

Baily's control of the situation meant that after the War *The Royal* became a satisfying blend of light romance, adventure and society fiction, the latter predominantly about the liberated woman. In presentation the magazine moved towards the *The Windsor*, but in content it was closer to *Nash's*, a woman's slick magazine in all but size. Elinor Glyn, Michael Arlen, Joseph Hergesheimer, May Edginton, Olive Wadsley and Fannie Heaslip Lea all wrote romances set in upper-class society, dominated by women. Magdalen King-Hall's "Frank Letters to Uncle Frank" (from Apr 1927) were the confessions of a modern society girl. Dale Collins, Achmed Abdullah and G.B. Lancaster wrote romantic adventure stories set in tropical or remote climes. Phyllis Denham and Margaret Kennedy brought romance closer to home in stories of domestic intrigue, to which Denis Mackail added the light touch. And the light touch was important. *The Royal* was filled with cartoons and humorous illustrations, especially the work of W. Heath Robinson, George Studdy, Mabel Lucie Atwell and Ernest Shepard. It was here that Shepard first drew Winnie the Pooh to accompany several of Milne's stories from June 1926 on (*right*).

KANGA COMES TO THE FOREST.
By A. A. Milne.
Illustrated by E. H. Shepard.

The Royal was ideal for the "cozy" mystery story. It was all but born here with Agatha Christie's Miss Marple in "The Tuesday Night Club" (Dec 1927-May 1928). Baily didn't mind a touch of the occult, either. Dion Fortune's psychic detective series "The Secrets of Dr. Taverner" ran from May 1922. Fortune, under her real name of Violet Firth, also delved into matters psychological in "How Does Your Mind Work?" (Oct 1926), while the French astronomer, Camille Flammarion, turned mystical for "Where the Soul Goes" (Sept 1924).

At the end of 1927 Frank Baily stepped down as editor, though remained a contributor. He was succeeded by Stuart Macrae and the change in content was rapid. Macrae kept some elements of the modern girl. Rebecca West contributed a series, "The Young Woman" (from Nov 1927). In "The Innocent Abroad" (Jan-Jul 1929), Dale Collins has a society girl set off round the world in search of trouble, and there was powerful feminist fiction from Storm Jameson and Pamela Frankau. But he also introduced more men's adventure and crime fiction. He imported Johnston McCulley's detective series about the "Crimson Clown" (from Feb 1929) from the American *Detective Story Magazine*. Gerard Fairlie continued the characters from his book *The Man Who Laughed*, with ex-Secret Service Agent Victor Caryll pitting his wits against a master criminal in "Octopus, the Master Crook" (Apr-Sept 1929). Although pulp writers Reginald Campbell, Achmed Abdullah, Bruce Norman and Albert J. Wetjen were also well in evidence, there was room for a rogue Peter Wimsey story by Sayers, "Copper Fingers" (Jan 1930). Also the lead feature, which had for years been photographs of stars of stage and screen, took a decidedly erotic turn with pictures of dancers and models. Macrae was clearly shifting the balance in the magazine away from the independent girl to the high-spirited man.

At this point, however, Pearson's muddied the waters. The end of the 1920s saw a fundamental change in magazines. They either remained predominantly fiction in the standard size and format, or they increased in size to the large flat format as wider general-interest magazines. Pearson's decided to have something in both camps. *Pearson's* remained in standard form but *The Royal*, renamed and relaunched as *The New Royal*, shifted to the new format. It did not go the full way and have high quality coated stock, but opted for a cheaper matt stock. Improved printing techniques allowed them to issue *The New Royal* at half the price. Macrae saw the change through but then stepped down.

John Reed Wade, who also edited *Pearson's*, took over and instigated further changes. *The New Royal* rapidly moved away from being a fiction magazine towards a celebrity-based magazine. The features on stage and screen grew and a film supplement was added from January 1932. It was a short step from that to being retitled *The Royal Pictorial* in June 1932. By May 1932 the magazine was down to running just three stories per issue, and the rest was given over to film coverage and general features. Although general fiction remained for a few more years, including light romances by Richmal Crompton, increasingly the fiction became adaptations of film stories.[3] In 1935 Wade handed the editorship to William J. Makin and the magazine became *The Royal Screen Pictorial*, shrunk six months later to *Screen Pictorial*. There were also Summer and Winter *Annual*s (1935-1939). By 1937 only the film adaptations remained. The magazine survived until September 1939 when it folded at the outbreak of War, but it had already long vanished as a fiction magazine.

---

[3] These include adaptations of "The Thin Man" (Nov 1934), "The Trail of the Lonesome Pine" (Oct 1936) and "Lost Horizon" (Oct 1937).

Frequency: Monthly.
Publisher: C. Arthur Pearson.
Editors: Peter Keary, Nov 1898-Apr 1901; Percy Everett, May 1901-Dec 1911; F. E. Baily, Jan 1912-Jun 1927; R. Stuart Macrae, Jul 1927-May 1932; John Reed Wade, Jun 1932-Dec 1934; William J. Makin, Jan 1935-1937; David Chancellor, 1937-Sept 1939.
Format/Size: Standard. Page count 96, dropped to 80, Jun 1899, rose to 84/88, Dec 1899 and 96, Apr 1901. Dropped to 80/84, May 1917, 72, May 1918; rose to 80/84, Feb 1919, 100/104, Aug 1922, 106/108, Nov 1927. With change to *The New Royal* became large flat semi-slick, 104 pages, dropped to 92, Jan 1931, 80, Apr 1931, 64/68, Dec 1931; 52, Jun 1932.
Price: 3d; rose to 4d, Nov 1899; 4½d, Jan 1912; 6d, May 1916, 7d, Feb 1917; 8d, Jan 1918; 9d, Mar 1918; 1/-, Jun 1918; dropped to 9d, Feb 1919; back to 1/-, Jan 1921. With change to *The New Royal*, dropped to 6d.
Holdings:
Complete run, UK. British Library (*Shelfmark*: PP.6018.tb).
Substantial run, UK. Bodleian has a near complete run of *The Royal Magazine*, missing only issue Jul 1930 (*Call Number*: Per. 2705 d.88); and has all issues of *The New Royal* and *The Royal Pictorial* (*Call Number*: Per. 2705 c.66). • Cambridge University Library has volumes 1-20, Nov 1898-Oct 1908 only (*Classmark*: L996.c.27). • National Library of Scotland has run Nov 1898-Nov 1930 (*Shelfmark*: Y.192.h).
Substantial run, US: New York Public Library has volumes 1-64, Nov 1898-Nov 1930.
Collecting points: Six-monthly Bound volumes in publisher's grey pictorial binding are common for the first few years but much less common from around 1910 onwards. Single issues are more common but erratic. Issues of *The New Royal* and *Royal Pictorial* are uncommon but *Screen Pictorial* remains common avidly collected by film buffs.

* * *

SIEVIER'S MONTHLY
23 issues. Volume 1, Number 1, January 1909 to Volume 2, Number 11, November 1910.

Robert Sievier does not seem the likeliest person to run a fiction magazine but during the heyday of magazine publishing many an individual entered the fray, building on the reputation of their name.[1] Sievier had been a soldier and all-round sportsman, even a successful actor, before he became a renowned racehorse owner. He founded the racing paper *The Winning Post* and it was through that enterprise that he launched his own monthly magazine.

Sievier's Monthly was a miscellany of short fiction, *bon mots*, sketches and verse, plus a fashion column, all liberally illustrated. In the early issues many stories were either anonymous or pseudonymous. Much was the work of the magazine's sub-editor, the young Marguerite Jervis who had already adopted the alias "Oliver Sandys". The magazine serialised her first novel, the episodic "The Woman in the Firelight" (from Jan 1909), and the series, "The Adventures of a Lady's Companion" (Jul 1909-Jun 1910), written as Olive Bree. Other main contributors were A. Kerr Bruce, Francis Headley and Ralph Stock, who was already producing stories of the South Seas. Sievier contributed his own romanticised autobiography, "Warned Off", from the first issue. From December 1909 the magazine ran a regular ghost story by Elliott O'Donnell.

---

[1] See also *Fry's Magazine* and *Sandow's Magazine* in Section 2.

Though no single issue of *Sievier's* was especially strong, its cumulative effect becomes rather pleasing, albeit erratic, partly due to Sandys's inexperience – she resigned in a tantrum after an argument with Sievier over the magazine's paste-up. Sievier continued for a while and then wound it up when it proved less than successful. It is one of those many short-lived, second-level magazines that has more to offer than is at first apparent.

Frequency: Monthly.
Publisher: Robert S. Sievier at The Winning Post.
Editor: Robert S. Sievier, with Oliver Sandys as sub-editor on first few issues.
Format/Size: Stunted standard (21cm x 17cm), 96 pages.
Price: 6d.
References: Oliver Sandys, *Full and Frank* (London: Hutchinson, 1941), pp. 64-72.
Holdings:
Complete run, UK. Bodleian (*Call Number*: Per. 2561 e.6490).
Substantial run, UK. British Library is missing issues May, Nov 1909, Sept, Oct 1910 (*Shelfmark*: PP.6018.tae).
Collecting points: Not as rare as one might expect but still uncommon, especially later issues.

***

THE SOVEREIGN MAGAZINE

88 issues. Volume 1, Number 1, November 1919 to Volume 13, Number 88, April 1927. Absorbed *The Regent Magazine* in May 1925 and was entitled THE SOVEREIGN AND REGENT MAGAZINE until November 1925.

The Sovereign began as a woman's orientated companion to *Hutchinson's Magazine*, but it soon developed into a magazine of adventure and romance. The opening serial was "The Golden Apple" by Kathlyn Rhodes, a society novel that becomes a desert romance. Also in the first issue was "The Trail of the Beast" by Achmed Abdullah, a detective novel set in France, featuring debonair American James Tennant, who prefers psychological deduction to forensic detection. Both novels oozed exotic escapism. They were bolstered by light romances by Berta Ruck, Charles Garvice, Mrs Baillie Reynolds and others.

The editors asked the readers to vote for their favourite story and the reader whose vote came closest to the overall result would win £50. The magazine was overwhelmed with responses, and it was a year before they revealed the most popular stories in the first six issues. Top of the list were Rhodes's and Abdullah's serials. The magazine printed the names of not only the prizewinner but the eighteen runners-up and all but one were women. During that first six months *The Sovereign* had published some top adventure stories. These included the latest series of Tarzan series by Edgar Rice Burroughs, "Tarzan the Untamed", of which the first story, "An Eye for an Eye" (Mar 1920), featured fourth on the readers' list. By contrast Sax Rohmer's exotic weird tale, "Tchériapin" (Apr 1920) did not figure in the list at all. Other top-rated authors included Sapper, Ruby M. Ayres and Anthony M. Rud, their work further emphasising the readers' delight in romantic adventure, mystery and intrigue.

Their desires came together in one novel that made its author's reputation, "Scaramouche" (Nov 1920-Sept 1921) by Rafael Sabatini. Although Sabatini had been contributing historical adventure stories to the magazines for over twenty years, which were always popular, it was this swashbuckler of the fight for justice during the French Revolution that captured the public imagination and soon became a major film (1923). *The Sovereign* did not capitalise on Sabatini's success, as he was in demand by other magazines; instead it shifted towards mystery stories and torrid romance.

At this stage there were few outright ghost stories, the magazine favouring occasional weird fiction in exotic settings. However from January 1922, as a result of an agreement between Hutchinson and the American publisher Bernarr Macfadden, material began to appear from Macfadden's magazines, accompanied by their posed photographs. Although *The Sovereign* still presented itself as a magazine of adventure and intrigue – featuring "The Black Gang" (Mar-Sept 1922), a new Bulldog Drummond serial by Sapper and "Shackled" (Apr-Jun 1924), another desert romance by Achmed Abdullah, and the earliest stories by Leslie Charteris – there was a significant growth in weird mysteries and ghost stories. There were home-grown authors, including Margery Allingham ("The Wind Glass", July 1924), Ursula Bloom ("The Curious Curse", February 1925), Agatha Christie ("The House of Dreams", Jan 1926) and Richmal Crompton ("Vision", Jan 1926), but most stories were from the American pulps, including *Weird Tales* and *Ghost Stories*. *The Sovereign* was in danger of becoming a copy of Hutchinson's *Mystery-Story*. It could be accused of betraying its readers, sacrificing the romantic adventure (which had been syphoned off to *Hutchinson's Magazine)* in favour of sensationalised mystery stories. One novel of interest at this time was "Colin II" (Apr-Jun 1925), the second of E. F. Benson's books about the victim of a curse. It is a profound character study by Benson into the nature of evil.

Then, in one of Hutchinson's characteristic whims, *The Sovereign* was converted into a humour magazine from the February 1927 issue. A few remnants from past issues remained, including "The Stolen Ghost" by Agatha Christie and two suspense series by William Le Queux and Johnston McCulley, but there was a marked shift to cartoons and jokes. In this form it saw only one further issue and then transformed into the humour magazine *The Jolly*. What had started with such promise had fallen victim to the publisher's erratic moods.

Frequency: Monthly, but combined issue June/July 1926.
Publisher: Hutchinson.
Editors: Uncertain; probably Eric Maschwitz, 1922-23; Miss G. Gilligan in 1925-26.
Format/Size: Standard pulp. Page-count 96, rose to 112, Feb 1920; 144, Dec 1923; dropped to 116/120, Oct 1925.
Price: 6d, rose to 9d, Feb 1920; 1/-, Dec 1923.
Holdings: *Complete run, UK.* Bodleian (*Call Number*: Per. 245611 d.80).
Substantial run, UK. British Library is missing issues Jun, Oct 1922, and Jun/Jul 1926 (*Shelfmark*: PP.6018.tba).
Collecting points: Extremely rare.

* * *

STANDARD STORIES

12 issues. Volume 1, Number 1, July 1925 to Volume 1, Number 12, June/July 1926. Merged with *Best-Story Magazine*.

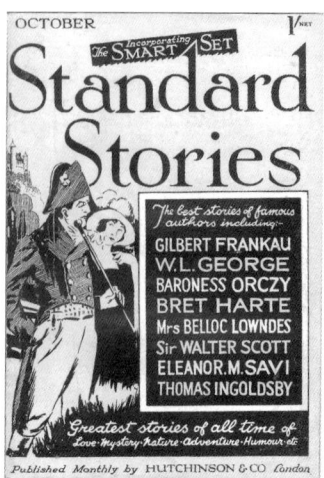

Clearly modelled on the American reprint magazine *Golden Book*, which had appeared in January 1925, *Standard Stories* credited itself as running "The World's Greatest Stories of Love, Mystery, Nature, Adventure, Humour". It built upon the feature common in many magazines of authors selecting their favourite amongst their own stories and explaining why. The authors' brief opening comments are the magazine's main appeal. In the first issue H. de Vere Stacpoole selected "The Girl at the Gate" because "it brings to me the light of other days." Anthony Hope chose "The Riddle of Countess Runa", a Ruritanianesque fable which he nevertheless felt was "one that corresponds to what I like best in life." Sir Philip Gibbs reason for selecting "Out of the Ruins" is at least refreshingly honest, as it was the story that he disliked the least. Thomas Burke selected "The Affair at the Warehouse" in the second issue, but commented that what he thought was his best story was "accidently destroyed in a spring-cleaning of my desk." Eden Phillpotts chose "The Skipper's Bible" (Nov 1925) claiming that it was "as good, though no better, than dozens of others."

One of the drawbacks of this feature is that an author can only be represented once, but before long many of the same names were reappearing but not under the "My Favourite Story" banner. The magazine also reprinted stories by authors long-dead, and before long it lost the edge that the author's involvement provided. It rarely carried any illustrations and priced at 1/- for just 96 pages, with no new fiction, was of questionable value. The magazine survived for twelve issues before being absorbed by *Best-Story Magazine*.

From its first issue *Standard Stories* proclaimed that it incorporated the British edition of *The Smart Set*. This made no difference to the contents and was simply a means to keep control over the title. It had none of the flair and style that had once been the province of *The Smart Set*. A better attempt at a reprint magazine was happening at Cassell's with *Argosy*.

Frequency: Monthly.
Publisher: Hutchinson.
Editor(s): Probably Evelyn Hornibrook.
Format/Size: Standard pulp, 92/96 pages.
Price: 1/-.
Holdings: *Complete run, UK*. Bodleian (*Call Number*: Per. 25612 d.56); Cambridge University Library (*Classmark*: L996.c.40).
Collecting points: Scarce but occasional issues do surface.

* * *

THE STORY-TELLER

367 issues. Two series. Volume 1, Number 1, April 1907 to Volume 59, Number 355, October 1936; 354 issues (there is no number 314). New series, Volume 1, Number 1, November 1936 to Volume 3, Number 13, November 1937; 13 issues.

The Story-Teller was the best all-round all-fiction magazine of its day. It was born following a purge conducted at Cassell's by new General Manager Arthur Spurgeon. The editors were rooted in the Victorian era and Spurgeon appointed Newman Flower as the "new broom". After a success with the *Penny Magazine*, Flower was asked to devise "a new magazine that would recapture the prestige and circulation that the firm's publications had enjoyed in the past."[1] The result was *The Story-Teller*.

It scarcely seems revolutionary. It was an all-fiction magazine, unillustrated, printed on cheap pulp-grade paper and selling for 4½d. There were already two magazines along these lines on the market, *The Grand* and *The Novel*, both of which sold for 4d, but *The Story-Teller* made up for this by being bigger, 176 pages instead of 144. *The Grand* had vacillated between fiction and non-fiction, whilst *The Novel* presented reprints and translations and work by many unknowns. Flower went for all new fiction mostly by big names. He outlawed serials at the outset, choosing instead connected story series and a long "complete novel" in each issue. These "novels" were usually between 20-30,000 words so were substantially longer than in other magazines.

The first issue led with a story by Hall Caine and included E. Phillips Oppenheim, Alice and Claude Askew, Marjorie Bowen, Oliver Onions and Tom Gallon. Historically, the most interesting item is the opening episode of "The Adventures of Arsène Lupin" by Maurice Leblanc. These stories of a master criminal who outwits the police but helps solve crimes had been a big hit in France and America.

To help gauge reader reaction Flower set a competition for readers to vote on their favourite stories and all those who nominated as first the one that topped the poll would be sent free a six-shilling novel. The most popular story was "Veronica's Victory" by Alice and Claude Askew. This was a romance with a twist, about how a woman saves a politician from sinking into crime. Flower kept this voting system going, awarding two guineas thereafter to whoever nominated the top three in their final order. Unfortunately he stopped printing the results after the first few responses.

Flower tried a few gimmicks at the outset, as all editors do. He created a series, "The Tenants of Toddington Terrace" (from May 1907), about a man who inherits a fortune along with the freehold to a terrace of houses. He decides to live in the terrace and study the people in the other houses. Flower then commissioned different authors to tell the stories of these residents, amongst them Tom Gallon, Fred M. White and William Le Queux. He also ran a story by a popular author but omitted the by-line, asking readers to identify him.

---

[1] Simon Nowell-Smith, *The House of Cassell* (London: Cassell, 1958), p. 201.

He soon found that he did not need the gimmicks. The magazine's strength was in its stories. Flower, and his sub-editor David Whitelaw (who had also provided the magazine's standard pastoral cover[2]), both knew what the public enjoyed. Although they published a range of fiction that would fall into several categories – sports stories, romances, mysteries, adventures, humour, supernatural – what was more important was that each story was inspiring. What Flower wanted were stories where humans had to show ingenuity and courage in overcoming unusual and sometimes extreme problems. He did not want straight love stories or slice-of-life dramas. He wanted what became known as "clever" stories, and this became the magazine's hallmark, remaining virtually unchanged but always refreshing for the next thirty years. In his final issues, Flower ran the popular series "The Careers of Bertram Barrington" by Norman Venner (from Dec 1927) about a man who pulls himself up by his bootstraps time after time after financial disaster.

The best examples, and those for which the magazine is remembered, were almost always mysteries. In December 1907 Flower launched the "Thinking Machine" stories by Jacques Futrelle in both *Cassell's* and *The Story-Teller*. These were complicated, seemingly impossible, crimes that only the remarkable intellect of Professor van Dusen can unravel. An early series by E. Phillips Oppenheim (who was a regular contributor throughout the magazine's life) was "The Long Arm of Mannister" (from Dec 1907), where the hero sets out to take revenge upon those who had wronged him. In each case his methods are original and varied. Years later Rudyard Kipling told Flower that "The Long Arm of Mannister" was "one of the finest series of stories you have had."[3]

Flower encouraged different stories by Rafael Sabatini, rather than straight historical swashbucklers. In "The Risen Dead" (Dec 1907), a man survives the gallows and is able to lead a different life. In "The Avenger" (Mar 1909), one of the longer "novels", we meet anti-hero Roger Galliphant, who takes the law into his own hands. The title of another series, "The League of the Watching Eye" by Grenville Hammerton [Frank H. Shaw] (from Apr 1910), refers to a secret society that works to stop criminals before they commit their crimes. There were similar clever stories and series by Mayne Lindsay, Katharine Tynan, Ward Muir – "The Man With the Ebony Crutches" (Feb 1908) about another master villain being a particular hit – Edgar Wallace, Headon Hill, William Hope Hodgson and Frank H. Shaw. Shaw would become the magazine's most prolific contributor, scarcely missing an issue. Most of his stories were sea adventures, of which the early short novel, "The Terror of the Seas" (Jun 1907) was especially popular. At the height of fascination with polar conquest his "The Frozen Vengeance" (Aug 1909), struck a chord.

But there were two series that stood head and shoulders above all others in the popularity of *The Story-Teller*'s early years: the Father Brown stories by G. K. Chesterton and the Fu Manchu stories by Sax Rohmer. Flower recognised the significance of Chesterton's stories which he announced as "the best detective stories of our time", hailing the September 1910 issue, in which "The Innocence of Father Brown" began, as the most important issue in the magazine's history. Chesterton had taken the impossible puzzle crime of Jacques Futrelle but instead of having them solved by a seeming human computer, he had chosen a meek and

---

[2] Whitelaw's pastoral and sylvan covers remained until November 1914. Thereafter each cover was pictorial, illustrating a story, with many painted by Albert Morrow.
[3] Newman Flower, *Just as It Happened* (London: Cassell, 1950), p. 29.

apparently harmless priest. These stories fitted one half of Flower's story policy precisely – the everyday innocent who comes up trumps and succeeds over adversity.

Fu Manchu was the opposite, and so fitted the other half of Flower's policy. Here was a fiendish, brutal, evil mastermind against whom the authorities seem powerless, and every story sees him matching wits against his Scotland Yard opponent, each time raising the stakes. The first series began with "The Zayat Kiss" in October 1912 and ran through to July 1913.

The unlikely partnership of Fu Manchu and Father Brown was the success formula for *The Story-Teller*. Sales in the first year had averaged 80,000 but by the end of the Father Brown series was up to 147,000 settling at around 130/140,000 for the next few years. This was almost double the sales of its stable-mate *Cassell's Magazine*, and resulted in that magazine being totally revamped into an all-fiction pulp. It also encouraged Cassell's to launch a further title, *The New Magazine*. The immediate success of *The Story-Teller* was the lure to other publishers and in quick succession came *The Red*, *Nash's* and *Everybody's*. Even *Pall Mall* added a special "story-book" section. Furthermore *The Story-Teller* saved Cassell's as a publisher. Newman Flower recalled the bold statistics:

> At a later stage Spurgeon declared that the firm lived on that magazine during its worst two years. All we could afford to spend on the first number – literary, publicity, everything – was £1,600, for we had nothing more in the till. Harmsworth's were spending £20,000 at that time for publicity alone, on every new publication they put out. But the God of battles was on our side. The *Story-Teller* blazed ahead; it was the child of my heart. When I gave up the editorship on its twenty-first birthday . . . I asked what the original investment of £1,600 had produced. The figures were got out. £262,000. Oh yes, the *Story-Teller* was ever my blue-eyed boy![4]

In the space of a few years *The Story-Teller* had changed the face of magazine publishing and established the niche for the all-fiction magazine that would thrive alongside its slick cousins well into the 1920s. During that period *The Story-Teller* changed little. Its page count fluctuated during the War, and its price rose rapidly, but its content remained true to the original formula. If there was any change during and after the War it was to recognise the growing female readership and include more stories of interest to women. This did not mean simple romance stories, though more of those did appear. Flower looked for stories of clever and intrepid women. Olive Wadsley set the standard with "Rosetime" (Aug 1914-Jan 1915) about an American barmaid who has to cope with becoming an heiress. Hugh Walpole's "March Square" (Sept 1914-Mar 1915) tells the escapades of a clever group of children. I.A.R. Wylie's "The Jonases" (Apr-Sept 1915) concerns a family where each member is forced to rebel to follow their scruples. Richard Marsh's "Judith Lee" (Jul-Dec 1915), won over from *The Strand*, is about a lip-reader whose skill gets her into and out of trouble.

Although *The Story-Teller* did publish war stories – two or three every issue, including headliners by Talbot Mundy, Warwick Deeping, E. P. Oppenheim, Allen Upward and Sapper – the preference remained for escapist, humorous or adventurous fiction. Andrew Soutar took us to the South Seas in "Rainbow Nights" (Feb 1915), Brinsley Moore introduced a humorous family in "Mrs Drake's Discoveries" (from Nov 1915) and Arnold Bennett provided several of

---

[4] Newman Flower, *Just as It Happened*, op. cit., p. 28. £262,000 is worth over £11 million at today's prices.

his sharp stories. Sax Rohmer had been lured away to *The Premier* for much of his fiction, but he returned to *The Story-Teller* with the "Si-Fan Mysteries" (Sept-Dec 1916) and other weird tales. Another regular was the poet Alfred Noyes whose contributions included the spiritually uplifting "The Hand of the Master" (Oct 1918), ideal for the end of the War. There was also a touching and rare short story by George Bernard Shaw, "The Emperor and the Little Girl" (Dec 1917). Shaw requested that his fee be donated to a Belgian charity for destitute children.

After the War, despite increased competition from a new batch of all-fiction magazines, *The Story-Teller* maintained its high circulation, hovering around the 100,000 mark. Its stories became, if anything, even more exotic. Warwick Deeping turned to ancient Egypt in "The Heart of Tua the Princess" (Feb 1920) and ancient Crete in "The Sacred Snakes" (Jan 1922). *The Story-Teller* did not escape the vogue for South Sea stories – Newman Flower even published his own, "The Island of 'God Forgets'" (Sept 1918). H. de Vere Stacpoole, Beatrice Grimshaw, Albert R. Wetjen and James Francis Dwyer all contributed exotic adventures during the 1920s.

In "Brethren All" (May-Jun 1920), Frank Shaw produced a series of masonic mysteries. Rudyard Kipling also turned to freemasonry for a series, starting with "In the Interests of the Brethren" (Dec 1918), about how Masonic principles could help rebuild the world. H. Rider Haggard contributed a rare story, "The Missionary and the Witch-doctor"[5] (Nov 1920); H. G. Wells turned in an equally rare post-war fantasy, "The Grisly Folk" (Apr 1921), whilst Sax Rohmer contributed an occasional tale of Chinatown. Flower secured a new series from Baroness Orczy, "The League of the Scarlet Pimpernel" (Feb-Apr 1919). Hugh Walpole began his candidly autobiographical "Jeremy" series (Dec 1918-Nov 1919). On the lighter side George Robey, contributed several humorous stories about a hen-pecked husband, starting with "A Moving Story" (Apr 1921).

G. K. Chesterton remained a regular contributor, even though some of the later Father Brown stories were sold to *Nash's*. In addition to a few one-off stories, he contributed several new intermittent series including "The Man Who Knew Too Much" (from Jul 1920), "Tales of the Long Bow" (from Jun 1924) and, in the thirties, the various puzzles of Mr Pond (from Jul 1935). Several major literary names contributed to *The Story-Teller* in the post-war decade. It published Arnold Bennett's final story, "Early Morning" (Jun 1932). Compton Mackenzie appeared with his novel of theatrical life, "The Vanity Girl" (Dec 1919-Nov 1920) and several stories in the Jenny Pearl series. There were also stories by Arthur Conan Doyle, Maxim Gorky, Sheila Kaye-Smith and John Galsworthy. *The Story-Teller* published an early story by Henry Williamson, "Aliens" (Sept 1922), and the only short story by the famed surgeon Frederick Treves, "Lady Margaret's Rose" (Dec 1925).

In December 1926 Cassell's magazine department was transferred to Amalgamated Press. Flower stayed at Cassell but, out of dedication to the "child of his heart", he remained as editor

---

[5] Included in *Smith and the Pharaohs* under the title "Little Flower".

of *The Story-Teller* until the May 1928 issue, to celebrate twenty-one years. He then handed it over to Clarence Winchester, who had worked as his sub-editor during the twenties.

Winchester sustained the individuality of *The Story-Teller*. If anything he enhanced it. He kept the same formula and mix of newcomers and major names. In his first two years he published work by James Hilton, F. Scott Fitzgerald and Vicente Blasco Ibanez alongside Eden Phillpotts, E. F. Benson, Francis Brett Young, Ernest Bramah and Thomas Burke. He soon added Dorothy L. Sayers, G. B. Stern, Martin Amstrong, C. S. Forester, Leslie Charteris, Stephen Vincent Benét and Paul Gallico. Under Flower he had acquired Agatha Christie's Harley Quin series, "The Magic of Mr Quin" (Dec 1926-May 1927), and now added the second series of her Miss Marple stories (Dec 1929-May 1930). He also published the enigmatic mysteries and weird stories of Vincent Cornier, including the remarkable series of impossible crimes, "The Brantyngham Riddles" (Apr-Oct 1929). He ran David Garnett's disturbing allegorical short novel, "The Grasshoppers Come" (Apr 1931), and John Galsworthy's final novel, "Over the River" (Jun-Nov 1933). The period 1928 to 1930 was especially powerful with every issue crammed with strong stories. The emphasis remained on mystery and exotic fiction, though by the mid-thirties a shift towards women's fiction became noticeable, led by Margaret Sangster's hospital romance "Night Call" (Oct 1935).

During Winchester's tenure several fiction magazines had merged with *The Story-Teller*, including *Cassell's* and *The New London*. *The Story-Teller* still stood proud. The magazine had been revamped in June 1932 with a new cover design and interior format, but Winchester felt there was scope to spread its wings further. From November 1936 the magazine was completely overhauled. It was converted into a slick, fully illustrated though keeping the old size. It incorporated non-fiction in the form of writers' adventures and experiences. Peter Fleming led the first issue with "Journey to Samarkand" whilst Antoine de Saint-Exupéry recounted his desert adventures in a three-part series. Later issues saw C. T. Stoneham's "Episode in Africa" (Feb 1937) and Edward Shackleton, son of the explorer, with "Arctic Hunter" (Apr 1937). The stories were jazzed up with modern-style artwork and cartoons were included, some in colour. The magazine now strongly resembled *Pearson's*.

The experiment was a short-lived disaster. After just six issues all non-fiction was dropped and the magazine reverted to the pulp format, with a price drop to sixpence. With the change the magazine lost its soul. The final few issues looked cheap and consisted primarily of reprints from American pulps. After seven issues it was merged with *The Red Magazine*.

The sudden failure of *The Story-Teller* was a strong message that the market for glossy magazines aimed at male readers was fading fast. Unlike other fiction magazines *The Story-Teller* did not adapt to the women's market, which led to its demise. Although a few magazines would continue up to and even into the first year of the War, one could argue that the real Age of the Fiction Magazine ended with the passing of *The Story-Teller*.

Frequency: Monthly, but combined issue for Jul/Aug 1926.
Publisher: Cassell to Apr 1927; thereafter Amalgamated Press.
Editors: Newman Flower, Apr 1907-May 1928; thereafter Clarence Winchester.
Format/Size: Standard pulp. Page count 176/180, dropped to 142/4, May 1916; 126, Mar 1918; 110/112, May 1918; 126, May 1919; 110/114, Apr 1920; rose to 140/144, May 1922; 148/152, Oct

1931. Turned standard slick, Nov 1936-Apr 1937, pagination shifting from 132 to 112. Reverted to standard pulp, 128 pages, May-Nov 1937.
Price: 4½d, rose to 7d, Feb 1917; 8d, Jun 1917; 9d, Feb 1918; 1/-, May 1918.
Holdings: *Substantial run, UK*. British Library run is on microfilm, missing issues for March 1923, Nov and Dec 1927 only. (*Shelfmark*: PP.6018.tab; *Microfilm*: Mic C/1838). • Bodleian has run Apr 1907-Jun 1929 (*Call Number*: Per. 2561 d.46).
Collecting points: Early volumes in publisher's pictorial binding are not uncommon but are undated and can only be identified by the number of stars on the spine. Single issues surface infrequently and are uncommon for the post-war years.

* * *

THE STRAND MAGAZINE

710 issues. Volume 1, Number 1, January 1891 to Volume 118, Number 711, March 1950; (issues 677/678 combined). Merged with *Men Only*.

The remarkable entrepreneur who launched *The Strand Magazine* was George Newnes (*left*), a north-countryman who started to build his publishing empire with a weekly paper, *Tit-Bits*, published in Manchester from 22 October 1881. Within a few years, Newnes's *pot-pourri* of human-interest snippets, fairly useless knowledge and serial fiction, aimed at lower-middle-class and "aspiring" working-class readers, had become very successful and he was able to move his offices to London – to Burleigh Street, just off the Strand. It was there, in the summer of 1890, that *The Strand Magazine* was conceived. For six months past, Newnes had collaborated with the well-known journalist W. T. Stead to produce a monthly called *The Review of Reviews*, intended (from Newnes's point of view) as a more up-market *Tit-Bits*; but there was a certain clash of wills and the partnership came to an amicable end when Newnes sold his share in that project to Stead. Relieved of that responsibility Newnes found himself with spare staff and printing capacity, so decided to produce another monthly. On his staff was a young man named Herbert Greenhough Smith, freshly arrived from the offices of the three-decades-old (and now declining) magazine *Temple Bar* where he had:

> hit on the idea of a magazine consisting of short stories translated from foreign authors. His proprietor turned it down, so he sent it to George Newnes who signed him on as assistant to him on *The Strand Magazine* to be.[1]

Greenhough Smith's idea obviously appealed to Newnes as one means of providing textual matter for his proposed new magazine, the main attraction of which, as far as Newnes was concerned, was that it would carry "a picture on every page."

Although *The Strand* was to be much more than a magazine of translated stories, the importance of Greenhough Smith's seed notion should not be underestimated. In the Britain of

---

[1] Reginald Pound, *A Maypole in the Strand*, pp. 89-90.

the 1880s, the short story as a distinct form of fiction was less common than overseas – particularly in Russia, France, and the United States of America. (It was an American critic of the 1880s, Brander Matthews, who did most to establish an English-language awareness of what he called "the true short-story" as opposed to "the more carelessly composed tale which happens to be brief.") Greenhough Smith was an admirer of Guy de Maupassant and other foreign masters, and as far as he was concerned one of the main purposes of *The Strand* in its early years was to introduce short stories of that type to a British audience. Hence the rule, which endured for the first five years, that the magazine would not follow the normal Victorian practice of serialising lengthy novels – every issue was to be complete in itself.

What Newnes, Greenhough Smith and their staff (principally the art editor, W. H. Boot) succeeded in creating was a new kind of magazine, one which had no exact precursor on either side of the Atlantic, and which was to become an important model for future periodical publishing. This may be termed the Standard Illustrated Popular Magazine. That descriptive phrase, although unwieldy, is chosen with care. The magazines in question were "standard" in size and format – about 170mm wide by 250mm tall, with spines and fore-and-aft advertising sections. They were copiously "illustrated" with line drawings or engravings, and soon with photographs, and it was in order to provide space for their illustrative matter that such magazines adopted the standard format in the first place (a size somewhat larger than the various book-like octavo formats which the majority of sparsely illustrated Victorian fiction magazines had clung to). And they were "popular" – that is to say, they were popularly priced in order to reach a mass audience, the rapid growth of which would greatly fuel advertising revenues. In Britain, in the 1890s, the typical price of these monthlies was sixpence; in America, it was ten cents.

The publication which provided the template for the Standard Illustrated Popular Magazine was *The Strand*, launched shortly before Christmas 1890, its first issue dated January 1891. To be clear, *The Strand* was not the first Standard Illustrated Magazine – that standard, both in terms of size and illustration, had been set in America, by *Harper's New Monthly Magazine* (which had evolved since 1850, with a European edition from 1880) and by the "quality" periodicals which emulated it, especially *The Century Illustrated Monthly Magazine* (from 1881) and *Scribner's Magazine* (from 1887), and it had already been introduced into Britain by *The English Illustrated Magazine* (from 1883). Nor was Newnes's *The Strand* the first monthly magazine to be popularly priced, at sixpence (half, or less than half, the price of most monthlies) – *Longman's Magazine*, mainly devoted to serial fiction, had also been priced at sixpence since its launch in November 1882. However, *Longman's* was a small "octavo" magazine, with no illustrations and a dull appearance. Newnes's simple *coup* was to combine the format of the American quality illustrated magazines with the low price-level of *Longman's*. Within a short space of time *The Strand* was able to achieve a circulation which was significantly greater than any previous monthly – sales in the region of 500,000 copies were claimed within the first few years of publication.[2]

Similar breakthroughs in circulation were to be achieved by *The Strand*'s first American emulators – three magazines which established their success during a price-war in 1893-94, a

---

[2] *The Cornhill* felt triumph when its early sales exceeded 100,000 in 1860, a peak it never again achieved, dropping to around 10,000 by the 1890s. In 1850 the weekly fiction paper *The London Journal* claimed sales of half-a-million. *The Strand*'s circulation figures included distribution in American.

tussle which resulted in the ten-cent American magazine (previously the usual price for a standard illustrated monthly had been 25 or even 35 cents). Those three were *McClure's Magazine* (from 1893), John Brisben Walker's *The Cosmopolitan* (cover price halved to 12½ cents in 1893) and *Munsey's Magazine* (from 1891, but a relative failure until it went to ten cents in 1893). McClure, Walker and Munsey all learned a crucial lesson from Newnes's British success: make your magazine large, plump and pleasing to look at, but also make it cheap, and you will succeed in attracting a new mass audience to monthly magazines.

Although "miscellanies," with many general-interest articles, all these magazines placed a heavy emphasis on fiction. Again, that was not new in itself – *Harper's Magazine* in America, and the Victorian shilling magazines in Britain, such as *The Cornhill* and *Temple Bar*, had run plentiful fiction, especially serialised novels – but what *was* new, especially in Britain, was the emphasis on the short story and the complete-in-one-issue novella, as opposed to the lengthy serial in twelve or more parts. Newnes changed that, producing a magazine of wide circulation which, initially, completely avoided serials and placed the emphasis on short stories.

At first Newnes and his editor, Greenhough Smith, filled *The Strand Magazine* with translated stories by Continental masters – Alphonse Daudet, Alexander Pushkin, Guy de Maupassant, Villiers de l'Isle-Adam – although there was also, from the outset, a sprinkling of original stories by English-language writers (Grant Allen, Stanley J. Weyman, E. W. Hornung

EDITORIAL OFFICE OF "THE STRAND MAGAZINE."

and others). No doubt drawing on his experience with *Tit-Bits*, Newnes believed that the new mass-market magazine reader would have a short attention-span and would prefer to absorb fiction in self-contained episodes. It was this surmise, combined with Greenhough Smith's strong liking for the short story, which lead to *The Strand*'s most crucial innovation in fiction – the short story *series*, conceived as such and run in consecutive issues of the magazine, which would give readers some of the pleasures of a continuing serial without that form's drawbacks. A reader could dip into a series at any point, soon become familiar with the continuing characters, and yet experience a sense of closure at the end of each episode. Without this innovation, *The Strand* might well have been just another fleetingly successful magazine – a triumph of marketing, destined to fade after a few years – but with the establishment of the short-story series, six months after the magazine's launch, it gained a second wind which was to make it the British market-leader for years to come (and a model for America).

That second wind was provided by a writer who was in the right place, at the right time, with the right idea, Arthur Conan Doyle, and his "continuing characters" were the consulting detective, Sherlock Holmes, and his medical amanuensis, Dr John Watson. The characters and their milieu were not even new, having made previous novella-length appearances in *Beeton's Christmas Annual* (1887) and the American periodical *Lippincott's Magazine* (February 1890), but the form in which Doyle now revived them for *The Strand* – the monthly short-story series – was so perfect, was so exactly what the moment and the magazine called for, that they might as well have been new-minted creations in July 1891. Having drawn little attention beforehand, the characters became world-famous almost overnight – and were to lose none of their fame in the century that followed. Doyle's "Adventures of Sherlock Holmes" appeared in twelve consecutive issues of *The Strand* (Jul 1891-Jun 1892), with a second series beginning, after a hiatus of a few months, in December 1892. The stories were syndicated to American newspapers by S. S. McClure, who went on to found his own *McClure's Magazine* in 1893 (with Conan Doyle as an investor). So Doyle must also receive credit for helping create the Standard Popular Illustrated Magazine, as should the enterprising editor, Greenough Smith and, for that matter, artist Sidney Paget, whose portrayals of Holmes and Watson did so much to fix the images in the public's mind (*below*).

The appearance of Conan Doyle's "Adventures of Sherlock Holmes" revolutionised English-language popular fiction – and not only in the field of the crime or detective tale (the vogue for which had been building throughout the 1880s, with translations of Emile Gaboriau's *feuilleton* novels and the success of "shilling shockers" like Fergus Hume's *The Mystery of a Hansom Cab*). What Doyle and *The Strand* gave to the world was the linked series of short stories, centred on recurring lead characters and conceived, in effect, as "situation comedy". Such series were comedic in the sense that each story tended to end happily; in the Sherlock Holmes series, most of the stories open with Holmes and Watson in their cosy rooms in Baker Street, and most end with them back there again, with the mystery solved, the status quo restored. With the exception of "The Final Problem", which was intended to put an end to it all, the stories can be read in any order. There may be hints of a chronological sequence, but it scarcely matters. That is the essence of sitcom: the repeatable formula *situation*, within which a potentially endless stream of stories may be slotted. This was a form which was to be imitated, very rapidly and fruitfully, in areas more wide-ranging than just detective fiction. For example, among Conan Doyle's staunchest admirers was the young P. G. Wodehouse (who was himself to become a mainstay of *The Strand* in later years). The turn-of-the-century story-series, on the Holmes-and-Watson (or Jeeves-and-Wooster) model, was to have a huge presence in the popular culture of the twentieth century, ranging across the contents of British and American popular magazines (both "slick" and "pulp"), through radio broadcasting to television.

The success of the Sherlock Holmes short stories was so stunning that, in a sense, *The Strand Magazine* never recovered from it. Ever after, for nigh on the 60 years of its existence, it was to be "Conan Doyle's magazine", at least in the estimation of the general reader. As one of the magazine's last editors, Reginald Pound, was to write forlornly:

Conan Doyle, I am told, was alone in being able to send up the circulation, which responded immediately a new story by him was announced... The power of his name to stimulate sales is said to have been considerable, and none of the other writers, it seems, had it.[3]

But of course there were many other successful ingredients in the magazine's mix. Apart from the stories and the copious illustrations, many of the non-fiction features proved popular and long-running, especially "Portraits of Celebrities at Different Times of their Lives" – brief picture galleries of famous people – and the "Illustrated Interviews". Interviewing was still a fairly new journalistic art, imported into Britain from America in the 1880s and made familiar in the pages of *The Pall Mall Gazette* when W.T. Stead was its editor. Most of the magazine's early interviews were the work of a regular Newnes employee, Harry How, and a collection was published in book form as *Illustrated Interviews* (1893). Among the interviewees in the magazine's first decade, alongside numerous aristocrats, politicians and churchmen, and figures from the arts and sciences and sports, were such popular writers as Marie Corelli, Conan Doyle (*left*), W. S. Gilbert, H. Rider Haggard and Jules Verne. True-life tales of heroism also appeared regularly, such as the "Stories of the Victoria Cross" feature which ran in early issues.

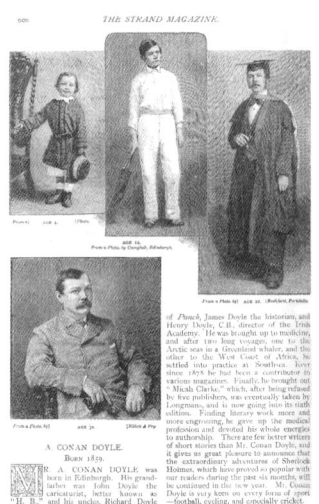

The fiction, however, was the main thing. The short stories in translation – by the likes of Pedro A. de Alarçon (Spanish), Björnstjerne Björnson (Norwegian), Moritz Jokaï (Hungarian) and Prosper Mérimée (French) – gradually faded away, and their place was taken by new stories from English-language authors, mostly British (or from Britain's Empire), although a few, such as W. L. Alden, Bret Harte and Frank R. Stockton, were American. Apart from Doyle, dependable contributors of fiction in the first few years included Walter Besant, Richard Dowling, George Manville Fenn, C. J. Cutcliffe Hyne, Richard Marsh, J. E. Preston Muddock (also known as "Dick Donovan"), David Christie Murray, "Rita" (Mrs Desmond Humphreys), W. Clark Russell and J. F. Sullivan (the last-named specialised in humorous fantasies). Rudyard Kipling appeared just once, with "The Lost Legion" (May 1892).

The first writer to produce an extended series of short stories, following Conan Doyle's success, was the little-known Charles J. Mansford (a schoolmaster, most notable elsewhere for his boys' school stories). His evocatively-titled "Shafts from an Eastern Quiver" series began in the July 1892 issue, at the beginning of the short hiatus following Doyle's twelfth tale, and ran for 12 consecutive issues. It was to be followed, three years later, by "Gleams from the Dark Continent" (Jul 1895-Mar 1896). With titles like "The Hindu Fakir of the Silent City" and "The Veiled Idol of Kor", these were imaginative stories of exploration and derring-do in exotic parts of the world, more in the spirit of Rider Haggard than Conan Doyle. More crucial to *The Strand*'s long-term success was another series-story writer, Mrs L. T. Meade. She first appeared as a collaborator with "Clifford Halifax", from the July 1893 issue, with a new series of medical mysteries, "Stories from the Diary of a Doctor". Most of Mrs Meade's were

---

[3] Pound, *A Maypole in the Strand*, p. 11.

presented as collaborations, although she did all the writing, and she soon became one of the magazine's most prolific contributors, with such further series as "The Adventures of a Man of Science" (Jul 1896-Feb 1897), "The Brotherhood of the Seven Kings" (Jan-Oct 1898), "Stories of the Sanctuary Club" (Jul-Dec 1899) and the aptly-titled "The Sorceress of the Strand" (Oct 1902-Mar 1903). All of Mrs Meade's series subsequently appeared in book form as episodic "novels", and were among the most widely visible titles in the growing field of late-Victorian and Edwardian crime fiction.

The event which, above all others, led to such an avalanche of story series by various hands was, of course, the appearance of Conan Doyle's "The Final Problem," his supposedly last Sherlock Holmes story (Dec 1893), which implied the great detective's death. The publication of that story, and Doyle's resolute refusal to write any more, posed a severe problem for Greenhough Smith and *The Strand*: could they continue to thrive without Sherlock? To fend off a possible decline in circulation, there were two obvious courses of action. One was to publish more non-Holmes fiction by Conan Doyle – indeed, *anything* by Doyle, in order to keep his name to the fore. The other was to encourage various writers to produce new short-story series, especially "detective" series, in the hope that some of them would prove hits with the public. The first of the post-Holmes series, "Martin Hewitt, Investigator", was provided by Arthur Morrison, commencing with "The Lenton Croft Robberies" (Mar 1894), and it ran for seven consecutive issues, complete with illustrations by Sidney Paget. They were clever stories, by a capable writer, but they did not quite have the Holmes magic. Nor were they to last long, as far as *The Strand* was concerned, because Morrison was poached by the later rival, *The Windsor Magazine* (where the second series of Martin Hewitt stories appeared from the first issue). By way of compensation, *The Strand* had a new series of Conan Doyle stories to run, although in a very different vein from Holmes: the historical comedies entitled "The Exploits of Brigadier Gerard" (Apr-Sept, Dec 1895).

To compensate for Morrison's defection, and to fill the gaps in between Doyle and L. T. Meade, an older writer, the Canadian-born Grant Allen (who had been a Newnes stalwart since his bestselling novel *What's Bred in the Bone* had run in *Tit-Bits* during 1891), was encouraged to try his hand at short mystery series. He came up with three, each consisting (in true Sherlockian fashion) of 12 stories: "An African Millionaire" (from Jun 1896), "Miss Cayley's Adventures" (from Mar 1898) and "Hilda Wade" (from Mar 1899). Alas, Grant Allen died before the third series was completed, and the final "Hilda Wade" story, "The Episode of the Dead Man Who Spoke" (Feb 1900), was finished for him by none other than Conan Doyle.

Such series dominated the magazine, but alongside them ran a considerable number of other stories by a cadre of newer authors who were beginning to build a collective strength as the 1890s wore on. They included, along with their first *Strand* appearance, Victor L. Whitechurch ("Stopping an Execution", Feb 1895), Max Pemberton ("The Cripple at the Mill", Sep 1895), Robert Barr ("The Understudy", Dec 1895), William Le Queux ("The Throne of the Thousand Terrors", Jul 1896), W. W. Jacobs ("A Safety Match", Feb 1898), Eden Phillpotts ("The Treasure of Nephron", Apr 1898), H. G. Wells ("Mr. Ledbetter's Vacation", Oct 1898), Edith Nesbit ("The Book of Beasts", Mar 1899), Kate and Hesketh Prichard ("The No-Good Britisher", May 1899) and Fred M. White ("The Purple Terror", Sep 1899). Of the foregoing, three – Jacobs, Nesbit and Wells – were to become significant contributors to the magazine.

A change of editorial policy occurred in January 1896, when the magazine commenced its first-ever continuous serialised novel. That first novel, run in twelve parts, was the historical adventure *Rodney Stone* by, once again, A. Conan Doyle. It is logical that Greenhough Smith should have broken his own rule for Doyle, above all other writers. Here is how Greenhough Smith announced the change, in the December 1895 issue (p. 615):

> Mr Conan Doyle has written a powerful Story which will succeed "Brigadier Gerard" in THE STRAND MAGAZINE, commencing with the January Number. It will be entitled "Rodney Stone" and will treat mainly of the period of George III, in a manner which has not hitherto been attempted. Though each instalment will, like "The Adventures of Sherlock Holmes" and "Brigadier Gerard", have separate incidents of its own, there will be a plot running through them all, and the publication of this important work will continue during the greater part of next year.

What contortions Greenhough Smith went through to avoid admitting that it was a serialised novel! But "Rodney Stone" proved a success and thereafter the editor had no compunction about serialising other novels he thought suitable. Apart from other considerations, this was a time of rising competition for *The Strand*. Not only *The Windsor Magazine*, which had begun in January 1895, but now *Pearson's Magazine* (from January 1896) was a direct imitator, and these interlopers were soon to be joined by others, at even cheaper prices, such as *The Harmsworth Magazine* (from July 1898) and *The Royal Magazine* (from November 1898), let alone changes in other titles like *Cassell's Magazine*, *English Illustrated Magazine* and *Ludgate Monthly* to turn them into *Strand* look-alikes. All these magazines published serial novels as well as short-story series.

The Strand's serials in the years following *Rodney Stone* included "The Tragedy of the Korosko" by Conan Doyle (May-Dec 1897), "A Master of Craft" by W. W. Jacobs (May 1899-Apr 1900), "The Brass Bottle" by F. Anstey (Jan-Sept 1900), "The First Men in the Moon" by H. G. Wells (Nov 1900-Aug 1901), "The Hound of the Baskervilles" by Conan Doyle (Aug 1901-Apr 1902), "The House Under the Sea" by Max Pemberton (Dec 1901-Jul 1902) and "The Psammead" by E. Nesbit (Apr-Dec 1902). The last, better known under its book title, *Five Children and It*, was the start of a wonderful ten-year run of children's fantasies by Edith Nesbit[4] – witty, stylish and imaginative tales which presumably were enjoyed as much by the adult readers of the magazine as by their offspring. By the early 1900s, with the arrival of Nesbit, *The Strand* had reached its peak as a fiction magazine. Not only was the magazine running serials and regular short-story series, but the serials were overlapping. In the August 1901 issue, for example, as Wells's "The First Men in the Moon" ended, so Conan Doyle's "The Hound of the Baskervilles" began. By all accounts, readers had to join long queues at the news-stands to buy a copy of that issue, for Doyle's new novel featured the long-awaited return of Holmes and Watson.

Many of the serials which *The Strand* ran in the early 1900s, from Anstey's comic fantasy "The Brass Bottle" through Nesbit's delightful "The Phoenix and the Carpet" (Jul 1903-Jun 1904), and well beyond, remain popular classics, still in print a century later, and still adapted for radio, television and film. Some of the magazine's serials have sunk without trace (who

---

[4] *The Strand* had included a children's story from the first issue, most illustrated by H. R. Millar, but Nesbit's became the best known, doubtless helped by Millar's ideal artwork.

now reads Jacobs's "A Master of Craft" or Pemberton's "The House Under the Sea"?) but the number of serials which became, and remained, long-term hits is astonishingly high. The list includes, gradually fading away towards the First World War, Nesbit's "The Amulet" (May 1905-Apr 1906), Conan Doyle's "Sir Nigel" (Dec 1905-Dec 1906), Rudyard Kipling's "Puck of Pook's Hill" (Jan-Oct 1906), Nesbit's "The Enchanted Castle" (Dec 1906-Nov 1907), A.E.W. Mason's "The Murder at the Villa Rose" (Dec 1909-Aug 1910) and Conan Doyle's Professor Challenger adventure, "The Lost World" (Apr-Nov 1912). *The Strand* may have been incorrigibly "middlebrow", and its fiction may not be rated as Great Literature, yet many of the works it first published have been remarkably enduring for all that.

Sir George Newnes (knighted in 1895) died on 9 June 1910, a month after King Edward VII. His passing did not much affect *The Strand*, as Greenough Smith was to remain in post for another 20 years. The magazine sailed on. Significant new writers it had attracted since the turn of the century included H. C. Bailey, J. J. Bell, Edgar Jepson, W. Somerset Maugham, E. Phillips Oppenheim, Edwin Pugh, Morley Roberts, Edith Somerville & Martin Ross, Horace Annesley Vachell, Valentine Williams and, above all, a young man named Pelham Grenville Wodehouse. He made his *Strand* debut with "The Wire-Pullers" (Jul 1905), having graduated to the magazine from a junior Newnes publication, *The Captain* (launched in 1899 to compete with the boys' papers of the day). Within a few years, the trickle of funny stories from Wodehouse's pen grew into a continuous stream, so that by 1910 he seemed to be contributing to every other issue. Most of the contents of his first "adult" collection, *The Man Upstairs and Other Stories* (Methuen, 1914), had appeared first in *The Strand*. His first novel to be serialised in the magazine's pages was "The Prince and Betty" (Feb-Apr 1912).

Among occasional contributors of stories were Arnold Bennett, Warwick Deeping and W. Pett Ridge. The bestselling novelist of the day, Hall Caine, wrote a serial, "The White Prophet" (Dec 1908-Nov 1909), and another bestseller, Rider Haggard, contributed a novella, "Smith and the Pharaohs" (Dec 1912-Feb 1913). Short-story series in the period from the turn of the century to the First World War included Conan Doyle's "The Adventures of Etienne Gerard" (from Aug 1902) and "The Return of Sherlock Holmes" (from Oct 1903), E. W. Hornung's "Stingaree Stories" (from Sep 1904), C.N. & A.M. Williamson's "The Scarlet Runner" (from Dec 1906), William J. Locke's "The Joyous Adventures of Aristide Pujol" (from Dec 1910), and Richard Marsh's "Judith Lee, Some Pages from Her Life" (from Aug 1911). But the author who continued to dominate the magazine was Conan Doyle. He followed the success of his science-fiction adventure serial "The Lost World" with a shorter, more Wellsian treatment of world cataclysm, "The Poison Belt" (Mar-Jul 1913), and a number of memorable short stories such as "The Horror of the Heights" (Nov 1913) and "Danger!" (Jul 1914). As War broke out, "The Valley of Fear", his first new Sherlock Holmes novel in over a decade, commenced serialisation (Sept 1914-May 1915).

The War years brought an increase in non-fiction to the magazine's pages, not least by Doyle, who contributed a long series of accounts of the conflict under the general title of "The

British Campaign in France" (from Apr 1916). But they also brought new writers of fiction. Edgar Wallace, already a prolific author elsewhere, contributed tales such as "The Despatch-Rider" (Dec 1914), and a serving officer named Cyril McNeile began writing war stories under what was to become his famous pseudonym of "Sapper" (starting with "Shrapnel", May 1916). F. Britten Austin became a frequent contributor, initially with war-related tales (such as "Panzerkraftwagen", Apr 1917), but later with more general adventure fiction. Another new author, regarded by some as one of the finest short-story writers the magazine ever published, was Stacy Aumonier (first appearance "The Match: To-day and Yesterday", Jul 1916). P. G. Wodehouse, domiciled in America, continued blithely on his own course as though the War had never happened, contributing sunny stories and serials, and creating, in the midst of those dark days, a pair of characters were introduced in "Extricating Young Gussie" (Jan 1916) who would become popular-fiction immortals – Bertie Wooster and his manservant Jeeves (*left*).

"JEEVES."

In the aftermath of the War *The Strand* entered its long Indian summer – once more fat with advertising, and with brighter, more colourful covers and more profuse internal illustration. Again, escapist fiction was to the fore. The post-war Christmas issues were remarkable artefacts. For example, the December 1920 number included Conan Doyle's article "Fairies Photographed" (about the infamous Cottingley fairies), "Mr Cray's Adventures", the second in a new story-series by E. Phillips Oppenheim, a story by W. W. Jacobs, still going strong after more than 20 years, plus new yarns by Sapper, F. Britten Austin, P. G. Wodehouse, Ethel M. Dell, Crosbie Garstin and Barry Pain. Similarly, the December 1921 issue contained yet more Austin, Doyle, Oppenheim, Sapper and Wodehouse, together with the ubiquitous Edgar Wallace – and a feature on Winston Churchill's paintings. Apart from the illustrated features, the contents were not very different from those of the better "pulp" magazines of the period. *The Strand*, although still printed on glossy paper, and still a highly entertaining product for its no-doubt loyal middle-class readers, had lost some of its cultural importance by the 1920s. The world had moved on: America, with its "big slick" magazines, now provided the main market for successful British writers like Doyle and Wodehouse – although both remained loyal to the old magazine, usually selling their UK serialisation rights to the Newnes company. *The Strand*, and the other remaining "gaslight" magazines such as *Pearson's*, was left beached, ever so gently subsiding. Some British magazines of the time, notably *Nash's–Pall Mall*, did become large-format slicks on the American model, but that was a transition *The Strand* never made.

D. H. Lawrence contributed a solitary story to the post-war magazine ("Tickets, Please!", Apr 1919), and so did Aldous Huxley ("A Deal in Old Masters", Feb 1923), but a more typical contributor of the interwar period was the prolific H. de Vere Stacpoole, still reworking the exotic matter of his 1908 bestseller, *The Blue Lagoon*, in serials such as "The Garden of God" (Jan-Apr 1923). Other regulars of the 1920s and 1930s were Michael Arlen, Thomas Burke, W. A. Darlington, C. S. Forester, Gilbert Frankau, Denis Mackail, Leonard Merrick, Roland Pertwee, Martin Swayne, and Hugh Walpole. Especially prominent was the thriller-writer

Sapper, with serials, story-series and one-off tales. But several of the old guard continued to sell to *The Strand*, right up to their deaths. Most notable among these was, of course, Conan Doyle, whose last Sherlock Holmes stories appeared sporadically during the 1920s. The final one was "The Adventure of Shoscombe Old Place" (Apr 1927), although Doyle was to carry on writing non-Holmes fiction such as the serial "The Maracot Deep" (Oct 1927-Feb 1928) and the short stories "When the World Screamed" (Apr-May 1928) and "The Disintegration Machine" (Jan 1929). Following his death, the magazine ran a fulsome obituary (Sept 1930) and reprinted the first Holmes short story from 1891, "A Scandal in Bohemia". Even then there was to be more fiction from Doyle, as a couple of his stories which had been published only in America made their first UK appearances, culminating in "The Last Resource" (Dec 1930). Appropriately, the same end-of-year issue which ran the very last Doyle story was also Greenhough Smith's last issue as editor. Bereft of his magazine's most celebrated author, Smith bowed out, aged 75, to live the last five years of his life in honourable retirement.

Others of the pre-1914 generation who continued to appear almost until their deaths were W. W. Jacobs ("The Visitor", Nov 1935) and Rudyard Kipling ("'Teem' – A Treasure Hunter", Jan 1936). And, although he had never been a frequent writer for *The Strand*, G. K. Chesterton contributed, posthumously, a final Father Brown story, "The Vampire of the Village" (Aug 1936). It was a time of farewells. The talented Stacy Aumonier had died, at the age of only 41, in 1928. Edgar Wallace passed away in 1932, as did Sapper, also prematurely, in 1937. With the departure of so many authorial mainstays, and a change of editorship, the magazine had to re-focus itself in the 1930s, slightly away from men's tastes and more towards women's. The new editor, Reeves Shaw, had a liking for the humorous and the romantic. He had been the editor of Newnes's *The Humorist* and *The Happy* since 1922. He continued to publish Wodehouse, in profusion; not just the stories of Jeeves and Wooster but those featuring Lord Emsworth, Mulliner, Ukridge and the Oldest Member. Shaw also ran much crime fiction – but many of the newer writers were female. Among those welcomed to *The Strand* were Margery Allingham, Dorothy L. Sayers and, most notably, Agatha Christie. The last was to become a dominant presence after Sapper's death. Almost the last numbered short-story series the magazine published was her "The Labours of Hercules" (Nov 1939-Sept 1940), featuring her popular sleuth Hercule Poirot.

By the time that Christie series appeared, World War II had broken out. The circulations of the more traditional magazines were in decline, and now paper shortages became severe. Many publications were axed. Sustained mainly by its prestige (the December 1940 issue carried a feature on "Fifty Years of *The Strand Magazine*", with a message of congratulation from its most famous non-fiction contributor, Winston Churchill), the magazine was allowed to continue, although with progressively fewer pages. Typical contributors of the period included detective-story writer John Dickson Carr and veteran historical swashbuckler Rafael Sabatini. But with effect from the October 1941 issue the magazine shrank to the so-called "digest" size, little more than half the previous dimensions. Reeves Shaw resigned and a temporary editor, R. J. Minney, oversaw the change. Minney was replaced by Reginald Pound, who worked under the supervision of another Newnes editor, Reginald Arkell.

With a much-reduced budget, Pound's brief was to make *The Strand* as much like Arkell's baby, the pocket-sized *Men Only*, as possible. That small magazine had been launched at the end of 1935, and was slanted, as its title indicated, towards the male reader. It was a success, especially in the early War years when its main readership seems to have been men in uniform. The Hulton company's competitor, *Lilliput*, started independently by Stefan Lorant in 1937, was an even bigger success, and the pressure was on *The Strand* to conform to the new model. The emphasis was on photographic features and brief, punchy articles; and the stories, in order to fit the small (and fewer) pages were reduced for the most part to sketches and vignettes. Some notable authors still appeared – for example, Lord Dunsany and Gerald Kersh, both of whom were in the October 1941 issue – but on the whole the change of policy was disastrous.

Pound kept the magazine going through the War years, an achievement in itself, but this period represented its lowest ebb. Probably for reasons related to the war, P. G. Wodehouse was suddenly gone from the magazine (his last appearance there was with "Bramley is So Bracing", Dec 1940). Without its most distinguished living contributor, the prospects for *The Strand* were not good. Agatha Christie continued to appear, at least until her story "A Case of Buried Treasure" (Jul 1944), and there was a sprinkling of other well-known crime writers, such as "Nicholas Blake" (C. Day-Lewis), as well as stories reprinted from America (e.g. Manuel Komroff's "Children of the Good Earth", Jul 1943, and even a drastic condensation of John Steinbeck's "The Moon is Down", Sep 1943), but the heart was gone from the magazine. Following the war, although the economic climate was still austere, the company decided to revamp the magazine, if in a slightly half-hearted way: from October 1946 it had more pages, new-look artwork, and a new editor, Macdonald Hastings. The reduced format remained the same, however. Hastings increased the fiction content once more, providing a series of humorous stories himself, the "Mr Quill" anecdotes, adorned with illustrations by Edward Ardizzone. Other new illustrators were Mervyn Peake and Ronald Searle, all of which contributed to making *The Strand* an imitation of *Lilliput* and no longer its own master.

Some old-time story-writers returned briefly to *The Strand* – Somerset Maugham (Nov 1946), A.E.W. Mason (May 1948) – and new literary stars appeared: Eric Ambler, Graham Greene, Georges Simenon and Evelyn Waugh, to name a few. The renowned Conan Doyle *aficionado*, Father Ronald A. Knox, was persuaded to write a Sherlock Holmes pastiche, "The Adventure of the First Class Carriage" (Feb 1947), with Sidney Paget type illustrations by Tom Purvis.

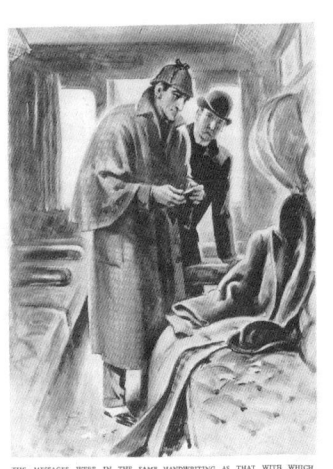

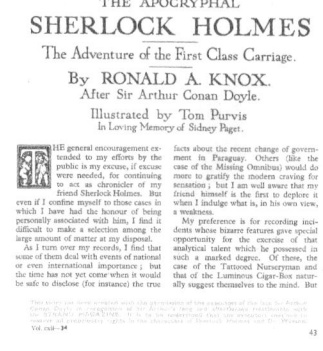

But it was not enough. The more typical fictional fare of the magazine at this time consisted of its last story-series, Richard Murdoch's BBC-radio-derived six-part "Chronicles of Much-Binding-in-the-Marsh" (Jan-Jun 1948), and its final serial, John Connell's "The Return of Long John Silver" (Dec 1948-Feb 1949), drastically reduced from its forthcoming book version.

The magazine's closure was announced at the end of 1949, and took effect immediately after the March 1950 issue, when it was merged with *Men Only*. Macdonald Hastings wore a black armband on the day the last issue went to press. An epitaph may be plucked from Benny Green's book, *P. G. Wodehouse: A Literary Biography* (1981, pp. 59-60):

> Wodehouse recalled with sad affection in 1949 when writing to Townend about the death of *The Strand*: "As practically everything I have written since July 1905 appeared in the *Strand*, I drop a silent tear, but I can't say I'm much surprised, for anything sicker-looking than the little midget it had shrunk to I never saw. Inevitable, I suppose, because of paper shortage. And in my opinion never anything worth reading in it, either, the last year or two."

Glancing through random samples of *Men Only* from the early 1950s, one can find a few faint after-flickers of *The Strand*. The February 1951 and March 1952 issues still state on the contents-page masthead: "*Men Only, incorporating The Strand Magazine*". The second of those issues even contains a Sherlock Holmes story, of sorts – "Last Word on Holmes" by W. F. Mikisch, a three-and-a-half page humorous squib of no great inspiration. At a later point, *Men Only* (which had also absorbed *Lilliput*, in 1960) was transformed into a large glossy soft-pornography magazine, in imitation of *Playboy* and *Penthouse*, and it still exists in that form today. If we are so minded, we could look at a current issue of *Men Only* on a newsagent's top shelf and muse, "there goes the last incarnation of *The Strand Magazine*..."[5]

Frequency: Monthly, but combined issue May/Jun 1947 (# 677/678).
Publisher: George Newnes.
Editors: H. Greenhough Smith, Jan 1891-Dec 1930 (with E. N. Sanders as assistant, 1899-1928; George Blake as Acting Editor, 1928-30); Reeves Shaw, Jan 1931-Sept 1941 (with Hugh Ross Williamson, acting editor, 1934-35); R. J. Minney, Oct 1941-May 1942, Reginald Pound, Jun 1942-Sept 1946, Macdonald Hastings, Oct 1946-Mar 1950.
Format/Size: Standard, to Sep 1941; thereafter small digest. Pagination, 108/12, rose to 120, Jan 1895, dropped to 112, Jan 1916; 104, May 1916; 96, May 1917; 88, Feb 1918; 76/80, Apr 1918; 86/90, rose to Feb 1919; 100/104, dropped to May 1919; 92/96, rose to Jun 1920; 100/108, Jan 1923; 110/112, May 1930; dropped to 104, Nov 1939; 88, Jun 1940; 72, Aug 1940; 68, Jun 1941. With change to digest size, 104, Oct 1941; dropped to 96, May 1942; rose to 112, Dec 1946; 120, May 1949.
Price: 6d, rose to 7d, Feb 1917; 8d, Aug 1917; 9d, Jan 1918; 1/-, Jun 1918; 1/3d, Jan 1941.
Other editions: A separate US edition ran from Jan 1891-Feb 1916 (302 issues) edited, until 1910, by James Walter Smith. Issues were dated one month later than the UK edition and were identical until the US issue for November 1895. Thereafter, although the core of the contents remained the same, stories were often shifted between issues and some stories (such as those by Arthur Conan Doyle and P. G. Wodehouse) were not reprinted if the US rights had been sold elsewhere. The

---

[5] *The Strand* has since been revived twice. Firstly in 1961 as a mixed fiction magazine and review called *The New Strand*, which ran for 15 issues (Dec 1961-Feb 1963). Towards the end it was edited by John Creasey primarily as a mystery magazine. More recently it was revived in the USA in 1998 as *The Strand*, almost wholly as a crime fiction magazine. It still appears on a two-or-three-issue per year basis.

editor frequently used new material and occasionally ran stories by regular contributors to the UK edition which appeared first (and sometimes only) in the US edition. The covers were always different and include some original portraits of Sherlock Holmes.

References: *The Life of Sir George Newnes* by Hulda Friederichs (London: Hodder & Stoughton, 1911), in particular chapter vii, "The 'Review of Reviews' and the 'Strand'". *A Maypole in the Strand* by Reginald Pound (London: Ernest Benn, 1948). *The Strand Magazine: 1891-1950* by Reginald Pound (London: Heinemann, 1966). *British Literary Magazines, Volume 3, The Victorian and Edwardian Age, 1837-1913* edited by Alvin Sullivan (Westport, CT: Greenwood Press, 1984). "A National Institution: *The Strand Magazine*" in *George Newnes and the New Journalism in Britain, 1880-1910: Culture and Profit* by Kate Jackson (Aldershot: Ashgate Publishing, 2001).

Indexes: *Index to the Strand Magazine, 1891-1950* by Geraldine Beare (Westport, CT: Greenwood Press, 1982) is a complete author, artist and subject index is. A more abbreviated issue index is *The Strand Magazine 1891-1950, a Selective Checklist* by J. F. Whitt (London: privately published, 1979).

Anthologies: Anonymous (editor), *Selections from The Strand Magazine, Vol. 1, 1891* (London: Vernon & Yates, 1966), facsimile reproduction, no other volumes known. Jack Adrian (editor), *Detective Stories from the Strand Magazine* (Oxford University Press, 1991), with Foreword by Julian Symons. Jack Adrian (editor), *Strange Tales from the Strand Magazine* (Oxford University Press, 1991), with Foreword by Julian Symons. Geraldine Beare (editor), *Crime Stories from the 'Strand'* (London: Folio Society, 1991), with introduction by H.R.F. Keating; *Short Stories from the 'Strand'* (The Folio Society, 1992), with introduction by Frank Delaney; *Adventure Stories from the 'Strand'* (The Folio Society, 1995), with introduction by Tim Heald.

Holdings:
Complete run, UK. The Bodleian (*Call Number*: Per. 2705 d.272).
Substantial run, UK. British Library is missing issues Jan, Feb, May-Jul 1917; Jan-Dec 1922; May 1925; Feb, Mar, May, Jun, Aug, Sep, Nov 1926; Jan-Dec 1929; Jul-Dec 1930; Jul-Dec 1931; Jan-Jun 1934; Jan–Oct 1935 (*Shelfmark*: PP.6004.glk). • Cambridge University Library has run, missing only volume 56, Jul-Dec 1918 (*Classmark*: L996.c.25). • National Library of Scotland has all issues except 102 (Oct 1941-Mar 1942).
Complete run, US: New York Public Library. • Free Library of Philadelphia (*Call Number*: 050 St8).
Substantial run, US: Library of Congress has run to Sep 1946 (*Call Number*: AP4.S75). University of Minnesota Libraries has several holdings split across various sites, in total vols. 1-42, 44-48, 50-91 (Jan 1891-Dec 1911, Jul 1912-Dec 1914, Jul 1915-Oct 1936), plus individual issues (in collection PR4623) 632 (Aug 1943), 661 (Jan 1946), 670 (Oct 1946), 674 (Feb 1947), 696-699 (Dec 1948-Mar 1949) and 711 (Mar 1950).
Substantial run, Australia: University of Queensland, Fryer Research unit, has all issues except Jun-Sept 1946 (*Reference*: AP4.S75).

Collecting points: The publisher's blue binding of six-monthly indexed volumes are very common up to the First World War though increasingly expensive for Sherlock Holmes content. Post-war volumes are also fairly common up to 1940 but only single issues surface thereafter. Some early volumes had dustjackets but are exceptionally rare. Early single issues were also bound in "Royal Edition" format in blue-silk boards. Single issues throughout the run are quite common, except during both World Wars, but long runs are rare.

***

THE SUNNY MAG.

95 issues. Volume 1, Number 1, July 1925 to Volume 16, Number 94, April 1933; plus one *Christmas Extra*, 1925. Incorporated *Gaiety* from February 1928 when title changed to THE SUNNY AND GAIETY MAG. on the cover only.

The Sunny was the companion to and direct copy of *The Happy Mag.*, though it lacked *The Happy*'s popular character, Richmal Crompton's William Brown. *The Sunny* started with a bang, serialising the new P. G. Wodehouse novel, "Sam the Sudden", which was appearing in America in the *Saturday Evening Post*. Wodehouse was ideal for *The Sunny* and, as a regular contributor to its companion *The Strand*, should have been easily available, but his presence was merely to kick start the magazine and he did not appear again. Nevertheless he set high standards.

Like *The Happy*, *The Sunny* was intended as a light, joyful magazine. It was not simply a humour magazine – it had a few pages of humorous anecdotes and rather more pages of cartoons and humorous sketches – but sought to be uplifting and positive. It was not averse to publishing stories that began downbeat, provided there was a happy ending. It carried most of the same contributors as *The Happy*, including C. C. Andrews, H. W. Leggett, Clare Thornton, Phyllis Hambledon, Evadne Price and K.R.G. Browne. Ursula Bloom and Michael Kent were also regulars, as were artists Arthur Ferrier, P. B. Hickling, Graham Simmons and Thomas Henry (who provided four full-colour William pictures in the 1925 Christmas Extra, and several covers featuring William). Richmal Crompton appeared twice in *The Sunny* but with non-William stories. Philip Atkey, who helped edit the magazine, also contributed under his alias Barry Perowne.

The fiction in the two magazines was virtually interchangeable. On balance *The Sunny* ran more romance stories and was marginally more serious. The editor secured a humorous serial from Edgar Wallace, "Barbara On Her Own" (Apr-Sept 1926), about the romantic destiny of an independent business girl. It also reprinted H. de Vere Stacpoole's "The Blue Lagoon" (from Jun 1929), along with its sequel "The Girl of the Golden Reef". It even published a western serial, "Lady Tenderfoot" by George F. Worts (Feb-Jun 1930). R. B. Saxe's stories about the "Princess", especially the serial "The Ragged Princess" (Jul-Dec 1930), are good examples of where the heroine suffers all that life throws at her and still comes up smiling.

From February 1928 *The Sunny* incorporated *Gaiety Magazine*, keeping the name alive on the cover, but incorporating none of that magazine's features. This formula could only last for so long and with the general downturn in people's fortunes in the 1930s – the very time they needed *The Sunny* – it was merged with *The Happy*.

Frequency: Monthly.
Publisher: George Newnes.
Editor: Reeves Shaw (assisted by Philip Atkey from 1925-27).
Format/Size: Standard pulp, 96 pages.

Price: 7d.
References: Mary Cadogan, *The William Companion* (London: Macmillan, 1990), p. 190.
Holdings:
Complete run, UK. British Library on microfilm (*Shelfmark*: PP.6018.tay; *Microfilm*: Mic.C.344).
Substantial run, UK. Bodleian has all issues except the last (Apr 1933) (*Call Number*: Per. 25612 d.50).
Collecting points: Issues are less common than *The Happy* but do surface occasionally as do volumes in pale blue publisher's binding.

* * *

TALES OF WONDER
16 issues. Number 1, [June] 1937 to Number 16, Spring 1942.

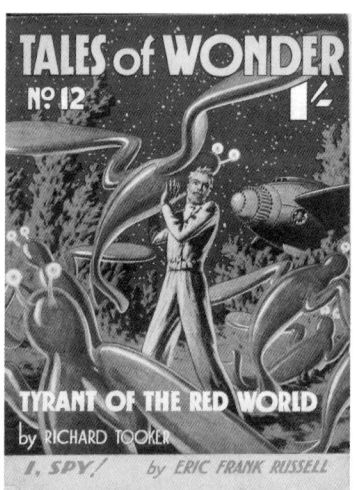

Tales of Wonder was the first serious British science-fiction magazine, following the ill-advised boys' story paper *Scoops*, which had appeared in 1934. Walter Gillings had been trying to interest British publishers for some years without success, but the development of the *Master Thriller* series of pulp fiction "anthologies" by World's Work opened a new line of enquiry. Although not part of that sequence, *Tales of Wonder* shared the same formula title and appearance. Gillings had followed the development of the science-fiction magazine in America almost from its birth in 1926. He had also issued his own amateur news and review magazine *Scientifiction* in printed form in January 1937. Being an enthusiast and a trained journalist Gillings was able to bring an expert eye to science fiction, something which had been woefully missing at *Scoops*, and the result was the start of a new era.

After the success of the first issue Gillings was able to provide a regular (albeit quarterly) market for British writers who hitherto had to rely on American magazines as their only outlet for what was still a specialist field. Gillings published new stories by John Russell Fearn, John Beynon (later to become famous as John Wyndham), Benson Herbert (who became better known for his psychic research) and William F. Temple. He also published the first professional work by Arthur C. Clarke, with his articles "Man's Empire of Tomorrow" (Winter 1938) and "We Can Rocket to the Moon—*Now!*" (Summer 1939).

This core of British writers was not enough to fill the magazine and Gillings found it difficult to acquire sufficient new material and fell back on reprinting stories from the American pulps. Authors included Edmond Hamilton, Jack Williamson, Stanton A. Coblentz, David H. Keller and Clark Ashton Smith and, having made contact Gillings acquired some new material from American writers. He also reprinted stories by Australian writer Coutts Brisbane which had appeared in *The Red Magazine* twenty years before.

The material was typical of the period, with the emphasis on ideas and super-science rather than on character and social implications, but *Tales of Wonder* was establishing a base from which British science fiction would grow. The War intervened and the magazine shrivelled due to paper rationing and then died because contributors, including the editor, were called-up for active service. It was not until after the War that *New Worlds* would pick up the pieces and provided stability to a growing field of British science fiction.

Frequency: Quarterly from second issue but irregular after 1939.
Publisher: The World's Work, Kingswood, Surrey.
Editor: Walter H. Gillings.
Format/Size: Standard pulp; page count 128, reducing to 96, Winter 1939; 80, Autumn 1940; 72, Spring 1941.
Price: 1/-.
References: Indexed in *Science Fiction, Fantasy & Weird Fiction Magazine Index (1890-2001)* by Stephen T. Miller and William G. Contento (Oakland: Locus Press, 2002).
Holdings:
Complete run, UK. British Library on microfilm (*Shelfmark*: PP.6018.thl; *Microfilm*: Mic.C.595); Bodleian (*Call Number*: Per. 254399 d.60).
Substantial run, UK. Leeds University Library, lacking only #15 (*Ref*: A/F A-0.01 TAL)
Substantial run, US: New York Public Library is missing only issue 15 (*Call Number*: ZAN-6100 on microfilm).
Collecting points: Still easy to find in science-fiction circles, especially the pre-war issues.

***

TIP TOP STORIES OF ADVENTURE AND MYSTERY

10 issues. Volume 1, Number 1, December 1923 to Volume 2, Number 10, March/April 1925. Retitled THE REGENT MAGAZINE from June 1924. Merged with *The Sovereign*.

The title of *Tip Top Stories* might suggest a boys' adventure magazine or a comic and there had been a series of short adventure novels called *Tip Top Tales* issued by Aldine up until 1914. There was also an American pulp called *Tip Top Semi-Monthly*, which had grown out of a dime novel series, *Tip Top Weekly* in 1915, aimed chiefly at the boys' market.

The British *Tip Top* promoted itself as a magazine of "adventure and mystery", a fact evident from its action covers by Dagnall Stocquart. It thereby set itself up in opposition to Hutchinson's who had just issued *Adventure-Story* and *Mystery-Story*. Like those titles, *Tip Top* drew heavily from the American pulps, reprinting stories from *Blue Book*, *Adventure*, *The People's Magazine*, *Telling Tales* and *Black Mask*. Its feature author was H. Bedford-Jones, one of the most prolific pulpsters. The publisher/editor – Board called the magazine "a one-man show" – came to an arrangement with Bedford-Jones for a package of new and second-run stories. Bedford-Jones was known for the thoroughness of his research. In *Twentieth Century Authors* (Wilson, 1942), Kunitz and Haycraft acknowledge him as not only one of the "best known" of the pulpsters but also "one of the better" writers.

In addition to Bedford-Jones, Board reprinted stories by George Allan England (his novel of the Far North, "The White Wilderness" was serialised from the first issue[1]), Vincent Starrett, Lemuel de Bra (whose work as a Secret Service agent in the Chinatown underworld of San Francisco provided plenty of material), Frederick C. Davis, and those doyens of the south-sea adventure, Beatrice Grimshaw and H. de Vere Stacpoole.[2] Board relied heavily on US reprints for his first few issues and the only other British writer of note was F.A.M. Webster, regarded by some as the natural successor to H. Rider Haggard. Webster began a new series, "The Companions of the Road" (from Apr 1924), another of his narratives of the outposts of Empire.

Judging from the editor's remarks sales of *Tip Top* were not high, a fact that he passed off, in the April 1924 issue, to "the General Election, Christmas, the railway strike and the docker's strike." They may have been contributory factors, but the title must also have been limiting, suggesting juvenile fiction rather than adult adventure. From the June 1924 issue, it became *The Regent Magazine*, and the covers became softer, depicting scenes of leisure and romance rather than adventure. The result was astonishing. Board proudly declared that the first new issue sold out within three days.

Despite the cover changes mystery fiction remained predominant, and the June issue began serialisation of Maurice Leblanc's new Arsène Lupin novel, "The Candlestick with Seven Branches".[3] However, by the September 1924 issue the editor was asking for more stories of romance. A change did become apparent over the next few issues. The covers emphasised women at play and leisure, and a few light romance stories appeared. But the contents remained primarily mystery with a growth in weird fiction and ghost stories. Marjorie Bowen, for instance, contributed "Florence Flannery" (Dec 1924) and "Kecksies" (Jan 1925).

Throughout its life the contents of *Tip Top/Regent* had been remarkably close to the magazines published by Hutchinson, especially *The Sovereign*, and the title change to *The Regent* may have been too close for comfort. With the February 1925 issue Hutchinson's took over the magazine, with no editorial comment or warning. They sustained it for just two issues and then merged it with *The Sovereign*. At the height of the fiction magazine boom the little minnows were soon swallowed up.

Frequency: Monthly.
Publisher: A.W. Board, until Jan 1925; then Hutchinson.
Editor: A.W. Board until Jan 1925.
Format/Size: Standard pulp, 96 pages.
Price: 1/-.
Holdings: *Complete run, UK*. British Library (*Shelfmark*: PP.6004.gox); Bodleian (*Call Number*: Per. 25612 d.25).
Collecting points: One of the rarest of British fiction magazines.

***

---

[1] Originally published in six parts in *The People's Magazine*, 1 July-15 September 1923.
[2] Selecting stories from US sources led to some anomalies. The first issue of *Tip Top* reprinted H. de Vere Stacpoole's "The Chilean Girl" from *The Popular Magazine* (7 Dec 1922), but this had already appeared in *Lloyd's Story Magazine*, July 1922. Likewise, Beatrice Grimshaw's "Forgotten Soul", from the *Red Book Magazine* (Feb 1923), had appeared in the December 1922 *Lloyd's Story Magazine*.
[3] Published in America as *The Memoirs of Arsène Lupin* (Macauley, 1925).

THE 20 STORY MAGAZINE

220 issues. Volume 1, Number 1, July 1922 to Volume 37, Number 220, October 1940.

20 Story was the unabashed all-fiction pulp companion to the more up-market *Pan*, though they shared a core of authors and a delight in adventure and mystery fiction. As the title suggests, each issue ran twenty stories crammed into 128 pages. There were occasional long stories, but only one serial, "The Quest of the Tweed Suit" by Albert Payson Terhune (Oct 1922-Feb 1923), a light fantasy about a suit made out of a cloth that brings success. Readers objected to serials and the editor acquiesced. Instead regular series stories abounded. There was a fair exchange of material from the American pulps during the 1920s, perhaps as much as fifty-fifty, but this faded during the 1930s when *20 Story* became one of the few remaining home markets for pulp fiction.

At the outset the magazine fell into the trap of presenting covers featuring young girls, which implied a romance or woman's magazine, and it was a year before they changed to more representative covers. The contents also suggest that some had been taken from submissions to *Pan* because they were set amongst high society or the well-to-do. It took *20 Story* some while to shed the English "country-house" image, and it never entirely did so. For most of its life it managed to walk the tightrope between presenting thoroughly British stories and hardboiled American (or Americanised) adventure fiction.

The first issue had a reasonably representative selection. The stories by Fannie Kilbourne, Douglas Newton and to some degree Will Scott, mix romance, fashion and big business. There's romance of the adventure kind in Bernard Masters's highwayman story "The Bully of York" whilst "Devil's Leap" by G. Ranger Wormser takes place in a circus.

Two other works in the first issue are a sign of things to come. The murder mystery, "The Rule of Three" by Francis Grierson, introduced the medical detective Professor Wells, and utilises an ingenious method of murder. During what many regard as the Golden Age of the classic murder mystery, *20 Story* would be a treasure trove.

Also present was L. Patrick Greene with "The Man With the Scar", one of his many African stories. British-born but, since 1913, resident in America, Greene spent several years in the colonial civil service in Rhodesia which provides background for his stories. Most fell into one of several series, including Trooper Drury, Commissioner Sykes or, the most popular, Aubrey St John Major, known as "the Major". He was an upper-class but street-wise (African-style) cove, whose illicit methods prove useful to the police. He first appeared in "Kruger's Gold" (May 1924). There are similarities between "the Major" and Edgar Wallace's Lieutenant Bones in the Sanders of the River series and Wallace contributed a series about Bones to *20 Story* later collected as *Bones of the River* (Newnes, 1923).

For the rest of the twenties and most of the thirties *20 Story* kept this balance between society romances, adventure and mystery. Sports stories were rare as were supernatural stories.

A. M. Burrage, a noted writer of weird fiction, was a frequent contributor but only a handful of these are strange stories, such as "The Case of Thissler and Baxter" (Oct 1924). Most are either light romances or mysteries. In the early years there were several animal stories. Guy Dent provided tense tales of the wild, but of greater significance is the appearance of Tarka the Otter in "Tarka's Last Hunt" (Jan 1925) by Henry Williamson.

In the early days many stories came from American magazines, with stories by Octavus Roy Cohen, H. Bedford-Jones, Achmed Abdullah, Carroll John Daly, Frederick C. Davis, Laurence G. Blochman, Arthur Dekker Savage and Jacland Marmur. F. Scott Fitzgerald was present with "Bernice Bobs Her Hair" (Oct 1922[1]), one of his early transitional tales of romance and high society. Arthur B. Reeve's Craig Kennedy, who put in a latter-day appearance in "The Radio Wraith" (Jul 1924). Lemuel de Bra appeared with his stories set in San Francisco's Chinatown. Chart Pitt contributed adventures set in the Arctic wastes. Albert Wetjen contributed many sea stories including a series about reckless adventurer Typhoon Bradley, starting with "Captain Typhoon" (Jan 1932).

Hugh Cave, another British-born American-resident writer recalled an interesting situation with his own submissions to *20 Story* which highlights both payment rates and publishing policy. He sent them tearsheets of four previously published stories, three of which had appeared under pen-names, though he had crossed these out and added his own. The editor bought all four and ran them all in the same issue, July 1932, and under the original pen names. Cave noted that after allowing for exchange rates his payment for all four stories came to just $60, then less than £20, even though they totalled over 15,000 words.[2] Clearly there was little value in American writers submitting new material.

Editor W. A. Williamson and his successors also developed a stable of British writers. The most prolific, at least during the 1920s, was Will Scott. He could turn his hand to anything, but most of his contributions are either humorous tales or mysteries. Amongst his mystery series are the characters of Detective Disher, starting in "The Footprints in the Sky" (Dec 1925) and the fiendishly clever criminal Dr Kent in "The Candid Crimes of Dr Kent" (from Mar 1928). Only a few of these stories have appeared in book form.

Leo Walmsley contributed a range of stories, many with African settings, and more or less took over when Greene's appearances faded. F.A.M. Webster was also known for his African stories. His best known series in *20 Story* was "The Man Who Knew" (from May 1926), about a planned uprising against the white races. Arlton Eadie, better remembered today for his stories in the American *Weird Tales*, contributed many mystery stories. The prolific Frank Shaw contributed nautical tales and mysteries. Stephen Phillips produced adventure, mystery and romance. There was an increase in romances during the 1930s with stories by Ursula Bloom, Clare Thornton, A. G. Greenwood and Ethel Mannin.

It is possible some of the contributors also appeared under pen names. The by-lines Robin Hood and Saxon Shore are obvious aliases, but there are others whose stories only seem to appear in *20 Story*. Green Howard was especially good at light mysteries. He had several regular characters of which the most interesting was schoolma'am detective Minnie Birch, a cross between Hildegarde Withers and Miss Marple, who first appeared in "Miss Birch Investigates" (Jun 1935). Van Harrison wrote many nautical tales – he had a series featuring

---

[1] This first appeared in *Saturday Evening Post*, 1 May 1920.
[2] See Hugh B. Cave, *Magazines I Remember* (Chicago: Tattered Pages Press, 1994), pp. 17-18.

sailor-of-fortune Captain Careless (from Sep 1936) – but he was also one of the few regular contributors of historical stories. "The Making of Barracuda" (Jan 1934) was the first in a series about piracy on the Spanish Main in the 1660s, whilst "Under the Moon" (from Dec 1934) pitted highwayman Galloping Larry against the Bow Street Runners.

Of the more recognisable names perhaps the most interesting is Edith Pargeter who appeared with some of her earliest stories, "Perfect Love" (Dec 1936) and a ghost story, "Brief Garland" (Apr 1937). Author and journalist Christopher St John Sprigg, who was killed in the Spanish Civil War, appeared with one of his last stories, "Four Friends and Death" (Mar 1935). "The Arm of Mrs Egan" (Jun 1935), a tale of spiritual revenge, was also one of the last stories by the noted writer of weird fiction, William Fryer Harvey. Stefan Lorant, who was in the process of launching *Lilliput*, appeared with "The Jockey Who Always Won" (Mar 1937). In the magazine's latter days it ran W. E. Johns's series of aviation mysteries featuring Dr Vane, beginning with "The Affair of the Barrage Balloons" (Apr 1940).

Other major names that appeared did so with reprints. The first of Agatha Christie's Tommy & Tuppence short stories appeared as "It Must Have Been a Fairy" (Jan 1930). Talbot Mundy had one solitary adventure story, "Black Flag" (May 1932) from the American pulp *Adventure*. Of particular interest are two appearances by Cornell Woolrich. "Borrowed Crime" (Oct 1939), a straight reprint from *Black Mask* (Jul 1939), and "The Corpse in the Statue" (May 1939) a heavily revised version of "Red Liberty" from *Dime Detective* (1 July 1935). It is closer to the version eventually included in *Violence* (1958), and suggests that Woolrich may have revised it for *20 Story*.

In its final year *20 Story* used a number of reprints, including several stories by Dorothy L. Sayers, though her early Peter Wimsey story, "The Adventure of the Cat in the Bag", was a *20 Story* original (May 1926). There was also a rare story by Vera Brittain, "Glamour" (Aug 1940), taken from the *St. Bartholomew's Appeal* volume published the previous year.

The fact that *20 Story* lasted for so long, and well into the War, showed the loyal support of its readers, but in the end wartime restrictions took their toll and the magazine was merged with *Parade* from November 1940. *Parade* was a digest miscellany much like *Lilliput* and it survived only another ten months. Despite a certain unevenness in content and quality, *20 Story* contains much that is worthy of attention and has not been reprinted. It is a particular goldmine for fans of British detective stories.

Frequency: Monthly.
Publisher: Odhams Press.
Editors: W.A. Williamson, 1922-27; Miss F.C. MacKenzie, 1927-34; E.C. Wray, 1935-40.
Format/Size: Standard pulp, 128 pages.
Price: 1/-.
Holdings:
Complete run, UK. British Library on microfilm, but issue for Jan 1928 is incomplete (*BL Shelfmark*: PP.6018.tar; *Microfilm*: Mic.C.349).
Substantial run, UK. Bodleian has run Jul 1922-Mar 1933 (*Call Number*: Per. 25612 d.9).
Collecting points: Becoming increasingly uncommon. Bound volumes have not been seen but occasional single issues surface. Long runs are scarce.

* * *

THE UNIVERSAL MAGAZINE

21 issues. Volume 1, Number 1, February 1900 to Volume 4, Number 21, January 1902. Merged with *The Ludgate* as THE UNIVERSAL AND LUDGATE MAGAZINE from March to November 1901, but reverted to THE UNIVERSAL MAGAZINE for last two issues.

Although the editor's introduction to the first issue of *The Universal* said that it was "designed to be a National Magazine, it has no exclusive field", it was overtly pretentious, clearly trying to appeal to the social climber. Features included "Peeps into Notable Homes" and "Our Public Schools", plus a "Ladies Page" and "The Stage". Marie Corelli provided the lead article, "Patriotism – or Self Advertisement?", and she remained the leader writer for several issues.

The emphasis was on features and fiction took second place with only Coulson Kernahan's hunting story, "A Bang at a Bruin", of any significance. However the editor made it clear that he wanted to expand his use of short fiction and over the next few issues he presented stories by Arthur Conan Doyle, Emile Zola, Bret Harte, Israel Zangwill and Robert S. Hichens.

The magazine's appearance, however, was uneven and did not maintain a regular schedule. De Beck established a company to publish the magazine himself, with Raymond Blathwayt as editor, and though it appeared regularly, it still looked a hurried operation. From March 1901 de Beck merged the magazine with *The Ludgate* under the cumbersome title *The Universal and Ludgate Magazine*, but he retained none of *The Ludgate*'s features or personality.

The impression remains that de Beck had brought out the magazine on impulse without a proper policy or plan and it was published constantly at a loss. There seems to have been acrimony between de Beck and his fellow directors, even a suspicion that de Beck may have been diverting funds. In the end the proprietors regained control of the magazine. In the December 1901 issue, which had reverted to the title *The Universal Magazine*, they announced that "The Proprietors hereby give notice that Mr. A. M. de Beck is no longer connected with the *Universal Magazine*." They managed to publish a special "New Year" issue for January 1902, but the company then ceased trading with debts of nearly £7,000.[1]

As a result *The Universal* has been completely forgotten and it contains little to make it memorable. Of most interest is Conan Doyle's story "The Confession" (Mar 1900), which was not included in any of Doyle's story collections during his lifetime. It is the story of a Jesuit priest's retreat to a convent and of his encounter with a woman from his past. Doyle's biographer, Owen Dudley Edwards, calls it "a work of considerable power"[2] and it is perhaps the most significant item in *The Universal*. Also of interest is Israel Zangwill's bohemian story of love, art and vanity, "The Woman Beater" (Dec 1900).

The Universal was a magazine with higher aspirations than it could achieve and its passing took with it the far more interesting *Ludgate*.

Frequency: Monthly, but no issues for Apr, Aug or Sep 1900.
Publishers: Horace Marshall to Oct 1900; then A. M. de Beck Ltd to December 1901.

---

[1] See *The Times*, 8 January 1902, p. 13 for details of the company's winding-up.
[2] Owen Dudley Edwards, *The Quest for Sherlock Holmes* (London: Penguin Books, 1984), p. 93.

Editors: Alexis Maria de Beck to Oct 1900, then Raymond Blathwayt.
Format/Size: Standard, 86 pages to Oct 1900; then 112 pages.
Price: 6d.
Holdings:
Substantial run, UK. British Library has up to Dec 1901 (*Shelfmark*: PP.6018.td). • Bodleian has up to Oct 1901 (*Call Number*: Per. 2705 d.129). • Cambridge University Library has volumes 1-2, May 1900-Apr 1901 only (*Classmark*: L900.c.84).
Complete run, US. Library of Congress (*Call Number*: AP4.U485).
Collecting points: Extremely rare.

* * *

THE VIOLET MAGAZINE

309 issues. Number 1, July 1922 to Number 309, November 1939. Thereafter incorporated in *Girls' Friend Library*.

The Violet was the romantic-fiction companion to the *Red Magazine* and *The Yellow*. It survived a surprisingly long time, though it is really a magazine with two lives. In the 1920s, when for most of the time it appeared fortnightly, it was a magazine full of fun, humour and romance in the broadest sense, incorporating suspense, love stories and even a few ghost stories. During the thirties it focused solely on love stories and developed other features such as knitting patterns, advice columns and recipes so that it read and looked more like a monthly version of *Woman's Weekly*. Early in the thirties it stopped running author's by-lines, unless they were major names such as Elinor Glyn or May Edginton, who appeared infrequently.

During the twenties the magazine drew heavily upon the same stable of Amalgamated Press writers who were appearing in the other magazines and story-papers. Alongside the female names – Madge Crichton, Maud Crawford, Amy Foskett and Margaret Peterson (some of which may well be pseudonyms for male writers[1]) – will be found many male authors – G. H. Teed, Ernest McKeag, J. Russell Warren, Lloyd Williams, Malcolm Saville, even Arnold Golsworthy. Ursula Bloom sold much early fiction here, and there was work by Phillippa Southcombe, Claire Pollexfen and Evadne Price. *The Violet* often dropped author credits. It is a shame that the series of stories told by a tenant at the Veevers' Arms hostelry was by-lined only "The Writing Gentleman" as these deserve better credit. The lack of major names is one reason why the magazine has virtually been forgotten. Furthermore the stories are formulaic, aimed primarily at young women, with little of import.

In the twenties *The Violet* was closer in content to Newnes's *Happy Mag.* than with women's magazines *per se*. It was certainly nothing like *Woman* or *The Home Magazine*. Although straight love stories accounted for over half the contents, it showed a remarkable

---

[1] Madge Crichton was probably the prolific H. Crichton Miln who may later have helped on the magazine.

ability for reworking standard themes. Many love stories were set in Japan or China or Africa – Margaret Peterson wrote an especially strong serial of African bewitchery in "The Witch Child" (17 Nov 1922-12 Jan 1923). There were several wild-west ranch romances – Crichton Miln was the main contributor. The magazine ran surprisingly few South Seas romances which dominated other magazines, but it eventually got round to these in the late twenties and again Crichton Miln obliged with "The Perfect Savage" (10 May-7 Jun 1929). Unlike Odhams's *Romance*, which was *The Violet's* closest comparison, the magazine never presented an image of escapism or forbidden romance. Its covers and illustrated contents page were more homely, with tennis courts and boating on the river or dancing. Only briefly during May to July 1929 did it present an image of distant castles and romantic islands, though the content changed little. It aimed at the young working girl with domestic romance and clearly secured a market.

Most mysteries were written by F. Addington Symonds (writing as Earle Danesford), Guy Trent and G. H. Teed. Teed contributed the more unusual stories including the weird tale "The Macaw" (18 February 1927) and stories set in the Wild West, Australian outback or India. There were few historical stories, though John Bolinbroke wrote of the romance of Nelson and Lady Hamilton in "Brave Heart and Fair Lady" (4 Mar 1927), and Ernest McKeag about Catherine the Great in "The Smiles of an Empress!" (30 Sep 1927). There was no sophistication in these stories however. They were told plain and simple. Amongst the more popular series, judging from the editorial comments, were W. Harold Thomson's long-running series about the clever dog, "Cracker!", and the uncredited "Adventures of Parker" (6 Jan-30 Mar 1928), about a domestic servant who inherits a fortune but keeps her wealth secret as she continues to observe the ways of the world as a housemaid. *The Violet* was really no more than a girl's illustrated story-paper and was never on a par with *The Red* or *The Yellow*.

Frequency: Monthly to Oct 1922; fortnightly to 3 Jan 1930; then monthly.
Publisher: Amalgamated Press.
Editors: Probably Leonard Pratt (under Reginald T. Eves) to Dec 1929; thereafter not known.
Format/Size: Small pulp, 112 pages.
Price: 7d (though dropped to 6d during 1926 until 4 Mar 1927).
Holdings: *Substantial run, UK*. British Library has a run complete to Aug 1938 on microfilm (*Shelfmark*: PP.6018.tat; *Microfilm*: Mic.C.618). • The Bodleian has a run to #175 (24 May 1929), lacking #86 (11 Dec 1925) (*Call Number*: Per. 25612 e.1207).
Collecting points: Very rare and 1930s issues extremely uncommon.

***

WAR STORIES

5 issues. Volume 1, Number 1, October 1935 to Volume 1, Number 5, February 1936.

The short-lived companion to Newnes's more succesful *Air Stories*. Both were edited by T. Stanhope Sprigg but whereas *Air Stories* was able to plug into the network of aviation devotees, the same wellspring was not there for war stories, especially when the magazine concentrated on stories of the First World War with nothing more recent or historical. Like *Air Stories* it was a mixture of real-life adventures and fiction from many of the same writers, including Arch Whitehouse and George Fielding Eliot. Eric Wood provided a series about the

Mascot Mob of crazy but creative warriors that began with "The Spooks of St Quentin" (Oct 1935), and which was only marginally above boys' adventure fiction.

The magazine began a series of personal reminiscences of the War, "This Was War!" which included an account by author Ernest L. McKeag of being torpedoed. Sprigg found the need to include several air-war stories, presumably taken from the *Air Stories* inventory, and naval stories. The more interesting items, however, are G. F. Eliot's story of betrayal at Gallipoli, "The Traitor of 'W' Beach" (Oct 1935) and C. T. Stoneham's exploit of a mounted infantry detachment in East Africa, "Last of the Old and Bold" (Feb 1936). There were also reprints of stories by F. Britten Austin and A. M. Burrage (as Ex-Private 'X'). The magazine ended abruptly and was superseded by the equally short-lived *Western Adventures*.

Frequency: Monthly
Publisher: George Newnes.
Editor: T. Stanhope Sprigg.
Format/Size: Standard pulp, 96 pages.
Price: 7d.
Holdings: *Complete run, UK*. British Library on microfilm (*Shelfmark*: PP.6018.thi; *Microfilm*: Mic.C.596).
Collecting points: Scarce.

* * *

WEEKLY TALE-TELLER
365 issues. Number 1, 8 May 1909 to Number 365, 29 April 1916.

Weekly Tale-Teller – or simply *Tale-Teller* as its editor, Isabel Thorne, called it – was one of many weekly story papers issued by Harry Shurey in Hind Court, off Fleet Street. It had been founded by Thorne and she infused it with her personality more than the other magazines and novelettes. She ran a weekly editorial column, "Concerning Ourselves", giving her personal views on current topics, stories and authors. She enjoyed all the stories she published, and the magazine glowed with her enthusiasm.

Like its elder sister, *Yes or No*, the magazine has suffered badly from the ravages of time and, being a disposable, penny magazine, few copies survive. Although *Weekly Tale-Teller* never matched *Yes or No* in circulation, it is generally regarded as the more significant magazine, and it often ran the bigger names. Oliver Onions, Max Rittenberg, Rafael Sabatini, George R. Sims Katharine Tynan and Stanley Waterloo all appeared within its pages, though not on a regular basis. Shurey's publications could not afford the high rates paid to major writers and though some of their appearances in *Weekly Tale-Teller* may have been with bottom-drawer material, this was not always the case. W. Pett Ridge's "Odd Trick to the Butler" (2 Mar 1912), one of those "clever" stories so abundant at the time, was written specially for the magazine and suggests that authors kept an eye on it as a market for original and different stories.

Thorne was constantly trying to discover new writers, because any writer of talent that she published invariably moved on to better paying markets. Her star discovery, or really rediscovery, was Edgar Wallace. He had been writing for ten years and had some success with *The Four Just Men* (1905), but by 1909 was in a rut. He had first met Thorne at Shurey's offices, where she had bought one story, "The Bandaged Hand" (15 May 1909), and told him what was wrong with another. A chance meeting with Thorne a few days later, when Wallace was going to a meeting of the Congo Reform Association, opened the floodgates and the character of Commissioner Sanders was created.[1] The first "Sanders of the River" story was "The Wood of Devils" (25 Sept 1909) and the series appeared regularly for the next five years. Wallace's book *Bones* is dedicated to Thorne.

Whereas *Yes or No* tended to go for the human interest story, the *Weekly Tale-Teller* preferred stories of action, intrigue and the unusual. Both overlapped in the types of stories they ran and occasionally a series from one magazine might switch to the other. Percy Brebner's stories about college professor and master detective, Christopher Quarles, for example, began in *Weekly Tale-Teller* in November 1912 and switched to *Yes or No* in 1914. But on the whole the *Tale-Teller* was what its title implied, a magazine of story-telling, with adventurous and stirring yarns.

The first issue contained seven stories (fairly typical for the magazine). Captain Frank H. Shaw opened with a nautical story, "The Man Who Extended the Empire". Shaw was one of the principle contributors, usually with stories of the sea. One of his most popular series involved nautical exploits in the Arctic, "North of 53°" (from 16 Dec 1911). Frederick Maxwell began the private-detective series "The Adventures of Courtenay Sykes". Sykes is perhaps too imitative of Sherlock Holmes, but surprisingly the series was never collected in book form. Almost every issue of *Weekly Tale-Teller* ran what it called "tales of the occult" or "unusual stories". The main contributors were Elsie Norris, herself something of a ghost hunter, Elliott O'Donnell and A. M. Burrage, though most of Burrage's appearances in the magazine were with light romances or historical stories. Oliver Onions's story of a ghostly encounter, "The Cigarette Case", later included in *Widdershins*, appeared in the issue for 13 August 1910. Probably the best known series of weird stories featured Aylmer Vance, Psychic Investigator, and were by Alice and Claude Askew[2] (from 4 Jul 1914). Historical fiction was another mainstay of the magazine and included many stories set in the Napoleonic and Regency periods. One of A. M. Burrage's most popular series, "Pistol and Spur" (from 24 February 1912), told of the exploits of highwayman Captain Jack Bishop.

Within a few years of its debut the circulation of *Weekly Tale-Teller* was reported as 77,000, just over half that of *Yes or No*, but though no further data were forthcoming, it is likely the circulation rose over time. Clearly the magazine must have been popular because in 1915, it increased its pagination, despite wartime restrictions. However, by April 1916 Thorne was voicing concerns over circulation, and within a year Shurey was forced to merge the magazine with *Yes or No*.

---

[1] See *Edgar Wallace, A Biography* by Margaret Lane (Heinemann, 1938), pp. 222-228.
[2] These have been collected as *Aylmer Vance: Ghost Seer* by Jack Adrian (Ash-Tree Press, 1998).

Frequency: Weekly.
Publisher: Shurey Publications.
Editor: Isabel Thorne.
Format/Size: Slim, large digest size; page count 48, rose to 56, 10 Apr 1915; back to 48, 25 Mar 1916.
Price: 1d.
Holdings:
Complete run, UK. British Library (*Shelfmark*: PP.6018.tag).
Substantial run, UK. The Bodleian has the following issues: 1-12 (8 May–24 Jul 1909), 46 (19 Mar 1910), 51 (23 Apr 1910), 55 (21 May 1910), 63 (16 Jul 1910), 66 (6 Aug 1910), 75 (8 Oct 1910), 81 (19 Dec 1910), 98 (18 Mar 1911), 103 (22 Apr 1911), 107 (20 May 1911), 128 (14 Oct 1911), 133 (18 Nov 1911), 157-160 (4-25 May 1912), 184 (9 Nov 1912), 238 (22 Nov 1913), 242-243 (20-27 Dec 1913), 261-262 (2-9 May 1914), 284-296 (10 Oct 1914-2 Jan 1915), 337 (16 Oct 1915) and 357 (4 Mar 1916) all with restricted access (*Call Number*: Hogan 896).
Collecting points: Extremely rare. Occasional single issues surface but never long runs.

* * *

WESTERN ADVENTURES
5 issues. Volume 1, Number 1, February 1936 to Volume 1, Number 5, June 1936.

The third of the pulp magazines published by Newnes under the editorship of T. Stanhope Sprigg, following *Air Stories* and *War Stories*. Unlike its companions, which featured mostly British writers, *Western Adventures* was almost entirely reprinted from American pulps. Authors included Frederick C. Davis, Charles Roy Cox and Lee Bond. Gerald Bowman flew the British flag. Not all the stories were stereotyped cowboy tales. "Trail of the Wolf" by Robert Pinkerton (Jun 1936) is set in the Canadian North-West. "When Calves Fly" by Robert McBlair (Apr 1936) may well be of British origin as it reads as much like trying to run a farm in Scotland as in Dakota. Western magazines have seldom fared well in Britain and *Western Adventures* was no different. It should be remembered, though, as the only original all-western British magazine.

Frequency: Monthly
Publisher: George Newnes.
Editor: T. Stanhope Sprigg.
Format/Size: Standard pulp, 96 pages.
Price: 7d.
Holdings: None known.
Collecting points: Rare.

* * *

THE WHITE MAGAZINE
3 issues. Number 1, March/April 1909 to Number 3, July/August 1909.

Inspired by the Franco-British Exhibition and the Olympic Games, both held at White City in West London in 1908, the long established firm of Simpkin, Marshall, Hamilton, Kent issued *The White Magazine* in the late winter of 1909. It may also have had one eye on the success of Amalgamated Press's *The Red Magazine*, but although it was likewise in pulp format and unillustrated, and even undercut *The Red* by a penny, it had none of that adventurous, exciting fiction of *The Red*. *The White* was hooked into the past and would not have looked out of place had it been published a decade or two earlier.

The White declared that "fiction will be the strongest characteristic", and that other subjects "grave and gay" will appear. Each issue ran between ten and twelve stories, plus a serial and a handful of poems. There was one main article, in the first two cases both with a military theme by Captain D. Renney-Presgrave, a children's story, and features on fashion and the theatre. Another on men's clubs began in the third issue. These features alone show that *The White* was aiming at a more cultured readership than the other all-fiction magazines. There was a token nod towards the more general reader with the start of a round-robin detective story, "The Scarlet Arrow", where each new episode was to be submitted by the readers. As the magazine was bi-monthly, there was time to do this, but that no reader was ever credited is suspicious, and the serial may have been continued by the original writer.

The stories were an uneven mixture. Headlining the first issue was George R. Sims, with a novelty item, "The Two Thousand Pounds Coupon". Mrs Barry Pain and S. Baring-Gould were the lead names in the other two issues. Aside from these, few authors of note appeared, although Arnold Golsworthy, May Edginton and Oliver Sandys all put in an appearance. Their stories were generally light romances or social dramas, products of their time. More unusual were two historical Viking sagas by Olaf Thorvaldsen – "Karen of Solvik" and "Gudrun" – reflecting a continued interest in that "northern thing", encouraged by William Morris.

The initial enthusiasm seems to have waned rapidly, and sales must have been poor, as the magazine disappeared after only three issues, the serial, "Proven" by Mrs Adams Acton, incomplete. Its bland white covers may not have helped, but the magazine lacked verve and with more exciting material around *The White Magazine* faded to grey.

*

Frequency: Bi-monthly.
Publisher: Simpkin, Marshall, Hamilton, Kent.
Editor(s): Not known.
Format/Size: Standard pulp, 112 pages.
Price: 3½d.
Holdings:
Complete run, UK. British Library (*BL Shelfmark*: PP.6018.taf); Bodleian (*Call Number*: Per. 2561 d.65).
Collecting points: Extremely scarce.

* * *

THE WINDSOR MAGAZINE

537 issues. Volume 1, Number 1, January 1895 to Volume 90, Number 537, September 1939.

The Windsor nailed its colours to the mast in the foreword to the first issue. It stated that "It is to the home that the *Windsor Magazine* desires specially to appeal", but this was rather lost in a three-page diatribe against women's suffrage. The powers behind *The Windsor*, the Lock family and their partner James Bowden, were evidently opposed to the "New Woman" who, they proclaimed, "is apt to be unlovely and to make her brief sojourn amongst us hideous with discordant cries."[1] *The Windsor* believed the woman's place was in the home and with the family, a view also held by Queen Victoria, and it was with the royal family, the British aristocracy and staunch British refinement and honour that *The Windsor* allied itself.

The magazine's foreword is important because it shows it was not launched as a clone of *The Strand*, then in its fourth successful year, even though it looked every inch the same. There was little need for Ward, Lock and Bowden to do so, because it already published a British edition of *Lippincott's Magazine*, one of the American magazines that had pioneered the popular illustrated general-interest magazine. *The Windsor* was looking for a different niche. Britain, in the mid-late Victorian period, had been awash with what were euphemistically called "home" magazines. These were devout Christian magazines that oozed upright living and sentimentality and were prone to preaching. Leading examples were *Good Words* and *The Quiver*. What *The Windsor* wanted to do was keep the upright morality but loosen the collar. It felt that stories and articles could remain ethical and still be fun. The editor explained:

> The chief purpose of the *Windsor Magazine* is to illuminate the hearth with genial philosophy, to widen its outlook, to give it a reasonable attitude of inquiry towards the problems of the time, to make it crackle with the good humour which is born of true tolerance and puts to flight the exaggerated self-consciousness of aggressive virtue.

It did not sound a bundle of fun, but it was seeking to appeal to the stolid Victorian middle-class family that had aspirations towards social status and to upholding the Victorian ethic that had made Britain the greatest power in the world. In other words it stood for traditional Victorian values, and was having nothing to do with feminism or socialism.

The Windsor also made clear that for its male readers there would be both serious articles and escapist adventure fiction, revealing the wonders of the world. It had a sideways dig at the success and therefore the imitation of the Sherlock Holmes stories by noting that "the world is not yet so completely cured of marvels that every novelist is reduced to evolving analytic

---

[1] "Foreword", *The Windsor Magazine*, January 1895, pp. 1-3. This was probably a swipe at the reputation of Rosamund Marriott Watson who (as Graham R. Tomson) had edited *The Windsor's* fore-runner *Sylvia's Journal* in 1892. The scandal caused by her divorce and remarriage and her association with the decadent movement had led Ward Lock to disassociate themselves from her. *Sylvia's Journal* had started life as the respectable *Young Englishwoman* in 1865, the true progenitrix of *The Windsor*.

significance from the buttons of the heroine's shoe!" In fact mystery and detective fiction would be a significant feature of *The Windsor*'s early years. For the magazine's female readers, it "will take a serious interest in educational questions and especially in a project which deeply concerns the welfare of women." This project was the magazine's crusade during 1895, the Marriage Insurance scheme, essentially an attempt to restore the dowry system. The scheme would allow fathers to take out a policy that paid a sufficient sum upon the marriage of a daughter or, if the daughter failed to marry, allow her an income in her later years. Henry Seton Merriman's serial, "The Grey Lady", conveniently underlined the perils of the day by tracing the consequences of a rich girl's fall from grace when her father's death leaves her penniless.

Other features that catered for the woman reader covered housekeeping, fashion and "home gossip", a romance story, and some rather saccharine poems. There were also plenty of features which pandered to the social climber such as "Children of Notable People", "Windsor: Castle and Home", "The Duchess of Bedford's Pets" and, in later months "Homes of Notable People". The cartoons by Louis Wain also found firm favour and he remained a regular contributor. There was also a series by H. D. Lowry, "Unknown London", who looked at the less salubrious areas that probably were "unknown" to the middle- and upper-class readers.

Yet, when the early issues of *The Windsor* are recalled, not just today, but soon after their appearance, none of these features are highlighted. The original plan for a decent and morally improving magazine was lost in the runaway success of two series – in fact two characters: Dr Nikola and Martin Hewitt.

Dr Nikola was the creation of Australian writer Guy Boothby, who had moved to Britain after the success of his book, *In Strange Company* (Ward, Lock, 1893). Nikola appeared in *The Windsor*'s opening serial, "A Bid for Fortune", illustrated by Stanley L. Wood. A complicated and serpentine plot allowed Boothby to keep the true character of Nikola (*left*), who was something of a scientific genius and possibly possessed psychic powers, in the shadows, so that when the book finished readers clamoured for more. The bizarre sequel, "Dr. Nikola", followed through 1896.

" The black cat looked through the smoke at the three men."

Martin Hewitt, the creation of Arthur Morrison, was a detective somewhat in the vein of Sherlock Holmes. Hewitt's first series had run in *The Strand* during 1894 to fill the void left by the end of the Holmes stories. Ward, Lock had managed to lure Morrison away and promptly ran three further series under the heading "The Chronicles of Martin Hewitt" during the first eighteen months. These two characters assured the success of *The Windsor*.

Evidently the readers of *The Windsor*, whilst appreciating the material relating to the upper classes, which was in itself a form of escapism, wanted escapist fiction, sport and humour, not

Sunday-school preaching. Ward, Lock rapidly rethought their policy. Stanhope Sprigg, who had helped develop *The Windsor*, was shuffled aside and David Williamson, who had assisted Clement Shorter at the *Illustrated London News* and *English Illustrated Magazine*, was brought in. Flora Klickmann, who had been the editor for the women's features, now became the assistant editor. The women's columns were dropped and Klickmann concentrated on writing her own articles and interviews and commissioning others, mostly about celebrities and royalty.

From the January 1896 issue, Williamson introduced an editorial persona in "The Editor's Scrap-Book". It rarely said anything about the magazine itself but served as a pot-pourri of humour, *bon mots*, poems and vignettes. With the September 1896 issue Williamson also ran "The Editor's Post Bag", the first time readers' letters were published (or in this case paraphrased) in a British popular monthly magazine. The feature was dropped when Williamson moved on to edit *The Temple Magazine*, but "The Editor's Scrap-Book" remained for the rest of the magazine's life.

Under Williamson *The Windsor* became more lively and exciting, especially in its fiction. There was historical fiction from S. R. Crockett and exotic adventure fiction from Charles J. Mansford, C. J. Cutcliffe Hyne and Arthur Conan Doyle. Alice Perrin portrayed the Anglo-Indian life. L. T. Meade joined Arthur Morrison with more mystery fiction. W. W. Jacobs provided his popular blend of homespun philosophy and quayside humour, as well as a particularly atmospheric ghost story, "Jerry Bundler" (Dec 1897), which the editor warned "all nervous readers to avoid". Barry Pain and Henry A. Hering lightened the tone with their wry observations on life, the unjustly forgotten Mayne Lindsay contributed several highly unusual stories whilst, with the serial "Captain Shannon" (Jul 1896), Coulson Kernahan highlighted the perils of socialism. There was even a cowboy story, "The Kid" (Nov 1896) by Owen Rhoscomyl, and artist Stanley L. Wood wrote a two-part feature on "A Tenderfoot in Texas" (Dec 1896-Jan 1897).

The Christmas issues of *The Windsor* were, as with most magazines, something special. The December 1895 issue ran a full colour frontispiece reproducing an early painting made by Queen Victoria when she was a princess in 1831. It also came with a free complete novel supplement, in this case a reprint of Conan Doyle's first Sherlock Holmes novel, "A Study in Scarlet", which Ward, Lock had originally published as a *Beeton's Christmas Annual*. The novel supplement remained a selling point for several years and the *Windsor* Christmas issues were always a sight to behold.

The articles in *The Windsor* were both educational and stimulating. In addition to the regular sporting features, there were interviews with authors and artists – including profiles of S. R. Crockett, Coulson Kernahan and Guy Boothby – and many articles on scientific achievement. The late Victorian period was one of considerable technological advance and *The Windsor* delighted in evaluating new achievements. This included travel and exploration and there were several articles on expeditions trying to reach the North Pole. There were also features on the royal family and the marvels of the British Empire.

By the time Arthur Hutchinson took over the editorial reins in June 1898, much of the character of *The Windsor* was already established and he needed only to build on that. This he did with relish. The month he took over he was able to start a new occult serial by Guy Boothby, "Pharos the Egyptian", and the first part of an account of Nansen's attempt to reach the North Pole. He ran two of the early Oswald Bastable stories by Edith Nesbit and Kipling's realistic public school series, "Stalky and Co." (Dec 1898-May 1899), illustrated by L. Raven-Hill. There was an article on the noted female traveller Lady Hester Stanhope in the same issue that another robust traveller, Cutcliffe Hyne, reported back on "Cave Dwellers in the Canary Islands" (Apr 1899). Of historical interest is a serial by Max Pemberton, "Pro Patria" (Jun-Nov 1900), part of which involves an attempt to build the Channel Tunnel. In keeping with the *fin de siècle* mood Robert Barr contributed an apocalyptic tale of the world engulfed in fire, "Within an Ace of the End of the World" (Dec 1900).

Hutchinson was able to report that over the previous few years the magazine had experienced a "rapid growth in popularity and a large circulation."[2] During its lifetime, the publishers never revealed any net sales figures, though claimed a "circulation" of around 150-170,000 with 200,000 for the Christmas issues. When the Advertisers' Protection Society suggested a more realistic 100,000 the publishers objected but provided no alternative. However, after the magazine's demise Edward Liveing, in his otherwise shallow history of Ward, Lock, revealed that "in most years the *Windsor*'s monthly sales ran between 110,000 and 115,000 and that 150,000 were always produced for its Christmas numbers."[3]

Hutchinson remained editor for almost thirty years, providing continuity and consistency. He had a broad range of interests. He not only adhered to Victorian values, thus satisfying the magazine's origins, but was open to change and fascinated with technological developments. His magazine, especially during the Edwardian period, scintillated with articles on scientific advances, such as "Marconi's Achievement" (May 1902) and "Edison's Latest Marvel" (Nov 1902). There were articles on the exploration of the ocean floor (Jul 1903), harnessing the power of the sun (Jun 1906), and venturing to the North Pole by airship (Sept 1907). Camille Flammarian wrote and illustrated "About the Moon" (Oct 1907) and Percival Lowell likewise revealed "More About Mars" (Mar 1908). This interest stimulated the growth in science fiction, particularly in tales of exploration, such as "The Secret of the South Pole" by Hamilton Drummond (Apr 1902) and "From Pole to Pole" by George Griffith (Oct 1904).

"It was the cross aussie, the Symbol of Life itself."

Hutchinson's interests in exploration and adventure stories set in remote places led to some interesting items. Upton Sinclair's "The Overman" (Dec 1906[4]) tells of a man who survives for over twenty years on a remote Pacific island and develops a psychic link with a new form of life. Beatrice Grimshaw, the queen of the tropical island romance, appeared with an occasional article such as "In the Cannibal New Hebrides" (Feb 1907). *The Windsor* published several of Rudyard Kipling's "Just So" stories, starting with "The Elephant's Child" (Feb 1902[5]) and, more significantly, the African adventures by H. Rider

---

[2] *The Windsor Magazine*, December 1898, p. 130.
[3] Edward Liveing, *Adventure in Publishing* (London: Ward, Lock, 1954), p. 74. The print run for the first issue was 100,000 and Ward Lock had to reprint an additional 50,000.
[4] Also published in *Harper's*, June 1906.
[5] First published in *Ladies' Home Journal*, April 1900.

Haggard. Haggard had contributed a few articles, including "Lost on the Veld" (Dec 1902), but *The Windsor*'s big scoop was to publish the sequel to *She*, "Ayesha", which began in the December 1904 issue, strikingly illustrated by Maurice Greiffenhagen (*opposite*).

The artwork and presentation of *The Windsor* was one of its main features and during the Edwardian decade its production values rose. Colour plates became a regular feature starting with the Christmas 1905 issue. Thereafter there was almost always a colour frontispiece in each issue until curtailed by wartime restrictions. The magazine led with a regular feature on works of art, written by Austin Chester. This ran for many years, first evaluating and reproducing the works of many Victorian and Edwardian artists and then surveying the works of major collections. Until it was rivalled by *Nash's Magazine* after Hearst took it over in 1911, *The Windsor* was undoubtedly the most polished of the standard monthly popular magazines.

The Windsor ran many stories from American magazines, mostly *McClure's*, and in so doing picked up two authors who became mainstays during the Edwardian period and War Years. Canadian author Charles G. D. Roberts contributed a long series of wildlife stories, most set in the wildernesses of North America, beautifully illustrated by Charles Livingston Bull. The other regular was the now forgotten Justus Miles Forman. He delighted in tales of romantic intrigue and adventure, and was a great admirer of Haggard. *The Windsor* serialised most of his novels, starting with "The Garden of Lies" (Dec 1903-May 1904), a twist on the Ruritanian theme. The novel was popular in England and adapted for the stage. Forman was paid amongst the highest rates for his work. He was killed when the *Lusitania* was sunk in the First World War. *The Windsor* published his last story, "The Gentleman Burglar" (Oct 1915). Other American writers who appeared at this time include Frank R. Stockton, Ellis Parker Butler, Jack London, Josephine Dodge Daskam and, perhaps surprisingly, the composer John Philip Sousa, with his mystical novella "The Fifth String" (Feb 1903).

Mystery fiction was a main component of *The Windsor* during most of its life. In this period it serialised such classic works as Richard Harding Davis's "In the Fog" (Mar-May 1902), Arnold Bennett's "The Loot of Cities" (Jun-Nov 1904) and Baroness Orczy's memoirs of defence lawyer Patrick Mulligan, known colloquially as "Skin o' My Tooth" (Jun-Nov 1903). *The Windsor* also published several of Robert Barr's stories featuring the pompous French detective Eugene Valmont, seen by some as a prototype of Hercule Poirot. These were spread over a period of time, starting with "The Mystery of the Five Hundred Diamonds" (Nov 1904). Some also appeared in *Pearson's Magazine*, but *The Windsor* published "The Absent-Minded Coterie" (May 1906), considered to be one of the cleverest of all early detective stories.

Although he would have seemed tailor-made for the magazine, *The Windsor* published only two stories by P. G. Wodehouse, both with public school settings: "The Fifteenth Man" (Dec 1906) and "The Guardian" (Sept 1908). Two major contributors, however, began to appear just before the outbreak of War: Edgar Wallace with "His Game" (Oct 1910) and Dornford Yates with "Busy Bees" (Sept 1911). Wallace remained a regular contributor for the next fifteen years, and hardly missed an issue during the War when he contributed many of his Bones and Sanders stories. Yates was an equally frequent contributor. His pre-War stories were collected as *The Brother of Daphne* (1914), but he would not settle into his rhythm until the twenties.

The War had the inevitable effect on *The Windsor*, but although page counts steadily dropped and the price rose, *The Windsor* retained its production quality throughout and never resorted to cheap paper. Although the colour frontispiece was dropped from September 1917, two months earlier it had upgraded its cover from the standard, stock sketch of Windsor Castle, to a pictorial full colour cover. Most of these depicted women at leisure and were painted by George Wilmshurst.

Although at the start of hostilities every issue was dominated by articles discussing every aspect of the War, *The Windsor* ran few war stories. Clearly the magazine wanted to provide those at home, and soldiers who were sent the magazine, something to take their minds away from the events. Most early stories were propaganda, such as L. G. Moberley's "An Ordinary Man" (Feb 1915), in which an everyday man becomes a hero. Over time the issues received more serious treatment. A. B. Cooper's "Facing the Guns" (Feb 1916) was one of the few to consider the horrors of the trenches, whilst Walter E. Grogan's "The Deserter" (May 1916) considered matters of guilt and cowardice. Otherwise most stories got away from the War. There were light romances by Keble Howard, historical romances by Marjorie Bowen, tales of Dartmoor by Eden Phillpotts, escapist adventures by James F. Dwyer and westerns by Crosbie Garstin. There was plenty of historical fiction, most of it set in the Regency or early Victorian period, and even a series of stories based on Icelandic sagas by Maurice Hewlett.

After the War, *The Windsor* soon got back to normal. One lyrical fantasy, "An Index to Dreams" by Charles L. Morgan (Apr 1919), which considered lost opportunities and the rebuilding of lives, seemed to close a door on the War and turn to matters new. *The Windsor* embraced the twenties as if it were coming home to an old friend. It had always striven to be a cut above its rivals, not just in the quality of its stories but in their very substance. Now *The Windsor* was able to present endless stories of golden days of British country life, the social set, weekend house parties, and the good life. This was when Dornford Yates came into his own, often appearing in many consecutive issues, invariably with one of his stories about Berry Pleydell and his family. Yates's good-natured, humorous, upper-middle class and above all thoroughly British characters typified all that *The Windsor* stood for and established a new reputation for it in the twenty years after the War. Other writers were soon contributing in a similar mode. Hugh Walpole, E. F. Benson, A. M. Burrage, Hugh de Sélincourt, Hylton Cleaver, Richmal Crompton, Horace Annesley Vachell and E. M. Delafield, all produced stories reflecting the formulaic chocolate-box village life in Britain in the twenties and thirties. It did not matter whether this reflected reality or not, it was the world that *The Windsor* wanted to project. It was the same in its articles. F.A.M. Webster produced a long-running series on "Our Great Public Schools" (from Nov 1929), a theme that had worked well for *The Ludgate* in the 1890s and worked again for the middle-class social climbers of the thirties.

Although Arthur Hutchinson died in August 1927 there was a seamless transition to his successor Harry Golding, who was of a similar age. Series stories proliferated in *The Windsor* at this time. Apart from Yates's work, and Barry Pain's stories about Mr Dumphry, that imitated Yates, *The Windsor* succeeded in acquiring H. C. Bailey's detective series featuring Reggie Fortune from *The London*, publishing them almost annually from 1928 onwards. Vachell provided one of the staple requirements of a good fiction magazine, the Club story, with "At the Sign of the Grid" (from Jul 1930). E. Temple Thurston's stories about John Boddy, subtitled "Leaves from a Constable's Notebook" began in June 1930. Kobold Knight contributed "Stories of the Secret Service" (from Oct 1930), in the same month that Laurence Meynell's series about Stanley Tredegar, Gentleman of Leisure, also began. There was also a rare return of Russell Thorndike's Dr Syn in "The Scarecrow Rider" (Aug 1933).

When not presenting humorous, criminous or light romance stories set in a near idyllic British countryside, *The Windsor* looked outwards towards the Empire. Garnett Radcliffe and Ganpat set their stories in the Indian Raj. Ralph Durand preferred darkest Africa, whilst Ralph Stock, H. de Vere Stacpoole and Evelyn Waugh had the whole world at their feet. Waugh's story, "Incident in Azania" (Dec 1933), was a spin-off from the novel *Black Mischief* (1932), and typified British colonialism.

Coloured pictures returned to *The Windsor* during 1933 and soon spread throughout the magazine. In some issues almost every story was illustrated all or partly in either full colour or two-tone. It may have been this passion for colour that made Caswell Garth, husband of actress Gretchen Franklin, write the unusual story "Black!" (May 1934) in which all colour drains out of the world into a uniform greyness. *The Windsor* had always had high production techniques and the use of colour now made it one of the most attractive magazines on the stalls. Although it never increased in size to match the glossy large format slicks like *Nash's* or *Harper's Bazaar*, it was a slick in every other form, and in some ways superior.

Although *The Windsor* always remained a family magazine, it consciously moved towards a stronger female readership in the thirties. A new column was introduced, "Woman's World" (Feb 1934), run by Judith Lynn Mabey, and there was an increase in romantic stories and light society tales with authors Berta Ruck, Eleanor Farjeon and Ethel Lina White. To some extent Vachell's stories about wily antiques dealer, Joe Quinney, fall into this category. There were also historical costume dramas by Jeffery Farnol, humorous tales by Barry Perowne, George Robey and Lord Dunsany and animal stories by C. T. Stoneham and Henry Williamson. Baroness Orczy contributed a series of articles on "Royal Romances" (from Oct 1934) and the covers, now mostly by John F. Campbell and Conrad Leigh, emphasised the grandeur and pageantry of British tradition.

The Windsor continued to attract new and established talent throughout the thirties. Naomi Mitchison, Winston Graham, Sax Rohmer, Oliver Onions, P. C. Wren and Thomas Burke all appeared in the last few years. The last new series was James Norman Hall's reminiscences of the old sea-dog Dr Dogbody during the Napoleonic era, starting with "Doctor Dogbody's Leg" (Dec 1938). The penultimate issue saw an article by British journalist and broadcaster Alistair Cooke, "A Briton's Surprises in America".

Had not the War intervened *The Windsor* might have continued for years. Its production costs must have been high and its circulation was almost certainly falling, along with most remaining fiction magazines, so its days were probably numbered, but it gave no impression of that. Nevertheless the fact that it was cut the moment War was declared, and did not wait for paper rationing, suggests that Ward, Lock felt it was opportune. It was the end of an era. *The Windsor* had been the benchmark for quality in fiction and magazine production for over forty years and it may be a cliché, but in *The Windsor*'s case it is true, its like was never seen again.

Frequency: Monthly.
Publisher: Ward, Lock & Co. (as Ward, Lock and Bowden until 1897).
Editors: Stanhope W. Sprigg, Jan-Dec 1895; David Williamson, Jan 1896-May 1898; Arthur Hutchinson, Jun 1898-Aug 1927; Harry Golding, Sep 1927-Sept 1939.
Format/Size: Standard; page count 116/120, dropped to 112, May 1917; 96/100, Nov 1917; returning to 112, Jul 1921; 120, Sep 1924.
Price: 6d, rose to 7d, Feb 1917; 8d, Sep 1917; 9d, Feb 1918, 1/-, Jun 1918.
References: Edward Liveing, *Adventure in Publishing. The House of Ward Lock, 1854-1954* (Ward Lock, 1954). Fiction until 1910 is indexed in *Indexes to Fiction in the Windsor Magazine 1894-1910*, compiled by Catharine Vaughan-Pow (University of Queensland, 2003).
Holdings.
Complete run, UK/Eire. British Library (*Shelfmark*: PP.6004.glw). • Bodleian (*Call Number*: Per. 2705 d.54). • Cambridge University Library (*Classmark*: L996.c.37). • Trinity College, Dublin (*Call Mark*: 37.p.1-170 up to 1930; E.Attic.D.5, 1930-39).
Substantial run, US: New York Public Library has full run lacking only issue Sep 1916.
Collecting points: The publisher's pictorial bound indexed volumes, in green cloth with Windsor Castle stamped in brown, are common up to 1914 but less common thereafter. Single issues surface frequently, especially from the 1930s. 1920s issues and volumes are least common. Bound volumes usually exclude the special Christmas supplements.

***

WINGS

10 issues. Volume 1, Number 1, Summer 1934 to Volume 2, Number 10, January 1936.

Wings was Britain's first aviation fiction magazine. It was issued by the publisher of Captain W. E. Johns's books and may have taken its title from Johns's own early novel, *Wings* (1931). Johns featured heavily in the magazine's first four issues with both stories and articles, as did Wilfrid Tremellen, Arch Whitehouse, J. Railton Holden and George Fielding Eliot. Johns also contributed a feature on the pioneers of flight, "The Dawn of Aviation" (Spring 1935). Much of the second issue was taken up by the German air ace, Haupt Heydemarck's account of his war experiences in the Balkans, "War Flying in Macedonia".

After a cautious start, when the editor admitted he did not believe he could acquire sufficient quality stories, and did not want to fill it with "wild American material", the magazine switched to a monthly schedule. It also changed from a thick pulp, to a slim large flat slick with plenty of photographs and illustrations. It now became an air enthusiast's dream as it ran a well documented "History of British Aviation, 1908-1914" by R. Dallas Brett and included a model aircraft section. It ran full colour covers by Stanley Bradshaw and included a free colour print with each issue. These later issues continued to run stories by Tremellen and Whitehouse, but Johns no longer appeared. George Rochester continued his series about the new-style aircraft, "The Flying Beetle" (Oct 1935) from *Boy's Own Paper*. The pseudonymous "Vigilant" looked ahead to a possible future war in "The Dress Rehearsal" (Oct 1935). M. E. Kahnert's serial, "Jagdstaffel 356" (Sept-Oct 1935) was a thinly disguised story of events in the First World War.

The magazine was an historical experiment – Britain's first specialist fiction slick magazine – but Daniels was unable to raise the advertising revenue to sustain it. He was reluctantly forced to cease publication with the January 1936 issue and though he promised to produce occasional future issues, none are known to have appeared.

Frequency: Quarterly to Spring 1935, then monthly from Aug 1935.
Publisher: John Hamilton.
Editor: Charles H. Daniels.
Format/Size: Standard pulp, 128 pages, to Spring 1935, then large flat slick, 64 pages.
Price: 1/-.
Holdings: *Substantial run, UK*. British Library has Winter and Spring 1935 only (*Shelfmark*: PP.6004.tal). • Bodleian has all except for Nov 1935 (*Call Number*: Per. 25305.d.2).
Collecting points: The first four issues in the publisher's plain red binding may still be found but the slick issues are increasingly uncommon.

* * *

WOMAN AT HOME

447 issues. Two series with title changes. Volume 1, Number 1, October 1893 to Volume 27, Number 190, July 1909. New series, Volume 1, Number 1, August 1909 to Volume 43, Number 257, January 1931. Retitled THE HOME MAGAZINE from June 1918; briefly retitled THE LADIES' HOME MAGAZINE from June to October 1922. The magazine absorbed *The Girl's Realm*, which was incorporated briefly into the title from December 1915 and *The Ladies' Field*, which was also incorporated into the title from August 1928. Merged with *Homes & Gardens*.

In her introduction to the first issue Annie Swan states that *Woman at Home* was the first popular fiction magazine to be aimed primarily at "the great mass of middle-class women".[1] That was not strictly true. There had been similar magazines where the woman (particularly mother) of the household had been the prime target, such as *Good Words*. Like that magazine, *Woman at Home* placed an emphasis on strong Christian values. Its founder, W. Robertson Nicoll, was a theologian and former church minister, but his views were not imposed as earnestly as in other "home" magazines. *Woman at Home* had a broader, more free-thinking attitude. It promoted itself as a magazine "for homely cultured women." It had been launched as "a female *Strand*",[2] an apt description, though one that Annie Swan could scarcely admit in her first editorial. She was correct in that there had been no magazine in Britain that ran a high quota of popular fiction aimed at the middle-class woman. There were many penny weeklies intended for the working-class woman and there would soon be several aimed at High Society, following the appearance of *The Lady's Realm* in 1896. There were also many magazines where the emphasis was on domestic and maternal advice, lead by *Housewife* in 1886. *Woman at Home* was the first to fill that niche for entertaining stories and articles.

---

[1] *Woman at Home*, Volume 1, October 1893, p. 62.
[2] Jane Stoddart, *My Harvest of Years* (Hodder & Stoughton, 1938), p. 76.

Nicoll built the magazine around the popularity of his fellow Scot Annie Swan. She had been writing regional fiction since 1878 and established her reputation with *Aldersyde* (1883) before turning to producing a steady diet of romantic fiction. Her name had sufficient status that Nicoll billed *Woman at Home* as "Annie S. Swan's Magazine" on the front of every issue and the magazine was an instant success. Swan recalls the magazine's origins:

> One day he [Nicoll] came to me with rather a startling proposition. He thought there was room for a new woman's magazine, and he wanted me to be associated with it – not as Editor, where I should have been a dismal failure (owing to the tendency to allow my heart to govern my head) but as chief contributor, and to have my name printed on the cover.[3]

The real editor at the outset was Nicoll's close associate, another fellow Scot, Jane T. Stoddart. She had assisted Nicoll in developing and launching *The British Weekly*, his flagship paper first issued in 1886, and Swan held her in high regard:

> She was far and away the most accomplished woman journalist I have ever met – widely read, mistress of several languages, author of many thoughtful and wise books.[4]

It was Stoddart who gave *Woman at Home* its high literary content, whilst Swan lent it a more homely element. About a quarter of each issue was given over to a "home" department which included, amongst the usual fare, a vigorous and innovative column on children and women's employment, encouraging women to work and have a degree of independence. Despite its title, *Woman at Home* supported the "new woman" without overtly encouraging the suffragette movement. The religious element of the magazine was catered for in "Sunday Readings".

Annie Swan contributed a monthly column, "Over the Teacups". Primarily an advice column, she responded to the many hundreds of letters received each month. She recalled:

> The effect on me at first was disastrous. I could not sleep at night, convinced by these poignant effusions that the whole of creation was groaning and travailing in anguish. It was quite a long time before I got inured to my task, which taught me more about the seamy side of life than I had imagined existed before.[5]

The remainder of the magazine was evenly split between fiction and articles. There were almost always articles on royalty or the nobility, and a regular society column, but many articles had a musical or literary interest. These included "How I Brought Liszt to London" (Nov 1893), "Among the Fjords with Edvard Greig" (Jan 1894) and "The Most Popular Singer of the Day" (Sept 1902) about Clara Butt. In an exact copy of *The Strand*, the magazine ran an occasional "Illustrated Interview", with subjects including Adelina Patti (Oct 1893), Paolo Tosti (Mar 1894) and Paderewski (May 1894). Literary articles and interviews abounded, including Robert Louis Stevenson (Feb 1894[6]), John Oliver Hobbes (Nov 1894), J. M. Barrie (Apr 1895), Mary E. Wilkins (Jan 1897), Mrs Gaskell (Jun 1897), Sir Walter Besant (Sept 1897) and Henrik Ibsen (Mar 1899) in the first few years. Annie Swan herself was the subject of an interview (May 1895) and a look at her new Hampstead home (Apr 1897). The larger

---

[3] Annie S. Swan, *My Life* (Ivor Nicholson & Watson, 1934) p. 80.
[4] Swan, *op. cit.*, p. 95.
[5] Swan, *op. cit.*, p. 81.
[6] This was credited as being by "One Who Knows Him", and was probably his wife, Fanny, who had already featured in the magazine with her own reminiscences, "A Backwoods Childhood" (Jan 1894).

Christmas issues gave room for a "gallery" of contributors and lady novelists. The Christmas 1897 issue, for example, had profiles and portraits of over twenty authors including Mary Braddon, Frances Hodgson Burnett, Lucy Clifford, Marie Corelli, Lucas Malet, Florence Marryat, L. T. Meade, Mary Molesworth, Ouida and Eliza Lynn Linton. Mrs Linton also contributed a series of articles (from Sep 1895) that amounted to a literary autobiography, recalling her meetings with George Eliot, Dickens, Thackeray, G. H. Lewes and others.

There were few articles on political or military matters, though occasionally the wife of a politician or military man would be interviewed or there homes illustrated. There were, though, plenty of opportunities for contributors to air their views in a number of symposia – another imitation of *The Strand* – looking at such issues as "Should Married Women Engage in Public Work?" (May 1895) or "Are Women Mean in Money Matters?" (Jun 1898).

Compared to the non-fiction features, the fiction was adequate with only occasional moments of inspiration. Annie Swan contributed to every issue, sometimes with two or three stories, including those under the alias David Lyall. She began with the story series "Elizabeth Glen, M.B." (from Oct 1893), about the experiences of a lady doctor (Swan's husband was a doctor and helped her with her advice columns), producing a sequel, "Mrs Keith Hamilton, M.B." (from Oct 1895), after Glen's marriage. Other series included "Memories of Margaret Grainger, Schoolmistress" (began Oct 1894) and "Miss Ferrar's Paying Guests" (from Oct 1897). All of these were framing devices to explore the lives and problems of families. Swan also contributed serials and children's stories, so it is not surprising that she looked back on this period as "the most productive years of my life."[7]

Few stories were outright romances. Most considered problems of daily life, but usually with a romantic element. Many were labelled "idylls", such as S. Baring-Gould's idylls of Dartmoor, starting with "Daniel Jacobs" (Jan 1894), or S. R. Crockett's idyll of love, "Across the March Dyke" (Jun 1894). Like *The Strand*, *Woman at Home* encouraged series. David Christie Murray contributed a private detective series, "The Investigations of John Pym" (from Jun 1894) which, for some reason, the magazine ran without credit. The main contributor was L. T. Meade starting with "Stories from the Diary of a Court Dressmaker" (from Jan 1895). She also added to her *Strand* success, "Stories from the Diary of a Doctor" with "The Mystery of Susanne Tankerville" (Dec 1901).

Most of the magazine's regular contributors – Katharine Lee, Ellen Thorneycroft Fowler, Sarah Grand, Flora Annie Steel and Q's sisters, Lilian and Mabel Quiller-Couch – penned stories of light romance and domestic life. Apart from Arthur Quiller-Couch's own stories, the magazine ran little historical fiction and kept supernatural fiction for the Christmas issues. Two of Nicolls's discoveries were contributors. J. M. Barrie appeared just the once with "A London Love Story" (Dec 1894) but "Ian Maclaren" (the Reverend John Watson) was a regular. His contributions included the popular serial "Kate Carnegie" (Jan-Dec 1896), regarded by many as his best work and which yielded several short-story sequels.

H. G. Wells was a one-off contributor with the obscure story, "A Perfect Gentleman on Wheels" (May 1897), a spin-off from his novel *The Wheels of Chance* (1896). A more surprising contributor was Guy Boothby with "Dr Nikola's Experiment" (Oct 1898-Apr 1899), the third in the series which had been the success of *The Windsor Magazine*. This novel, of a

---

[7] A weekly companion *Annie S. Swan's Penny Stories* was launched on 15 July 1896 to which she also regularly contributed.

mysterious mastermind and his efforts to discover rejuvenation suggests that *Woman at Home* was attracting male readers, a point that Annie Swan noted in "Over the Teacups" regarding the number of letters for advice received from men. Other notable male contributors included Barry Pain, W. Pett Ridge, F. Frankfort Moore, William Le Queux, Max Pemberton and A.E.W. Mason, whilst notable female authors were Gertrude Atherton, May Sinclair, Mrs Alfred Sidgwick, Edith Nesbit, Arabella Kenealy, Mrs C. N. Williamson and Marie A. Belloc.

With the end of the Victorian era there was a further relaxing of limits in the magazine and it began to run more sensational fiction, such as Max Pemberton's serial "Doctor Xavier" (Oct 1902-Sept 1903), oriental fiction, such as Carlton Dawe's "The Beggar Woman of Shansi" (Jun 1903) and stories of intrigue by E. Phillips Oppenheim and William Le Queux. Two of Somerset Maugham's early and otherwise forgotten stories appeared at this time, "The Course of True Love" (Aug 1904) and the macabre "Told in the Inn at Algeciras" (Feb 1905). Phyllis Bottome also contributed some early work. However, the summer of fiction was all too brief and rapidly faded towards the end of the Edwardian era. The occasional literary article still appeared, such as those on Baroness Orczy (Jun 1908) and Charles Kingsley (Jul 1908) but the magazine was becoming increasingly filled with domestic non-fiction.

A big change came in the summer of 1909. Hodder & Stoughton decided they could no longer issue the magazine alone and established a joint company with George Newnes. The latter had the controlling interest and became the publisher of record, but it had a separate board of directors, under the guiding hand of Newnes's managing director, Sir George Riddell. At this point Jane Stoddart stood down as editor and in her place came Alice Mary Head. Head had previously worked as an assistant at *Country Life* and had a somewhat troubled period at *The Academy* before becoming Riddell's personal assistant. Under her editorship the magazine shifted towards being a women's domestic magazine. It was almost a magazine of two halves. The main magazine ran to 96 pages whilst the "home" supplement now expanded to over 50 pages. Annie Swan stepped down from contributing the advice column. The main magazine also ran mostly non-fiction on such subjects as poultry keeping, arts and crafts, needlework, childhood illnesses, wood-carving and gardening.

Although fiction remained, it usually consisted of a serial and two or three stories, one of which was always by Annie Swan. Major names continued to appear – Lucas Malet, Ethel L. White, Ward Muir, Mrs Baillie Reynolds, Bertram Atkey, Hugh Walpole, Mary Wilkins-Freeman. The strength was in the serials, which included "Mrs Ames" by E. F. Benson (Jan-Dec 1912), "Unto Caesar" by Baroness Orczy (Mar 1913-Feb 1914) and "Laddie" by Gene Stratton Porter (Mar-Oct 1914).

The War inevitably influenced what little fiction remained – Berta Ruck set that ball rolling with "The War Baby" (Jan 1915) – but most women were concerned about supporting the War effort, considered by May Sinclair in "Women's Sacrifices for the War" (Feb 1915). There were still items of interest: a feature on "The Art of Arthur Rackham" (Jan 1915), Rebecca West writing on her "Apprenticeship to Literature" and a personal account by Will Owen, "With the YMCA at the Front" (Oct 1917). From December 1915 the magazine had absorbed *The Girl's Realm* and a separate section for young women was introduced into the magazine.

As the War progressed Alice Head noted that, regarding her magazine, "periodical journalism of that type became a matter of no importance. Lord Riddell was completely occupied with public work and I seldom saw him, the staff was depleted, air-raids shattered our nerves and the lack of food sapped our vitality."⁸ At the end of 1917 Head was presented with an opportunity as assistant editor at *Nash's* and, with her departure, further changes were made. Head's work at *Woman at Home* would stand her in good stead for the development of the British edition of *Good Housekeeping* in 1922, and had laid the groundwork for the modern women's-interest magazine. That same thinking was now followed at Newnes. During the spring of 1918 the magazine's title was phased over to become *The Home Magazine* from June.

The Home Magazine took a while to settle down. It changed its size, format and name twice before November 1922 when it became permanently *The Home Magazine* in the large flat, slick format under the editorship of Beatrice Goodwin. During this interim period it launched a fictional character who would become immortal: schoolboy William Brown. The author, Richmal Crompton, had first appeared in *The Home Magazine* with her second story sale, "The First Arrow" (Aug 1918), a simple love story under her full name, R. C. Lamburn. "One Crowded Hour" (Oct 1918) featured a prototype of the William character and it was the third story, "Rice-Mould" (Feb 1919) that introduced the immortal eleven-year-old. The second story in the series, "The Outlaws" (Mar 1919), was the first to be illustrated by Thomas Henry, the start of a 42-year partnership. The William stories appeared on an almost monthly basis until October 1922, forty-one in total, before they transferred to *The Happy Mag*.

That shift saw the change in *The Home Magazine* to an up-market slick, seeking to rival the newly successful *Good Housekeeping*. It ran the full range of fashion, health, beauty and domestic features and sported beautiful covers by Lucie Attwell, showing an appeal as much to the mother as the housewife. There was much fiction of interest. E. F. Benson resurrected his first great society character, Dodo, in "The Brick" (Mar 1923). Michael Arlen contributed several of his suave stories of relationships such as "The Vermilion Orchid" (Sept 1923) and F. Scott Fitzgerald appeared with a somewhat sexist story (for a woman's magazine), "Gretchen's Forty Winks" (Jun 1925).⁹ There were serials by May Sinclair and W. B. Maxwell and stories by Marjorie Bowen, Warwick Deeping and G. B. Lancaster, but at its heart *The Home Magazine* was a women's magazine. Much of the fiction was light, frothy romances from Ethel M. Dell, Ruby M. Ayres, Fanny Heaslip Lea and G. B. Stern, all overshadowed by heavily illustrated features and articles.

By the late 1920s, *The Home Magazine* was no longer a fiction magazine at heart and as each issue passed it moved further away from fiction, losing it all together in its final months. It merged with *Homes and Gardens* in February 1931.

Frequency: Monthly.
Publisher: Hodder & Stoughton Oct 1893-Jul 1909; George Newnes Aug 1909-Feb 1931.
Editors: Jane T. Stoddart, Oct 1893-Jun 1909; Alice M. Head, Jul 1909-May 1918; Miss M. Cruickshank, Jun 1918-1921; Beatrice Goodwin, 1921-29; Elsie H. Shand, 1930-31.

---

⁸ Alice M. Head, *It Could Never Have Happened* (London: Heineman, 1939), p. 52.
⁹ Originally published in the *Saturday Evening Post*, 15 March 1924.

Format/Size: Standard to Feb 1920, and also Sept 1920-May 1922. Page count 76/80, rose to 92/96, Oct 1898; dropped to 88, Feb 1918; 76, Jun 1918; back to 96, Feb 1919. Became large flat slick, 72/76 pages, Mar-Aug 1920, and again from Jun 1922 onwards. Page count rose to 88, Sept 1920.
Price: 6d, dropped to 4d, Oct 1905, rose to 4½d, Aug 1909; 6d, Jan 1912; 7d, Feb 1917; 8d, Oct 1917; 9d, Jun 1918; 10d, Feb 1920; 1/-, Mar 1920.
Holdings:
Complete run, UK. Bodleian (*Call Number*: Per. 2705 d.45).
Substantial run, UK. British Library has issues Oct 1893-Mar 1905, Apr-Sept 1908; New series, Aug 1910-Jul 1915, Jul-Dec 1917 (*Shelfmark*: PP.6004.od). It has no issues of *The Home Magazine*. • Cambridge University Library has volumes 1-25, Oct 1893-Sept 1908 (*Classmark*: L900.c.96).
Collecting points: Early bound volumes remain fairly common but volumes after 1910 are rare. Volumes or single issue of *The Home Magazine* are scarce and avidly collected by "William" fans.

***

WORLD STORIES
86 issues. Number 1, April 1928 to Number 86, May 1935.

World Stories consisted entirely of reprints from American pulp magazines, initially from the Clayton Magazine empire. At the outset the contents were predominantly westerns, all of which were also reprinted from the Clayton pulps, mostly *Ace High Magazine*. It was an image reflected on the covers, some of which were by the much admired artist Nick Eggenhofer. A small proportion of the magazine consisted of adventures in the Far North, Africa or the Orient, and there were also occasional war stories and aerial adventures so that it mimicked *Frontier Stories* (later *Empire Frontier*) issued by Atlas's rival, World's Work. After a year a greater number of crime stories appeared, almost entirely from *Clues*, which introduced stories by Erle Stanley Gardner, Johnston McCulley and Lemuel de Bra. During 1930-1932, when Clayton also published *Strange Tales* and *Astounding Stories*, the magazine reprinted some science fiction and weird stories, but the emphasis remained on westerns. Amongst these, authors of note include Hapsburg Liebe and S. Omar Barker. Other writers include L. Patrick Greene, F. van Wyck Mason, Theodore Roscoe, Hugh B. Cave, Sewell Peaslee Wright and, in the magazine's final days, L. Ron Hubbard. The magazine continued beyond the collapse of Clayton's business in 1933 but folded soon after.

Frequency: Monthly.
Publisher: Atlas Publishing & Distributing Co. Ltd.
Editor: Not known.
Format/Size: Standard pulp, 196 pages to Jan 1932, thereafter 128.
Price: 1/- to Jan 1932; thereafter 6d.
Holdings: *Substantial run, UK.* British Library has a run on microfilm, missing issues Jun 1928, Dec 1930, Feb 1934 (*Shelfmark*: PP.6018.thg; *Microfilm*: Mic.C.395) • Bodleian has issues for Nov 1933–Apr 1934 only (*Call Number*: Per. 25613 d.43).
Collecting points: Extremely rare. Issues hardly ever surface and no complete run is known.

***

THE YELLOW MAGAZINE
130 issues. Number 1, 23 September 1921 to Volume 20, Number 130, 17 September 1926.

The Yellow was a stablemate of *The Red Magazine*. Both on a fortnightly schedule, they appeared on alternate Fridays so that in effect they were one weekly magazine. In the first issue the editor took pains to note that "Although companion magazines it is intended that both *The Red* and *The Yellow* shall be quite apart and distinct from each other." There was, though, little to tell them apart aside from the different coloured covers. They both shared the same stable of authors and artists and both had the same mixture of adventure, light romance and humorous stories. If there is anything to distinguish them it is that during its existence *The Yellow* took the lion's share of adventure and off-trail fiction away from *The Red* leaving the latter with more mundane fiction, but even this balance changed towards the end of *The Yellow*'s life.

The main contributor was Australian-born Coutts Brisbane who also wrote as Reid Whitley. Most of his stories were humorous, such as "The Teeth of Chance" (2 Jun 1922, as Whitley) where an old man loses his false teeth and borrows a set which starts making him say things uncontrollably. Most of his science fiction was satirical, but there were exceptions. "Where It Was Dark" (16 Dec 1921), for instance, is unusual for its day in being set on Mercury. Brisbane wrote several stories warning of the devastation of future wars. In "As It Was in the Beginning" (16 Nov 1923) a war wipes out civilisation and Britain returns to savagery. *The Yellow* published several such warning stories, most significantly "Atoms" by T. C. Wignall and G. D. Knox (20 Oct-29 Dec 1922) about the harnessing of atomic power.

Adventure fiction appeared in most issues with stories set in virtually every remote part of the world. The main contributors were Douglas Newton, Edmund Snell, Ralph Durand and John Austin. Newton's stories include "The Woman Out of the Bush" (24 Feb 1922) about the reappearance of a girl lost in the Amazon jungle for a year, and the unusual "The Hub of All Hate" (30 May 1924), that explained all the evil in the world. Africa was a common setting for many stories, none so atmospheric as Stephen Phillips's romance, "The Pool of Beautiful Ghosts" (16 Nov 1923). Most of these stories betrayed the racial prejudices and stereotypes of the period, but a refreshingly different series was "Toro of the Little People" by Leo Walmsley (from 2 Apr 1926), about the exploits of a clever and resourceful pygmy. "The Golden Gates" by Ralph Durand (20 Oct 1922), is an inspirational story of survival in the Siberian wastes. James Barr wrote several stories set in the Canada of his youth including one of the most violent stories to appear in *The Yellow*, "The Vengeance of the Madman" (3 Nov 1922).

There was a surprising lack of sports stories in *The Yellow*, and hardly any serious historical stories, though there were several stories set in pre-history. Of particular interest was the intermittent series by Charles G. D. Roberts, "Overlords of Earth" (from 18 Apr 1924), which follows the development of a tribe of early humans. It was a sequel to *In the Morning of Time* (Hutchinson, 1919) but was not itself published in book form.

There were a number of naval stories, mostly by Owen Oliver and Stuart Martin, and H. de Vere Stacpoole contributed a couple of unusual serials. "Golden Ballast" (18 Apr-11 Jul 1924) concerns a man who inherits sufficient money to buy a boat which he learns, too late, has a sinister reputation. "City Under the Sea" (7 Aug-27 Nov 1925) is set in Greece and involves an ancient city preserved off the coast of an island.

Humour pervaded all issues of *The Yellow*, and was the primary image projected by the bright covers, mostly by Hawley Morgan. The main contributors were Coutts Brisbane, A. E. Ashford and F. Morton Howard. Ashford contributed an Atkey-like series, "The Ramblings of Mr Niggs" (18 Apr-11 Jul 1924) about a wayfarer and optimist who always believes he will land on his feet. J. Russell Warren contributed "The Interventions of Professor Telepath" (3 Nov-12 Jan 1922) about a stage act where the Professor has invented a device to read thoughts which leads to all manner of predicaments. A. M. Burrage provided two series of which "The Knightly Adventures of Sir Archibald" (24 Feb-5 May 1922), set in the Arthurian world, allowed for a rash of satirical farce.

Most of the romances were light, slice-of-life stories. There were no torrid love stories; such, if any, were saved for *The Yellow*'s companion *The Violet*. There were, though, some stronger character-driven stories that considered the tensions of the day. Especially powerful were two similar but unconnected serials by Anthony Carlyle, "The Tavern and the Arrows" (13 Jan-24 Mar 1922) and "The Eden Tree" (25 Aug-20 Oct 1922). Both concern families in financial straits where the daughter is forced into a marriage she does not want. Both explore post-war middle class values and the need for advancement and respectability.

In *The Yellow*'s final year the emphasis shifted more to stories of romance and adventure, and the covers changed to present a stronger image of women's stories. For whatever reason, possibly the departure of John Stock, it was decided to replace *The Yellow* with *All-Story,* a more up-market women's magazine. Most of the stories in *The Yellow* were meant as passing entertainment, and few of the stories are of any lasting significance. But there are enough that were sufficiently different or unusual to make *The Yellow* worthy of further consideration.

Frequency: Fortnightly.
Publisher: Amalgamated Press.
Editor: John Stock.
Format/Size: Small standard pulp, 112 pages.
Price: 7d.
References: George Locke, "Fantasy and Mystery in The Yellow Magazine", *Search & Research*, June 1974, pp. 23-27.
Holdings:
Complete run, UK. Bodleian (*Call Number*: Per. 25612 e.534).
Partial run, UK. British Library has the first seven issues only (*Shelfmark*: PP.6018.tao).
Complete run, Australia. University of Queensland (*Reference*: PR1309.S5 Y46).
Collecting points: Increasingly uncommon with few single issues surfacing.

***

YES OR NO

798 issues. Two series. Number 1, 21 March 1904 to Number 737, 27 April 1918. Revived, Number 1, 28 February 1921 to Number 61, 24 April 1922; 61 issues.

The oddly titled *Yes or No*, which bore the sub-title "The Saturday Magazine", was one of several weekly story papers issued by Harry Shurey out of Hind Court, London. The business had been started by his father Charles and, after a few moderate successes, they had struck lucky with the romantic story papers *The Duchess Novelette* in 1894 (later retitled *Smart Novels*) and *The Empress Novelette* in 1897 (retitled *Dainty Novels*). These, along with *Sketchy Bits* and *Home Bits*, were all similar: thin booklets of 32 or 48 pages printed on cheap paper, running a long lead story plus a serial in many short episodes and perhaps a vignette or two. This was much the same with *Yes or No*. It started in tabloid format, like *Tit-Bits*, its 24 pages filled with a host of short features, competitions, serials and very short stories, none with author credits. The first serial, "The Terror of the Road", was typical of the high action, formulaic material that filled these papers.

After 72 unpreposessing issues it changed, cutting its size in half to a large digest (230mm x 150mm) and increasing its page count to 64. The small font and minimal use of illustrations meant that it could cram up to 40,000 words into each weekly issue, enough for a long serial episode, a long lead story and four or five shorter stories. *Yes or No* differed from most other story papers in that it was aimed at the whole family, rather than the young domestic or shop-girl, and ran a wide range of stories. An editorial announcement clarifies the requirements:

> Authors are invited to submit MSS., payment for which will be made within a week of acceptance. I want strong, dramatic stories of mystery, crime, love and adventure of from three to six thousand words in length; clever humorous stories up to four thousand words, and human interest stories up to five thousand words. Problem, dialect, or sexual stories of those which strain for feminine interest, I have no opening for. Strong plot, clearness of style in writing and sustained interest throughout, essential.[1]

The new editor, Isabel Thorne, was shrewd and observant, fully aware of the interests and demands of her readers. She took over the editorial reins of all of Shurey's weekly publications during 1905/6 and tailored each one for a range of markets. Her success is evident from the sales figures. Average circulation data for 1907[2] shows *Smart Novels* selling 200,331 copies, *Yes or No* 142,726, *Dainty Novels* 117,738 and *Sketchy Bits* 95,498, and they sustained these levels over many years.

Despite these figures very few copies survive. They were disposable weekly fodder, read, perhaps shared round the family, and then discarded. Paper drives and two world wars have also taken their toll to the extent that no complete run is known and the full scale of its contents

---

[1] Taken from the issue for 28 August 1915.
[2] See *The A.P.S. Monthly Circular*, May 1908, pp.5-6.

can no longer be assessed. Sufficient can be drawn from existing copies, however, to appreciate the general nature of the magazine.

Every issue was a good mixture of stories, usually one rousing adventure story, one or two mystery stories, a humorous and/or a "clever" tale, a love story, possibly a sports story or a story of the stage, and a "human interest" story. The serials were usually mystery or adventure stories, allowing for good dramatic pace and a cliff-hanger ending. The magazine had other regular features, including a question-and-answer column (where readers responded to other readers' queries), a letter column, an editorial (rare amongst story-papers and evidence of Thorne's personal interest) and later a humour column. It also published occasional articles. One unusual series was "Ongwe-Honwe" (from 23 May 1908), a Mohawk Indian's views about the Native American Indians and their relationship with the "whites".

The stories were seldom sophisticated, the characters usually stereotyped and the plots imitative, but they were only intended as escapist light relief from the daily toil and they served this purpose admirably. Most of the writers were regular hacks, even if some were from the landed gentry. Sir William Magnay may have been the son of the Lord Mayor of London and a Baronet, but he churned out blood-and-thunder adventure yarns like the best of them, and his wicked tale of sinister goings on in the peerage, "A Corner in Jewels" (from 28 Mar 1908), was typical of much that the magazine published.

But it was not all formulaic hackwork. Thorne had an eye for talent and was good at attracting and developing new writers. She published the first stories by Edwy Searles Brooks ("Mr. Dorian's Missing £2,000", 13 Jul 1907) and Douglas Newton (the series "The Fortunate Adventures of Lord Felix Suerte", 1 Feb 1908-28 Mar 1908) and probably plenty of others if details were available. She published many stories by E. R. Punshon and also took Edgar Wallace under her wing and gave him a new start when his early outlets began to fade. His main work was for *The Weekly Tale-Teller* but he had several pieces in *Yes or No*, including the serial "The Man Who Bought London" (Jul/Aug 1914). Other regulars include C. Randolph Lichfield, Frank Shaw, Arthur Applin, Tom Gallon, Fenton Ash and his son, writing as F. St Mars, Kitty Lofting, A. M. Burrage and George S. Surrey. Surrey wrote many adventure stories, and was the magazine's leading contributor of westerns. Amongst Richard Marsh's contributions was the serial "Helen: the Romance of a Woman's Life" (from 31 Oct 1914).

Yes or No published at least two interesting detective series. During 1914 it ran the exploits of Christopher Quarles, a college professor turned detective, written by Percy Brebner, later collected as *Christopher Quarles: College Professor and Master Detective* (Dutton, 1914) and *The Master Detective* (Dutton, 1916). Of special interest are the stories featuring Garnett Bell by Cecil H. Bullivant. Bell is a complete Sherlock Holmes clone, even down to his Baker Street lodgings. Indeed *Yes or No* promoted him as "the <u>new</u> Sherlock Holmes". These stories appeared intermittently during 1915 and 1916 and were not collected in book form until 1920 in a volume that is now exceedingly rare.

The First World War took its toll on the Shurey publications. *Yes or No* absorbed both *Sketchy Bits* and *Weekly Tale-Teller* and its pagination had halved by May 1917, though it kept its price at one penny. At some stage, possibly as early as 1910, Thorne had delegated the routine editorial work on *Yes or No* to Arthur Sarl, but she remained at the editorial helm and revived the magazine in February 1921. It soon regained its market, selling 120,000 copies in April 1921, and yet the magazine was dropped after little more than a year. It is not known why, as Thorne continued to edit the other Shurey publications until they were sold to William Stevens in 1932. Harry Shurey himself died in 1924.

Yes or No may have been a working-class magazine with formula stories, but its rarity mitigates against a proper analysis of its contents and the chance to assess its full contribution to popular fiction.

Frequency: Weekly.
Publisher: Harry Shurey.
Editors: Charles Shurey, 21 Mar 1904-31 Jul 1905; Isabel Thorne, 5 Aug 1905-24 Apr 1922 (assisted by Arthur J. Sarl, perhaps 1910-18).
Format/Size: Tabloid, 24/28 pages until #72 (31 Jul 1905); thereafter slim, large digest, 64 pages, dropped to 48, by Aug 1916, and 32, May 1917.
Price: 1d.
Holdings: *Partial run, UK.* British Library has an incomplete run of only 64 issues in volumes 1, 2 and 3 for 1904 and 1905 only. They are missing issues 1, 3, 14, 16, 30, 32, 33, 40, 60 and all from 73 on (*Shelfmark*: PP.5998.be).
Collecting points: Extremely rare with no complete run known. Less common than *Weekly Tale-Teller*.

* * *

SECTION TWO

OTHER MAGAZINES

The following briefer entries cover those magazines which, whilst they do not qualify under the criteria for the main section, are nevertheless of merit in the promotion and publication of fiction during the "Age of the Storytellers". The majority were also monthlies, but several weekly publications have been included where fiction was an important part of their profile (marked [W]). In most cases fiction constituted less than half the content of these magazines, but it was still a significant selling point. See also the note at the end regarding British editions.

The Argosy December 1865-September 1901, 418 issues
One of the many magazines to appear following the success of *The Cornhill*. *The Argosy* was intended as an informative but unsensational magazine, but the strait-laced Strahan got cold feet following the reception to the first serial, Charles Reade's tale of bigamy, "Griffith Gaunt". The magazine was taken on by Mrs Henry Wood whose reputation was high following her sensation novel *East Lynne*. *The Argosy* became a major vehicle for her works, with at times half the magazine consisting of her writings, including fourteen novels and the long running "Johnny Ludlow" series of country tales. It also published the works of Helen Prothero Lewis, Jean Ingelow, Sarah Doudney, William Allingham, George MacDonald, and early poems by Edith Nesbit. Mrs Wood conducted *The Argosy* successfully for twenty years but following her death in 1887 her son, Charles (who contributed most of the travel articles) failed to develop the magazine, taking the backward step of raising the price from 6d to 1/- in 1895. Despite a facelift under its final publisher it ran little more of significance, though it did print "Manacled" (Aug 1900), one of Stephen Crane's last stories.
Publishers: Alexander Strahan (1865-67); Charles W. Wood (1867-71); Richard Bentley (1872-97); Macmillan (1897-99); George Allen (1900-1).
Editors: Isa Craig (1865-67); Mrs Henry Wood (1867-86); Charles W. Wood (1887-98); Herbert Morrah (1899-1901).

Atalanta October 1887-September 1898, 132 issues
A standard size, 64-page monthly, *Atalanta* was the successor to *Every Girl's Magazine*, which had been founded by Routledge in 1878 and taken over by Hatchards in 1885. It was intended primarily for mature girls and young ladies. *Atalanta* lacked the overall impact of *Every Girl's* (such as the colour plates by Kate Greenaway) but it was still heavily illustrated and there was a constant drive by its editors to make it the most appealing of all girls' magazines. Clearly

influenced by the *Boy's Own Paper*, it was part of the transition towards the popular illustrated magazine soon to be dominated by *The Strand*. Despite the strong didacticism of the magazine, which even sponsored an Atalanta Scholarship, it ran copious amounts of fiction including many serials, of which the best known is Robert Louis Stevenson's sequel to *Kidnapped*, "David Balfour" (1892-3), in book form as *Catriona*. Other works of interest include the serials "A Tale of Three Lions" (1887) by H. Rider Haggard, "The White Man's Foot" (1888) by Grant Allen, "The Werewolf" (1890-1) by Clemence Housman and "Sir Robert's Fortune" (1893-4) by Mrs. Oliphant, plus stories by F. Anstey, Frances Hodgson Burnett, Edith Nesbit and Mrs Molesworth. In June 1892 the magazine was taken on by Marshall Brothers and from December 1892 incorporated their lady's *Victorian Magazine*. This later formed *Atalanta*'s subtitle, reflecting its image in upholding Victorian values and morals. Later issues are more strait-laced but generally it was more appealing than most other morally improving magazines.
Publishers: Hatchards (1887-90); Trischler & Co. (1890-92); Marshall Brothers (1892-98).
Editors: L. T. Meade (1887-92) with co-editors Alicia A. Leith (1887) and John C, Staples (1888-92); A. B. Symington (1892-96); Edwin Oliver (1896-98).

Badminton Magazine August 1895-January 1923, 330 issues
Primarily a sports magazine, issued in standard illustrated format. Early issues ran two or three stories and the occasional serial, reducing to around one story per issue after 1903. Most focused on the sporting life or outdoor activities. Its best known series was "Some Experiences of an Irish R.M." (1898-9) by Edith Œ. Somerville and Violet Martin (as "Martin Ross"). It published the first "Don Q" story by Kate & Hesketh Prichard (1898) that later developed into a series in *Pearson's Magazine*, and ran a long series "Strange Stories of Sport" (1905-9) by Frank Savile and others. Watson edited the magazine for the rest of his life, and it folded soon after his death. Under its final publisher it was a companion to *Lloyd's Magazine*.
Publishers: Longmans, Green (1895-1900), Heinemann (1900-2); The 1900 Publishing Syndicate (Jan-Jun 1903); Sphere & Tatler (1903-11); Hulton (1911-16); John E. Chandler (Jul-Oct 1916); H. Reiach for Badminton Magazine (1916-21); United Newspapers (1921-23).
Editor: Alfred Edward Thomas Watson.

Belgravia November 1866-June 1899, 392 issues, plus Christmas and Holiday Annuals
Launched by John Maxwell after selling *Temple Bar*, *Belgravia* became a vehicle for both the fiction and editing talents of Maxwell's lover, Mary E. Braddon. At the height of her notoriety, following the success of *Lady Audley's Secret*, Braddon's name was a major sales factor, and *Belgravia* serialised fourteen of her novels plus many short stories. It milked the vogue for the sensation novel, publishing stories by George Manville Fenn, George Augustus Sala, Florence Marryat and Sheridan Le Fanu amongst others. Although one of the better *Cornhill* imitations, sales were not as high as hoped and the magazine was taken over by Chatto and Windus. The quality of writers improved to include Wilkie Collins, Bret Harte, James Payn, Charles Reade and most notably Thomas Hardy ("The Return of the Native", 1877-8). Chatto & Windus also initiated the popular *Belgravia Annual*, which was always a feast of seasonal fare. However sales continued to dwindle, even after it became an all-fiction magazine in 1886. It did not respond to advances amongst other magazines and fared no better under later publishers. Nevertheless *Belgravia* should not be lightly dismissed. Even as a second-tier magazine, with low pay rates, it provided a haven for new and rising authors becoming a fertile training ground

for the popular magazines of the 1890s. It published the early stories by Grant Allen, Algernon Blackwood, E.W. Hornung, Richard Marsh, Alice Perrin, Eden Phillpotts and Braddon's son W.B. Maxwell. It was partial to weird fiction running "The Haunted Hotel" by Wilkie Collins (1878-9) and "The Frozen Pirate" by W. Clark Russell (1887-8) as well as stories by Grant Allen, A. Conan Doyle, James Grant and M. P. Shiel.
Publishers: John Maxwell (1866-76); Chatto & Windus (1876-89); F. V. White (1889-97); Biggs & Co. (Apr-Dec? 1897); May, Wyatt & Co. (Jan?-Oct 1898), A. F. May (1898-99).
Editors: Mary E. Braddon (1866-76); Andrew Chatto (1876-89); thereafter probably Braddon again.

Black & White [W] 6 February 1891-13 January 1912, 1,093 issues; merged with *The Sphere*
A high quality, large format magazine in the style of *The Graphic*. Whilst it was a token newspaper with discussion of current affairs the emphasis was on art and literature. Beautifully illustrated by all the major artists, including Walter Crane, L. Raven-Hill, Linley Sambourne, Sidney Sime, and Maurice Greiffenhagen, it also featured fiction by the popular authors of the day. These included J. M. Barrie, Henry James, Arthur Quiller-Couch and H. G. Wells plus newcomers Robert Barr, Jerome K. Jerome, William Le Queux, A.E.W. Mason, E. Nesbit, Ralph Stock and Bram Stoker. One feature, started in 1892, was a short story told entirely in dialogue, a selection of which was collected by Crawfurd as *Dialogues of the Day* (Chapman & Hall, 1895) with contributions by Anthony Hope, Mrs Crackanthorpe, Ada Leverson and Violet Hunt. In similar vein was its development of the dramatised documentary. The serial "The Great War of 1892" (1892), published anonymously – but by seven authors, including Rear-Admiral Philip Colomb, Captain F. N. Maude and D. Christie Murray – presented an account of a European War in the form of newspaper reports, telegraph despatches and eyewitness accounts, which proved highly influential. The later "The Franco-German War" (1906-7) is similar. Especially valued are the magazine's Christmas issues. An annotated checklist of fiction is in draft and planned for private publication.
Publisher: Black and White.
Editors: Charles N. Williamson (1891-92?); Oswald Crawfurd (1892?-95); James Nicol Dunn (1895-97); W.D. Ross (1897-1900); Arthur Mee (1901-3); J. M. Gibbon (1903-5); Spencer Arnold (1906-12).

The Black Cat February 1898-March 1900, 26 issues
This should not be confused with the American *Black Cat*, published in Boston from Oct 1895-Mar 1922, though there are similarities. Both were slim booklets of around 56/64 pages, and sold for the same small amount. Both sported a docile black cat on their covers – in neither case symbolic of sinister or supernatural fiction – and both aimed to publish original and different short stories. However, unlike its American counterpart, the British *Black Cat* did not establish a reputation for clever and unusual stories, nor did it launch any major careers.
The quality of the fiction was a cut above the usual penny magazine, and included a new mystery story by Fergus Hume ("The Miracle of the Holy Mother", Feb 1898) and an early poem by John Cowper Powys ("To a Black Cat", Jul 1898). Most of the contents, though, were by a small group of individuals common to the penny magazines: Agnes M. Biddle, Mrs Ernest Cresswell and Agnes Neville with various series of modern life, Hiram K. Wells with a war story and J. Colne Dacre [Mary Stuart Boyd] with an overly melodramatic mystery serial, "Dead Man's Drive" (Feb-Apr 1898). Among the more original stories was "The Awakened

Soul" (May 1899) by Bernard Clements-Henry, which began a series about a doctor who uses hypnotism to cure his patients. Otherwise editor George Dusart dominated the magazine, revealing his literary and musical interests in "Notes and Jottings" and "Musical Notes". He also provided a children's page and a column for women. The tone of the magazine shows that it was aimed at the growing number of middle-class woman, unlike most penny magazines of the period, which catered for the working class. The magazine was liberally illustrated with line drawings, most of which appear to be the work of *Punch* artist E. J. Wheeler.

The extent of the advertising matter suggests that the magazine was successful. Dusart was able to publish a double-size Christmas issue (Jan 1899), still costing a penny, which sold out within five days. However, from July 1899 it was taken over by New Century Press, becoming a companion to *Crampton's Magazine*. It is not known whether Dusart continued as editor or whether it came under the aegis of Oswald Crawfurd. Although the format did not change, and the emphasis remained on stories for women, the magazine became slimmer with more reliance on reprints and translations. New Century's staff artist, Jim Swift, became the main illustrator, but his work was basic and less ornate. Over the next few months the flair that Dusart had created, vanished. From January 1900 the title became *The Black Cat Penny Stories* and the content changed to one long melodramatic novelette supported by one or two short stories, like most other penny magazines. In this form the magazine survived only two more issues.
Publishers: London & Brighton: John Davis, to Jun 1899; thereafter New Century Press.
Editor: George C. Dusart to at least Jun 1899.

Blackwood's (Edinburgh) Magazine   April 1817-December 1980, 1,982 issues
One of the most important Victorian magazines, entitled *The Edinburgh Monthly Magazine* for first six issues. It set the standard and format for the first generation of literary reviews. Early authors of note include John Galt, John Gibson Lockhart, James Hogg, Samuel Warren and Edward Bulwer Lytton. George Eliot's first fiction appeared here in 1857. Margaret Oliphant was one of its most prolific contributors from 1852-98.

During the "Age of the Storytellers" *Blackwood's*, or *Maga* as it was affectionately known, was in the hands of two Blackwoods, William and his nephew George William. Both had been born in India and brought an Imperial perspective to the magazine. It has been argued that *Blackwood's* was read by more people across the globe than in Britain itself. Two authors who epitomise that outlook were Joseph Conrad and John Buchan. Conrad's "Heart of Darkness" and "Lord Jim" were both serialised in 1899. Buchan also first appeared in 1899 ("No-Man's-Land"). He contributed many articles on the British in various parts of the globe, though his best known work was "The Thirty-Nine Steps" (1915). In like vein were the works of Hugh Clifford, J. Storer Clouston and Perceval Gibbon. *Blackwood's* published the early novels of Ian Hay whose "The First Hundred Thousand" (1914-16), about a subaltern in Kitchener's army, had a huge impact in Britain and America. In contrast, Henry Newbolt looked back to an idealised medieval Britain in the serials "The New June" (1908-9) and "Aladore" (1914) whilst equally atmospheric were the near mystical stories of life in the Highlands and Isles by Neil Munro including the serials "Doom Castle" (1900-1) and "Children of the Tempest" (1902-3). *Blackwood's* was symbolic of Britain and Empire, but though its circulation rose during both World Wars, its image had become stale by the 1950s and it struggled in a diminishing market offering little but a haven for those yearning for a different age.

An index of contents from 1825-1900 (omitting poetry) is in Volume 1 of *The Wellesley Index to Victorian Periodicals*, whilst post-1900 is in *An Index to Blackwood's Magazine, 1901-1980* by David Finkelstein (Scolar Press, 1995). Finkelstein hosts a website on *Blackwood's* at <http://mcdept.qmuc.ac.uk/Blackwoods/blackwoods.html>
Publisher: William Blackwood & Sons, Edinburgh.
Editors: James Cleghorn & Thomas Pringle (Apr-Sept 1817); William Blackwood (1817-34); Alexander Blackwood (1834-45); John Blackwood (1845-79); William Blackwood (1879-1912); George William Blackwood (1912-42); James Hugh Blackwood (1942-48); George Douglas Blackwood (1948-76); David Fletcher (1976-79); Michael Blackwood (1980).

Boy's Own Paper, The [W] 18 January 1879-February 1967, 2,511 issues
Perhaps best known in its annual bound form, the *Boy's Own Paper* (or *B.O.P*) was a byword to many English-language readers. Originally a weekly paper, when it was under the guiding hand of G. A. Hutchison, it became monthly in 1913 under sundry editors until its demise in 1967, which was extraordinarily late for a Victorian publication. Although the product of an evangelical publishing firm, it aimed to entertain as well as to instruct its boy readers, and lively fiction, both in the form of serialised novels and shorter stories, was an important part of the mix from the outset. Its first major serial was W.H.G. Kingston's "From Powder Monkey to Admiral; or, The Stirring Days of the British Navy" (1879), and such muscular tales, dealing with history, war, seafaring and empire-building, were long a staple from the hands of a host of writers working in Kingston's tradition. However, the author who dominated the first decade or so of the paper was a purveyor of gentler fare. Talbot Baines Reed began as the anonymous author of short tales about "Parkhurst School", and soon graduated to full-length serials which bore his name, including "The Adventures of a Three-Guinea Watch" (1880) and "Tom, Dick and Harry" (1892). They were, in the main, school stories, a long-lived genre which Reed did much to establish. His premature death in 1893 robbed the paper of its most popular and characteristic contributor, but by that time it was sufficiently established to survive the blow.

Serials translated from the French were important to the paper's success, notably the works of Jules Verne, as were the exciting tales of homegrown (frequently Scottish) lesser-knowns such as Gordon Stables, the young Arthur Conan Doyle ("The Mystery of Uncle Jeremy's Household", 1887) and David Ker. As it moved into the twentieth century, *B.O.P.*'s fiction remained much the same, with newer regulars such as Tom Bevan, H. Mortimer Batten, Captain Charles Gilson and Percy F. Westerman. It ran the first ever published piece by Leslie Charteris (Feb 1919). In the 1920s, yarns of exploration, war, sport and adventure still dominated, although tales of boarding-school life remained a constant. Later, one can find such unexpected iitems as "Camping with the Soviet Pioneers" (Apr 1936) by Geoffrey Trease, but on the whole the magazine remained patriotic and imperialist. Perhaps the most famous writer of the later years, during and after World War II, was Captain W. E. Johns, with tales of his air-ace hero Biggles. When the *B.O.P.* staggered to its death in 1967 (it had become a slim digest in 1942) it felt to many like the passing of a great British institution.
Publishers: Religious Tract Society to 1939; Lutterworth Press, 1939-1963; Purnell from 1963.
Editors: James Macauley (1879-97); George Andrew Hutchison (1897-1912); Arthur L. Haydon (1912-24); Geoffrey Pocklington (1924-33); George Northcroft (1933-35); Robert Harding (1935-42); Leonard Halls (1942-46); Jack Cox (1946-67).

OTHER MAGAZINES

Britannia and Eve May 1929-January 1957, 333 issues
This beautiful top quality slick arose from the merger of two lesser weeklies: *Eve*, which was predominantly a women's fashion and general-interest magazine, founded in 1919 by Edward Huskinson, and *Britannia*, "conducted" by Gilbert Frankau, which Heitner (one of the directors of British National Newspapers) had created in a shake-up of the company in September 1928. *Britannia* was a politically orientated magazine aimed more at men than women. From issue five it featured a regular "Britannia Short Story" slot, with work by A. M. Burrage, Marten Cumberland, Elinor Mordaunt and C. J. Cutcliffe Hyne, but it was a lacklustre affair. Heitner merged the two titles, injected considerable money and style, and created one of the most attractive magazines of the 1930s. It was a companion to *The Sketch* and *Illustrated London News*, but ran more fiction than either. Besides the usual home section, fashion and topical articles there were often five or six stories per 120-page issue. Rather then concentrate on women's fiction *per se* (a direction that it took in the post-war years), it ran much romantic and exotic mystery and adventure fiction. Authors included Agatha Christie, Lord Dunsany, James Francis Dwyer, Beatrice Grimshaw, Sax Rohmer, Edgar Wallace and Dennis Wheatley. Artists included Steven Spurrier and Fortunio Matania. Matania wrote and illustrated his series "Old Tales Retold".
Publisher: British National Newspapers. *Editor:* Jesse Heitner.

Butterfly, The May 1893-February 1894, 10 issues; March 1899-February 1900, 12 issues
A literary magazine with the emphasis on art and humour. The first series had a narrow format (228x127mm) with 64 pages. In content it was similar to *The Idler*, but in presentation was more like a shrunken *Fun*. It ran two or three stories per issue, plus poems and wit, the best of the latter being by editor Golsworthy. In more serious tone the first series ran work by Yvan Lavor, W. W. Jacobs and historical stories by John Gray and Clotilde Graves. Most artwork was by Oscar Eckhardt, Edgar Wilson, Maurice Greiffenhagen and Raven-Hill himself. After the first series, Raven-Hill experimented with a weekly, *The Unicorn*, which lasted only three issues (11-25 September 1895) and *The Minster* (see Section 1), before starting a new series of *The Butterfly*, in standard but slimmer format, which saw the magazine at its most fanciful. It ran art by the original team plus Max Beerbohm, Dion Clayton Calthrop and Sidney Sime, plus stories and features by Arthur Morrison, Baron Corvo, Laurence Housman and Barry Pain. In the words of James Thorpe (in 1935) it was "the most artistic periodical we have ever had."
Publishers: Walter Haddon (Mar-Oct 1893); Morland, Judd (Nov 1893-Feb 1894); Grant Richards (Mar-Sep 1899); New Century Press (Oct 1899-Feb 1900).
Editors: L. Raven-Hill and Arnold Golsworthy.

Captain, The April 1899-March 1924, 300 issues
Sometimes miscalled a "boys' weekly", *The Captain* was never that; rather, it was a juvenile males' monthly magazine, perhaps best regarded as a little brother of the same publisher's *The Strand*. In addition to stories, each issue contained a quantity of non-fiction sport, wildlife, stamp-collecting, chess, etc., plus reviews of boys' books, illustrated with covers. There was a regular miscellaneous editorial column, usually spread over five or six pages at the rear of each issue and, unfortunately, headed "The Old Fag"; here, editor Warren Bell and his successors ruminated on various topics of interest to Edwardian boys. Like the genuine boys' papers such

as *Boy's Own Paper* and *Chums*, it was noted for its school stories and adventure yarns, many of which were by the same authors as contributed to those flimsier organs – including Harold Avery, H. Mortimer Batten, Richard Bird, Captain Frank H. Shaw, Captain Charles Gilson, Gunby Hadath and T.C. Bridges. One distinguished *Captain* regular who rarely contributed to the rival publications (although he was later to loom large in *The Strand*) was the young P.G. Wodehouse. His first serial was "The Gold Bat" (1903), and he contributed a further seven, most, like the first, public-school yarns, including "Jackson Junior" (1907) and "The Lost Lambs" (1908) – better known in book form as *Mike at Wrekin* and *Mike and Psmith*. Another famous serial was John Buchan's rousing African tale "The Black General" (1910) – in book form as *Prester John*.
Publisher: George Newnes.
Editors: R. S. Warren Bell (1899-1910); Reeves Shaw (1910-22); Augustus Baker (1922-24).

Chambers's (Edinburgh) Journal [W] 4 February 1832-December 1956, 4,143 issues
The second longest-running popular magazine after *Blackwood's*. At the outset it pitched itself to a readership below the literary acumen of *Blackwood's*, but in later years the two magazines came closer together. It was founded by the brothers William and Robert Chambers who had started a publishing business in 1823. Whilst they shared the desire to stimulate and educate the developing middle class, they had differing views of how to achieve it, William believing the magazine must eschew anything sensational whilst Robert believed that such would attract readers. It was Robert, who had the more direct involvement with the magazine, whose approach tended to prevail, but it was this tension that made *Chambers's* accessible without becoming either too highbrow or commonplace. It was initially priced at a penny-halfpenny. The circulation rose to around 80,000 in its first few years. It appeared as a weekly, a tradition that remained even after it issued a four-weekly compilation in 1854 (retitled *Chambers's Journal of Popular Literature, Science and Arts*). It finally converted to a monthly in 1897, as *Chambers's Journal*, but up to the last issue it retained an individual weekly issue number.

For the first twenty years the magazine consisted chiefly of essays, most by William and Robert or their sub-editors Thomas Smibert and Leitch Ritchie, but it also published George Meredith's first work, the poem "Chillianwallah" (Jul 1849). It was not until the third series started in 1854 that fiction gained a higher profile. Serials became the focal point with work by Mayne Reid, James Payn and Ritchie himself. Payn's melodramatic "Lost Sir Massingberd" (1864), which launched the fourth series, was reputed to have increased circulation by 20,000, even though William Chambers believed it too sensational. It was during Payn's editorship that Thomas Hardy made his first professional appearance, with an article "How I Built Myself a House" (18 Mar 1865). During the editorship of Robert Chambers, Jr. *Chambers's* significance as a market for fiction increased. It published the first stories by Stanley Weyman ("My Scouts", 25 Nov 1876) and Arthur Conan Doyle ("The Mystery of the Sasassa Valley", 6 Sept 1879), David Christie Murray's first novel, "A Life's Atonement" (1880), and early work by Max Pemberton, E.W. Hornung, William Le Queux and W. W. Jacobs.

Chambers's continued to foster new talent and present a representative cross-section of the work of established writers. The late Victorian and Edwardian periods saw stories and serials by Mrs Oliphant, W. Clark Russell, Grant Allen, Walter Besant, Anthony Hope, John Buchan and Guy Boothby. It published many works by authors either born in or who spent much time in the colonies so that *Chambers's*, like *Blackwood's*, projected a strong feeling of Empire. Its refusal to publish illustrations caused *Chambers's* to suffer in comparison to the illustrated monthlies of the 1890s, but its steadfastness and integrity always guaranteed it a bedrock of readers. It continued to encourage new talent, amongst them Sax Rohmer ("The Leopard Couch", 30 January 1904) and most surprisingly Raymond Chandler, his first published work being the poem "The Unknown Love" (19 December 1908). It also launched the career of Maurice Walsh with his novel "The Key Above the Door" (1925) and published the early short fiction of Pierre Audemars. Throughout its life, even into the 1950s, *Chambers's* maintained its original purpose, providing a miscellany of informative articles and items interspersed with entertaining, if no longer morally improving, stories. It outlasted most of its rivals but eventually succumbed to the general demise of the popular fiction magazines.

An affectionate memoir of its first century is "A Hundred Years Old: *Chambers's Journal*" by W. Forbes Gray in the December 1932 issue. *Indexes to Fiction* by Sue Thomas (University of Queensland, 1989) covers the years 1854-1910.

Publisher: W. & R. Chambers, Edinburgh.

Editors: William (1832-37) with Robert Chambers (1833-58) assisted by Thomas Smibert (1837-42), William H. Willis (1842-44) and Leitch Ritchie (1845-58); Leitch Ritchie alone (1858-62); James Payn (1858-73); Robert Chambers, Jr. (1873-88), Charles E. S. Chambers (1888-1935); J. Liddell Geddie (1935-47); John M. Dickie (1947-56).

Chums [W]   12 September 1892-July 1934, 2,101 issues. Continued as *Annual*, 1935-1941

Launched by Cassell into an already overcrowded field, *Chums* became the chief rival to the *Boy's Own Paper*. Success was not instantaneous and it has been claimed that it was not until editor Max Pemberton ran an adventure serial of his own, "The Iron Pirate" (1892-1893), followed by a reprint of Robert Louis Stevenson's decade-old "Treasure Island" (1894), that the paper really took off. The mix was similar to that of the *B.O.P.*, although perhaps slightly less preachy, with a strong emphasis on historical tales, imperial derring-do, and public-school stories. Aside from Pemberton in its first decade, a handful of very competent authors dominated the paper throughout its 42-year run: D. H. Parry, who provided the first serial "For Glory and Renown"(1892) and was still writing for it as late as 1930; S. Walkey, whose first serial was "In Search of Sheba's Treasure" (1895-6) and who likewise was still producing the goods in the paper's last days; and sea-story writer Captain Frank H. Shaw, whose exciting serials such as "The Peril of the Motherland: The Great War With Russia" (1908) tended towards future-war scenarios and scientific romance. Other regulars included John Bloundelle-Burton, Andrew Soutar, Alfred Judd, Maxwell Scott, L. J. Beeston, Frank Howel Evans and T. C. Bridges. Postwar regulars included many of the above, plus Captain Oswald Dallas ("The Lake of the Purple Flames", 1919), John Hunter (mainly sports stories), Eric W. Townsend, Captain F.A.M. Webster, Hylton Cleaver (mainly school stories) and Eric Wood (i.e. F. Knowles Campling). The last-named's serial "The Lost Planet" (1921) and its sequel "The Drowned Planet" (1921) were indicative of a rise in the quantity of science fiction published by *Chums* in the 1920s, although it was never to dominate the paper. Serials like Lt.-Colonel F. S. Brereton's "Scouts of the Baghdad Patrols" (1921) were more typical of the overall tone.

The transfer of Cassell's magazines to the Amalgamated Press had little immediate effect, but by the early 1930s the paper was looking old-fashioned. It switched to a monthly schedule

in July 1932, and finally was absorbed by the more up-to-date *Modern Boy* in 1934. New *Chums* annuals continued to appear until 1940, containing work by many of the familiar names, and older yearly collations continued in circulation worldwide. Among well-known authors who have testified to being raised on "old *Chums* annuals" are Leslie Charteris (born 1907, in Singapore) and J. G. Ballard (born 1930, in Shanghai). It may be that the spirits of Pemberton, Parry, Walkey and Shaw had a wider and more enduring influence than is generally realised.
Publishers: Cassell 1892-1927; thereafter Amalgamated Press.
Editors: Max Pemberton (1892-94); Ernest Foster (1894-1907); Ernest H. Robinson (1907-15); F. Knowles Campling (1915-18); A. Donnelly Aitken (1918-20); Clarence Winchester (1920-24); Arthur L. Hayward (1924-26); Draycot M. Dell (1926-39); William B. Home-Gall (1939-40).

Colour 3 series: August 1914-September/October 1924 (120 issues); January 1925-January 1927 (11 issues); November 1928-May 1932 (42 issues). Total 173 issues
An unusual magazine which existed predominantly as a vehicle for the printing of fine and contemporary art, mostly in colour, with the work of Frank Brangwyn, Edmund Dulac, W. Russell Flint, Augustus John, Austin O. Spare, Jack B. Yeats and many more. The artwork seldom related to the text, though there were occasional articles about art and artists. Many articles were reflective pieces, though there were specific essays such as Elliott O'Donnell's "The Language of Animals" (Nov 1914). No expense was spared on the reproduction of art – Frank Salisbury's "The Muse of Art" (Mar 1916) was mostly in gold – and the magazine retained a high quality coated stock throughout the War. It was expensive – one shilling for 38 pages (rising to two shillings in the 1920s) – but evidently had a market. Throughout the magazine's early years the editor was buoyant about the circulation.

What was unusual about *Colour* was how much fiction it ran. The editor commented in the November 1915 issue that *Colour* "is becoming known for its remarkably clever little stories" and went on to admit that "we are not strictly speaking an art journal at all." It seldom ran more than three stories per issue, sometimes brief mood pieces or stream of consciousness, often modern in treatment, and rarely material you would find elsewhere (the closest might be *The Smart Set* or the reviews). Authors included J. H. Rosny aîné, R. Murray Gilchrist, Alan Griff, Phyllis Mégroz, Louis Golding, E. Charles Vivian and George Manning Sanders. By the post-war years *Colour* was running serials, including two by Eden Phillpotts, "The Treasures of Typhon" (1923-4) and "The Apes" (1929-30). There fiction often favoured the fantastic or unusual. A complete run provides one of the more unusual marriages of art and fiction. Wilson-Barrett kept the magazine going through several changes of publisher, eventually establishing his own company to run it. Costs would have been high and the increasing rivalry from the slick magazines must have eroded his market.
Publishers: William Dawson (1914-24); Suttley & Silverlock (1925-27); New Colour (1928-32).
Editor: Alfred Wilson-Barrett (initially with E. A. Hoppé as Art Director).

Cornhill Magazine, The January 1860-Spring 1975, 1,084 issues
The Cornhill was the premier literary magazine of the High Victorian period, dominating the scene between 1860 and the 1890s. It had its competition, notably from *Macmillan's* and those inspired by *The Cornhill*, such as *Temple Bar* and *Longman's*, but in terms of quality and prestige none rivalled it. It was the first of the illustrated shilling monthlies intended, by publisher George Smith, to broaden the market for the quality periodical. To help him he

appointed Thackeray, then second only to Dickens as Britain's leading novelist. The combination of Thackeray's influence and Smith's vision was unbeatable and the magazine soared to a paid circulation of 110,000. There was scarcely a writer of note who did not seek publication in *The Cornhill* during its first twenty years. In addition to Thackeray, during the first decade the magazine ran stories and serials by Anthony Trollope (including "The Small House at Allington", 1862-3), George Eliot ("Romola", 1862-3 – for which she was offered, though not paid, the sum of £10,000), George MacDonald, Mrs Gaskell ("Cousin Phillis", 1863-4; "Wives and Daughters", 1864-5), Wilkie Collins ("Armadale", 1864-6), Harriet Beecher Stowe, Charles Reade and George Meredith.

The magazine also presented a wide range of notable articles with George Augustus Sala, Matthew Arnold, George Crabbe and Harriet Martineau amongst the essayists in the early years, though it was in this territory that Thackeray was reproved. He had to stop publication of John Ruskin's series "Unto the Last" (1860), which challenged the Victorian conservative status quo, and was criticised for publishing Robert Bell's account of a séance with the medium Daniel Douglas Home, "Stranger than Fiction" (Aug 1860).

Leslie Stephen developed the non-fiction element of *The Cornhill*, which included a young Robert Louis Stevenson discussing matters French, but none of this was at the expense of fiction for it was Stephen who serialised "Far from the Madding Crowd" (1874) by Thomas Hardy, "Daisy Miller" (1878) and "Washington Square" (1880) by Henry James, plus works by R. D. Blackmore, Eliza Lynn Linton and Mrs Oliphant. Surprisingly Stephen did not take his readers with him as by the end of his editorship circulation had dropped to around 12,000. James Payn injected more vitality, reducing the price to sixpence from July 1883 and introducing the type of middlebrow fiction which had typified his work at *Chambers's Journal*. He published work by F. Anstey, Grant Allen, David Christie Murray, Stanley J. Weyman (it was really *The Cornhill* that launched Weyman's career), S. Baring-Gould, H. Rider Haggard and Arthur Conan Doyle ("The White Company", 1891). It was in *The Cornhill* that the mystery of the *Mary Celeste* acquired legendary status through Doyle's story "J. Habakuk Jephson's Statement" (Jan 1884). Alas Payn rejected the first Sherlock Holmes story, "A Study in Scarlet" as being both "too long & too short" for the magazine.

Despite the impressiveness of this line-up it attracted no new readers and alienated many so that circulation still fell. Smith was determined to save his brainchild. After a brief period with Strachey as editor, when the magazine returned to a shilling review, *The Cornhill* entered a period of stability under Smith's son-in-law, Reginald Smith, who struck a balance between the literary and the popular. Though he placed emphasis on non-fiction, with essays by Andrew Lang, Stephen Gwynn, A. C. Benson and Sidney Lee, he ran much popular fiction, including work by those becoming established in the illustrated monthlies, such as E. W. Hornung, Kate and Hesketh Prichard, Horace Annesley Vachell, Bernard Capes and A.E.W Mason, plus one of the earliest stories by William Hope Hodgson.

After Reginald Smith's death in 1916 his company, Smith, Elder, was taken over by John Murray who continued the magazine even though its circulation was as low as 5,000. Murray chose to consolidate the magazine's strengths for its existing readership, so it became rather elitist. Unlike *Blackwood's* or *Chambers's Journal*, its closest compatriots, *The Cornhill*, preferred to heighten a national identity than foster an imperial one. Its stories and essays are staunchly British and the magazine shifted more into the territory of the literary review. It continued to publish fiction – the literary imperative now encouraging unusual often macabre treatments. Contributors under Murray's first two editors include J. D. Beresford, H. Rider Haggard, Stanley Weyman, John Drinkwater, Nugent Barker and Ann Bridge. Huxley published the first work by Angela Thirkell and early work by Barbara Euphan Todd.

Murray suspended the magazine from 1939 to 1944 and when it returned it was as a quarterly review. It still ran fiction (H. E. Bates, Elizabeth Bowen, William Sansom) but the emphasis was on the literary essay.
Publishers: Smith, Elder (1860-1916), John Murray (1917-75).
Editors: William Makepeace Thackeray (1860-62); Frederick Greenwood and G. H. Lewes (1862-64); Greenwood alone (1864-68); Edward Dutton Cook and G. H. Lewes (1868-71); Leslie Stephen (1871-82); James Payn (1883-96); John St. Loe Strachey (1896-97); Reginald Smith (1898-1916); Leonard Huxley (1917-33); Lord Gorell (1933-39); Peter Quennell (1944-51); John Murray & Osyth Leeston (1951-75).

Eureka / The Favorite Magazine April 1897-1903 (?), 52 (?) issues.
An erratic magazine that began as a theatre and entertainment guide but soon converted under Sime to a miscellany of artwork and fiction, rather like *The Butterfly*. It ran prose by Frank Aubrey, Arnold Golsworthy and Marie Corelli. After Sime's brief editorship, during which the title mutated to *The Favorite Magazine* (spelling is correct) the magazine rather lost its way. It presented some major names by reprinting stories by H. G. Wells and E. Phillips Oppenheim but the magazine clearly lacked finances. It is believed to have survived to 1903 but only copies up to November 1901 (#52) have been seen.
Publisher: The Favorite Publishing Company (Paul Naumann).
Editors: Paul Naumann (with Sidney H. Sime, 1897-8).

Fry's Magazine April 1904-August 1914, 125 issues.
C. B. Fry was a champion cricketer, famed footballer, co-holder of the world long-jump record and generally all-round sporting hero. His magazine, started as *C.B. Fry's Magazine* (until Mar 1911) concentrated on sporting matters but ran one or two stories per issue, not all of a sporting nature. It published early stories by Bertram Atkey, several Klondike stories by Jack London, and Guy Thorne produced a series of sporting stories set in classical times. It ran several serials, including "Heronhaye" by K. & H. Prichard. Fiction was less common after 1911.
Publishers: George Newnes (1904-11); Fry's Magazine, Ltd (1911-14).
Editors: C. B. Fry with Bertram Atkey (1904-11?) and Walter Burton Baldry (1911-14).

Gaiety December 1921-November 1927, 72 issues.
A Humour Magazine. Almost half the contents were sketches or cartoons, sometimes two-page spreads, with work by H. M. Bateman, Fred Bennett, Alfred Bestall (pre-Rupert), Charles Crombie, L. R. Brightwell, Thomas Henry, Alfred Leete, Will Owen, W. Heath Robinson and Graham Simmons. The other half was filled with four or five stories or satirical articles. These were not solely by humorists, although Americans Ellis Parker Butler and Stephen Leacock and Britain's Barry Pain were regulars. Other contributors included Stacy Aumonier, H. C. Bailey, George A. Birmingham, Francis Gribble, Holloway Horn, Bruno Lessing and W. J. Makin.

Items of special interest include Gerald du Maurier's caustic views on Sapper's Bulldog Drummond (Dec 1921); Richard Connell's clever "The Martyr to Mystery" (May 1922), about a man whose incessant questioning creates a puzzle where none previously existed; and E.V. Odle's humorous Jewish fantasy, "The Curse Upon Isaac Knockabout" (Apr 1923). There is a short-story version of Noël Coward's first play, "I'll Leave it to You" (Mar 1923). Anthony Armstrong lampooned various characters in his series "Loose in the Library" including the Scarlet Pimpernel (Nov 1926), Sherlock Holmes (Dec 1926) and, unusually, Edgar Rice Burroughs's Martian novels (Sep-Oct 1926).

Gaiety was produced by a small independent company and though it attained a circulation of around 40,000 in its first year, this tailed off amidst the virulent competition in a decade of humour magazines. It was acquired by Newnes who merged it with *The Sunny Mag.* but kept the title alive on the cover.
Publisher: Gaiety Magazine. *Editors*: T. A. Price to 1926, then Arthur M. Turner.

Good Housekeeping March 1922-*current* (1000th issue June 2005).
The original American edition of *Good Housekeeping* had started in May 1885 but its influence began when it was taken over by William Randolph Hearst in 1911. He converted it to a large flat quality slick magazine and though he retained the original service elements for house-keeping, fashion and lifestyle, he bolstered the fiction content. The same mix was retained for the British edition launched in 1922 as a companion to *Nash's–Pall Mall*. In his editorial McPeake emphasised that "fiction is one of the pleasures of most women's leisure" and assured that only the very best would be published. The opening serial was "The Tale of Triona" by William J. Locke, then one of Britain's most popular authors. Fiction remained a key part of the magazine until well into the 1970s, usually a serial or two and four or five short stories. Although there was always a bed-rock of romantic fiction, mostly by Fanny Heaslip Lea, May Edginton and I.A.R. Wylie, there was much else besides. McPeake relied on a core of British authors, mostly J. D. Beresford, W. L. George and Horace Annesley Vachell, but also reprinted from the American Hearst magazines, with work by F. Scott Fitzgerald, Emma-Lindsay Squier (her stories often featured historical or exotic settings) and James Oliver Curwood, with stories of the Canadian wilderness. This diversity increased under Head. There were contributions by Rudyard Kipling (his retelling of the Adam and Eve story in "The Enemies to each Other" [Aug 1924] illustrated by Edmund Dulac), Hugh Walpole, E. M. Delafield, John Galsworthy, Achmed Abdullah, Jacland Marmur, L.A.G. Strong, Edison Marshall and Rafael Sabatini. 1935 saw Mary Pickford's first story, "Little Liar", whilst 1936 saw serials by Mary Roberts Rinehart, R. C. Sherriff and A. J. Cronin.

Good Housekeeping was heavily illustrated with occasional colour features, such as Edmund Dulac's paintings to Hugh Ross Williamson's series on Greek myths (1931-2) later issued in book form as *Gods and Mortals in Love* (1934). There was also exotic work by John R. Flanagan and Elizabeth Montgomery. Until 1934 the covers were by Jessie Willcox Smith, most being known as the "Water Babies" series because they all portrayed young children. The magazine also ran colour cartoons for children and had an arrangement with Walt Disney Studios to reproduce his "Silly Symphonies" series. This agreement reaped dividends when Disney's feature-length cartoons were released as *Good Housekeeping* ran adaptations of "Snow White" (Jan 1938) and "Pinocchio" (Dec 1939) with stills reproduced from the films.

Rebecca West, Lady Bonham-Carter, Marie Belloc Lowndes were regular advice columnists in the 1920s. During 1931-2 Virginia Woolf provided an occasional series on "The

London Scene", whilst the April 1932 issue ran a symposium on "If Christ Should Come" with contributions by G. K. Chesterton, Aldous Huxley and J.B.S. Haldane. At times it seemed that were it not for the service section, *Good Housekeeping* would have been a duplicate of *Nash's Pall Mall*. It was perhaps no surprise when from October 1937 the two magazines merged. Until the war years this bolstered *Good Housekeeping*'s fiction bringing contributions by James Hilton, Alec Waugh, Mazo de la Roche, Somerset Maugham and others.

After 1939 Head handed the editorship to Oliver Robinson (son of W. Heath Robinson) and during the War years, when the magazine had to slim down to digest size (from August 1942), there was a shift to more sentimental stories, which remained after the War. Thereafter *Good Housekeeping* moved wholly into the women's market, but between 1922 and 1939 it was one of the premier fiction-carrying magazines in Britain.

Publisher: National Magazine Company.
Editors: J. Y. McPeake (1922-24); Alice Maud Head (1924-39); Oliver Robinson (1940-67); Laurie Purden (1967-72); Charlotte Lessing (1973-86); Noëlle Walsh (1987-91); Sally O'Sullivan (1992-95); Pat Roberts Cairns (1996-98); Lindsay Nicholson (1999-).

Good Words January 1860-April 1906, 556 issues.
Purportedly the most popular fiction magazine of the mid-Victorian period, until *The Strand*, with a circulation of around 160,000 in mid-1860s and 130,000 in the 1870s. It remains one of the easiest magazines to collect, evidence not only of its circulation but of how many copies were retained by its dedicated readers. It created the marketing niche of the Sunday magazine: that is a magazine for Sunday reading. The contents were morally improving, even pious. The Macleod brothers, particularly Donald, were sufficiently flexible to allow a wide range of fiction and articles, though they were challenged by the more strict authoritarians on the grounds that fiction would lead young minds astray. Macleod doubted that, but was known to edit or reject works for being "too worldly", most notably Trollope's "Rachel Ray" (Chapman & Hall, 1863). Even so he published much quality High Victorian fiction, including the serials "Hereward the Wake" (1865) by Charles Kingsley, "Kept in the Dark" (1882) by Anthony Trollope, "Fated to be Free" (1875) Jean Ingelow's sequel to her popular *Off the Skelligs*, "The Trumpet Major" (1880) by Thomas Hardy, "The Little Minister" (1891) by J. M. Barrie and "The Half-Hearted" (1899-1900) by John Buchan. Other contributors include S. Baring-Gould, R. D. Blackmore, Mrs Craik, Amelia B. Edwards, George MacDonald and Mrs Oliphant. The popular Christmas editions were entitled *Good Cheer*.

The magazine later suffered from Strahan's financial difficulties. Circulation dwindled in the 1890s partly from rivalry with other magazines but also as Sunday observance faded. In 1906 it passed into the hands of the Amalgamated Press and was merged with the *Sunday Magazine* as a weekly tabloid and thereafter ceased to make any impression, folding in 1911.

Publishers: Alexander Strahan (1860-72); William Isbister (1873-1904); Pitman's (Jan-Oct 1905); Amalgamated Press (1905-1911).
Editors: Norman Macleod (1860-72); Donald Macleod (1872-1906); Hartley Aspden (1906-11).

Graphic, The [W] 4 December 1869-14 July 1932, 3,266 issues; merged with *The Sphere*.
Established as a rival to the *Illustrated London News*, it placed similar emphasis on portraying the news in highly illustrated form, but it also published fiction. Initially only in its special Christmas issues but, from January 1873, it serialised novels starting with "Innocent" by Mrs.

Oliphant. Short fiction appeared only occasionally outside the Christmas and (from 1878) Summer issues until 1879 when at least one story appeared in most issues until World War I. Amongst its more notable serials were "Phineas Redux" (1873-4) and "Marion Fay" (1881-2) by Anthony Trollope, "The History of a Crime" (1877-8) by Victor Hugo, "The Mayor of Casterbridge" (1886) and "Tess of the D'Urbervilles" (1891) by Thomas Hardy, "She" (1886-7) and "Montezuma's Daughter" (1893) by H. Rider Haggard, "When the Sleeper Awakes" (1899) by H. G. Wells and "The Three Hostages" (1924) by John Buchan. Although the volume of fiction dwindled in later years, the Christmas issues still excelled in quality names and could count Edgar Wallace, Lord Dunsany and Vita Sackville-West amongst their number. It was retitled *National Graphic* from 28 April 1932 and almost all fiction dropped.

The Victorian Fiction research Guide #29 (University of Queensland, 2001) compiled by Graham Law, indexes the fiction in *The Graphic* from 1869 to 1901.

Publishers: E. J. Mansfield (1869-93); G. R. Parker (1894-1903); The Graphic (1903-32).

Editors: H. Sutherland Edwards (1869-70); Arthur Locker (1870-91); Thomas Heath Joyce (1891-1906); W. Comyns Beaumont (1906-09); John M. Bulloch (1909-24); Frank Le Couteur (1924-26); Alan J. Bott (1926-32).

Home Chimes   2 series: weekly, 2 January 1884-26 December 1885; monthly, January 1886-December 1894; 212 issues.

Originally a penny weekly then a fourpenny-monthly, this miscellany was dominated by fiction, mostly by little-known authors. Robinson encouraged new writers including the young Jerome K. Jerome and *Home Chimes* serialised both "Idle Thoughts of an Idle Fellow" (1886) and "Three Men in a Boat," (1888-9). It published early works by J. M. Barrie, J. S. Fletcher, W. W. Jacobs, Richard Marsh, Eden Phillpotts and Edith Nesbit. Unlike Robinson's own work, which was often heavily religious or set amongst the poor, the stories in *Home Chimes* were light and often amusing. Forgotten amongst the plethora of rival magazines that mushroomed about it, *Home Chimes* was a key predecessor of the popular fiction magazine.

Publisher: Richard Willoughby.
Editor: F. W. Robinson.

Horlicks Magazine   January 1904-March 1905, 15 issues.

Despite its name, *Horlick's Magazine* was not a trade journal but a literary magazine issued under the auspices of the malted milk company. It replaced a promotional medium in the colonies and, as a consequence, regularly featured items grouped in the index as "Colonial Articles and Stories". The cover, depicting a Regency gentleman surrounded by books and studying a picture, gave the impression of an antiquarian magazine, which the contents did little to dissuade. It was unillustrated, sold for 6d, and its 96 pages were printed on thick book paper. Waite had sold the idea to James Horlick as a ladies' magazine but, apart from some minor items, the overall tone was very different. Waite, a leading adept in the magical order the Golden Dawn, used the magazine as a vehicle for mystical and hermetical writings and it is these that have kept the magazine's name alive. Among its contributors were Arthur Machen, Edgar Jepson, Evelyn Underhill and Waite himself. Its most memorable story is Machen's "The White People" (Jan 1904). It also serialised Machen's biographical "A Fragment of Life" (from Mar 1904) and "The Garden of Avallaunius" (from Jul 1904) and Edgar Jepson's

pantheistic "The Horned Shepherd" (from Aug 1904). Some of the articles also had a mystical bent, such as Waite's "The Legend of the Holy Grail" (Jan 1904), but there were other more prosaic items. Many of the Colonial stories were set in Burma, painting a surprisingly ordinary existence against an otherwise alien landscape. *Horlick's Magazine* has more historical value today than any reader interest it sustained at the time.
Publisher: James Elliott & Co. *Editor*: A. E. Waite.

Illustrated London News [W] 14 May 1842-*current*, over 7,150 issues plus Christmas and other specials.
The first and, for many years, the pre-eminent weekly illustrated newspaper, issued in tabloid format, priced 6d. Its files are regarded by many as the best recorded history of the Victorian era. Circulation peaked at about 300,000 in 1860s. One of its engravers, Frank Leslie, took the concept to the USA in 1848, launching what became *Frank Leslie's Illustrated Newspaper*, the forerunner of *The American Magazine*. Although the *Illustrated London News* (*ILN*) ran the occasional serial and short story in its early years, particularly in its Christmas numbers, it did not feature fiction regularly until 1883, spurred on by the success of *The Graphic*. It ran serials by James Payn, Mrs Riddell, Walter Besant, Bret Harte, Hall Caine, Gilbert Parker and Stanley J. Weyman, but its best known were "Cleopatra" (1889) and "Nada the Lily" (1892) by H. Rider Haggard, "The Wonderful Adventures of Phra the Phoenician" (1890) by Edwin Lester Arnold, "Uma" (1892) by Robert Louis Stevenson, "The Pursuit of the Well-Beloved" (1892) by Thomas Hardy and "The Other House" (1896) by Henry James. From 1897 it dropped serials in favour of short stories or novellas, running one or two per issue, notably the works of Arthur Quiller-Couch, Edith Nesbit ("The Would-be-goods" series, 1900-1) and Joseph Conrad ("Amy Foster", 1901). G. K. Chesterton wrote a regular weekly column, "Our Notebook", from 1905 till his death in 1936, when it was taken over by Arthur Bryant. After Shorter's editorship the volume of fiction decreased, save for the Christmas issues, being switched to *ILN*'s companions *The Sketch* and later *Britannia and Eve*. The Christmas issues were highly illustrated, especially in the 1920s, which featured the work of Kay Nielsen, Edmund Dulac, W. Heath Robinson, E. H. Shepard, Fortunio Matania and Mabel Lucie Attwell. Authors in the 1920s and 1930s included E. F. Benson, Freeman Wills Croft, Ethel Mannin and Daphne du Maurier. It became a monthly magazine in May 1971 and quarterly in 1990.
The Victorian Fiction Research Guide #29 (University of Queensland, 2001) by Graham Law, indexes the fiction from 1869 to 1901. A website of interest is www.ilnpictures.co.uk
Publishers: Joseph Clayton (1842); William Little (1843-57); George C. Leighton (1858-83); Ingram Brothers (1884-1905); Illustrated London News & Sketch (1905-1961); Thomson Organisation (1961-1985); Illustrated London News Group (since 1985).
Editors: F.W.N.Bayley (1842-46); John Timbs (1846-52); Charles Mackay (1852-59); John Lash Latey (1859-90); Clement Shorter (1891-1900); Bruce Ingram (1900-63); Hugh Ingram (1963-65); Tim Green (1965-67); John Kisch (1967-70); James Bishop (1970-94); Mark Palmer (since 1995).

Imp, The June 1907-November 1911, 54 issues.
The Imp was issued with a refreshing honesty, Arthur Greening proclaiming that it "is not designed to fill a long-felt need; it will be content to create one." This slim journal was really an in-house organ, the publisher using it to promote his books. Greening had a remarkable track record of developing new authors – Sax Rohmer and Baroness Orczy being his greatest

triumphs. Orczy was present in several issues, writing about herself in the first number and contributing the serial "The Nest of the Sparrowhawk" (1909-10). The bumper Christmas 1907 issue is of special interest for its portrait gallery of authors, many of whom were rarely photographed, including Gerald Biss, Robert W. Cole, J. B. Harris-Burland and Clive Pemberton. *The Imp* is a treasure trove of rarities. There are stories by Gerald Biss, R. Andom, Beatrice Heron-Maxwell, Elliott O'Donnell and Winifred Graham amongst the more collectable names. Greening was more of a book-lover than a publisher and eventually went out of business, but left behind an interesting legacy. A detailed study of the magazine will be found in the small-press book *Marked by the Macabre* by Ethan Barlass (Lamorna: Cove Press, 2002).
Publisher and *Editor:* Arthur Greening.

Lambert's Monthly January 1890-May 1891, 17 issues plus Summer 1890 special.
A 64-page penny miscellaneous story paper issued on cheap newspulp. It ran a wide range of second-rate yet popular sensationalistic material. Authors included George Manville Fenn, James Grant, Florence Marryat, G. A. Henty, Edmund Yates, L. T. Meade, Ouida and George R. Sims. It reported sales of 72,000, but copies today are very rare. It was superseded by *The Ludgate Magazine*. There was an attempt to revive it in 1898, but only one issue appeared.
Publisher: F. J. Lambert. *Editors:* Sir Gilbert Campbell; later Philip May.

London Society February 1862-December 1898, 441 issues plus Christmas specials.
Subtitled "an illustrated magazine of light and amusing literature for the hours of relaxation", *London Society* was one of the better *Cornhill* imitations that flourished in the 1860s. It was copiously illustrated with line drawings and engravings and ran the whole range of fiction, essays and poetry. Unfortunately most contributions were anonymous or identified solely by initials and many remain unidentified. The original proprietor was James Hogg, son of the Ettrick Shepherd, and he produced a middle-brow magazine of diversity and diversion. Its extra Christmas and Holiday numbers were especially prized. Known contributors includes Walter Besant, James Grant, Tom Hood, Mary Howitt, Henry Kingsley, Mark Lemon, Florence Marryat (who briefly assisted Hogg as editor), Mrs J. H. Riddell, Edmund Yates and Jules Verne (whose "Michael Strogoff" was serialised in 1876 with much publicity),. It published the first story by Abraham [Bram] Stoker, "The Crystal Cup" (Sep 1872) and the second story by Conan Doyle "An American's Tale" (Christmas 1879). It also published the earliest sketches by Randolph Caldecott. Other artists include George Cruikshank, Jr., Frank Dicksee, Harry Furniss and Linley Sambourne. Like *Belgravia* and *Tinsley's Magazine* (1867-92) it served as a good training ground for short-story writers.
Publishers: Kelly & Co. (1862-71); Sampson, Low (1872-80); London Society (1881-86); F. V. White (1887-96); Arliss Andrews (1897-98).
Editors: James Hogg (1862-86?), assisted by Florence Marryat (1872-76); later editors unidentified.

Longman's Magazine November 1882-October 1905, 276 issues.
Introduced by Longman's as a successor to *Fraser's Magazine*, with the idea of publishing a non-political unillustrated magazine of fiction and popular articles. Apart from Andrew Lang's column "At the Sign of the Ship", which ran monthly from January 1886, there was no editorial personality. It seems that from the outset Longman fell under the influence of Andrew Lang and perhaps Robert Louis Stevenson to produce a magazine that favoured the romantic in

fiction over the realist. This was already evident in such contributions as "The Three Strangers" by Thomas Hardy (Mar 1883) and the article "The Pageant of Summer" by Richard Jefferies (Jun 1883) but came to a head in Stevenson's response to Henry James's article "The Art of Fiction" (Sep 1884). In "A Humble Remonstrance" (Nov 1884) Stevenson argued that fiction was not a recording of history but the creation of an artistic vision. Lang supported this view and as a consequence much that appeared in *Longman's* was larger than life. This included "Allan Quatermain" (1887) by H. Rider Haggard, "A Gentleman of France" (1893) by Stanley J. Weyman, and Stevenson's own "Prince Otto" (1885) and various "Fables". It also published early material by F. Anstey, Margaret Oliphant, Edith Nesbit and Rudyard Kipling. *Longman's* thus captured the mood of the time which would be developed by *The Strand* and *Pearson's*, but seemed unable to capitalise on it itself. Perhaps had *Longman's* become an illustrated magazine like its rivals it might have survived but in its final issue the publishers admitted that they had no desire to change. *Longman's* always looked old-fashioned and thus never represented what it offered.

Publisher: Longman, Green & Co. *Editor:* Charles J. Longman, assisted by Andrew Lang.

Lovat Dickson's Magazine November 1933-June 1935, 20 issues
A late entry into the fiction magazine market, it was Dickson's intention to remind readers of the short story as an "art form" rather than the formulaic popular story or the politicised variety with which Dickson had grown so frustrated when editing *The Fortnightly Review*. It was part of a movement in the late thirties that drew a curtain across the "age of the storyteller". Similar markets were Blackwell's *New Stories* (1934-6) and John Lehmann's *New Writing* (1936-46), all encouraged by the success of the American *Story* (first series, 1931-48). Dickson used the magazine chiefly to promote his publishing company but also to attract writers and in this regard he believed the magazine a success, though it apparently never made a profit. The magazine concentrated on short fiction plus the occasional literary essay such as H. E. Bates's "A Note on the English Short Story" (Feb 1934). Bates was one of the leading contributors of fiction along with Arthur Calder-Marshall, L.A.G. Strong, John Collier, Neil Bell, and Walter de la Mare. As the magazine progressed Dickson encouraged more literary reminiscences and digressions and sought unusual, non-commercial work, perhaps best typified by William Saroyan's non-story, "Seventy Thousand Assyrians" (Jan 1935), itself a reprint from *Story*. Other contributors of note include Pearl S. Buck, Ernest Hemingway, Vladimir Nabokov, V. S. Pritchett and John Steinbeck. The contents are indexed (by author only) in *Comprehensive Index to Little Magazines 1890-1970* by Marion Sader (Kraus-Thomson, 1976).
Publisher: Lovat Dickson.
Editors: P. Gilchrist Thompson (Nov 1933-Sept 1934); Lovat Dickson (Oct 1934-Mar 1935); L.A.G. Strong (Apr-Jun 1935).

Macmillan's Magazine November 1859-October 1907, 546 issues
The first of the literary shilling monthlies (though unillustrated) appearing just two months before *The Cornhill*, which remained its closest rival. Whilst *The Cornhill* was always superior in its fiction, *Macmillan's* earned a reputation for the quality of its articles. Of special note were Francis Galton's pieces on hereditary genius (1865), Richard Burton's "Articles on Rome" (1874-5), A. R. Wallace's "The Colours of Animals and Plants" (1877), George

Saintsbury's essays on English literature and various classical studies by Walter Pater. In its early years *Macmillan's* published some noted poetry, including the work of Tennyson and Christina Rossetti. Its serials were generally rather lightweight, starting with Thomas Hughes's "Tom Brown at Oxford" (1859-60) – it had been the success of *Tom Brown's Schooldays* that had prompted Macmillan to launch a magazine – and Henry Kingsley's "Ravenshoe" (1861-2). Its classic early serial was Charles Kingsley's "The Water-Babies" (1862-3), which thereafter associated the magazine with the Sunday "Home" periodicals. Consequently *Macmillan's* subsisted for many years on a safe diet of Charlotte M. Yonge and Mrs Craik, though it did run R. D. Blackmore's novel of London lowlife, "Cardock Nowell" (1865-6). It was not until the 1880s that it published its two heavyweight serials, "Portrait of a Lady" (1880-1) by Henry James and "The Woodlanders" (1886-7) by Thomas Hardy. It failed to respond to the changes in magazine publishing in the 1890s and soon looked antiquated. It final editor, Morris, became renowned for his inflexibility, with his one bow to trends being Winston Churchill's Ruritanian novel "Savrola" (1899). A half-hearted attempt in 1905 to transform the magazine into a sixpenny monthly, still unillustrated, probably hastened its end. An index of contents to 1900 is in Volume 1 of *The Wellesley Index to Victorian Periodicals* whilst a detailed study is *Macmillan's Magazine, 1859-1907* by George J. Worth (Ashgate, 2003).
Publisher: Macmillan.
Editors: David Masson (1859-68); George Grove (1868-83); John Morley (1883-85); Mowbray Morris (1885-1907).

Magazine of Short Stories *see Short Stories*

Master Thriller Series [July] 1933 to [December] 1939, 32 volumes
A quarterly (later monthly) pulp anthology selecting material from Doubleday's and Dell's US pulps and later from various British sources plus the occasional new story. Each issue followed a set theme, starting with *Tales of the Foreign Legion*, and the more popular selections saw second or third compilations. Others, like *Tales of Mystery and Detection*, generated their own separate magazine. At the outset the series selected material by several major names, amongst them Somerset Maugham, Algernon Blackwood, L. Patrick Greene and P. C. Wren, but over time, and as budgets tightened, the stories came from second-tier British and American pulpsters. The quality is variable but the variety of themes makes the overall package of greater value than individual issues. The full run of titles and dates is as follows.
1. *Tales of the Foreign Legion* (Jul 1933); 2. *Tales of the North-West Mounted Police* (Sep 1933); 3. *Tales of the Seven Seas* (Dec 1933); 4. *Tales of Mystery and Detection* (Mar 1934); 5. *Tales of the Foreign Legion 2* (Jun 1934); 6. *Tales of the Uncanny* (Sep 1934); 7. *Tales of African Adventure* (Dec 1934); 8. *Tales of the Orient* (Mar 1935); 9. *Tales of the Jungle* (Jul 1935); 10. *Tales of the Foreign Legion 3* (Oct 1935); 11. *Tales of the Sea* (Jan 1936); 12. *Tales of Valour* (Apr 1936); 13. *Tales of the Levant* (Jul 1936); 14. *Tales of the Air* (Sep 1936); 15. *Tales of the Foreign Legion 4* (Jan 1937); 16. *Tales of Adventure* (Apr 1937); 17. *Tales of Terror* (Jul 1937); 18. *Tales of East and West* (Oct 1937); 19. *Tales of the Underworld* (Jan 1938); 20. *Tales of the Uncanny 2* (Apr 1938); 21. *Tales of Crime and Punishment* (Jul 1938); 22. *Tales of the Grand Express* (Oct 1938); 23. *Tales of the North-West Mounted Police* (Jan 1939); 24. *Tales of Outlawry* (Apr 1939); 25. *Tales of the Great Dominion* (May 1939); 26. *Tales of the Far Frontier* (Jun 1939); 27. *Tales of the Underworld 2* (Jul

1939); 28. *The Far-Flung Coasts of Crime* (Aug 1939); 29. *Tales of the Foreign Legion 5* (Sep 1939); 30. *Tales of the Jungle 2* (Oct 1939); 31. *Tales of Gangsters and G-Men* (Nov 1939); 32. *Tales of Ghosts and Haunted Houses* (Dec 1939).

Two other titles associated with the series but not officially part of it were *Fireside Ghost Stories* (Dec 1937) and *Ghosts and Goblins* (Jan 1938). See separate entries on *Mystery and Detection*, *Mystery Stories* and *Tales of Wonder* in Section 1.
Publisher: The World's Work, Kingswood, Surrey. *Editor*: H. Norman Evans.

Nash's Illustrated Weekly 14 June 1919-10 July 1920, 41 issues
This heavily illustrated tabloid weekly paper heralded Eveleigh Nash's return to the magazine world five years after he had sold *Nash's Magazine* to the Hearst empire. Although it ran topical articles and features on fashion and cookery, suggesting its primary market was women, the emphasis was on a wide range of fiction, including several weird tales by William Hope Hodgson (the later Carnacki stories) and Algernon Blackwood. Amongst its serials were the spiritualist novel, "Mrs. Marden" by Robert Hichens, "Teach" by Cutcliffe Hyne, "Queen Lucia" by E. F. Benson and "Black Bartlemy's Treasure" by Jeffery Farnol.
Publishers: Periodical Publishing Company to 10 Apr 1920; thereafter Hutchinson.
Editor: Eveleigh Nash to 10 Apr 1920; thereafter not known.

Osborne, The November 1896-May 1897, 7 issues
Taking its name from Queen Victoria's residence on the Isle of Wight, this slim magazine was of the "Home" type, presumably designed not to upset Her Majesty. In its short life it ran a serial by S. R. Crockett and a series by Charles J. Mansford, but was otherwise uninspired.
Publisher: S. W. Partridge. *Editor:* Not known.

Outward Bound October 1920-March 1924, 42 issues.
Mathews had been the Editorial Secretary of the London Missionary Society from 1910-1919. In 1920 he established Far and Near Publications to publish works that encouraged a greater understanding of the world, its people and cultures. *Outward Bound* was the principal publication. It was a standard size, 100-page slick, selling for one shilling. Although there were the usual photographs and articles on peoples and places, initially almost half the magazine was fiction, with an historical serial by John Buchan, "The Path of the King" and a south-seas story by John Russell. Mary Ovington's long serial "The Shadow" (1921) was an important study of the black culture in the southern United States. H. de Vere Stacpoole was a regular contributor, including his serial "Vanderdecken" (1922). In later issues the emphasis shifted towards non-fiction but there were occasional tales of local legends and folklore. Unfortunately financial problems and Mathews's resignation brought an end to an otherwise worthy venture.
Publisher: Far and Near Publications. *Editor:* Basil Mathews.

Passing Show, The [W] 2 series: 20 March 1915-19 March 1932 (918 issues); 26 March 1932-25 February 1939 (362 issues); total 1,280 issues.
The first series was a slim, small tabloid humour magazine which ran a few short stories but concentrated mostly on light articles, gossip, amusing experiences and cartoons. It was completely revamped in 1932 to produce a highly illustrated weekly tabloid with the emphasis on adventure and mystery fiction and sensational feature articles. It ran many serials, some

reprinted from American periodicals such as "Lost on Venus" (1933) by Edgar Rice Burroughs and "When Worlds Collide" (1934) by Edwin Balmer and Philip Wylie. In similar vein by home-grown talent were "The Madness of Professor Pye" (1934) by Warwick Deeping, "Stowaway to Mars" (1936) by John Beynon [John Wyndham] and the Savaran series (1936-8) by Douglas Newton. The proliferation of exotic adventure fiction allowed for some of the best artwork by Fortunio Matania. Its most prolific contributor was Will Scott, who had also appeared regularly in the first series, and produced a remarkable array of humorous and mystery stories. The magazine retained a centre-page cartoon feature which included work by Mabel Lucie Attwell and Bruce Bairnsfather. One of the brightest fiction papers of the thirties.
Publisher: Odhams Press.
Editors: W. Comyns Beaumont (1915-19); Augustus Muir (1920-24); W.A. Williamson (1925-39).

Pearson's Story-Teller [W] 9 October 1895-22 February 1896 or after; at least 21 issues
Although details are given in the companion *Pearson's Weekly* no copies of this story paper have been found. It was announced as a story magazine consisting entirely of serials, listing ones by Winifred Graham, George Griffith, Iza Duffus Hardy and George C. Wallis amongst others. By January it was running a complete "novel" as well as serials but thereafter all reference ceases and it may have merged with the novella-based *Pearson's Library*.
Publisher: Pearson. *Editor:* C. Arthur Pearson.

Pearson's Weekly [W] 26 July 1890-1 April 1939, 2,540 issues
The tabloid magazine that established Pearson's publishing company when he and Peter Keary left Newnes. Though similar to *Tit-Bits*, which Keary had edited, with many competitions and prize stories, it placed a stronger emphasis on serials and short fiction. It had particular success with the future-war stories by George Griffith, "The Angel of the Revolution" (1893), "The Syren of the Skies" (1893-4) and "Briton or Boer?" (1896). It also serialised "Heart of the World" by H.Rider Haggard (1894-5), "The Final War" by Louis Tracy (1895-6) and "The Invisible Man" by H. G. Wells (1897), and also ran many railway detective stories by Victor L. Whitechurch. It published the first story by A. Sarsfield Ward (Sax Rohmer), "The Mysterious Mummy" (Christmas 1903). Other regulars were Arthur Applin, Arnold Golsworthy and Ladbroke Black. Fiction in later issues was mostly trivial or reprints. A complete index to the fiction with assorted material is *Pearson's Weekly, A Checklist of Fiction 1890-1939* by George Locke (Ferret Fantasy, 1990).
Publisher: Pearson.
Editors: Peter Keary (1890-1915); Frank J. Lamburn (1915?-32?); William J. Makin (1933?-35); J.B. Platnauer (1936-39).

Physical Culture *see Sandow's Magazine*

Quiver, The 2 series: 7 September 1861-16 September 1865; new series, 23 September 1865-June 1956; total 1284 issues
A religious-orientated magazine that concentrated on articles and fiction of a highly moral and improving nature, "designed for the defence of Biblical truth and the advancement of religion." Edited initially by a succession of Church ministers, the magazine was, for its first forty years or so, overwhelmingly pious, offering a constant diet of Bible interpretations, church lectures,

and accounts of good deeds. In its first incarnation as an unillustrated penny weekly (small tabloid, 24 pages), it was unsuccessful and was revamped by Cassell, shortly before he died, as an illustrated monthly, still issued in weekly parts (like *Chambers's Journal*) until 1879. The only fiction of note in the first series were the serials by Mrs Henry Wood, though F. W. Farrar, the author of *Eric, or Little by Little* (1858), was a contributor of both fiction and non-fiction for forty years from 1863. Other regulars during the Victorian period were Sarah Doudney, Annie Swan, L. T. Meade and Katharine Tynan, bright moments in a magazine that was otherwise too saccharine for its own good. It was a reputation that its later editors tried hard to counter. Herbert Williams, who did the most to reinvigorate the magazine under the reforms of the new Managing Director Arthur Spurgeon, railed against charges of "harmless insipidity" and declared "we will not tolerate 'goody-goodyism' and mere sentimentalism." Under Williams *The Quiver* retained the moral highground – it ran a special "Chivalry" issue in May 1916 – whilst adapting to the changing world. There was no better example of this in its fiction than E. F. Benson's novel "Michael" (1915-16) which explored divided loyalties and duty. More atypical was one of H. Rider Haggard's final attempts to recapture the world of fantastic adventure, "When the World Shook" (1918-19), a novel more suited to *Cassell's*. Also of interest at this time was Jerome K. Jerome's last novel "Anthony Strong'th'arm" (1922-3) and Warwick Deeping's series "The Green Caravan" (1926) both of which explored the change in post-war society. By the 1920s *The Quiver* had shifted its base from a religious to a woman's magazine, albeit with strong moral overtones. Alongside serials and stories by Sophie Kerr, Mary Wiltshire, Michael Kent and H. Mortimer Batten, plus a wide range of articles, it retained a crusading zeal with its "Army of Helpers", seeking funds for all manner of good deeds. In this way it survived the war, reducing in size in August 1940, and ending its days looking like a parish magazine. Apart from *Argosy,* it was the last of Cassell's original titles to close. It was absorbed into the *Sunday Companion*.

Publishers: Cassell to January 1927, then Amalgamated Press.
Editors: John Cassell (1861-63); Charles Wright (1863); John Willis Clark (1863-64); Teignmouth Shore (1864-65); Bonavia Hunt (1865-1905); David Williamson (1905-9); Herbert Dakin Williams (1909-53); John Erskine Tuck (1953-56).

Sandow's Magazine [Physical Culture] 2 series, April 1898-27 December 1906; new series, 3 January-25 July 1907; total 212 issues. Continued as *Sandow Health Magazine*.

Eugene Sandow was a national celebrity in the 1890s for his strength and physique and he launched this magazine to educate people in all forms of physical culture – its title was *Physical Culture* until March 1899. Rather incongruously it published one or two stories per issue which had nothing to do with fitness but were adventure or mystery fiction, including work by Cutcliffe Hyne, Fred T. Jane, Herbert Russell and C. Ranger Gull. Of special interest amongst the non-fiction were two pieces on physical exercises by William Hope Hodgson (Aug 1901, August 1903) and an article on boxing by P. G. Wodehouse (Jul 1902). Fiction was dropped when it became a 20-page twopenny weekly in January 1905. The American health fanatic Bernarr Macfadden was sufficiently inspired to bring out his own version of *Physical Culture* in America from March 1899, which launched his publishing empire.

Publisher: Harrison & Sons. *Editor:* Eugene Sandow.

OTHER MAGAZINES

Savoy, The January-December 1896, 8 issues
Noted "decadent" magazine and rival to the *Yellow Book*, it is renowned for its controversial artwork by Aubrey Beardsley plus his much expurgated erotic Wagnerian novel "Under the Hill" (Jan-Apr). It was Symons's intention to provide a magazine of art in all its forms and thus in addition to its illustrations it featured poetry and mood pieces as well as essays. Amongst the fiction is work by W. B. Yeats (notably "Rosa Alchemica", April), Hubert Crackanthorpe, Ernest Dowson, Fiona Macleod and Ernest Rhys. After two quarterly issues Symons overreached himself by publishing the magazine monthly. Falling sales aggravated by W. H. Smith refusing to stock later issues led to its early demise. Holbrook Jackson regarded the magazine as "the most satisfying achievement of *fin de siècle* journalism in England."
Publisher: Leonard Smithers. *Editor:* Arthur Symons.

Scoops [W] 10 February-23 June 1934, 20 issues
This weekly story paper was Britain's first all science-fiction magazine. Unfortunately it pandered to a juvenile readership, the editor being unaware of the adult science fiction in American magazines. Most of the stories, published anonymously, were by regular writers for boys' magazines, such as Bernard Buley, Reginald Thomas and George E. Rochester, with stories of renegade robots and mutated monsters. It reprinted Conan Doyle's "The Poison Belt" (5 May-9 Jun) but otherwise most fiction was new and included the serial "Space" (17 Feb-21 Apr) by Professor A. M. Low (book, *Adrift in the Stratosphere*, Blackie, 1937). Once Britain's mature-sf writers – including John Russell Fearn, W. P. Cockcroft and Maurice Hugi – began contributing, the quality steadily improved but too late for any discerning readership. The magazine remains a sad reminder of a lost opportunity.
Publisher: C. A. Pearson. *Editor:* Haydn Dimmock.

Search Light, The March 1892-September 1894, 31 issues plus Christmas 1892 special
In the same vein as Stead's *Review of Reviews*, *The Search Light* sought to reprint in more permanent form the best stories and journalism appearing in the daily and weekly newspapers and other ephemeral press. Its contents were therefore entirely reprint, but the likelihood of finding all of the original sources extant today is remote. The bulk of the contents were articles, though these include much of literary and artistic interest, such as profiles on or interviews with Frances Hodgson Burnett, Alphonse Daudet, Kate Greenaway, Andrew Lang, Maurice Maeterlinck, George du Maurier, Jules Verne, Edmund Yates and Emile Zola. Most of the short stories, of which there were three or four per issue, were anonymous but included translations from many countries probably seeing their first appearance in English. Curiously the magazine displayed boldly on the cover and running head the sub-title *Pearson's Monthly* which would, in due course, supersede this magazine in its own right.
Publisher: Pearson. *Editor:* C. Arthur Pearson.

Short Stories [W] 12 January 1889-18 June 1904, 807 issues. Continued as *Smith's Weekly* until 10 August 1907.
One of the more important weekly all-story magazines. It was originally a compendium entitled *Magazine of Short Stories* from E. & H. Bennett where the stories were either anonymous or signed by initials, with many reprints. It ran serials but also many brief, minor items. Had this been its only existence it would have been of no interest. However in July 1893 it was taken

over by C. Arthur Pearson as a companion to his already popular *Pearson's Weekly*. Pearson shortened the title to *Short Stories* but, rather paradoxically, placed greater emphasis on serials. In addition to light romance by Winifred Graham and Blanche Eardley, historical adventures by Mary Fermor and Rafael Sabatini, and mysteries by Headon Hill the magazine ran many science fiction and future war serials, most notably "The Outlaws of the Air" (1894) by George Griffith, "The Last King of Atlantis" (1896-7) by George C. Wallis and "The Empress of the Earth" (1898) by M. P. Shiel. *Short Stories* reprinted many items from American sources with the title and authors' names changed. The magazine was originally a 16-page tabloid but shrank to a smaller tabloid format with 32 pages in August 1895. The final issue announced that it would continue as *Smith's Weekly* and is recorded under that title for a further three years but no copies are known to survive[1]. An advertisement in *Pearson's Weekly* tells us that it began with a serial by Arthur Applin.

Publishers: E.& H. Bennett to 8 Jul 1893; then C. A. Pearson
Editors: E.& H. Bennett to 8 Jul 1893; then C. Arthur Pearson to 17 Feb 1900; thereafter probably Percy Everett

Sketch, The [W] 1 February 1893-17 June 1959, 2,989 issues
The companion to, and somewhat modelled on, the *Illustrated London News*, *The Sketch*, encased in its shell of adverts, consisted mostly of society photographs, art studies, theatre and (later) cinema features. It usually published only one story per issue, including the series "Tales With a Sting", which featured stories by Marjorie Bowen, Barbara Cartland, E. M. Delafield, Douglas Newton G. B. Stern and Ralph Stock. It can lay claim to publishing the first short stories by Walter de la Mare ("Kismet", 7 Aug 1895) and Agatha Christie (the series "The Grey Cells of M. Poirot", from 7 Mar 1923). It also promoted the early artwork of W. Heath Robinson (from 1905), and created something of a national icon in the shape of G. E. Studdy's lovable puppy Bonzo (from 1921). It ran many illustrations by Sidney H. Sime including those to illustrate a series by Lord Dunsany (1910/11) that became *The Book of Wonder*. Besides other Agatha Christie series it also ran a Clubfoot series by Valentine Williams (1923), and further stories about Algernon Blackwood's "Dudley & Gilderoy" (1930). L. P. Hartley contributed the column "The Literary Lounger" in the 1930s.
Publisher: Illustrated London News & Sketch
Editors: Clement Shorter with J. M. Bulloch (1893-99); John Latey (1899-1902); John Keble Bell (1902-04); Bruce Ingram (1905-59, assisted by Harry Hearson to 1955 and Hazel Rogers to 1959).

Smith's Weekly *see Short Stories*

The Sphere [W] 27 January 1900 to 27 January 1964, 3,343 issues
One of the brash new illustrated weeklies created by Clement Shorter (along with *The Tatler*) after he left the *Illustrated London News*. Like its close rival, *The Graphic*, which it eventually absorbed, *The Sphere* focused on news stories and society features and though it ran fiction – usually only one or two stories per issue – it was never a main feature. It initially published work by Hall Caine, Robert W. Chambers, Marie Corelli, Thomas Hardy, A.E.W. Mason,

---

[1] It should not be confused with the Australian newspaper of that name which ran from 1 March 1919 to 28 October 1950.

Katherine Mansfield and Edith Nesbit, amongst others, but it subsequently confined fiction to its beautiful Christmas issues.
Publisher: Illustrated Newspapers.
Editors: Clement Shorter (1900-26, assisted by John M. Bulloch to 1909); Jesse Heitner (1926-60); John Oliver (1960-64).

Sunday Journal/Story Journal, The [W]   8 March 1909-31 August 1914, 287 issues
A story paper remembered today solely because Edgar Wallace was briefly its editor. It ran many of his stories, starting from the first issue with his serialised soldier's love story "O.C." Initially in small tabloid format as *The Sunday Journal*, with colour covers, the change of name (from 6 Sep 1909) may have been to avoid confusion with the religious papers. Whilst its contents did include a number of sentimental romances it ran much else besides, though frequently one-pagers or short stories of incident rather than anything substantial. It switched to a standard tabloid format from issue #84 (10 October 1910), pitching into the story-paper market rather than the slimmer novelettes. Regular contributors included L. J. Beeston, Clare Thornton and Katharine Tynan.
Publisher: London Publishing (Edward Hulton).
Editors: Many, including Edgar Wallace during summer of 1913.

Sunday Strand, The   January 1900-June 1910, 126 issues.
Not to be confused with *The Strand* of which this was its more sedate companion. It had an independent life publishing material intended for Sunday reading. It incorporated Newnes's previous weekly *Home Magazine* from January 1901. It ran material by many of *The Strand*'s regulars including L.T. Meade, Edith Nesbit, Fred M. White and William Le Queux and was attractively illustrated by Charles Robinson, Arthur Rackham and Paul Hardy. It favoured historical stories (such as "Tales of Early Christians" by S. N. Sedgwick) or light humour and seldom ran stories of stern moralising. It serialised some charming children's fantasies including "The Dwindleberry Zoo" (1906-7) by G. E. Farrow. Its non-fiction was primarily religious, promoting the wonders of God's creation, and included a life of Christ by Ian Maclaren. It finally merged with *Woman at Home*.
Publisher: Newnes.
Editors: George Clarke (1900-3); Alfred B. Cooper (1903-8); W. Llewelyn Williams (1908-10).

T. P.'s Magazine   October 1910-July 1912, 22 issues
T.P.O'Connor was renowned in his day both as an Irish Nationalist MP and a radical journalist. He founded what many regard as the first modern newspaper, *The Star*, in 1887, followed by *The Sun* (1893) and *T.P.'s Weekly* (1902). He briefly flirted with the standard popular magazine but *T.P.'s Magazine*, was too much like his other publications to make any additional impact and the monthly schedule gave little opportunity for topical articles. Each issue ran two or three short stories, of which the only memorable item was "The Strange Man" by Maurice Leblanc (Dec 1910).
Publisher: T.P.'s Magazine
Editors: T. P. O'Connor, with Wilfred Whitten (1910-11) and George Holbrook Jackson (1911-12).

Temple Bar December 1860-December 1906, 553 issues
One of the more successful shilling monthlies that erupted in imitation of *The Cornhill*. It was the usual mixture of fiction, poetry and articles. Under Sala and Yates the fiction favoured sensational serials such as Sala's own "The Seven Sons of Mammon" (1861) and Mary E. Braddon's "Aurora Floyd" (1863). In 1866 it was taken over by Richard Bentley and soon incorporated *Bentley's Miscellany*, one of the better early Victorian magazines. It now featured several of Bentley's more renowned authors, including Wilkie Collins and Charles Reade and also attracted work from Robert Louis Stevenson, Florence Marryat and Anthony Trollope. Amongst the short fiction were two of Arthur Conan Doyle's early stories, plus work from Mrs Henry Wood, Rhoda Broughton, Amelia B. Edwards and George Gissing. Although *Temple Bar* prospered under Bentley it never achieved the circulation heights of its early years (estimated at 30,000) and by 1896 was as low as 8,000. The magazine passed to Macmillan's, under Bentley's editorship, but fared no better. It ran serials and stories by E. F. Benson, D. K. Broster, Agnes & Egerton Castle, S. R. Crockett, Beatrice Grimshaw and, more significantly, the first fiction by Arthur Ransome ("The Pipe from the Rue Pignon", Feb 1906), who was assistant editor in the magazine's final year. However none of this, nor a half-hearted attempt to convert it to a sixpenny monthly in 1906, improved sales. An index of contents to 1900 is in Volume 3 of *The Wellesley Index to Victorian Periodicals*.
Publishers: Ward and Lock for Proprietors John Maxwell (1860-62) and George Augustus Sala (1862-66) Richard Bentley (1866-98); Macmillan (1898-1906).
Editors: George Augustus Sala (1860-63); Edmund Yates (1863-67); George Bentley (1867-95); Richard Bentley (1895-1900); Gertrude Mayer (1901-6).

Temple Magazine, The October 1896-September 1903, 84 issues
The Temple was the brainchild of Silas K. Hocking intended, in his words, "for the home, the church and the school." Effectively it was yet another Sunday magazine, in the style of *The Quiver*, issued as a sixpenny monthly (80 pages) profusely illustrated with artwork and photographs. Fiction accounted for about 40% of the contents, and included work by Arthur Quiller-Couch, Hocking himself and his brother Joseph, S. Baring-Gould, L. T. Meade, Gilbert Parker, Katharine Tynan, G. A. Henty and other Sunday magazine regulars. Little of its fiction has survived the test of time but its articles retain a scholarly interest, and occasional features such as a symposium started by Robert Barr on "How to Write a Short Story" (Mar 1897), with contributions by Arthur Morrison, L.T. Meade and George Manville Fenn and others, are of literary value. The magazine went through a rapid succession of editors but otherwise remained consistent. James Thorpe was a little unfair when he categorised the magazine amongst the "great unwanted" but it is true that it offered nothing that was not available elsewhere.
Publisher: Horace Marshall.
Editor: Frederick A. Atkins (1896-98); David Williamson (1898-99); John Foster Fraser (1899-1900); Charles Herbert (1900-3).

Thriller, The [W] 9 February 1929-10 May 1940, 589 issues
Although crime and detective fiction had long been a staple of the Amalgamated Press's boys' papers, *The Thriller* was a departure in that it was devoted to the type of mystery/adventure yarn chiefly associated with the 1920s' most popular author, Edgar Wallace (the word "thriller", a replacement for the older "shocker", was new in the twenties, and Wallace was the

prince of thriller-writers). It was the brainchild of Monty Haydon, supervising editor of a group of the A.P.'s papers, including the *Magnet*, *Gem*, *Union Jack* and *Detective Weekly*. With *The Thriller*, Haydon and editor Len Pratt succeeded in creating the British crime-fiction story paper which most closely resembled the American pulp magazines (in content, not format). Although mainly for boys, many of its stories were reprinted in book form for the adult market. Edgar Wallace was present in the first issue, with his novella "Red Aces" and he followed this with a couple more original novellas in the succeeding months – but thereafter all Wallace stories were reprints. Most of the fiction, which usually consisted of a 25,000-word novella plus a serial segment or short story per issue, was provided by a stable of less famous authors which included Anthony Skene, Hugh Clevely, Edmund Snell, Ladbroke Black, Gerard Fairlie, Sydney Horler, John Hunter, Barry Perowne (who revived E. W. Hornung's gentleman jewel-thief, A. J. Raffles, for this weekly), John G. Brandon, Roland Daniel, Bruce Graeme, John Creasey, Peter Cheyney, Edwy Searles Brooks (usually writing as Berkeley Gray), Geo. E. Rochester and Captain W. E. Johns. There were occasional women writers, such as Margery Allingham and Evadne Price. Perhaps the most distinguished contributor was Leslie Charteris, who developed his laughing desperado character "the Saint" for *The Thriller* (from "The Five Kings", May 4, 1929) – and thus did most to set the tone for this fondly-remembered paper. It was retitled *War Thriller* for its last 11 issues.
Publisher: Amalgamated Press.
Editor: Leonard Pratt (with Percy Montague Haydon as Supervising Editor).

Thrills Undated [1939], 1 issue
A standard adventure pulp with stories reprinted from American magazines. Not all sources for the stories have been traced but they may mostly be from magazines once published by William Clayton. *Thrills* looked like an attempt by the publisher to revive *World Stories* but hopes of a second issue was dashed by the onslaught of World War II.
Publisher: Atlas Publishing. *Editor:* None credited; possibly Paul Imbush.

Tit-Bits [W] 22 Oct 1881-9 June 1984, 5,107 issues
Newnes's first magazine, the success of which laid the foundation for Newnes's empire and the birth of *The Strand*. It was always planned as a miscellany incorporating fascinating "tit-bits" of news, gossip and stories, initially extracted from other newspapers but soon editorially written or contributed. The circulation grew on the back of prize contests and insurance offers and early short stories were mostly anonymous and trivial. The real success came with the £1000 prize-winning serial "What's Bred in the Bone" (1891) by Grant Allen, whilst J. E. Preston Muddock's "For God and the Czar" (1892) was another circulation builder. *Tit-Bits* continued to be a money winner and to publish short fiction throughout much of its life but its importance to the development of the fiction magazine faded rapidly during the 1890s. There was a related weekly *Tit-Bit Novels* (239 issues, 15 Jul 1911-5 Feb 1916) which usually ran one short novel per issue with occasional filler short fiction when necessary.
Publisher: Newnes.
Editors: George Newnes (1881); Peter Keary (1882-90); Galloway Fraser (1890-1918); Leonard Crocombe (1918-46); Trevor Henley (1946-64); Eric Grimshaw (1965); R. T. Payne (1966); H. Weisbloom (1967-68); Perrot Phillips (1969).

To-Day [W] 11 November 1893-19 July 1905, 611 issues. Incorporated with *London Opinion*. *To-Day* was a twopenny weekly literary paper founded by Robert Barr and W.A. Dunkerley in the hope of regaining *The Idler* to themselves (*see Section 1*). However Jerome handled both publications with equal aplomb, assisted by Ernest Bramah. He introduced into *To-Day* a regular supply of fiction from Robert Louis Stevenson, Rudyard Kipling, Bret Harte, W. Clark Russell, Mary E. Braddon, Israel Zangwill and others. The paper was an instant success and was Jerome's delight, but following a libel case the paper was sold to Horatio Bottomley. Thereafter it became politically orientated and lost the sparkle that had made it popular. The title was re-used by Holbrook Jackson when he renamed *T.P.'s Weekly* in 1916 and then launched an entirely new magazine as *To-Day* in March 1917 as a sixpenny monthly. Though it was promoted as running fiction it was generally a literary and political review. It ran for 58 issues until December 1923.
Publishers: W. A. Dunkerley (1893-97); Horatio Bottomley (1897-1905).
Editors: Jerome K. Jerome (1893-97); Barry Pain (1897-99); George Wedlake (1900-1); Frank Rutter and Ladbroke Black (1902-4), Black alone (1904-5).

Woman April 1924-July 1929, 64 issues
A high quality 96-page flat-format shilling slick magazine issued to celebrate the world of the "New Woman". It was a fitting companion to the recently upgraded *Hutchinson's Magazine*. It was always attractive with bright art-deco covers by Rilette and copious internal artwork. There were regular features by Lady Cynthia Asquith, Marie Belloc Lowndes and Lady Eleanor Smith. Fiction was a key element with a serial and four or five stories per issue. Cosmo Hamilton was the most represented author; other regulars include Michael Arlen, E.F. Benson (with several 'spook stories' leaching over from *Hutchinson's*), Marjorie Bowen, Richmal Crompton, Margery H. Lawrence, Elinor Mordaunt, Baroness von Hutten and Alec Waugh. There were serials by E. F. Benson, Mary Borden, George Moore and May Sinclair. The magazine was merged with *Hutchinson's Story Magazine*. It is not connected to the present-day weekly magazine *Woman* started in 1937 by Odhams Press.
Publisher: Hutchinson. *Editors:* Miss Jerome; Ida Lascelles.

Woman's Journal November 1927-February 2002, 889 issues. (Retitled *Woman's Home Journal* from June 1967-February 1969.)
A hefty 192-page women's slick magazine, priced one shilling, set up to rival *Good Housekeeping*, *Woman* and *Home Magazine*. Given the strap line "A Magazine of Home Interests", there were the inevitable sections on fashion, cooking, and domestic issues, which filled almost a third of each issue, but there were always four or five stories plus one or two serials, plus occasional articles of literary interest. Warwick Deeping had the honour of the lead serial in the first issue with "Old Pybus" whilst the back-up serial was "Octavia" by Margot Oxford (her first novel) plus stories by Pamela Frankau, Fannie Hurst and Ring Lardner, amongst others. April 1928 started John Galsworthy's last Forsyte novel "Swan Song" whilst the June 1928 issue included one of A. A. Milne's Pooh stories, "Eeyore Joins the Game" not only illustrated by E. H. Shepard but with a photograph of Christopher Robin and Piglet. That same issue has J. B. Priestley writing on how he creates his characters. It was difficult to maintain this high quality but even well into the 1930s, when the magazine had slimmed to 132

pages, fiction still took pride of place on the contents page. Although the type of story had slipped to more routine women's fare on the whole – with authors Vicki Baum, Fanny Hurst, Phyllis Bottome and Sophie Kerr – it could still present a new thriller serial by Dornford Yates ("Storm Music") and a complete novel by Margaret Turnbull. Fiction remained a key content until the 1960s, when H. E. Bates was a contributor, but thereafter it faded in significance.
Publisher: Amalgamated Press (later IPC).
Editor: Harold W. Snoad (until 1944); Dorothy M. Sutherland (1946-64); Ailsa Garland (1965-66); Edith Teague (1967-69); Kathleen Jones (1970-78); Laurie Purden (1978-88); Deirdre Vine (1989-97); Marcelle d'Argy Smith (1998); Elsa McAlonan (1999-2002).

World & His Wife, The November 1904-May 1910, 67 issues
A large tabloid slick sixpenny monthly described as a "magazine for the home". It was issued with a children's supplement, *Playbox*, which became a separate annual from 1911. Although the emphasis was on fashion and society gossip, each issue ran four or five short stories and a serial. Contributors in the first few volumes included E. F. Benson, Keble Howard, Arthur Morrison, W. Pett Ridge and J. J. Bell. Later years included Oliver Onions, Georgia Pangborn, James Barr, Morley Roberts, Gouverneur Morris and J. M. Barrie ("The O'Reilly", Jan 1909). H. de Vere Stacpoole had a serial "The Drums of War" (1908-9) and Edgar Jepson contributed his series "Garthoyle Gardens" (from Mar 1909). There was work by most leading artists including W. Russell Flint, Cyrus Cuneo, Mabel Lucie Attwell and Fred Pegram and early issues reprinted American covers by Jessie Willcox Smith.
Publisher: Amalgamated Press. *Editor:* Laurence Clarke, 1908-1910 (and possibly all issues).

Yellow Book April 1894-April 1897, 13 issues
The most memorable of the literary and artistic periodicals of the 1890s, and a major part of the aesthetic movement. It was published quarterly in hardcover priced at 5 shillings (the equivalent today of over £20). It is best remembered for its artwork by Aubrey Beardsley which resulted in the magazine being vilified during the Oscar Wilde trial. At that time (from issue 5) Beardsley's work was dropped. The degree of fiction in the magazine and the range and importance of the authors is often overlooked. Contributors included Henry James (3 stories starting with "The Death of the Lion", Apr 1894), H. G. Wells ("A Slip Under the Microscope", Jan 1896), John Buchan ("A Journey of Little Profit", Apr 1896), Baron Corvo ("Stories Toto Told Me", Apr 1896), plus the first story by Arnold Bennett ("A Letter Home", 1895). There were also poetry and other contributions by W. B. Yeats, Edmund Gosse, Max Beerbohm, George Gissing, E. Nesbit, Richard Le Gallienne and sub-editor Ella D'Arcy, plus artwork by Walter Sickert, Laurence Housman and Charles Conder. The magazine was initially a success but folded with the adverse public reaction following the Wilde trial. It nevertheless outlived its rival *The Savoy*. A complete index is *The Yellow Book: A Checklist and Index* by Mark Samuels Lasner (Eighteen Nineties Society, 1998).
Publisher: John Lane (with Elkin Matthews for first four issues).
Editor: Henry Harland.

*

Note on British editions.

Background

The unsatisfactory position regarding international copyright in the nineteenth century meant that it was easy for material published in British magazines to be pirated in America and elsewhere. In Europe the matter was controlled when most of the leading nations signed the Berne Convention in 1886, but the United States withheld (it did not become a signatory until 1988). In Britain the Society of Authors (created in 1884 by Walter Besant) brought pressure upon the United States so that in 1891 the US introduced the International Copyright Treaty which agreed (in theory more than practice) to respect British copyright. Nevertheless, for British copyright to be protected it was usually necessary for an item to be published in the United States within thirty days of its British appearance, which led to a rapid exchange of material between British and American magazines.

Some publishers had already acceded to copyright protection, most notably the Harper Brothers. They had originally pirated British material just like other US publishers for the early issues of *Harper's New Monthly Magazine*, started in June 1850. Within a couple of years, though, the Harpers came to an agreement with British authors and publishers to run "advance sheets" from British sources, but it was still several years before this settled down. Starting from December 1880, a European edition of *Harper's* was published in London. Volume 62 of the US edition became volume 1 of the European. It was printed from the American plates, except for the columns of the "Editor's Easy Chair" and the record of recent events called the "Historical Record" where the English publisher, Sampson, Low, made their own notes. *Harper's* acquired world serial rights which allowed them to publish the European edition. On those occasions when they were unable to acquire these rights the item would be dropped from the European edition and an original item inserted. Generally, though, the European and American editions were the same. During its first two decades it ran several significant serials by British authors including "A Laodicean" (1881) and "Jude the Obscure" (1894-5) by Thomas Hardy (the latter under the title "Hearts Insurgent") and most notably "Trilby" (1894) by George du Maurier, the most popular novel of the 1890s. The European edition was taken over by Osgood, McIlvaine (a subsidiary of Harper's) in June 1891 and in 1897, after Osgood's death, the firm was absorbed back into Harper's. There remained a distinct European edition, published directly by Harper's, until May 1918.

Amongst other leading American magazines establishing British editions at this time, the most notable was *Lippincott's* in 1890 with Ward, Lock as the British publisher. It was renowned for publishing the second Sherlock Holmes story "The Sign of the Four" (February 1890) and Oscar Wilde's "The Picture of Dorian Gray" (July 1890). Also of import were *The Century* in 1881 from Frederick Warne (later run by T. Fisher Unwin from 1886, Macmillan from 1895 and Hodder & Stoughton from 1910) and *Scribner's* in 1887, also from Frederick Warne, and which serialised Stevenson's "The Master of Ballantrae" from November 1888. These magazines sold for a shilling. The first to compete directly with the sixpenny illustrated monthlies was *McClure's Magazine*, launched in May 1893, but it found competition difficult and the London office closed within a year. *McClure's* had originally been planned as an American edition of *The Idler* and the two magazines had a brief exchange arrangement.

OTHER MAGAZINES

During the 1890s it became common for American publishers to establish their own London office for simultaneous publication of their magazines. This was especially true with the growing number of cheap magazines, including many pulps, such as those published by Street and Smith in New York starting with *Smith's Magazine* from April 1905. Until the outbreak of the Second World War, most of the British editions were identical to the American save only for the cover price and advertisements. It was not until the 1920s that a few magazines, like *The Smart Set*, introduced some original fiction, whilst others, most notably *Good Housekeeping* and *Harper's Bazaar*, had independent British editions with autonomous control over original contents.

Definition.
This brings us to the need to distinguish between various types of "British edition".
(1) British and American editions are identical in every respect except that the front cover bears a British price and usually has a British address on the back cover. This was the prevailing practice by the end of the 1890s and continued generally into the 1930s. Such magazines are not covered here.
(2) This is similar to the above except that the British edition runs different advertisements and the editor may have discretion to run different editorial matter or small filler items. This was the case with the European edition of *Harper's* and became more common in the 1920s.
(3) This is where the British publisher has more autonomy and may change contents between issues or even introduce occasional new material. The main example covered below is *The Smart Set*. The practice became common after the outbreak of the Second World War when import restrictions and paper rationing limited the magazine's size. This applies to most of the pulp magazines issued in Britain from 1939 to 1963, which is generally outside the scope of this book but includes some magazines (*Short Stories*, *West*, *Astounding Science Fiction*) which were already circulating in Britain during the 1920s and 1930s.
(4) This is where the British publisher has complete autonomy and the magazine takes on an existence independent from its American parent linked by a common name and some share of contents. The main example covered in this volume is *Good Housekeeping*. The same later happened to *Harper's Bazaar*, which is covered below.

Schedule of Titles
The following lists the British editions of American magazines in addition to those already noted above. It cites only those magazines known to have had a British edition prior to 1940, omitting those under definition (1) above and some minor or ephemeral titles. Dates are given for the British printings but reference is made to the run of the parent edition and of any significant differences. See separate entries in Section 1 for *Frontier Stories* and *The Golden West* and the listing above for *Good Housekeeping*.

Action Stories (Apr 1923-Jan 1928, 58 issues). Published by Hutchinson on behalf of Fiction House (New York). Parent magazine ran from Sep 1921-Fall 1950. Standard pulp.

All-Star Detective Magazine (Jul-Sep 1933, 3 issues; then became *All Detective Magazine*, an identical reprint of US original). Published by World's Work on behalf of Dell Magazines

(New York). Parent magazine ran from Nov 1932-Jan 1935. British edition continued the slot held by *All Star Western & Frontier Magazine* – see under *Empire Frontier* (Section 1).

Astounding Science-Fiction (Aug 1939-Aug 1963, 288 issues; retitled *Analog* from February 1961). Published by Atlas Publishing & Distributing on behalf of Street & Smith (New York). The parent magazine began in Jan 1930 and continues to this day as *Analog*. British edition was an abridged version of the US original reprinting partial issues six or seven months later.

Black Mask (Nov 1939-Nov 1953, 120? issues). Published by Atlas Publishing & Distributing on behalf of Pro-Distribution (New York) and Popular Publications (New York) from 1940. Parent magazine ran from Apr 1920-Jul 1951. Noted crime fiction pulp.

The Golden Book Magazine (Aug 1927-May/Jun 1928, 10 issues). Published by The Fleetway Press for the London office of The Golden Book. British reprint of the American pulp (and sometime semi-slick) of the same name which had started in Jan 1925. Its contents were entirely reprint, selected from a wide range of world literature, and endorsed by an advisory panel. It was the same with the British edition. Hugh Walpole worked with American editor Henry Lanier and an Advisory Board consisting of Somerset Maugham, Laurence Binyon, J. B. Priestley and A. E. Coppard, though most contents were drawn from the US edition. The magazine was similar to the British *Argosy* which survived for far longer.

Harper's Bazaar (Oct 1929-Oct 1970, 493 issues; merged with *Queen* as *Harpers & Queen*). Autonomous British offspring of the US magazine which began as a weekly in Nov 1867 (as *Harper's Bazar*), converting to monthly from May 1901. Initially published by Harper's it was taken over by the Hearst Corporation in 1913. The US title changed to *Harper's Bazaar* at the same time as the British edition was launched by Hearst's National Magazine Co. in London as a large format monthly sophisticated slick, priced 2/-, and a companion to *Nash's Pall Mall* and *Good Housekeeping*. General Editor was Phyllis Joyce Reynolds with Alan Y. McPeake as art and fiction editor. The emphasis was on fashion and society, but it ran one or two stories per issue and included work by Elizabeth Bowen, John Collier, Lord Dunsany, Richard Hughes, Rose Macauley, Dorothy L. Sayers, L.A.G. Strong, Hugh Walpole, Evelyn Waugh and Virginia Woolf. It also serialised Somerset Maugham's "Cakes and Ale" (1930). Anne Scott-James took over as editor from 1945-1951.

The New Magazine (Nov 1910-Aug 1915, 58 issues). Published by the London office of La Salle Publishing (Chicago) until Jan 1912 and then by the London branch of Street & Smith (New York). Successor to *Gunter's Magazine*. A direct reprint of the US parent magazine which ran from Nov 1910-Nov 1915. Listed so as to avoid confusion with Cassell's home-grown *New Magazine* which appeared at the same time (*see Section 1*).

Short Stories (Mar 1920-Jun 1955, 640 issues). Published by World's Work on behalf of Doubleday (New York). Parent magazine began in June 1890 but was revamped as a pulp and ran from Dec 1909-Sep 1954 with later short-lived revivals. The British edition consisted initially of complete reprints of the US edition but dated some eight months later. It was published twice a month between 1922 and 1939. During and after the War the issues became increasingly abridged reducing to a slim 64 pages by the final issues.

OTHER MAGAZINES

The Smart Set (May 1901-Jun 1925, 290 issues). Published by the London Office of Smart Set Publishing until December 1913 then by W. H. Dawson (Jan 1914-Apr 1918), Rolls House Publishing (May 1918-Nov 1922), J.W. Milne (Dec 1922-Sep 1923) and Hutchinson (Oct 1923-Jun 1925). The parent magazine ran from March 1900-Jul 1930. The British edition was initially a straight but reduced reprint, but from 1905 it ran minor new material, mostly fashion, photographs and social notes. Under Hutchinson's it ran more original material, including a serial by E. Temple Thurston, and became heavily illustrated with art-deco covers. Standard size but became large-flat format from Dec 1924. Editors were W. J. Thorold (1905-1911), H. J. Gillespie (1911-1915), James W. Milne (1915-1923) and Kitty Shannon (1923-1925).

Unknown/Unknown Worlds (Sep 1939-Win 1949, 41 issues). Published by Atlas Publishing & Distributing on behalf of Street & Smith (New York). Parent magazine ran from Mar 1939-Oct 1943 (retitled *Unknown Worlds* from Oct 1941; British edition from Mar 1942). Fantasy fiction pulp. The British edition was abridged and was sufficiently popular that it outlived its parent and eked out the contents to survive a further six years.

West (Aug 1926-Feb 1954, 492? issues). Published by World's Work on behalf of Doubleday (New York). Parent magazine ran from 5 Jan 1926-Fall 1953. The British edition consisted initially of complete reprints of the US edition but dated some eight months later. It was published monthly to Feb 1928, twice monthly from Mar 1928-Oct 1939, then monthly. During and after the War the issues became increasingly abridged reducing to a slim 64 pages by the final issues. It merged with *Short Stories* from May 1954.

Western Story Magazine (Sep 1939-Apr 1962, at least 180 issues). Published by Atlas Publishing & Distributing on behalf of Street & Smith (New York). The parent magazine ran from Jul 1919-Jul/Aug 1949 but was revived by Popular Publications from Oct 1952-Jun 1954. The British edition was an abridged version which managed to continue long after the parent magazine's demise. It switched to digest format in Oct 1957.

SUMMARY OF EDITORS AND PUBLISHERS

The following is an alphabetical listing of editors and publishers covered in Sections 1 and 2. Wherever possible the issue months are given for editorial tenure. Editors are listed only if their tenure falls within the period 1880-1950. All roles are as editor unless otherwise noted.

1. Editors

Aitken, A. Donnelly (1892-1962)
 Chums, 1918-1920

Anderson, Alderson
 The Grand Magazine, Feb 1905-1910; *The Magpie*, Aug 1912–Dec 1914

Applin, Arthur (1873-1949)
 The Novel Magazine, 1914

Arnold, Spencer
 Black and White, 1906-1912

Aspden, Hartley (1858-1940)
 Good Woods and Sunday Magazine, 5 May 1906-8 Apr 1911

Atkey, Bertram (1880-1952)
 Assistant *Fry's Magazine*, 1904-1911?

Atkey, Philip (1908-1985)
 Assistant *The Happy Mag.* and *The Sunny Mag.*, 1925–1927

Atkins, Frederick A(nthony) (1864-1929)
 The Temple Magazine, Oct 1896-Sept 1898

Baily, F(rancis) E(vans) (1887-1962)
 The Royal Magazine, sub-editor 1906-1911; editor Jan 1912-Jun 1927 (with gap for War Service, 1917-1918)

Baker, Augustus
 Editorial assistant at Newnes including *The Captain*, 1910-1924

Baldry, Walter Burton (1888-1940)
 Fry's Magazine, Apr 1911-Aug 1914

Barr, Robert (1850-1912)
 The Idler Feb 1892-Jul 1895; Dec 1897-Sept 1898; Oct 1902-Mar 1911

Beaumont, (William) Comyns (1879-1955)
 The Graphic, 1906-1909; *The London Magazine*, 1909-1911; *The Passing Show*, 1915-1919; *Pan*, 1919-1920

Bell, John Keble (*aka* Keble Howard 1875-1928)
 The Sketch, 1902-1904

Bell, Robert Stanley Warren (1871-1921)
 The Captain, Apr 1899-1910

Bennett, E. and H.
 Publishers and probable editors of *Short Stories*, 12 Jan 1889-8 Jul 1893

Bennett, (Joseph) Hannaford (1867- ?)
 The English Illustrated Magazine, Oct 1901-Mar 1903

SUMMARY OF EDITORS AND PUBLISHERS

Bennett, K. Maud,
  The Lady's Magazine, probably all issues, Jan 1901-Mar 1905

Bentley, George (1828-1895)
  Temple Bar, Oct 1867-May 1895

Bentley, Richard (1854-1936)
  Temple Bar, Jun 1895-Dec 1906

Besier, Rudolf (1878-1942)
  Assistant *The Royal Magazine*, probably 1905-1906

Black, Ladbroke [Lionel Day] (1877-1940)
  To-Day, 1902-1905 (joint editor until 1904)

Blackwood, Alexander (1806-1845)
  Blackwood's Magazine, Oct 1834-Apr 1845

Blackwood, George Douglas (1909-1997)
  Blackwood's Magazine, 1948-1976

Blackwood, George William (1876-1942)
  Blackwood's Magazine, 1912-1942

Blackwood, James H. (1878-1951)
  Blackwood's Magazine, 1942-1948

Blackwood, John (1818-1879)
  Blackwood's Magazine, May 1845-Oct 1879

Blackwood, William (1776-1834)
  Blackwood's Magazine, Oct 1817-Sept 1834

Blackwood, William [III] (1836-1912)
  Blackwood's Magazine, Nov 1879-1912

Blake, George (1893-1961)
  Acting editor *The Strand*, 1928-1930

Blathwayt, Raymond (1855-1935)
  The Universal (& Ludgate) Magazine, Nov 1900-Jan 1902

Board, A. W.
  Tip Top Stories/The Regent Magazine, Dec 1923-Jan 1925

Bott, Alan John (1893-1952)
  The Graphic, 1926-1932

Braddon, Mary Elizabeth (1835-1915)
  Belgravia, Nov 1866-Apr 1876 and Jan 1890?

Bramah, Ernest (1868-1942)
  The Minster, Jan-Mar 1896

Broadwell, Albert H. (1871- ?)
  Co-editor *The Red Magazine*, at least to 1909

Brown, Ivor (John Carnegie) (1891-1974)
  Associate editor, *Pall Mall*, Jan-Sept 1929

Bullivant, Cecil H(enry) (1882-1981)
  Managing editor, *The Captain*, 1911-1912

Bulloch, John Malcolm (1867-1938)
  Assistant *The Sketch*, 1893-1899; *The Sphere*, 1900-1909; editor, *The Graphic*, 1909-1924

Campbell, Sir Gilbert (1833-1899)
  Lambert's Monthly, Jan 1890- ?

Campling, F. Knowles (d. 1940)
  Chums, 1915-1918

Carr, J(oseph) W(illiam) Comyns (1849-1916)
  The English Illustrated Magazine, Oct 1883-Sept 1889

Cassell, John (1817-1865)
Founder of Cassell's Publishing, from 1846
  Cassell's Illustrated Family Paper, 1855-Autumn 1859; *The Quiver*, 1861-1863

Chambers, Charles Edward Stuart (1859-1936)
  Chambers's Journal, 1888-1935

Chambers, Robert (1802-1871)
Co-founder of W. & R. Chambers, 1832
  Chambers's Journal, 1833-1858

Chambers, Robert, Jr. (1832-1888)
  Chambers's Journal, 1873-1888

Chambers, William (1800-1883)
Co-founder of W. & R. Chambers, 1832
  Chambers's Journal, 1832-1837

Chancellor, David (1913-1955)
Screen Pictorial, 1937-Sept 1939
Assistant *The Strand* 1940-1946

Chatterton, E(dward) Keble (1878-1944)
The Lady's Realm, in 1904-1906

Chatto, Andrew (1841-1913)
Editor *Belgravia*, Apr 1876-Sept 1889

Clarke, Austin (1897-1974)
Assistant *Argosy*, 1929-1930

Clarke, George (1856-1921?)
The Sunday Strand, Jan 1900- 1903

Clarke, Laurence (Ayscough)
The World & His Wife, 1908-1910 (and possibly all issues from 1904)

Cook, Edward Dutton (1829-1883)
Co-editor *The Cornhill*, 1868-Mar 1871

Cook, Oscar (1889-1952)
Adventure-Story Magazine, 1925; *Mystery-Story Magazine*, 1925

Cooper, Alfred B(enjamin) (1863-1936)
The Sunday Strand, 1903-1908

Cox, John Roberts ["Jack"] (1915-1981)
Boy's Own Paper, 1946-1967

Craig, Isa (1831-1903)
The Argosy, Dec 1865-Sept 1867

Crawfurd, (John) Oswald (Frederick) (1834-1909)
Black and White, 1892?-1895; *Chapman's/Crampton's Magazine*, May 1895-Sept 1900?

Crawfurd-Price, Walter Harrington (1881-1967)
Britannia, Sept 1928-Apr 1929.

Crocombe, Leonard (Cecil) (1890-1968)
Sub-editor *Pearson's Magazine*, 1910
Tit-Bits, 1918-1946

Cruickshank, Miss M.
Home Magazine, Jun 1918-1921

Daniels, Charles H.
Wings, Summer 1934-Jan 1936

de Beck, A(lexis) M(aria) (1863/4- ?)
The Universal Magazine, Feb-Oct 1900

Dell, Draycot M(ontagu) (1888-1940)
Chums, 1926-1939

Dickie, John M(ackinley) (1895- ?)
Chambers's Journal, 1947-1956

Dickson, (Horatio Henry) Lovat (1902-1987)
Lovat Dickson's Magazine, Oct 1934-Mar 1935 (see also under Publishers)

Dilnot, George (1883-1951)
The Detective Magazine, 24 Nov 1922–8 May 1925; *Hush*, Jun 1930–Jun 1931

Dimmock, (Frederick) Haydn (1895-1955)
Scoops, 10 Feb-23 Jun 1934

Dixon, Meredith Vibart (1898- ?)
Adventure-Story, 1926; *Mystery-Story*, 1926; *Hutchinson's (Story) Magazine*, in 1926/7

Doran, George H. (1869-1956)
Nash's and Pall Mall Magazine, 1930-1933

Dunn, James Nicol (1856-1919)
Black & White, 1895-1897; *The Ludgate*, Nov 1895-1897

Dusart, George C(harles) (1864- ?)
The Black Cat, Feb 1898–Jun 1899 (at least) and possibly to Feb 1900

Edwards, Henry Sutherland (1828-1906)
The Graphic, 1869-1870

Evans, H. Norman
Editor at World's Work who may have had all or partial responsibility for *The Master Thriller Series*, [Jul] 1933-[Dec] 1939; *Modern Stories*, Aug 1934-1941 (?); *Mystery*

SUMMARY OF EDITORS AND PUBLISHERS

and Detection, [Autumn] 1934-Oct 1935; *Mystery Stories*, Mar 1936-Feb 1942

Everett, [Sir] Percy W(inn) (1870-1952)
Pearson's Magazine, Jan 1900-Dec 1911; *The Royal Magazine*, May 1901-Dec 1911; *The Novel Magazine*, 1905-1912; probable editor *Short Stories*, 24 Feb 1900-18 Jun 1904.

Fitchew, (Edward) Hubert (1851- ?)
Pall Mall Magazine, Jan 1913-Aug 1914.

Flower, [Sir] (Walter) Newman (1879-1964)
Joined Cassell as editor of *Penny Magazine*, 1906; became a Director in 1915, Proprietor and Managing Director, May 1927, Chairman, 1943 *The Story-Teller*, Apr 1907-May 1928; *The New Magazine*, Apr 1909-1922; *Cassell's Magazine of Fiction*, Apr 1912-1922 (?)

Foster, Ernest (1852-1919)
Chums, 1894-1907

Frankau, Gilbert (1884-1952)
Director, *Britannia*, Sept 1928-Apr 1929

Fraser, Galloway (1861?-1925)
Tit-Bits, 1890-1918

Fraser, (Sir) John Foster (1868-1936)
The Temple Magazine, Oct 1899-Sept 1900

Fry, Charles B(urgess) (1872-1956)
Proprietor and Editorial Director of *Fry's Magazine*, 1904-1917

Geddie, John Liddell (1881-1969)
Chambers's Journal, 1935-1947 (assistant from 1915)

Gibbon, J. M.
Black and White, 1903-1905

Gillespie, H. J.
The Smart Set (BRE), Sept 1911-Mar 1915

Gilligan, Miss G.
The Sovereign Magazine, in 1925/6; *Adventure-Story Magazine*, 1927; *Mystery-Story Magazine*, 1927; *Adventure & Mystery Story Magazine*, 1927-1929; *The Jolly Mag.*, May 1927-Dec 1929; *Hutchinson's (Story) Magazine*, in 1929

Gillings, Walter H(erbert) (1912-1979)
Tales of Wonder, [Jun] 1937-Spring 1942

Goddard, Ernest Hope (1879-1939)
Assistant *The Sketch*, 1905-1939 and *Illustrated London News*, 1909-1939 (and acting editor 1916-1918)

Golding, Harry (1871-1947)
The Windsor Magazine, Sept 1927-Sept 1939

Golsworthy, Arnold (1865-1939)
co-editor *The Butterfly*, May 1893-Feb 1900

Goodwin, Beatrice
The Home Magazine, 1921-1929

Gorell, Lord [Ronald Gorell Barnes] (1884-1963)
The Cornhill, Jun 1933-1939

Graves, Charles L. (1856-1944)
Acting editor, *Cornhill Magazine*, 1898-1899

Greening, Arthur C. (1865- ?)
The Imp, Jun 1907-Nov 1911

Grove, George (1820-1900)
Macmillan's Magazine, May 1868-Apr 1883

Halkett, George R(oland) (1855-1918)
Pall Mall Magazine, Jan 1901-Jun 1905

Halls, Leonard (1893- ?)
Boy's Own Paper, 1942-1946

Hamilton, Lord Frederick (1856-1928)
Pall Mall Magazine, May 1893-Dec 1900

Hammerton, [Sir] John Alexander (1871-1949)
The London Magazine, 1905-1907

Harding, Robert (1897- ?)
Boy's Own Paper, 1935-1942

Harland, Henry (1861-1905)
The Yellow Book, Apr 1894-Apr 1897

Harmsworth, Cecil (1869-1948)
Harmsworth's Magazine, Jul 1898-1902

Hastings, Macdonald (1909-1982)
The Strand, Oct 1946-Mar 1950

Haydon, Arthur Lincoln (1872-1954)
Boy's Own Paper, 1912-1924

Haydon, Percy Montague ["Monty"] (1895-1971)
The Thriller, 9 Feb 1929-19 May 1940

Hayward, Arthur Lawrence (1885-1967)
Chums, 1924-1926

Head, Alice Maud (1886-1981)
The Woman at Home, Aug 1909-May 1918; *Nash's and Pall Mall Magazine*, 1924-1930 (assistant from 1918); *Good Housekeeping*, 1924-1939

Heitner, Jesse (1893-1965)
Director of British National Newspapers Ltd. (later Illustrated Newspapers Ltd.), 1926-1961
Acting Editor *The Graphic*, 1927
Britannia and Eve, 1929-1957; *The Sphere*, 1926-Jun 1960
Editorial Director *The Sketch*, 1958-1959

Henley, (Herbert Francis) Trevor (b. 1906)
Tit-Bits, 1946-1964

Henson, Leslie (1891-1957)
Nominal editor, *The Merry Mag.*, Jul 1924-Jun 1925

Herbert, Charles
The Temple Magazine, Oct 1900-Sept 1903

Higginbottom, Frederick James (1859-1943)
Managing editor, *Pall Mall Magazine*, Jan 1901-Dec 1912

Hocking, Silas K(itto) (1850-1935)
Founder and primary editor of *The Temple Magazine*, 1896

Hogg, James (1806-1888)
Founder and Proprietor *London Society*, 1862-1886 (?)

Home-Gall, William Bolinbroke (1894-1982)
Chums Annual, 1939-1940

Hoole, J.
Romance, 1926-7?

Hornibrook, Evelyn
Possible editor *Standard Stories*, Jul 1925-May 1926; *Best-Story Magazine*, Aug 1926-Apr 1929; *Hutchinson's Magazine*, 1927-29

Hunt, Bonavia (1847-1917)
The Quiver, Jul 1865-1905; *Cassell's Family Magazine*, Dec 1874-Nov 1896

Hutchinson, Arthur (1870-1927)
The Windsor Magazine, Jun 1898-Aug 1927

Hutchinson, A(rthur) S(tuart) M(enteith) (1879-1971)
Assistant *The Royal Magazine*, 1903-1904

Hutchison, George Andrew (1841-1913)
Acting editor *Boy's Own Paper*, 1879-1897; full editor, 1897-1912

Huxley, Leonard (1860-1933)
The Cornhill, Feb 1917-May 1933

Hyatt-Woolf, Charles (1863-1938)
The Ludgate, 1898/9-Feb 1901

Imbush, Paul
Possible editor of *Thrills*, 1939

Ingram, [Sir] Bruce (Stirling) (1877-1963)
The English Illustrated Magazine, Sept 1899-Sept 1901
Editor-in-Chief *Illustrated London News*, 6 Jan 1900-Jan 1963; *The Sketch*, 1905-Jun 1959.

Jackson, George Holbrook (1874-1948)
Acting editor *T.P.'s Magazine*, 1911-Jul 1912

SUMMARY OF EDITORS AND PUBLISHERS

Jerome, Jerome K(lapka) (1859-1927)
The Idler, Feb 1892-Nov 1897; *To-Day*, 1893-1897

Jerome, Miss
Woman, dates unknown

Johns, W(illiam) E(arle) (1893-1968)
Pearson's Magazine, May-Sept 1939

Joyce, Thomas Heath (1850-1925)
The Graphic, 1891-1906

Keary, Peter (1865-1915)
Joint Managing Director and co-Proprietor of C. Arthur Pearson, Ltd., 1890-1915.
Tit-Bits, 1881-1890; *Pearson's Weekly*, 1890-1915; *The Royal Magazine*, Nov 1898-Apr 1901

Kennedy, (Miss) N. W.
The Novel Magazine, 1923-1937

Kinloch-Cooke, Clement (1854–1944)
The English Illustrated Magazine, Oct 1889-Sept 1893

Klickmann, (Emily) Flora (1867–1958)
Assistant *The Windsor Magazine*, 1895-1908; Editor *Everybody's* (later *Everyone's*) *Story Magazine*, Nov 1909-Apr 1914

Lamburn, Frank J.
Pearson's Weekly, 1915?-1932?

Lascelles, Ida
Woman, by 1926

Latey, John (1842-1902)
The Sketch, 1899-1902

Latey, John Lash (1808-1891)
Illustrated London News, 1859-1890

Lawrence, Arthur (1870- ?)
The Idler, May 1899-Aug 1900

Le Couteur, Frank (1887-1950)
The Graphic, 1924-1926

Leggett, H(arry) W(illiam) (1888- ?)
Acting editor *The Grand Magazine*, 1927-1931; full editor 1932-1940

Leith, Alicia A(my) (1851-1945)
Joint editor *Atalanta*, Oct 1887-Sept 1888

Lewes, George Henry (1817-1878)
Joint editor *The Cornhill*, Jun 1862-1864 and 1868-Mar 1871

Liddell, Walter Scott
Acting editor *Nash's and Pall Mall Magazine*, 1915-1917

Locker, Arthur (1828-1893)
The Graphic, 1870-1891

Longman, Charles J(ames) (1852-1934)
Longman's Magazine, Nov 1882-Oct 1905

Lowry, H(enry) D(awson) (1869-1906)
The Ludgate, 1897-1898/9

Lunn, Erle (1895- ?)
Production Manager, Hutchinson & Co., and probable editor *Hutchinson's Story Magazine*, 1919-1921

Macauley, James (1817-1902)
Founder and Supervising editor *Boy's Own Paper*, 1879-1897

MacKenzie, Miss F. C.
Romance, 1925-1926; *20 Story Magazine*, 1927-1934

Macleod, Donald (1831-1916)
Good Words, Jul 1872-Apr 1906

Macleod, Norman (1812-1872)
Good Words, Jan 1860-Jun 1872

McPeake, Alan Young (1899-1987)
Art and Fiction editor *Nash's Pall Mall* and *Good Housekeeping* from 1923; *Pall Mall Magazine*, 1927-29; *Harper's Bazaar* from 1930

McPeake, J(ames) Y(oung) (1868-1924)
Manager Director, *Nash's Magazine/Nash's Pall Mall*, Feb 1911-Sept 1924; *Good Housekeeping*, Mar 1922-Sept 1924

Macrae, R(obert) Stuart (1900- ?)
The Royal/New Royal Magazine, Jul 1927-May 1932

Makin, William J(ames) (1894-1944)
Assistant *Pearson's Weekly*, 1926-1932; *Royal Magazine/Screen Pictorial*, 1926-1934 Editor, *Pearson's Weekly*, 1933?-1935?; *Screen Pictorial*, Jan 1935-1937

Marshall, A(rthur) C(harles) (1879?-1945)
The Crusoe Magazine, Jun 1924-May 1926; and probably *The Golden Mag.*, Jun 1926-Jun 1927 and *The Golden West*, Jul-Dec 1927.

Maschwitz, Eric (1901-1969)
Hutchinson's (Story) Magazine, 1922-1923; *The Sovereign Magazine*, 1922-1923

Masson, David (1822-1907)
Macmillan's Magazine, Nov 1859-Apr 1868

Mathews, Basil (Joseph) (1879-1951)
Outward Bound, Oct 1920-Mar 1924

Maxwell, Perriton (1878-1947)
Nash's Magazine, 1911-1915

May, Philip
Lambert's Monthly, ? - May 1891; *Ludgate Monthly*, May 1891-Apr(?) 1894

Mayer, Gertrude Townshend (1839-1932)
Temple Bar, Jan 1901-Dec 1906 (and assistant from 1898)

Meade, L(illie) T(homasina) (1854-1915)
Atalanta, Oct 1887-Sept 1892

Meadland, Richard L(ewis) (1902-1958)
Nash's–Pall Mall Magazine, 1933-Sept 1937

Mee, Arthur (1875-1943)
Black and White, 1901?-1903

Milne, James W.
The Smart Set (BRE), Apr 1915-Sept 1923 (and Publisher, Dec 1922-Sept 1923)

Minney, R(ubeigh) J(ames) (1895-1979)
The Strand, Oct 1941-May 1942

Morley, Charles (1847-1916)
Pall Mall Magazine, Jul 1905-Dec 1912

Morley, John (1838-1923)
Macmillan's Magazine, May 1883-Sept 1885

Morrah, Herbert (1870-1939)
The Argosy, 1899-1901

Morris, Mowbray (1847-1911)
Macmillan's Magazine, Oct 1885-Oct 1907

Muir (Charles) Augustus (1892-1989)
The Passing Show, 1920-1924

Nash, James Eveleigh (1873-1956)
Publisher and editor *Nash's Magazine*, Apr 1909-Jan 1911; *Nash's Weekly*, 14 Jun 1919-10 Apr 1920

Naumann, Paul (1862- ?)
Publisher and editor *Eureka/Favorite Magazine*, 1897-1903.

Newnes, [Sir] George (1851-1910)
Proprietor and Managing Director, George Newnes, Ltd., 1881-1910; founding editor of *Tit-Bits* (1881), *The Strand Magazine* (1891) and *The Grand Magazine* (1905)

Nicholson, Ivor (Percy) (1891-1937)
Assistant *Nash's and Pall Mall Magazine*, 1924-1928; full editor *Pall Mall Magazine*, May 1927-Sept 1929

Northcroft, George J. H. (1868- ?)
Boy's Own Paper, 1933-1935

O'Connor, T(homas) P(ower) (1848-1929)
Founder and editor *T.P.'s Magazine*, Oct 1910-Jul 1912

SUMMARY OF EDITORS AND PUBLISHERS

Odle, E(dwin) V(incent) (1890-1942)
The Argosy, 1926-1935

O'Donnell, W. A.
Possible editor *All-Story Magazine*, 1926-1927; editor *The Red Magazine*, 1927-1931

O'Farrell, Philip (Howard Handley)
Pearson's Magazine, Jan 1912-Dec 1919

Oliver, Edwin (1866-1950)
Atalanta, Oct 1896-Sept 1898; *The Idler*, Oct 1898-Apr 1899; possibly *The Charing Cross Magazine*, Jan-Aug 1900

Pain, Barry (1865-1928)
To-Day, 1897-1899

Parker, Oscar
The English Illustrated Magazine, Mar 1905-Aug 1913

Parker, Percy Livingstone (1867-1925)
Harmsworth's (London) Magazine, Feb 1899-1902 (assistant from Jul 1898)

Payn, James (1830-1898)
Chambers's Journal, 1858-1873 (jointly to 1862); *The Cornhill*, Jan 1883-Jun 1896

Pearson, [Sir] C(yril) Arthur (1866-1921)
Proprietor and Managing Director of C. Arthur Pearson, Ltd., 1890-1921
Pearson's Weekly, 1890; *The Search Light*, Mar 1892-Sept 1894; *Short Stories*, 15 Jul 1893-17 Feb 1900; *Pearson's Story-Teller*, 9 Oct 1895-at least Feb 1896; *Pearson's Magazine*, Jan 1896-Dec 1899

Pemberton, Max (1863-1950)
Cassell's (Family) Magazine, Dec 1876-Nov 1905; *Chums*, 1892-1894

Perris, George Herbert (1866-1920)
Crampton's Magazine, Oct 1900-Nov 1901

Peters, A(ugustus) D(udley) (1892-1973)
Pan, 1920-1921

Platnauer, J. B.
Pearson's Weekly, 1936-1939

Pocklington, Geoffrey Richard (1879-1958)
Boy's Own Paper, 1924-1933

Poole, Reginald (Heber) (1885-1959)
Fiction Editor United Newspapers, 1921-1923

Pound, Reginald
The Strand, Jun 1942-Sept 1946

Pratt, Leonard E(rnest) (1889-1966)
Probable editor *The Violet Magazine*, Jul 1922-Dec 1929

Preston, Miss Philippa
Romance, 1923 (formerly *Everywoman's*)

Price, T. A.
Gaiety, until 1926

Quennell, Peter (1905-1993)
The Cornhill, 1944-1951

Ransome, Arthur (1884-1967)
Assistant *Temple Bar*, 1905-1906

Raven-Hill, Leonard (1867-1942)
Founder and joint-editor *The Butterfly*, May 1893-Feb 1900; Publisher, *The Minster*, Jan-Mar 1896

Reynolds, Phyllis Joyce (1898- ?)
Harper's Bazaar, 1929-1944

Rittenberg, Max (1880- ?)
Possible editor *The Lady's Realm*, Jul 1911-May 1916 (?); *The Club Room*, 1913-1914 (?)

Robinson, Ernest H(erbert) (1880-1947)
Chums, 1907-1915

Robinson, Frederick William (1830-1901)
Home Chimes, Jan 1884-Dec 1894

Robinson, Oliver (1908- ?)
Good Housekeeping, 1940-1967

Rosman, Alice Grant (1887-1961)
Assistant, *The Grand Magazine*, 1923-1927

Ross, W. D.
Black and White, 1897-1900

Rutter, Frank (1876-1937)
Co-editor *To-Day*, 1902-1904

Sanders, E. N.
Assistant *The Strand*, 1899-1928

Sandow, Eugene [real name Friedrich Wilhelm Mueller] (1867-1925)
Founder/editor-in-chief *Physical Culture/Sandow's Magazine*, Apr 1898-Jul 1907

Sandys, Oliver (real name Marguerite Jervis, 1890?-1964)
Sub-editor *Sievier's Monthly*, Jan 1909 (and a few thereafter)

Sarl, Arthur J. (1880–1946)
Yes or No, possibly 1910-1918

Scott, Eric Clement
The London Magazine, 1907-1909

Scott-James, Anne (b. 1913)
Harper's Bazaar, 1945-1951

Sellicks, Frank
The Blue Magazine, Jul 1919-?

Shackleton, [Sir] Ernest (Henry) (1874-1922)
Assistant *The Royal Magazine*, 1902-1903

Shand, Elsie H.
The Home Magazine, 1930-1931

Shannon, Kitty
The Smart Set (BRE), Oct 1923-Nov 1924 (and possibly to Jun 1925)

Shaw, Herbert
The Happy Mag., 1932-1940.

Shaw, (Percy) Reeves (1886-1952)
Editorial assistant at C. Arthur Pearson, Ltd., 1903-1910; Editor at George Newnes, Ltd., from 1910, rising to Chief editor 1930-1941
The Captain, 1910-1922; *The Grand Magazine*, 1920-1931; *The Happy Mag.* Jun 1922-1931; *The Crusoe Magazine*, Jun 1924-May 1926; *The Sunny Mag.*, Jul 1925-Apr 1933; *The Golden Mag.*, Jun 1926-Jun 1927 and possibly *The Golden West*, Jul 1927-Dec 1928; *The Strand*, Jan 1931-Sept 1941

Shorter, Clement King (1857-1926)
Illustrated London News, 1891-1900; *The Sketch*, 1893-1899; *The English Illustrated Magazine*, Oct 1893-Aug 1899
Director of The Sphere and the Tatler Company, 1900-1926, where edited both *The Sphere* and *The Tatler*

Shurey, Charles (1859-1935)
Co-Proprietor, with Harry Shurey (1860-1924), and chief editor, Shurey Publications, 1892-1933

Sievier, Robert (1860-1939)
Sievier's Monthly, Jan 1909-Nov 1910

Sime, Sidney H(erbert) (1867-1941)
Eureka, autumn 1897-Feb 1898; *The Idler*, Sept 1900-Feb 1901 (also Art Editor from May 1899)

Sisley, Charles P(ercival) (1867-1934)
The London Magazine, 1902-Dec 1905

Smith, George (1824-1901)
Head of Smith & Elder, 1846-1901
Publisher and chief editor of *The Cornhill Magazine*, 1860-1897

Smith, H(erbert) Greenhough (1851-1935)
The Strand, Jan 1891-Dec 1930; *The Grand Magazine*, 1905

Smith, James Walter (1868-1931)
US edition of *The Strand*, 1896-1908; *Cassell's Magazine*, Dec 1908-Mar 1912

Smith, Reginald John (1857-1916)
Head of Smith, Elder & Co., 1901-1916
The Cornhill Magazine, 1897-1916

SUMMARY OF EDITORS AND PUBLISHERS

Smith, Vere (1871- ?)
Proprietor *The Lady's Realm*, May 1910-May 1916; editor, 1907-1911 and possibly beyond

Smith, (Henry) Wood (1865-1906)
Assistant, *The London Magazine*, 1906

Snoad, Harold W.
Woman's Journal, 1927?-1944; *The Argosy*, Feb 1940-1944?

Sprigg, Stanhope W(illiam) (1867-1932)
The Windsor Magazine, Jan-Dec 1895
Assistant *Cassell's Magazine*, 1909-1910

Sprigg, T(heodore) Stanhope (1903-1977)
Air Stories, May 1935-Apr 1940; *War Stories*, Oct 1935-Feb 1936; *Western Adventures*, Feb-Jun 1936 ; *Fantasy*, [Jul] 1938-[Jul] 1939

Spurgeon, [Sir] Arthur (1861-1938)
General Manager/Managing Director, Cassell & Co., 1905-1922

Staples, John C.
Joint editor *Atalanta*, Oct 1888-Sept 1892

Stephen, (Sir) Leslie (1832-1904)
The Cornhill Magazine, Apr 1871-Dec 1882

Stock, John A(lexander) (1875-?)
The Red Magazine, 1908?-1926?; *The Green Magazine*, 7 Nov 1922-18 Dec 1923; *The Yellow Magazine*, 23 Sept 1921-17 Sept 1926

Stoddart, Jane T(homson) (1863-1944)
The Woman at Home, Oct 1893-Jul 1909

Strachey, John St. Loe (1860-1927)
The Cornhill Magazine, Jul 1896-Dec 1897

Straight, Sir Douglas (1844-1914)
Joint editor, *Pall Mall Magazine*, May 1893-Aug 1896

Strong, L(eonard) A(lfred) G(eorge) (1896-1958)
Lovat Dickson's Magazine, Apr-Jun 1935

Sutherland, Dorothy M.
The Argosy, 1945?-1964; *Woman's Journal*, 1946-1964

Symington, A. B.
Joint editor *Atalanta*, Oct 1892-Sept 1896

Symons, Arthur (1865-1945)
The Savoy, Jan-Dec 1896

Thompson, John
Assistant *Pearson's Magazine*, 1908-1912

Thompson, P(iers) Gilchrist (1893-1969)
Lovat Dickson's Magazine, Nov 1933-Sept 1934

Thorne, Isabel (Mary)
Yes or No, 5 Aug 1905-24 Apr 1922; *Weekly Tale-Teller*, 8 May 1909-29 Apr 1916

Thorold, William James (1871-1942)
The Smart Set (BRE), 1905-Aug 1911

Tremayne, Harold (1861?-1908)
Crampton's Magazine, Dec 1901-Dec 1902

Turner, Arthur M.
Gaiety, 1926-1927

Vickers, Roy (William Edward) (1889-1965)
Novel Magazine, 1915-1918

Vincent, Louis (1876- ?)
Assistant *The London Magazine*, 1908 (exact dates unknown); editor *Lloyd's Magazine*, probably all issues 1917-1923

Vivian, Charles
Assistant *Pearson's Magazine*, 1910-1912
editor *The Novel Magazine*, 1912-1914 and 1919-1922; *Cassell's Magazine of Fiction*, 1922-1924; *The Corner Magazine*, Sept 1922-1924; *The New Magazine*, 1922-1924

Vivian, E(velyn) Charles (1882-1947)
Adventure-Story Magazine, 1922-1924; *Mystery-Story Magazine*, 1922-1924

Wade, John Reed (1880?- ?)
  Assistant *Short Stories*, probably 1900-1904
  Editor *Pearson's Magazine*, Jan 1920-Apr 1939; *The New Royal Magazine/Royal Pictorial*, Jun 1932-Dec 1934

Waite, A(rthur) E(dward) (1857-1942)
  Horlick's Magazine, Jan 1904-Jun 1905

Wallace, (Richard Horatio) Edgar (1875-1932)
  The Story Journal, during summer 1913;
  Nominal editor, *Hush*, Jun 1930-Jun 1931

Walpole, (Sir) Hugh (Seymour) (1884-1941)
  The Golden Book (BRE), Aug 1927-May 1928

Ward, Francis (1889- ?)
  Sub-editor *The London Magazine*, 1910-1912;
  Assistant 1912-1931; editor 1931-1933
  The Red Magazine, 1933-1935

Watson, Alfred Edward Thomas (1849-1922)
  Badminton Magazine, Aug 1895-Dec 1922

Wedlake, George (1848- ?)
  To-Day, 1900-1901

Whitelaw, David (1876-1971)
  Assistant *The Story-Teller*, 1907-1910
  Editor *The London Magazine*, 1911-1931; *The Premier Magazine*, May 1914-Mar 1931; *The Red Magazine*, 1932

Whitten, Wilfred ["John O'London"] (1863-1942)
  T. P.'s Magazine, Oct 1910-1911

Wilkins, William Henry (1860-1905)
  The Lady's Realm, Nov 1896-Oct 1902

Williams, Herbert Dakin (1882- ?)
  The Quiver, 1909-Aug 1953

Williams, W. Llewelyn (1867-1922)
  The Sunday Strand, 1908-1910

Williamson, C(harles) N(orris) (1859-1920)
  Black and White, 1891-1892?

Williamson, David (1868-1955)
  Assistant, *English Illustrated Magazine* and *Illustrated London News*, 1893-1895
  Editor *The Windsor Magazine*, Jan 1896-May 1898; *The Temple Magazine*, 1898-1899; *Cassell's Magazine*, Dec 1905-Nov 1908; *The Quiver*, 1905-1909

Williamson, Hugh Ross (1901-1978)
  Acting editor, *The Strand*, 1934-1935

Williamson, W(illiam) A(lan) (1893- ?)
  Pan, Apr 1921-May 1924; *20 Story Magazine*, 1922-1927; *Romance*, 1923-1924; *Passing Show*, 1925-Feb 1939

Wilson-Barrett, Alfred
  Colour, Aug 1914-May 1932

Wimbury, Harold
  The New Magazine, 1924-1927

Winchester, Clarence Arthur (1895-1981)
  Assistant Chief Editor at Cassell. 1925-1927;
  Chief Editor, Amalgamated Press, 1927-1940
  Editor *Chums*, 1920-1924; *The Corner Magazine*, May 1925-Feb 1935; *Cassell's Magazine*, 1925 (?)-Dec 1932; *The Argosy*, Jun 1926-Jan 1940; *The New Magazine*, 1927-1930; *The Story-Teller*, Jun 1928-Nov 1937; *The Red Magazine*, 1936-1939

Wingham, C(harles) W(ing) (1882- ?)
  The Grand Magazine, 1911-1920

Wood, Charles William (1845-1919)
  Publisher *The Argosy*, Dec 1867-Dec 1871, and editor from Jan 1887-Dec 1898

Wood, Mrs Henry [Ellen] (1814-1887)
  The Argosy, Oct 1867-Dec 1886

Wray, E. C.
  20 Story Magazine, 1935-1940.

*

SUMMARY OF EDITORS AND PUBLISHERS

2. Publishers

The following is an alphabetical listing of the Publishing Companies (not the Company Head) in both Sections 1 and 2. All Companies are based in London unless otherwise stated. (The abbreviation BRE below refers to BRE.)

Allen, George
The Argosy, Jan 1900-Sept 1901

Amalgamated Magazine Company
The Lady's Realm, Nov 1910-May 1916; *The Club Room*, Nov 1913-? (May 1914?)

Amalgamated Press
(formerly Harmsworth Brothers; became Amalgamated Press from Aug 1901; Fleetway Publications from Oct 1959 and incorporated within IPC Magazines in Feb 1969)
The Harmsworth/London Magazine/New London Magazine, Jul 1898-May 1933; *The World and His Wife*, Nov 1904-May 1910; *Good Words*, Nov 1905-8 Apr 1911; *The Red Magazine*, Jun 1908-Sept 1939; *The Premier Magazine*, May 1914-Mar 1931; *The Yellow Magazine*, 23 Sept 1921-17 Sept 1926; *The Violet Magazine*, Jul 1922-Nov 1939; *The Green Magazine*, 7 Nov 1922-18 Dec 1923; *The Detective Magazine*, 24 Nov 1922-8 May 1925; *The Merry Mag.*, Jul 1924-Aug 1927; *All-Story Magazine*, Oct 1926-Jan 1928; *The Quiver*, Feb 1927-Jun 1956; *Argosy*, Mar 1927-Feb 1974; *Cassell's Magazine*, Mar 1927-Dec 1932; *Chums*, Mar 1927-Jul 1934; *The Corner Magazine*, May 1927-Feb 1935; *The New Magazine*, May 1927-Dec 1930; *The Story-Teller*, May 1927-Nov 1937; *Woman's Journal*, Nov 1927-Feb 2002; *The Thriller*, 9 Feb 1929-10 May 1940

Arliss-Andrews, William
London Society, Jan 1897-Dec 1898

Arnold, Edward
English Illustrated Magazine, Oct 1892-Sept 1893

Artistic Publishing Company
The Minster, Jan-Mar 1896

Atlas Publishing & Distributing Co. Ltd.
World Stories, Apr 1928-May 1935; *Thrills*, 1939; *Astounding/Analog Science Fiction* (BRE), Aug 1939-Aug 1963; *Unknown/Unknown Worlds* (BRE), Sept 1939-Win 1949; *Western Story Magazine* (BRE), Sept 1939-Mar 1953; *Black Mask* (BRE), Nov 1939-Apr 1941

Bennett, E. & H.
Short Stories, 12 Jan 1889-8 Jul 1893

Bentley, Richard
Temple Bar, Apr 1866-Aug 1898; *The Argosy*, Jan 1872-Jun 1897

Biggs & Co.
Belgravia, Apr-Dec 1897

Blackwood & Sons, William [Edinburgh]
Blackwood's Magazine, Apr 1817-Dec 1980

Board, A W.
Tip-Top Stories/The Regent Magazine, Dec 1923-Jan 1925

Bottomley, Horatio
To-Day, 1897-1905

British National Newspapers
Britannia and Eve, May 1929-Jan 1957

Cassell & Company
The Quiver, 7 Sept 1861-Jan 1927; *Cassell's Magazine*, Apr 1867-Feb 1927; *Chums*, 12 Sept 1892-Feb 1927; *The Story-Teller*, Apr 1907-Apr 1927; *The New Magazine*, Apr 1909-Apr 1927; *The Corner Magazine*, Sept 1922-Apr 1927; *Argosy*, Jun 1926-Feb 1927

Central Publishing
English Illustrated Magazine, Mar 1905-Aug 1913

Chambers, W. & R. [Edinburgh]
Chambers's [Edinburgh] Journal, 4 Feb 1832-Dec 1956

Chandler, John E.
The Badminton Magazine, Jul-Oct 1916

Chapman & Hall
Chapman's Magazine, May 1895-Oct 1898

Chatto & Windus
Belgravia, May 1876-Sept 1889; *The Idler*, Feb 1892-Jan 1898, Oct 1902-Sept 1906

Collins, William
Hush, Jun 1930-Jun 1931

Constable & Co.
Scribner's Magazine (European edition), Jun 1912-Jan (or Mar?) 1917

David, John [Brighton]
The Black Cat, Feb 1898-Jun 1899

Dawbarn & Ward
The Idler, Mar 1901-Sept 1902

Dawson, William
The Smart Set (BRE), Jan 1914-Apr 1918; *Colour*, Aug 1914-Sept/Oct 1924

de Beck, Ltd., A. M.
The Universal [& Ludgate] Magazine, Nov 1900-Dec 1901

de Meray, Jules
The Ludgate, Nov 1900-Feb 1901

Dent, J. M.
The Idler, Feb-Jul 1898

Dickson, Lovat
Lovat Dickson's Magazine, Nov 1933-Jun 1935

Elliott & Co., James
The Horlick's Magazine, Jan 1904-Mar 1905

Ess Ess Company/Smart Set Company
The Smart Set (BRE), Mar 1900-Dec 1913

Everett & Co.
The Magpie, Aug-Oct 1912

Far and Near Publications
Outward Bound, Oct 1920-Mar 1924

Favorite Publishing Company, The
Eureka/The Favorite Magazine, Apr 1897-1903?

French, Samuel
Gunter's Magazine (BRE), Feb 1905-Oct 1910

Greening, Arthur
The Imp, Jun 1907-Nov 1911

Haddon, Walter
The Butterfly, May-Oct 1893

Hamilton, John
Wings, Summer 1934-Jan 1936

Harmsworth Brothers *see under* Amalgamated Press

Harrison & Sons
Physical Culture/Sandow's Magazine, Apr 1898-27 Dec 1906

Hatchards
Atalanta, Oct 1887-Sept 1890

Heinemann, William
The Badminton Magazine, Jan 1901-Dec 1902; *Scribner's Magazine* (European edition), Jul 1904-Jun 1906

Hodder & Stoughton
Woman at Home, Oct 1893-Jul 1909; *Century Magazine* (BRE), Nov 1910-Nov 1913

Hulton, Edward (*see also* London Publishing]
The Badminton Magazine, Aug 1911-Jun 1916

Hutchinson
The Lady's Realm, Nov 1896-Oct 1909; *English Illustrated Magazine*, Apr 1903-Feb 1905; *Hutchinson's [Story] Magazine*, Jul 1919-Dec 1929; *The Sovereign Magazine*,

SUMMARY OF EDITORS AND PUBLISHERS

Nov 1919-Apr 1927; *Nash's Illustrated Weekly*, 17 Apr-10 Jul 1920; *Adventure-Story*, Sept 1922-Sept 1927; *Mystery-Story Magazine*, Feb 1923-Sept 1927; *Action Stories* (BRE), Apr 1923-Jan 1928; *The Smart Set* (BRE), Oct 1923-Jun 1925; *Woman*, Apr 1924-Jul 1929; *The Regent Magazine*, Feb-Mar/Apr 1925; *Standard Stories*, Jul 1925-Jun/Jul 1926; *The Jolly Magazine*, May-Dec 1927; *Adventure & Mystery-Story Magazine*, Oct 1927-Jun 1929; *Best-Story Magazine*, Aug 1926-Apr 1929

Iliffe & Sons
Pall Mall Magazine, Jan 1913-Aug 1914

Illustrated London News [Ingram Brothers]
Illustrated London News, 1884-1961; *The Sketch*, 1 Feb 1893-17 Jun 1959; *English Illustrated Magazine*, Oct 1893-Sept 1901

Illustrated Newspapers
The Sphere, 27 Jan 1900-27 Jan 1964

Innes, A. D.
The Minster, Jan-Dec 1895

Isbister, William
Good Words, Jan 1873-Dec 1904

Lambert, F. J.
Lambert's Monthly, Jan 1890-May 1891; *The Ludgate Monthly*, May 1891-Apr 1894

Lane, John
The Yellow Book, Apr 1894-Apr 1897 (with Elkin Matthews for first four issues)

Link House
The Blue Magazine, Sept 1928-Aug 1929

London Publishing [Edward Hulton]
The Sunday/Story Journal, 8 Mar 1909-31 Aug 1914

Longmans, Green & Co.
Longman's Magazine, Nov 1882-Oct 1905; *Badminton Magazine*, Aug 1895-Dec 1900

Macdonald & Martin
The Realm, Apr-Sept 1904

Macmillan and Company
Macmillan's Magazine, Nov 1859-Oct 1907; *English Illustrated Magazine*, Oct 1883-Sept 1892; *Century Magazine* (BRE), May 1895-Oct 1910; *The Argosy*, Jul 1897-Dec 1899; *Temple Bar*, Sept 1898-Dec 1906

Magazine Publishing Company, The
The Holborn Monthly Magazine, Apr 1903-Apr 1904

Mansfield, E. J.
The Graphic, Dec 1869-Dec 1893

Marshall Brothers (Marshall Russell & Co)
Atalanta, Jun 1892-Sept 1898

Marshall, Horace
Ludgate Illustrated Magazine, May 1894-Oct 1895; *Temple Magazine*, Oct 1896-Sept 1903; *Universal Magazine*, Feb-Oct 1900; *The Idler*, Aug 1900-Feb 1901; *The Magpie*, Nov 1912-Dec 1914

May, Wyatt & Co., [A. F. May from Nov 1898]
Belgravia, Jan 1898-Jun 1899

Monckton, W. J. P.
The Ludgate, Nov 1895-Mar 1898 (on behalf of Black & White)

Morland, Judd & Co.
The Butterfly, Nov 1893-Feb 1894

Murray, John
The Cornhill Magazine, Jan 1917-Spring 1975

Nash, Eveleigh (*see also* Periodical Publishing Company)
Nash's Magazine, Apr 1909-Jan 1911

National Magazine Company
Nash's Magazine, Feb 1911-Sept 1914; *Nash's--Pall Mall*, Oct 1914-Sept 1937; *Pall Mall Magazine*, Sept 1914; May 1927-Sept 1929; *Good Housekeeping*, from Mar 1922; *Harper's Bazaar*, Oct 1929-Oct 1970; *Nash's Annual*, Sum 1938; Dec 1946-Winter 1949/50

New Century Press
Crampton's Magazine, Nov 1898-Sept 1900; *The Black Cat*, Jul 1899-Mar 1900; *The Butterfly*, Oct 1899-Feb 1900; *The Charing Cross Magazine*, Jan-Aug 1900

New Colour, Ltd.
Colour, Nov 1928-May 1932

Newnes, George
Tit-Bits from 22 Oct 1881; *The Strand Magazine*, Jan 1891-Mar 1950; *The Captain*, Apr 1899-Mar 1924; *The Sunday Strand*, Jan 1900-Jun 1910; *Fry's Magazine*, Apr 1904-Mar 1911; *The Grand Magazine*, Feb 1905-Apr 1940; *Woman at Home/The Home Magazine*, Aug 1909-Feb 1931; *The Happy Mag.*, Jun 1922-May 1940; *The Crusoe Mag.*, Jun 1924-May 1926; *The Sunny Mag.*, Jul 1925-Apr 1933; *The Golden Mag.*, Jun 1926-Jun 1927; *The Golden West*, Jul 1927-Dec 1928; *Air Stories*, May 1935-Apr 1940; *War Stories*, Oct 1935-Feb 1936; *Western Adventures*, Feb-Jun 1936; *Fantasy*, Summer 1938-Summer 1939

1900 Publishing Syndicate, The
The Badminton Magazine, Jan-Jun 1903

Odhams Press
The Passing Show, 20 Mar 1915-25 Feb 1939; *Pan*, Feb 1919-May 1924; *Film Fiction*, Aug 1921; *The 20 Story Magazine*, Jul 1922-Oct 1940; *Romance*, Feb 1923-Jan 1927

Osgood, McIlvaine
Harper's Magazine (BRE), Jun 1891-Nov 1897

Parker, G. R.
The Graphic, 1894-1903

Parsons, F. J.
The Blue Magazine, Jan 1927-Jul/Aug 1928; *Romance*, Jan-Jul 1927

Partridge, S. W.
The Osborne, Nov 1896-May 1897

Pearson, C. Arthur
Pearson's Weekly, 26 Jul 1890-1 Apr 1939; *The Search-Light*, Mar 1892-Sept 1894; *Short Stories*, 15 Jul 1893-18 Jun 1904; *Pearson's Story-Teller*, 9 Oct 1895-*at least* 22 Feb 1896; *Pearson's Magazine*, Jan 1896-Nov 1939; *The Royal Magazine,* Nov 1898-Nov 1930; *The Lady's Magazine/The Home Magazine*, Jan 1901-Feb 1905; *The Novel Magazine*, Apr 1905-Dec 1937; *The New Royal Magazine/Royal Pictorial/Screen Pictorial*, Dec 1930-Sept 1939; *Scoops*, 10 Feb-23 Jun 1934

Periodical Publishing Company
Nash's [Illustrated] Weekly, 14 Jun 1919-10 Apr 1920

Pitman's
Good Words, Jan-Oct 1905

Reiach, Herbert
Badminton Magazine, Nov 1916-Apr 1921

Religious Tract Society
Boy's Own Paper, 1879-1939; *Everybody's/Everyone's Story Magazine*, Nov 1909-Apr 1914

Richards, Grant
The Butterfly, Mar-Sept 1899

Rolls House Publishing Company
The Smart Set (BRE), May 1918-Nov 1922

Routledge, George
Pall Mall Magazine, May 1893-Dec 1912

Russell, W. R.
The Idler, Aug 1898-Jul 1900; *Crampton's Magazine*, Nov 1898-Sept 1900 (on behalf of New Century Press)

Sampson, Low
London Society, Jan 1872-Dec 1880; *Harper's Magazine* (BRE), Dec 1880-May 1891; *Scribner's Monthly*, Jan 1892 to Jun 1904

SUMMARY OF EDITORS AND PUBLISHERS

Shurey Publications
Yes or No, 21 Mar 1904-27 Apr 1918; 28 Feb 1921-24 Apr 1922; *Weekly Tale-Teller*, 8 May 1909-29 Apr 1916

Sievier, Robert S.
Sievier's Monthly, Jan 1909-Nov 1910

Simpkin, Marshall, Hamilton, Kent
The White Magazine, Mar/Apr-Jul/Aug 1909

Smith, Elder & Co.
The Cornhill Magazine, Jan 1860-Dec 1916

Smithers, Leonard
The Savoy, Jan-Dec 1896

Southern, William
The Blue Magazine, Jul-Dec 1926

Sphere and Tatler (*see also* Illustrated Newspapers)
Badminton Magazine, Jul 1903-Jul 1911

Stanley Paul
The Lady's Realm, Nov 1909-Oct 1910

Strahan, Alexander
Good Words, Jan 1860-Dec 1872; *The Argosy*, Dec 1865-Nov 1867

Suttley & Silverlock
Colour, Jan 1925-Jan 1927

Treherne, Anthony
Crampton's Magazine, Dec 1901-Dec 1902

Trischler & Co.
Atalanta, Oct 1890-May 1892

United Newspapers
Lloyd's [Story] Magazine, Jul 1917-Jan 1923; *Badminton Magazine*, May 1921-Jan 1923

Unwin, T. Fisher
Century Illustrated Magazine (BRE), May 1886-Apr 1895; *English Illustrated Magazine*, Oct 1901-Mar 1903

Walbrook, H. M.
The Blue Magazine, Jul 1919-Jun 1926

Ward, Lock & Co.
Temple Bar, Dec 1860-Mar 1866; *Lippincott's Monthly* (BRE), Jan 1890-Jun 1895; *The Windsor Magazine*, Jan 1895-Sept 1939

Warne, Frederick
Century Illustrated Magazine (BRE), Nov 1881-Apr 1886; *Scribner's Monthly* (BRE), Jan 1887- Dec 1891

White, F. V.
Belgravia, Oct 1889-Mar 1897; *London Society*, Jan 1887-Dec 1896; *The Ludgate*, Apr 1898-Oct 1900

Willoughby, Richard
Home Chimes, 2 Jan 1884-26 Dec 1885

World's Work, The (Kingswood, Surrey)
Short Stories (BRE), Mar 1920-Jun 1955; *The Frontier/Frontier Stories* (BRE), Apr 1925-Jul 1929; *West* (BRE), Aug 1926-Feb 1954; *Empire Frontier*, Aug 1929-Jun 1932; *All Star Western and Empire Frontier Magazine*, Jul 1932-Jun 1933; *All-Star Detective Magazine*, from Jul 1933; *Master Thriller* series, Jul 1933-Dec 1939; *Modern Stories*, from Aug 1934; *Mystery and Detection*, Sept 1934-Oct 1935; *Mystery Stories*, Mar 1936-Feb 1942; *Tales of Wonder*, Jun 1937-Spring 1942

BIBLIOGRAPHY

The primary source of data for this Guide is the magazines themselves. A wide range of secondary sources were also consulted in whole or in part and are recommended to the reader interested in further information on this period, its writers and magazines.

Adcock, A. St. John, *Gods of Modern Grub Street*, London: Sampson Low, Marston, 1923
Adcock, A. St. John, *The Glory That Was Grub Street*, London: Sampson Low, Marston, 1928
Allen, Walter, *The Short Story in English*, Oxford: Oxford University Press, 1981
Baines, Jocelyn, *Joseph Conrad, A Critical Biography*, London: Weidenfeld & Nicolson, 1993.
Beare, Geraldine, *Index to the Strand Magazine, 1891-1905*, Westport, CT: Greenwood Press, 1982.
Bloom, Clive, *Bestsellers: Popular Fiction Since 1900*, London: Palgrave Macmillan, 2002
Bonavia-Hunt, Noel A., *Irons in the Fire*, London: Musical Opinion, 1959
Bourne, Richard, *Lords of Fleet Street*, London: Unwin Hyman, 1990
Braithwaite, Brian and Barrell, Joan, *The Business of Women's Magazine*, revised edition, London: Kegan Paul, 1988
Brome, Vincent, *Frank Harris*, London: Cassell, 1959
Brome, Vincent, *H.G. Wells*, London: Longmans, 1952
Burgin, G. B., *Many Memories*, London: Hutchinson, 1922
Butler, William Vivian, *The Durable Desperadoes*, London: Macmillan, 1973
Cadogan, Mary, *Richmal Crompton, The Woman Behind William*, London: Allen & Unwin, 1986
Cadogan, Mary, *The William Companion*, London: Macmillan, 1990
Campbell Thomson, Christine, *I Am a Literary Agent*, London: Sampson Low, Marston, 1951
Carpenter, Humphrey, *Secret Gardens: The Golden Age of Children's Fiction*, London: Allen & Unwin, 1985
Carr, J. Comyns, *Some Eminent Victorians*, London: Duckworth, 1908
Carr, Mrs. Comyns, *J. Comyns Carr, Star Memories*, London: Macmillan, 1920
Clark, Alan, *Dictionary of British Comic Artists, Writers and Editors*, London: The British Library, 1998
Clarke, Austin, *A Penny in the Clouds*, London: Routledge & Kegan Paul, 1968
Cockburn, Claud, *Bestseller: The Books That Everyone Read, 1900-1939*, [London: Sidgwick & Jackson, 1972] Harmondsworth: Penguin, 1975
Cohen, Morton, *Rider Haggard: His Life and Work*, London: Macmillan, 1960. Revised ed., 1968
Cox, Jack, *Take a Cold Tub, Sir!: The Story of The Boy's Own Paper*, London: Lutterworth, 1982
Dark, Sidney, *The Life of Sir Arthur Pearson*, London: Hodder & Stoughton, 1922
Darlington, W. A., *I Do What I Like*, London: Rockliff, 1950
Dell, Penelope, *Nettie & Sissie*, London: Hamish Hamilton, 1977
Donaldson, Frances, *P. G. Wodehouse, A Biography*, New York: Alfred A. Knopf, 1982

BIBLIOGRAPHY

Doran, George H. *Chronicles of Barabbas, 1884-1934*, London: Methuen, 1935
Doubleday, F. N., *The Memoirs of a Publisher*, Garden City, New York: Doubleday, 1972
Dwyer, James Francis, *Leg-Irons on Wings*, Melbourne: Georgian House, 1949
Edwards, Owen Dudley, *The Quest for Sherlock Holmes: A Biographical Study of Sir Arthur Conan Doyle*, Harmondsworth: Penguin Books, 1984
Engel, Matthew, *Tickle the Public: One Hundred Years of the Popular Press*, London: Gollancz, [1996] 1997
Ellis, Peter Berresford, *H. Rider Haggard, A Voice from the Infinite*, London: Routledge & Kegan Paul, 1978
Ferris, Paul, *The House of Northcliffe*, New York: World Publishing, 1971
Flower, Newman, *Just as It Happened*, London: Cassell, 1950
Friederichs, Hulda, *The Life of Sir George Newnes, Bart.*, London: Hodder & Stoughton, 1911
Glyn, Elinor, *Romantic Adventure*, London: Ivor Nicholson, 1936
Green, Benny, *P. G. Wodehouse: A Literary Biography*. London: Pavilion Press, 1981
Green, Roger Lancelyn, *Andrew Lang: A Critical Biography*, London: Ward, 1946
Green, Roger Lancelyn, *Tellers of Tales: Children's Books and Their Authors*, London: Kaye & Ward, [1946]. Revised ed., 1965
Gross, John, *The Rise and Fall of the Man of Letters: English Literary Life Since 1800*, London: Weidenfeld & Nicolson, 1969
Hamilton, Lord Frederic, *My Yesterdays*, Garden City, NY: Doubleday, Doran, 1930
Hammerton, J. A., *Books and Myself*, London: Macdonald, 1944.
Head, Alice M., *It Could Never Have Happened*, London: Heinemann, 1939
Heneage, Simon and Ford, Henry, *Sidney Sime, Master of the Mysterious*, London: Thames and Hudson, 1980
Higgins, D. S., *Rider Haggard, the Great Storyteller*, London: Cassell, 1981
Horne, Alan, *The Dictionary of 20th Century British Book Illustrators*, Woodbridge: Antique Collectors' Club, 1994
Houfe, Simon, *The Dictionary of 19th Century British Book Illustrators*, Woodbridge: Antique Collectors' Club, 1978, revised, 1996
Howarth, Patrick, *Play Up and Play the Game: The Heroes of Popular Fiction*, London: Eyre-Methuen, 1973
Hyne, C. J. Cutcliffe, *My Joyful Life*, London: Hutchinson, 1935
Jackson, Kate (editor), *George Newnes and the New Journalism in Britain, 1880-1910*, Aldershot: Ashgate, 2001
James, Louis, *Fiction for the Working Man*, London: Oxford University Press, 1963
Jerome, Jerome K., *My Life & Times*, London: John Murray, 1926
Joseph, Michael, *The Magazine Story*, London: Hutchinson, 1928
Joseph, Michael, *Short Story Writing for Profit*, London: Hutchinson, 1923
Joseph, Richard, *Master of Words*, Southampton: Ashford Press, 1986
Keating, Peter, *The Haunted Study: A Social History of the English Novel 1875-1914*, London: [Secker & Warburg, 1989] Fontana, 1991
Keir, David, *The House of Collins*, London: Collins, 1952
Kemp, Sandra, with Mitchell, Charlotte and Trotter, David, *Edwardian Fiction*, Oxford: Oxford University Press, 1997
Lane, Margaret, *Edgar Wallace*, London: Heineman, 1938

Law, Graham, *The Illustrated London News (1842-1901), The Graphic (1869-1901), Indexes to Fiction*, Australia: University of Queensland, 2001

Law, Graham, *Serializing in the Victorian Press*, Basingstoke: Palgrave, 2000

Le Gallienne, Richard, *The Romantic '90s*, new edition, London: Putnam & Company, 1951

Liveing, Edward, *Adventure in Publishing, The House of Ward Lock, 1854-1954*, London: Ward, Lock, 1954

Locke, George, *Pearson's Weekly, A Checklist of Fiction, 1890-1939*, London: Ferret Fantasy, 1990

Locke, George, *The Premier Magazine 1914 to 1931, An Annotated Checklist*, London: Ferret Fantasy, 1999

Locke, George, *A Spectrum of Fantasy*, London: Ferret Fantasy, 1980, and subsequent volumes, 1994, 2002

Lofts, W.O.G. and Adley, D. J., *The British Bibliography of Edgar Wallace*, London: Howard Baker, 1969

Lofts, W.O.G. and Adley, D. J., *The Men Behind Boys' Fiction*, London: Howard Baker, 1970

Lusty, Robert, *Bound to be Read*, London: Jonathan Cape, 1975

McClure, S. S., *My Autobiography*, New York: Magazine Publishers, 1914

McLynn, Frank, *Robert Louis Stevenson: A Biography*, London: [Hutchinson, 1993] Pimlico, 1994

Martell, Edward (editor), *The Author's and Writer's Who's Who*, London: Shaw Publishing, 1934, and subsequent editions

Maschwitz, Erc, *No Chip on My Shoulder*, London: Ferbert Jenkins, 1957

Meredith, Mark, *Who's Who in Literature*, Liverpool: Literary Year Books Press, 1924

Mordaunt, Elinor, *Sinabada*, London: Michael Joseph, 1937

Morgan, Charles, *The House of Macmillan, 1843-1943*, London: Macmillan, 1943

Mumby, F. A., *The House of Routledge, 1834-1934*, London: Routledge, 1934

Nash, Eveleigh, *I Liked the Life I Lived*, London: John Murray, 1941

Nowell-Smith, Simon, *The House of Cassell, 1848-1958*, London: Cassell, 1958

O'Brien, Edward J. and Cournos, John, *The Best British Short Stories of 1922*, Boston: Small, Maynard, 1923 and subsequent annual editions

Orwell, George, *The Penguin Essays of George Orwell*, Harmondsworth: Penguin, 1984

Oxenham, Eric, *Scrap-Book of J.O.*, London: Longmans, Green, 1946

Page, Norman, *A Kipling Companion*, London: Macmillan, 1984

Pearce, Joseph, *Wisdom and Innocence: A Life of G. K. Chesterton*, London, Hodder & Stoughton, 1996

Peterson, Theodore, *Magazines in the Twentieth Century*, Urbana: The University of Illinois Press, 1956

Pound, Reginald, *A Maypole in the Strand*, London: Ernest Benn, 1948

Pound, Reginald, *The Strand Magazine, 1891-1950*, London: Heinemann, 1966

Pringle, David, *Imaginary People: A Who's Who of Modern Fictional Characters*, London: Grafton, 1987. 2nd edition, Scolar Press, 1996

Quigly, Isabel, *The Heirs of Tom Brown: The English School Story*, London: Chatto & Windus, 1982

Reed, David, *The Popular Magazine in Britain and the United States, 1880-1960*, London: The British Library, 1997

Richards, Grant, *Author Hunting; Memories of Years Spent Mainly in Publishing*, London: The Unicorn Press, 1934

Sandys, Oliver, *Full and Frank*, London: Hutchinson, 1941

BIBLIOGRAPHY

Scott, J. W. Robertson, *The Story of the Pall Mall Gazette*, London: Oxford University Press, 1950

Shaw, Captain Frank H., *Seas of Memory*, London: Oldbourne Book Co., 1958

Shepherd, C. W., *Let's Walk Down Fleet Street,* London: Gerald Swan, 1947

Sillars, Stuart, *Visualisation in Popular Fiction, 1860-1960*, London: Routledge, 1995

Stacpoole, H. de Vere, *Men and Mice*, London: Hutchinson, 1942; and *More Men and Mice*, London: Hutchinson, 1945

Stead, W. T. *Index to the Periodicals of 1890* [to] *1902*, London: Review of Reviews, 1891-1903

Stewart, R. F, *...And Always a Detective: Chapters on the History of Detective Fiction,*. Newton Abbot: David & Charles, 1980

Stoddart, Jane T., *My Harvest of Years*, London: Hodder and Stoughton, 1938

Stott, Raymond Toole, *The Writings of William Somerset Maugham*, London: Bertram Rota, 1956

Stringer, Jenny (editor), *The Oxford Companion to Twentieth-Century Literature in English*, Oxford: Oxford University Press, 1996

Sullivan, Alvin (editor). *British Literary Magazines, The Victorian and Edwardian Age, 1837-1913*, Westport, CT: Greenwood Press, 1984; and *British Literary Magazines, The Modern Age, 1914-1984*, Westport, CT: Greenwood Press, 1986

Sutherland, John, *The Longman Companion to Victorian Fiction*, London: Longman, 1988

Swan, Annie S., *My Life*, London: Ivor Nicholson & Watson, 1934

Thesing, William B. and Lewis, Becky, *Indexes to Fiction in The Idler (1892-1911),* Australia: University of Queensland, 1994

Thomas, Sue, *Cassell's Family Magazine, Indexes to Fiction,* Australia: University of Queensland, 1987

Thomas, Sue, *Indexes to Fiction in The Harmsworth Magazine,* Australia: University of Queensland, 1984

Thomas, Sue, Versteeg, M. and Huddleston, Joan, *The Lady's Realm, Indexes to Fiction,* Australia: University of Queensland, 1981

Thomas, Sue, *Pall Mall Magazine, Indexes to Fiction,* Australia: University of Queensland, 1983

Thorpe, James, *English Illustration: The Nineties*, London: Faber, 1935

Thorpe, James, *Happy Days*, London: Gerald Howe, 1933

Turner, E. S., *Boys Will be Boys*, [London: Michael Joseph, 1948] Revised ed. Harmondsworth: Penguin, 1975

Usborne, Richard, *Clubland Heroes: A Nostalgic Study of Some Recurrent Characters in the Romantic Fiction of Dornford Yates, John Buchan and Sapper*, London: Constable, 1953

Usborne, Richard, *Wodehouse at Work to the End* (Revised ed.), London: Barrie & Jenkins, 1976

Vachell, Horace Annesley, *Distant Fields,* London: Cassell, 1937

Walker, Nancy A. (editor), *Women's Magazines 1940-1960*, Boston: Bedford/St. Martin's, 1998

Ward, A. C., *Longman Companion to Twentieth Century Literature*, London: Longman, 1970

Waugh, Arthur, *A Hundred Years of Publishing*, London: Chapman & Hall, 1930

Wells, H. G., *Experiment in Autobiography*, London: Gollancz and The Cresset Press, 1934

Whistler, Theresa, *Imagination of the Heart: The Life of Walter de la Mare*, London: Duckworth, 1993

White, Cynthia L., *Women's Magazines, 1693-1968,* London: Michael Joseph, 1970

Whitelaw, David, *A Bonfire of Leaves*, London: Geoffrey Bles, 1937

Williams, Valentine, *The World of Action*, London: Hamish Hamilton, 1938

Williamson, David, *Before I Forget*, London: Sampson Low, Marston, 1932

INDEX

The index is to all authors, editors and magazines discussed. Magazine titles are in italics. Pages for the main entries are in bold type. Pages for illustrations are in italics, plus reference to the relevant Plate number for colour covers between pages 38 and 39. A page number followed by 'n' means the reference is in a footnote.

Abdullah, Achmed 57, 134, 171, 172, 185, 186, 188, 189, 214, 253
Ace High Magazine 236
Action Stories 40, 271
Acton, Mrs Adams 222
Adams, Samuel Hopkins 140
Adventure (comic) 9
Adventure (US pulp) 40, 83, 211, 215
Adventure & Mystery-Story Magazine 33, 41-2
Adventure-Story Magazine 12, 14, 31, 33, **40-2**, *41*, 64, 127, 129, 211, *Plate 5*
Adventure Trails 68
Advertisers' Protection Society 19, 76, 92, 98, 115, 122, 139n, 143, 162, 170n, 226, 239
Agnus, Orme 116
Air Stories 14, 35, 36, **42-4**, *43*, 79, 218-9, 221, *Plate 8*
Aitken, A. Donnelly 250, 274
Alan, A. J. 116
Alcock, C. W. 72
Alden, W. L. 95, 96, 125, 160, 200
Alexander, R. W. 127
All-Star Detective Magazine 69, 271-2
All Star Magazine 34, 69; as *All Star Western & Frontier Magazine* 35, 69
All-Story (US magazine) 171n
All-Story Magazine 32, 33, **45-6**, 64, 238, *Plate 7*
All the Year Round 22, 52
Allen, George 242, 285
Allen, Grant 24, 54, 70, 95, 198, 201, 243, 248, 251, 267
Allerton, Mark 107
Allingham, Herbert 123, 124
Allingham, Margery 15, 189, 205, 267
Allingham, William 242
Alma-Tadema, Laurence 70
Altson, Abbey 148, *148*, 163

Ambler, Eric 206
American Magazine, The 256
Andersen, Hans Christian 4n
Anderson, Alderson 82, 85, 122-3, 274
Anderson, William Ashley 134
Andom, R. 257
Andrews, C. C. 209
Andrews, E. C. 165
"Andrul" *see* Begbie, Arundel
Anstey, F. 5, 14, 75, 133, 202, 243, 251, 258
Answers 7, 21, 111, 160
Applin, Arthur 51, 84, 144, 146, 240, 261, 264, 274
Archer, William 150
Ardizzone, Edward 206
Argosy, The (Victorian magazine) 24, 47, **242**,
Argosy, The (UK) 32, 33, 36, **46-9**, *47*, 85, 179, 190, 262, 272, *Plate 7*
Argosy, The (US) 8n, 40, 46-7, 68
Arkell, Reginald 206
Arlen, Michael 15, 85, 158, 185, 204, 235, 268
Armstrong, Anthony 100, 166, 253
Armstrong, Martin 195
Arnold, Edwin Lester 95, 256
Arnold, Matthew 251
Arnold, Spencer 244, 274
Arrowsmith, publisher, 5, 6
Ash, Fenton *see* Atkins, Frank, Sr.
Ashford, A. E. 177, 238
Ashton-Wolfe, H. 167
Askew, Alice and Claude 56, 107, 143, 191, 220
Aspden, Hartley 254, 274
Asquith, Cynthia 268
Astor, William Waldorf 133, 147-52 *passim*, 154, 159
Astounding Stories/Science Fiction 236, 272
Atalanta 21, 23, **242-3**

Atherton, Gertrude 135, 234
Atkey, Bertram 27, 29, 60, 83, 88, 140, 166, 176, 177, 234, 252, 274
Atkey, Philip *see* Barry Perowne
Atkins, Frank, Jr., as F. St Mars 83, 115, 165, 177, 240
Atkins, Frank, Sr., as Fenton Ash 10, 240; as Frank Aubrey 252
Atkins, Frederick A. 266, 274
Atlas Publishing 236, 267, 273, 285
Attwell, Mabel Lucie 11, 26, 163, 185, 235, 256, 261, 269
Aubrey, Frank *see* Atkins, Frank, Sr.
Audemars, Pierre 249
Aumonier, Stacy 15, 33, 47, 48, 51, 91, 128, 140, 157, 167-8, 204, 205, 252
Austin, F. Britten 83, 106, 116, 123, 165, 204, 219
Austin, John 237
Avery, Harold 248
Ayres, Ruby M. 64, 83, 91, 143, 145, 146, 179, 181, 184, 189, 235

Bacon, J. M. 175
Bacon, Josephine Daskam *see* Daskam, Josephine Dodge
Badminton Magazine, The 22, 31, 162, **243**
Bailey, H. C. 15, 83, 84, 126, 152, 203, 228, 252
Baily, F. E. 183, 184-5, 187, 274
Baird, John Logie 168
Bairnsfather, Bruce 261
Baker, Augustus 248, 274
Baldry, Walter Burton 252, 274
Ballantyne, R. M. 8, 95
Ballard, J. G. 250
Balmer, Edwin 261
Bangs, John Kendrick 140
Baring-Gould, S. 111, 222, 233, 251, 254, 266
Barker, Nugent 252

294

INDEX

Barker, S. Omar
Barr, James 142, 175, 176-7, 237, 269
Barr, Robert as author 28, 54, 89, 94, 95, 99, 113, 160, 162, 164, 201, 226, 227, 244, 266; as editor 25, 93-100, 176, 268, 274
Barrett, Frank 53
Barrie, J. M. 9, 70, 75, 94, 143, 232, 233, 244, 254, 255, 269
Barrington, E. *see* Beck, L. Adams
"Bartimeus" *see* Ricci, Lewis
Bateman, H. M. 84, 100, 157, 165, 252
Bateman, May 108
Bates, H. E. 9, 137, 252, 258, 269
Batten, H. Mortimer 86, 165, 177, 246, 248, 262
Baum, Vicki 269
Bayley, Donovan 83
Bayley, F. W. N. 256
Beard, Freda 155
Beardsley, Aubrey 23, 96, *147-8*, 148, 263, 269
Beaufoy, P. 62
Beaumont, W. Comyns 114, 117, 156-7, 159, 255, 261, 274
Bechdolt, Frederick 134
Bechdolt, Jack 81
Beck, L. Adams 117
Becke, Louis 61, 164
Bedford-Jones, H. 40, 57, 63, 174, 211, 214
Beeding, Francis 32, 64
Beerbohm, Max 150, 247, 269
Beeston, L. J. 83, 157, 171, 249, 265
Beeton's Christmas Annual 6, 21, 198, 225
Begbie, Arundel ("Andrul") 62
Belgravia 24, 58, **243-4**, 257
Bell, J. J. 98, 101, 113, 139, 142, 203, 269
Bell, John Keble *see* Keble Howard
Bell, Neil 258
Bell, O'Brien 127
Bell, Robert Stanley Warren 247-8, 274
Belloc, Hilaire 115, 133, 153, 170
Belloc, Marie A. *see* Lowndes, Marie Belloc
Benét, Stephen Vincent 116, 158, 195
Bennett, Arnold 25, 34, 46, 47, 48, 57, 93, 114, 115, 117, 132, 135, 151, 152, 154, 193-4, 203, 227, 269
Bennett, Edward 75
Bennett, Fred 64, 170, 252
Bennett, Hannaford 76, 274
Bennett, K. Maud 103, 275
Benson, A. C. 251

Benson, E. F. 14, 49, 59, 92, 93, 96, 103, 105, 110, 152, 189, 195, 234, 235, 256, 260, 262, 266, 268, 269
Benson, R. H. 133
Bensusan, S. L. 165
Bentley, George 266, 275
Bentley, Richard 242, 266, 275, 285
Bentley's Miscellany 266
Beresford, Charles 95
Beresford, J. D. 45, 109, 135, 172, 252, 253
Beresford, Leslie 84, 88, 171, 177, 179, 180
Bernay, Robert 136
Bernhardt, Sarah 84
Berry, William and Gomer 57
Besant, Walter 60, 95, 120, 160, 200, 232, 248, 256, 257, 270
Besier, Rudolf 183, 275
Best-Story Magazine, The 32, 33, **49**, 190, *Plate 7*
Bestall, Alfred 13, 252
Bevan, Tom 246
Biddle, Agnes M. 244
Bierce, Ambrose 143
Biggers, Earl Derr 106, 158
Binyon, Laurence 272
Bird, Richard 248
Birkenhead, Lord 93, 128, 135
Birmingham, George A. 122, 252
Bishop, James 256
Biss, Gerald 172, 257
Björnson, Björnstjerne 200
Black and White 21, 28, 58, 120, 143n, **244**
Black Cat, The (UK) 23, 24, 61, **244-5**
Black Cat, The (US) 59, 244
Black Mask 211, 215, 272
Black, Dorothy 45, 85
Black, Ladbroke 261, 267, 268, 275
Black, William 71
Blackmore, R. D. 54, 251, 254, 259
Blackwood & Sons 245-6, 275, 285
Blackwood, Algernon 14, 115, 126, 150, 162, 243, 259, 260, 264
Blackwood's Magazine 11, 16, 17, 24, 28, 29, **245-6**, 248, 251
Blake, George 207, 275
Blake, Stacey 65, 80, 116
Blasco Ibanez, Vicente 195
Blathwayt, Raymond 216, 275
Blochman, Lawrence G. 214
Bloom, Ursula 129, 145, 178, 189, 209, 214, 217
Blow, George 44
Blue Book Magazine 40, 80, 128, 130, 211

Blue Magazine, The 12, 14, 30, 34, **50-2**, 64, 110, 181, *Plate 4*
Blumenschein, E. S. 163
Blyton, Enid 133
Board, A. W. 211-2, 275, 285
Bodkin, M. McDonald 144, 184
Bond, Lee 221
Bonham-Carter, Lady 185, 253
Boot, W. H. 197
Boothby, Guy 22, 26, 124, 182, 224, 225, 233-4, 248
Borden, Mary 268
Bosanquet, Eva M. 143
Bott, Alan John 255, 275
Bottome, Phyllis 78, 105, 234, 269
Bottomley, Horatio 97, 180n, 185, 268, 285
Bowden, James 223
Bowen, Elizabeth 252, 272
Bowen, Marjorie 46, 49, 51, 84, 108, 117, 140, 145, 153, 181, 191, 212, 228, 235, 264, 268
Bowman, G. M. 43, 221
Boys' Friend, The 9
Boy's Own Paper, The 7, 7-8, 9, 10, 20, 28, 37, 77, 78, 230, 243, **246**, 248, 249
Braddon, Mary E. 29, 53, 82, 104, 114, 149, 233, 243-4, 266, 268, 275
Bradshaw, Stanley 44, 230
Brady, Cyrus T. 98, 163
Bramah, Ernest 59, 60, 78, 96n, 105, 125, 140, 152, 195, 268, 275
Brand, Max 64, 84
Brandon, John G. 86, 267
Brangwyn, Frank 96, 250
Brebner, Percy 220, 240
Bree, Olive *see* Sandys, Oliver
Brett, George Ira 59
Brett, R. Dallas 230
Brice, Alfred 120
Bridge, Ann 252
Bridges, T. C. 66, 248, 249
Brightwell, L. R. 92, 252
Brisbane, Coutts 176, 177, 210, 237, 238
Britannia 33, 247; see also *Britannia and Eve*
Britannia and Eve 15, 33, **247**, 256
British Weekly 20
Brittain, Vera 215
Broadwell, Albert H. 176, 275
Brock, C. E. 36, 110
Brock, H. M. 64, 170
Brontë, Charlotte 132
Brooks, Edwy Searles 240, 267
Broster, D. K. 266
Broughton, Rhoda 266

295

Brown, Hilton 41
Brown, Ivor 136, 137, 155, 275
Brown, Royal 124
Browne, Gordon 170
Browne, K. R. G. 80, 87, 141, 209
Bruce, A. Kerr 187
Bryant, Arthur 256
Buchan, John 9, 14, 29, 36, 49, 116, 125, 154, 245, 248, 254, 255, 260, 269
Buck, Pearl S. 258
Bucke, R. M. 162
Buckingham, George 105
Buley, Bernard 263
Bull, Charles Livingston 163, 227
Bullen, Frank T. 113
Bullivant, Cecil H. 109, 240, 275
Bulloch, John M. 255, 264, 265, 275
Bulwer-Lytton, Edward 4n, 71n, 245
Bunter, Billy 9
Burgess, Gelett 102
Burgin, George 94
Burgoyne, Alan 165
Burke, Thomas 49, 110, 126, 152, 190, 195, 204, 229
Burne-Jones, Edward 70
Burnett, Frances Hodgson 104, 133, 134, 233, 243, 263
Burrage, A. Harcourt 10
Burrage, A. M. 51, 65, 80, 84, 87, 109, 110, 116-7, 123, 144, 170, 174, 212, 219, 220, 228, 238, 240, 247
Burroughs, Edgar Rice 88, 188, 253, 261
Butler, Ellis Parker 102, 145, 163, 227, 252
Butt, Clara 232
Butterfly, The 22, 24, 61, **247**, 252
Byrd, Richard 166
Bystander, The 25, 36

Cabell, James Branch 113
Cable, Lindsay 92, 124, 157
Cady, Harrison 87
Caine, Hall 14, 24, 34, 95, 101, 132, 203, 256, 264
Cairns, Pat Robert 254
Caldecott, Randolph 70, 257
Calder-Marshall, Arthur 258
Calthrop, Dion Clayton 247
Campbell, (Sir) Gilbert 257, 275
Campbell, John F. 229
Campbell, Reginald 167, 181, 186
Campling, F. Knowles 250, 275; as Eric Wood 218-9, 249
Cannan, Joanna 45
Capes, Bernard 105, 251
Captain, The 9, 24, 31, 84, 203, **247-8**

Carlyle, Anthony 238
Carmarthen, Katherine 148
Carr, J. W. Comyns 29, 70-2, 76, 275
Carr, John Dickson 15, 205
Carre, Colin 120
Carroll, Lewis 48
Carruthers, D. F. Seton 163
Carter, Howard 166
Cartland, Barbara 264
Cassell, John 52, *52*, 53, 262, 275
Cassell's (Family) Magazine 8, 12, 14, 23-8 *passim*, 33, 34, **52-8**, *53*, 55, 56, 63, 118, 139, 145, 150, 152, 193, 195, 202, Plate 1
Cassell's Illustrated Family Paper 52
Cassell's Popular Magazine 32
Cassell's Saturday Journal 7, 20, 30, 53
Cassell's Winter Annual 56n
Castle, Agnes and Egerton 266
Cave, Hugh B. 68, 214, 236
Cecil, Edward 109
Central Publishing Company 75, 285
Century Illustrated Magazine, The 2, 10, 72, 149, 197, 270
Chambers, Charles E. S. 249, 275
Chambers, Robert, Jr. 248-9, 275
Chambers, Robert W. 27, 35, 46, 48, 56, 57, 74, 99, 115, 131-2, 173, 178, 264
Chambers, William and Robert 248-9, 275-6, 286
Chambers's (Edinburgh) Journal 16, 17, 26, 71, **248-9**, 251
Chancellor, David 187, 276
Chandler, Raymond 26, 249
Chapbook, The 59
Chapman and Hall 58-9, 61, 286
Chapman, Frederic 58
Chapman's Magazine 22, *58*, **58-61**, Plate 2; as *Crampton's Magazine* 23, 24, 25, *60*, 60-1, 245
Charing Cross Magazine, The 24, **61-2**, Plate 2
Charteris, Leslie 9, 15, 136, 154, 189, 195, 246, 250, 267
Chase, Frank 153
Chatterton, E(dward) Keble 105, 106, 276
Chatto and Windus 98, 99, 243-4, 286
Chatto, Andrew 244, 276
Chester, Austin 227
Chester, George Randolph 109, 131, 132
Chesterton, G. K. 14, 25, 30, 32, 35, 55, 75, 98-9, 125, 132-5 *passim*, 148, 150-1, 194, 254, 256; Father Brown 12, 27, 56, 126, 153, 170, 192, 205

Cheyney, Peter 15, 31, 64, 128, 267
Chidsey, Donald Barr 168
Child, Richard Washburn 135
Christie, Agatha 12, 15, 31, 32, 41, 84, 93, 125, 145, 167, 189, 205, 215, 247, 264; Miss Marple 33, 90, 136, 185, 195, 206; *see also* Poirot, Hercule
Christie, Vera 148
Christy, Chandler 131
Chums 9, 21, 35, 53, 248, **249-50**
Churchill, Winston 112, 135, 168, 204, 205, 259
Chute, Margaret 142
Clark, John Willis 262
Clarke, Arthur C. 36, 210
Clarke, Austin 47, 276
Clarke, George 265, 276
Clarke, Laurence 269, 276
Clayton, William 69, 236, 267
Cleator, P. E. 79
Cleaver, Hylton 228, 249
Cleaver, Reginald 92
Cleghorn, James 246
Clements-Henry, Bernard 245
Clevely, Hugh 267
Clifford, Guy 120
Clifford, Hugh 245
Clifford, Lucy 71, 233
Clode, E. J. 168
Cloete, Stuart 137
Clouston, J. Storer 109, 245
Club Room, The 2, 28, **62-3**, Plate 4
Clues 236
Cobb, Irvin S. 134
Cobden-Sanderson 70
Coblentz, Stanton A. 210
Cohen, Octavus Roy 66, 174, 181, 214,
Cole, G. D. H. and M. 90
Cole, Robert W. 257
Collier, John 258, 272
Collier's Weekly 109, 113, 158n,
Collingwood, Harry 10
Collins, William 90, 286
Collins, Dale 157, 185
Collins, Wilkie 4n, 52, 72, 243, 244, 251, 266
Colomb, Rear-Admiral Philip 244
Colour 28, 34, **250**
Comic Cuts 111
Compton, Fay 181
Connell, F. Norreys 121
Connell, John 16, 207
Connell, Richard 158, 252-3
Conrad, Joseph 24, 26, 32, 55, 92, 108, 114, 115, 151, 152, 153, 245, 256

INDEX

Conway, Hugh [Frederick John Fargus] 5-6, 71
Cook, Edward Dutton 252, 276
Cook, Frederick A. 60
Cook, Oscar 41, 42, 128, 276
Cooke, Alistair 229
Cooke, Clement Kinloch see Kinloch-Cooke, Clement
Cooper, Alfred B. 228, 265, 276
Coppard, A. E. 9, 85, 272
copyright 270
Corelli, Marie 31, 95, 103, 104, 113, 133, 200, 216, 233, 252, 264
Corner Magazine, The 31, 32, 33, 35, 46, *63*, **63-5**, Plate 5
Cornhill Magazine, The 5, 7, 10, 17, 58, 71, 197n, 198, 242, 243, **250-2**, 257, 258, 266
Cornier, Vincent 126, 167, 195
Coronet 13
Corvo, Baron 247, 269
Cosmopolis 23
Cosmopolitan 10-11, 109n, 131-2, 136, 198
Couch, Sir Arthur Quiller see Quiller-Couch, Arthur
Country Life 23, 234
Courier 35
Courtney, W. L. 58
Coward, Noël 48, 181, 253
Cox, Charles Roy 221
Cox, George 75
Cox, John R. ["Jack"] 246, 276
Crabbe, George 251
Crackanthorpe, Hubert 263
Crackanthorpe, Mrs 244
Craig, Elizabeth 179
Craig, Gordon 125
Craig, Isa 242, 276
Craik, Mrs 70, 254, 259
Cram, Mildred 84
Crampton's Magazine see *Chapman's Magazine*
Crandell, Bradshaw 136
Crane, Stephen 22, 59, 60, 74, 98, 242
Crane, Walter 29, 70, 244
Crawford, F. Marion 27, 72, 104
Crawfurd, Oswald 27, 58-61, 244, 245, 276
Creasey, John 207, 267
Crellin, H. N. 95
Cresswell, Mrs Ernest 244
Crockett, S. R. 14, 59, 83, 120, 225, 233, 260, 266
Crocombe, Leonard 267, 276
Croft, Freeman Wills 256
Croker, B. M. 59, 60, 101, 130
Crombie, Charles 11, 65, 80, 252

Crompton, Richmal 15, 100, 145, 166, 173, 186, 189, 209, 228, 268; William stories 2, 29, 65, 80, 87-8, 209, 235
Cronin, A. J. 136, 253
Crosland, T. W. H. 157
Crowley, Aleister 99
Cruickshank, Miss M. 235, 276
Cruikshank, George (Jr.) 257
Crusoe Mag., The 32, *65*, **65-6**, 80, Plate 6
Cumberland, Marten 247
Cumberland, May 119
Cuming, E. W. D. 128
Cuneo, Cyrus 169, 269
Curtis, Wardon Allan 161
Curwood, James Oliver 46, 81, 134, 158, 177, 181, 253
Curzon, (Lord) George 148
Cust, Henry 147

Dacre, J. Colne 244
Daily Chronicle 107
Daily Express 163, 183
Daily Mail 111
Daily Mirror 111
Dainty Novels 239
Dallas, Oswald 249
Daly, Carroll John 214
Dane, Clemence 47
Danger Trail 68
Daniel, Roland 267
Daniels, Charles H. 230-1, 276
D'Arcy, Ella 269
Dark, Sidney 61
Darlington, W. A. 141, 156, 166, 204
Daskam, Josephine Dodge 98, 102; as Josephine Daskam Bacon 134, 227
Daudet, Alphonse 11, 198, 263
Davies, W. H. 47
Davis, Frederick C. 212, 214, 221
Davis, Richard Harding 158, 227
Dawbarn, Clement 99
Dawe, Carlton 234
Dawn of Day, The 89n
Day-Lewis, C. 206
de Alarçon, Pedro A. 200
de Beck, Alexis M. 121, 216-7, 276
de Bra, Lemuel 128, 212, 214, 236
de Crespigny, Mrs Champion 172
de la Mare, Walter 22, 47, 105, 150, 152, 258, 264
de la Roche, Mazo 136, 254
de l'Isle-Adam, Villiers 198
de Meray, Jules 121, 286
de Polo, Harold 40
de Saint-Exupéry, Antoine 195
de Sélincourt, Hugh 228

Deeping, Warwick 37, 57, 64, 85, 93, 125, 136, 193, 194, 203, 235, 261, 262, 268
Delafield, E. M. 15, 125, 228, 253, 264
Dell, Draycot M. 77, 250, 276
Dell, Ethel M. 15, 24, 36, 64, 91, 121, 140, 143, 176-9 *passim*, 204, 235
Denham, Phyllis 185
Dent, Guy 214
Dent, J. M. 97, 286
Detective Library 66
Detective Magazine, The 14, 31, 32, **66-7**, 86, 127, 173, Plate 6
Detective Story Magazine 63, 127, 185
Detective Weekly 9, 267
Dickens, Charles 4n, 52, 132, 233, 251
Dickie, John M. 249, 276
Dicksee, Frank 257
Dickson, Lovat 258, 276, 286
Dilnot, George 66-7, 90, 173, 276
Dime etective 215
Dimmock, Haydn 263, 276
Dingle, Captain 174
Dixon, Meredith Vibart 41, 42, 93, 128, 129, 276
Doran, George H. 46, 136, 137, 276
Doubleday, F. N. 68, 136
Doudney, Sarah 242, 262
Dowling, Richard 200
Dowson, Ernest 263
Doyle, Arthur Conan 2, 5, 6, 9, 10, 11-12, 13-14, 21, 34, 48, 53, 55, 61, 82, 95, 108, 114-5, 120, 133, 143, 149, 162, 165, 194, 198-205, *200*, 216, 225, 244, 246, 248, 251, 257, 263, 266; see also Holmes, Sherlock
Doyle, Captain John E. 43
Drigin, Serge R. 44
Drinkwater, John 47, 252
Drummond, Hamilton 226
du Maurier, Daphne 15, 256
du Maurier, George 22, 120, 263, 270
du Maurier, Gerald 252
Dulac, Edmund 135, 151, 155, 250, 253, 256
Dundas, Ralph 77
Dunkerley, William 94-7, 268; as John Oxenham 37
Dunn, J. Allan 40, 63
Dunn, James Nicol 120, 121, 244, 276
Dunne, F. P. 98, 133
Dunsany, Lord 14, 206, 229, 247, 255, 264, 272
Durand, Ralph 229, 237
Dusart, George C. 245, 276

Dwyer, James Francis 85, 167, 171, 172, 177, 194, 228, 247

Eadie, Arlton 127, 214
Eardley, Blanche 264
Eckhardt, Oscar 247
Edginton, Daisy Mace 184
Edginton, May 84, 87, 177, 184, 185, 217, 222, 253
Edison, Thomas A. 132, 161, 226
Edmunds, Kay 157
Edwards, Amelia B. 254, 266
Edwards, Hamilton 175
Edwards, Henry Sutherland 255, 276
Eggenhofer, Nick 236
Eliot, George 233, 245, 251
Eliot, George Fielding 43, 218, 219, 230
Ellery Queen's Mystery Magazine 13
Empire Frontier 34, **67-9**, 68, Plate 7
England, George Allan 212
English Illustrated Magazine, The 2, 5, 10, 12, 20, 21, 22, 25, 28, **70-7**, 147, 150, 163, 197, 202, 225, Plate 1
English Review 40, 41
Ervine, St John 135
Eureka (The Favorite Magazine) 23, **252**
Eustace, Robert 54
Evans, H. Norman 126, 260, 276-7
Evans, (Frank) Howel 51, 124, 138, 176, 249
Eve 30, 33, 247; see also *Britannia and Eve*
Evening News (London) 111
Evens, R. H. 65
Everett, [Sir] Percy W. 141-4 *passim*, 146, 160, 164, 168, 183, 187, 264, 277
Every Girl's Magazine 242
Everybody's (US magazine) 78
Everybody's Story Magazine 12, 27, 28, 77, **77-8**, 193, Plate 4; as *Everyone's* 78
Everyone's Story Magazine see *Everybody's Story Magazine*
Everywoman's Weekly 31, 180
Eves, Reginald T. 218
Evesham Monthly Magazine, The 89, 89

Fairlie, Gerald 185-6, 267
Fane, Violet 105
Fantasy 36, 42, 43, 79, **79-80**, Plate 8
Fargus, Frederick John *see* Conway, Hugh
Farjeon, Eleanor 229
Farjeon, J. Jefferson 86

Farmer, Lucy 53
Farnol, Jeffery 14, 83, 229, 260
Farrar, F. W. 262
Farrow, G. E. 265
Favorite Magazine, The see *Eureka*
Fawcett, E. Douglas 73
Fayant, Frank 98
Fearn, John Russell 79, 210, 263
Fenn, George Manville 8, 27, 52-3, 57, 200, 243, 257, 266
Ferber, Edna 133, 140, 179
Fermor, Mary 264
Ferrier, Arthur 87, 124, 209
Fiddler, Henry J. 144
Field, Julian 148
Finn, Frank 105
Fireside Ghost Stories 260
Firth, Violet *see* Fortune, Dion
Fischer, Anton O. 131
Fisher, Harrison 35, 131, 136
Fitchew, Hubert 153, 155, 277
Fitzgerald, F. Scott 179, 195, 214, 235, 253
Flammarion, Camille 114, 185, 226
Flanagan, John R. 134, 253
Fleming, Peter 195
Fletcher, David 246
Fletcher, Guy 64
Fletcher, J. S. 90, 113, 143, 152, 255
Flint, W. Russell 250, 269
Flower, Newman 28, 47, 52, 55-6, 57, 139, 191-5 *passim*, 277
Flying 40, 42
Flying Aces 43
Flynt, Josiah 98
Forbes, Archibald 159
Forbes, Rosita 166
Forester, C. S. 15, 137, 195, 204
Forman, Henry 115
Forman, Justus Miles 29, 102, 227
Forster, E. M. 152
Fortnightly Review, The 58, 258
Fortune, Dion (*r.n.* Violet Firth) 31, 185
Foskett, Amy 217
Foster, Ernest 250, 277
Foster, Will 131
Fowler, E. Thorneycroft 104, 233
Francis, Henry 75
Frankau, Gilbert 84, 91, 117, 204, 247, 277
Frankau, Pamela 136, 185, 268
Fraser, Galloway 267, 277
Fraser, (Mrs) Hugh 104
Fraser, John Foster 115, 266, 277
Fraser's Magazine 257
Freeman, R. Austin 14, 23, 26, 54, 126, 143-4, 152, 164, 178, 183

Freeman, William 77, 123
Frith, Henry 53
Froest, Frank 171
Frontier, The/Frontier Stories 34, 67, 68, 236; see also *Empire Frontier*
Fry, C. B. 252, 277
Fry's Magazine 25, 29, 187n, **252**
Furniss, Harry 32, 70, 75, 257
Futrelle, Jacques 28, 55, 139, 176, 192

Gaiety 30, 33, 34, 209, **252-3**
Gainsborough, Thomas 70
Gale, Norman 160
Gallico, Paul 195
Gallon, Tom 139, 175, 191, 240
Galsworthy, John 34, 35, 47, 129, 133, 194, 195, 253, 268
Galt, John 245
Galton, Francis 258
"Ganpat" 229
Gardiner, Florence May 119
Gardner, Erle Stanley 181, 236
Garland, Ailsa 269
Garland, Hamlin 163
Garnett, David 195
Garnett, Mayn Clew 144
Garnett, Richard 74
Garstin, Crosbie 204, 228
Garth, Caswell 229
Garvice, Charles 30
Gaskell, (Mrs) Elizabeth 4n, 232, 251
Gaunt, Mary 59
Geddie, John Liddell 249, 277
Gem, The 9, 267
George, W. L. 106, 253
Ghosh, A. Sarath Kumar 162
Ghost Stories 41, 127, 128, 189
Ghosts and Goblins 260
Gibbon, J. M. 244, 277
Gibbon, Perceval 135, 245
Gibbons, Stella 15, 137
Gibbs, Philip 91, 135, 190
Gibson, Charles Dana 88, 131, 163
Gielgud, Val 64
Gilbert, W. S. 150, 200
Gilchrist, R. Murray 250
Gill, Tom 45
Gillespie, H. J. 273, 277
Gilligan, Miss G. 41, 42, 93, 128, 129, 189, 277
Gillings, Walter 210-11, 277
Gilson, Captain Charles 246, 248
Gingold, Hermione 51, 129
Girls' Crystal, The 9
Girls' Friend, The 9
Girl's Own Paper, The 9, 77, 78
Girl's Realm, The 234

INDEX

Gissing, George 59, 74, 75, 97, 124, 266, 269
Gladwin, Peter 66
Glossop, Reginald 65, 124
Glyn, Elinor 33, 37, 84, 104, 122, 124, 133, 135, 145, 154, 181, 185, 217
Goble, Warwick 11, 37, 162
Goddard, Ernest Hope 277
Golden Book Magazine 46, 190; British edition 33, 46n, 272
Golden Mag., The 32, 66, *80*, **80-1**, *Plate 7*; as *The Golden West* 33, 80-1, *Plate 7*
Golden West, The see *The Golden Mag.*
Golden West Magazine (US pulp) 81
Golding, Harry 33, 228, 277
Golding, Louis 47, 250
Goller, Izak 92
Golsworthy, Arnold 75, 217, 222, 247, 252, 261, 277
Good Cheer 254
Good Housekeeping, 13, 15, 31, 36, 92, 106, 129, 134-7 *passim*, 154, 155, 235, **253-4**, 271
Good Words 26, 223, 231, **254**
Goodwin, Beatrice 235, 277
Gordon, Leslie H. 110
Gorell, Lord 252, 277
Gorki/Gorky, Maxim 75, 194
Gosse, Edmund 269
Grace, W. G. 72, 119
Graeme, Bruce 15, 32, 57, 63, 140, 141, 267
Graham, Winifred 83, 142, 144, 257, 261, 264
Graham, Winston 229
Grahame, Kenneth 14
Grahame-White, Claude 78
Grand Magazine, The 2, 10, 26, 27, 28, 31, 36, 61, 68, **81-6**, *81*, *85*, 122, 130, 141-2, 146, 191, *Plate 3*
Grand, Sarah 233
Grange, A. Demaine 108
Grant, Gerald 83
Grant, James 244, 257
Graphic, The 20, 21, 24, 34, 244, **254-5**, 256, 264
Graves, Charles L. 277
Graves, Clotilda 247
Gray, John 247
Graydon, Robert Murray 9
Grayle, ubert 119
Green Magazine, The 31, **86-7**, 177, 178, 179, *Plate 5*
Green, Anna Katherine 102, 142
Green, Edward 43

Green, Roger Lancelyn 1, 3, 5, 6, 13
Greenaway, Kate 242, 263
Greene, Graham 15, 206
Greene, L. Patrick 15, 68, 145, 181, 213, 236, 259
Greening, Arthur C. 256-7, 277, 286
Greenup, Joseph 167
Greenwood, Anthony 177, 214
Greenwood, Frederick 252
Greenwood, James 118
Greiffenhagen, Maurice 34, 244, 247
Greig, Edvard 232
Grey, Zane 57, 80, 109, 166
Grierson, Francis D. 128, 213
Griff, Alan 250
Griffith, George 26, 160, 161, 226, 261, 264
Griffiths, Arthur 75
Grimshaw, Beatrice 26, 41, 84, 85, 109, 145, 164, 166, 171, 172, 174, 194, 212, 226, 247, 266
Grimshaw, Eric 267
Grogan, Walter E. 228
Grossmith, George 6, 95
Grove, George 259, 277
Groves, Joseph 62
Gülich, John 94
Gull, C. Ranger *see* Thorne, Guy
Gunter's Magazine 272
Gurdon, John E. 43
Gwynn, Stephen 251

Hadath, Gunby 10, 248
Haddon, Walter 247, 286
Haggard, H. Rider 1, 4, 9, 13-14, 20, 21, 32, 41, 54, 55, 91, 93, 95, 104, 130, 149, 153, 164, 178, 194, 200, 203, 226-7, 243, 251, 252, 255, 256, 258, 261, 262
Haldane, J. B. S. 254
Halkett, George R. 24, 150-1, 155, 277
Hall, James Norman 36, 229
Halls, Leonard 246, 277
Hambledon, Phyllis 100, 145, 177, 209
Hamilton, Cosmo 89, 268
Hamilton, Edmond 210
Hamilton, John 231, 286
Hamilton, Lord Frederick 23, 147-50 *passim*, 155, 277
Hammerton, J. A. 113-4, 117, 277
Hammond, Laurence 48
Hannigan, D. F. 119
Hanshew, T. W. 56
Happy Mag., The 14, 31, 36, 65, 84, 87, **87-8**, 123, 205, 209, 217, *Plate 5*
Harcourt-Smith, Sir Cecil 93

Harding, Robert 246, 277
Hardy, Dudley 94
Hardy, Iza Duffus 261
Hardy, Paul 162, 265
Hardy, Thomas 20, 21, 33, 48, 71, 75, 113, 132, 149, 150, 151, 243, 248, 251, 254, 255, 256, 258, 259, 264, 270
Hare, Cyril 168
Harland, Henry 269, 277
Harmsworth, Alfred (Lord Northcliffe) 7, 9, 31, 111-4, 153.
Harmsworth, Cecil 111-2, 117, 278
Harmsworth, Harold 112
Harmsworth's Magazine see *The London Magazine*
Harper, Harry 78
Harper's Bazaar 34, 155, 229, 271, **272**
Harper's (New) Monthly Magazine 2, 10, 22, 72, 197, 198, 226, 270; European edition 72, 149, 197, 270
Harris, Frank 58, 168
Harris, Joel Chandler 74
Harris, John Beynon ("John Wyndham") 79, 210, 261
Harris-Burland, J. B. 173, 257
Harrison, Van 214
Harte, Bret 11, 59, 72, 95, 151, 160, 162, 200, 243, 256, 268
Hartley, L. P. 264
Harvey, William Fryer 215
Harwood, John Berwick 53
Hastings, Basil Macdonald 157, 174
Hastings, Macdonald 206, 207, 278
Hatchards 242-3, 286
Haweis, Hugh R. 52-3, 57
Hawthorne, Julian 74
Hay, Ian 28, 245
Haydon, Arthur L. 246, 278
Haydon, Percy Montague ["Monty"] 267, 278
Hayward, Arthur Lawrence 250, 278
Head, Alice Maud 32, 135-6, 137, 234-5, 254-5, 278
Headley, Francis 187
Heard, Gerald 137
Hearst, William Randolph 131, 134, 153, 253
Heather, Roy 180
Heinemann, William 148, 150, 243, 286
Heitner, Jesse 247, 265, 278
Hemingway, Ernest 136, 258
Henderson, James 3
Henley, Trevor 267, 278
Henley, William Ernest 4, 5, 16, 25, 75, 148, 151

Henry, Charles 77
Henry, O. 27, 47, 99, 122, 176
Henry, Thomas 65, 80, 87, 141, 209, 235, 252
Henson, Leslie 123-4, 166, 278
Henty, G. A. 8, 257, 266
Herbert, A. P. 158
Herbert, Benson 210
Herbert, Charles 266, 278
Hergesheimer, Joseph 185
Hering, Henry A. 54, 55, 225
Herman, Henry 119
Heron-Maxwell, Beatrice 51, 60, 78, 83, 181, 257
Hersey, John 137
Hewlett, Maurice 228
Heydemarck, Haupt 230
Heyer, Georgette 15, 67, 88
Hichens, Robert S. 14, 22, 37, 49, 85, 91, 140, 148, 154, 216, 260
Hickling, P. B. 124, 209
Higginbottom, Frederick 150, 278
Hill, Headon 192, 264
Hilton, James 93, 168, 195, 254
Hird, Frank 120
Hitchcock, Alfred 57
Hitler, Adolf 136
Hobbes, John Oliver 82, 89, 232
Hocking, Joseph 77, 266
Hocking, Silas K. 107, 266, 278
Hodder & Stoughton 234, 235, 270, 286
Hodgson, William Hope 51, 82, 99, 115, 130, 171, 177, 192, 251, 260, 262
Hogg, James (Jr) 257, 278
Hogg, James (Sr) 11n, 245
Holborn Monthly Magazine, The 25, **89** *Plate 2*
Holden, J. Railton 230
Holland, Clive 102
Holmes, Sherlock 2, 6, 10, *11*, 11-12, 21, 22, 33, 85, 98, 160, 198-9, *199*, 201, 203, 205, 208, 225, 251, 270; parodies or pastiches 67, 77, 95, 128, 132, 162, 173, 206, 207, 220, 223-4, 240, 253
Home Chimes 6, 21, **255**
Home Magazine (weekly) 265
Home Magazine, The see *Woman at Home*
Home Magazine (of Fiction), The see *The Lady's Magazine*
Home-Gall, William B. 250, 278
Hood, Tom 257
Hoole, J. 181, 278
Hope, Anthony 6, 9, 14, 54, 97, 120, 124, 130, 150, 160, 190, 244, 248

Hopkins, R. Thurston 126
Hoppé, E. A. 250
Hopwood, Avery 64
Horler, Sidney 64, 267
Horlick's Magazine 25, 26, **255-6**
Horn, Holloway 87, 109, 252
Hornibrook, Evelyn 49, 93, 190, 278
Hornibrook, J. L. 112
Hornung, E. W. 14, 59, 178, 198, 203, 244, 248, 251; Raffles 23, 54, 67, 151, 267
Household, Geoffrey 136
Housman, Clemence 243
Housman, Laurence 98, 247, 269
How, Harry 200
Howard, F. Morton 45, 87, 123, 124, 141, 145, 173, 174, 177, 238
Howard, Green 214
Howard, Keble (r.n. John Keble Bell) 88, 108, 145, 157, 228, 264, 269, 274
Howard-Burleigh, Florence 177, 179
Howitt, Mary 257
Hubbard, Elbert 29, 132
Hubbard, L. Ron 236
Hueffer, Oliver Madox 41, 67, 122, 153
Hughes, Richard 128, 272
Hughes, Thomas 7, 259
Hugo, Victor 151, 255
Hull, E. M. 15, 30, 32, 134, 166, 180
Hulme-Beaman, Emeric 75
Hume, Fergus 6, 49, 95, 199, 244
Hume, Martin 130
Humorist, The 84, 205
Humphreys, Mrs Desmond ("Rita") 61, 200
Hunt, Bonavia 29, 53, 55, 57, 262, 278
Hunt, Violet 59, 60, 74, 244
Hunter, John 65, 80, 249, 267
Hurst, Fannie 45, 134, 145, 268, 269
Hush 14, 34, **90**, *90*, *Plate 7*
Huskinson, Edward 247
Hutchinson, A. S. M. 152, 183, 278
Hutchinson, Arthur 225-8, 230, 278
Hutchinson, George (artist) 94,
Hutchinson, George (publisher), 103
Hutchinson, Walter 15, 40-2, 49, 91, 92-3, 103
Hutchinson's (Story) Magazine 2, 14, 30, 32, 33, 34, **91-3**, *92*, 167, 189, 268, *Plate 4*
Hutchinson's Mystery-Story Magazine see *Mystery-Story Magazine*
Hutchison, George Andrew 246, 278
Huxley, Aldous 136, 204, 254

Huxley, Leonard 132, 252, 278
Huxley, T. H. 70
Hyatt-Woolf, Charles 121, 278
Hyne, C. J. Cutcliffe 14, 24, 48, 53, 54, 74, 111, 113, 114, 142, 149, 150, 152, 160-1, 165, 183, 200, 225, 226, 247, 260, 262; Captain Kettle 12, 22, 116, 160

Ibsen, Henrik 232
Ideas 152
Idler, The 21-7 *passim*, 59, 73, 82, **93-100**, *95*, *97*, *99*, 120, 247, 268, 270, *Plate 1*
Ignatius, Father 95
Iliffe & Sons 152-3, 155, 287
Illustrated London News 73-4, 225, 247, 254, **256**, 264
Imbush, Paul 267, 278
Imp, The 26, 28, **256-7**
Ingelow, Jean 242, 254
Ingram, Bruce 74-5, 76, 256, 264, 278
Ingram, Hugh 256
Ingram, William 73
Irving, Sir Henry 96
Irwin, Wallace 45
Isbister, William 254, 287

Jackson, Holbrook 263, 265, 268, 278
Jacobs, W. W. 14, 37, 47, 48, 75, 82, 97, 113, 125, 133, 201-5 *passim*, 225, 247, 248, 255
James, Henry 71, 244, 251, 256, 258, 259, 269
James, M. R. 148
Jameson, Storm 154, 185
Jane, Fred T. 73, 262
Jefferies, Richard 258
Jenkins, Herbert 123, 166
Jenks, Tudor 102
Jepson, Edgar 14, 51, 85, 122, 143, 177, 182, 203, 255-6, 269
Jepson, Selwyn 45, 117, 177
Jerome, Jerome K(lapka) as author 6, 14, 21, 33, 47, 59, 99, 133, 171, 244, 255, 262; as editor 22, 93-7, 268, 279
Jerome, Miss 268, 279
Jesse, F. Tennyson 83, 99, 117, 126, 172, 181
Jewett, Sarah Orne 98
John Bull 156, 180n
John o'London's Weekly 29
John, Augustus 250
Johns, W. E. 10, 15, 43, 168, 215, 230, 246, 267, 279
Johnson, Amy 146
Johnson, Morgan 180

INDEX

Johnson, Owen 77
Johnson, Pamela Hansford 136
Jokaï, Moritz 200
Jolly Mag., The 14, 33, 87, **100**, 189, Plate 7
Joseph, Michael 128
Joyce, Thomas Heath 255, 279
Judd, Alfred 249

Kahnert, M. E. 230
Kaye-Smith, Sheila 134, 194
Keary, Peter 29, 160, 183, 187, 261, 267, 279
Keeler, Harry Stephen 41, 67
Keene, Norman 124
Kelland, Clarence B. 67
Keller, David H. 210
Kenealy, Annesley 105
Kenealy, Arabella 104, 234
Kennedy, Margaret 185
Kennedy, (Miss) N. W. 145-6, 279
Kent, Michael 46, 84, 87, 144, 145, 177, 209, 262
Ker, David 246
Kernahan, Coulson 216, 225
Kerr, Sophie 262, 269
Kersh, Gerald 15, 206
Kilbourne, Fannie 213
King, Basil 133
King-Hall, Magdalen 185
King-Hall, Stephen 168
Kingsley, Charles 7, 234, 254, 259
Kingsley, Henry 257, 259
Kingston, Charles 64
Kingston, W. H. G. 8, 246
Kinloch-Cooke, Clement 72, 76, 279
Kinsella, E. P. 88
Kipling, Rudyard 4, 9, 11, 13-14, 22, 23, 24, 26, 35, 54, 57, 75, 94, 95, 96, 97, 113, 115, 116, 118, 130, 133, 135, 162, 164, 192, 194, 200, 203, 205, 225-6, 253, 258, 268
Kisch, John 256
Klickmann, Flora 77-8, 225, 279
Knight, Kobold 140, 228
Knox, G. D. 237
Knox, Ronald A. 206
Komroff, Manuel 206
Kruger, Paul 75

Ladies' Home Journal, The 101
Ladies' Home Magazine 31
Lady's Magazine, The 24, 25, *101*, **101-3**, *Plate 2*; as *The Home Magazine of Fiction* 26, 102, 141
Lady's Realm, The 23, 27, 29, 62, 75, 101, *103*, **103-106**, 231, *Plate 2*
Lady's World, The 174

Lagerhof, Selma 104
Lambert, F. J. 121, 257, 287
Lambert's Monthly 21, 118, **257**
Lamburn, Frank J. 261, 279
Lancaster, G. B. 45, 185, 235
Landon, Herman 63
Lane, Jeremy 180
Lang, Andrew 4, 14, 75, 95, 251, 257-8, 263
Lardner, Ring 268
Lascelles, Ida 268, 279
Latey, John 264, 279
Latey, John Lash 256, 279
Lavor, Yvan 247
Lawrence, Arthur 24, 97, 99, 279
Lawrence, D. H. 34, 92, 154, 204
Lawrence, Margery 49, 92, 128, 268
Layard, Arthur 97
Layard, George 148
Laye, Evelyn 181
Le Couteur, Frank 255, 279
Le Fanu, Joseph Sheridan 4n, 52, 243
Le Gallienne, Richard 269
Le Queux, William 9, 33, 54, 83, 97, 108, 111, 128, 130, 139, 169, 171, 172, 175, 184, 189, 191, 201, 234, 244, 248, 265
Lea, Fannie Heaslip 84, 110, 134, 185, 235, 253
Leacock, Stephen 100, 135, 140, 252
Leblanc, Maurice 26, 114, 139, 154, 191, 212, 265
Lee, Katharine 233
Lee, Sidney 251
Leeston, Osyth 252
Leete, Alfred 87, 110, 252
Leggett, H. W. 84-5, 209, 279
Leigh, Conrad 229
Leinster, Murray 81
Leith, Alicia A. 243, 279
Lemon, Mark 257
Leno, Dan 112
Leroux, Gaston 64, 92, 176
Leslie, Frank 256
Lessing, Bruno 78, 131, 132, 134, 252
Lessing, Charlotte 254
Level, Maurice 158
Leverington, A. C. 44
Leverson, Ada 244
Levetus, Celia 97
Lewes, George Henry 233, 252, 279
Lewis, Henry Prothero 242
Lewis, Sinclair 135-6
Ley, Willy 79
Lichfield, C. Randolph 56, 240
Liddell, Walter Scott 279
Liebe, Hapsburg 236
Lilliput 13, 16, 36, 206, 207, 215

Lindsay, Mayne 192, 225
Linton, Eliza Lynn 233, 251
Lippincott's Magazine 10, 21, 149, 198, 223, 270
Liszt, Franz 232
Little Folks 53
Little, Arthur 168
Lloyd, Edward 107
Lloyd, Marie 61
Lloyd's (Story) Magazine, 29, 30, 31, *107*, **107-10**, 212n, 243, *Plate 4*
Locke, William J. 9, 34, 46, 133, 153, 203, 253
Locker, Arthur 255, 279
Lockhart, John Gibson 245
Lofting, Kitty 240
London, Jack 29, 83, 98, 105, 115, 131, 132, 133, 151, 152, 163, 176, 227, 252
London Magazine, The 1, 16, 25, 26, 56, 68, 86, *111*, **111-8**, 134, 169, 170, 172, 175; as *Harmsworth's Magazine* 12, 23, 111-2, 181-2, 202, *Plate 2*; as *The New London Magazine* 34, 35, *117*, 117, 195
London Mercury, The 30, 36
London Opinion 268
London Society 23, 257
Longman (publisher) 5, 6, 243, 287
Longman, Charles J. 258, 279
Longman's Magazine 20, 21, 26, 58, 197, 250. **257-8**
Loos, Anita 135
Lorant, Stefan 206, 215
Lovat Dickson's Magazine 35, **258**
Lovell, John 52, 57
Low, A. M. 263
Low, David 136
Low, Sir Ernest 86
Lowell, Percival 226
Lowndes, Marie Belloc 27, 57, 82, 84, 128, 130, 253, 268; as Marie Belloc 102, 234
Lowry, H. D. 121, 224, 247, 279
Ludgate Monthly, The 21, 22, 23, 24, *118*, **118-22**, 202, 216, 228, 257, *Plate 1*
Ludgate Weekly, The 21, 119
Lunn, Erle 91, 279
Lytton, Earl 71

Mabey, Judith Lynn 229
Macauley, James 246, 279
Macauley, Rose 272
McBlair, 221
McClure, S. S. 74, 98, 198, 199
McClure's Magazine 74, 98, 163n, 198, 199, 227, 270

301

McCormack, Helen 134
MacCreagh, Gordon 41
McCulley, Johnston 40, 42, 63, 100, 185, 189, 236
MacDonald, George 4n, 26, 242, 251, 254
Macfadden, Bernarr 41, 127, 128, 189, 262
MacGrath, Harold 98, 143
Machen, Arthur 14, 59, 255
Mackail, Denis 166, 185, 204
Mackay, Charles 256
McKeag, Ernest 217, 218, 219
Mackenzie, Compton 15, 122, 133, 140, 153, 194
McKenzie, F. A. 115, 215
MacKenzie, Miss F. C. 181, 279
Mackinlay, M. 92
Maclanachan, William 43
Maclaren, Ian 233, 265
Macleod, Donald 254, 279
Macleod, Fiona *see* Sharp, William
Macleod, Norman 254, 279
MacManus, Seamus 89
Macmillan (publisher) 72, 242, 270, 287
Macmillan, Alexander 70
Macmillan's Magazine 26, 70, 71, 151, 250, **258-9**
McNeile, H. C. ["Sapper"] 2, 15, 30, 36, 40, 83, 91, 92, 110, 116, 139, 167, 189, 193, 204, 205; Bulldog Drummond, 2, 30, 91, 93, 116, 189, 252
McPeake, Alan Y. 135, 155, 272, 279
McPeake, J. Y. 32, 131, 135, 137, 253, 154, 280
Macrae, Stuart 185-6, 187, 280
Maeterlinck, Maurice 263
Magazine of Short Stories see *Short Stories*
Maginn, William 49
Magnay, Sir William 240
Magnet, The 9, 26, 267
Magpie, The 28, 62, 122, **122-3**, *Plate 4*
Maitland, F. W. 70
Major, Dagney 62
Makin, William J. 167, 168, 186, 187, 252, 261, 280
Malet, Lucas 233, 234
Malloch, G. R. 79, 167
Mannin, Ethel 45, 51, 100, 145, 214, 256
Mansfield, Katherine 265
Mansford, Charles J. 119, 200, 225, 260
Marc, Elizabeth 166

Marchmont, A. W. 182
Margerison, John 83, 116, 184
Marky, Alexander 168
Marmur, Jacland 214, 253
Marriott, William 164
Marriott Watson, H. B. 176
Marriott Watson, Rosamund ("Graham R. Tomson") 223n
Marryat, Florence 118, 233, 243, 257, 266
Marryat, Frederick 8
Marsh, Ngaio 15
Marsh, Richard 29, 61, 111, 112, 193, 200, 203, 240, 243, 255
Marshall Brothers 243, 287
Marshall, A. C. 66, 280
Marshall, E. Forster 78
Marshall, Edison 40, 174, 253
Marshall, Horace 99, 121, 122, 123, 216, 266, 287
Martin, David 43
Martin, J. Sackville 143
Martin, Stuart 43, 177, 238
Martineau, Harriet 251
Maschwitz, Eric 41, 51, 91, 181, 189, 280
Masefield, John 136, 152
Mason, A. E. W. 14, 37, 54, 84, 91, 113, 114, 130, 155, 203, 206, 234, 244, 251, 264
Mason, F. van Wyck 236
Masson, David 259, 280
Master Thriller series 35, 36, 126, 210, **259-60**
Matania, Fortunio 117, 247, 256, 261
Mathews, Basil 260, 280
Maton, Grenville 121
Matthews, Brander 59, 74
Maude, Captain F. N. 244
Maugham, W. Somerset 23, 25, 31, 32, 45, 68, 85, 134, 135, 146, 152, 166, 203, 206, 234, 254, 259, 272
Maupassant, Guy de 11, 47, 197, 198
Maxwell, Frederick 220
Maxwell, John 243, 266
Maxwell, Perriton 131, 137, 280
Maxwell, W. B. 235, 244
May, Phil (artist) 25
May, Philip 118-9, 121, 257, 280
Mayer, Gertrude 266, 280
Meade, L. T. 14, 53, 54, 200-1, 225, 233, 243, 257, 262, 265, 266, 280
Meadland, Richard L. 136-7, 280
Mee, Arthur 244, 280
Mégroz, Phyllis 250
Men Only 16, 35, 37, 206, 207
Meredith, George 75, 149, 248, 251
Mérimée, Prosper 200

Merrick, Leonard 176, 204
Merriman, Henry Seton 14, 54, 224
Merry Mag., The 32, 34, 87, *123*, **123-3**, 179, *Plate 6*
Meynell, Laurence 228
Michael, A. C. 152
Middleton, Jessie A. 102
Midnight Mysteries 127
Mighels, Philip Verrill 75
Millar, H. R. 11, 96, 130, 170, 202
Miller, John L. 44
Million, The 21
Mills, (Lady) Dorothy 166
Mills, J. Dewar 180
Miln, (Mrs) George Crichton 105, 106
Miln, H. Crichton 217n, 218
Milne, A. A. 15, 137; Winnie the Pooh 15, 116, 185, 268
Milne, James W. 273, 280
Miniter, Edith 140
Minney, R. J. 205-6, 207, 280
Minster, The 22, **124-5**, 247, *Plate 1*
Mitchison, Naomi 229
Moberly, L. G. 102, 107, 228
Modern Boy, The 9, 250
Modern Stories 35, **125**, *Plate 8*
Moffett, Cleveland 161-2
Molesworth, Mary 72, 233, 243
Moore, Brinsley 184, 193
Moore, F. Frankfort 96, 101, 104, 176, 234
Moore, George 75, 150, 151, 268
Mordaunt, Elinor 41, 45, 46, 50, 157, 247, 268
Morgan, Charles L. 228
Morgan, Hawley 178, 238
Morley, Charles 26, 151-3, 155, 280
Morley, John 151, 259, 280
Morrah, Herbert 242, 280
Morris, Gouverneur 122, 133, 134, 269
Morris, Mowbray 259, 280
Morris, William 21, 71, 74
Morrison, Arthur 4, 14, 22, 113, 122, 152, 201, 224, 247, 266, 269
Morrow, Albert 64, 70, 139, 192n
Morton, J. B. 157
Muddock, J. E. Preston ("Dick Donovan") 200, 267
Muir, Augustus 66, 261, 280
Muir, Ward 192, 234
Mulford, Clarence E. 81
Mundy, Talbot 28, 63, 83, 115, 139, 144, 184, 193, 215
Munns, Bernard 75
Munro, Neil 245
Munsey, Frank A. 8n, 198

INDEX

Munsey's Magazine 198
Murdoch, Richard 207
Murray, Andrew 86
Murray, D. Christie 72, 200, 233, 244, 248, 251
Murray, John 251-2, 287
Murray, Marr 63
Mussolini, Benito 136
Mystery and Detection 35, **126**, *Plate 8*
Mystery Stories 35, 37, **126**, *Plate 8*
Mystery-Story Magazine 10, 14, 31, 40, *127*, **127-9**, 189, 211, *Plate 6*

Nabokov, Vladimir 258
Nash, Eveleigh 129-31, 137, 260, 280, 287
Nash's Annual 36, 37, 137
Nash's Illustrated Weekly 30, **260**
Nash's Magazine 2, 27, 28, 33, *129*, **129-137**, 227, *Plate 3*; as *Nash's and Pall Mall* 13, 18, 31, 33, 34, 36, 45, 57, 68, 85, 92, 98, 109n, 110, *131*, *136*, 153, 154, 185, 193, 194, 204, 229, 235, 253, 254, 260
Naumann, Paul 252, 280
Neish, Rosalie 101-2
Nesbit, Edith 14, 26, 31, 60, 113, 130, 150, 151, 152, 178, 201, 202-3, 225, 234, 242, 243, 244, 255, 256, 258, 265, 269
Neville, Agnes 244
New Century Press 60, 61, 62, 245, 247, 288
New Century Review 60, 61
New London Magazine, The see *The London Magazine*
New Magazine, The (UK) 14, 27, 28, 32, 33, 34, 50, 57, 63, *138*, **138-41**, *Plate 4*
New Magazine, The (US) 272
New Penny Magazine, The 23, 32, 191; as *P. M.* 32
New Review, The 22
New Stories 35, 258
New Strand, The 207
New Worlds 79, 211
New Writing 35, 36, 258
Newbery House Magazine, The 124
Newbolt, Henry 245
Newman, Ronald M. 128
Newnes, [Sir] George 7, 10, 11, 27, 72, 81, 95, 159, *196*, 196-8, 203, 267, 280
Newsom, J. D. 68
Newton, Douglas 42, 45, 86, 108, 157, 167, 170, 213, 237, 240, 261, 264

Nicholls, Beverly 136
Nicholson, Ivor 36, 135-6, 137, 155, 280
Nicholson, Lindsay 254
Nicoll, W. Robertson 231-2
Nielsen, Kay 256
Norfield, Edgar 168
Norman, Bruce 186
Norman, Philip 74
Normanby, Henry 82
Normanton, Helena 154
Norris, Elsie 220
Norris, Frank 101
Norris, W. E. 72
Northcliffe, Lord see Harmsworth, Alfred
Northcroft, George J. H. 246, 280
Norton, Roy 176, 177, 179
Novel Magazine, The 2, 12, 26, 31, 36, 61, 81, 82, 85, 102-3, 130, 138, **141-6**, *142*, *145*, 166, 184, 191, *Plate 3*
Novello, Ivor 181
Noyes, Alfred 47, 56, 140, 194

O'Brien, E. J. 46, 166
Observer, The 152
O'Connor, T. P. 153, 265, 280
Odell, Maude 184
Odhams Press, 156, 159, 181, 268, 288
Odle, E. V. 47, 253, 281
O'Donnell, Elliott 92, 98, 127, 144, 172, 187, 220, 250, 257
O'Donnell, W. A. 46, 179, 281
O'Farrell, Philip 168, 281
Ogilvie, Charles
"Ole-Luke-Oie" see Swinton, Colonel Ernest
Oliphant, Margaret 4n, 23, 72, 243, 245, 248, 251, 254-5, 258
Oliver, Edwin 62, 97, 99, 243, 281
Oliver, John 265
Oliver, Owen 86, 107, 238
Onions, Oliver 49, 126, 152, 176, 191, 219, 220, 229, 269
Oppenheim, E. Phillips 12, 37, 46, 57, 74, 84, 108, 126, 133, 134, 145, 191, 192, 193, 203, 204, 234, 252
Orczy, Baroness 14, 37, 91, 129, 138, 142, 162, 172, 182, 227, 229, 234, 256-7; Old Man in the Corner 24, 183; Lady Molly 27, 55, 170; Scarlet Pimpernel 56, 83, 84, 140, 194, 253
Ormsby, Fritz 62
Osborne, The 23, **260**
Osbourne, Lloyd 83
O'Sullivan, Sally 254

O'Sullivan, Vincent 171
Ottolengui, Rodriguez 95
Ouida 54, 233, 257
Outward Bound 30, 31, **260**
Ovington, Mary 260
Owen, Will 87, 88, 163, 234, 252
Oxenham, John see Dunkerley, William
Oxford, Margot 268
Ozaki, Yei Theodora 105

Packard, Frank L. 40, 56, 63, 78
Paderewski, Ignatz 232
Paget, Sidney 11, 26, 199, 201
Pain, Barry 14, 75, 82, 95, 96, 97, 115, 120, 122, 124, 133, 157, 176, 204, 225, 228, 234, 247, 252, 281
Pain, Mrs Barry 222
Paine, Albert Bigelow 81, 163
Pall Mall Gazette 147, 149, 151, 200
Pall Mall Magazine, The 1, 22, 23, 24, 25, 26, 27, 28, 33, 59, 73, 133, 135, **147-56**, *154*, 163, 168, *Plate 1*
Palmer, Mark 256
Pan 29, 30, 31, 145, *156*, **156-9**, 180, 213, *Plate 5*
Pangborn, Georgia 269
Pankhurst, Sylvia 164
Parade 36, 37, 215
Pargeter, Edith 215
Parker, Gilbert 14, 48, 72, 74, 96, 114, 148, 256, 266
Parker, Oscar 75, 76, 281
Parker, Percy L. 112, 117, 281
Parry, D. H. 249, 250
Passing Show, The 29, 34, 36, 156, **260-1**
Pater, Walter 259
Patti, Adelina 232
Payn, James 59, 71, 124, 243, 248, 249, 251, 252, 256, 281
Payne, R. T. 267
Peake, Mervyn 206
Pearson, C. Arthur 7, 30, 101, 114, 159-63 passim, 168, 181, 183, 261, 263, 264, 281
Pearson's Magazine 1, *12*, 13, 14, 16, 22-7 passim, 30, 31, 32, 35, 36, 74, 79, 92, 110, 113, 114, 116, 144, *159*, **159-69**, *166*, 182, 195, 202, 204, 243, 258, *Plate 2*; US edition 161, 163, 168
Pearson's Story-Teller 22, **261**
Pearson's Weekly 7, 21, 23, 36, 159, 161, 183, **261**, 264
Peary, Robert 89, 130
Peattie, Elia W. 78
Pechey, Archibald ("Valentine") 50

303

Pedler, Margaret 178, 179
Pegram, Fred 94, 269
Pemberton, Clive 257
Pemberton, Max 23, 37, 53-5, 57, 82, 100, 109, 124, 140, 162, 170, 201, 202, 203, 226, 234, 248, 249, 250, 281
Pendarves, G. G. 127
Penny Magazine, The see *The New Penny Magazine*
Penny Pictorial Magazine, The 24, 113
People's Magazine, The 211, 212n
Percival, Stanley 121
Perowne, Barry (*r.n.* Atkey, Philip) 80, 88, 166, 209, 229, 267, 274
Perrin, Alice 45, 46, 60, 143, 173, 179, 225, 243
Perris, George 60, 61, 281
Pertwee, Roland 139, 158, 166, 204
Peters, A. D. 159, 281
Peterson, Margaret 217, 218
Petrie, Flinders 70
Philips, Austin 66
Phillips, Henry Wallace 98
Phillips, Stephen 174, 214, 237
Phillpotts, Adelaide 110
Phillpotts, Eden 46, 47, 59, 95, 96, 97, 100, 110, 117, 120, 125, 152, 190, 195, 201, 228, 244, 250, 255
Physical Culture see *Sandow's Magazine*
Piccadilly Magazine, The 170n
Pickford, Mary 253
Pinero, Arthur Wing 150
Pinkerton, Robert 221
Pirkis, C. L. 22, 119
Pitt, Chart 214
Pizer, H. 157
Platnauer, J. B. 261, 281
Pocklington, Geoffrey R. 246, 281
Poe, Edgar Allan 11
Pogany, Willy 105
Poirot, Hercule 15, 30, 31, 84, 85, 138, 205, 227, 264
Pollexfen, Claire 140, 217
Pollock, Walter Herries 160
Poole, Reginald 109, 281
Pope, Jessie 184
Popular Magazine, The 68, 144n, 212n
Porter, Gene Stratton 234
Post, Malville Davisson 64, 174
Pound, Reginald 9, 199-200, 206, 207, 281
Powys, John Cowper 244
Praed, Mrs Campbell 105
Prater, Ernest 120-1

Pratt, Ambrose 113
Pratt, Leonard E. 218, 267, 281
Premier Magazine, The 2, 14, 28, 29, 30, 31, 32, 34, 66, 86, 116, *169*, **169-74**, *172*, 179, 194 *Plate 4*
Prescott, Augusta 184
Preston, Philippa 181, 281
Price, Evadne 87, 145, 174, 209, 217, 267
Price, T. A. 253, 281
Prichard, Kate and Hesketh ["E. & H. Heron"] 12, 162, 164, 201, 243, 251, 252
Priestley, J. B. 15, 167, 268, 272
Pringle, Thomas 246
Pritchard, Alfred H. 44
Pritchett, V. S. 137, 258
Prothero, J. K. 102
Protheroe, Ernest 77
Pugh, Edwin 121, 203
Punch 6, 27
Punshon, E. R. 60, 128, 144, 152, 240
Purden, Laurie 254, 269
Purvis, Tom 157, 206
Pushkin, Alexander 11, 198

Quail, Jesse 175
Queen, The 31
Queen, Ellery 102, 136, 137, 183
Quennell, Peter 252, 281
Quiller-Couch, Arthur ["Q"] 14, 96, 114, 148, 150, 170, 233, 244, 256, 266
Quiller-Couch, Lilian 233
Quiller-Couch, Mabel 62, 233
Quirk, Violet 84, 144
Quiver, The 2, 16, 33, 36, 52, 53, 55, 223, **261-2**, 266

Rackham, Arthur 102, 151, 163, 265
Radcliffe, Garnett 126, 166, 229
Railton, Herbert 70
Raleigh, H. M. 166, 168
Ramsay, Alicia 167
Ransom, H. C. 143
Ransome, Arthur 15, 26, 266, 281
Raphael, John N. 165
Rath, E. J. 88
Raven-Hill, Leonard 125, 226, 244, 247, 281
Read, Sheridan P. 60
Reade, Charles 52-3, 242, 243, 251, 266
Reader's Digest, The 13, 18
Realm, The 25, **174-5**, *Plate 3*
Red Book 138, 158n, 212n
Red Magazine, The 12, 14, 26, 27, 29, 34, 36, 48, 50, 64, 86, 112n, 124,
130, 169, 172, 174, **175-9**, *176*, *178*, 193, 195, 210, 217, 222, 237, *Plate 3*
Reed, Talbot Baines 5, 7-8, 246
Reeve, Arthur B. 28, 66-7, 90, 131, 132, 214
Regent Magazine, The see *Tip Top Stories*
Reid, C. Lestock 41, 50, 181
Reid, Stephen 97
Reid, T. Mayne 8, 248
Reid, Wemyss 53, 55
Renard, Maurice 165n
Review of Reviews, The 10, 196, 263
Reynolds, Mrs Baillie see G. M. Robins
Reynolds, Phyllis Joyce 272, 281
Reynolds, Warwick 11, 32, 92, 110, 115, 116, 165
Rhodes, Kathlyn 45, 145, 188
Rhoscomyl, Owen 225
Rhys, Ernest 263
Ricci, Lewis ("Bartimeus") 83
Richards, Frank 10
Richards, Grant 247, 288
Richtofen, Manfred Von 56
Riddell, (Sir) George 234
Riddell, Mrs J. H. 119, 256, 257
Ridge, W. Pett 14, 75, 76, 106, 203, 219, 234, 269
Ridley, Arnold 128
Rilette 268
Rinehart, Mary Roberts 64, 110, 140, 253
"Rita" *see* Mrs Desmond Humphreys
Ritchie, Leitch 248, 249
Rittenberg, Max 62, 63, 106, 115, 122, 219, 281
Robbins, H. N. 148
Roberts, Charles G. D. 115, 152, 153, 163, 177, 184, 227, 237-8
Roberts, Morley 74, 171, 203, 269
Robertson, Morgan 142
Robey, George 64, 140, 165, 194, 229
Robins, G. M. 104-5; as Mrs Baillie Reynolds 188, 234
Robinson, B. Fletcher 102, 142
Robinson, Charles 151, 265
Robinson, Ernest H. 250, 281
Robinson, F. W. 255, 281
Robinson, Oliver 254, 281
Robinson, W. Heath 11, 37, 84, 92, 105, 145, 151, 166, 185, 252, 254, 256, 264
Rochefort, Henri 95
Rochester, George E. 230, 263, 267
Rockey, Howard P. 62
Rodin, August 132
Roe, Vingie E. 145

INDEX

Rohmer, Sax (*r.n.* A. Sarsfield Ward) 2, 14, 25, 28, 45, 48, 49, 56, 57, 64, 84, 93, 107, 108, 115, 117, 128, 129, 139, 140, 162, 169, 171, 172, 183, 188, 194, 229, 247, 249, 256, 261; Fu Manchu 2, 15, 28, 56, 139, 192-3
Rolt, L. T. C. 126
Romance 14, 31, 33, 157, *180*, **180-1**, 218, *Plate 6*
Roscoe, Theodore 236
Rosman, Alice Grant 84, 85, 167, 281
Rosny, aîné, J.-H. 51, 60, 250
Ross, W. D. 244, 282
Rossetti, Christina 259
Rossetti, Dante Gabriel 70
Rountree, Harry 37, 105, 165
Rousseau, Victor 68
Routledge, George 147, 149, 155, 242-3, 288
Royal Magazine, The 12, 15, 23, 24, 31, 32, 33, 90, 110, 116, 117, 138, 144, 166, **181-6**, *182*, 202, *Plate 2*; as *The New Royal Magazine* 34, 186, *186*; see also *The Royal Pictorial* and *Screen Pictorial*
Royal Pictorial, The 34, 35, 186, *186*
Royal, Mayne 83
Rubinstein, Stanley 67
Ruck, Berta 64, 84, 91, 98, 100, 141, 145, 146, 181, 184, 188, 229, 234
Rud, Anthony M. 40, 189
Runyon, Damon 81, 136
Ruskin, John 251
Russell, Eric Frank 79
Russell, Fox 184
Russell, John 85, 134, 260
Russell, W. Clark 28, 72, 74, 95, 200, 244, 248, 268
Russell, W. R. (publisher) 61, 99, 288
Rutter, Frank 268, 282
Ryland, Henry 70

Sabatini, Rafael 14, 23, 29, 37, 48, 56, 64, 84, 89, 92, 112, 113, 114, 121, 142, 152, 153, 162, 171, 175, 176, 182, 192, 205, 219, 253, 264; Captain Blood 2, 167, 169, 172; Scaramouche 30, 40, 136, 189
Sackville-West, Vita 255
St Aubyn, F. J. 123
St Clair, Francis 62
St Mars, F. *see* Atkins, Frank, Jr.
Saintsbury, George 258-9
Sala, George Augustus 243, 251, 266
Sale, Mark 59
Salisbury, Frank 250
Sambourne, Linley 124, 147, 244, 257

Sanders, E. N. 207, 282
Sanders, George Manning 250
Sandow, Eugene 262, 282
Sandow's Magazine (*Physical Culture*) 23, 24, 26, 187n, **262**
Sandys, Oliver 26, 84, 88, 142, 187-8, 222, 282
Sangster, Margaret 195
Sansom, William 252
"Sapper" *see* H. C. McNeile
Sarl, Arthur J. 240, 241, 282
Saroyan, William 258
Saturday Evening Post, The 12, 66, 109, 143, 214n, 235n
Savage, Arthur Dekker 214
Savile, Frank 163, 243
Saville, Malcolm 217
Savory, Isabel 105
Savoy, The 22, 23, **263**
Saxby, Charles 179
Saxe, R. B. 209
Sayers, Dorothy L. 15, 32, 85, 126, 167, 186, 195, 205, 215, 272
Schisgall, Oscar 174
Schooling, J. Holt 162
Scientifiction 210
Scoops 35, 79, 210, **263**
Scott, Eric Clement 114, 117, 175, 282
Scott, Maxwell 249
Scott, Will 87, 157, 158, 213, 214, 261
Scott-James, Anne 272, 282
Screen Pictorial 35, 186, *186*; see also *The Royal Magazine*
Scribner's Monthly 10, 72, 149, 197, 270
Scrymsour, Ella 51, 146
"Seamark" (Austin J. Small) 109, 158, 180
Search Light, The 21, 22, 159, **263**
Searle, Ronald 206
Sedgwick, S. N. 265
Sellicks, Frank 50, 51, 282
Selous, F. C. 175
Seltzer, Charles Alden 81
Seton, Paul 119, 120
Seton-Thompson, Ernest 101
Seyler, Athene 181
Shackleton, Edward 195
Shackleton, Ernest 115, 164, 183, 282
Shand, Elsie H. 235, 282
Shannon, Kitty 273, 282
Sharp, William 150; as "Fiona Macleod" 152, 263
Shaw, Frank H. 56, 63, 138-40 *passim*, 192, 194, 214, 220, 240, 248, 249, 250

Shaw, George Bernard 71, 75, 82, 133, 194
Shaw, Herbert 88, 282
Shaw, Reeves 81, 84, 85, 88, 205, 207, 209, 248, 282
Shepard, Ernest H. 11, 32, 151, 170, 185, 256, 268
Shepherd, J. A. 11
Shepstone, Harold 114
Sherriff, R. C. 253
Shiel, M. P. 24, 59, 75, 148, 183, 244, 264
Shields, Leonard 124
Shore, Teignmouth 262
Short Stories (UK) 25, 161, **263-4**; as *Magazine of Short Stories* 21, 22, 263
Short Stories (US) 67-8, 69n, 272
Shorter, Clement King 32, 73, 74, 76, 225, 256, 264, 265, 282
Shorthouse, John H. 71
Shurey, Charles 241, 282
Shurey, Harry 219, 239, 241
Sibson, Francis H. 126
Sickert, Walter 269
Sidgwick, Mrs Alfred 234
Sieveking, Lance 41, 128
Sievier, Robert 187-8, 282, 289
Sievier's Monthly 27, **187-8**, *Plate 3*
Sime, Sidney H(erbert) as artist 11, 119, 125, 151, 244, 247; as editor 24, 97-8, 99, 252, 264, 282
Simenon, Georges 206
Simmons, Graham 87, 124, 209, 252
Sims, George R. 95, 130, 219, 222, 257
Sinclair, May 133, 234, 235, 268
Sinclair, Upton 115, 123, 143, 226
Sisley, Charles P. 112-3, 117, 282
Sitwell, Osbert 136
Skene, Anthony 267
Sketch, The 22, 31, 74, 84, 247, 256, **264**
Sketchy Bits 239, 240
Small, Austin J. *see* "Seamark"
Smart Novels 239
Smart Set, The 122; British edition 190, 250, 271, **273**
Smibert, Thomas 248, 249
Smith, Clark Ashton 210
Smith, Eleanor 268
Smith, George 250-1, 282
Smith, Herbert Greenhough 35, 82, 196-8, *198*, 202, 203, 205, 207, 282
Smith, James Walter 55, 57, 207, 282
Smith, Jessie Willcox 253, 269
Smith, Reginald 251, 252, 282
Smith, Vere 105-6, 283

305

Smith's Magazine 271
Sneddon, Robert W. 128, 144
Snell, Edmund 41, 50, 91, 92, 126, 166, 174, 179, 237, 267
Snoad, Harold W. 48, 269, 283
Somervell, E. L. 164
Somerville, Edith Œ. 122, 203, 243
Sousa, John Philip 227
Soutar, Andrew 117, 139-40, 174, 193, 249
Southcombe, Philippa 84, 217
Sovereign Magazine 30, 32, 33, 40, 45n, 100, *188*, **188-9**, 212, *Plate 5*
Spare, Austin Osman 250
Spence, Lewis 92, 127, 163
Sphere, The 24, 28, 74, 157, 244, **264-5**
Spilsbury, Bernard 66
Spofford, Harriet Prescott 74
Sprigg, Christopher St John 42, 215
Sprigg, Stanhope W. 42, 55, 57, 225, 230, 283
Sprigg, T. Stanhope 42-4, 79, 80, 218-9, 221, 283
Spurgeon, Arthur 36, 55-6, 191, 193, 262, 283
Spurrier, Steven 11, 157, 247
Squier, Emma-Lindsay 153
Stables, Gordon 8, 246
Stacpoole, H. de Vere 14, 26, 48, 56, 68, 84, 85, 90, 91, 92, 105, 109, 115, 116, 122, 144, 153, 165, 166, 171, 172, 178, 190, 194, 204, 209, 212, 229, 238, 260, 269
Stafford, J. H. 43
Standard Stories 32, **190**, *190*, *Plate 6*
Stanhope, Lady Hester 226
Stanlaws, Penrhyn 89
Staples, John C. 243, 283
Star, The 265
Star Magazine, 69; see also *All Star Magazine*
Starr, Richard 123
Starrett, Vincent 212
Stead, W. T. 10, 11, 28, 133, 196, 200
Steel, Flora Annie 59, 101, 130, 233
Steinbeck, John 206, 258
Stephen, (Sir) Leslie 251, 252, 283
Stephens, Dorothy 149
Stern, G. B. 195, 235, 264
Stevens, James H. 44
Stevenson, Robert Louis 1, 3-5, *4*, 6, 8, 11, 13, 16, 20, 22, 65, 70, 95, 150, 151, 164, 232, 243, 249, 251, 256, 257-8, 266, 268, 270
Stewart, Oliver 43
Steyn, Stella 155
Stock, John A. 87, 176, 179, 238, 283

Stock, Ralph 187, 229, 244, 264
Stockley, Cynthia 134
Stockton, Frank R. 59, 74, 82, 113, 200, 227
Stocquart, Dagnall 211
Stoddart, Jane T. 232, 234, 235, 283
Stoddart, Joseph 10
Stoker, Bram 14, 28, 47, 77, 149, 244, 257
Stoneham, C. T. 195, 219, 229
Story 258
Story [Sunday] Journal, The 27, 28, **265**
Story-Teller, The 2, *2*, 10, 12, 14, 26-36 *passim*, 46, 55, 56, 57, 61, 81, 82, 92, 114, 117, 130, 138, 139, 140, 153, 167, 169, 170, 172, 175, 179, *191*, **191-6**, *194*, *Plate 3*
Stowe, Harriet Beecher 251
Strachey, John St. Loe 251, 252, 283
Strahan, Alexander 242, 254, 289
Straight, Sir Douglas 147-9, 155, 283
Strand Magazine, The 1-2, *1*, 7, 9, 10-12, 13, 14, *15*, 16, 17, 21, 22, 24, 26, 29, 33, 37, 56, 59, 72, 73, 74, 81-2, 84, 85, 94, 110, 112, 118, 129, 130, 147, 150, 160, 168, 182, 193, **196-208**, *203*, *205*, 223, 247, 254, 258, 265, *Plate 1*; influence of 12, 54, 104, 111, 116, 119, 159, 163, 198, 202, 231, 233; US edition 55, 207-8
Strang, Herbert 10
Strange Tales 236
Street and Smith (publisher) 127, 271
Strong, L. A. G. 253, 258, 272, 283
Studdy, G. E. 37, 157, 166, 185, 264
Sullivan, J. F. 160, 200
Sumner, Heywood 70
Sun, The 265
Sunday Journal, The see *The Story Journal*
Sunday Strand, The 24, 27, **265**
Sunny Mag., The 32, 33, 66, *209*, **209-10**, 253, *Plate 6*
Sunset 181
Surrey, George S. 240
Sutcliffe, Halliwell 54, 158, 162
Sutherland, Dorothy M. 48, 269, 283
Sutherland, Halliday 79
Swan, Annie 78, 231-4, 262
Swayne, Martin 108, 204
Swift, Jim 245
Swinburne, Algernon 70, 75
Swinton, Colonel Ernest ("Ole-Luke-Oie") 83
Sykes, Charles 105
Sylvia's Journal 223
Symington, A. B. 243, 283

Symonds, F. Addington 218
Symons, Arthur 263, 283

Tales of Wonder 14, 35, 36, 37, 79, *210*, **210-11**, *Plate 8*
Tanacre, Robert 83
Tarkington, Booth 133
Tatler, The 36, 74, 264
Teague, Edith 269
Teed, G. H. 217, 218
Telling Tales 211
Temple Bar, 4, 7, 26, 196, 198, 243, 250, **266**
Temple Magazine, The 23, 25, 55, 225, **266**
Temple, William F. 210
Templeton, Herminie 98, 102
Tennyson, Alfred, Lord 259
Terhune, Albert Payson 57, 77, 145, 169-70, 173, 174, 213
Tesla, Nikolai 161
Thackeray, William Makepeace 233, 251, 252
Thirkell, Angela 252
Thomas, Reginald 263
Thomas, William Moy 52, 57
Thompson, Dorothy 136
Thompson, P. Gilchrist 258, 283
Thomson, Christine Campbell 41, 128
Thomson, Hugh 70
Thomson, W. Harold 218
Thorndike, Russell 228
Thorne, Guy (*r.n.* C. Ranger Gull) 51, 86, 108, 121, 171, 252, 262
Thorne, Isabel 219-21, 239-41, 283
Thornton, Clare 145, 167, 209, 214, 265
Thorold, William James 273, 283
Thorvaldsen, Olaf 222
Thurston, E. Temple 228, 273
Thurston, Katherine 104
Thriller, The 9, 33, 36, **266-7**
Thrills 267
Tinsley's Magazine 21, 257
Tip Top Stories 31, *211*, **211-2**, *Plate 6*; as *The Regent Magazine* 32, 188, 212, *Plate 6*
Tit-Bit Novels 267
Tit-Bits 7, 20, 53, 159, 196, 198, 261, **267**
To-Day 22, 26, 96, 97, **268**
Todd, Barbara Euphan 252
Tomson, Graham R. *see* Marriott Watson, Rosamund
Torry, E. Norman 177, 179
Tosti, Paolo 232
Townend, W. 139
Townsend, Eric W. 249

INDEX

T. P.'s Magazine 27, 28, **265**
T. P.'s Weekly 265, 268
Tracy, Louis 102, 142, 261
Train, Arthur 171
Travers, Ben 155
Travers, Sydney 121
Treherne, Anthony 61, 289
Tremayne, Harold 60-1, 283
Tremellen, Wilfrid 43, 230
Trent, Guy 218
Treves, Frederick 194
Tristram, W. Outram 70
Trollope, Anthony 11n, 251, 254, 255, 266
Troubridge, Lady 108
True Story Magazine 127
Tuck, John Erskine 262
Turnbull, Margaret 269
Turner, Arthur M. 253, 283
Twain, Mark 27, 94, 95, 104
20-Story Magazine, The 10, 12, 14, 31, 32, 36, 68, 145, 157, 158, *213*, **213-5**, *Plate 5*
Tynan, Katharine 74, 109, 130, 192, 219, 262, 265, 266

Udet, Ernst 44
Underhill, Evelyn 255
Unicorn, The 247
Union Jack, The 9, 267
Union Jack Library, The 66
United Newspapers 107, 109, 110, 243, 289
Universal Magazine, The 24, 25, 121, **216-7**, *Plate 2*
Unknown/Unknown Worlds 273
Unwin, T. Fisher 75, 270, 289
Upward, Allen 160, 162, 165, 193

Vachell, Horace Annesley 54, 57, 109-10, 140, 149, 203, 228, 229, 251, 253
Vaizey, Mrs George de Horne 77
Valentine *see* Pechey, Archibald
Van de Water, Virginia 132
Van Loan, Charles 109
Venner, Norman 192
Verlaine, Paul 148
Verne, Jules 8, 11, 73, 200, 246, 257, 263
Vickers, Roy 35, 122, 144-5, 146, 167, 283
Victorian Magazine 243
Vignon, Paul 75
Vincent, Lady Kitty 157
Vincent, Louis 108, 109, 110, 283
Violet Magazine, The 31, 36, 86, 123, 178, 179, 217, **217-8**, 238, Plate 5

Vivian, Charles 57, 65, 141, 144-5, 146, 283
Vivian, E. Charles 40-1, 42, 86, 92, 127-9, 250, 283
von Hutten, Baroness 101, 152, 268

Wade, John Reed 165, 166-8, 186, 187, 284
Wadsley, Olive 139-40, 179, 185, 193
Wagner, Leopold 118
Wain, Louis 36, 60, 70, 89, 96224
Waite, A. E. 255-6, 284
Wakefield, H. R. 42
Walker, Emery 70, 71
Walker, John Brisben 10-11, 198
Walkey, S. 64, 139, 140, 249, 250
Wallace, Alfred Russell 75, 258
Wallace, Edgar 14, 26, 27, 34, 46, 63, 66, 84, 88, 90, 107, 124, 126, 129, 136, 140, 144, 145, 152, 154, 158, 181, 192, 204, 205, 209, 213, 220, 227, 240, 247, 255, 265, 266-7, 284
Wallis, George C. 79, 261, 264
Walmsley, Leo 214, 237
Walpole, Hugh 15, 29, 46, 48, 49, 85, 193, 194, 204, 228, 234, 253, 272, 284
Walsh, Maurice 249
Walsh, Noëlle 254
Walters, J. Cuming 75
Walton, Francis 98
War, effect of, Boer War 183; First World 13, 29, 133-4, 139, 153, 165-6, 170, 172, 193, 228, 234-5, 245; Second World 16, 18, 44, 79, 205-6, 215, 245
War Stories 35, 42, **218-9**, 221, *Plate 8*
Ward, Francis 117, 179, 284
Ward, H. Snowden 99
Warren, J. Russell 42, 217, 238
Warren, Samuel 11, 245
Warrington, Peter 124
Warwick, Countess of 103
Wassilief, Sophie 96
Watanna, Onoto 89, 102
Waterloo, Stanley 219
Watson, Alfred E. T. 243, 284
Waugh, Alec 51, 137, 146, 167, 254
Waugh, Arthur 59, 125, 268
Waugh, Evelyn 35, 206, 229, 272
Webster, F. A. M. 41, 50, 63, 108, 109, 126, 128, 181, 212, 214, 228, 249
Wedlake, George 268, 284
Weekly Tale Teller 27, 29, *219*, **219-21**, 240, *Plate 4*
Weeks, Edward Olin 161

Weird Tales 127, 189
Wells, Carolyn 142
Wells, H. G. 13-14, 22, 23, 24, 26, 37, 48, 49, 56, 75, 82, 83, 97, 105-6, 113, 116, 125, 134, 135, 136, 147-51 *passim*, 152, 160, 161, 194, 201, 202, 233, 244, 252, 255, 261, 269
Wells, Hiram K. 244
West 68, 273
West, Rebecca 136, 185, 234, 253
Westerman, Percy F. 10, 246
Western Adventures 35, 42, 219, **221**, *221*, *Plate 8*
Western Story Magazine 273
Westrup, Margaret 99
Wetjen, Albert R. 41, 57, 63, 68, 140, 145, 166, 173, 186, 194, 214
Weyman, Stanley J. 14, 21, 41, 59, 71, 74, 97, 120, 124, 149, 198, 248, 251, 252, 256, 258
Wheatley, Dennis 85, 247
Wheeler, E. J. 245
White Magazine, The 27, **222**, *Plate 3*
White, Ethel Lina 84, 110, 158, 167, 184, 229, 234
White, Fred M. 54, 56, 61, 162, 165, 191, 201, 265
White, Stewart Edward 98
Whitechurch, Victor L. 183, 201, 261
Whitehouse, Arch 42-3, 218, 230
Whitelaw, David 114-7, 169-74 *passim*, 179, 192, 284
Whitten, Wilfred 265, 284
Whymper, Charles 70
Wignall, T. C. 237
Wilcox, Ella Wheeler 132
Wild, Harold W. 62
Wilde, Oscar 10, 14, 21, 24, 48, 71, 92, 269, 270
Wilder, Thornton 47
Wilkins, Mary E. 59, 74, 102, 232, 234
Wilkins, William H. 103-4, 106, 284
Wilkinson, Gilbert 87, 157
Williams, Ben Ames 40, 134
Williams, Herbert Dakin 262, 284
Williams, Lloyd 217
Williams, Valentine 30, 66, 84, 154, 172, 203, 264
Williams, W. Llewelyn 265, 284
Williamson, Alice M (Mrs C. N.) 102, 203
Williamson, Charles N. 203, 234, 244, 284
Williamson, David 55, 57, 225, 230, 262, 266, 284
Williamson, Henry 15, 31, 32, 136, 158, 165, 194, 214, 229, 284

307

Williamson, Hugh Ross 207, 253
Williamson, Jack 210
Williamson, W. A. 145, 157, 158-9, 181, 214, 215, 261, 284
Wilmshurst, George 228
Wilson, Edgar 247
Wilson, John 11n
Wilson-Barrett, Alfred 250, 284
Wimbury, Harold 141, 284
Winchester, Clarence 48, 57, 65, 141, 179, 194, 250, 284
Windmill, The 61
Windsor Magazine, The 1, 12, 13, 22, 23, 25, 33, 35, 36, 42, 53, 55, 92, 116, 160, 164, 168, 182, 185, 201, 202, *223*, **223-30**, *229*, *Plate 1*
Wingham, Charles 83, 85, 284
Wings 35, 42, **230-1**, *Plate 8*
Winter, Charles A. 131, 132
Wishaw, Fred 97
Wister, Owen 135
Withers, Hartley 108
Withers, Pearkes 123
Wizard, The 9
Wodehouse, P. G. 14, 15, 25, 82, 84, 85, 115, 125, 141, 142, 153, 155, 157, 158, 163, 199, 203-7 *passim*, 209, 262; Jeeves and Wooster 12, 29, 204-5; school stories 9, 143, 162, 183, 203, 227, 248; imitators 166, 177
Woman 15, 31, 33, 45, 92, **268**
Woman at Home, The 14, 22, 27, 101, 104, 135, *231*, **231-6**, 265, *Plate 1*; as *The Home Magazine* 2, 15, 18, 29, 30, 31, 34, 87, 106, 134, *235*, 235
Woman's Home Companion 179
Woman's Journal 33, **268-9**
Wood, Charles William 242, 284
Wood, Eric *see* Campling, F. Knowles
Wood, Lawson 11, 64, 84, 87, 130, 141, 163
Wood, Mrs Henry [Ellen] 242, 262, 266, 284
Wood, Robert W. 171
Wood, Stanley L. 11, 64, 94, 113, 163, 224, 225
Wood, Starr 157
Wood, Walter 116, 175, 184
Woodrow, Mrs Wilson 66
Woodward, Edward 51, 64, 87, 123
Woolf, Virginia 253-4, 272
Woollcott, Alexander 136
Woolrich, Cornell 215
World & His Wife, The 25, 27, **269**
World Stories 33, 35, 67, **236**, 267, *Plate 7*
Wormser, G. Ranger 213
Worrell, H. T. Webster 75
Worts, George F. 209
Wray, E. C. 215, 284
Wren, P. C. 14, 37, 50, 85, 116, 125, 155, 166, 229, 259
Wright, Charles 262
Wright, Sewell Peaslee 145, 174, 236
Wylie, I. A. R. 45, 56, 85, 105, 134, 139, 143, 184, 193, 253
Wylie, Philip 261
Wyndham, John *see* Harris, John Beynon
Wynne, May 107, 108, 152
Wynne-Tyson, Esmé 51

Yarcott, W. C. 99
Yates, Dornford 15, 27, 164, 227, 228, 269
Yates, Edmund 257, 263, 266
Yeates, V. M. 43
Yeats, Jack B. 250
Yeats, W. B. 4, 47, 75, 263, 269
Yellow Book, The 22, 23, 59, 149, 263, **269**
Yellow Magazine, The 30, 32, 45, 86, 178, 179, 217, *237*, **237-8**, *Plate 5*
Yes or No 25, 29, 30, 31, 219, 220, *239*, **239-41**, *Plate 3*
Yonge, Charlotte M. 71, 259
Young Folks 3, 7, 20
Young, Francis Brett 78, 85, 195

Zangwill, Israel 95, 132, 148, 149, 216, 268
Zec, Philip 136
Zola, Emile 216, 263
Zweig, Stefan 47